Far from the madding crowd: the estuary at Portmeirion, North Wales

The Business of Tourism

The Business of Tourism

SEVENTH EDITION

J Christopher Holloway

with Neil Taylor

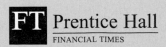 Prentice Hall
FINANCIAL TIMES

An imprint of **Pearson Education**
Harlow, England • London • New York • Boston • San Francisco • Toronto • Sydney • Singapore • Hong Kong
Tokyo • Seoul • Taipei • New Delhi • Cape Town • Madrid • Mexico City • Amsterdam • Munich • Paris • Milan

Pearson Education Limited
Edinburgh Gate
Harlow
Essex CM20 2JE
England

and Associated Companies throughout the world

Visit us on the World Wide Web at:
www.pearsoned.co.uk

First published 1983

© Pearson Education Limited 1983, 2002, 2006

ISBN-13: 978-0-273-70161-3
ISBN-10: 0-273-70161-4

British Library Cataloguing-in-Publication Data
A catalogue record for this book is available from the British Library

Library of Congress Cataloging-in-Publication Data
A catalogue record for this book is available from the Library of Congress

10 9 8 7 6 5 4 3 2 1
10 09 08 07 06

Typeset by 35 in 9/12pt Stone serif
Printed by Ashford Colour Press Ltd, Gosport

The publisher's policy is to use paper manufactured from sustainable forests.

Contents

Part II   The travel and tourism product

Part V Case studies

2   Strategies for national and local audience development at the Currency Museum
    of the Bank of Canada   634
3   Brilliant Weekends: the concept and development of a new holiday programme   640
4   Marketing Michigan's Heritage Route   644
5   Ensuring visitor satisfaction at Warwick Castle   654
6   Steppes Travel: a mid-size operator facing the challenge of change   657
7   Ludlow Marches Food and Drink Festival   661
8   Crime, safety and security: tourists' perceptions of South Africa   668

    Bibliography   679
    Index   697

Preface to the seventh edition

The previous edition of this text was completed just weeks before the outrage of September 11 2001, which was to impact massively not only on tourist movements and tourism, but on world events generally. Life was never likely to be quite the same again. This edition was in the final stages of preparation when the bombers struck twice in London, in July 2005, closely followed by a terrorist attack in the popular resort of Sharm el-Sheikh in Egypt. The long-term repercussions of these and subsequent attacks are still to be determined. In the first five years of this century we have also witnessed foot-and-mouth outbreaks in Britain, the SARS and avian flu scares in Asia, the 2004 tsunami disaster affecting popular beach resorts in the Far East, and within the year the virtual eradication by hurricane Katrina of beach resorts in Mississippi and the popular tourist city of New Orleans.

Each edition of this text has re-emphasized the challenges facing the tourism industry, as world events impact on travel; yet the industry and the travel market both prove remarkably resilient, and the growth of tourism moves remorselessly upwards. As it does so, concern rises about the impact of the sheer volume of people travelling, and the critics question whether such long-term growth is sustainable. Certainly, sustainability is a critical issue in tourism today, even if some sectors of the industry prefer to disregard it, and the subject receives appropriate coverage in this edition.

The new edition continues to stress the diversity of the industry, and the search for new destinations and activities associated with the travel and stay of the global population. Less than half a century ago, mass tourism was largely confined to a handful of global regions, resorts, landscapes and cities; ultimate adventure was defined as a visit to Timbuktu in Mali, a destination available exclusively to the true explorer, inconceivably remote. Today, Timbuktu is firmly on the tourist map, while overland expeditions to similar sites are becoming commonplace. Other tourists with time and money venture even further afield. Depending on taste, these trips will take them snorkelling in the Maldives, hiking in the Himalayas or penetrating the depths of Antarctica. Skimming through these chapters, I see references to Chobe and Okavango, while even closer to home, budget airlines like Ryanair are generating tourism to regional airports at such unpronounceable destinations as Rzeszów and Bydgoszcz. Today, it has to be acknowledged that virtually any point of the globe can become a tourist destination.

A concern expressed in earlier editions of this text regarding congestion and pollution, as the developing nations generate their own overseas tourism, is becoming realized as

China and Russia become prominent generators, and as extrapolation of trends in global air traffic indicate a sharpening geometric increase in travel. Many environmentalists are now arguing in favour of stronger emphasis on domestic travel, and a switch from air services to high-speed rail networks, in order to reduce this impact. Such issues will occupy the minds of the movers and shakers of the industry in the coming years, and are just some of the many challenges which tourism faces.

It is a pleasure to welcome Neil Taylor to this edition as a contributing author. As a former Managing Director of Regent Holidays in the UK, Neil has made many useful suggestions to the content of former editions of this text, and his greater involvement, and useful contemporary experience of the industry, will be invaluable in this and future editions. My thanks go out to others who have made suggestions, or offered help, in the preparation of this new edition, and in particular to Frances Tuke, Public Relations Manager at ABTA, who has helped in updating many of the statistics. My thanks also to those who have contributed case studies and photographs to this new edition.

Chris Holloway

List of abbreviations

AA	Automobile Association
AAA	American Automobile Association
ABTA	Association of British Travel Agents
ABTAC	Association of British Travel Agents' Certificate
ACD	Automatic Call Distribution
ACE	Association of Conference Executives
ACTE	Association of Corporate Travel Executives
ADS	Approved Destination Status
AIC	Airbus Integrated Company
AIEST	Alliance Internationale d'Experts Scientifiques de Tourisme
AIT	Air Inclusive Tour
AITO	Association of Independent Tour Operators
ALVA	Association of Leading Visitor Attractions
APEX	Advance Purchase Excursion Fare
APT	Advanced Passenger Train
ARTAC	Association of Retail Travel Agents' Consortia
ASEAN	Association of South East Asian Nations
ASTA	American Society of Travel Agents
ATB	Automated Ticketing and Boarding Pass
ATC	Air Traffic Control
ATOC	Association of Train Operating Companies
ATOL	Air Travel Organizer's Licence
ATTF	Air Travel Trust Fund
ATTT	Association of Tourism Teachers and Trainers (formerly ATT Association of Teachers of Tourism)
AUC	Air Transport Users' Council
AVE	*Alta Velocidad Espagnola* (Spanish high-speed train)
B2B	Business to business
B2C	Business to consumer
BA	British Airways
BAA	Organization operating airports, now privatized, formerly publicly owned British Airports Authority
BABA	Book a bed ahead

B&B	Bed and breakfast
BACD	British Association of Conference Destinations (Formerly British Association of Conference Towns, BACT)
BCG	Boston Consulting Group
BEA	British European Airways, later merged with BOAC to form British Airways
BHA	British Hospitality Association
BH&HPA	British Holiday and Home Parks Association
BHTS	British Home Tourism Survey
BITOA	British Incoming Tour Operators' Association, now renamed UKInbound
BITS	Bureau International de Tourisme Sociale
BNTS	British National Travel Survey
BOAC	British Overseas Airways Corporation, later merged with BEA to form British Airways
BRA	British Resorts Association
BTA	British Tourist Authority, now VisitBritain
BTI	Business Travel International
BWB	British Waterways Board
CAA	Civil Aviation Authority
CAB	Civil Aeronautics Board (USA)
CBI	Confederation of British Industry
CECTA	Central European Countries Travel Association
CGLI	City and Guilds of London Institute
CIM	Chartered Institute of Marketing
CIMTIG	Chartered Institute of Marketing Travel Industry Group
CIT	Chartered Institute of Transport
CLIA	Cruise Lines Industry of America
COTAC	Certificate of Travel Agency Competence
COTAM	Certificate of Travel Agency Management
COTICC	Certificate of Tourist Information Centre Competence
COTOP	Certificate of Tour Operating Practice
CPT	Confederation of Passenger Transport
CRN	Countryside Recreation Network
CRS	Computer Reservations System
CTC	Certified Travel Counsellor
CTT	Council for Travel and Tourism
DCMS	Department for Culture, Media and Sport
DMO	Destination Management Organization
DTI	Department of Trade and Industry
EADS	European Aeronautic Defence and Space Company
EC	European Commission
ETB	English Tourist Board (later, the English Tourism Council)
ETC	(1) English Tourism Council (now integrated with VisitBritain) (2) European Travel Commission
EU	European Union
FFP	Frequent Flyer Programme
FIT	Foreign Inclusive Tour

FTO	Federation of Tour Operators
GBTA	Guild of Business Travel Agents
GDP	Gross Domestic Product
GDS	Global Distribution System
GISC	General Insurance Standards Council
GIT	Group inclusive tour-basing fare
GNE	Global New Entrant
GNP	Gross National Product
HCIMA	Hotel and Catering International Management Association
Htf	Hospitality Training Foundation
IAE	International Aero Engines
IATA	International Air Transport Association
IBTA	International Business Travel Association
ICAO	International Civil Aviation Organization
IFAPA	International Foundation of Airline Passenger Associations
IFTO	International Federation of Tour Operators
II	Interval International
IIT	Independent Inclusive Tour
ILG	International Leisure Group
IPS	International Passenger Survey
ISIC	International Standard Industrial Classification
ISP	Internet Service Provider, a company providing information on the Internet for commercial payment
IT	(1) Inclusive Tour
	(2) Information Technology
ITM	Institute of Travel Management
ITS	International Tourist Services
ITT	Institute of Travel and Tourism
ITX	Inclusive tour-basing excursion fare
IUOTO	International Union of Official Tourist Organisations (now UNWTO)
LAI	Local Area Initiative (formerly Tourism Development Action Plan, TDAP)
LCLF	Low cost low fare
LDC	Lesser Developed Countries
LTU	Lufttransport-Unternehmen
MIA	Meetings Industry Association
MOMA	Museum of Modern Art, New York
MMC	Monopolies and Mergers Commission (now Competition Commission)
MTAA	Multiple Travel Agents' Association
MTOW	Maximum take-off weight
NAITA	National Association of Independent Travel Agents (later Advantage, now part of Triton)
NBC	National Bus Company
NCVQ	National Council for Vocational Qualifications
NGO	Non-governmental Organization
NITB	Northern Ireland Tourist Board
NPTA	National Passenger Traffic Association

NTB	(1) National Tourist Boardw
	(2) former National Training Board of ABTA
NTO	National Tourist Organization
NUR	Neckermann und Reisen
NVQ	National Vocational Qualifications
OECD	Organization for Economic Cooperation and Development
PATA	Pacific Area Travel Association
P&O	Peninsular and Oriental Steam Navigation Company
PNR	Passenger Name Record
PSA	Passenger Shipping Association
RAC	Royal Automobile Club
RCI	Resort Condominiums International
RDAs	Regional Development Agencies
RFF	Reseau Ferré de France (French equivalent of Britain's Network Rail, responsible for operating the national rail track)
RTB	Regional Tourist Board
RV	Recreational Vehicle
SAS	Scandinavian Airlines System
SIC	Standard Industrial Classification
SME	Small to medium-sized enterprise
SNAT	Societé Nouvelle d'Armement Transmanche
SNCF	Societé National de Chemins de Fer
SOLAS	Safety of Life at Sea
SPR	Size to passenger ratio
SSSI	Site of Special Scientific Interest
STB	Scottish Tourist Board (now VisitScotland)
STOL	Short take-off and landing
TAC	Travel Agents' Council
TDAP	Tourism Development Action Plan
TGV	Train à Grande Vitesse
TIC	Tourist Information Centre
TIM	Tourism Income Multiplier
TIP	Tourist Information Point
TIQ	Tourism Intelligence Quarterly
TOC	Tour Operators' Council
TOMS	Tour Operators' Margin Scheme
TOP	Thomson Holidays' computer reservations system
TOSG	Tour Operators' Study Group (now FTO)
TRIPS	Tourism Resource Information Processing System
TSA	Tourism Satellite Account
TTC	The Travel Training Company
TTENTO	Travel, Tourism and Events National Training Organization
TUI	Touristik Union International
UATP	Universal Air Travel Plan
UBR	Uniform Business Rate
UKTS	United Kingdom Tourism Survey

UN	United Nations
UNESCO	United Nations Educational, Scientific and Cultural Organization
UNWTO	United Nations World Tourism Organisation
VAT	Value Added Tax
VFR	Visiting Friends and Relatives
VTOL	Vertical take-off and landing
WISE	Wing-in-surface effect
WPC	Wave-piercing catamaran
WTB	Wales Tourist Board
WTO	World Tourism Organization
WTTC	World Travel and Tourism Council
WWW	World Wide Web

Part 1 Defining and analyzing tourism and its impacts

1 An introduction to tourism

Objectives

After studying this chapter, you should be able to:

- define what is meant by tourism, both conceptually and technically, and distinguish it from travel, leisure and recreation
- identify the composition and major characteristics of tourism products
- outline the various forms of tourist destination, and their appeal
- explain why destinations are subject to changing fortunes.

Defining tourism

The economic benefits of tourism, however real and significant they may be, do not constitute the only criteria for a state to encourage tourism. . . . The opportunity for a citizen to know his own environment, a deeper awareness of national identity, and a sense of belonging to a culture are all major reasons for stimulating domestic and international tourism.

Philip Cooke, UK Tourism: It's all in the balance,
Tourism, No. 119, Winter 2004

This book is about tourism: its nature, its appeal, its phenomenal growth and impact on our and other societies, and its steady institutionalization – that is to say, the manner in which tourism has become commercialized and organized since its inception, and more especially since the mid-nineteenth century. It will also be about travel, but only those forms of travel specifically undertaken within the framework of a tourism journey.

A good starting point for any textbook which sets out to examine the tourism business is to try to define what is meant by the terms 'tourist' and 'tourism', before going on to look at the many different forms which tourism can take. While an understanding of the term's meaning is essential, in fact the task of defining it is none too easy. It is relatively easy to agree on technical definitions of particular categories of tourism or tourist, but the wider concept is ill defined.

First, it is important to recognize that tourism is just one form of activity under-taken during a period of *leisure*. Leisure is defined as *free time*, or *time at one's disposal*[1] and therefore can be taken to embrace any activity apart from work and obligatory duties. Leisure can therefore entail active engagement in play or recreation, or more passive pastimes such as watching television, or even sleeping. Sports activities, games, hobbies, pastimes – and tourism – are all forms of recreation and discretionary uses of our leisure time.

We can go on to say that the tourist is one who engages in tourism. Tourism, as one element of leisure, involves the movement of a person or persons away from their normal place of residence: a process that usually incurs some expenditure, although this is not *necessarily* the case. Someone cycling or hiking in the countryside on a camping weekend in which they carry their own food may make no economic contribution to the destination in which they travel, but can nonetheless be counted as a tourist. Many other examples could be cited in which expenditure by the tourist is minimal. We can say, then, that tourism is one aspect of leisure which usually, but not invariably, incurs some expenditure of income – and that further, money spent has been earned within the area of normal residency, rather than at the destina-tion. Even this latter criterion could be challenged, however, were the tourist to have retired and to be spending income earned, saved and repatriated while working abroad.

The term tourism is further refined as the movement of people away from their *normal* place of residence. Here we find our first problem. Should shoppers travelling from, say, Bristol to Bath, a distance of twelve miles, be considered tourists? And is it the *purpose* or the *distance* which is the determining factor? Just how far must people travel before they can be counted as tourists for the purpose of official records? And what about that growing band of people who are travelling regularly between their first and second homes, sometimes spending equal time at each? One group of people commonly overlooked are children travelling to visit estranged parents at weekends or half-terms, where they will be living away from their usual place of residence and are often taken out on leisure trips during their visits – yet this growing group, again, would not normally be included in the statistics for tourism.

Clearly, our definition must be specific. In the United States, the National Resources Review Commission in 1973 established that a domestic tourist would be 'one who travels at least 50 miles (one way)', and this was confirmed by the US Census Bureau, which defined tourism eleven years later as a round trip of at least 100 miles. However, the Canadian government defines it as a journey of at least 25 miles from the bound-aries of the tourist's home community, while the English Tourism Council proposed a measure of not less than 20 miles and 3 hours' journey time away from home to con-stitute a leisure trip, so consistency has by no means yet been achieved.

One of the first attempts to define tourism was that of Professors Hunziker and Krapf of Berne University, in 1942. They held that tourism should be defined as 'the sum of the phenomena and relationships arising from the travel and stay of non-residents, in so far as they do not lead to permanent residence and are not connected to any earning activity'. This definition helps to distinguish tourism from migration, but it makes the assumption that both *travel* and *stay* are necessary for tourism, thus precluding day tours. It would also appear to exclude business travel, which is connected with earnings, even if that income is not earned in the destination country. Moreover, distinguishing between business and leisure tourism is in many cases extremely difficult, since most business trips will combine elements of leisure activity.

Earlier still, in 1937 the League of Nations recommended adopting the definition of a 'tourist' as one who travels for a period of at least 24 hours in a country other than that in which he usually resides. This was held to include persons travelling for pleasure, domestic reasons or health, persons travelling to meetings or otherwise on business, and persons visiting a country on a cruise vessel (even if for less than 24 hours). The principal weakness in this definition is that it ignores the movement of domestic tourists. Later, the United Nations Conference on International Travel and Tourism, held in 1963, considered recommendations put forward by the IUOTO (later the World Tourism Organization), and agreed to use the term 'visitor' to describe 'any person visiting a country other than that in which he has his usual place of residence, for any reason other than following an occupation remunerated from within the country visited'. This definition was to cover two classes of visitor:

1   Tourists, who were classified as temporary visitors staying at least 24 hours, whose purpose could be categorized as leisure (whether for recreation, health, sport, holiday, study or religion), or business, family, mission or meeting.

2   Excursionists, who were classed as temporary visitors staying less than 24 hours, including cruise travellers but excluding travellers in transit.

Towards an agreed definition

Once again, these definitions fail to take into account the domestic tourist. The inclusion of 'study' in this definition is an interesting one, since it is often excluded in later definitions, as are longer courses of education.

A working party for the proposed Institute of Tourism in Britain (which later became the Tourism Society) attempted to clarify the issue, and reported in 1976:

> Tourism is the temporary short-term movement of people to destinations outside the places where they normally live and work, and activities during their stay at these destinations; it includes movement for all purposes, as well as day visits or excursions.

This broader definition was reformulated slightly, without losing any of its simplicity, at the International Conference on Leisure-Recreation-Tourism, organized by the AIEST and the Tourism Society in Cardiff in 1981:

> Tourism may be defined in terms of particular activities selected by choice and undertaken outside the home environment. Tourism may or may not involve overnight stay away from home.

Finally, the following definition devised by the WTO was endorsed by the UN Statistical Commission in 1993 following an International Government Conference held in Ottawa, Canada in 1991:

Tourism comprises the activities of persons travelling to and staying in places outside their usual environment for not more than one consecutive year for leisure, business or other purposes.

These definitions have been quoted at length because they reveal how broadly the concept of tourism must be defined in order to embrace all forms of the phenomenon, and how exceptions can be found for even the most narrowly focused definitions. Indeed, the final definition could be criticized on the grounds that, unless the activities are more clearly specified, it could be applied equally to someone involved in burglary! With this definition, we are offered guidance neither on activities undertaken nor distance to be travelled. In fact, with the growth of second-home owners, who in some cases spend considerable periods of time away from their main homes, and time-share owners, it could be argued that a tourist is no longer necessarily 'outside the home environment'. It is also increasingly recognized that defining tourists in terms of the distances they have travelled from their homes is unhelpful; locals can be viewed as 'tourists' within their own territory if they are engaged in touristic activity, and certainly their economic contribution to the tourism industry in the area is as important as that of the more traditionally defined tourist.

Figure 1.1 illustrates the guidelines produced by the WTO to classify travellers for statistical purposes. Some loopholes in the definitions remain, however. Even attempts to classify tourists as those travelling for purposes unconnected with employment can be misleading if one looks at the social consequences of tourism. Ruth Pape[2] has drawn attention to the case of nurses in the United States who, after qualifying, gravitate to California for their first jobs, since employment is easy to find and they can thus enjoy the benefits of the sunshine and leisure pursuits for which the state is famous. They may spend a year or more in this job before moving on, but the point here is that they have been motivated to come to that area not because of the work itself, but because of the area's touristic attractions. People increasingly buy homes in areas where they can enjoy walking, skiing or other leisure activities, so that tourism is literally on their doorsteps – yet this growing group of 'resident tourists' is not taken into consideration for statistical purposes. Indeed, the division between work and leisure is further blurred today by the development of electronic mail and websites which offer immediate access from wherever a worker happens to be spending time. This has led many to buy second homes in the countryside from where work may be engaged in, between bouts of leisure and relaxation. Internet cafes, or personal laptop computers, allow workers to keep in touch with their business while away from home, further blurring the distinction between travel for work and for leisure. Many examples could also be given of young people working their way around the world (the contemporary equivalent of the Grand Tour?), or workers seeking summer jobs in seaside resorts.

Finally, we must consider the case of pensioners who choose to retire abroad in order to benefit from the lower costs of living in other countries. Many Britons have moved to southern Spain or the Canary Islands after retirement, while Americans similarly gravitate to Mexico; they may still retain their homes in their country of origin, but spend a large part of the year abroad. Canadians and Americans living in northern states, known as 'snowbirds' because of their migrant behaviour, also come down in their mobile trailers to the sunshine states of the US southwest during the winter

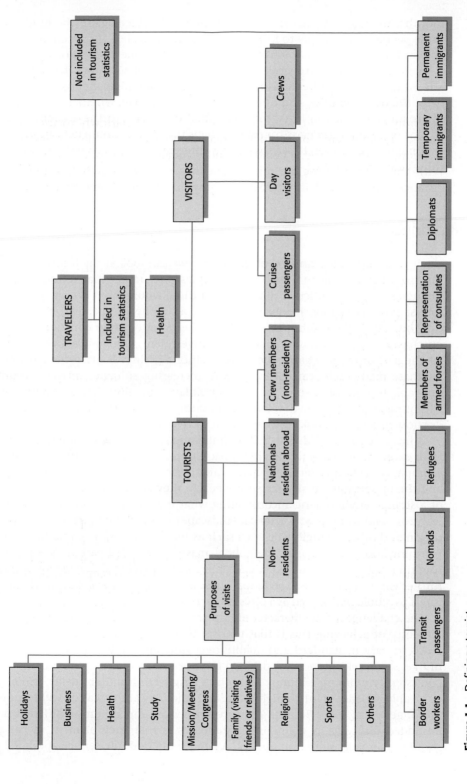

Figure 1.1 Defining a tourist
(Courtesy: The U.N. World Tourism Organization)

months, to escape the harsh winters of the north. Once again, the motive of all of these people is not simply to lower their costs of living, but also to enjoy an improved climate and the facilities which attract tourists to the same destinations.

Conceptually, then, to define tourism precisely is an all but impossible task. To produce a technical definition for statistical purposes is less problematic. As long as it is clear what the data comprise, and one compares like with like, whether inter-regionally or internationally, we can leave the conceptual discussion to the academics. With the advent of modern-day mass tourism, perhaps the most accurate definition of a tourist is 'someone who travels to see something different, and then complains when he finds things are not the same'!

The tourist product

Having attempted a definition of the tourist, we can look at the tourist product itself. The first characteristic to note is that this is a service rather than a tangible good. The intangibility poses particular difficulties for those whose job it is to market tourism. A tourist product cannot, for example, be inspected by prospective purchasers before they buy, as can a washing machine, video recorder or other consumer durable. The purchase of a package tour is a speculative investment, involving a high degree of trust on the part of the purchaser, the more so since a holiday is often the most expensive purchase made each year (although with increasing affluence, many consumers are now able to purchase two or more such holidays annually). The necessary element of trust is heightened by the development of sales via the World Wide Web and the introduction of ticketless booking for much air travel.

It has often been said that 'selling holidays is like selling dreams', and this is to a great extent true. When tourists buy a package tour abroad, they are buying more than a simple collection of services, such as an airline seat, hotel room, three meals a day and the opportunity to sit on a sunny beach; they are also buying the temporary use of a strange environment, incorporating what may be, for them, novel geographical features – old-world towns, tropical landscapes – plus the culture and heritage of the region and other intangible benefits such as service, atmosphere and hospitality. The planning and anticipation of the holiday may be as much a part of its enjoyment as is the trip itself; recalling the experience later, and reviewing slides, videos or photos are further extensions of the experience. These are all part of the product, which is therefore a psychological as well as a physical experience.

The challenge for the marketer of tourism is to match the dream to the reality. The difficulty of achieving this is that tourism is not a homogeneous product, that is, it tends to vary in standard and quality over time and under different circumstances, unlike, say, a television set. A package tour, or even a flight on an aircraft, cannot be consistently uniform; a bumpy flight, or a long technical flight delay, can change an enjoyable experience into a nightmare, and a holiday at the seaside will be ruined by a prolonged rainy spell. Because a tour comprises a compendium of different products, an added difficulty in maintaining standards is that each element of the product should be broadly similar in quality. A good room and fine service at a hotel may be spoilt by poor food, or the flight may mar an otherwise enjoyable hotel stay. An element of chance is always present in the purchase of any service, and where the purchase must precede the actual consumption of the product, as with tourism, the risk for the consumer is increased.

The introduction of *dynamic packaging*, which is rapidly overhauling the traditional package tour, is beginning to obfuscate this analysis. Where tourists themselves put their packages together through Internet suppliers, uncertainty about the uniformity of the product is heightened – and even when packages are tailor-made by the travel agent or other retailer in a similar manner, the lack of a single tour operator or supplier to oversee the final package threatens to undermine the concept of a 'standard quality' product.

Another characteristic of tourism is that it cannot be brought to the consumer; rather, the consumer must be brought to the product. In the short term, at least, the supply of this product is fixed; the number of hotel bedrooms available at a particular destination cannot be varied to meet the changing demands of holidaymakers during the season. The unsold hotel room or aircraft seat cannot be stored for later sale, as is the case with tangible products, but is lost forever. Hence the great efforts that must be made by those in the industry to fill empty seats or rooms by last-minute discounting or other techniques. If market demand changes, as it does frequently in the business of tourism, the supply will take time to adapt. A hotel is built to last for many years, and must remain profitable over that period. These are all problems unique to tourism, and call for considerable marketing ingenuity on the part of those in the business.

The nature of tourism

Now that we have made an attempt to define what is meant by tourism, let us look at this topic systematically. It is useful to examine the characteristics of a tour under the following five broad categories.

The motivation for a trip

Motivation identifies first the purposes of a visit. These fall into three distinct categories:

- holidays (including visits to friends and relatives, known as VFR travel)
- business (including meetings, conferences etc.)
- other (including study, religious pilgrimages, sport, health etc.).

It is important to be aware of the underlying purpose behind the tourist's travels, because each of these categories will reveal a different set of characteristics. Let us consider, for example, how business travel differs from leisure travel. The business traveller will have little discretion in choice of destination or the timing of the trip. In general, destinations will bear little similarity with the destinations of the leisure traveller, since enjoyment of the attractions and facilities do not form part of the purpose of the trip (even if those that exist may be enjoyed as an adjunct to the trip). Business trips frequently have to be arranged at short notice, and for specific and brief periods of time – often as short as a day, even where substantial journey time is involved. For these reasons, business travellers need the convenience of frequent, regular transport, efficient service and good facilities (in terms of accommodation and catering) at the destination. Because the company will usually be paying for all the travel arrangements, business travellers will be less concerned about the cost of travel than if they were paying for it themselves. Higher prices are not likely seriously to deter travel, nor will lower prices encourage more frequent travel. We can say, therefore, that business travel is relatively *price inelastic*. Holiday travel, however, is highly *price elastic*; lower prices for holidays to a particular destination will tend to lead to an increase in the aggregate number of travellers, as tourists find the holiday more affordable, while others may be encouraged by the lower prices to switch their planned destination. Leisure travellers will be prepared to delay their travel, or will book well in advance of their travel dates, if this means that they can substantially reduce their costs.

While these generalities continue to hold, we must also recognize the fact that growing disposable income among the populations of the developed world is having the effect of reducing price elasticity for many holidaymakers, as up-market winter sports holidays, cruising, special interest and long-haul travel attract a greater percentage of the mass market travellers (especially the growing numbers taking second and third holidays every year). For these travellers, service is becoming more important than price. At the same time, narrowing profits in the business world are driving up elasticity among business travellers. In the latter case, the growth of the low-cost air carriers has made discounted air travel so attractive by comparison with fares on the established carriers (particularly first and business class) that low-cost airlines now claim that a large proportion of their passengers are travelling on business.

Beyond price, we must also identify other reasons why a specific type of holiday or resort is chosen. Different people will look for different qualities in the same destination; a particular ski resort, for example, may be selected because of its excellent slopes and sporting facilities, its healthy mountain air, or the social life which it offers to skiers and non-skiers alike.

The characteristics of a trip

These define what kind of visit is made and to where. First, one can differentiate between *domestic* tourism and *international* tourism. The former refers to travel taken exclusively within the national boundaries of the traveller's home country. The decision to take one's holidays within the borders of one's own country is an important one economically, since it will have an impact on the balance of payments, and reduce the outflow of money from that country. The British Government is keen to reverse the present trend towards overseas holidays and encourage more British residents to holiday in their own country, in order to aid the economy.

Next, what kind of destination is being chosen? Will travel be to a seaside resort, a mountain resort, a country town, a health spa or a major city? Is it to be a single-centre visit, a multi-centre one (involving a stopover at two or more places) or a longitudinal tour which will involve extensive travel with brief overnight stays along the route? Or if a cruise is to be taken, statisticians have to decide whether to count this as international travel if the vessel visits foreign ports, and if so, whether to count each country visited as a separate visit to a foreign country, or to include only the main port visited. Does a one-night stopover in Miami before boarding a cruise vessel bound for the Caribbean count as a separate visit to the USA?

Next, what length of time is being spent on the trip? A visit that does not involve an overnight stay is known, as we saw earlier, as an excursion, or is frequently referred to as a 'day trip'. Expenditure by day trippers is generally less than that of overnight visitors, and statistical data on these forms of tourism are often collected separately. A visitor who stops at least one night at a destination is termed a 'tourist', but can, of course, make day trips to other destinations; these could even involve an international trip. For instance, a visitor staying in Rhodes may take a trip for the day by boat to the Turkish mainland; another in Corfu can take an excursion to the nearby coastal resorts of Albania. For the purposes of Turkey's and Albania's records, that visitor will be recorded as an excursionist.

Finally, in order to maintain accurate records, some maximum length of time must be established, beyond which the visitor can no longer be looked upon as a tourist. There are different approaches here, some using a low figure of three months, others six months and in some cases a full year is viewed as the maximum period.

Modes of tour organization

This further refines the form which the travel takes. A tour may be *independent* or *packaged*. A package tour, for which the official term is 'inclusive tour' (IT), is an arrangement in which transport and accommodation are purchased by the tourist at an all-inclusive price. The price of individual elements of the tour cannot normally be determined by the purchaser. The tour operator which puts together the package will buy transport and accommodation in advance, generally at a lower price because each of the products is being bought in bulk, and the tours are then sold individually to holidaymakers, either directly or through travel agents. Agents and operators can also package independent inclusive tours by taking advantage of special net fares and building the package around the specific needs of the client.

As we saw earlier, the emerging *dynamic package* is now producing a hybrid form of tour, as holidays are increasingly put together as tailor-made programmes, whether by the operator, the retailer or even by the holidaymakers themselves. This form of holiday package is rapidly overhauling the standard inclusive tour, although it is not thought that this will lead to the demise of the traditional package; rather, operators are adjusting their products to make them more flexible by means of tailor-made alterations to duration and arrangements.

The composition of the tour

This consists of the elements comprising the visit. All tourism involves travel away from one's usual place of abode, as we have seen, and in the case of 'tourists', as opposed to 'excursionists', it will include accommodation. So we must here identify the form of travel – air, sea, road or rail – that is to be used. If air transport is involved, will this be by charter aircraft or scheduled flight? If an overnight stay, will this be in a hotel, guesthouse, campsite or self-catering facility? How will the passenger travel between airport and hotel – by coach, private taxi or airport limousine? A package tour will normally comprise transport and accommodation, often with transfers to and from the accommodation included, but in some cases additional services will be provided in the programme, such as car hire at the destination, excursions by coach or theatre entertainment.

The characteristics of the tourist

Analysis of tourism must include analysis of the tourist. We have already distinguished between the holidaymaker and the business traveller. Now we must identify the tourist in terms of nationality, social class, sex, age and lifestyle. What stage of their life cycle are they in? What type of personality do they have?

Such information is valuable not only for the purpose of record-keeping; it will also help to shed light on the reasons why people travel, why they select certain destinations and how patterns of travel differ between different groups of people. Research is now focusing much more intently on personality and lifestyle as characteristics which determine the choice of holidays, rather than looking simply at social class and occupation. The more that is known about such details, the more effectively can those in the industry produce the products that will meet the needs of their customers, and develop the appropriate strategies to bring the products to the attention of their customers.

The tourist destination

We can now examine the tourist destination itself. The nature of destinations will be explored in some depth in Chapter 9, but at this early point in the book an initial understanding about what attracts tourists to different destinations will be helpful. This is quite a complex topic, as a destination can be a particular resort or town, a region within a country, the whole of a country or even a larger area of the globe: for example, a package tour may embrace visits to three separate countries in Latin America whose attractions are quite distinct – say, an initial visit to Peru to see the cultural life of the Peruvian Indians and the ruins at Macchu Pichu, followed by a flight to Buenos Aires, Argentina, for a typical capital city experience of shopping and night life, returning home via Cancun, Mexico for a few days' recuperation at a beach resort. This 'pick and mix' approach to the varieties of destination and their relative attractiveness is becoming increasingly common, with the earlier concept in which one is expected to choose between a beach holiday, cultural holiday, short-break city tour or some other uniform package arrangement no longer holding true. Cruise companies have recognized this, and now commonly market a fortnight's combination holiday consisting of several days' cruise preceded or followed by a few days at a beach resort close by the seaport.

In the case of cruising, for many tourists the 'destination' is the ship itself, and its actual ports of call may be secondary to the experience of life on board – indeed, it is by no means unusual for regular cruise passengers to fail to disembark at ports of call, preferring to enjoy the company of the cruise staff and entertainment on board while the ship is in port. In other examples the destination and accommodation are inseparable, as in the case of a resort hotel which provides a range of leisure facilities on site. In such cases, it may be the tourist's objective to visit the hotel purely and simply because of the facilities the hotel provides, and the entire stay will be enjoyed without venturing beyond the precincts of the hotel grounds. This is a characteristic which is commonly found among certain old-established resort hotels in the USA, but an example more familiar to UK holidaymakers would be the Sandals all-inclusive resorts in the Caribbean (see Plate 5).

All destinations share certain characteristics. Their success in attracting tourists will depend upon the quality of three essential benefits that they offer the tourist: attractions, amenities (or facilities) and accessibility (or ease of getting to the destination). At this point we will do no more than outline the variety of destinations attractive to tourists, before considering their attractions, amenities and accessibility. In Chapter 9, the nature of tourist destinations will be examined in detail.

Varieties of destination

Destinations are of two kinds: they may be either 'natural' or 'constructed'. Most are 'managed' to some extent, whether they are natural or constructed; national parks, for example, are left in their natural state of beauty as far as possible, but nevertheless have to be managed, through the provision of access, parking facilities, accommodation (such as caravan and campsites), litter bins, and so on.

Figure 1.2
The 'managed' wilderness. Attractive look-out points have been constructed within the Darling National Wildlife Refuge on Sanibel Island, Florida, an otherwise pristine natural environment. Note the ramp provided for disabled access

(Photographed by the author)

Broadly, we can categorize destinations by delineating them according to geographical features, under the following three headings:

- *Seaside tourism* This will include seaside resorts, natural beaches, boating holidays along coasts, coastal footpaths etc.
- *Rural tourism* This will include the most common category of lakes and mountains, but also countryside touring, 'agritourism' such as farm holidays, visits to vineyards, gardens, visits and stays at villages or rural retreats, river and canal holidays, wildlife parks and national parks
- *Urban tourism* This will include visits to cities, towns, capitals.

Health resorts, including spas (which are important to the tourist industries of many countries) may be based in rural, seaside or urban areas. Adventure holidays and active holidays, such as winter sports, are commonly associated with rural sites, but if one thinks of the appeal of towns such as St Moritz in Switzerland, Aspen in Colorado or Jackson Hole, Wyoming in the United States, which developed primarily to attract winter sports enthusiasts, it must be recognized that pigeonholing all forms of tourism within one of these three types of destination is inappropriate.

All destinations can suffer from overuse, and for the most popular, this is a growing problem. The difficulties created by over-demand, and the need for careful management of city centres, beaches and natural countryside, are subjects to be discussed in Chapters 6 and 7.

Attractions, amenities and accessibility

All destinations require adequate attractions, amenities and accessibility if they are to appeal to large numbers of tourists. In this section, we will look at these issues.

The more attractions a destination can offer, the easier it becomes to market that destination to the tourist. Listing and analyzing attractions is no easy matter, especially when one recognizes that what appeals to one tourist may actually deter another.

In looking at the list of destinations above, it will become clear that many of the attractions of a destination will depend upon its physical features: the beauty of mountains, the fresh air of a seaside resort and the qualities of a particular beach, the historical architecture, shopping and entertainment opportunities and 'atmosphere' of a great city. To these can be added numerous purpose-built attractions to increase the pulling power of the destination. For example, Blackpool maintains its lead among the seaside resorts in Britain by investing in indoor entertainments, a conference centre and other features which will appeal to a cross-section of tourists. Key cities and capitals build new museums, art galleries or exhibition centres (in which impressive contemporary design is playing an increasingly important part in attracting the urban tourist – see Figure 1.3), while former stately homes or castles are transformed by development into focal points for visits by tourists and day trippers alike. Sometimes, the constructed attraction becomes a destination in its own right, as is the case with theme parks like the Disney complexes in Anaheim (California), Orlando (Florida), near Paris, France and in the Far East. The success of many spa towns on the Continent rests on their ability to combine constructed attractions such as casinos with the assumed medical

Figure 1.3
Contemporary design appeals to the cultural market. The Salvador Dali Museum in St Petersburg, Florida

(Photographed by the author)

benefits of the natural springs, while the popular ski resort must provide adequate ski runs, ski lifts and après-ski entertainment to complement its combination of suitable weather and mountain slopes.

The operation of managed visitor attractions is dealt with in some detail in Chapter 10. At this point, it will be sufficient to draw the reader's attention to certain distinctions in the nature of attractions.

First, attractions may be either *site* or *event* attractions. Site attractions are permanent by nature, while event attractions are temporary, and are often mounted in order to increase the number of tourists to a particular destination. Some events have a short time-scale, such as an air display by the famed Red Devils close-formation flyers, as part of a one-day event; others may last for many days (e.g. the Edinburgh Festival) or even months (the Floriade Garden Festival in Holland). Some events occur at regular intervals – yearly, biennially (the outdoor sculpture exhibition at Quenington in the Cotswolds – see Figure 1.4), four-yearly (the Olympic Games) or even less frequently (The Oberammergau Passion Play in Germany, or the Floriade Festival mentioned above, occur only once every ten years), while other festivals are organized on an ad hoc basis, and may indeed be one-off events. A destination which may have little to commend it to the tourist can in this way succeed in drawing tourists by mounting a unique exhibition, while a site destination can extend its season by mounting an off-season event such as a festival of arts.

Second, destinations and their attractions can be either *nodal* or *linear* in character. A nodal destination is one in which the attractions of the area are closely grouped geographically. Seaside resorts and cities are examples of typical nodal attractions, making

Figure 1.4
A biennial event: the outdoor sculpture exhibition at Quenington, Gloucestershire, is held against a backdrop of classic Cotswold architecture

(Photographed by the author)

them ideal for packaging by tour operators. This has led to the concept of 'honeypot' tourism development, in which planners concentrate the development of tourism in a specific locality. Whistler in Canada is an example of a purpose-built nodal tourism resort, erected largely to satisfy the growing needs of winter-sports enthusiasts, which, with its superb range of accommodation, attractions and amenities, now draws high-spend tourists from all over the world. Linear tourism, on the other hand, is that in which the attraction is spread over a wide geographical area, without any specific focus. Examples include the Shenandoah Valley region in the United States, the Highlands of Scotland or the so-called 'romantische Strasse' (romantic trail) through central Germany – all ideal for touring holidays, rather than just 'stay-put' holidays. Motels or bed-and-breakfast accommodation spring up to serve the needs of the transient tourist, who may spend only one or two nights at a particular destination. Cruising is another form of linear tourism, currently enjoying growing popularity as it enables tourists to see a multitude of different sites conveniently and with minimal disruption.

Readers are reminded that much of the attraction of a destination is intangible, and greatly depends upon its image as perceived by the potential tourist. India may be seen by one group of travellers as exotic and appealing, while others will reject the destination because of its poverty or its unfamiliar culture. Images of a destination, whether favourable or unfavourable, tend to be built up over a long period of time, and once established are difficult to change. Britain, for instance, is still seen by many as a fog-engulfed, rain-battered island with friendly but rather reserved inhabitants – an image frequently stereotyped in foreign media. Overcoming such stereotyping is an important task of the country's national tourist board.

Amenities are those essential services catering for the needs of the tourist. These include accommodation and food, local transport, information centres and the necessary infrastructure to support tourism – roads, public utility services and parking facilities. Naturally, such amenities will vary according to the nature of the destination itself: it would clearly be unsuitable to provide an extensive infrastructure in an area of great scenic beauty such as a national park, and those planning to visit such a destination will recognize that the availability of hotels and restaurants must inevitably be limited. Such sites are likely to attract the camper and those seeking only limited amenities.

It should also be recognized that on occasion the amenity itself may be the attraction, as was discussed earlier in the case where a resort hotel offers a comprehensive range of *in situ* attractions. Similarly, a destination like France, which is famed for its regional foods, will encourage tourists whose motive in travelling may be largely to enjoy their meals. In this case, the amenity is its own attraction.

Finally, a destination must be accessible if it is to facilitate visits from tourists. While the more intrepid travellers may be willing to put themselves to great inconvenience in order to see some of the more exotic places in the world, most tourists will not be attracted to a destination unless it is relatively easy to reach. This means, in the case of international travel, having a good airport nearby, regular and convenient air transport to the region at an affordable price, and good local connections to the destination itself (or at very least, good car-hire facilities). Cruise ships will be attracted by well-presented deep-water ports with moorings available at reasonable cost to the shipping

Figure 1.5
The less accessible destination. Plockton, Ross-shire, owes much of its charm to its isolated location in the far north of Scotland

(Photographed by the author)

line, and situated at a convenient distance from major attractions in the area. Cities such as Helsinki, Stockholm and Tallinn have the great advantage of providing deep-water moorings close to the very heart of the capital. Other travellers will be drawn by good access roads or rail services, and coach links.

On the other hand, if access becomes too easy, this may result in over-demand and resultant congestion, making the destination less attractive to the tourist. The building of motorways in Britain opened up the Lake District and the West Country to millions of motorists, many of whom now find themselves within a two-hour drive of their destination. This has led to severe congestion from weekend day trippers and summer holidaymakers during the peak tourist months.

It should be noted that the *perception* of accessibility on the part of the traveller is often as important as a destination's actual accessibility. In particular, the development of the low-cost airlines operating often to less familiar destinations on the Continent from the UK has led many people in Britain to perceive many Mediterranean destinations as being more accessible than Cornwall or the Scottish Highlands, in terms both of cost and travelling time. Such perceptions will undoubtedly affect decision-making when tourists are making travel plans.

Notes

1 *Concise Oxford English Dictionary*
2 Pape, R, Touristry – a Type of Occupational Mobility, *Social Problems*, 2/4 Spring 1964

Questions and discussion points

1 How important is the annual holiday to you, and to your family? How important is it that this holiday is taken abroad, and what are the principal reasons for this preference? Is price a key factor in making the decision between holidaying in your own country and going abroad?

2 Inadequate accessibility can hinder tourism, but there are circumstances where isolation and the difficulty of reaching a destination can be part of its appeal. Identify destinations about which this might be true (in your own country, and globally), and give reasons for their attraction.

3 Intangibility is a characteristic of the tourism product, requiring the tourist to trust the supplier. How do suppliers go about building this trust?

4 Look at the picture in Plate 1. How would you classify these tourists? What are their holiday needs, and how does the industry go about satisfying those needs?

There are two ways of getting up Snowdon: by mountain railway, or a lengthy, although none too challenging, trek to the top. Which would you prefer to take, and why? What are your views about building mountain railways to allow access to the tops of mountains for more people?

5 Some resorts have directly opposing images, according to who is evaluating them. Faliráki in Greece and Ibiza in the Balearic Islands are two examples. Can you think of others? Are the conflicting views justified, are they misconceptions or is it simply a matter of demographics of the consumer – age, personality or other personal characteristics? What are your own views of these destinations?

Assignment topics

1   As research assistant in the tourist office of a region of your choice, you have been asked to evaluate the appeal of the principal destinations within the region, according to the markets they attract. Identify the markets these attract, and the needs of each. How well do the destinations currently meet these needs, and can you identify any significant gaps? Why haven't these been bridged already – is this merely an oversight, poor management, political sensitivity or lack of funds?

Taking any one weakness you have identified, consider how funding might be raised to enhance the destination. Would this attract more tourists, or merely prevent a decline in the present visitors? What effect would it have on the expenditure by tourists in the region?

Produce a brief report for your employer which:

(a)   looks at trends in the numbers and type of market served by the region;
(b)   compares this with statistics for tourism to the country as a whole, explaining any discrepancies;
(c)   outlines suggestions on how tourism can be boosted to the region, and which markets it would be best to focus on, justifying your choices.

Your report should specifically indicate the shortcomings you find in the amount and quality of the statistical data you seek, and what further research you think may be needed to guide the tourist office in its planning.

2   As a tourism researcher, examine trends in direct booking via the World Wide Web in your country, and how this varies between domestic and foreign holiday booking.

Undertake a random sample of people in the area who have taken holidays in the past year, both domestic and foreign, and find out what proportion used the Internet to search for information, to make formal enquiries, and to make a booking. Why did they choose this means of booking?

Can dynamic packaging by retailers reduce this trend? What evidence can you amass to indicate that this might be happening? It may be possible to conduct some research among travel agents to get a general feel for this, but you should also produce a report to your employer which summarizes your findings and identifies the sources of secondary evidence you have produced to support your case. What are the principal shortcomings in finding secondary evidence about methods of booking?

2 The development and growth of tourism to the mid-twentieth century

Objectives

After studying this chapter, you should be able to:

- explain the historical changes which have affected the growth and development of the tourism industry from its earliest days
- understand the relationship between technological innovation and tourism development
- explain why particular forms of travel and destinations were chosen by the early tourists
- identify and distinguish between enabling conditions and motivating factors affecting tourism demand.

Introduction: the early years

Hadnakhte, scribe of the treasury, came to make an excursion and amuse himself on the west of Memphis, together with his brother, Panahkti, scribe of the vizier

Inscription on an Egyptian pyramid, dated to 1244 BC.
Quoted in Lionel Casson, *Travel in the Ancient World*,
George Allen and Unwin 1974, p 32.

A study of the history of tourism is a worthwhile occupation for any student of the tourism business, not only as a matter of academic interest, but because there are lessons to be learned which are as applicable today as in the past. One thing we learn from history is that the business of tourism from its earliest days some three thousand years ago shared many of the characteristics of the business as we know it today. Many of the facilities and amenities demanded by modern tourists were provided – albeit in a more basic form – from the earliest days of travel: not just accommodation and transport, but also catering services, guides and souvenir shops.

The earliest forms of travel can be traced at least as far back as the Babylonian and Egyptian empires, some three millennia BC, but these originated for business purposes rather than leisure. People travelled largely out of obligation, for reasons of government administration, for trade, or for military purposes. However, there is also evidence of significant movements of religious tourists to the sites of sacred festivals, from the very earliest days of travel. Leisure travel took a little longer to develop, traceable as far back as c. 1500 BC, when the Egyptians began to travel to visit their pyramids, partly for reasons of religion but largely out of curiosity or for pleasure[1]. Most travel, however, entailed very little pleasure, and was viewed as a stressful necessity by travellers – indeed, the origin of the word 'travel' is to be found in its earlier form of *travail*, literally a painful and laborious effort.

Even earlier than this, around 1900 BC, we find the first extant example of western travel literature, the classic *Epic of Gilgamesh*, in which the eponymous hero king is obliged to travel as both a challenge and an educational experience – perhaps the first example of what became known much later as the Grand Tour[2].

While some limited travel along the coasts and rivers of these ancient empires must have occurred even earlier than these dates, travel was greatly facilitated when ship-wrights first designed vessels capable of travelling safely and relatively comfortably over open water, some time after 3000 BC[3]. These would primarily have been for the carriage of freight, but would also have been capable of carrying a limited number of passengers. One of the earliest recorded journeys for the purposes of tourism was that of Queen Hatshepsut, from Egypt to the land of Punt (now Somalia) in around 1490 BC[4]. In landlocked areas transport was at the time limited to donkey riding pending the introduction – probably by the Sumerians at first – of solid-wheeled wagons drawn by oxen or onagers (a type of wild ass), also from around 3000 BC.

In the first millennium BC the world was to change dramatically, as new empires grew, fought and died. Most forms of transport around this time (such as the chariot) were first developed for military purposes, but this soon led to the use of horse-drawn wagons for the carriage of goods and people. Horse riding also appeared at first in military guise, as warriors from Asia swept down from the Steppes, but from about 500 BC was adopted by the western nations, firstly in the form of cavalry but later as a more peaceful form of transport.

A museum of 'historic antiquities' was opened to the public in the sixth century BC in Babylon, while, as we have noted, the Egyptians held many religious festivals attract-ing not only the devout, but many who came to see the famous buildings and works of art in the cities. To provide for these throngs during the festivals, services of all kinds sprang up: street vendors of food and drink, guides, hawkers of souvenirs, touts and prostitutes. Some early tourists took to vandalizing buildings with graffiti to record their visit and Egyptian graffiti dating back to 2000 BC have been found.

From about the same date, and notably from the third century BC, Greek tourists travelled to visit the sites of healing gods. Because the independent city-states of ancient Greece had no central authority to order the construction of roads, most of these tourists travelled by water, and since most freight also travelled in this fashion, the seaports prospered. The Greeks, too, enjoyed their religious festivals, which in time became increasingly oriented to the pursuit of pleasure, and in particular, sport. Already by the fifth century BC Athens had become an important destination for travellers visiting major sights like the Parthenon, and inns – often adjuncts of the temples – were established in major towns and seaports to provide for the travellers'

Figure 2.1
The first Olympic Games were held in Greece in 776 BC. Their importance was such that during the event wars stopped and roads became toll free

(Courtesy: The Greek National Tourist Organization)

needs. Innkeepers of this period were known to be difficult and unfriendly, and the facilities they provided very basic: a pallet to sleep on, but no heating, no windows and no toilet facilities. Courtesans 'trained in the art of music, dance, conversation and making love' were the principal entertainment offered.

Early guides and guidebooks

Around 500 BC, some travellers took to recording their observations. Aristedes, for example, made reference to the appalling conditions of the highways in Asia Minor in his *Sacred Discourses*. But we have the writings of Herodotus, who lived between c. 484 and 424 BC, to thank for much of what we know of travel around this period. A noted historian and early traveller who can be accurately described as one of the world's first significant travel writers, he has recorded extensively, and with some cynicism, the tall stories recounted to him by the travel guides of the day. It appears that these guides varied greatly in the quality and accuracy of the information they provided. The role of guides was divided between those whose task was to shepherd the tourists around the sites (the *periegetai*) and those whose function it was to provide information for their charges (the *exegetai*). Liberties with the truth included the story that the great pyramids at Giza extended downwards into the earth to the same extent as their height, and that the perfection of the dazzling white marble used in the greatest statues was such that viewers risked damaging their eyesight unless they averted their gaze. The philosopher Plutarch wrote to complain, a century before the birth of Christ, that guides insisted on talking too much about the inscriptions and epitaphs found at the sites, choosing to ignore the entreaties of the visitors to cut this short.

Guidebooks, too, made their appearance as early as the fourth century BC, covering destinations such as Athens, Sparta and Troy. Pausanias, a Greek travel writer, produced a noted 'Description of Greece' between 160 and 180 AD which, in its critical evaluation of facilities and destinations, acted as a model for later writers. Advertisements, in the form of signs directing visitors to wayside inns, are also known from this period.

However, it was under the Roman Empire that international travel first became important. With no foreign borders between England and Syria, and with the seas safe from piracy owing to the Roman patrols, conditions favouring travel had at last arrived. Roman coinage was acceptable everywhere, and Latin was the common language of the day. Romans travelled to Sicily, Greece, Rhodes, Troy, Egypt – and, from the third century AD, to the Holy Land. The Romans, too, introduced their guidebooks (*itineraria*), listing hostels with symbols to identify quality in a manner reminiscent of the present-day Michelin Guides. The Roman poet Horace published an anti-travel ode following his travel experiences from Rome to Brindisi in 38–37 BC.

It is interesting to note, too, the growth of travel bureaucracy from the earliest stages of travel. Reference to passport-type documents can be traced back at least as far as 1500 BC, and there are biblical references to 'letters' allowing passage for travellers relating to the period around 450 BC[5]. Later, exit permits were required to leave by many seaports, and a charge was made for this service. The Roman *tractorium* is an early example of a passport-type document, issued during the reign of Augustus Caesar. Souvenirs acquired abroad were subject to an import duty, and a customs declaration had to be completed.

The Roman Empire, too, suffered its share of 'cowboy operators', both at home and abroad. Among the souvenirs offered to Roman travellers were forgeries of Greek statues, especially works bearing the signature of Greece's most famous sculptor, Praxiteles. Popular souvenirs of the day included engraved glass vials, while professional stonecutters offered their services to inscribe graffiti on tourist sites. Roman writers of the day complained of Athens being a 'city of shysters', bent on swindling the foreign tourist.

Domestic tourism flourished within the Roman Empire's heartland. Second homes were built by the wealthy within easy travelling distance of Rome, occupied particularly during the springtime social season. The most fashionable resorts were to be found around the Bay of Naples, and there is evidence of early market segmentation between these destinations. Naples itself attracted the retired and intellectuals, Cumae became the resort of high fashion, Puteoli attracted the more staid tourist, while Baiae, which was both a spa town and a seaside resort, attracted the down-market tourist, becoming noted for its rowdiness, drunkenness and all-night singing. As the Roman philosopher Seneca put it, 'Why must I look at drunks staggering along the shore, or noisy boating parties?'

The distribution of administrators and the military during the days of the Roman Empire led to Romans making trips abroad to visit friends and relatives, setting a precedent for the VFR movements of the present day. The rapid improvement in communications which coincided with the Roman conquests aided the growth of travel; first-class roads, coupled with staging inns (precursors of the modern motels), led to comparatively safe, fast and convenient travel unsurpassed until modern times. There is even recent evidence of leisure cruises taken by super-rich Romans: a 150-foot cruise ship, designed to provide luxurious travel along the coastal waters of the Mediterranean, was discovered by divers off the Sicilian coast in 2000. The ship was fitted with bedroom suites and even passenger lounges for social interaction.

Travel in the Middle Ages

Following the collapse of the Roman Empire, and the onset of the so-called Dark Ages, travel became more dangerous, difficult and considerably less attractive, and more synonymous with the concept of *travail*. The result was that most pleasure travel was undertaken close to home, though this is not to say that international travel was unknown. Adventurers sought fame and fortune through travel, merchants travelled extensively to seek new trade opportunities, strolling players and minstrels made their living by performing as they travelled (the most famous of these must be Blondel, a native of Picardy and friend of King Richard I, the 'Lion-Heart', whom he is reputed to have accompanied during the latter's Crusade to the Holy Land). However, all these forms of travel would be identified either as business travel, or travel from a sense of obligation or duty. In order for people to travel for pleasure, the conditions that favour travel must be in place.

Nonetheless, closer to home, holidays played an important role in the life of the public. The word 'holiday' has its origin in the old English *haligdaeg*, or 'holy day', and from earliest times religion provided the framework within which leisure time was spent. For most people, this implied a break from work, rather than a movement from one place to another. The village 'wakes' of the Middle Ages, held on the eve of patronal festivals, provide an example of such 'religious relaxation'. Such public holidays were, in fact, quite numerous, and far more so than today – up until as recently as 1830 there were as many as 33 Saint's days in the holiday calendar, dispelling the myth of peasants engaged almost constantly in hard manual labour. For the pious, intent on fulfilling a religious duty, pilgrimages would be undertaken to places of worship, notably including Canterbury, York, Durham and, by the thirteenth century, Walsingham Priory in Norfolk. Chaucer's tales of one pilgrimage to Canterbury provide evidence that there was a pleasurable side to this travel too.

Religious travel was not limited to the home country at this time. Once political stability was achieved on the Continent and in Britain following the Norman invasion of Britain in 1066, pilgrimages to important sacred sites abroad became increasingly commonplace. Among the most notable were Santiago de Compostela (where the ever-increasing flow of pilgrim tourists led to the creation of relatively sophisticated travel facilities along the pilgrim route by the fifteenth century), Rome, and the Holy Land itself. Visits to the latter countries were generally routed via Venice, which itself became a wealthy and important stopover point as a trading centre for the pilgrims. In twelfth-century Rome, a marketing-orientated Pope of the day encouraged the sale of badges bearing images of Saints Peter and Paul, iconic souvenirs of their visit[6].

Developments in road transport in the seventeenth to early nineteenth centuries

Before the sixteenth century, those who sought to travel had three modes in which to do so: they could walk (many who were too poor to afford any form of transport had to do so, regardless of the distance involved), they could ride a horse, or they could be carried, either on a litter (carried by servants, and restricted largely to the aristocracy) or on a carrier's wagon. This horse-drawn vehicle was slow and appallingly uncomfortable, being without springs. The roads of the time were poorly surfaced, pot-holed and in winter deeply rutted by the wagon wheels which churned the road into a sea of mud, making the journey an endurance test for passengers. The journey was also unsafe: footpads and highwaymen abounded on the major routes, posing an ever-present threat to wayfarers. Apart from royalty and the court circle, who were always well guarded, only a handful of wealthy citizens, such as those with 'country seats' (second homes in the country) travelled for pleasure until well into the eighteenth century.

The development of the sprung coach was a huge advance for those who were obliged to travel. The invention in its most primitive form is traced to the Hungarian town of Kocs in the fifteenth century (from which the word 'coach' originates), and by the mid-1600s coaches were operating regularly in Britain, with a daily service recorded between London and Oxford. The concept of the stagecoach, for which teams of horses would be used and changed at regular points along the route, greatly aided mobility. These appeared in England as early as the seventeenth century, and were in use widely throughout Continental Europe by the middle of the eighteenth century (Austria, for example, introduced its first services in 1749). The construction of these coaches, in which the body of the coach was 'sprung' by being suspended from primitive leather straps, encouraged travel by offering a greater measure of comfort. In the eighteenth century the introduction of turnpike roads, which provided improved surfaces for which tolls would be charged, enabled stage coaches carrying between eight and fourteen passengers to cover upwards of 40 miles a day during the summer. However, this still meant that a journey to Bath from London would take some three days, while the 400 miles to Edinburgh took fully ten days. The later introduction of metal, leaf-spring suspension added to comfort. Stagecoaches also greatly aided the development of the North American colonies, with a service between Boston and New York introduced in 1772, and other routes serving Providence (Rhode Island), Philadelphia and Baltimore. However, mail coaches, which were to provide additional passenger accommodation, were not to make an appearance until the 1780s in Europe and the USA.

Travel of some distance requires accommodation. At this time, such accommodation was basic. Inns sprang up to serve the needs of overnight guests and to provide fresh horses, while lodgings or 'chambers' were available for rent to visitors when they arrived at their destinations.

Around 1815, the discovery of tarmacadam revolutionized the road systems of Europe and North America. For the first time, a hard surface less subject to pitting and ruts enabled rapid increases to be made in the average speed of coach services. Charabancs, public coaches drawn by teams of horses, with rows of transverse seats facing forward, have been identified as far back as 1832; the term was later applied to the first motor-coaches used for leisure travel in the early twentieth century. By the 1820s, the horse-drawn omnibus was a common sight in London and Paris, greatly improving local city transport. Mail coaches were now covering the distance between London and Bath in twelve and a half hours, and the London–Brighton run was reduced to a little over five hours.

The Grand Tour

From the early seventeenth century, a new form of tourism developed as a direct outcome of the freedom and quest for learning heralded by the Renaissance. Under the reign of Elizabeth I, young men seeking positions at court were encouraged to travel to the Continent to finish their education. This practice was soon adopted by others high in the social circle, and it eventually became customary for the education of a gentleman to be completed by a 'Grand Tour' (a term in use as early as 1670) of the major cultural centres of Europe, accompanied by a tutor and often lasting three years or more. Travel for reasons of education was encouraged by the fact that under Elizabeth I a special licence had to be obtained from the Crown in order to travel abroad, though universities had the privilege of granting licences themselves for the purpose of scholarship. The publication in 1749 of a guidebook by Dr Thomas Nugent entitled *The Grand Tour* gave a further boost to the educational tour, and some intrepid travellers ventured as far afield as Egypt. While ostensibly educational, as with the spas the appeal soon became social, and pleasure-seeking young men of leisure travelled, predominantly to France and Italy, to enjoy the rival cultures and social life of cities such as Paris, Venice and Florence. By the end of the eighteenth century, the custom had become institutionalized for the gentry.

As a result, European centres were opened up to the British traveller. Aix-en-Provence, Montpellier and Avignon became notable bases, especially for those using the Provence region as a staging post for travel to Italy. When pleasure travel followed in the nineteenth century, eventually to displace educational tours as the motive for Continental visits, this was to lead to the development of the Riviera as a principal destination for British tourists, aided by the introduction of regular steamboat services across the Channel from 1821 onwards. However, the advent of the Napoleonic wars early in the nineteenth century inhibited travel within Europe for some 30 years. By the time of Napoleon's defeat, the British had taken a greater interest in touring their own country.

Example The rise of Nice as a popular tourism destination

Nice was seen initially as an unpleasant stopover point for those undertaking the Grand Tour. It was poor, had few facilities for the visitor, and the roads along the Mediterranean coast were appalling. However, it was convenient geographically, and, gradually, the number of

English visitors grew. By the end of the eighteenth century a small colony of English invalids would winter in the town. The reputation of the town soon spread. Between 1860 and 1914 Nice was one of the fastest growing European cities; entertainments proliferated, including shooting and roller skating. Gradually, adjacent villages along the Côte d'Azur began to benefit from the prosperity of Nice. Not only the English, but wealthy Russians, too, were choosing to spend their winter in a more temperate climate. However, by the early twentieth century newer resorts like Antibes and Cannes had begun to entice visitors away from the town, and its importance as a tourism base declined.

Authorization to travel

Travel outside the boundaries of one's country had often been subject to restrictions, as we have seen from constraints imposed by the state under the Roman Empire, and by even earlier authorities. In fact, at various times some states have even imposed limitations on travel between towns and regions within their own territory; in eighteenth century France, for example, internal passports were needed to travel between towns, while prior to the war of independence in America (1776–81) similar internal passports were required to move between states.

The first use of the term 'passport' in law in Britain is thought to have occurred in 1548[7]. Such passports hark back directly to the medieval *testimoniale*, a letter from an ecclesiastical superior given to a pilgrim to avoid the latter's possible arrest on charges of vagrancy. Later, papers of authority to travel were more widely issued by the state, particularly during periods of warfare with neighbouring European countries.

Prior to the eighteenth century few people travelled any great distance, and those who did so were generally involved with affairs of state. Monarchs were suspicious of intrigues and alliances with foreign states, and vetted such travel carefully, issuing letters of authority to members of court, ostensibly to facilitate travel but equally to ensure that they were familiar with the movements of their subjects. In Britain, it was the prerogative of the monarch to control any movements of their subjects overseas, and throughout the sixteenth and seventeenth centuries applications had to be made for a 'licence to pass beyond the seas'. Such 'licences' became more frequent in the eighteenth and nineteenth centuries, but were prohibitively expensive for all but the wealthy – in 1830, a British passport had cost £2/7/6 (or around £2.37 in today's decimal currency), then a high weekly wage. Demand was to cut this figure to just 2/- (or 10 pence) by 1858 – still equivalent to a daily wage for many.

Nevertheless, from the late eighteenth century on travel demand was growing, to a point where it became impossible to issue passports based on traditional practice by the mid-nineteenth century. In Britain, it had been the practice for the Foreign Secretary to issue all passports, based on his personal knowledge of the applicant, but this was clearly no longer practical. Curiously, around this period, countries such as France and Belgium were even willing to issue passports to non-citizens; Lloyd[8] recounts the story of the poet Robert Browning, eloping with Elizabeth Barrett Browning in 1846, who travelled on a French passport.

Consequently, by the mid-nineteenth century many European countries began to abandon most passport requirements other than in times of war. This paralleled policy in the United States, which made no requirement for passports except during the Civil War (following the War of Independence, individual states, as well as the Department of Foreign Affairs, had been permitted to issue passports for foreign travel). Regulations were introduced in 1846 in the UK for the movement of merchants and diplomats, but those travelling purely for leisure were no longer obliged to carry formal documentation.

Once travel documents are no longer deemed necessary, it becomes difficult to reimpose their requirement. When Belgium sought to oblige visitors to present passports for inspection in 1882, there was widespread indignation in the British press. The First World War was to change all this. New passports, accompanied by a photograph of the bearer, were widely introduced, and the League of Nations standardized their design in 1921. Britain made passports compulsory in 1916, although by 1924 Belgium was again allowing Britons to travel on no-passport excursions to the Continent.

The institution of a formal immigration service in the UK is also a twentieth-century phenomenon, having been established under the Aliens Act 1905.

Other political hindrance to travel

Many other essentially political factors will affect the movement of tourists between countries. A critical one is the political relationship between the generating and destination countries. All through history the European nations have been at war with one another; and clearly the desire to travel in the territories of a recent or former enemy will be limited, just as willingness to visit those of former allies will be enhanced. At times of tension, border controls will inhibit travel; some nationalities may be excluded, while at the very least, visas or other documentary requirements may be imposed on less friendly nations. It has also been common, particularly in recent history, for countries to refuse entry to visitors who have travelled to or through a nation with which the destination country is in conflict.

Decisions concerning the value of a currency relative to others, even where economically motivated, are nonetheless political. Such decisions directly affect the buying power of tourists travelling abroad, and will either discourage travel or switch travellers to destinations where exchange rates are more favourable. Of course, the use of common currencies in different countries facilitates travel. As we have seen, under the Roman Empire the universal acceptance of Roman coinage greatly encouraged travel, by contrast with the vast range of currencies to be found, even within individual countries, in the Middle Ages. Fynes Moryson, an academic who travelled extensively on the Continent, was to write in 1589 of finding over 20 different coinages in Germany, five in the Low Countries and as many as eight in Switzerland. Moneychangers cheated the visitor as a matter of course, and were sometimes difficult to find. The adoption of the euro as a common currency throughout most of the 25 countries within the European Union – the first such common currency since the days of the Roman Empire – has been a motivating factor in generating inter-European tourism, but it also has its downside, as we shall see in the next chapter.

Further political hindrance occurs in the form of taxation, which has affected travel from the very earliest periods of tourism history. The opportunity to enhance a nation's coffers at the expense of the foreign tourist was also widely recognized in the Middle Ages; the first spa tax is known to have been introduced in Bad Pyrmont, Saxony, as early as 1413. But history also reveals how tourists react to high taxation by switching to other destinations where costs are lower, so measures to tax tourists are always subject to economic sensitivity.

The development of the spas

Spas were already well established during the time of the Roman Empire, but their popularity, based on the supposed medical benefits of the waters, had lapsed in subsequent centuries. They were never entirely out of favour, however; the sick continued to visit Bath throughout the Middle Ages. Renewed interest in the therapeutic qualities of mineral waters can be traced to the influence of the Renaissance in Britain and other European centres.

In 1562, Dr William Turner published a book drawing attention to the curative powers of the waters at Bath and on the Continent. Bath itself, along with the spa at Buxton, had been showing a return to popularity among those 'seeking the cure', and the effect of Dr Turner's book was to establish the credibility of the resorts' claims. In 1626, Elizabeth Farrow drew attention to the qualities of the mineral springs at Chalybeate in Scarborough, which became the first of a number of new spa resorts. In the same year, Dr Edmund Deane wrote his *Spadacrene Anglica* which drew attention to what he claimed were 'the strongest sulphur springs in Great Britain' at Harrogate. This rapidly led to the popularity of the town as a spa resort, a role it continues to enjoy today. Soon, an astonishing number of spa resorts sprang up, sometimes in unlikely places: Streatham in south London, for instance, became briefly fashionable following the discovery of mineral springs there in 1659. Between 1560 and 1815, at one time or another as many as 175 different spas were operating in England, although only three of these – at Bath, Buxton and Hotwells, in Bristol – actually incorporated thermal springs in their cures. By 1815, seven of the spas had purpose-built theatres to provide entertainment.

'Taking the cure' rapidly developed social status, and the resorts changed in character as pleasure rather than health became the motivation for visits. Bath in particular became a major centre of social life for high society during the eighteenth and early nineteenth centuries, aided by visits from the monarchs of the day. Under the guidance of Beau Nash at the beginning of the eighteenth century, it soon became a centre of high fashion, deliberately setting out to create a select and exclusive image. The commercial possibilities opened up by the concentration of these wealthy visitors were not overlooked; facilities to entertain or otherwise cater for these visitors proliferated, changing the spas into what we would today term holiday resorts rather than watering places. The building of a Pump Room as a focal point within Bath was a key development leading to the town's success as a resort, while Harrogate similarly benefited by the construction of its own Pump Room in 1841–42.

Eventually, in the early nineteenth century, the common characteristic of resorts to go 'down-market' through their life cycle led to a changing clientele, with the landed gentry replaced by wealthy merchants and the professional class. By the end of the eighteenth century, the heyday of the English spas was already over, although they were to have a far longer life cycle on the Continent (see Figure 2.2).

The popularity of the spas on the Continent may be ascribed to the belief in their efficacy by the general public, supported by members of the medical profession, to an extent where public funding was, and still is in some cases, provided by the state for those needing treatment. The town of Spa in Belgium gave its name to the concept of a centre for the treatment of illness through taking, or bathing in, the mineral waters (or later, by the application to the body of mud or other substances with perceived healing qualities). Spas rapidly became popular in Germany (town names with the appendage Bad or Baden all owe their origins to their spas), Italy and middle European countries like Hungary and Czechoslovakia.

There are interesting parallels between the decline of the English spas and that of the English seaside resorts one hundred and fifty years or so later. The spa towns were seen as attractive places in which to live, and residents gradually supplanted visitors. These residents tended to be older, and their demand for more passive and traditional

Figure 2.2
The Continental spa: the baths at Spa, Belgium

(Photographed by the author)

entertainment, with a preference for entertaining at home rather than seeking commercial entertainment, hastened the spas' economic decline. However, it was the rise of the seaside resorts (see Plate 2) which did much to undermine the success of the inland spas, just as later it would be the rise of the Mediterranean resorts which would lead to the decline of the British seaside resort.

The rise of the seaside resort

Until the Renaissance, bathing in the sea found little favour in Britain. Although not entirely unknown before then, such bathing as did occur was undertaken unclothed, and this behaviour conflicted with the mores of the day. Only when the sea became associated with certain health benefits did bathing gain popularity. The association of sea water with health did not find acceptance until the early years of the eighteenth century, and initially the objective was to drink it rather than bathe in it. It is perhaps to be expected that health theorists would eventually recognize that the minerals to be found in spa waters were also present in abundance in sea water. By the early eighteenth century, small fishing resorts around the English coast were beginning to attract visitors seeking 'the cure', both by drinking sea water and by immersing themselves in it. Not surprisingly, Scarborough, as the only traditional spa bordering the sea, was one of the first to exploit this facility for the medical benefits it was believed to offer, and both this town and Brighton were attracting regular visitors by the 1730s (see Plate 3). But it was Dr Richard Russell's noted medical treatise *A Dissertation on the Use of Sea Water in the Diseases of the Glands, particularly the Scurvy, Jaundice, King's Evil, Leprosy, and the Glandular Consumption*, published in 1752 (and two years earlier in Latin), which is credited with popularizing the custom of sea-bathing more widely. Soon Blackpool, Southend and other English seaside resorts were wooing bathers to their shores. Blackpool, in fact, had attracted some categories of sea bather well before its growth as a resort: workers in the area are known to have travelled there by cart in order to wash off the accumulation of dirt resulting from their jobs. The heyday of these 'Padjamers', as they were known, was in the century between 1750 and 1850.

The growing popularity of taking the cure, which resulted from the wealth generated by the expansion of trade and industry in Britain at the time, meant that the inland spas could no longer cater satisfactorily for the influx of visitors they were attracting. By contrast, the new seaside resorts offered almost boundless opportunity for expansion. Moral doubts about exposing one's body in the sea were overcome by the invention of the bathing machine, and the resorts prospered.

Undoubtedly, the demand for seaside cures could have been even greater in the early years if fast, cheap transport had been developed to cater for this need. But in the mid-eighteenth century, it still took two days to travel from London to Brighton, and the cost was well beyond the reach of the average worker, at the equivalent of six weeks' wages. Accommodation provision, too, grew only slowly, outpaced by demand. But all this was to change in the early nineteenth century.

First, the introduction of steamboat services reduced the cost and time of travel from London to the resorts near the Thames Estuary. In 1815, a service began operating between London and Gravesend, and, five years later, to Margate. The popularity of these services was such that other pleasure boat services were quickly introduced to more distant resorts. This development required the construction of piers to provide landing stages for the vessels; the functional purpose of the seaside pier was soon overtaken by its attraction as a social meeting-point and a place to take the sea air.

However, it was also the introduction of steamboat services linking Britain and Continental Europe which posed the first threat to the British seaside resorts. Brighton established a ferry link with Dieppe as early as 1761, and later this was followed by links from Shoreham and Newhaven to France. It has been estimated that by the 1820s some 150,000 visitors a year were travelling from Britain to mainland Europe, many for the purposes of visiting coastal resorts. At first, from about 1780 onwards, travel was concentrated along the Riviera, between the mouth of the Var and the Gulf of Spezia. The Italian resorts benefited from direct steamer services from London and Liverpool to Genoa. Before the advent of the railways, stagecoaches or hired carriages took three weeks to travel from London to Rome, but direct steamboats to Italy were to reduce this by half. Soon, French resorts were attracting British visitors along the north coast between Boulogne and Cherbourg. The British visitors insisted on facilities which met their particular needs, including churches of favourite denominations, and British shops, chemists, physicians and newspapers; the more successful French resorts quickly provided these. From 1880 onwards, the Train Bleu offered wealthy British visitors elegant sleeping accommodation from Paris to the Riviera, popularizing not only summer but also winter holidays to escape the cold of the British climate.

Seaside resorts were also finding favour with the nobility and wealthy of other countries by this time. Aristocratic Russians travelled to the Crimea, the Baltic and the South of France for their holidays, and wealthy Americans on the Eastern seaboard frequented the first resorts developed along the New Jersey, New York and New England coastlines, with the most wealthy of them building second homes in the nineteenth century along the Rhode Island shores.

Conditions favouring the expansion of travel in the nineteenth century

From this brief history of travel from earliest times to the nineteenth century, we can see that a number of factors have been at work to encourage travel. We can divide these into two categories: factors that make travel possible (*enabling* factors), and factors that persuade people to travel (*motivating* factors).

In order for travel to be possible at all, people must have adequate time and money to undertake it. However, throughout most of history, and until very recently, both of these have been the prerogative of a very few members of society. Leisure time for the masses was very limited; workers laboured from morning to night, six days a week, and were encouraged to treat Sundays (and the not infrequent Saint's days) as days of rest and worship. Wages were barely adequate to sustain a family and pay for the basic necessities of life. The idea of paid holidays was not even considered until the twentieth century.

Equally important, the development of pleasure travel depends upon the provision of suitable travel facilities. The growth of travel and of transport is interdependent:

travellers require transport that is priced within their budget and that is fast, safe, comfortable and convenient. As we have seen, none of these criteria began to be met until the latter half of the eighteenth century, but from the early nineteenth century onwards rapid improvements in technology led to transport that was both fast and moderately priced.

The development of transport during the nineteenth century will be examined in greater detail shortly. But good transport must be complemented by adequate accommodation at the traveller's destination. The traditional hospices for travellers in the Middle Ages were the monasteries, but these were dissolved in Britain during the reign of Henry VIII and the resulting hiatus acted as a further deterrent to travel for everyone apart from those planning to stay with friends or relatives. The gradual improvement in lodgings that accompanied the introduction of the mail coaches and stagecoaches went some way to correcting this shortcoming. However, the general inadequacy of facilities away from the major centres of population meant that towns such as London, Exeter and York, with their abundant social life and entertainment as a magnet, were to become the first centres to attract large numbers of visitors for leisure purposes.

Other constraints awaited those prepared to ignore these drawbacks to travel. In cities, public health standards were low, and travellers risked disease, a risk compounded in the case of foreign travel. Exchange facilities for foreign travel were unreliable, rates of exchange were inconsistent and travellers risked being cheated, so they tended to carry large amounts of money with them, making them prey to highwaymen. Foreign currencies were, in any event, chaotic, as we have noted earlier – in the sixteenth century, for instance, Germany, with its multiplicity of small states, had no fewer than 20 coinages as well as the Reich's Dollar, while there were similar multiple coinages in other European countries. Before unification, Italy, a popular venue for the cultural tourist, boasted 16 different coinages. As we have also seen, travel documents of some kind were generally necessary, and at times not easy to come by. Political suspicion frequently meant long delays in obtaining permission to travel.

Removing these constraints will encourage growth in travel. However, the real motivation for travel must be intrinsic, a wish to travel for its own sake, to get away from one's everyday surroundings and become acquainted with other places, cultures and people. It was the rapid urbanization of the population in Great Britain which provided the impetus for travel in the nineteenth century. The industrial revolution had led to massive migration of the population away from the villages and countryside and into the industrial cities, where work was plentiful and better paid. This migration was to have two important side effects on the workers themselves. First, workers became conscious of the beauty and attractions of their former rural surroundings for the first time. Cities were dark, polluted and treeless. Formerly, workers had little appreciation of their environment – living in the midst of the natural beauty of the countryside, they accepted it without question. Now, they longed to escape from the cities in what little free time they had – a characteristic still evident among twenty-first-century city dwellers. Second, the type of work available in the cities was both physically and psychologically stressful. The comparatively leisurely pace of life in the countryside was replaced by monotonous factory work from which any change of routine and pace was welcome.

The expansion of the British economy which took place as a result of the increased productivity created by the industrial revolution led to growth in real purchasing power for every worker, while worldwide demand for British goods created a huge business travel market. Increased wealth stimulated rapid growth in the population at this time too.

In short, Britain at the beginning of the nineteenth century stood poised on the threshold of a considerable escalation in the demand for travel. The introduction of modern transport systems at this point in history was to translate this demand into reality.

The age of steam

The railways

Two technological developments in the early part of the nineteenth century were to have a profound effect on transport and the growth in travel generally. The first of these was the advent of the railway.

The first passenger railway was built in England, between Stockton and Darlington, in 1825. It was to herald a major programme of railway construction throughout the world, and a major shift in the facility to travel. We have noted the problems of travelling by road up to that point; and, although travel by canal had become possible by 1760, it was too slow a mode to attract travellers, being used essentially for the carriage of freight. As a means of transport for all purposes, it was to suffer a rapid decline after 1825, when railways made travel at 13 mph possible for the first time – at least three miles an hour faster than the fastest mail coaches. *Invicta*, the first steam driven passenger train (based on the design of Stephenson's *Rocket*) made the first passenger journey between Whitstable Bay and Canterbury on the 3rd May, 1830, carrying day trippers. In the decade following the introduction of a rail link between Liverpool and Manchester in the same year, trunk routes sprang up between the major centres of population and industry in Britain, on mainland Europe and throughout the world; in the USA, for example, passenger services on the east coast were being built from the 1820s, and by 1869 a transcontinental link was in place. One of the last great rail routes, the Trans-Siberian, opened in 1903, connecting Moscow with Vladivostok and Port Arthur (now Lüshun).

In the UK, after their initial function to serve the needs of commerce, new routes emerged linking these centres to popular coastal resorts like Brighton, bringing these within reach of the mass of pleasure travellers for the first time. On the whole, however, the railway companies appeared to be slow to recognize the opportunities for pleasure travel offered by the development of rail services, concentrating instead on providing for the needs of business travellers. Certainly, in the 1840s, the growth of regular passenger traffic was enough to occupy them; between 1842 and 1847, the annual number of passengers travelling by train rose from 23 million to 51 million. Competition between the railway companies was initially based on service rather than price, although from the earliest days of the railways a new market developed for short day trips. Before long, however, entrepreneurs began to stimulate rail travel by organizing excursions for the public at special fares. In some cases, these took place on regular train services, but in others, special trains were chartered in order to take travellers to their destination, setting a precedent for the charter services by air which were to become so significant a feature of tour operating a century later. As an indication of the speed with which these opportunities were put into place, within twelve days of the rail line to Scarborough being opened in 1845, an excursion train from Wakefield was laid on to carry a thousand passengers to the seaside.

Thomas Cook, contrary to popular opinion, was not, in fact, the first entrepreneur to organize tours for the public. Sir Rowland Hill, who became chairman of the Brighton Railway Company, is sometimes credited with this innovation (others have suggested that the first package tour can in fact be traced to a group of tourists taken from Wadebridge to Bodmin to witness a public hanging!), and there were certainly excursion trains in operation by 1840. However, Cook was to have by far the greatest impact on the early travel industry. In 1841, as secretary of the South Midland Temperance Association, he organized an excursion for his members from Leicester to Loughborough, at a fare of one shilling (the equivalent of five pence) return. The success of this venture – 570 took part – encouraged him to arrange similar excursions using chartered trains, and by 1845 he was organizing these trips on a fully commercial basis.

The result of these and similar ventures by other entrepreneurs led to a substantial movement of pleasure-bound travellers to the seaside. In 1844, it is recorded that almost 15,000 passengers travelled from London to Brighton on the three Easter holidays alone, while hundreds of thousands travelled to other resorts to escape the smoke and grime of the cities. The enormous growth in this type of traffic can be appreciated when it is revealed that by 1862 Brighton received 132,000 visitors on Easter Monday alone.

Supported by a more sympathetic attitude to pleasure travel by public authorities such as the Board of Trade, the railway companies themselves were actively promoting these excursions by the 1850s, while at the same time introducing a range of discounted fares for day trips, weekend trips and longer journeys. By 1855, Cook had extended his field of operations to mainland Europe, organizing the first 'inclusive tours' to the Paris Exhibition of that year. This followed the success of his excursions to the Great Exhibition in London in 1851, which in all had welcomed a total of three million visitors.

Cook was a man of vision in the world of travel. The success of his operations was due to the care he took in organizing his programmes to minimize problems; he had close contacts with hotels, shipping companies and railways throughout the world, ensuring that he obtained the best possible service as well as cheap prices for the services he provided. By escorting his clients throughout their journeys abroad he took the worry out of travel for the first-time traveller. He also made the administration of travel easier by introducing the hotel voucher in 1867, which allowed tourists to prepay their hotel accommodation and to produce evidence to the hotels that this had been done. In 1874 he introduced the 'circular note', the precursor to today's traveller's cheque, a promissory note which could be exchanged abroad for local currency. This greatly helped to overcome the problems arising from the many different coinages in use in Europe. The latter was not a totally new concept; a certain Robert Herries set up the London Banking Exchange Company in 1772 in order to issue similar documents, but it was Cook (and later in North America, American Express, which introduced the first traveller's cheque in 1891) who popularized these ideas, which made travel far more tolerable for the Victorian traveller.

The coincidental invention of photography in the mid-nineteenth century further stimulated overseas travel for reasons of prestige. For the first time, visitors abroad could be photographed against a background of the great historical sites of Europe, to the envy of their friends.

The expansion of the railways was accompanied by a simultaneous decline in the stagecoaches. Some survived by providing feeder services to the nearest railway stations, but overall road traffic shrank, and with it the demand for the staging inns. Those situated in the resorts were quick to adapt to meet the needs of the new railway travellers, but the supply of accommodation in centres served by the railways was totally inadequate to meet the burgeoning demand of this new market. A period of hotel construction began, in which the railway companies themselves were leaders, establishing the great railway terminus hotels which came to play such a significant role in the hotel industry over the next hundred years. The high capital investment called for by this development led to the formation of the first hotel chains and corporations.

Social changes in the Victorian era all encouraged travel. The new-found interest in sea-bathing meant that the expanding rail network favoured the developing resorts, accelerating their growth. At the same time, Victorian society placed great emphasis on the role of the family as a social unit, leading to the type of family holidays for which the seaside was so well suited. The foundations of traditional seaside entertainment were soon laid – German bands, 'nigger minstrels' and pierrots, Punch and Judy shows, barrel organs, donkey rides and the seaside pier all became essential components of the seaside holiday. Resorts began to develop different social images, partly as a result of their geographical location: those nearer London or other major centres of population developed a substantial market of day trippers, while others deliberately aimed for a more exclusive clientele. These latter generally tended to be situated further afield, but in some cases their exclusivity arose from the desire of prominent residents to resist the encroachment of the railways for as long as possible. Bournemouth, for example, held out against the extension of the railway from Poole until 1870. Some areas of early promise as holiday resorts were quickly destroyed by the growth of industry – Swansea and Hartlepool, for example, and Southampton, where beaches gave way to the development of docks.

Health continued to play a role in the choice of holiday destinations, but the emphasis gradually switched from the benefits of sea-bathing to those of sea air. Climate became a feature of the resorts' promotion. Sunshine hours were emphasized, or the bracing qualities of the Scarborough air, while the pines at Bournemouth were reputed to help those suffering from lung complaints. Seaside resorts on the Continent also gained in popularity and began to develop their own social images – Scheveningen near the Hague, Ostend, Biarritz and Deauville offered the same magic for British holidaymakers as the Mediterranean resorts were to provide a century later. Some overseas resorts flourished in reaction to middle-class morality in Victorian England; Monte Carlo, with its notorious gambling casino, was a case in point. This desire to escape from one's everyday environment was as symptomatic of nineteenth-century life as it was to become in the middle of the twentieth century. Of course, these destinations on the Continent were to attract only the relatively well off, and the railways produced the service to cater for these high-spend tourists. Trains such as the Blue Train, which entered service between Paris and the Côte d'Azur and Rome in 1883, and the Orient Express of the same year, operating from Paris to the Black Sea, provided unsurpassed levels of luxury for rail travellers on the Continent. Long-distance rail services became possible with the introduction of sleeping cars, invented in the USA by George Pullman in 1864 and introduced into Europe by the French Wagon-Lits company in 1869. These luxury carriages were even operating on the London to Brighton run by 1881.

Other forms of holiday-making, opened up by the advent of the railways on the Continent, arose from the impact of the Romantic Movement of mid-Victorian England. The Rhine and the French Riviera benefited from their new-found romantic appeal, while the invigorating mountain air of Switzerland, combining the promise of better health with opportunities for strenuous outdoor activities, was already drawing tourists from Britain by the 1840s. Mountaineering became a popular pastime for the British in the 1860s, and was later spurred on by the introduction into Switzerland of skiing. The origins of skiing are lost in antiquity, but using skis as a sport is credited to a certain Bjorland Blom, Sheriff of Telemark in Norway, in the 1660s. By the beginning of the 1890s a number of individual British visitors to that country had transported the sport to Switzerland, while Mathias Zdardsky similarly brought skis to his native Austria in 1890. Sir Henry Lunn, the British travel entrepreneur, is credited with the commercialization of winter ski holidays in Switzerland, having organized packages to Chamonix before the end of the nineteenth century. The railways made their own contributions to these developments, but above all they encouraged the desire to travel by removing the hazards of foreign travel that had formerly existed for travellers journeying by road.

Early tourism in North America

Just as tourism was growing within Europe during the nineteenth century, parallel patterns of tourism were developing across the Atlantic. At first, in the early part of the century, the first seaside resorts grew up to cater for tourists from the major North American conurbations within the thirteen States. Fashionable resorts developed at Newport, Rhode Island, Cape May and Atlantic City in New Jersey and along the Massachusetts coast, while more popular resorts closer to New York City, such as those on the coast of New Jersey and on Long Island, catered to the needs of the masses, who could reach these on day trips. Spa resorts were also developing at this time, with Saratoga Springs in upstate New York becoming particularly popular. Others, in resorts such as French Lick, Indiana, White Sulphur Springs in West Virginia (popular with early US presidents), Hot Springs, Arkansas and Glenwood Springs, Colorado, prospered, and these still owe some economic dependence to their attraction as tourism resorts today. Interest in rugged landscapes, especially mountain tourism, ran parallel with this development in Europe, with travellers visiting the mountainous regions of eastern USA by the 1820s. The less adventurous could visit the mountain ranges across

New England. The Catskill Mountains, in upstate New York, were popular, an especial draw being the accommodation at the Mountain House, which flourished from 1824 until the 1930s (an early example of the accommodation and destination being inseparable). A short time later, Niagara Falls became the travellers' target, soon to be popularized by improved accessibility with the development of paved roads and railways. Canadian tourism, meanwhile, was developing to cater to the needs of expanding populations in and around Toronto and Montreal; visits to the St Lawrence Seaway, Niagara Falls and the Maine coast soon became popular. The absence of any border formalities between Canada and the USA, and the common language (at least, for the large part of Canada), facilitated the movement of tourists between the countries, giving holidaymakers the comforting sense of reassurance with the familiar while 'travelling abroad' – a characteristic which continues to enhance travel in North America to this day.

Steamships

Just as the technological developments of the early nineteenth century led to the development of railways on land, so was steam harnessed at sea to drive new generations of ships. Here, necessity was the mother of invention. Increasing trade worldwide, especially with North America, required Britain to develop faster, more reliable forms of communication by sea with the rest of the world. Although, as we have seen, ferry services were operating as early as 1761 between Brighton and Dieppe, the first regular commercial cross-Channel steamship service was introduced in 1821, on the Dover–Calais route. The railway companies were quick to recognize the importance of their links with these cross-Channel ferry operators, and by 1862 they had gained the right to own and operate steamships themselves. Soon after, control over the ferry companies was in the hands of the railways, which rapidly expanded cross-Channel services.

Deep-sea services were introduced on routes to North America and the Far East; the Peninsular and Oriental Steam Navigation Company (later P&O) is credited with the first regular long-distance steamship service, beginning operations to India and the Far East in 1838. This company was soon followed by the Cunard Steamship Company which, with a lucrative mail contract, began regular services to the North American continent in 1840. Britain, by being the first to establish regular deep-sea services of this kind, came to dominate the world's shipping in the second half of the century, although it was soon to be challenged by other leading industrial nations on the popular North American route. This prestigious and highly profitable route prospered not only from mail contracts but also from the huge demand from passengers and freight as trade with the North American continent expanded. Later, the passenger trade would be boosted by the flow of emigrants from Europe (especially Ireland) and a smaller but significant number of American visitors to Europe. Thomas Cook played his part in stimulating the package tour market to North America, taking the first group of tourists in 1866. In 1872, he went on to organize the first round-the-world tour, taking twelve clients for 220 days at a cost of some £200 – more than the average annual salary at the time.

The Suez Canal, opened in 1869, stimulated demand for P&O's services to India and beyond, as Britain's Empire looked eastwards. The global growth of shipping led, in the latter part of the century, to the formation of shipping conferences, which developed cartel-like agreements on fares and conditions applicable to the carriage of traffic. The aim of these agreements was to ensure year-round profitability in an unstable and seasonal market, but the result was to stifle competition by price, and eventually led to excess profits which were to be enjoyed by the shipping companies until the advent of airline competition in the mid-twentieth century.

Other late-nineteenth-century developments

As the Victorian era drew to a close, other social changes came into play. Continued enthusiasm for the healthy outdoor life coincided with the invention of the bicycle, and cycling holidays, aided by promotion from the Cyclists' Touring Club, which was founded in 1878, enjoyed immense popularity. This movement not only paved the way for later interest in outdoor activities on holiday, but also may well have stimulated the appeal of the suntan as a status symbol of health and wealth, in marked contrast to the earlier association in Victorian minds of a fair complexion with gentility and breeding. The bicycle offered for the first time the opportunity for mobile rather than centred holidays, and gave a foretaste of the popularity of motoring holidays in the early years of the following century.

Political stability in the final years of the nineteenth century and opening years of the twentieth also allowed the expansion of travel. Significantly, no conflicts occurred on the European Continent between 1871 and 1914, one of the longest peacetime stretches in history, and a Europe at peace was becoming an attractive place to visit, both for Europeans and for tourists from further afield, like the United States.

As tourism grew in the later years of the century, so the organizers of travel became established institutionally. Thomas Cook and Sir Henry Lunn (who founded Cooperative Educational Tours in 1893, and whose name was retained until very recently in the company Lunn Poly, now renamed Thomson by its TUI owner) are two of the best-known names of the period, but many other well-known companies became established at this time. Dean and Dawson appeared in 1871, the Polytechnic Touring Association (the other half of the Lunn Poly name) in the following year, and Frames Tours in 1881. In the United States, American Express (founded by, among others, Henry Wells and William Fargo of Wells Fargo fame) initiated money orders and traveller's cheques, although the company did not become involved in making holiday arrangements until early in the twentieth century.

Mention has already been made of the impact of photography on nineteenth-century travel. As the century drew to a close, the vogue for photography was accompanied by the cult of the guidebook. No British tourist venturing abroad would neglect to take a guidebook, and a huge variety of these soon became available on the market. Many were superficial and inaccurate, but the most popular and enduring of those published were those of John Murray, whose Hand-books appeared from 1837 onwards, and Karl Baedeker, who introduced his first guidebook (of the Rhine) in 1839. By the end of the century Baedeker had become firmly established as the leading publisher of guidebooks in Europe.

1900–1950 and the origins of mass tourism

In the opening years of the twentieth century, travel continued to expand, encouraged by the gradually increasing wealth, curiosity (inspired to some extent by the introduction in Britain of compulsory education under the Education Act 1870), the outgoing attitudes of the post-Victorian population, and by the steady improvement in transport. Travellers had become safer from disease and physical attack, mainland Europe was relatively stable politically, and documentation for British travellers uncomplicated – since 1860, passports had generally not been required for travel to any European country. The popularity of French Riviera resorts as places for wealthier British visitors to spend the winter is evidenced by the fact that immediately before World War I (1914–18) some 50,000 UK tourists are estimated to have been wintering on the coast.

Disastrous though it was, the Great War proved to be only a brief hiatus in the expansion of travel, although, as we have seen, it led to the widespread introduction of passports for nationals of many countries. The prosperity which soon returned to Europe in the 1920s, coupled with large-scale migration, meant unsurpassed demand for travel across the Atlantic, as well as within Europe. The first-hand experience of foreign countries by combatants during the war aroused a sense of curiosity about foreign travel generally among less well-off sectors of the community for the first time. These sectors were also influenced by the new forms of mass communication which developed after the war – the cinema, radio and ultimately television, all of which educated the population and encouraged an interest in seeing more of the world.

Forms of travel also began to change radically after the war. The railways went into a period of steady decline, following the introduction of the motor car. Motorized public road transport and improved roads led to the era of the charabanc – at first, adapted from army surplus lorries and equipped with benches to provide a rudimentary form of coach. These vehicles achieved immense popularity in the 1920s for outings to the seaside, but their poor safety record soon resulted in licensing regulations governing road transport. For those who could afford superior public transportation, more luxurious coaches also made an appearance. The coach company Motorways offered Pullman coaches, generally accommodating fifteen people in comfortable armchairs with tables, buffet bars and toilets. These coaches operated to many parts of Europe and North Africa, were used on safaris in East and Central Africa, and even provided a twice weekly service between London and Nice, taking a relaxing five to six days for the trip.

However, it was the freedom of independent travel offered by the private motor car which contributed most to the decline of the railways' monopoly on holiday transport. The extensive use of the motor car for holidaying has its origins in the United States, where, in 1908, Henry Ford introduced his popular Model T at a price which brought the motor car within reach of the masses. By the 1920s, private motoring was a popular pastime for the middle classes in the United States, and soon, camping and caravanning followed. Caravans, or trailers in American terminology, arrived by the 1930s; over 100,000 owners were taking them on holiday in the first year of that decade[9]. Equally, by the 1930s private motoring had arrived on a large scale in Britain, and the threat to domestic rail services was clear, although Continental rail services survived and prospered until challenged by the coming of the airlines. In an effort to stem the decline, domestic rail services in Britain were first rationalized in 1923 into four major companies – the London, Midland and Scottish Railway (LMS), the London and North Eastern Railway (LNER), the Great Western Railway (GWR) and the Southern Railway (SR) – and later nationalized following World War II, remaining under public control until again privatized in the mid-1990s.

While long voyages by sea were popular as means of leisure travel, the concept of cruising caught on only slowly. Among early examples of ship voyages treated essentially as a cruise, the Matson Line services between the US West Coast and Hawaii were to open up those islands to tourism. The Royal Hawaiian Hotel, built to accommodate visitors in the 1920s to those then exotic islands, was one of the first to offer what we today know as 'all-inclusive' holidays, although hotels along the French Riviera and in Switzerland were to follow suit. Hawaii was to remain an up-market destination until mass package tours arrived with air services in the 1950s.

The era of the Great Depression

The 1930s are generally thought of as a period when the economic collapse in the Western world was similarly accompanied by the collapse of the international tourist market. While it is true that travel was severely curtailed, the Depression hit Europe rather later than the USA, and in the early 1930s there remained a substantial market of those with sufficient wealth to travel. However, in Britain government-imposed limits on foreign exchange for travel abroad proved a severe constraint. The ever-resilient travel industry reacted with typical enterprise. The formation of the Creative Tourist Agents' Conference (CTAC) in the early 1930s brought together the leading travel agents (who were by this time also tour operators), including Thomas Cook, Dean and Dawson, Hickie Borman and Grant, Frames, Sir Henry Lunn, Pickfords, Wayfarers' Touring Agency, the Workers' Travel Association and the Polytechnic Touring Association (PTA). These formed what amounted to a cartel to hold down and fix prices for foreign excursions. The PTA was instrumental in persuading the Continental railways to discount their fares for bulk purchases – a move the railways had always resisted in the past. Soon, special rail charters were being organized to Germany, Italy, the Riviera and Spain, and by 1938 the PTA were operating their own regular train charters to Switzerland, then one of the most popular destinations on the Continent. This agency also packaged one of the first air charters, approaching Imperial Airways (who were in financial difficulties) in the opening years of the decade to charter a Heracles to carry 24 passengers from Croydon Airport to Basle, Switzerland and Paris[10]. By 1932 the company was carrying nearly 1,000 passengers by air to the Continent, mainly then as a means of avoiding foreign currency payments to rail and bus companies abroad, and the following year it organized a 14-day air cruise to seven European capitals. Doubtless these air charters would have been continued, but the partial recovery of Imperial Airways' financial situation led the carrier to withdraw charter privileges, ending these first entrepreneurial modern package tours – and making the point that tour operators of the future would have to avoid dependence on suppliers over whom they had no control, a lesson that the first large-scale operators were quick to learn.

Cruising remained a popular holiday for those who could afford it. The formation of the Soviet Union after World War I had led that country to build up a strong fleet of cruise vessels, and these carried some 5,000 tourists from Britain to Russia in 1932, curious to learn about the country and its new political system. By 1938, it was claimed as many as one million holidaymakers were cruising on 139 cruise ships[11].

The growth of the airline industry

The arrival of the airline industry signalled the beginning of the end, not only for long-distance rail services but, more decisively, for the great steamship companies. British shipping lines had been under increasing threat from foreign competition throughout the 1920s, with French, German and US liners challenging British supremacy on the North Atlantic routes particularly. The first commercial air routes were initiated – by Air Transport & Travel, the forerunner of British Airways – as early as 1919, from Hounslow Airport, London, to Paris. The infant air services were expensive (nearly £16, equivalent to several weeks' average earnings) and uncertain (passengers were warned that forced landings and delays could occur). Consequently, initial growth in air services was limited to short-haul flights, over land. It was many years before air services achieved the reliability and low price which would make them competitive with world shipping routes. Pan American Airways introduced transatlantic air services in the 1930s (initially using flying boats), but in addition to their expense the aircraft proved unreliable and uncomfortable by modern standards, and long-distance journeys necessitated frequent stopovers. In the early years, commercial aviation was more important for its mail-carrying potential than for the carriage of passengers. Only with the technological breakthroughs in aircraft design achieved during and after World War II did air services prove a viable alternative to shipping for intercontinental travel. As for air package holidays, although the PTA reintroduced limited air charters in 1947, the holiday market would have to wait until the 1950s before this form of transport came into its own.

The arrival of the holiday camp

Among the major tourism developments of the 1930s, the creation of the holiday camp deserves a special mention. Aimed at the growing low-income market for holidays, the camps set new standards of comfort, offering 24-hour entertainment at an all-inclusive price; they were efficiently operated, with the added benefit of child-minding services – a huge bonus for young couples on holiday with their children. This was in marked contrast to the lack of planned activities and the often surly service offered by the traditional seaside boarding houses of the day.

The origin of these camps goes back to early experiments by organizations in Britain like the Co-operative Holidays Association, the Workers' Travel Association and the Holiday Fellowship (although summer camps for boys such as that run by Joseph Cunningham on the Isle of Man have been dated as early as 1887). In the USA, summer camps for children were already a strong institution by the early twentieth century. However, their popularity and widespread acceptance by the adult public have commonly been ascribed to the efforts and promotional flair of Billy (later Sir Billy) Butlin. Supposedly, Butlin, who built his first camp at Skegness in 1936, met a group

Figure 2.3
The early days of the holiday camp: Butlin's luxury holiday camp at Clacton-on-Sea, 1940s

(Courtesy: Butlins)

of disconsolate holidaymakers huddled in a bus shelter to avoid the rain on a wet summer afternoon (although it is thought he was also influenced by a visit to Trusville Holiday Village in Mablethorpe, Lincolnshire, which had been opened and operated successfully by Albert Henshaw since 1924). Butlin determined to build a camp with all-weather facilities, for an all-in price. The instant success of the concept led to a spate of similar camps built by Butlin and other entrepreneurs such as Harry Warner and Fred Pontin in the pre-war and early post-war years. On the Continent, pre-war Germany had introduced the concept of the highly organized and often militaristic health and recreation camp which enabled many to enjoy holidays, who would otherwise have been unable to afford them.

In France, the *villages de vacance* arose from similar political and social influences. The success of this concept of all-in entertainment was later to be copied by hotels – and we have already noted that the all-inclusive hotel with its own leisure complex had originated in the United States even earlier. Between the two World Wars (and into the 1960s), Grossingers resort hotel in the Catskills flourished as a popular all-inclusive destination in its own right, targeting principally the New York Jewish market.

Interest in outdoor holidays and healthy recreation was also stimulated by the Youth Hostels Association in 1929 (the French equivalent opened in the same year), which provided budget accommodation for young people away from home.

Figure 2.4
Swallow Falls,
Betws-y-Coed,
North Wales
have been
a popular
attraction since
the nineteenth
century, for
visitors travelling
by both rail
and road

(Photographed by the author)

The popular movement to the seaside

In spite of the rising appeal of holidays abroad to those who could afford them, mass tourism between the wars and in the early post-World War II era remained largely domestic. This period saw the seaside holiday become firmly established as the traditional annual holiday destination for the mass of the British public. Suntans were for the first time seen as a status symbol, allied to health and time for leisure. Blackpool, Scarborough, Southend and Brighton consolidated their positions as leading resorts, while numerous newer resorts – Bournemouth, Broadstairs, Clacton, Skegness, Colwyn Bay – grew rapidly in terms of both visitors and residential population. Until the Great Depression of the 1930s, hotels and guesthouses proliferated in these resorts. The tradition of the family holiday, taken annually over two weeks in the summer, became firmly established in Britain at this time.

The growing threat of competition from the European mainland was already apparent, for those who chose to take note of it. From the 1920s onwards, the Mediterranean Riviera had begun to attract a summer, as well as a winter, market from the UK, while the resorts of northern France were seen as cheaper and began to offer competition for the popular south coast resorts of Brighton, Hove, Folkestone and Eastbourne. These nearby French resorts, however, were seen primarily as places for short summer holidays, rather than the longer winter stays which had been popular with a wealthy British clientele in the nineteenth century.

The growth of public involvement

It was in this period that Britain experienced the first stirrings of government interest in the tourism business. Britain was well behind other European countries in this respect; Switzerland, for example, had long recognized the importance of its inbound tourism and was actively involved in both tourism promotion overseas and gathering statistics on its visitors.

The British Travel and Holidays Association was established by the government in 1929, but with the theme 'travel for peace', its role was seen as essentially promotional, and its impact on the industry relatively light, until a change in status some forty years later. By the outbreak of World War II in 1939, the British government had at least recognized the potential contribution tourism could make to the country's balance of payments; equally, it had recognized the importance of holidays to the health and efficiency of the nation's workforce. The French government had already introduced holidays with pay in 1936; publication of the Amulree Report in 1938 led to the first Holidays with Pay Act for Britain in the same year. This encouraged voluntary agreements on paid holidays and generated the idea of a two-week paid holiday for all workers. Although this ambition was not fulfilled until several years after the end of World War II, by the outbreak of war some 11 million of the 19 million workforce were entitled to paid holidays – a key factor in generating mass travel.

In this chapter we have seen how social and, in particular, technological change had begun to make mass travel feasible. In Chapter 3 we will see how contemporary mass tourism developed, with further advances in technology and, above all, improved standards of living throughout the developed world.

Notes

1 Casson, L, *Travel in the Ancient World*, George Allen and Unwin, 1974, p 32
2 Leed, E J, *The Mind of the Traveller: From Gilgamesh to Global Tourism*, Basic Books, 1991
3 Casson, L, *op cit*, p 21
4 McIntosh, R W and Goeldner, C R, *Tourism Principles, Practices, Philosophies*, Wiley, 4th edn 1984
5 Lloyd, M, *The Passport: the History of Man's Most Travelled Document*, Sutton Publishing, 2003
6 Footbinding Protest Badge, *The Times*, 4 August 2004
7 Lloyd, M, *op cit*, p 25
8 Lloyd, M, *op cit*, p 10
9 Löfgren, O, *On Holiday: a History of Vacationing*, Berkeley, University of California Press, 1999, p 37
10 Studd, R G, *The Holiday Story*, Percival Marshall, 1950, pp 145, 196/7
11 Ibid, p 146

Further reading

Brodie, A, Sargent, A and Winterby, G, *Seaside Holidays in the Past*, English Heritage, 2005
Burke, T, *Travel in England: From Pilgrim and Packhorse to Light Car and Plane*, Batsford, 1942
Feifer, M, *Going Places: the Ways of the Tourist from Imperial Rome to the Present Day*, Macmillan, 1985
Hern, A, *The Seaside Holiday: the History of the English Seaside Resort*, Cresset Press, 1967
Perrottet T, *Route 66 AD: Pagan Holiday on the Trail of Ancient Roman Tourists*, Random House, 2003
Pimlott, J A R, *The Englishman's Holiday: a Social History*, Harvester Press, 1947
Swinglehurst, E, *Cook's Tours: the Story of Popular Travel*, Blandford Press, 1982
Ward, C and Hardy, D, *Goodnight Campers! The History of the British Holiday Camp*, Mansell Publishing, 1986

Websites

The History of the British Seaside Holiday   www.seasidehistory.co.uk

Questions and discussion points

1   The horse was the principal means of transport on land during the Middle Ages and until the nineteenth century. Horses still play a role in tourism today – for example, horse-drawn traditional gypsy caravans can be hired out to tourists in Ireland for holidays. What other examples can you find of the use of horses in tourism today, and how important are they in terms of revenue creation? What other beasts of burden perform similar roles in Britain, and in other countries?

2   George Washington visited Natural Bridge in Virginia, and carved his initials deeply into the archway of this natural wonder. The initials are now carefully preserved. How old must graffiti be – or how historically significant – before it becomes acceptable for preservation? Should old graffiti be removed (where feasible) from historical monuments, ignored, or brought to visitors' attention as an interesting feature?

3   We have seen in this chapter that a common language and currency greatly facilitated travel 2,000 years ago. To what extent is this comparable with the wide knowledge of the English language, and a common currency, the euro, in use in many European Union countries, today? Does this point to clear advantages if Britain were to adopt the euro, or are there potential (tourism-related) disadvantages to this action?

4   What comparisons can be made between length of travel time relative to distance travelled between travellers in the nineteenth century and in the twenty-first century?

5   What evidence is there for a renewed interest in cultural travel reminiscent of the European grand tours (apart from compressed time) in present day international travel? What analogies can be made between the nineteenth century Grand Tour and cultural tours of the twenty-first century?

Assignment topics

1   In the early twentieth century, it was considered unfashionable to cultivate a suntan. Today, in spite of health warnings, it remains unfashionable to be white, and to deliberately refrain from tanning when on a beach holiday.

Undertake some research, using a questionnaire, among the population where you live or study to determine attitudes towards the suntan, awareness of the dangers of skin cancer resulting from sun worship, and the extent to which holidaymakers are responding to the warnings disseminated widely by the medical profession, magazines and other media.

Categorize your results according to age, gender, social class or other variables, and produce a short report summarizing your conclusions.

2   Prepare notes for a short talk to be given at a meeting of an all-women's organization (such as the Women's Institute) in your region, summarizing the key issues which have led to the growth of tourism since the early nineteenth century.

Undertake some research into the role of women travellers and explorers over this period, and, following your talk, be prepared to discuss with your audience how far these women have helped others to overcome their fear of travel and encourage tourism in the past 200 years.

3 The era of popular tourism: 1950 to the twenty-first century

Objectives

After studying this chapter, you should be able to:

- describe the factors giving rise to mass tourism after 1950
- explain the origins and development of the package holiday
- understand the significance of rapid change in political, social and economic circumstances giving rise to the current uncertainties facing the tourism industry.

Tourism since World War II

Those who wish to see Spain while it is worth seeing must go soon.

Rev Henry Christmas, The Shores and Islands of the Mediterranean; including a visit to the Seven Churches of Asia, (1851) quoted in Löfgren, O, pp 184–5

In the aftermath of World War II, the long and deprived war years led to an increased desire to travel to foreign destinations, although the ability to do so was limited for many, restricted by both political barriers and inadequate finance. In Britain, as in other lands in Europe, there were also strict limits to the availability of foreign currency, a major barrier to cross-border travel. Nevertheless, the war had given rise to a curiosity among many British travellers to witness the sites of battles such as those fought on the Normandy beaches and at St Nazaire, while North Americans and Japanese alike felt similarly drawn to sites of conflict in the Pacific like Iwo Jima and Guadalcanal – although it was to take some 40 years or more before interest in these historic military sites was to approach the level of those of World War I. Interest was also limited to the sites of battle on the Western Front in Europe; the horrors of warfare on the eastern front were such that neither side showed much inclination to visit the former battlefields, many of which were, in any case, banned to visitors until after the fall of the Soviet Government. The extensive theatre of war had introduced the many combatants not only to new countries but also to new continents, generating new friendships and an interest in diverse cultures. Another outcome of the war, which was radically to change the travel business, was the advance in aircraft technology which was soon to lead to a viable commercial aviation industry for the first time. With the ending of the war in 1945, the first land-based commercial transatlantic flight took place between New York and Bournemouth, calling at Boston, Gander and Shannon. This flight, operated by American Overseas Airlines using a Douglas DC4, served to point the way ahead, although cost and the time involved, necessitated by the frequent stops, ensured that long-haul flights would not become popular until the advent of the jet age.

The surplus of aircraft in the immediate post-war years, a benevolent political attitude towards the growth of private-sector airlines, and the appearance on the scene of air travel entrepreneurs like Harold Bamberg (of Eagle Airways) and Freddie Laker aided the rapid expansion of air travel after the war. But more significantly for the potential market, aircraft had become more comfortable, safer, faster and, in spite of relatively high prices in the early 1950s, steadily cheaper by comparison with other forms of transport. The war had seen many new airports built in Europe to serve the military, and these were later adapted for civilian use. This was to prove particularly valuable in opening up islands in the Mediterranean that were formerly inaccessible or time-consuming to reach by sea. Commercial jet services began with the ill-fated Comet aircraft in the early 1950s (withdrawn from service after crashes resulting from metal fatigue), but advances in piston-engine technology were already beginning to impact on price. With the introduction of the commercially successful Boeing 707 jet in 1958, the age of air travel for the masses had arrived, hastening the demise of the great ocean liners. The number of passengers crossing the Atlantic by air exceeded those by sea for the first time in 1957, and although the liners continued to operate across the Atlantic for a further decade, their increasingly uncompetitive costs, high fares (saddled by conference agreements on routes across the Atlantic and Pacific which banned discounting), and the length of the journey time resulted in declining load factors from one year to the next. The new jets, with average speeds of 800–1,000 kph, compared with older propeller-driven aircraft travelling at a mere 400 kph, meant that an air traveller could reach a far more distant destination within a given time (the key New York to London route fell from 18 hours in 1949 to just 7 hours in 1969). This was particularly valuable for business journeys where time was crucial.

The early 1970s saw the arrival of the first supersonic passenger aircraft, the Anglo-French Concorde. Never truly a commercial success (the governments wrote off the huge development costs), it nevertheless proved popular with business travellers and the wealthy. Travelling from London or Paris to New York in three and a half hours, it allowed business people for the first time to complete their business on the other side of the Atlantic and return home without incurring a hotel stopover. The limited range and carrying capacity (just over 100 passengers) of the aircraft, and restrictions against sonic booms over land, acted as severe constraints on operable routes, and the fatal crash near Paris of a chartered Concorde in 2000 sealed the aircraft's fate, leading to its withdrawal from service. It is thought unlikely that any further supersonic aircraft development will take place within the next twenty years.

The development of the package tour

Inclusive tours by coach soon regained their former appeal after the war. The Italian Riviera was popular at first, French resorts proving too expensive, and resorts like Rimini became affordable for the North European middle market. The inclusive tour by air, or package tour as it has become known, was soon to follow. Cheap packages by air depend upon the ability of tour operators to charter aircraft for their clientele, and to buy hotel beds in bulk, driving down costs and allowing prices to be cut. Initially, UK government transport policy had restricted air charters to the movement of troops, but as official policy became more lenient, the private operators sought to develop new forms of charter traffic. Package holidays were the outcome, as the smaller air carriers and entrepreneurs learned to cooperate. In the late 1950s the larger airlines began to purchase the new jets, allowing smaller companies to buy the stock of second-hand propeller-driven aircraft coming on to the market, which were then put into service for charter operations. For the first time, holiday tourists could be transported to Mediterranean destinations faster than, and almost as cheaply as, trains and coaches. These new charter services soon proved highly profitable. Meanwhile, across the Atlantic, the first stirrings of an air package holiday industry emerged as regional operators began chartering aircraft from so-called 'supplemental' carriers, on routes between major cities in the USA and Canada and the Caribbean Islands.

Although there are instances of charter flights as early as the 1920s (Thomas Cook, for example, had organized an escorted charter, believed to be the first, to take fans from New York to Chicago in 1927 to see the Dempsey–Tunney heavyweight title fight), and the National Union of Students is known to have been organizing charter flights for its members as early as 1949, Vladimir Raitz is generally credited with founding the mass inclusive tour business using air charters, as we know it today. In 1950, under the Horizon Holidays banner, he organized an experimental package holiday trip using a charter flight to Corsica. By chartering the aircraft and filling every seat instead of committing himself to a block of seats on scheduled air services, he was able to reduce significantly the unit cost of his air transport and hence the overall price to his customers. He carried only 300 passengers in the first year, but repeated the experiment the following year and was soon operating profitably. Other budding tour operators, both in Britain and on the Continent, were soon copying his ideas (Club Méditerranée being among the best-known of the early entrepreneurs), and by the early 1960s the package holiday to the Mediterranean had become an established product for the mass holiday market.

The Spanish coastline and the Balearic Islands were the first to benefit from the new influx of mass tourism from Britain, Germany and the Scandinavian countries, carried by the workhorse Douglas DC-3 aircraft. First, the Costa del Sol, then other coasts along the eastern seaboard, the islands of Majorca, Ibiza and, finally by the 1970s, the Canaries became in turn the destination for millions. By 1960, Spain was already welcoming 6 million tourists every year, and this was to grow to 30 million by 1975. Italy, Greece and other Mediterranean coastal regions all benefited from the 'rush to the sun'; Greece in particular, although slower to develop than Spain, provided a cheaper alternative as prices in the latter country rose; only 50,000 visited in 1951, but a decade later this had grown to 500,000, and by 1981 Greece was vying with

Spain, welcoming 3,500,000). The Nordic countries were also soon setting up their own package holiday arrangements to the Mediterranean, and began to compete with Britain and their southern counterparts for accommodation along the Mediterranean coast. In Denmark, Pastor Eilif Krogager conducted a group of package tourists by coach to Spain in 1950, using the name of his village, Tjaereborg, as the company name. In 1962, Tjaereborg Travel moved into the air charter market with the formation of Sterling Airways, which soon became Western Europe's largest privately owned charter airline of the period.

In Britain, difficulties in the economy forced the government to impose ever tighter control over foreign exchange. By the late 1960s the foreign currency (V-form) allowance for travel abroad had been cut to only £50 per person, although for business travellers, additional funds (under T-form regulations) were permitted. There was, however, a silver lining to this particular cloud: it encouraged people to take package holidays rather than travel independently, and the industry continued to flourish. Air transport costs were payable in sterling, and as only the foreign currency element of the tour – the *net* costs of accommodation and transfers – had to be paid out of the allowance, the benefits of dealing with an operator became clear. The limits were relaxed from 1970 onwards, and with further liberalization of air transport regulations, and longer paid holidays, which encouraged a growing number of tourists to take a second holiday abroad each year, a new winter holiday market emerged in the 1970s. With a more even spread of package holidays throughout the year, operators found that they were able to reduce their unit costs still further, and package holiday prices continued to fall, boosting off-season demand. Britain was not alone within Europe in

Figure 3.1
A wide-bodied
jumbo jet

Source: The Flight Collection/Alamy

Figure 3.2
The linear tour:
an example of
the 'milk run'
around Britain

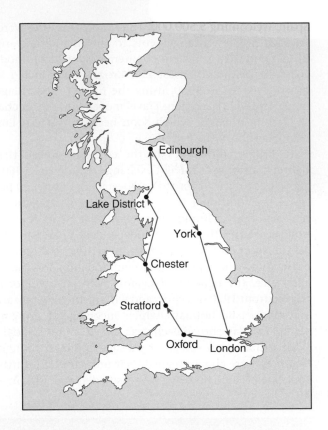

imposing currency restrictions during these early post-war years; indeed, exchange controls were not totally abolished in France until as recently as 1990.

A further technological breakthrough in air transport occurred in 1970, when the first wide-bodied jets (Boeing 747s), capable of carrying over 400 passengers, appeared in service (Figure 3.1). The unit cost per seat fell sharply, and the result was an increased supply of seats at potentially cheaper fares. This innovation meant that once again the aviation industry had to unload cheaply a number of obsolescent, although completely air-worthy, smaller aircraft, and these were quickly pressed into service for charter operations.

The innovation coincided with a steady increase in demand by North American visitors to Europe for basic tours of Britain and the Continent, hitting as many 'high spots' as possible in a ten to fourteen day visit. This gave rise to the concept of the 'milk run', a popular route which would embrace the top attractions in one or more countries in a limited time-scale for the first time visitor (see Figure 3.2).

The movement to the sun

By the 1960s, it was clear that the future of mass market leisure travel was to be a north–south movement, from the cool and variable climates of North America and northern Europe, where the mass of relatively well-off people lived, to the sunshine

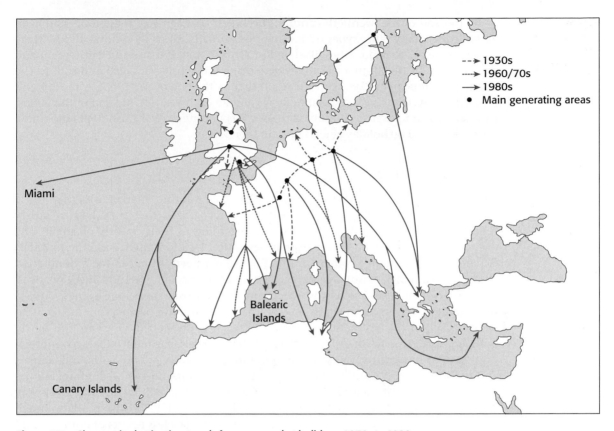

Figure 3.3 Changes in destination trends for mass-market holidays, 1930s to 1980s

and warmth of the temperate to tropical lands in the southern part of the northern hemisphere (see Figure 3.3). These southern countries were also for the most part less developed economically, and offered low-cost opportunities for the formation of a tourism industry. The new breed of tourism entrepreneurs involved with packaging tours recognized this trend very early on. Major hotel corporations, too, were quick to seize the opportunities for growth in these countries, and chains such as Sheraton and Hyatt in the USA quickly expanded into Mexico and the Caribbean, as well as into Florida and Hawaii, the states offering the most attractive climates for tourism development. Hawaii in particular proved popular as an 'overseas' destination, following its incorporation into the USA; from 100,000 visitors in 1955, the flow of tourists increased to 2 million in 1970 (and 6.5 million by 1990). In Europe, British and German tour operators such as Thomson and TUI developed bulk inclusive tours to the Mediterranean and North Africa, and with increasing volume were able to charter jumbo jets for the first time, bringing prices still lower. As transport costs fell, operators were also able to attract a mass market for long-haul travel on chartered jumbo jets. Florida, boosted particularly by the attractions of Disney World and Miami Beach, has become almost as popular a destination for Europeans as the major Mediterranean destinations.

By the end of the twentieth century, the expert packaging of these tours had been extended to many other types of destinations. Initially, tours to cultural and heritage sites, city breaks to major cities like London, Paris, Rome, Brussels and Amsterdam and river cruises on the Rhine or Danube were being efficiently packaged and sold to the northern European market, with the result that by the end of the 1960s, some 2.5 million Britons were taking packaged holidays abroad each year. By the end of the 1980s, this had grown to over 11 million, with over 70 per cent of the British population having been abroad on holiday at least once in their lives.

Identikit destinations

One important result of the growth of the mass tourism market was that those responsible for marketing tourist destinations recognized that they had to satisfy tourists sharing broadly similar aspirations, regardless of their country of origin. The destinations accepted that, apart from geographical location, there was little to differentiate one resort from another, and that consumer needs were centred around good climate and beaches, reasonable standards of food and accommodation and low prices. Consumers themselves cared little which country they were in, as long as these criteria were fulfilled. The larger the mass market, the less distinctive destinations are likely to be, especially if the destination is small and recently developed. One can find newly built 'marina' type resorts with yachting basins, hotel/apartment/villa accommodation, similar restaurants, cafes and shops, and golf, tennis, water sports, folk singers and barbecue nights in any one of a dozen countries around the Mediterranean, the Caribbean, North Africa and the South Pacific. Vernacular architecture has given way to the standard monobloc development typical of all beach resorts from Miami Beach to Australia's Gold Coast, by way of Benidorm and the faceless resorts of Rumania and Bulgaria (including the optimistically named 'Golden Sands' and 'Sunny Beach').

This is also true even where business travellers attending conferences abroad are concerned. A convention centre, for example, is today likely to be a multi-purpose venue, containing facilities for conferences and committee/lecture rooms, and including modern single or twin bedded hotel rooms with private facilities, restaurants with banqueting rooms, bars, exhibition space, a leisure centre with pool, indoor and outdoor sports facilities and good scheduled transport links. The location may be Birmingham, Barcelona or Brisbane – once inside their hotel or conference centre, delegates may not even notice where they are. Indeed, one can find ubiquitous furniture of identical design (e.g. *faux Regency* chairs spray-painted in gold) in conference centres and hotels throughout the world. The term *identikit destination* will be used to define and identify this form of resort. Each has emerged following comprehensive market research among various generating markets to find products with guaranteed mass demand. They may be contrasted with the piecemeal development of resorts two or three generations ago whose attractions may have been developed with very different aims and markets in mind.

This is not to say that all identikit destinations are chasing identical markets. Many may be 'down-market' in their attractiveness – that is, they may offer cheap tourism to a large number of people, with the image of great popularity – while others may offer a more up-market, but nonetheless uniform, image, offering the perception of higher

Figure 3.4
The ultimate 'identikit' mass tourist destination: high-rise apartment blocks and hotels spring up along Miami Beach, Florida

(Photographed by the author)

quality, and thus more expensive services, to fewer visitors. In the former category we may think of Benidorm, Magaluf, Benitses in the Mediterranean, Miami Beach in Florida, or Seefeld in Austria, while in the latter category we may think of Tahiti, Fiji, Malindi in Kenya, or Barbados. Many identikit destinations have been developed through the activities of multinational tour companies such as the all-inclusive resorts run by Sandals in the Caribbean, France's Club Méditerranée, Germany's Robinson Club or the United States' Sheraton Hotel chain. Within their establishments the mass tourist will find a comforting degree of uniformity.

Mass tourism has therefore demanded, and been supplied with, products designed specifically for its needs as revealed through the process of market research, that is, products which are *user-oriented* as opposed to *resource-oriented* (that is, based on the resources available at a destination).

However, many of these identikit destinations are now finding themselves at a disadvantage as the world tourism market becomes more sophisticated. Research by the former English Tourism Council revealed that one of the weaknesses of many English seaside resorts has been their failure to project a unique image. Those that have succeeded, notably Blackpool and a handful of other major or minor resorts, have done so through a combination of significant investment and differentiation from other, often similar, resorts. Those resorts unable to make the investment needed to change their image are faced with the prospect of decline, or have to appeal to newer, generally lower-spend markets. The later years of the last century found several of the formerly popular Mediterranean resorts attracting new tourists from the central European countries to replace the gradual decline in Western European visitors. One saving grace for those identikit destinations which developed around the core of an established town has been the ability to retain and improve the original 'old town', which is now promoted as a core attraction in its own right.

Private motoring and holidays

After a slow post-war recovery, standards of living rose steadily in the 1950s and after. Many people could contemplate buying their first motor car, even if it were second-hand. For the first time, the holiday masses had the freedom to take to the roads as a family in their own private car, and in Britain the popular routes between London and the resorts on the south coast were soon clogged, in these pre-motorway days, with weekend traffic.

The flexibility which the car offered could not be matched by public transport services, and both bus and rail lost the holiday traveller. In 1950 some two out of every three holidaymakers took the train for their holidays in Britain; this fell to one in seven by 1970. In this period, private car ownership in Britain rose from 2 million to over 11 million vehicles, while by the end of the 1980s it had risen to some 20 million.

This trend led in turn to a growth in camping and caravanning holidays. Ownership of private caravans stood at nearly 800,000 by the end of the 1980s (excluding static caravans in parks), while 13 million holidaymakers in the UK took their holidays in a caravan. This development was a cause for some concern, however; the benefits to a region of private caravan tourism are considerably less than most other forms of tourism (owners can bring most of their own food with them, and do not require accommodation), and caravans tend to clog the holiday routes in summer. Both mobile caravans and static caravans on site are perceived as something of an eyesore too.

The switch to private transport led to new forms of accommodation to cater for this form of travel. Britain saw the development of its first motels, modelled on the American pattern, the contemporary version of the staging inn catering for transit passengers. The construction of a new network of motorways, and other road improvements, brought the more distant resorts closer to centres of population, in some cases changing both the nature of the market served and the image of the resort itself. The ever resourceful tour operators met the private car threat to package holidays by devising more flexible packages like fly–drive programmes, with the provision of a hire car at the airport on arrival. Hotels, too, spurred on by the need to fill their rooms off-peak, devised their own programmes of short-stay holidays tailored to the needs of the private motorist. Demand for car rental abroad rose sharply, as the overseas holidaymaker was emboldened to move away from the hotel ghettos, and car rental businesses in popular areas profited accordingly.

The shipping business in the post-war period

By contrast with other elements of the travel business, passenger-shipping companies, hit by rising prices and competition from the airlines, were struggling to survive. Forced to abandon their traditional liner routes by the 1960s, some attempted to adapt their vessels for cruising. In this, they were far from successful; vessels purpose-built for long-distance, fast, deep-sea voyages are not ideally suited for cruising, either economically or from the standpoint of customer demand. Many were incapable of anchoring alongside docks in the shallow waters of popular cruise destinations such as the Caribbean islands. Companies that failed to embark on a programme of new construction, either due to lack of resources or lack of foresight, soon ceased trading. Others, such as the Cunard Line, were taken over by conglomerates outside the travel or transport industries. American cruise lines, beset by high labour costs and strong unions, virtually ceased to exist. However, many new purpose-built cruise liners, of Greek, Norwegian and later Russian registry soon appeared on the market to fill the gaps left by the declining maritime powers. These vessels, despite their registry, were based primarily in Caribbean or Mediterranean waters. British shipping was not entirely without innovations at this time, however; Cunard initiated the fly–cruise concept in the 1960s, with vessels based at Gibraltar and Naples, where passengers flew out to join their cruise in chartered aircraft.

The rapid escalation of fuel and other costs during the 1970s threatened the whole future of deep-sea shipping, but, although declared dead by the pundits, this sector refused to lie down. Gradual stabilization of oil prices and control of labour costs (largely by recruiting from Third World countries) enabled the cruise business to stage a comeback in the 1980s and 90s, led by entrepreneurial shipping lines like Carnival Cruise Line, the American operator which set out to put the fun back into cruising. More informality, to appeal to more youthful family markets, helped to turn the business round so that by the end of the twentieth century cruising had again become a major growth sector. Carnival absorbed many of the traditional carriers, including British companies Cunard and P&O, and had the financial backing necessary to make substantial investment in new vessels. Chapter 13 will reveal the current healthy status of the passenger-shipping world.

By contrast with the cruise business, ferry services achieved quite exceptional levels of growth between the 1950s to the end of the century. This largely resulted from the increased demand from private motorists taking their cars abroad, influencing particularly routes between Scandinavian countries and Germany, and between Britain and Continental Europe. Growth in demand was also better spread across the seasons, enabling vessels to remain in service throughout the year with respectable load factors (although freight demand substantially boosted weak passenger revenue in the winter period). Regular sailings, with fast turnarounds in port, encouraged bookings, and costs were kept down by offering much more restricted levels of service than would be expected on long-distance routes. Hovercraft and jetfoil services were introduced across the Channel, although their success was limited by technical problems and their limitations in severe weather. Reliable fast ferry services did not appear until the advent of the catamarans in the 1990s.

Government policy in the mass-market era

In Britain, the end of the 1960s was marked by a new direction in government policy towards tourism, with the introduction of the 1969 Development of Tourism Act. This Act, the first in the country specifically and uniquely devoted to tourism, established a new framework for public-sector tourism, which took into account the industry's growing importance to the British economy. For the first time, also, conservation became an issue, as the number of foreign visitors to Britain leapt. The former laissez-faire attitude of successive governments gave way to recognition of the need for adequate planning and control in order to balance supply and demand, to maintain the quality of the tourist product, and to safeguard consumers' rights. Thus, the government introduced licensing for tour operators for the first time in the 1970s, and government incentives were introduced for the construction of hotels and other tourist facilities. The first serious efforts were made to categorize and register the accommodation sector, although resistance by hoteliers eventually led to a voluntary form of registration only. The failures of public-sector planning and control in other countries (notably Spain), where exceptionally high growth rates in visitors were recorded, added fuel to the government's concern.

By the 1980s, the Conservative government (and later the Labour government, when it returned to power in 1997) revealed changing attitudes to tourism, offering passive encouragement rather than active financial support. Grants provided under the terms of the 1969 Act were discontinued in England (although limited grants remained available in Wales and Scotland), and policy became one of encouraging partnerships between the private and public sectors. Responsibility for tourism was subject to frequent transfers between the Department of Trade and Industry, the Department of Employment, and finally the newly created Department of National Heritage, whose name was changed in 1997 to the Department for Culture, Media and Sport (within which a Minister for Film and Tourism reports to the Secretary of State). Some efforts were made to coordinate the various government departments' interests in tourism through the establishment of committees such as the Inter-Departmental Tourism Coordinating Committee. On the whole, however, the government adopted a 'market forces' and hands-off approach to tourism development, and regulation became increasingly the prerogative of the European Union (EU) after the 1980s. The EU responded through the introduction of a number of measures designed to liberalize air and road transport, to harmonize hotel classification, to ease frontier controls and to harmonize sales tax and duty-free regulations throughout the region. Most importantly, from the standpoint of the consumer, however, there were measures aimed at providing greater protection for the traveller buying package holidays. These measures will be discussed at greater length in Chapter 15.

By the early years of the twenty-first century, a number of crises had hit global tourism, necessitating some government intervention to rescue the industry. These will be outlined in the closing section of this chapter.

The growing importance of business travel

The growth in world trade in these decades saw a steady expansion in business travel, individually and in the conference and incentive travel fields, although recession in the latter part of the century caused cutbacks in business travel as sharp as those in leisure travel. As economic power shifted between countries, so emerging nations provided new patterns of tourism generation: in the 1970s, Japan and the oil-rich nations of the Middle East led the growth, while in the 1980s, countries such as Korea and Malaysia expanded both inbound and outbound business tourism dramatically. The introduction of eight Eastern European nations (together with Malta and Cyprus) into the EU in May, 2004 is leading to new growth areas in the movement of tourists during the first decade of the century, and the rise of a new, free-spending elite within the Russian community and adjacent countries has also resulted in these nationalities being among the fastest growing in international tourism, albeit from a low base. Meanwhile, uncertainty in the Western world, particularly the fall and slow recovery of the stock market since the events of September 2001, continued to limit the recovery of business and leisure travel well into the twenty-first century.

Nevertheless, business travel of all kinds remains of immense importance to the tourism industry, not least because the per capita revenue from the business traveller greatly exceeds that of the leisure traveller. Motivational factors involving business travel are discussed in the next chapter, but here it must be stressed that business travel often complements leisure travel, to spread the effects of tourism more evenly in the economy. A major factor is that business travellers are not generally travelling to areas that are favoured by leisure travellers (other than in the very particular case of the conference market); business people have to go to locations where they are to conduct business, and this generally means city centres, often in cities that have little to attract the leisure tourist. Travel also takes place all year round, with little peaking, and hotel demand occurs between Mondays and Fridays, encouraging the more attractively situated hotels to target the leisure market on weekends. Often, spouses will travel to accompany the business traveller, and their leisure needs will have to be taken into consideration; thus, in practice it becomes difficult to distinguish between business and leisure tourism.

Although business travel is less price-elastic than leisure travel, it has already been pointed out that efforts to cut costs in the world of business today are ensuring that business travellers no longer spend as freely as formerly. Fewer business travellers now travel first class or business class on airlines (many are making use of the new budget airlines to minimize costs), less expensive hotels are booked and there is even a trend to travel on weekends to reduce prices. Companies are buying many more tourism products, particularly air tickets, through the Internet, where they can shop around for the cheapest tickets. These changes are not seen as short-term trends, and in future any distinction between the two major tourist markets is likely to become less apparent.

The conference and incentive travel business

Conferences and formal meetings have become very important to the tourism industry, both nationally and internationally, with continued growth from the 1960s to the end of the century. The British conference market alone is responsible for the organization of some 700,000 individual conferences each year, the very large majority lasting just one or two days, and as most of these are held in hotels, this market is vital to the accommodation sector. Low-cost carriers, having broken the traditional carriers' imposition of conditions requiring a weekend stop-over to gain low fares, changed business protocol and began to win a share of these important markets. Major conferences, such as that of the American Bar Association, which accounts for up to 25,000 delegates each year travelling all over the world (the 2000 conference was held in London), impact on all sectors of the industry, from hotels to the destination itself, which will benefit from expenditure in shops, theatres, nightclubs and other centres of amusement. To serve the needs of the largest conferences, international conference centres seating up to 5,000 or more delegates have been built in major cities like London and Berlin, but the number of conferences of this size is inevitably limited, and the competition to attract them intense. The logistics of organizing these and other major events are generally in the hands of professional events organizers, most of whom in Britain will belong to the Association of Conference Executives (ACE). As international conferences generally have English as the common language (although simultaneous translations are always available where necessary), countries like Britain and the USA greatly benefit from this market.

Exhibitions also account for another form of business travel. Major international exhibitions can be traced at least as far back as the Great Exhibition, held at Crystal Palace in London in 1851, and World Fairs have become common events in major cities around the globe as a means of attracting visitors and publicizing a nation's culture and products. Many national events are now organized on an annual basis, some requiring little more than a field and marquees or other temporary structures – the Royal Bath & West agricultural show being one example of a major outdoor attraction, held annually in the UK's West Country. As these events have grown and become more professionally organized, so have they, too, become an important element in the business of tourism.

The all-inclusive holiday

Mention has already been made of the trend to *all-inclusive* holidays. As the term indicates, this holiday includes everything – food, alcoholic drinks, water sports and other entertainment at the hotel. The attractions of this form of tourism are obvious – it is seen by tourists as offering better value, because they can pay up front for the holiday, know what their budget will be well in advance, and be unconcerned about changes in the value of foreign currency, or the need to take large sums of money abroad. For the more timid foreign traveller, or those who are concerned about being badgered by local souvenir sellers and 'beach salesmen', there is the added reassurance that they do not even have to leave the hotel complex to enjoy their holidays. Critics argue that the growth of all-inclusive holidays has implications for the local economy, as local bars, shopkeepers and others no longer stand to benefit to the same extent from visitors, while greater profits flow back to the operators in generating countries who control the leisure site. In this sense, one may question whether all-inclusive tourism can be judged sustainable; however, operators themselves would refute this, arguing that by keeping tourists in 'ghettos' they are in fact helping to reduce the negative impact of tourism on locals.

In its modern form, this type of tourism originated in the Caribbean, and up-market tour operators such as Sandals have promoted these programmes very successfully to the US and European markets. However, the concept later moved down-market and became popular in the more traditional European resorts such as those of the Balearic Islands. Further expansion is seen as a direct threat to the livelihood of many in the traditional coastal resorts.

Mass-market tourism in its maturity

Southern European mass-market tourism can be said to have entered a period of maturity by the 1980s. Although still showing steady growth, expansion was not on the scale found between the 1950s and 1970s. Short-haul travel was changing geographically, with tourists seeking new resorts and experiences. Portugal, having an Atlantic rather than a Mediterranean coast, wisely kept an up-market image for its developments in the Algarve, while the Canaries, being within the crucial four hours' flying time from northern European airports, were the closest destinations which offered guaranteed warm winter sunshine, and prospered with year-round appeal. Other, rather more exotic destinations attracted the up-market winter holidaymaker: Tunisia, Morocco, Egypt and Israel pitched for the medium-haul beach markets. As prices rose in the traditional resorts, tourists moved on to cheaper, and less developed, destinations still close at hand; Turkey, seen as cheap, uncontested and mildly exotic, boomed in the 1980s, proving an attractive alternative to Greece. The Yugoslavian Adriatic Coast provided charming architecture and cultural attractions in their seaside resorts, although good sandy beaches were missing. Malta had always had an appeal with the more conservative British tourist, but Crete and Cyprus began to attract larger numbers (especially following the war in Lebanon). Spain woke up to the despoliation of its resorts, and made efforts to up-grade them, especially on the island of Majorca and in popular coastal towns like Torremolinos. But by the end of the century, it was becoming clear that seaside tourism was moving in a new direction. Visitors were no longer willing simply to lie on a beach; they sought activities and adventure. For the young, this meant action from sports to bungee jumping and discos; taking over popular resorts on Ibiza and in Greece, they encouraged the family holiday market to move on. For the older tourist, it meant more excursions inland to cultural sites and attractive villages.

The long-haul market was changing, too. Attempts to sell some long-haul destinations as if they were merely extensions of the Mediterranean sunshine holidays failed to take into account the misunderstandings that could occur between hosts and guests, first in the Gambia, then in the Dominican Republic. Cruising, dormant for so long, suddenly found a new lease of life. Long-haul beach holidays in Kenya and Thailand, marketed at costs competitive with those in Europe, attracted Western tourists.

The American and Northern European markets were joined by a rising flow of tourists from other parts of the world. The Asian market has become a leading source of business for the travel industry, in the West as well as throughout Australasia. The flow of Japanese tourists to Australia is noteworthy; travel time to Australia is shorter than to Europe and, equally importantly, because the travel is largely within the same longitude, there is no time change or jet lag to face. With typically only eight days of holiday, avoidance of jet lag becomes an attractive bonus for the market, and makes Australia doubly attractive to the Japanese. Absence of jet lag is also helping to accelerate tourism to South Africa from the European nations, although uncertainty over crime and the country's political future remains.

Destinations in the Pacific began to attract Europeans in significant numbers, just as they have long attracted the Japanese and Australian markets. However, a large proportion of these visitors were using the Pacific islands as stopover points for a night or two, rather than as a holiday base. The impact of technology can be seen when for the first time aircraft became capable of flying direct between the USA and Sydney, with the introduction of the Boeing 747-400SP aircraft. Tahiti, slightly off the direct route between these continents and long established as an attractive stopover point but expensive for longer holidays, immediately suffered a sharp decline in visitors as the airlines concentrated their promotion on direct services between Los Angeles and Sydney or Auckland.

Further reading

Bray, R and Raitz, V, *Flight to the Sun: the Story of the Holiday Revolution*, Continuum, 2001
Brodie, A, Sargent, A and Winterby, G, *Seaside Holidays in the Past*, English Heritage, 2005
Franco, V, *Club Méditerranée*, Shepheard-Walwyn, 1972
Löfgren, O, *On Holiday: a History of Vacationing*, University of California Press, 1999
Grant, G, *Waikiki Yesteryear*, Mutual Publishing, Honolulu, 1996

Questions and discussion points

1 In 1984, McIntosh and Goeldner, in their classic text *Tourism Principles, Practices, Philosophies*, made a number of predictions about the future of the travel business by 2009, among which were the following:

   ■ red tape problems in travel would be largely eliminated
   ■ fast and comfortable room-to-room service available
   ■ all data of interest and all reservations by instantaneous home video
   ■ consistent travel planning by weather, weeks ahead. Resorts with controlled environment
   ■ tourist pollution receding as a controversial issue, largely controlled by local option and improved management
   ■ real-time pictures available from point-of-destination agencies
   ■ tourism and leisure stabilizing, but options growing, with diverse specialized tourism. Extensive world-wide travel, with some space travel available
   ■ working week typically 20 hours
   ■ business travel partly or largely superseded by new telecommunications
   ■ third-generation supersonic aircraft in operation, many various and big jets, guided surface transport with rail services operating between 200–400 mph and cars with auto control operating at 100–200 mph.

How far have these predictions been fulfilled? Are those currently unfulfilled likely to come to pass within the next few years? What reasons would you give for the failure of the authors to accurately predict events in the first decade of the twenty-first century?

2　Battleground sites of World War I have always had strong appeal for tourists, even today, while the appeal of similar sites from World War II is far more limited. What would account for this, in your view?

3　Is there an inevitable clash between the concept of sustainable tourism and the demand for all-inclusive holidays? What are the pros and cons of this form of holiday package?

4　Will the growth of Internet bookings by customers mean a further decline in the appeal of iden-tikit destinations, or are other factors causing this decline?

Assignment topics

1　New Wave tours is an organization that prides itself on being at the cutting edge of new holiday trends, catering to demand from more adventurous holidaymakers who are always looking for something new. As a research assistant in their marketing department, you have been asked to prepare a report identifying the most promising trends in holiday-taking patterns, which will allow the company to develop small, niche-market tailor-made packages for their customers. Your report should identify destinations, forms of activity and the characteristics of the potential market, including age range, social class (in terms of income and employment) and consumer patterns based on personality factors.

2　The sheer numbers of passengers now travelling by air from the major airports in generating countries is making travel by air an ordeal for many holidaymakers. As a member of the planning team of a large tour operator, you have been asked to look into the faltering demand of airports like Heathrow and Gatwick, and the preference for travel direct to destinations from UK provincial airports. Develop a research programme to test the sensitivity of the market to a choice of these alternatives, considering price differentials, convenience and other relevant factors. A survey using a questionnaire could be employed in the first instance, but give consideration to more qualitative forms of research to gain a better insight into customer preferences, and provide your employer with proposals for a research exercise to elicit this information.

4 The demand for tourism

Objectives

After studying this chapter, you should be able to:

- distinguish between motivating and facilitating factors
- understand the nature of the psychological and sociological demand for tourism
- recognize how the product influences consumer demand
- be aware of some of common theories of consumer behaviour, such as decision-making and risk avoidance
- be aware of the factors influencing demand and how demand is changing in the twenty-first century.

Introduction

We live in an era when there are increasing numbers of people of a certain age (usually 45-plus) who have different requirements from a holiday: they have a desire to experience new and alien cultures but see no need to compromise their creature comforts to do so.

Karen Exell, *Times Higher Education Supplement*, 27 Aug 2004

An understanding of why people buy the holidays or business trips they take, how they go about selecting their holidays, why one company is given preference over another, and why tourists choose to travel when they do is vital to those who work in the tourism industry. Yet curiously, we still know relatively little about tourist motivation, and although we gather numerous statistics which reveal a great deal about who goes where, the reasons for these choices are not well understood. This is not entirely the result of a lack of research, because many large companies do commission research into the behaviour of their clients, but as this is 'in-house' research, and the information it reveals is confidential to the company concerned, it seldom becomes public knowledge.

Motivation and purpose are closely related, and earlier in this book the principal purposes for which tourists travel were identified. These are classified into three broad categories: business travel, leisure travel and miscellaneous travel, which would include, *inter alia*, travel to visit friends and relatives (VFR), travel for one's health and religious travel. However, simply labelling tourists in this way only helps us to understand their general motivation for travelling; it tells us little about their specific motivation, or about their needs and wants which reflect that travel, and how these needs and wants are met and satisfied. It will be the purpose of this chapter to explain these terms, and the complex interrelationship between the factors which go to make up the choice of trips taken by tourists of all kinds.

The tourist's needs and wants

If we ask the prospective tourist why they want to travel to a particular destination, they will offer a variety of reasons, such as 'it's somewhere I've always wanted to visit', or 'some friends recommended it very highly', or 'it's always good weather at that time of the year, and the beaches are wonderful; we've been going there regularly for the past few years'. Interesting as these views may be, they actually throw very little light on the real motivation of the tourists, because they have not helped to identify the tourists' *needs* and *wants*.

People often talk about their 'needing' a holiday, just as they might say they need a new carpet for their lounge, a new dress or a better lawnmower. Are they in fact expressing a need, or a want? 'Need' suggests that the products we are asking for are necessities for our daily life, but this is clearly seldom the case with these products. We are merely expressing a desire for more goods and services, a symptom of the consumer-oriented society in which we live.

Occasionally, a holiday (or at least, a break from routine) can become a genuine need, as is the case with those in high stress occupations, where a breakdown can occur if relief from stress is not achieved. Families and individuals suffering severe deprivation may also need a holiday, as shown by the work of charitable organizations like the Family Holiday Association.

Let us start by examining what it is we mean by a need.

Example   Wants versus needs

A London hotel undertook research in 2004 to find out the specific requirements of its clientele of varying nationalities. Some of these wants proved to be quite detailed. German tourists preferred mixer taps, rather than individual hot and cold taps, in their bathrooms; Americans wanted fixed head, not hand held, showers. Italian guests asked for menus available around the clock, including pizza, while the Japanese visitors were pleased if they could be given tabi (socks) with their bathrobes.

Figure 4.1
Maslow's
hierarchy of
needs

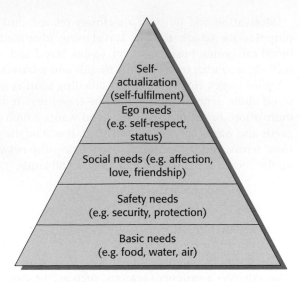

(From *Motivation and Personality* by A Maslow (1987). Reprinted by permission of Pearson Education, Inc., Upper Saddle River, NJ 07458)

People have certain physiological needs, which are essential for their survival: they need to eat, to drink, to sleep, to keep warm and to reproduce – all needs which are essential to the survival of the human race. Beyond these needs, we also have psychological needs which are important for our well-being, such as the need to love and be loved, the need for friendship, and the need to value ourselves as human beings and to have others value and respect us. Many people believe we also have inherently within us the need to master our environment, and to understand the nature of the society in which we live. Abraham Maslow conveniently grouped these needs into a hierarchy (see Figure 4.1), suggesting that the more fundamental needs have to be satisfied before we seek to satisfy the higher-level needs.

The difficulty in exploring these needs is that many people may actually be quite unaware of their needs, or how to go about satisfying them. Others will be reluctant to reveal their real needs; for example, few people would be willing openly to admit that they travel to a particular destination to impress their neighbours, although their desire for status within the neighbourhood may well be a factor in their choice of holiday and destination.

Some of our needs are *innate*, that is, they are based on factors inherited by us at birth. These include biological and instinctive needs such as eating and drinking. However, we also inherit genetic traits from our parents which are reflected in certain needs and wants. Other needs and wants arise out of the environment in which we are raised, and are therefore *learned*, or socially engineered. The early death of parents, or their lack of overt affection towards us, may cause us to have stronger needs for bonding and friendship with others, for example. As we come to know more about genomes, following the discovery of the human genetic code early in the twenty-first century, so we are coming to appreciate that our genetic differences are in fact very slight, indicating that most of our needs and wants are conditioned by our environment.

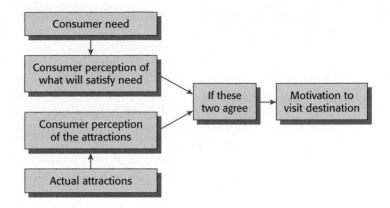

Figure 4.2
The motivation process

Travel may be one of several means of satisfying a need, and although needs are felt by us, we do not necessarily express them, and we may not recognize how travel actually satisfies our particular needs. Consequently, if we re-examine the answers given earlier to questions asking why we travel, it may be that in the case where respondents are confirming the desire to return to the same destination year after year, they are actually expressing the desire to satisfy a need for safety and security, by returning to the tried and tested. The means by which this is achieved, namely a holiday in a resort well known to them, reflects the respondents' 'want', rather than their need.

The process of translating a need into the motivation to visit a specific destination or to undertake a specific activity is quite complex, and can best be demonstrated by a diagram (see Figure 4.2).

A potential consumer must not only recognize that they have a need, but also understand how a particular product will satisfy it. Every consumer is different, and what one consumer sees as the ideal solution to the need, another will reject. A holiday in Benidorm, which Mr A thinks will be something akin to paradise would be for Mr B an endurance test; he might prefer a walk in the Pennines for a week, which Mr A would find the nearest thing to purgatory. It is important that we all recognize that each person's perception of a holiday, like any other product, is affected by their experiences and attitudes. Only if the perception of the need and of the attraction match will a consumer be motivated to buy the product. The job of the skilled salesperson behind a travel agent's desk is to subtly question clients in order to learn about their interests and desires, and find the products to match. Those selling more expensive holidays may need to convince their clients that the experience on offer is worth the extra payment above what they would expect to pay for a regular holiday.

General and specific motivation

We have established that motivation arises out of the felt wants or needs of the individual. We can now go on to explain that motivation is expressed in two distinct forms, known as *specific motivation* and *general motivation*.

General motivation is aimed at achieving a broad objective, for example that of getting away from the routine and stress of the workplace in order to enjoy different surroundings and a healthy environment. Here, health and relief of stress are the broad motives reflecting the needs discussed above. If the tourist decides to take their holiday in the Swiss Alps, where they will be able to take walks in fresh mountain air and enjoy varied scenery, good food and total relaxation, these are all specific objectives, reflecting the means by which their needs will be met. Marketing managers sometimes refer to these two forms of motivation as 'push' factors and 'pull' factors; the tourist is being pushed into a holiday by the need to get away from their everyday environment, but other factors may be at work to pull, or encourage, them to travel to a specific destination. For this reason, marketing staff realize that they will have to undertake their promotion at two distinct levels, persuading the consumer of the need to take a holiday, and also to show those consumers that the particular holiday or destination the organization is promoting will best satisfy that need.

If we look at the varied forms of leisure tourism which have become a part of our lives in the past few years, we will quickly see that certain types of holiday have become popular because they best meet common, and basic, needs. The 'sun, sea and sand' holiday, which caters to the mass market, is essentially a passive form of leisure which entails nothing more stressful than a relaxing time on the beach, enjoyment of the perceived healthy benefits of sunshine and salt-water bathing, good food and reasonably priced alcohol (another relaxant). The tendency among certain groups of tourists

Figure 4.3
Getting away from the everyday: hikers at Dunkery Beacon in Exmoor National Park, Somerset

(Photographed by the author)

abroad to drink too much, and to misbehave generally, is again a reflection of need, even if the result is one which we have come to deplore because of its impact on others. Such tourists seek to escape from the constraints of their usual environment, and to enjoy an opportunity to 'let their hair down', perhaps in a more tolerant environment than they would find in their own home country. Those travelling on their own might also seek opportunities to meet other people, or even find romance (thus meeting the need to belong and other social needs). In the case of families, parents can simultaneously satisfy their own needs while also providing a healthy and enjoyable time for their children on the beach; parents may also be given the chance to get away and be on their own while their children are being cared for by skilled childminders. What is provided is therefore a 'bundle of benefits', and the more a particular package holiday, or a particular destination, can be shown to provide the range of benefits sought, the more attractive will that holiday appear to the tourist compared with other holidays on offer. In this case, the bundle will be made up of benefits which are designed to cater to both general and specific needs and wants.

Today, there is a growing demand for holidays which offer more strenuous activities than are to be found in the traditional 'three S' holidays, such as trekking, mountaineering or yachting. These appeal because they attract those whose basic needs for relaxation have already been satisfied (and their desk-bound jobs may involve mental, rather than physical, strain); they are now seeking something more challenging. Strenuous activities provide opportunities for people to test their physical abilities, and while this may involve no more than a search for health by other means, there may also be a search for competence, another need identified by Maslow. Because these holidays are also purchased by like-minded people, and are often provided in small groups, they can also help to meet other ego and social needs.

Figure 4.4
Contrasts in holidaymaking 1: a stag party in Warsaw, Poland

(Courtesy: Vamos Travel)

The growing confidence and physical fitness of many tourists (and not just the young!) has put extreme sports on the agenda of many holiday companies. Formerly limited to winter sports such as skiing and snowboarding, and summer white-water rafting, adventure holidays now embrace off-piste skiing, snowboarding, windsurfing, BMX biking, paragliding, heli-skiing, kitesurfing, kitebuggying, landboarding and base-jumping (leaping off tall buildings with parachutes – seldom available as a legal activity!), and the range of activities increases each year.

Example Destinations which offer the appropriate topography for extreme sports, and have developed organized programmes to support them, include:

- The coast of Kauai, Hawaii (cliffside kayaking)
- Bolivia, and Morzine in the French Alps (downhill cycling)
- Shaggy Ridge Mountains, Papua, New Guinea (jungle hacking)
- Yucatan, Mexico (underwater cave diving)
- Utah Canyonlands, USA, and the Himalayas (trekking)

It must also be recognized that many tourists are constantly seeking novelty and different experiences. However satisfied they might be with the former holiday, they will be unlikely to return to the same destination, but are forever seeking something more challenging, more exciting, more remote. This is in part an explanation for the growing demand for long-haul holidays. For other people, these increasingly exotic tourist trips satisfy the search for status.

Example The shock of the new

My holiday wanderlust (which, fortunately, my husband shares) is by no means a symptom of dissatisfaction. It's not as if we are restlessly searching for somewhere better than the year before. In fact, some of the places we've visited over the past couple of decades are close to perfection. . . . for us, it is their very novelty which makes them so appealing.

Mary Ann Sieghart, writing in *The Times*, 12 Aug 2004

The writer in the above quote was reacting to news of research which revealed that almost fifty per cent of Italian tourists choose to return to the same hotel in the same destination for their annual holidays over a period of at least ten years.

The need for self-actualization can be met in a number of ways. At its simplest, the desire to 'commune with nature' is a common trait among many tourists, and can be achieved through scenic trips by coach, by fly–drive packages in which routes are identified and stopping-off points recommended for their scenic beauty, by cycling

Figure 4.5
Contrasts in
holidaymaking
2: a cultural tour
in Sardinia

(Courtesy: Andante Travel)

tours, or by hiking holidays. Alternatively, the quest for knowledge can be met by tours such as those offered to cultural centres in Europe, accompanied by experts in particular fields such as archaeology (see Figure 4.5). Self-actualization can be aided through packages offering painting or other artistic 'do-it-yourself' holidays. Some tourists seek more meaningful experiences through contact with foreign residents, where they can come to understand the local cultures. This process can be facilitated through careful packaging of programmes arranged by organizers, who build up suitable contacts among local residents at the destination. Local guides, too, can act as 'culture-brokers' in overcoming language barriers or helping to explain local culture to inquisitive tourists, while at the same time reassuring more nervous travellers.

As people come to travel more, and as they become more sophisticated, or better educated, so will their higher-level needs predominate in their motivation for a particular holiday. Companies in the business of tourism must always recognize this and take it into account when planning new programmes or new attractions for the tourist.

Segmenting the tourism market

So far in this chapter we have looked at the individual factors that give rise to our various needs and wants. In the tourism industry, those responsible for marketing destinations or holidays will be concerned with both individual and *aggregate*, or total, demand for a holiday or destination. They find it convenient to categorize and segment demand according to four distinct sets of variables, namely: geographic, demographic, psychographic and behavioural. These categories are examined in more detail in a companion book to this text[1], but will be briefly summarized here.

Geographic variables are determined according to the areas in which consumers live. These can be broadly defined by continent (e.g. North America, Latin America, Asia, Africa), by country (e.g. Britain, France, Japan, Australia), or according to region, either broadly (e.g. Nordic, Mediterranean, Baltic States, US mid-western States) or more narrowly (e.g. Tyrol, Alsace-Lorraine, North Rhine-Westphalia, UK Home Counties). It is appropriate to divide areas in this way only where it is clear that the resident population's buying or behaviour patterns reflect commonalities, while differing from those of other areas in ways that are significant to the industry. The most obvious point to make here is that chosen travel destinations will be the outcome of factors such as distance, convenience and price to reach the destination; Europeans will find it more convenient, and probably cheaper, to holiday in the Mediterranean, North Americans in the Caribbean, Australians in Pacific islands like Fiji and Bali. But differing climates in the generating countries will also result in other variations in travel demand.

Demographic variables include such characteristics as age, gender, family composition, stage in life cycle, income, occupation, education and ethnic origin. The type of holiday chosen is likely to differ greatly between 20 to 30 year olds, and 50 to 60 year olds, to take one example. Changing patterns will also interest marketers – declining populations, increasing numbers of elderly consumers, greater numbers of individuals living alone and taking holidays alone, or increases in disposable incomes among some age groups, will all affect the way holidays are marketed. Significant factors in travel demand in the British market in recent years have been the rise in wealth among older sectors of the public, as their parents – the first generation to have become property owners on a major scale – died, leaving significant inheritances to their offspring. This, and the general rise in living standards, fuelled demand for second homes both in Britain and abroad, changing leisure patterns and encouraging the growth of low-cost airlines to service the market's needs.

Demographic distinctions are among the most easily researched variables, and consequently provide readily available data. Market differentiation by occupation is one of the most common ways of categorizing consumers – not least because it offers the prospect of a ready indication of relative disposable incomes. Occupation also remains a principal criterion for identifying social class. The best-known socio-economic segmentation in Britain was introduced after World War II, and is still widely used in market research exercises, including those conducted under the aegis of the National Readership Surveys (NRS). Using this tool, the consumer market is broken down into six categories on the basis of the occupation of the head of household (see Figure 4.6).

Figure 4.6
Social classification by employment, previous version

- A   Higher managerial, administrative or professional
- B   Middle managerial, administrative or professional
- C1   Supervisory or clerical, junior managerial
- C2   Skilled manual workers
- D   Semi- and unskilled manual workers
- E   Those at lowest levels of subsistence

Table 4.1 Social classification by employment, new version

Class	% of UK population	Occupations	Examples include
1	8	large employers, higher managerial and professional	doctors, clergy
2	19	lower managerial and professional	writers, artists
3	9	intermediate managerial and professional	medical, legal secretaries
4	7	small employers and own account workers	hotel, restaurant managers
5	7	lower supervisory and technical	plumbers, mechanics
6	12	semi-routine occupations	sales assistants, chefs
7	9	routine occupations	waiters, couriers

This attempt to distinguish between market segments on the grounds of social class arising from occupation can be criticized today as increasingly anachronistic, as society becomes more egalitarian. Patterns of purchase or behaviour are now less clearly determined by social class – although these categories may well offer some indication of the *ability* to purchase, on the grounds of income. The proportion of those travelling on holiday each year is, as one would expect, far higher among the higher income brackets than the lower. However, in an era where plumbers and electricians may earn up to twice as much as university lecturers, new forms of guidance are necessary to meet the need of the market researchers.

Various attempts have been made in recent years to overcome this stigmatic characterization by occupation. A new system of social classification was introduced in Britain in 2001 (see Table 4.1).

However, the new classification leaves some 29 per cent unaccounted for, including the long-term unemployed, students and those never employed. It also perpetuates the belief that behaviour can be ascribed largely to occupation, which, given the changes taking place in twenty-first century society, can be a misleading fallacy.

Nevertheless, categorizing demand for a company's products by social class can be of some value in helping to determine advertising spend and the media to be employed. Similarly, breaking down demand by age group is also helpful, and even vital if the aim is, say, to develop holidays with particular appeal to young people. But market research in recent years has been transformed by the efforts of researchers to bring together both geography and demography, through a process of pinpoint *geo-demographic* analysis. This is based on combining census data and postal codes to reveal that fine-tuning by region can produce a picture of spend and behaviour which will be common to a large proportion of the population of that region. Among the best known of these systems is ACORN (A Classification of Residential Neighbourhoods) operated by CACI Information Services, which takes into account such factors as age, income, lifestyle and family structure. However, even with the sophistication and refinement of this approach, this will not be sufficient to explain all of the variation in choice between different tourist products, and for this we must look to consumer psychographics for further enlightenment.

Psychographic variables are those which allow us to note the impact of aspirational and lifestyle characteristics on consumer behaviour. Beyond simple demographic distinctions, as buyers we are heavily influenced by those immediately surrounding us (our so-called *peer groups*), as well as those we most admire and wish to emulate (our *reference groups*). In the former case, while we may develop choices favoured by our parents and teachers in early life, as we become more independent we prefer to emulate the behaviour of our immediate friends, fellow students, colleagues at work or others with whom we come into regular close contact. In the latter case, the influence of celebrities is becoming paramount, as the holiday choices and behaviour of pop idols, cinema and TV 'personalities' and those in the media and modelling worlds come increasingly to influence buying patterns, particularly those of younger consumers. In short, the way that significant others live and spend their leisure hours exerts a strong influence on holiday consumerism among all classes of client. Swan's Cruises have marketed themselves for many years on the basis that their passengers will mingle with the great and the good, and the Caribbean island of Mustique successfully promoted itself as an exclusive hideaway for the rich, largely because Princess Margaret had been a frequent visitor.

As members of society, we tend to follow the norms and values reflected in that society. We all like to feel that we are making our own decisions about the products we choose, without always realizing how other people's taste influences our own, and what pressures there are on us to conform. When we claim that we are buying to 'please ourselves', what exactly is this 'self' that we are pleasing? We are, in fact, composed of many 'selves'. There is the self that we see ourselves as, often highly subjectively; the ideal self, representing how we would like to be; there is our self as we believe others see us, and the self as we are actually seen by others; yet none of these can be construed as our real self – if, indeed, a real self can be said to exist outside of the way we interact with others. Readers will be aware that they put on different 'fronts' and act out different roles according to the company in which they find themselves, whether family, best friend, lover, employer. Do any of these relationships truly reflect our real self?

The importance attached to this theory of self, from the perspective of this text, is the way in which it affects those things we buy and with which we surround ourselves. This means that in the case of holidays we will not always buy the kind of holiday we think we would most enjoy, or even the one we feel we could best afford, but instead we might buy the holiday which we feel will give us status with our friends and neighbours, or will reflect the kind of holiday we feel that 'persons in our position' should take. Advertisers will frequently use this knowledge to promote a destination as being suited to a particular kind of tourist, and will perhaps go further, using as a model in their advertisements some well-known TV personality or film star, who will reflect the 'typical tourist at the destination' with whom we can then mentally associate ourselves.

In the same way, status becomes an important feature of business travel, as business travellers are aware that they are representing their company to business associates and must therefore create an impression. Since the company also accepts this view and is paying their bills, it can be seen why business travel generates more income per capita than does leisure travel!

Finally, *behavioural variables* allow us to segment our markets according to their usage of the products. This is a much simpler concept, and facts about consumer purchasing can be ascertained quite readily through market research. The frequency of product purchase, the quantities we purchase, where we choose to buy (from a retailer, or direct, for example) and the sources from which we obtain information about products, are of great interest to marketers who, armed with this knowledge, will be able to shape their strategies more effectively in order to influence purchases. A key element in this is to know which benefits a consumer is looking for when they purchase a product. The motives for buying a lakes-and-mountains holiday, for example, can vary substantially: some may be seeking solitude and scenic beauty, perhaps to recover from stress or to enjoy a painting or photography holiday, some will seek the social interaction of small hiking groups, or evening chats in the bar of their hotel with like-minded guests, others will be looking for more active pastimes such as water-skiing or mountaineering. Only when the organization arranging the holiday knows which elements of the product are appealing to their customer, can an effective sale take place.

The consumer process

If all consumers responded in the same way to given stimuli, the life of marketing managers would become a great deal easier. Unfortunately it has to be recognized that, while research continues to shed more light on our complex behaviour, the triggers that lead to this behaviour are still poorly understood. However, we can make some generalizations, based on research to date, which assist our understanding of consumer processes and, in particular, those of decision-making. Marketing theorists have developed a number of models to explain these processes. Perhaps the best known, as well as the simplest model, is known as AIDA (see Figure 4.7).

This model recognizes that marketing aims to move the consumer from a stage of unawareness, either of the product (such as a specific destination or resort) or the particular brand (such as an individual package tour company, or a hotel), through a number of stages to a point where the consumer is persuaded to buy a particular product and brand. The first step in this process is to move the consumer from unawareness to awareness. This entails an understanding about the way in which the consumer learns about new products.

If you, the reader, think for a moment about how you came to learn about a particular destination you have visited, you will quickly recognize how difficult it is to pinpoint all the influences – many of which you may not be consciously aware of. Every day, consumers are faced with hundreds of new pieces of knowledge, including information about new products. If we are to retain any of this information, the first task of marketing is to ensure that we perceive it, that is, become conscious of it.

Perception is an important part of the process by which we learn. It involves the selection and interpretation of the information which is presented to us. As we cannot possibly absorb all the messages with which we are faced each day, many are

Figure 4.7
The AIDA model

- Awareness
- Interest
- Desire
- Action

consciously or unconsciously 'screened out' from our memories. If we are favourably predisposed towards a particular product or message, there is clearly a greater likelihood that we will absorb it. So, for example, if our best friend has just returned from a holiday in the Cayman Islands, and has enthusiastically talked to us about the trip, if we then spot a feature on the Cayman Islands on television this may arouse our interest, even if, up to the point our friend mentioned the place, we had never even heard of it. If what we see on the television programme reinforces the image of the destination which we gained from our friend, we might be encouraged to seek further information on the destination, perhaps by searching the Web, or contacting the tourist office representing the destination. At any point in this process, we might be put off by what we find – for instance, if we perceive the destination as being too far away, too expensive, or too inaccessible for the length of time we are contemplating a trip, we may search no further. If, on the other hand, the search process leads us to form a positive image of the destination, we may start mentally comparing the destination with others towards which we were favourably disposed. The process of choice involves constant comparison, weighing up one destination against others, estimating the benefits and the drawbacks of each as a potential holiday destination. As this process goes on, three things are happening.

The tourism 'image'

First, we are developing an image of the destination in question. This image may be a totally inaccurate one, if the information sources we use are uninformed, or deliberately seek to distort the information they provide. We may then find that we become confused about the image itself. For example, in the early 1990s the British media carried inflated reports of muggings carried out against tourists in the Miami area, while the destination itself continued to try to disseminate a positive image of the resort, and brochures of the tour operators likewise concentrated on selling the positive benefits with little reference to any potential dangers faced by tourists.

Images are built around the unique attributes which the destination can claim. The more these help to distinguish the destination from other similar destinations, the greater the attraction of the destination to the tourist. Those destinations which offer truly unique products, such as the Grand Canyon in the USA, the Great Wall of China near Beijing, or the Pyramids at Giza, Egypt, have an inbuilt advantage – although in time the attraction of such destinations may be such that it becomes necessary to 'de-market' the site to avoid over-popularity. In the early 1990s the Egyptian Tourist Office also faced the problem of negative publicity associated with attacks against tourists by Islamic fundamentalists, soon after a large influx of Western tourists, many of whom failed to conform to the proprieties expected in an Islamic country. A major objective among tourist offices in developing countries is to generate a long-term positive image of the destination in their advertising, to give it an edge over its competitors.

By contrast with those destinations offering unique attractions, many traditional seaside resorts, both in Britain and increasingly elsewhere, suffer from having very little to distinguish them from their competitors. The concept of the identikit destination as the popular choice for tourists is becoming outdated, and simply offering good beaches, pleasant hotels and well-cooked food in an attractive climate is no longer enough in itself. In some way, an image must be *induced* by the tourist office to distance the resort from others, so that, for example, if changes in exchange rates or inflation rates work against the destination, it may still be seen as having sufficient 'added value' to attract and retain a loyal market.

Attitudes to the product

So much for image. Next, we find we are developing an attitude towards the destination. Several theorists suggest that an individual's lifestyle in general can best be measured by looking at their activities (or attitudes), interests and opinions – the so-called 'A–I–O Model'. Attitude is a mix of our emotional feelings about the destination and our rational evaluation of its merits, both of which together will determine whether we would consider it a possible venue for a holiday. It should be stressed at this point, however, that while we may have a negative image of the destination, we may still retain a positive attitude towards travel there, because we have an interest in seeing some of its attractions, or learning about its culture. This was often the case with travel to the Communist Bloc countries before the collapse of their political systems at the end of the 1980s, and, notwithstanding the increasing strains in the early twenty-first century in relationships between Western nations and countries with large Islamic populations, interest in these countries' tourist sites and cultures remains high. In fact, media coverage of some previously little known countries will have helped to expand curiosity about these countries, and not purely on the grounds of 'dark tourism' (see Chapter 10).

Risk as a factor in tourism choice

Finally, there is the issue of risk to consider when planning to take a trip. All holidays involve some element of risk – whether of illness, of bad weather, of being unable to get what we want if we delay booking, of being uncertain about the product until we see it at first hand, about its representing value for money. We will be asking ourselves what risks we are running, whether there is a high likelihood of their occurrence, whether the risks are avoidable, and how significant the consequences would be. Some tourists, of course, will relish a degree of risk, as this gives an edge of excitement to the holiday, so the presence of risk is not in itself a barrier to tourism. Others, however, are 'risk averters' and will studiously avoid risk wherever possible. Clearly, the significance of the risk will be a key factor; there will be much less concern with the risk of poor weather than with the risk of crime. Risk averters will book early; they may choose to return to the same resort they have visited in the past, knowing its reliability; they will book a package tour, rather than travel independently. The American Hilton and Holiday Inn chain hotels have been eminently successful throughout the world by offering some certainty about standards, in countries where Americans could feel at risk from 'foreign' food, poor plumbing or other inadequacies of a tour which can become preventable by good forward planning. Travel businesses such as cruise lines, which offer a product with a reassuring lack of risk, can – and do – make this an important theme in their promotional campaigns.

Risk is also a factor in the methods chosen by customers to book their holidays. There is evidence that much of the continuing reluctance shown by tourists to seek information and make bookings through Internet providers can be attributed in part

Figure 4.8
Personality
and travel
destination
choice: the
allocentric–
psychocentric
scale

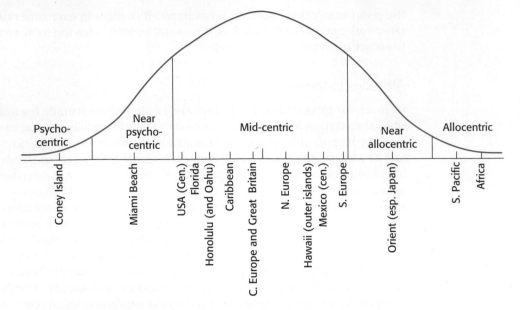

to the lack of face-to-face contact with a trusted – and, hopefully, expert – travel agent, and in part to the suspicion that information received through the Internet will be biased in favour of the information provider.

The extent to which risk is a product of personality is an issue which has been addressed by a number of tourism researchers, most notably Stanley Plog[2]. Essentially, Plog attempted to determine the relationship between introvert and extrovert personalities and holiday choice, and his theories have been widely published in tourism texts (see Figure 4.8).

Plog's theory attempted to classify the United States population by distinguishing between those judged *allocentrics*, being those seeking variety, self-confident, outgoing and experimental, and *psychocentrics*, those who tend to be more concerned with themselves and the small problems of life. The latter are often anxious, and inclined to seek security. The theory would suggest that psychocentrics would be more inclined to return to resorts with which they are familiar, to stay closer to home and to use a package holiday for their travel arrangements. Allocentrics, by contrast, would be disposed to seek new experiences, in a more exotic destination, travelling independently. Of course, these are polarized examples, and in practice most holidaymakers are likely to fall somewhere between the extremes, as *mid-centrics*. Those tending towards the psychocentric were found by Plog to be more commonly from lower-income groups, but it is equally these groups who are more constrained financially as to the kind of holiday they can afford to take. Whether Plog's findings are similarly applicable to European markets is by no means certain.

Plog recognized that personalities change over time, and that given time the psychocentric may become allocentric in their choice of holiday destination and activity, as they gain experience of travel. It has long been accepted that many tourists actually seek novelty from a base of security and familiarity. This would enable the psychocentric to enjoy more exotic forms of tourism, which can be achieved, for instance, by tourists travelling through unfamiliar territories by coach in their own 'environmental bubble'. The provision of a familiar background to come home to after touring, such as is offered to Americans at Hilton Hotels or Holiday Inns (referred to earlier in this chapter) is a clear means of reassuring the nervous while in unfamiliar territory.

It is a point worth stressing that extreme pyschocentrics (or indeed, those unable to travel through disabilities) may benefit from experiences of virtual travel, as increasingly sophisticated computers can replicate the experience of travel to exotic locations with none of the risk or difficulties associated with such travel. Already, armchair travellers can benefit from the experience second-hand of travel abroad through the now numerous holiday programmes and travelogues available via the television screen, a popular form of escapism.

Taking the decision

The process of sorting through the various holidays on offer and determining which is the best to choose is inevitably complex, and individual personality traits will determine how the eventual decision is arrived at. Some people undertake a process of *extensive problem solving*, in which information is sought about a wide range of products, each of which is evaluated and compared with similar products. Other consumers will not have the patience to explore a wide variety of choices, and will deliberately restrict choice, with the aim of 'satisficing' rather than trying to guarantee they buy the best possible product. This is known as *limited problem solving*, and will provide the benefit of saving time. Many consumers engage in *routinized response behaviour*, in which choice changes relatively little over time. This is a common pattern among brand-loyal consumers, for example, and some holidaymakers who have been content with a particular company or destination in the past may opt for the same experience again. Finally, some consumers will buy on *impulse*. While this is more typical of products costing little, it is by no means unknown among holiday purchasers, and is in fact a pattern of behaviour which is becoming increasingly prevalent – to the dismay of the operators, who have less scope for forward planning and reduced opportunity to gain through investing deposits in the short term. Impulse purchasing is a valuable trait where 'distressed stock' needs to be cleared at short notice, and can be stimulated by late availability offers particularly.

Fashion and taste

Many tourism enterprises, and above all, destinations, suffer from the effect of changing consumer taste, as fashion changes and as 'opinion leaders' find new activities to pursue, new resorts to champion. It is difficult to define exactly what it is that causes a particular resort to lose its popularity with the public – although clearly, if the resources it offers are allowed to deteriorate, the market will soon drift away to seek better value for money elsewhere.

Sometimes, however, it is no more than the movement of fashion which causes tourism to fall off. This is most likely to be the case where the site was a 'fashionable' attraction in the first place. This happened to Bath after its outstanding success as a resort in the eighteenth century, and can be seen again in the case of several seaside resorts in the late twentieth century, such as St Tropez (fashionable in the 1960s and 1970s after film star Brigitte Bardot chose to reside there). It is the case, however, that

Figure 4.9
The life cycle of a resort

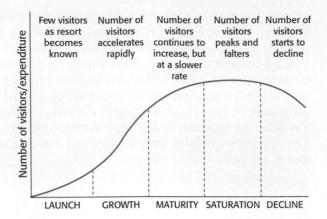

all products, including tourism, will experience a life cycle of growth, maturity, saturation and eventual decline if no action is taken to arrest it (see Figure 4.9). Generally, this will entail some form of innovation or other investment helping to revitalize the product.

In the earlier historical chapters we looked at some of the ways in which tourism has changed over time owing to changes in consumer behaviour. Fashion, of course, is a critical element in this process. In recent years there has been a swing towards better health and well-being which has affected the type of holiday chosen. As a direct consequence, most large hotel chains now incorporate a health centre as an element in their facilities.

Physical fitness already plays a larger role in our lives, and is directly responsible for the growth in activity holidays. Tour operators have learned to cater for this changing demand pattern. Greater concern about what we eat has led to better quality food, better preparation, better hygiene and a cuisine which caters for increasingly segmented tastes, from veganism and vegetarianism to low glycemic index and fat-free diets. Similarly, the growing interest in personal development and creativity, and the desire to lead a full, rich life promises well for those planning special-interest and activity holidays of all kinds, especially the arts.

Better health, of course, includes greater concern about the danger of contracting skin cancer as a result of exposure to the sun. These dangers are already well documented[3]; annually, some 1,700 people are dying from malignant melanoma in Britain alone. Melanoma is caused by sudden and intensive exposure to the sun, typically as a result of sunbathing. Cases of carcinoma, a cancer which develops through more gradual exposure to sunlight over a much longer period of time, occurs far more frequently, although if treated in its early stages will seldom prove fatal. Carcinoma does, however, affect many employees in the travel industry, due to their frequent exposure to the sun while at work (consider, for instance, the jobs of resort representative, lifeguard, ski instructor or coach driver). In Australia, where love of the sun is inbuilt in the culture, the number of new cases of skin cancer diagnosed each year runs into the hundreds of thousands, of which around 1,000 prove fatal; as a result, the authorities there launched a nationwide, and highly effective, campaign to reduce cancer by encouraging sun lovers to cover up and use sunscreens. As the depletion of

Figure 4.10
A thalassotherapy health centre links the Ibis and Novotel Hotels in le Touquet, France, both owned by Accor Hotels

(Photographed by the author)

the ozone layer heightens risk, so tourists will be forced to reconsider the attraction of the beach holiday – at least, in the form in which it has been offered up to the present. The fashion for suntans may well disappear; this was, after all, a twentieth-century phenomenon, as until the early part of this century tans were disparaged by the middle class as indicative of those working outside, i.e. 'the labouring classes'. However, in spite of widespread media coverage on this subject in Great Britain, it is proving difficult to change long-standing attitudes, and it is recognized that younger readers will be slow to absorb this lesson!

Example   Bavarian barmaids

In 2005, the media gave widespread coverage to an EU proposal that would require barmaids, who serve tankards of beer outdoors (particularly at the popular beer festivals) wearing traditional Bavarian costume, to 'cover up' their bare shoulders and *décolletage* to avoid potential skin damage from the sun. Employers were warned that they could face compensation claims if barmaids were to suffer illness resulting from exposure. In the event, the European Parliament voted instead to allow individual EU states to determine whether employers should be required to protect their outdoor workers from solar radiation.

The motivation of business travellers

What we have examined in this chapter applies mainly to the leisure traveller. Those travelling on business may well have different criteria to be considered.

We noted earlier that business travellers are in general less price sensitive and more concerned with status. They are motivated principally by the need to complete their travel and business dealings as efficiently and effectively as possible within a given time frame – this reflects their company's motivation for their trip. They will, however, also have personal agendas to take into account. Through the eyes of their company, then, they will be giving consideration to issues such as speed of transport and convenience in getting to their destination, the punctuality and reliability of the carrier, and the frequency of flights so that they can leave at a time to suit their appointments and return as soon as their business is completed. Decisions about their travel are often taken at very short notice, so arrangements may have to be made at any time of the day or night. They need the flexibility to change their reservations at minimal notice, and are prepared to pay a premium for this privilege. However, the arrival of the low-cost airlines has persuaded many to stick with a booking, since savings of hundreds of pounds can be achieved, even for a flight within Europe. Travel needs to be arranged on weekdays rather than weekends – most business people like to spend their weekends with their families. Above all, business people will require those that they deal with – agents, carriers, travel managers – to have greater in-depth knowledge of travel products. It is known that many business travellers will undertake their own searches on-line for information, frequently competing with their own travel managers for data on prices and flights, in the belief that their own research ability is superior to the travel experts'.

Personal motivation enters the scene when the business traveller is taking a spouse or partner with them, and when leisure activities are to be included as an adjunct to the business trip. A business person may also be interested in travelling with a specific carrier in order to take advantage of frequent flyer schemes which allow them to take a leisure trip with the airline when they have accumulated sufficient miles. This may entail travelling on what is neither the cheapest nor the most direct route.

Factors such as these can cause friction between the traveller and their company, since the decision about whether to travel, and how and when, may not rest with the traveller themselves, but rather with a senior member of the company, whose concern may have more to do with ensuring the company receives value for money than any considerations of comfort or status.

It was believed that when videoconferencing facilities were introduced a few years ago, this would herald the decline of business travel. In fact, the reverse has occurred; traditional meetings continue, while conferences and trade shows are continuing to expand.

Motivators and facilitators

We have dealt up to now with the factors that motivate tourists to take holidays. However, in order to take a holiday, the tourist requires both time and money. These factors do not motivate in themselves, but they make it possible for prospective tourists to indulge in their desires. They are known for this reason as facilitators.

Facilitators play a major role in relation to the specific objectives of the tourist. An increase in disposable income, for instance, means that the tourist can enjoy a wider choice of destination. Better accessibility to the destination, or more favourable exchange rates against the local currency, easier entry without political barriers, and friendly locals speaking the language of the tourist, all act as facilitators as well as motivating the choice of destination.

A growing characteristic within wealthier countries in this new century is the presence of 'cash rich, time poor' consumers who are prepared to sacrifice money to save time. The implications of this phenomenon are significant for the industry. Those who can offer the easiest and fastest means of communicating opportunities, prices and booking facilities, couple with reliability and good service, can gain access to a wealthy, rapidly expanding market. Whether this race will be won by the direct sell organizations using websites and call centres, or by retailers using new sales techniques (such as experienced travel counsellors prepared to call on their customers in the latter's own time and home, including evenings and weekends), remains to be seen.

Factors influencing changes in tourism demand

It is fitting to complete this chapter by recognizing that patterns of demand in tourism are affected by two distinct sets of factors. First, we have factors which cannot be predetermined or forecast but which influence changes, sometimes with very little advance warning. The second set of factors will include cultural, social and technological changes going on in society, many of which can be forecast and for which there is time to adapt tourism products to meet new needs and expectations.

In the first category we must include changes influenced by economic or political circumstances, climate and natural or artificial disasters. Economic influences will be examined more thoroughly in the following chapter but here it will be salutary to look at just some of the factors which have impacted so severely on demand for foreign tourism in recent years.

Undoubtedly, the outbreak of war has been the single greatest threat to foreign travel for the past half century. Millions of tourists visited the former Yugoslavia every year during the 1980s, but this market virtually disappeared in the 1990s when civil wars broke out. The Vietnam War and its aftermath killed off much tourism to South-East Asia in the 1960s–70s, and the various wars in the Middle East curtailed travel there, if for a shorter time. Civil war and ethnic strife have long inhibited the development of tourism in many African countries.

More recently, it has been the threat of terrorist attacks, actual or perceived, which is inhibiting global travel: both Western fear of travel to Muslim countries and a general fear of travel to cities threatened by Islamic extremists. While terrorism was responsible for a number of crises in the 1980s (notably the attack on the US Marine barracks at Beirut in October 1983, Air India flight 182 off Ireland in 1985 and the disaster of Pan Am flight 103 over Lockerbie in December 1988), attacks have escalated in the 1990s and early twenty-first century, and it is sobering to recall some of the key events in these years (see Table 4.2).

Table 4.2 A decade of violence: major global terrorist attacks 1995–mid-2005

Date	Site	Death toll
19 April 1995	Oklahoma	169
23 November 1996	Ethiopian Airlines over Indian Ocean	127
7 August 1998	Nairobi, Kenya and Dar es Salaam, Mozambique (US Embassy complexes)	253
11 September 2001	Twin towers, New York	2,749
12 October 2002	Bali, Indonesia	202
11 March 2004	Madrid, Spain	191
7 July 2005	London, England (followed by a series of failed attacks two weeks later)	56
23 July 2005	Sharm el-Sheikh, Egypt	c.88

These figures do not take account of the several serious attacks on Russian soil by Chechen separatists, or smaller attacks by Islamic extremists on Jordan, Tunisia, Yemen and Kenya in 2002, and on sites in Casablanca, Morocco; Jakarta, Indonesia; Riyadh, Saudi Arabia; and Istanbul, Turkey in 2003. The escalation in the number of attacks, together with the near-certainty by officials that further attacks will take place, especially in the USA and UK, has led to long-term uncertainty about growth prospects for global travel.

The second factor recently undermining world travel growth has been the Iraqi War which began in March 2003, and the subsequent destabilization during the occupation of that country. Coupled with on-going conflict following war in Afghanistan, these two conflagrations show no signs of leading to peaceful conclusions at the time of writing, restricting travel demand and adding to uncertainty for the travel industry.

No less serious for global travel has been the threat posed by the rising impact of disease on a world-wide scale. The emergence of more virulent and vaccine-resistant forms of malaria in Africa and Asia has discouraged tourists from visiting these areas. Countries in Asia suffered the double blow of a serious outbreak of SARS (severe acute respiratory syndrome) early in 2003 which led to the cancellation of many flights and tourist movements – travel to China virtually ceased, apart from that by adjacent neighbours, for a period of some six months. During this period, Britain was also severely hit by outbreaks of disease; first, with the discovery of BSE in British herds which, although with only limited ability to cross the species to humans, scared away many potential visitors; and subsequently by an outbreak of foot-and-mouth disease which, while far less dangerous to human beings, received massive negative publicity through scare stories in the foreign press (to some extent the result of inept and draconian control measures in the UK which were perceived as actively discouraging tourists from visiting rural areas). In 2005, China and Vietnam were both hit by outbreaks of virulent Asian bird flu which has the potential to cross the species and create a pandemic among humans.

Finally, one must include the issue of climate change, which is contributing to natural disasters affecting tourist destinations globally. Areas already prone to heavy rainfall or hurricanes are witnessing conditions which are leading to catastrophe for locals and tourists alike, crowned by the disasters of the tsunami in the Far East at the end of 2004 and the impact of Hurricane Katrina on New Orleans and the US Gulf Coast in 2005.

Few of these events were predictable in advance. The lesson for the industry has been that, wherever possible, companies must be prepared for rapidly changing circumstances, often at very short notice, building up an organization and products which are flexible and adaptable to cope with change. The lesson for government has been that the tourism industry is vital to the UK economy, and recovery should be supported with public funds if small firms are to remain viable. In terms of demand for foreign travel, undoubtedly these events compound fear of foreign travel generally, and those most averse to risk-taking – our psychocentrics – are likely to choose to spend their holidays nearer to home, or at very least in countries viewed as being safer.

Social change is easier to predict, as are long-term trends in travel patterns. All too often, however, the industry has been slow to respond to these indicators. We know, for example, that only one family in four in the UK now conforms to the stereotypical family of two parents and two children, and that increasing numbers of people are living alone or bringing up children as single parents, yet the 'untypical' composition of families is not welcomed by operators whose pricing structure may weigh unfairly against such tourists. With increasing life expectancy, rise in divorce and fall in marriage rates, there are now some seven million single-person households in Britain, yet high additional charges for single tourists in package tours remain the norm, and demand for single accommodation is often difficult to meet. Other notable changes in British society include an increase in spending power among working women, and earlier maturation of children leading to demand for more adult holidays. Children now exert much more influence in travel decisions, and are tending to travel more with friends than in the traditional family group.

Perhaps most notable has been the impact of a growing market of seniors who are active, have high spending power and are looking for new experiences in their travels (for those who write off the senior market as unadventurous, it's worth bearing in mind that Dennis Tito, the world's first space traveller, was over 60 when he took his space flight in 2001). The over-50s today account for one-third of all the disposable income in the UK. While the total population of Britain is expected to fall in the medium term, it is estimated there will be a 31 per cent increase in the over-55s by 2020, with many seniors taking early retirement to spend the inheritances arising from the sale of their parents' properties on long-haul and cruise holidays. By 2017 there will be more people aged over 65 in Britain than under 16. It has been estimated that this will lead to seniors enjoying an additional five million holidays a year by 2020 – many of these far more active than the erstwhile 'sitting on the beach with a knotted handkerchief on the head' stereotype so popular with the media.

Another fast growing market is the gay/lesbian so-called 'pink market'. Members of this group in the UK typically take one domestic and two foreign holidays each year, earning more – and spending more – than the average traveller. They particularly enjoy travelling to destinations where their orientation is unquestioned, such as Montreal, Bangkok and the Sydney Mardi Gras festival.

Example   Catering for the pink pound

The UK's first call centre aimed at the gay/lesbian market opened in 2004. Outlet 4 Travel, a member of the Freedom Travel Group, planned to include programmes to destinations outside the obvious ones, inspired by dedicated gay agencies in the USA. The agency claims, 'Most gay men and women have to spend a lot of time looking on the Internet to book a holiday, unless they want to go to the usual places. They have to put it together themselves, which often works out more expensive'.

Source: *The Observer* travel news, 29 Aug 2004

This market has already been successfully tapped in the USA, where travel propensity is high: 91 per cent take annual vacations (54 per cent overseas) compared with a national average of only 64 per cent (9 per cent overseas).

Travellers of all kinds are now both sophisticated and demanding, often being more familiar with world travel destinations and attractions than those selling the products. This produces a new kind of challenge for a professional level of service which the industry is still a long way from meeting.

There are many other clear social trends in the industry in the opening years of the twenty-first century for which suppliers and agents must learn to cater. Greater choice in consumer purchasing of all kinds is leading to demand for more flexible packages of differing duration; many will require tailor-made approaches to packaging, and companies are establishing divisions specifically for this purpose. This has led to the phenomenon of *dynamic packaging*, in which agents and operators put together individual elements of the package, usually by a search of websites. This process, however, is labour intensive and requires greater product knowledge.

Earlier in this text, reference was made to the way in which the mass demand for passive beach holidays has given way to demand for more active holidays of all kinds, even from those in the upper age brackets among tourists. Special-interest holidays now cater for the widening range of interests of a leisure-oriented society. Adventure holidays, both domestic and foreign, are now packaged by operators to appeal to a range of markets.

In the latter years of the last century tour operators attempted to gain market share by cutting prices and making budget offers which often fell below the quality levels anticipated by consumers. Selling on price rather than quality became the keynote for the industry. Consumers were encouraged to buy on price and seek out the cheapest. Inevitably the rising toll of complaints forced companies to reconsider value for money and quality assurance, although deep discounting remains the bugbear of the industry, both for traditional package tours and for the cruise market.

In the format of package tours, we find demand moving in two distinct directions. On the one hand, self-catering has become increasingly popular, partly as a cost-saving exercise but equally as a means of overcoming the constraints imposed by package holidays in general and the accommodation sector in particular. Set meals at set times gave way to 'eat what you please, where you please, when you please'. In reply, the package tour industry provided the product to meet this need: the French *gîte* holidays became popular and across Southern Europe self-catering villas and apartments flourished, while in the UK demand moved from resort hotels and guest houses to self-catering flats. Hundreds of thousands of Britons invested in time-share property in order to own their own 'place in the sun', or increasingly found their own accommodation abroad, while the operators provided 'seat-only' packages on charter aircraft to cater for their transport needs. But perhaps the most significant development has been the increase in second-home ownership. Government figures reveal that 177,000 English households owned homes abroad in 2004 (a 14 per cent increase over the previous year), while second homes in the UK increased by 11 per cent to over 229,000 in the same year. Other sources put UK property ownership abroad far higher, with some estimates suggesting that as many as 500,000 Britons own properties in France alone. This has fuelled the growth of the low-cost airlines from and to regional airports on the Continent.

The other side of the coin is reflected in the growth in demand for all-inclusive holidays, which we looked at earlier in this chapter. This particular type of holiday is likely to experience continuing demand both for short- and long-haul destinations.

The market for short-break holidays of between one and three nights has also expanded rapidly, becoming frequently an addition to the principal holiday. The British tourism industry has benefited, as many of these breaks are taken within the UK, helping to make up for the decline in traditional two-week summer holidays at the seaside. The choice in short-break destinations abroad has also widened, with the traditional destinations of Paris, Amsterdam, Brussels, Barcelona and Rome being joined by Budapest, Prague, Kraców, Reykjavik, Carcassonne, Graz, Kaunas, Trieste and even New York.

Long-haul traffic is set to continue its rise as growing disposable incomes are matched by ever-reducing air fares, especially across the Atlantic. Holidays to the USA boomed, especially to Florida where many Britons also now own second homes, not only along the coast but also within easy driving distance of Orlando, where the popular Disney World theme park attracts millions eager to rent self-catering accommodation during their stay.

All this is not to say that the traditional sun, sea, sand holiday is in terminal decline; but those still loyal to this form of holiday are seeking more activities, including cultural visits inland from the popular resorts of Spain and Greece. Nor are these traditional holidaymakers content merely to seek out the familiar beaches of the Mediterranean; many are now travelling as far afield as Pattaya Beach and Phuket in Thailand, Goa in India and Mombasa in Kenya, to enjoy their beaches in more exotic surroundings.

The traditional 'law of tourism harmony', in which every aspect of the tour would be broadly of similar standard and quality, has given way to a 'pick and mix' approach, in which savings may be effected in one area in order to indulge oneself in another. Tourists may decide, for example, to choose cheap B&B accommodation while eating out in expensive restaurants; others are booking cheap flights on the low-cost airlines and a luxury hotel at their destination, on the grounds that the flight lasts a mere couple of hours, while they intend to stay several days in the hotel, so standards here are more important.

Example   Mixed-status leisure

Raymond Blanc's famed restaurant in Oxfordshire, *Le Manoir au Quat' Saisons*, is notably luxurious – and expensive – as is the accommodation in the associated hotel. However, an alternative 'package' has become available; rival accommodation in the form of a small campsite near the restaurant is now catering for those prepared to pay for the meal – among the most expensive in Britain – but not the cost of an overnight stay in the hotel.

By contrast, the term 'Hilton Hippies' has been used to describe those who may want to engage in rough activities such as mountain biking by day, but who look for luxury in their overnight accommodation. This is another example of the more flexible approach to holidays for which the travel industry must learn to cater.

In most developed countries, those in work are forecast to enjoy increased disposable incomes and a higher propensity to travel abroad. On the other hand, there will continue to be a relatively high number of unemployed in the population, most of whom will be unable to take holidays of any kind. In the past, those with spouses who have not wished to travel abroad have tended not to do so themselves, but lifestyle changes could mean that an increasing number of happily married couples will choose to holiday separately, each 'doing their own thing'.

Those charged with the task of marketing to tourists must be fully familiar with patterns of tourist behaviour, and with any trends which might suggest these are changing. Some of these changes will be generated by tourists themselves, others will come about as a result of changes taking place in the business environment, and in society as a whole. What must be recognized is that the pace of change in the tourism world is speeding up all the time, requiring entrepreneurs to react faster than they have needed to do in the past. Of equal importance is the requirement for industry to recognize that protection of the environment and the indigenous populations in the destination countries must also be taken into account, and companies will have to ensure that any new initiatives do not depart from the obligation to ensure products are sustainable. The days of 'slash and burn' tourism exploitation are over.

Notes

1 Holloway, J C, *Marketing for Tourism*, Prentice Hall, 4th edn 2004
2 Plog, S, Why Destination Areas Rise and Fall in Popularity, paper presented to the Southern Chapter of the Travel Research Association, 1972
3 For example, research conducted by Mount Vernon Hospital, London, in 2003

Further reading

Carey, S, Why It Just Got a Little Bit Harder to See the World, *Wall Street Journal*, 20 November 2003, p 1

Krippendorf, J, *The Holiday Makers: Understanding the Impact of Leisure and Travel*, Heinemann, 1984

Ross, G, *The Psychology of Tourism*, Hospitality Press (Melbourne), 1994

Ryan, C, *Recreational Tourism: a Social Science Perspective*, Routledge, 1991

Questions and discussion points

1   In 2005, Contiki Holidays announced their intention of launching a new style of holiday aimed at the youth market, based on the resort of Mykonos. The aim was to move away from the negative image associated with the 18–30's drink and sex market.

> Times have changed, and today's younger market lives a much healthier and more discerning lifestyle, and no longer wants to spend a week in basic accommodation getting hammered.
> Simon O'Flynn, Marketing Manager,
> quoted in *Travel Weekly*, 11 March 2005

Are young people looking for a different kind of holiday? What activities would you recommend to introduce to the programme, and how would you put over the message in your marketing campaigns?

2   Is there a parallel between risk avoiders and those leisure travellers unwilling to visit countries where terrorist acts have been committed? How do factors such as age, nationality or personality influence decisions?

When terrorist attacks were launched in Bali, the British Foreign and Commonwealth Office advised UK residents against visiting for well over a year, while a similar strike in Spain was largely disregarded. Are government recommendations governed by political sensitivities, or by safety considerations for their electorate? Should such recommendations (which affect a tourist's ability to obtain travel insurance) be applicable, allowing governments to restrict the freedom to travel? Should the non risk-averse tourist ignore such warnings and demonstrate their right to travel freely?

3   In a group, discuss your own personal preferences for a holiday destination and activity. How far do these reflect your own personality? Would you sometimes choose a holiday that appears an allocentric choice, and sometimes one that appears more like a psychocentric choice? What might account for this?

Assignment topics

1   You are working with a local authority tourism department which is planning a marketing drive to the region. They want to know what qualitative data are available about tourists who currently visit the region, and have asked you to prepare a short report giving as much detail as you can obtain about visitors presently coming to the region. Your sources of information should be listed, with brief comments on the value of each. Conclude your report by advising your employers what further research could be carried out by the local authority, within reasonable cost limits,

that would enhance the data you have obtained and would help in drafting a series of television advertisements to the region.

2   Do tourists behave differently when they go on holiday abroad? In what ways? As a tourism researcher, undertake a series of depth interviews (at least ten) with people who have holidayed abroad in the preceding two years, which will help to throw light on this. Your interviews should be conducted with the aid of a list of key questions centring on the topics on which you would like them to elaborate. Classify the information you receive into categories of behaviour, and produce a conclusion which would offer guidelines on how the information you have obtained could be useful to those in the industry. The issue of sustainability should underpin at least some of your questioning.

5 The economic impact of tourism

Objectives

After studying this chapter, you should be able to:

- identify the economic benefits of tourism for a nation, both nationally and regionally
- be aware of the principal trends in tourism, as they affect Britain specifically, and the world generally
- understand how tourism is measured statistically
- recognize the limitations of statistical measurement.

Introduction

> Tourism is an increasingly competitive industry. If we are to keep pace with world travel fore-casts, we must be aiming for a £100 billion industry as a minimum by 2010.
>
> Tessa Jowell, Secretary of State for Culture,
> Media and Sport, May 2004 Report

Tourism is a human activity which arises from the economic circumstances and preferences of consumers. It also has economic consequences, both good and bad, for nations and their regions. For both these reasons, we need to study and understand the economic nature of tourism. This is a topic which is complex, and can only be touched on in this text; readers who wish to examine the subject in depth are referred to texts designed for this purpose, such as Bull (1995). The aim of this chapter will be primarily to explore the economic impact of tourism resulting from national and international tourist flows, and the ways in which this is measured and recorded. In later chapters, the economics of the firm, the industry and its various sectors will be examined.

First, however, we will look at the movement of tourists internationally, and some of the economic factors influencing these flows.

The international tourist market

Travel and tourism is probably the single most important industry in the world. It currently accounts for at least 6 per cent of the world's gross domestic product (GDP), and employs 127 million people around the world, one job in every fifteen. According to the most recent estimate by the World Tourism Organization, some 763 million international trips were taken in 2004 (against 691 million in the previous year), with provisional worldwide tourism receipts (excluding the cost of international fares) reaching $622 billion ($524 billion in 2003). These figures do not include the vast number of people taking trips within their own country; probably six times this number will take a domestic trip lasting at least four nights (see Table 5.1).

The rapid increase in international travel during the early post-war years, exceeding 10 per cent per annum from 1950 to 1960, could not be permanently sustained, of course, and it reflected the pent-up demand which the war years, and the slow economic recovery after the war, had constrained. However, it is worth noting that apart from the odd hiccup, from 1970 to the 1990s annual growth ran above 4 per cent, even in the early 1990s when there was a global recession. The WTTC estimates the annual growth in 2004 as having continued this trend, with the tourism industry generating some $6.2 trillion globally. The good news for the tourism industry is therefore that, although the rate of increase in arrivals in some recent years has faltered – scarcely surprising, given the world events since September 2001 – the long-term trend continues upwards. As controls over the freedom of movement of populations in many countries are gradually lifted, many are seeking the opportunity for the first time to travel outside their own borders, not least residents of China, now the seventh biggest generator of overseas tourist expenditure. The WTO therefore continues to take an optimistic

Table 5.1 A profile of international tourist arrivals and receipts, 1950–2004

Year	Arrivals (m)	Receipts (US $bn)
1950	25.3	2.1
1960	69.3	6.9
1970	165.8	17.9
1980	278.2	106.5
1990	445.8	272.9
1995	544.9	410.8
1996	575.3	446.0
1997	597.8	451.0
1998	617.4	448.6
1999	641.1	459.7
2000	685.5	476.4
2001	683.8	464.4
2002	702.8	482.3
2003 (P)	690.9	524.2
2004 (P)	763.0	622.0

Note: Excludes international fares. (P) provisional.
Source: from *Yearbook of Tourism Statistics*. Published by World Tourism Organization

Table 5.2 Leading tourism-generating countries, 2003 (based on provisional tourism expenditure)

	Country	Expenditure (US$ billion)
1	Germany	64.7
2	USA	56.6
3	UK	48.5
4	Japan	29.0
5	France	23.6
6	Italy	20.5
7	China	15.2
8	Netherlands	14.6
9	Canada	13.3
10	Russian Federation	12.9

Source: 'Leading tourism-generating countries, 2003 (based on provisional tourism expenditure' from *Yearbook of Tourism Statistics*. Published by World Tourism Organization

view of the long term, estimating that tourism will continue to increase for the foreseeable future.

International tourism is generated for the most part within the nations of Europe, North America and Japan, the result of low prices, frequent flights, and large, relatively wealthy populations (see Table 5.2). Japan in particular has been growing strongly as a tourism-generating country in recent years, due to its wealth and a growing willingness on the part of its population to take holidays. Traditionally, the Japanese work ethic militated against their taking all the holidays to which they are entitled, but with government encouragement and changes in attitude to work and loyalty to their firms, the Japanese have taken to travelling abroad in greater numbers and for longer periods of time. As a result, Japan is now fourth among the top ten generating countries which together are responsible for well over half the total expenditure on foreign travel.

It is interesting to note the changes occurring over time among the generating countries. While the leading half-dozen countries change little from one year to another, China has joined the top ten as the country enjoys relatively more freedom of movement, with some 20 million currently travelling abroad each year (mainly to adjacent countries). Estimates suggest that even given existing conditions, some 50 million Chinese have an income which would allow them to travel further afield (estimates for domestic holidays taken in China in 2003 are as high as 870 million), and VisitBritain expects 200,000 of these to be visiting Britain by 2010, following the granting of Approved Destination Status. Hong Kong, which enjoys special status within China, already lies thirteenth in overseas expenditure. The Russian Federation is also rising sharply in the list as the wealthy elite choose to spend their holidays abroad, while Poland and other former Eastern Bloc countries are all showing strong growth. The so-called tiger economies of the Pacific region, including Taiwan, the Republic of Korea, Thailand, Singapore and Malaysia, have also experienced a major upsurge in foreign travel, only briefly interrupted when the Thai baht collapsed in the summer of 1997. Germany replaces the United States to become again the leading generating country, and although a popular destination country also, its balance of payment on the tourism account remains in substantial deficit, as does that of the UK. The popularity of the USA as a destination helps to off-set the high spend abroad by US residents.

Looking at the flow of international tourism over the long term, one can conclude that the tourism business is surprisingly resilient. Whatever short-term problems emerge – acts of terrorism, medical emergencies like SARS and fowl disease, the 2004 Asian tsunami – tourists eventually return in ever greater numbers.

Eastern Europe is growing in popularity as a destination too. Hungary and Poland are now eleventh and fourteenth in terms of visitor numbers, and the Russian Federation takes twentieth place. China is rapidly rising in popularity, with an estimated 41.8 million visitors in 2004, which puts it into fourth place ahead of Italy. The Russian Federation and South Africa both have great potential for growth as destination countries, but the political picture for these two is clouded. Uncertainty about security and the political situation in South Africa hinders expansion (see the case study at the end of this text), while Russia still demands expensive visas for tourists from Western countries (and complicated paperwork to obtain them), a major drawback in attracting visitors, especially those visiting briefly from cruise ships; while the Baltic States of Estonia, Latvia and Lithuania, by contrast, require none, and have experienced massive growth since their return to democracy and subsequent integration into the EU. The capital, Tallinn, in Estonia, has also benefited from its seaboard location 1 hour and 40 minutes by fast ferry from Finland's capital, Helsinki, resulting in a huge flood of tourists travelling between these cities. The open-skies policy within the EU, and resultant expansion of no-frills airlines operating within the new borders, has also helped fuel this boom, and the city is now popular as a destination for young singles.

Simply looking at receipts (see Table 5.3) will not give a sound picture of the value of tourism to an economy. The countries with the highest per capita receipts are those where prices are highest, including Sweden, Denmark and Japan, with the UK well down the list. The highest spend per capita by tourists coming to Britain tends to be among the Scandinavians, especially Icelandic visitors, while those from Eastern Europe spend least. In economic terms, the financial value of tourism to a country is more important than the number of tourists it receives, so it is important to assess the

Table 5.3 Leading tourism-receiving countries, 2003 (based on provisional international tourist arrivals in millions)

	Country	Receipts (US$ billion)
1	France	75.0
2	Spain	51.8
3	USA	41.2
4	Italy	39.6
5	China	33.0
6	UK	24.7
7	Austria	19.1
8	Mexico	18.7
9	Germany	18.4
10	Canada	17.5

Source: 'Leading tourism-generating countries, 2003 (based on provisional tourism expenditure' from *Yearbook of Tourism Statistics*. Published by World Tourism Organization average daily spend of tourists from different countries, and the average length of time tourists from a particular country spend when visiting a country. One must also always take account of factors likely to lead to the growth or decline of tourism from each country. The potential for growth is high for those living in Eastern Europe, whose income, for the most part, is rising strongly since the fall of Communism. The entry of several of these countries into the EU in 2004 has already boosted tourism in both directions within Europe. The potential from Japan remains high also, as only a small proportion of the population travels abroad, and those that do are relatively free spenders. This is partly accounted for by their high spend on shopping and souvenirs for friends and relatives. Australians are also high spenders, together with tourists from Thailand, Taiwan and Singapore. In spite of the high revenues received from Americans travelling abroad, only a small minority of the population actually possess a passport; most American tourists tend to travel to adjacent countries which do not require them to carry passports, and because of the size and diversity of their own landscape, many are content to take their holidays within their own country – so the *propensity* to take holidays abroad is another important characteristic to take into account. The propensity to take foreign holidays varies considerably within Europe too. It is high among the Scandinavians – no doubt in part due to the long winters and lack of sunshine – while only a quarter of Italians share this desire for foreign travel. Italians are surprisingly unadventurous in travel; nearly half of those travelling on holiday are content to return to the same resort, and even the same hotel, every year for a decade. The French, too, prefer to travel within their own country, often to second homes in the countryside, rather than to venture abroad. Although Britons have a reputation for travelling abroad, a third of the population take no holidays at all during the year (but not necessarily the same third every year).

We should also recognize that, while tourism expenditure in aggregate will be highest from wealthy countries having large populations, the high disposable income among the populations of smaller nations with a significant proportion of wealthy residents, such as Switzerland or Luxembourg, will tend to lead to higher levels of participation in international tourism – and where international borders are so close to places of residence, as is the case with these two countries, this will significantly increase the propensity to travel abroad.

While (as we have seen earlier in this book) there are many factors which motivate people to travel abroad, the major factor will be the relative cost, compared with their income. Since greater demand also leads to lower prices, with transport and accommodation costs falling for each additional person booked, there is a direct relationship between cost, price and demand (see Figure 5.1).

Figure 5.1
The relationship between cost, price and demand

This helps to explain the vicious price wars in the travel industry, designed to capture market share and increase numbers, which have been so much a feature of competition in the travel industry over the past twenty years. One report claims the cost of international travel has fallen 55 per cent in real terms in the past 25 years[1]. As new no-frills airlines are founded every year, and several are embarking on longer-haul services, this trend is likely to continue, unless sharply curtailed by rising fuel prices or the imposition of fuel taxes to off-set pollution.

Other factors to take into account include attitudes to the use of leisure time. In the USA, some 30 per cent of the workforce take less than half the holiday time to which they are entitled – and this is in a country where the average paid holiday is still only two to three weeks, compared with the four to five weeks now standard throughout Europe. The Japanese, as we have seen, seldom take their full entitlement; with average holiday lengths of 17 days, they typically take only 9.5 days. Even in the UK, roughly a quarter of the working population fails to take its full entitlement.

Britain's place in world tourism

Britain has enjoyed comparable growth, both in its outbound and inbound markets, with other Western nations. At the beginning of the 1950s, Britons were only taking some 5.5 per cent of their holidays abroad; but by the end of the century this had risen to 46 per cent. In 2004, British residents took nearly 64.2 million trips abroad, with many travelling abroad two or more times. UK visitors to Spain, at 13.8 million, exceed those to France, at 11.6 million, but the proportion of those on package tours is far greater in the case of the former destination. France's appeal, because of its proximity to England and the nature of its tourist attractions, is for self-drive holidays in particular, and the Eurotunnel services between Folkestone and Calais, as well as improvements to cross-Channel ferry services, have facilitated this movement. Easier communications (especially low-cost air carrier routes to regional airports) have also led to many Britons buying second homes in France. The growth in long-haul holidays has also been marked, particularly to the United States, which was the third most popular destination for British holidaymakers, who numbered over 4 million in 2004.

The propensity of the British to take a holiday – that is, the ratio of those taking holidays out of the total population – is high (see Table 5.4). Around 60 per cent of Britons take a holiday of four nights or more, and this figure has remained relatively unchanged for many years, having peaked in 1980 at 62 per cent.

In most respects, future trends for British travel appear healthy. The British have now firmly adopted the habit of taking an annual holiday. Not only are disposable incomes growing; inherited wealth is also having an impact on holiday spending, as those in middle age inherit properties from the first generation of parents to own their own homes on a wide scale. Many older people enjoy good health and leisure time, having retired early. On the other hand, pensions are now worth less as they are no longer linked to increases in average earnings, and the government is moving towards upping the retirement age. Workers are encouraged to invest a greater proportion of their income into saving for pensions. Savings have to be increased, or insurance taken

Table 5.4   Trends in British holiday taking: foreign holidays and inclusive tours, 1994–2004

Year	Holidays	Inclusive tours
	(000s)	(000s)
1994	27,337	15,164
1995	27,808	15,166
1996	26,765	13,901
1997	29,138	15,394
1998	32,306	17,437
1999	35,023	19,077
2000	36,685	20,055
2001	38,670	20,631
2002	39,902	20,638
2003	41,197	19,515
2004	42,912	19,803

Source: Business Monitor MQ6. © Crown copyright

out, to pay for possible nursing-home care in old age. These factors, common throughout the developed world, have persuaded forecasters that while holidays will become more frequent, they will be of shorter duration, and spread more evenly throughout the year.

Britain received 27.8 million visitors from abroad in 2004, spending over £13 billion. Of these, around 9.3 million were tourists on holiday. The number of British tourists travelling abroad on holiday is therefore nearly five times greater than the number of foreign holidaymakers visiting Britain. The WTO has forecast that the inbound numbers will double by 2020. However, the gap between expenditure by British residents travelling abroad for all tourist-related purposes and expenditure in Britain by visitors from abroad continues to widen, with the result that there is an expanding balance of payments deficit on tourism account over the past decade (see Figure 5.2). Moreover, no account at the time of writing can be taken of the impact of the terrorist strikes in London in July 2005, which may impact upon anticipated numbers for the coming year.

However, Britain does benefit substantially from incoming and domestic tourism. In 2004, British residents took some 121 million domestic holidays, spending £76 billion. The industry gives employment to around 2.1 million people, working either in tourism or a closely related activity; this represents some 7 per cent of all those employed. Tourism accounts for some 4.5 per cent of all export earnings (and nearly a quarter of all services exports). This compares with over 20 per cent in Spain, which, in view of the volatile nature of the business, might appear to many observers to be an over-dependence upon tourism in the economy. However, some economists have argued that these figures grossly underestimate the actual value of tourism to Britain; the World Travel and Tourism Council has put Britain's annual earnings in excess of £105 billion for travel and tourism and related businesses, more than 12 per cent of GDP, and has forecast that this could rise to £174 billion by 2010.

Figure 5.2
Britain's balance
of payments on
tourism account,
1970–2004

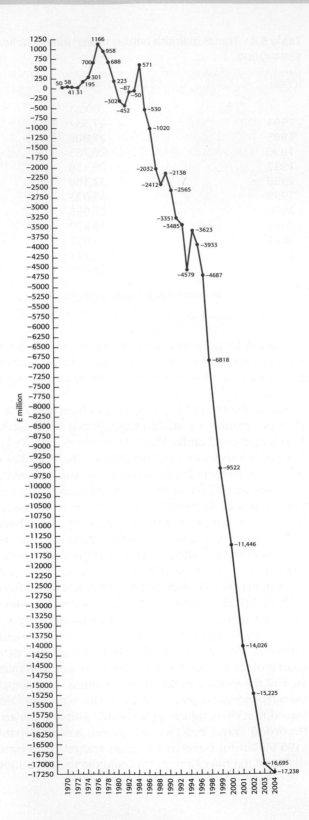

One must also take account of many other forms of tourism from which the UK benefits. London in particular has always benefited from an influx of wealthy foreigners, particularly African, Arab and more recently Russian and Chinese, occupying second homes. The importance of foreign students coming on short or extended visits to Britain to learn the language (quite apart from those engaged in full-time academic study who are not included in tourist statistics) should also be borne in mind. The award of the Olympic Games to London in 2012 will be a major factor in boosting tourism revenue to the UK, both in that year and in subsequent years, as the country gains a higher international profile.

The value of economic data

Gathering data on tourists is a vital task for the government of a country, both for use by its own national tourist office and for the benefit of the providers of tourism services. Governments need to know the contribution which tourism makes to the economy in terms of income, employment, investment and the balance of payments. Concern with regional development requires that these statistics be sufficiently refined to allow them to be broken down by region. Governments will also wish to compare their tourism performance with that of other countries, as well as to establish their performance in attracting tourists to the country over a period of time.

Tourism organizations, whether in the public or the private sector, need such data to enable them to forecast what will happen in the future. This means identifying trends in the market, patterns of growth and changing demand for destinations, facilities or types of holiday.

On the basis of this knowledge, future planning can be undertaken. The public sector will make recommendations and decisions regarding the *infrastructure* and *superstructure* needed to support growth. Infrastructure will include, for example, the building of new airports and seaport terminals or the expansion of existing ones, the provision of new or improved roads to the growth destinations, and the improvement of other services such as public utilities including water and electricity, which will be needed to cope with the expected expansion of tourism. Some of these plans may take many years to implement. The discussions surrounding the building of a fifth terminal at London's Heathrow airport took place over more than a decade, and will take several more years before the terminal comes into use. Similar debates are taking place regarding expansion at Gatwick, Luton and Stansted Airports. In the meantime, congestion in the air encourages carriers to switch air traffic to alternative airports. Schiphol in the Netherlands is one such airport which has actively promoted itself as an alternative to Heathrow, using the hub-and-spoke system, given that it offers services to around a dozen UK airports. Similarly, the new fast rail track for Eurotunnel's service from London to the Channel Tunnel took many years before approval was granted, and will not be fully operational before 2007. This will encourage a greater flow of tourists between London, Brussels and Paris and beyond, as well as diverting more air traffic to rail.

Superstructure comprises the tourist amenities needed – hotels, restaurants, shops and other services tourists take for granted when they visit. It cannot necessarily be assumed either that these services will be provided by developers in the private sector. If a new destination is being developed, there will be a degree of risk involved while the destination becomes established, and developers may be reluctant to invest in such projects as hotels until there is proven demand for the destination. Governments or local authorities can themselves undertake the construction of hotels, as often occurs in developing countries, or they can encourage hotel construction by underwriting costs or providing subsidies of some kind until the destination becomes established. Similarly, private companies can use the statistics which demonstrate growth or market change by extending or adapting their products to meet the changing needs of the marketplace.

To show how this information can be used, let us take the example of a destination such as London, which attracts a high volume of overseas visitors. The flow of these visitors will be affected by a great many different factors: if tourists can purchase more pounds sterling for their own currency, or if air fares have fallen to the destination, or if a major event such as an international exhibition is being organized, this will encourage tourism to the city. Outbreaks of foot-and-mouth disease among farmyard animals in the countryside, and terrorist activity in the capital (as in July 2005) affected decisions to come to Britain, while events abroad – war in Iraq and SARS (severe acute respiratory syndrome) in 2003, avian flu in 2004/5, and terrorist threats and actions around the world in 2004 and 2005 – have all left their mark on international travel plans in recent years. US tourists are particularly sensitive to the threat of terrorism, and will revert to holidaying at home if they sense that the risk of foreign travel is increasing. Negative first impressions, such as air pollution in the city, extensive littering, a decaying and overcrowded public transport system, even large numbers of homeless people on the streets, can affect tourism adversely, and tourists may decide to go elsewhere, or recommend to their friends that they do so.

Recessions may be hitting countries to a different extent, so that in one year the forecast might be for a reduced number of tourists from the USA, but a growth in the number from Japan. In the third quarter of 2000 the pound fell sharply against the dollar, while remaining relatively strong against European currencies. This would have encouraged Americans to travel to Britain, and the British to visit the Continent, while tourists from countries like Germany and France would have been dissuaded from coming to Britain and fewer Britons would have visited the USA. In 2004/5 the dollar weakened against both sterling and the euro, increasing travel from Britain and the Continent to the US (and, incidentally, further heightening the demand for second homes in Florida for the British). This uncertainty about currency movements makes forward planning difficult, adding another element of risk to product pricing, although this can be offset to some extent by the forward purchasing of foreign currencies. If Britain does eventually join the euro, one benefit will be help in stabilizing the travel business, and it will also allow British travellers to share with their counterparts in other EU countries the benefits of using a single currency across several countries, leading to a substantial saving on foreign exchange when calculating the costs of a holiday abroad. Such savings are less likely to be welcomed by those in the industry who provide foreign exchange facilities, however!

Companies and tourist offices will have to take all of these factors into account when drawing up their promotional campaigns – and may need to consider employing staff with the appropriate languages to deal with any new incoming markets. On the basis of the forecasts made, organizations must decide where they will advertise, to whom, and with what theme. International tourism depends on more than merely economic behaviour of tourists, however; as we noted in the previous chapter, it will also be influenced by motivation arising from the tourists' efforts to meet their psychological or sociological needs.

The economic impact of tourism

It is the concern of this chapter to examine the economic effects of tourism, and how these are measured. As in other industries, tourism affects the economy of those areas – whether regions, countries or continents – where it takes place. These are known as tourist *destinations*, or *receiving areas*, and many become dependent upon an inflow of tourism to sustain their economy. This is especially true of developing countries, some of which are largely or almost totally dependent upon tourism. The areas from which the tourists come to visit these destinations are known as *generating areas*, and, of course, as the tourists are taking their money with them to spend in other places, this represents a net loss of revenue to the generating area, and a gain to the receiving area. We can say that incoming tourist spend is an *export*, while outgoing tourist spend is an *import*.

The flow of tourists between generating and receiving areas can be measured in four distinct ways. We must examine the effect on *income*, on *employment*, on the area's *balance of payments* and on *investment and development*. Let us look at each of these in turn.

Income

Income is generated from wages and salaries, interest, rent and profits. In a labour-intensive industry such as tourism, the greatest proportion is likely to be derived from wages and salaries paid to those working in jobs either directly serving the needs of tourists or benefiting indirectly from the tourists' expenditure. Income will be greater in those areas which generate large numbers of tourists, where visitors tend to stay for longer periods, where the destination attracts an up-market or more free-spending clientele, and where there are many opportunities to spend. A destination such as the Côte d'Azur, for example, satisfies most of these criteria, attracting not only many overseas visitors for a fairly long season (even through the winter some tourists will be attracted to the milder climate) but also bringing in many domestic tourists from other areas of France. A number of up-market resorts such as Nice, Cannes, Antibes, St Tropez and Juan les Pins provide a good range of relatively expensive hotels; there are also expensive shops and restaurants, casinos, night-clubs and discos where the high-spend tourists can be relieved of their money. There are opportunities for water-based activities such as yachting or fishing, with marinas to attract the wealthy motor yacht owners, and there are numerous attractions nearby which bring in the day excursionists by coach or private car. Finally, the area is also well served with conference and exhibition halls, which attract high-spend business tourists. All these services are labour intensive, and thus invaluable in providing local employment.

It is important to recognize that while income may be greatest where wage levels are high, and there is relatively little unemployment in the area, tourism may in fact be of greater value in those areas where there are few other opportunities for employment. Tourism is the main income generator for one-third of the developing nations[2], but is also a major income generator in the Western world. In Britain, to take one example, tourism is of prime importance in areas where there is little industry, such as in the Scottish Highlands, western Wales and Cornwall. While tourism jobs are often seen as low-wage, and based on seasonal employment, many are neither seasonal nor temporary. As to low-wage jobs, one must take into account that without tourism, many workers would have no source of income at all, given that tourism often takes place in areas where there is little alternative work, forcing workers to move away from the area.

Income is also generated from interest, rent and profits on tourism businesses. This could include, for example, the interest paid on loans to an airline in order to buy aircraft, or rent paid to a landowner for a car park or campsite near the sea. We must also count taxation on tourism activities, such as value added tax (and occasionally additional room taxes) on hotel bills, duty and taxation on petrol used by tourists, and other direct forms of taxation which countries may choose to levy on tourists to raise additional public income. In Austria, to give one example, there is a *Kurtaxe* imposed on accommodation to raise money for the local authority. Most countries, including the UK, levy a *departure tax* on all passengers travelling by air, while in the USA airline taxes are levied on both departing and arriving travellers.

Example VAT on tourist facilities

The Czech Republic was admitted to the EU in 2004. As a direct result, it raised VAT on restaurant meals from 5 per cent to 19 per cent; VAT on hotel accommodation also increased to the same level in the following year. The industry has argued against common VAT policies in the EU, on the grounds that it would tend to discourage international tourists, but it provides governments with a substantial tax bonus.

The sum of all incomes in a country is called the national income, and the importance of tourism to a country's economy can be measured by looking at the proportion of national income created by tourism. In Britain this is estimated to be about 3.4 per cent, including income from accommodation, tourist transport and all kinds of extras for which tourists pay. This may seem a small percentage, but even engineering, the country's largest industry, only contributes about 8 per cent to the national income. By contrast, some regions of the world, particularly the Caribbean countries, are heavily dependent upon the income from tourism, as one study undertaken in 1997 reveals (see Table 5.5). Some might see this as an unhealthy overdependence upon one rather volatile industry.

Table 5.5 Percentage of national income represented by tourism in selected countries, 1997

Country	Percentage
Antigua and Barbuda	87
Maldives	82
Balearics	81
St Lucia	46
Barbados	33
Bermuda	29

Source: *Spiegel* Special, 'Urlaub Total' No. 2 1997

Attempts to measure the impact of tourism are always difficult, because it is difficult to distinguish the spend by tourists and the spend by others in restaurants or shops, for example. In resorts, even such businesses as laundromats – which we would not normally associate with the tourism industry – might be highly dependent upon the tourist spend where, for instance, a large number of visitors are camping, caravanning or in self-catering facilities. Furthermore, tourism's contribution to the income of an area is enhanced by a phenomenon known as the *tourism income multiplier* (TIM). This arises because money spent by tourists in the area will be re-spent by recipients, augmenting the total. The multiplier is the factor by which tourist spend is increased in this process. This is easiest to demonstrate by way of the following example.

Example   The tourism income multiplier

A number of tourists visit Highjinks on Sea, spending £1,000 in hotels and other facilities there. This amount is received as income by the hoteliers and owners of the facilities, who, after paying their taxes and saving some of the income, spend the rest. Some of what they spend goes to buy items imported into the area, but the rest goes to shopkeepers, suppliers and other producers inside the area. These people in turn pay their taxes, save some money and spend the rest.

Let us assume that the average rate of taxation is 20p in the pound and that people are saving on average 10p in the pound of their gross income, and are therefore left to spend 70p in the pound on goods and services. Let us further assume that of this 70p in the pound spend, 20p is spent on goods and services imported from other areas, while the remaining 50p is retained within the local community. The original £1,000 spent by the tourists will then circulate in the local community as shown in Figure 5.3, in the category 'first circulation'.

Of the 50p spent within the community, some will go to local suppliers of such items as food. The shopkeepers or restaurateurs then pay their employees, who in turn shop in other shops locally, although some of what they purchase will have been brought into the region from outside. This second circulation will be further spent by the recipients, and so the cycle goes on, with a declining expenditure at each level of circulation. These cycles are illustrated in Figure 5.3, under the categories of second circulation, third circulation, and so on.

▶

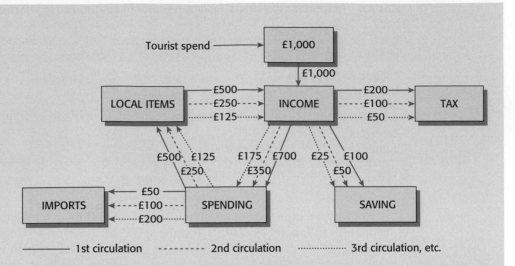

Figure 5.3
The tourism income multiplier at work

———— 1st circulation   - - - - - - - 2nd circulation   ··········· 3rd circulation, etc.

Each time the money is circulated in this way, some will be lost to the area. Taxes paid are transmitted outside the area, some of the savings may be similarly removed from the area, and some of the spend has gone to pay for goods imported into the area from other regions of the country or even from abroad. Expenditures in which the money is lost to other areas are known as *leakages* from the system. Leakages in this sense can therefore be regional or national, the latter being a loss of revenue to the country as a whole.

So far, how much income has been created? From Figure 5.3 we can see that it is £1,000 + £500 + £250 + £125 + ... A progression is developing, and by adding up all the figures or by using the appropriate mathematical formula, we will find that the total sum is £2,000. The original injection of £1,000 by tourists visiting the area has multiplied by a factor of 2 to produce an income of £2,000.

It is possible to forecast the value of the multiplier if one knows the proportion of leakages in the local economy. In the example above, tax was 20/100ths of original income, savings were 10/100ths of income and imports were 20/100ths of income. Total leakages therefore amount to 50/100ths, or half the original income. The multiplier can be found by applying the formula:

$$\text{Multiplier} = \frac{1}{\text{Proportion of leakages}}$$

In the example given, the multiplier was 1/0.5, or 2.

So in an economy with a high proportion of leakages, such as high tax rates (although we must remember that the government may choose to reinvest this tax money in the local economy, so much of it may not be lost for all time), or where many of the goods demanded by consumers are imported, TIM may be quite low, and the economy will not benefit greatly from tourism. Local hotels may also be foreign-owned, so that profits achieved are then transmitted to the hotel chain's head office and so lost to the area. This might be true of other tourist facilities in the area, and even local ground-handling agents or coach operators may be owned by companies based elsewhere, leading to further losses in the multiplier effect. On the other hand, where many firms are in the hands of locals, and leakages are minimized in this way, the TIM may be quite high, and tourism will contribute far more than the amount originally spent by the tourists themselves. The principal reasons for leakages include:

- cost of imported goods, especially food and drink
- foreign exchange costs of imports for the development of tourist facilities
- remittance of profits abroad
- remittance of wages by expatriates
- management fees or royalties for franchises
- payments to overseas carriers and travel companies
- costs of overseas promotion
- additional expenditure on imports resulting from the earnings of those benefiting from tourism.

Many studies have been undertaken of the TIM in different areas, ranging from individual resorts such as Eastbourne and Edinburgh to entire countries such as Barbados and Fiji. In most cases, the multiplier has varied between 1 and 2.5 (estimates have put it at about 1.7 for Britain as a whole, and around 1.2–1.5 for individual towns and regions in the UK), although in the case of some destinations in the developing world which depend heavily on outside investment and must import much of the food and other commodities demanded by tourists, the figure may be well below 1. Barbados, for instance, has been estimated at 0.60. Leakages in Western developed nations are generally estimated at around 10 per cent of tourism income, while in developing economies with strong tourism dependency such as Fiji, the Cook Islands, Mauritius and the Virgin Islands, estimates suggest that imports consume between 36 and 56 per cent of gross tourism receipts.

Figure 5.4
Leakage of foreign exchange earnings: sixteen countries

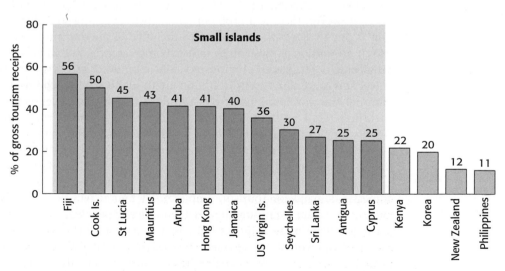

(Courtesy: The World Tourism Organization)

Employment

The WTO has estimated that around 260 million people work in jobs directly related to tourism around the world, and according to one source, by the end of 2005 tourism will have represented some 8.3 per cent of total world employment[3]. Its importance to many economies as a generator of employment will therefore be clear. Several of the leading tourism destinations in the world are developing countries, and in some tourism-dependent economies like the Caribbean, as many as 25 per cent of all jobs are associated with the tourism industry. Estimates suggest that some three million tourism jobs will be created in the ten nations which joined the European Union in 2004; most of these are expected to be in Poland and Hungary. Jobs are created in travel agencies, tour operators and other intermediaries who supply tourist services in both the generating and destination areas. Transport companies such as airlines will also employ staff to serve tourists in both areas. But the bulk of employment will be in the destination country, with jobs ranging from hotel managers to deckchair attendants, from excursion-booking clerks to cleaners employed in the stately homes that are open to the public, or maintenance staff who maintain the rides at leisure centres or theme parks in the resort.

Many of these jobs are seasonal or part-time, so that tourism's contribution to full-time employment is considerably less than its contribution to 'job-hours'. While this is a criticism of the industry in economic terms, and one that has resulted in large sums of money being spent in an effort to lengthen the tourist season in many resorts, one must be reminded that these jobs are often being created in areas where there is little alternative employment. It is also worth making the point that many of the jobs attract those who wish to work seasonally, such as students seeking jobs as resort representatives during the summer, or householders who wish to open their house for summer periods only as bed-and-breakfast establishments.

Earlier, it was pointed out that Britain has around two million workers involved in 'tourism or an associated activity'. This represents around 7 per cent of the British labour force. However, there is a problem about measuring the so-called 'related activities'. How is one to determine what is to be included in the tourism employment statistics? A high proportion of jobs will be in hotels and catering, not all of which are concerned with tourists. Estimates of those actually employed in the more narrowly defined 'travel and tourism industry' in Britain are thought to be much lower. In 1991, ABTA's National Training Board undertook a study of the travel services sector, embracing tour operating, retail travel and business travel, which concluded that around 80,000 were directly employed in these fields, of which perhaps 12,000 were in management posts (*An Occupational Mapping of the Travel Services Industry*, 1991[4]). This figure was estimated to have risen to approximately 122,600 by the end of the last century.

Clearly, for countries which are major receiving destinations or which enjoy a strong domestic demand for tourism, employment figures will be far higher. On balance, tourism as a form of employment is economically beneficial, although efforts must be made to create more full-time jobs in the industry. The extent to which tourism benefits employment can be seen when it is appreciated that, given the figure quoted earlier, roughly one job in twelve in the world is directly ascribed to tourism. The

World Travel and Tourism Council research identifies tourism as generating over 10 per cent of worldwide GDP – a measure of the total value of goods and services produced by the world's economy. Tourism is considered by many to be the largest industry in the world, and it is certainly the fastest growing.

Just as tourism is globally important, so it is important for regions within an economy. The multiplier which affects income in a region affects employment in the same way. If tourists stay at a destination, jobs are directly created in the tourism industry there. These workers and their families resident in the neighbourhood must also buy goods and services locally, their families require education and need medical care. This in turn gives rise to jobs in shops, schools and hospitals to serve these needs. The value of the employment multiplier is likely to be broadly similar to that of the TIM, assuming that jobs with average wage rates are created.

However, recent developments in technology are threatening labour opportunities in tourism. For example, computer reservations systems (CRS) are rapidly replacing manual reservations systems, and as a result many booking clerk jobs in large companies such as airlines, tour operators and hotel chains are disappearing. Similarly, the trend towards online bookings via the Internet threatens jobs in travel agencies and suppliers. Call centres are replacing branch shops, and increasingly these are set up abroad, in low-wage countries like India. Fortunately for the future of the industry, at the 'sharp end', where the tourist seeks a high level of personal service at the destination, the nature of the tourist experience should ensure that technology cannot replace many jobs (although even the key job of resort representative has been sharply curtailed in recent years). However, the success of tourism in a country will be in part dependent upon an adequate supply of skilled labour, with the right motivation towards employment in the industry and appropriate training. Here, Britain has some way to go. Turnover of labour is high (attributable to relatively poor salaries and working conditions compared with many other fields of business); training, while having improved considerably over recent years, still lags behind that of many other countries; and attitudes towards working in a 'service industry', where many people in Britain still equate service with servility, make recruitment of good staff difficult. Furthermore, as many as nine out of ten tourism jobs are in SMTEs – small to medium size tourism enterprises, with turnover lower than €40 million. The EC defines these as micro enterprises if employees are fewer than eleven, small if between eleven and fifty, and medium-sized if between 51 and 250. Firms at the lower end of this scale tend to have fewer qualified staff, fewer training facilities, and poorer management, as well as paying poorer salaries, thus making careers in tourism less attractive to high flyers, and impacting on ability to compete with other organizations.

Balance of payments

In a national context, tourism may have a major influence on a country's balance of payments. International tourists are buying tourist services in another country, and these payments are noted in a country's accounts as 'invisibles'. A British resident going on holiday to Spain will be making an invisible payment to that country which is a debit on Britain's balance of payments account and a credit to Spain's balance of payments. The money spent by an American visitor to Britain is credited to Britain's balance of payments, becoming an invisible receipt for Britain, while it is debited as a payment against the American balance of payments. It is important to remind readers at this point that the outflow of British money being spent abroad by British residents counts as an *import*, while the inflow of foreign holidaymakers' money spent in Britain counts as an *export*.

The total value of receipts minus the total payments made during the year represents a country's *balance of payments on the tourism account*. This is part of the country's entire invisible balance, which will include other services such as banking, insurance and transport. This latter item is of course also important for tourism. If an American visitor to Britain decides to travel on a British airline, then a contribution is made to Britain's invisible receipts, while if a Briton going on holiday to Spain does so on Iberia Airlines, that fare is credited to Spain, and represents a payment on the British balance of payments account. Of course, with the demise of flag carriers and the growth of global integration, it may no longer be the case that the leading airlines will in the future be so clearly identified with their country of origin, and if the majority shareholding is to be found abroad, ultimately the profits, if not the earnings, will find their way to other countries in the form of leakages.

Throughout the 1970s, Britain enjoyed a surplus on its tourism balance, reaching a peak during 1977, the year of the Queen's Silver Jubilee. Since then, however, spending by British tourists travelling abroad has increased faster than receipts the country has gained from overseas tourists, with the result that, as we have seen, there has been a net, and steadily increasing, deficit since 1986 (see Figure 5.2).

For a country like Britain, which has experienced a steady decline in the terms of trade (amount of our goods sold abroad, compared with the amount of goods we import), it is important to try to redress the balance by a better showing on our invisible exports. As can be seen, however, tourism is not producing a net gain for Britain either – a matter about which we should be concerned. The government will attempt to resolve this deficit by encouraging more visitors to visit Britain, through the marketing efforts of the national tourist boards, or encouraging more Britons to stay at home and enjoy their holidays in their own country. However, the lure of the sun is a strong magnet for British tourists, and the tourist boards may find it easier to attract the overseas tourist to Britain. Some countries, particularly developing countries, could not afford this kind of drain on their financial resources, and would be forced to impose restrictions either on the movement of their own residents, or on the amount of money which they may take abroad with them. Other countries suffer severe deficiencies in their tourism balance of payments, but can offset this with manufacturing exports. Germany and Japan have in the past been examples of countries heavily in deficit on the tourism balance of payments, but which have nevertheless enjoyed a surplus overall through the sale of goods overseas. With both countries now finding it increasingly difficult to compete against low-wage economies in the industrial sector, they are now seeking to boost their own inbound tourism to compensate for this net outflow on the tourism account. By contrast, Spain and Italy both enjoy a strong surplus on their tourism balance of payments as they are popular receiving countries with fewer residents going abroad for their own holidays.

Investment and development

One factor helping to determine the success or otherwise of tourism in a region is the level of investment, whether private or public, in the industry. Unfortunately, tourism, and leisure generally, are seen by private investors as high-risk investments. Banks are reluctant to lend money for tourism projects, and developers are less willing to take investment risks. This will often mean that tourism cannot take off until the public sector is prepared to 'kick-start' the economy: that is, to invest risk capital in order to encourage tourism development. This might take the form of grants or low-interest loans to private developers, or in some more centrally planned economies it may mean that government itself builds and operates facilities such as hotels for tourists.

Example   Disney Resort, Paris

A good example of this 'partnership' between the public and private sectors is the development of the Disney Resort site near Paris, involving investment of many hundreds of millions of dollars. The French government, in order to ensure that the Disney Corporation built in France rather than in competitive European countries, provided subsidies to attract the company to the site near Paris which was eventually selected.

Investment is something of a 'chicken and egg' situation. There may be an unwillingness to invest until a flow of tourists to the area can be demonstrated, while the area will in turn attract few tourists until they can see evidence of sufficient facilities to attract them. However, once tourism is shown to be successful, private developers or government agencies are often willing to invest even further in the area – in short, success breeds success. Economists refer to this as the *accelerator* concept. Areas which have benefited from this phenomenon include Spain and the Mexican East Coast in the 1960s, Hawaii, Tunisia and the Languedoc-Roussillon region of France in the 1970s, and Turkey and Greece in the 1980s and 1990s. Naturally, the attraction of these regions to tourists will also attract other industries, which will recognize the benefits to be gained from a large inflow of consumers, and the attraction of a pleasant working environment for staff. Resorts such as Bournemouth and Brighton in Britain, or the fast-expanding resorts of Florida in the USA and the Gold Coast in Queensland, Australia, have all benefited from this process.

Unfortunately, the relationship between tourism growth and economic development is uneven, owing to other complicating factors such as the rate of inflation, the ability of an area to diversify and attitudes to work among the local labour force. Often, key workers are brought in from outside the area, in cases where the local labour force is either unwilling or unable to adapt to the needs of the tourism industry. Consequently, risk in investment remains high, as it does in many other areas of the economy.

Statistical measurement of tourism

Gathering data on tourism is a vital task for the government of a country. Governments need to know the contribution which tourism makes to the economy in terms of income, employment, balance of payments and investment. Figures must be available in sufficient detail to know how they have affected regional as well as national economies. Governments will wish to examine trends over time, not only within the country, but also in comparison with the performance of other, competing countries. National tourist offices will use this information to forecast growth, to plan for tourism in their areas, and as a guide to their promotional campaigns.

Information must be both quantitative and qualitative in nature; that is, data should be provided not only about the numbers and composition of tourists but also about their nature and purpose. For example, British statistics should include:

- the number of visitors to Britain
- how these are distributed over the months of the year
- the countries generating these tourists, and the number of tourists they generate as a proportion of the whole
- the growth, year on year, of these tourists
- their spend in Britain, in absolute terms and how they distribute the spend between accommodation, transport, shopping, catering etc.
- their mode of travel, i.e. what form of transport they use, whether they are travelling independently or on an inclusive tour
- the duration of their visit
- the type of accommodation they use
- the purpose of their visit; whether leisure, business, VFR etc.
- demographic profiles: age, group composition, social class
- sociographic profiles: personality, lifestyle, interests and activities
- what these tourists seek, and the extent to which they are satisfied with what they find.

This is a great deal of information, and when one remembers that it must also be collected for British residents travelling abroad and for British residents taking their holidays within Britain, the task of collecting the data is daunting. However, it is vital that governments undertake this collection of data, and that, as far as is possible, the data that are collected are based on commonly defined criteria, so that meaningful comparisons can be made between countries. If the collection of data allows the nation to know what trends are developing over time, what patterns of growth are taking place, and how tastes and preferences are changing over time, this information will enable governments to determine where to site roads and airports, where to plan for expansion in local government plans, and in what countries to increase or decrease the spend on advertising (as well as how to redirect the theme of advertisements, when it is found that new types of tourist are being reached). The private sector will benefit from this information in deciding whether and where to invest in hotels or tourist attractions, and the form these facilities should take. Similarly, those in the industry require an understanding of the propensity to take holidays – that is, the proportion of the population choosing to take a holiday each year, and in particular a holiday abroad, or to take more than one holiday a year – and how this propensity is affected by a growth in disposable income. Public-sector planners must be aware of the multiplier effect, which will call for sophisticated research techniques if measurement is to be accurate.

We will examine the most commonly used measurements of tourism here, under two categories: international surveys and national surveys.

International surveys

Statistics of intra-European and transatlantic tourist flows were collected even before World War II. However, the systematic collection of tourism data on a global scale can be dated to the early post-war years, and methods of measurement have been gradually refined and improved in recent years, particularly in those developed countries which have seen tourism expand rapidly.

Global tourism statistics, covering traffic flows, expenditure and trends over time, are produced and collated annually by the UNWTO and the Organization for Economic Cooperation and Development (OECD). Figures are published in the UNWTO's *World Tourism Statistics Annual Report* and *Tourism Compendium*, and in the OECD's annual *Tourism Policy and International Tourism*. These statistics, however, are not always strictly comparable, as data-gathering methods vary and differences in definition of terms remain.

In Britain, information on travel into and out of the country is obtained in a variety of ways. Until the early 1960s, most basic data on incoming tourism were obtained from Home Office immigration statistics, but as the purpose of gathering such data was to control immigration rather than to measure tourism, the data had major weaknesses, including failure to distinguish the purpose of travel – obviously a key statistic in surveying tourists. The government therefore decided to introduce a regular survey of visitors entering and leaving the country. The *International Passenger Survey* (IPS) has enabled data to be collected on tourists since 1964, and the survey, which is undertaken by the Office of National Statistics for the Department for Culture, Media and Sport and the national tourist boards, interviews a representative sample (258,000 people in 2004) of all international travellers, recording the number of visitors, the purpose of their visit, the geographical region visited, their expenditure, mode of travel, transport used and duration of stay. Information is based on country of residence; so, for example, the large number of British visitors living in America and travelling to visit friends and relatives in Britain each year would be counted as American visitors. This information is published quarterly, and compounded annually, in the government's *Business Monitor* series (MQ6, *Overseas Travel and Tourism*). The IPS is a random sample of all visitors travelling into or out of the UK via the major seaports and airports and the Channel Tunnel, stratified by port of arrival or departure, time of day and mode of transport used.

Other surveys are undertaken to provide additional data on tourism volume and expenditure, although reduced resources have led to cutbacks in the collection of data by the public-sector bodies, so supplementary information is now largely collected by private organizations. STATS MR, for example, carry out substantial research on overseas tourism and make the results available on subscription to businesses.

National surveys

In Britain, as in other countries in Europe, surveys are regularly carried out on tourism flows within the country. The most important of these is the *UK Tourism Survey* (UKTS). This survey has been carried out in recent years on a monthly basis by NOP Consumer Market Research on behalf of VisitBritain, VisitScotland and the Wales and Northern Ireland Tourist Boards (although due to be renegotiated in 2006). Between 1989 and 1999, residents of the UK over the age of 15 were interviewed in their homes, again using stratified random sampling. To reduce costs, since 2000, data collection has been based on telephone sampling, based on random digital dialling, with around 50,000 people interviewed over the course of each year. Information is collected on the volume and value of all trips involving at least one overnight stay, and includes the purpose of the trip, accommodation and transport used, activities engaged in, the method of booking and demographic details of respondents. This is now the only national survey carried out on a regular basis since the *British National Travel Survey* (BNTS), which researched holidays only, was dropped in 1998.

Information on day visitors is less complete. A GB Leisure Day Visits Survey is carried out on an ad hoc but infrequent basis. Sponsored by a number of bodies, including DCMS and the National Boards, it excludes figures for Northern Ireland. Individual members of the Countryside Recreation Network, particularly the Countryside Agency, have also conducted occasional day-visit surveys in the past.

The national boards also collect information on hotel occupancy, in the UK Occupancy Survey, which is updated regularly. Among national surveys that have been abandoned is the annual Holiday Intentions Survey, which was carried out by the former English Tourist Board and the European Travel Commission, to determine how people in Britain intended to spend their forthcoming summer holidays.

Techniques and problems of tourism measurement

From the descriptions of the methods of gathering UK tourist statistics outlined above, it can be seen that most research employs quantitative methods in order to provide descriptive information about issues such as when and where tourists travel, where they come from, how long they stay and how much they spend. In some cases, this information is available in considerable detail; for instance, expenditure can be broken down into sector (shopping, food, accommodation etc.) and data on visits can be identified by tourism region within the country. Although the data collected are not above criticism, by and large there is a sufficient body of information on which to make decisions.

However, research dealing with why people travel is far more limited. This is beginning to change, as organizations become more concerned with understanding the behaviour of tourists: how they choose their destinations, what they do when they arrive and why, what satisfies them, their purchasing patterns (preference to book directly rather than through an agent, or to book early rather than close to departure time). None of these questions is easily answered by use of the structured question-naire, and a more qualitative approach to research is needed. This can involve lengthy interviews in the home, or in 'panels' or groups of up to eight consumers who will talk about their behaviour under the guidance of a skilled interviewer. Some information is best obtained by observation rather than questioning, for example, by watching how customers visiting a travel agency choose their brochures from the racks. All these types of research are expensive, and time-consuming to administer. What is more, unlike quantitative methods, they cannot be subjected to tests of statistical probability in order to 'prove' the accuracy of the findings, no matter how carefully and scienti-fically the information is collected. Many organizations are therefore reluctant to commission research involving qualitative methods, although a growing number of research experts now recognize that they may produce richer and more complete data than the more common survey. After all, the information provided by the use of questionnaires will only be as accurate as the honesty of the answers, and it is particu-larly difficult to know if respondents are answering questionnaires honestly or with sufficient thought about the questions. This problem is compounded where mailed questionnaires are used.

Asking questions of arriving passengers at a destination is in reality an 'intention survey' rather than an accurate picture of what those passengers will actually engage in while in the country, while surveys carried out on departing travellers will require recall – at best, guesswork, especially where the aim is to assess the expenditure which the tourist has incurred.

Even if common definitions are used, direct comparisons may be misleading. An international journey may require an American resident to make a trip of several hundred kilometres, or to cross a stretch of water, which will usually mean forward planning, while a resident of Continental Europe may live within a couple of kilo-metres of an international border and think nothing of crossing it regularly for shopping or a meal out. In some cases, it is difficult to think of border crossings as international; the Schengen Agreement eradicated any border controls between several of the EU countries, with the result that monitoring visitors has become much harder. Some countries still use hotel records to estimate the number of visitors – a system known to be notoriously inadequate, because visitors travelling from one hotel to another are double counted, while those visiting friends and relatives will be omitted entirely from the count.

While international standards for methods of data collection and definition of terms have become widely accepted, particularly among the developed countries, small variations continue to make genuine comparison difficult, not only between countries but within a country over a period of time. Above all, if specific types of tourist activity are being examined, as part of a larger sample of general tourists, limits of confidence may fall sharply. Some survey data in the past have produced results that are accurate only to within 20 per cent either way, owing to the small number of respondents in the particular category being examined.

Accurate measures of tourist expenditure are equally difficult to make. Shopping surveys have problems distinguishing between residents and tourists, and tourists themselves frequently under- or over-estimate their expenditure. Above all, much of the real tourist expenditure is lost to statistical collection, especially in developing countries, because it is not taken into account. This includes secondary spend by recipients of tourist monies, and even direct spend by tourists in shops and other outlets. In countries where cash, rather than credit cards, is still the normal means of payment, and bargaining normal for even the smallest of items, reliable spending patterns are particularly difficult to calculate.

In an effort to provide more accurate assessment, the UNWTO has introduced the concept of the *tourism satellite account* (TSA). This technique attempts to include all these indirect expenditures and their resultant contribution to GDP, employment and capital investment. The technique was approved as an international standard by the United Nations Statistical Commission in 2000. However, its implementation is fraught with difficulties; it is not only expensive and time-consuming to employ, but accepts all tourism expenditure as beneficial, disregarding the question of sustainability. Neither can the results revealed in one country or region necessarily be transposed to another. Each situation is unique, and there is no magic formula which will allow estimates of statistical measure to be obtained without full-scale research within the area.

At present, the UK is not well geared up to collect and collate the basic information required to complete TSAs. The Office for National Statistics (ONS) is not directly involved in collecting tourism data other than those collected in the IPS, and surveys are inconsistent – for example, there were no leisure day-visitor surveys between 1998 and 2002/3, and these surveys are unlikely to be repeated in their present form. The UKTS is to be re-contracted in 2006, and while it is hoped that subsequent surveys may contain more data of relevance for the establishment of TSAs, consistency with earlier surveys is uncertain.

The issue of sustainability is a critical one here. It can be argued that we are far too concerned with measuring the economic impact of tourism on a region at the expense of the social or environmental impact. The industry's sole concern with growth in annual trends may conceal the very real danger that the number of tourists visiting a region will eventually exceed the number which the region can comfortably contain. Statistics on the ratio of tourists to residents, for example, or the number of tourists per square kilometre would provide some guidance on the degree of congestion experienced by the region. However, the social impact of tourism is also the outcome of many other variables, and statistical measurement is still a comparatively recent art which will require continual refinement in the future for the purposes of both economic and social planning.

Notes

1 It's Goodbye to Luxury, *The Observer*, 13 April 2003, p 21
2 *Developments* No 27, 3/2004, Department for International Development (DfID)
3 Tourism Concern *Campaign*, Spring 2005
4 ABTA NTB *An Occupational Mapping of the Travel Services Industry*, ABTA, 1991

Further reading

Bull, A, *The Economics of Travel and Tourism*, Longman, 2nd edn 1995

Lennon, J (ed), *Tourism Statistics: International Perspectives and Current Issues*, Continuum, 2003

Sinclair, M T and Stabler, M, *The Economics of Tourism*, Routledge, 1997

Tribe, J, *The Economics of Leisure and Tourism*, Butterworth Heinemann, 2nd edn 1999

Veal, A J, *Research Methods for Leisure and Tourism: a Practical Guide*, Longman, 2nd edn 1997

OECD *Tourism Policy and International Tourism in OECD Member Countries* (annual)

UNWTO *Compendium of Tourism Statistics* (annual)

UNWTO *Yearbook of Tourism Statistics* (annual)

UNWTO *World Tourism Barometer* (monthly)

Websites

World Tourism Organization	www.world-tourism.org
UK Research Liaison Group	www.staruk.org.uk
British Government Statistics	www.statistics.gov.uk
Business Monitor MQ6 series Overseas Travel and Tourism	
	www.statistics/gov.uk/statbase/product.asp? vlnk=1905&POS=&colRank=1&Rank=240
Civil Aviation Authority	www.caa.co.uk/default.aspx?categoryid=80
DFID	www.developments.org.uk
Strathclyde University (includes access to Business Monitor MQ6 statistics)	
	www.lib.strath.ac.uk/govpub/statstourism.htm
Internet marketing resources center	www.newcreationmarketer.com

Questions and discussion points

1 We have seen that the British Government needs to increase domestic tourism, in order to reduce the balance of payments deficit on the tourism account. Yet the ETC has been integrated into VisitBritain, and there is no longer a separate marketing board to promote England within the UK. Further, grants to VisitBritain have been frozen for several years. Given that VisitBritain claims £30 of revenue is produced for every £1 invested in tourism promotion, consider why the Government is so reluctant to increase financial support to the promotional bodies.

2 Would you welcome Britain joining the European common currency? Apart from other economic arguments for and against this move, would joining be beneficial for both incoming and outbound tourism?

3 What are the main purposes behind the collection of tourism statistics? What other information could be obtained at the time passengers are interviewed for the IPS which would be helpful for tourism executives?

4 Should visa charges be waived, or reduced, to encourage more tourists from the developing world to visit the UK? Can charges be justified, and if imposed should they merely seek to recover the administrative costs of issuing them?

Assignment topics

1   Using figures from the UNWTO or alternative sources, examine how tourism statistics have changed for the Balkan countries since 1980 to the present day. Include in your study all the countries which previously formed part of Yugoslavia, together with Albania, Bulgaria and Romania. How have political changes affected the economies of these countries in terms of in-bound tourism? Suggest possible reasons for the changing fortunes of these countries, based on historical reports from the world's press on events affecting them. Produce a report of your findings which draws conclusions about the future prospects for tourism in each of these countries, and makes recommendations about how best each country can take advantage of improved relations with the rest of the world to develop and expand tourism to the area.

2   At the time of writing, there are proposals from leading members of the tourism industry for a new Act to replace the 1969 Development of Tourism Act in Britain, and soundings are being taken about what this Act should include. As a researcher employed on behalf of the Committee set up to lobby the Government on the contents of the Act, produce a report which makes recommendations on the areas of priority which should be the focus of the new Act, concentrating on the economic benefits which would flow from the adoption of your recommendations.

6 The sociocultural impact of tourism

Objectives

After studying this chapter, you should be able to:

- understand the various ways in which tourism can impact on the populations of both destination and generating countries
- identify and evaluate different approaches to finding solutions to these problems
- understand the concept, and the importance, of sustainable tourism, in a socio-cultural context
- recognize the need for adequate planning, and for cooperation between the private and public sectors, as means of overcoming problems.

Introduction

We . . . Assume that you, like us, want to be a responsible traveller. You want to create the minimum negative impact on the places you pass through. As far as possible, you want your money to go into hands of the people who actually provide the service.

Chris Parrott, Marketing Director,
Journey Latin America 2004 brochure editorial

Up to this point, it has been generally accepted that tourism is, for the most part and with relatively few exceptions, beneficial to both generating and destination countries. But this is only half the story. In this chapter we will look at a different, and in many ways a darker, side of the tourism business – its impact (other than in purely economic terms) on those who participate in tourism, and on the residents of countries subjected to tourist flows. This will mean looking at both sociocultural issues affecting hosts and tourists and the impact of tourism on the individual tourist's health – quite an important issue, with growing concern over the effects of the sun on tourists and workers in the tourist industry, the global spread of AIDS and the increasing impact of tropical and sexual diseases on ever more adventurous mass tourists.

As we have seen in the previous chapter, tourism can be a potent force for economic good, creating employment and wealth. Equally, it can be argued that tourism provides a basis for widening our understanding of other societies, developing and maintaining links, reducing tensions and even avoiding conflicts; indeed, in the first half of the twentieth century tourism was seen, and actively promoted by the authorities in many countries, as a force for good. But while the interplay between tourist and host was seen initially as a means of stabilizing relations between nations, it readily became apparent that foreign visitors with a curiosity about other cultures could, through their enthusiasm, ensure the survival of those very cultural attractions which might otherwise have withered away for lack of support. This book contains numerous examples of the way in which in-coming tourism has benefited the culture and traditions of a particular country or region. In Britain, many great buildings, particularly those serving the needs of eighteenth- and nineteenth-century industry, would have been lost had it not been possible to convert those same factories, mills and warehouses into living and working museums for the tourist. With the increasing secularization of Western societies, arguably it is also the tourist who will eventually ensure that our great cathedrals survive, since the costs of maintaining these buildings for dwindling numbers of worshippers can no longer be borne by the ecclesiastical authorities alone. Whole inner cities and dockland areas have been restored and developed to make them attractive as tourist sites. Even a city like London would be a poorer place without the tourist; 40 per cent of West End theatre tickets are bought by tourists, and undoubtedly the cornucopia of theatres available to Londoners (together with residents of New York and other great cultural cities) owes much to patronage by visitors. In London, as with

Figure 6.1
El Mesquida
Cathedral,
Cordova, Spain
suffers from
excess demand
by visitors

(Photographed by the author)

other major cities, tourists' use of public transport enables residents to enjoy a better and cheaper service than would otherwise be possible. In rural areas and small seaside resorts, many heritage attractions such as local museums, art galleries and provincial theatres would be forced to close without tourist support, impoverishing the lives of local residents. Country crafts, pubs, even the restoration of traditional pastimes (such as morris dancing in England), all owe their survival to the presence of the tourist.

However, the rapid growth of tourism during the twentieth century produced problems, as well as opportunities, on a vast scale for both developed and developing countries. Authorities in these countries came to realize that unrestrained and unplanned tourist development could easily aggravate problems to a point where tourists would no longer wish to visit the destination – and residents no longer wish to receive them. This is, therefore, not just an environmental issue; a point is reached where residents can feel swamped by sheer numbers of tourists at peak periods of the year, resulting in disenchantment and eventually alienation, with growing altercations taking place between residents and visitors. In short, without adequate planning tourists could well destroy what they had come to see. The problem accelerates as long-haul travel to previously unaffected destinations increases.

Legislation and guidance protecting the tourism destination

Awareness of the need for planning is the first step in attempting to control the worst effects of mass tourism. However, in the early stages of awareness authorities failed to make the distinction between cultural and environmental impacts, with concern for sustainability initially concentrating largely on environmental issues. The origins of sustainable tourism legislation to cover both cultural and environmental impacts will therefore be examined at this point, while specifically environmental issues will be examined in the following chapter.

Broad awareness of the problems which tourism creates can be traced back at least as far as the 1960s, but it was another twenty years before these problems began to be addressed, with legislation introduced to dampen its impact. Influential voices made themselves heard, calling for a new tourism, variously described as 'sustainable tourism', 'eco-tourism', 'green tourism', 'soft tourism' and, eventually, 'responsible tourism'. Proponents of sustainability argued that responsible tourism should be defined as underpinning a properly thought out management strategy, with collaboration between the private and public sectors, to prevent irreparable damage to the environment before it was too late.

One of the early expressions of concern was manifested when the WTO and the United Nations Environment Programme issued a joint declaration in 1982, calling for the rational management of tourism to protect, enhance and improve the environment. In the following year these bodies suggested employing zoning strategies to concentrate tourists in those regions which could best absorb them, and to disperse them where environments were viewed as too fragile to sustain mass tourism.

It is important to recognize that not all tourists are seeking the same forms of tourism, just as the terms used above to describe the new tourism are not necessarily synonymous.

Eco-tourism in its early days was described (by the environmentalist Hector Ceballos-Lascurain) as, 'that tourism that involves traveling to relatively undisturbed natural areas with the specific object of studying, admiring and enjoying the scenery and its wild plants and animals, as well as any existing cultural aspects (both past and present) found in these areas. Ecotourism implies a scientific, esthetic or philosophical approach'[1]. This is clearly not a description of the activities of the vast masses of tourists who go on holiday each year, nor does the definition specifically embrace sustainability. It is appropriate to argue that all forms of tourism should be 'sustainable', and that they should not destroy the destination to which the tourist is attracted. Perhaps a better definition is that offered by the International Ecotourism Society itself: 'Ecotourism is responsible travel to natural areas that conserves the environment and improves the well-being of local people'[2]. This definition makes clear that responsible tourism includes responsibility to both the environment and the indigenous populations.

Tourism must be environmentally compatible, as the World Travel and Tourism Council proposed in its ten-point guideline (see Figure 6.2). It will be noted that only two of the ten points refer specifically to issues that can be defined as sociocultural.

By comparison, a ten-point set of principles established by Tourism Concern[3] in 1992 appears to achieve a more equal balance between sociocultural and environmental elements.

The issue of sustainability was boosted by the concern expressed by the UN General Assembly in the mid-1980s, which established a commission to look in depth at the

Figure 6.2
A guideline for sustainable tourism

1 Identify and minimize product and operational environmental problems, paying particular attention to new projects.
2 Pay due regard to environmental concerns in design, planning, construction and implementation.
3 Be sensitive to conservation of environmentally protected or threatened areas, species or scenic aesthetics, achieving landscape enhancement where possible.
4 Practise energy conservation, reduce and recycle waste, practise freshwater management and control sewage disposal.
5 Control and diminish air emissions and pollutants.
6 Monitor, control and reduce noise levels.
7 Control, reduce and eliminate environmentally unfriendly products, such as asbestos, CFCs, pesticides and toxic, corrosive, infectious, explosive or flammable material.
8 Respect and support historic or religious objects and sites.
9 Exercise due regard for the interests of local populations, including their history, traditions and culture and future development.
10 Consider environmental issues as a key factor in the overall development of travel and tourism destinations.

(Courtesy: World Travel and Tourism Council)

Table 6.1   Ten principles of sustainable tourism

1	Using resources sustainably
2	Reducing over-consumption and waste
3	Maintaining diversity
4	Integrating tourism into planning
5	Supporting local economies
6	Involving local economies
7	Consulting stakeholders and the public
8	Training staff
9	Marketing tourism responsibly
10	Undertaking research

Source: Tourism Concern, www.tourismconcern.org.uk, Eber, S. (ed)

planet's people and their resources, and to make recommendations on ways to achieve long-term sustainable development. The Brundtland Commission presented its report, *Our Common Future*[4], in 1987, adopting the definition of sustainable development as: 'Development that meets the needs of the present without compromising the ability of future generations to meet their own needs'.

The influence of this paper soon led to the UN's organizing a major international conference on the topic. This Conference on Environment and Development (the so-called *Earth Summit*) was held at Rio de Janeiro in 1992. Although tourism neither appeared as an issue in the original Brundtland Report, nor was included in the agenda of the Rio meeting, the industry's planning and development have been heavily influenced by the recommendations emerging from these two sources, most notably by the conference's Agenda 21, a guide for local government action to reconcile development and sustainability of the environment. The year 1992 was a momentous one for sustainability: the hospitality industry launched its International Hotel Environment Initiative (IHEI), designed to reduce the impact of staying visitors on the environment, while in the same year the charitable pressure group Tourism Concern set out its own guidelines (outlined in Table 6.1), and began actively to lobby the private sector to take more account of the need for sustainable planning. This voluntary-aided organization has been a leader in drawing the UK industry's attention to the issue of sustainability, which, first perceived as an irrelevant and esoteric subject, is now taken more seriously by those responsible for planning and marketing.

By the start of the twenty-first century, the concept had become familiar both within the industry and among the travelling public. The United Nations Environmental Programme (UNEP) introduced its Initiative for Sustainable Tourism, aimed at tour operators and adopted in 2000, and this was followed by a UN declaration to designate 2002 as the International Year of Ecotourism (IYE). A World Summit on Sustainable Development was also held in Johannesburg in 2002, and for the first time this took into account the importance of sustainability in the tourism industry; however, a world eco-tourism summit at Quebec in the same year appears to have had relatively little impact. Nonetheless, 2002 proved to be the year when the industry in Britain began to take active interest. As a direct result of the Johannesburg summit, the British Foreign Office introduced a Sustainable Tourism Initiative, to which over 40 companies (including the leading four tour operators) subscribed. The result was the formation of The Travel Foundation, strongly supported both by commercial and environmental organizations and industry bodies such as ABTA, AITO and FTO. The Foundation's stated aims are to change the practice of tourism to ensure it makes a greater contribution to the welfare of the environment and populations of tourist destinations.

Other organizations with links to industry, such as the UNWTO and the World Travel and Tourism Council (WTTC), have added their support for the principles of sustainable development which will minimize damage to the environment, wildlife and local indigenous populations. These organizations have particularly recommended the use of local building materials for tourist sites, the recycling of waste and water and the recruitment of locals for jobs within tourism. Together with the Earth Council, the two bodies also published a report, *Agenda 21 for the Travel and Tourism Industry: Towards Environmentally Sustainable Development*[5], encouraging the industry to take the lead in preserving the environment in the areas they develop.

Example   The Travel Foundation

Two of the Travel Foundation's early activities to support sustainable tourism both centred on sociocultural issues. In Cyprus, tour operators were encouraged to develop small group tours to the interior of the island, to comparatively unspoilt villages, allowing the villagers to benefit both commercially and socially from interaction with tourists. The organization supported tours by SAVE (Support Abandoned Villages and their Environments), which were designed to encourage tours away from the coastal resorts. Aiming to show visitors a true picture of Cypriot rural life, the tours have encouraged shops and other tourist facilities to open, and labour forces to seek jobs in their villages rather than migrating to the coast.

In the Gambia, traders found it difficult to sell direct to customers, who resented being hassled on the beaches to buy what were often viewed as inferior products. The Foundation helped local traders sell their products direct to tourists by overseeing quality control, and compiling a directory of local businesses meeting the improved standards. In 2002, the Gambia introduced a tax on all visitors arriving at Banjul Airport to raise revenue for tourism advertising and environmental improvements.

While joint action of this kind is invaluable, many businesses, particularly the smaller, independent companies which were quick to recognize the value of selling the concept of sustainable tourism to their sophisticated markets, introduced their own policies to support sustainability. AITO, the Association of Independent Tour Operators, has shown great enthusiasm for its members embracing responsible tourism, offering a series of guidelines, including:

1   protection of the environment – flora, fauna, landscapes;
2   respect for local cultures – traditions, religions, and the built heritage;
3   economic and social benefits for local communities;
4   conservation of natural resources, from the office to the destination;
5   minimizing pollution caused by noise, waste disposal and congestion.

The organization awards from one to three gold stars to member companies in recognition of efforts to ensure that tours are planned and operated responsibly. One star is awarded for the appointment of a Responsible Tourism Manager, acceptance of the AITO guidelines and advice to customers in published information; another star is awarded for specific action in undertaking an environmental review and developing a company policy towards responsible tourism; and a third star goes to companies engaged in specific initiatives at destinations.

One specialist long-haul operator and member of AITO with notable success in this field has been Journey Latin America, which has been awarded two stars by AITO.

Example Journey Latin America

In the Andes, JLA has worked with reputable local agents to protect porters and the environment on the Inca Trail. In 2003, the company ran a clean-up campaign in the Cordillera Blanca, Northern Peru (where as yet there is little legislation to protect the environment). The company has stated its intention to help protect the integrity of indigenous populations, with particular reference to those in the Amazon basin where adventure holidays are offered. They have also cooperated with Climate Care to off-set the effect of carbon dioxide emissions in the flights which transport their staff travelling on business.

The sociocultural effects of tourism

With this overview of legislation and directives encouraging a more sustainable approach to tourism development, we can go on to examine the specific cultural and social impacts on a host country which result from the influx of large numbers of people, sharing different value systems and away from the constraints of their own environment. In the following chapter we will address the issue of environmental impacts.

The sociocultural impact of mass tourism is most noticeable in less developed countries, but is by no means restricted to these; tourism has contributed to an increase in crime and other social problems in such diverse centres as New York and London, Hawaii and Miami, Florence and Corfu.

Any influx of tourists, however few, will make some impact on a region, but the extent of the impact is dependent not just upon numbers but also on the kind of tourists which the region attracts. The mass tourist is less likely to adapt to the local cultures, and will seek amenities and standards found in the home country, while the independent traveller or backpacker will adapt more readily to an alien environment. This has been exemplified in a model devised by Valene Smith (see Table 6.2).

Explorers, or tourists whose main interest is to meet and understand people from different cultures and backgrounds, will fully accept and acclimatize to the foreign culture. These travellers will generally travel independently, and be as little visible as possible. However, as increasingly remote areas of the world are 'packaged' for wealthy

Table 6.2   Adaptation of tourists to local norms

Type of tourist	Numbers of tourists	Adaptation to local norms
Explorer	Very limited	Adapts fully
Elite	Rarely seen	Adapts fully
Off-beat	Uncommon, but seen	Adapts well
Unusual	Occasional	Adapts somewhat
Incipient mass	Steady flow	Seeks Western amenities
Mass	Continuous influx	Expects Western amenities
Charter	Massive arrivals	Demands Western amenities

Source: Valene Smith, *Hosts and Guests*, 1992, © Blackwell Publishers Ltd

tourists, and as ever larger numbers of tourists travel further afield to find relaxation or adventure, these tourists bring with them their own value systems, either expecting or demanding the lifestyle and facilities to which they are accustomed in their own country.

At its simplest and most direct, this flow of comparatively wealthy tourists to a region will attract petty criminals, as evidenced by increases in thefts or muggings – a problem that has become serious in some areas of the Mediterranean, in Florida, Latin America, the Caribbean and Russia. As tourism expands in Eastern Europe, taxi drivers in Poland, the Czech Republic and Hungary have been found to overcharge gullible tourists, in some cases by manipulating their meters. Tourists may also be seen as easy prey when making purchases in shops or from street vendors. This has become a noted problem in London, where street vendors have overcharged tourists for items such as ice cream. A familiar anecdote in Continental European nations is that the pricing policy of shop goods in resort regions falls into three bands: the cheapest price is available to locals, a slightly higher price is demanded from visitors with sound know-ledge of the local language, and the highest price is applied to visitors with little or no knowledge of the language (some argue that a fourth tier is applicable for gullible Americans!). Where gambling is a cornerstone of tourism growth, prostitution and organized crime often follow – and there are already concerns about the proposed un-limited expansion of Las Vegas-style mega-casinos in British cities following relaxa-tion of the gaming laws in 2005. Certain countries which have more relaxed laws on sexual behaviour than those in the West attract tourists for sexual encounters, with governments turning a blind eye, and in some cases condoning even organized child abuse. In some countries, notably Germany and Japan, tour operators organize sexu-ally oriented package tours to destinations like the Philippines and Thailand. This public promotion of commercial sex, especially where it involves sex with minors, has come under increasing criticism in the Western world from organizations like the World Council of Churches and Tourism Concern. Britain, following the example of other western countries, has passed legislation to enable paedophiles to be prose-cuted in their home country for offences committed abroad.

There are a number of less direct, and perhaps less visible, effects on tourist localities, including the phenomenon known as 'relative deprivation'. The comparative wealth of tourists may be resented or envied by the locals, particularly where the influx is seen by the latter as a form of neo-colonialism, as in the Caribbean or some African countries. Locals come to experience dissatisfaction with their own standards of living or way of life, and seek to emulate that of the tourist. In some cases, the effect of this is marginal, as in the adoption of the tourists' dress or fashions, but in others the desire to emulate the tourist can threaten deep-seated traditions in the community, as well as leading to aspirations which are impossible to meet.

Job opportunities and the higher salaries paid to workers in the tourist industry will attract workers from agricultural and rural communities who, freed from the restrictions of their families and home environments, may abandon their traditional values. This can result in an increase in promiscuity, and the breakdown of marriages.

The problem of interaction between the host and tourist is that any relationships which develop are fleeting and superficial, and are often conducted for commercial ends. A report by UNESCO in 1976 identified four characteristics of host–guest relations in tourism:

1   relations are transitory and superficial;
2   they are undertaken under constraints of time and space, with visitors compacting sights into as limited amount of time as possible;
3   there is a lack of spontaneity in relations; meetings tend to be prearranged to fit tour schedules, and involve mainly financial transactions;
4   relations are unequal and unbalanced, due to disparities in wealth and status of the participants.

Most tourists visiting a new country for the first time, who may be spending no more than a week in that country and do not expect to return, will be eager to condense their experiences, to a point where each tends to be brief and superficial. Add to this an initial fear of contact with locals, and tourists' comparative isolation – hotels often being dispersed away from centres of local activity – and opportunities for any meaningful relationship become very limited. Few relationships are spontaneous; contact is generally with locals who work within the tourism industry, or else it is mediated by couriers. Language may form an impenetrable barrier to genuine local contact, and this limitation can lead to mutual misunderstanding. The relationship is further unbalanced by the status of the visitor, not only in terms of wealth but the fact that the tourist is on holiday while the local is likely to be at work, often being paid to serve the needs of the tourist.

Sometimes, locals are exploited as 'tourist objects'. In picturesque localities such as villages, local residents can be annoyed by coachloads of tourists descending on the village to peer through cottage windows, or to swamp local bar and pubs in order to 'get a flavour' of the local life. A more extreme example is to be found in Thailand, where on the border with Myanmar (Burma), Padaung tribeswomen from across the border have been forced into 'human zoos' as objects of curiosity for tourists; only outcries in the international press have helped to release some of these women from virtual slavery.

Exploitation of this kind can result in both sides seeing any contact in purely commercial terms. In Kenya's Masai Mara region, the Masai tribespeople extract payment for photographs, of themselves or of a 'real' (but specially constructed) village.

Charging for photographs has become a norm in many parts of the world. In exchange, feeling themselves exploited, tourists feel that it becomes acceptable to steal the towels from their hotel; the host–guest relationship has changed to one of supplier and customer.

Photography itself is a sensitive issue for many. Tourists from the West expect to be permitted to take what may often be intrusive photographs at will, yet seldom feel it necessary to seek permission from their subjects. In some lesser developed countries it is viewed as offensive to take any pictures of people (the author witnessed a tribesman on horseback in Uzbekistan deliberately turn his horse's backside to the camera, much to the bemusement of the would-be photographer); while in others care must be exercised to avoid taking photographs of landscapes which include military or quasi-military installations (a group of British plane-spotters were recently arrested, prosecuted and jailed for just such as activity at a Greek airport, and released only after the intercession of the British Government. Plane-spotting is an unknown, not to say eccentric, activity in Greece). Bird-watchers have similarly been arrested in some countries when using binoculars close to militarily sensitive areas.

In these situations, the role of the courier or representative as a 'culture broker' becomes vital. These members of the industry enjoy local knowledge (and are often from the local community), help to avoid misunderstandings, interpret the local culture for visitors and explain what is appropriate and inappropriate behaviour for the guests. Interpretation plays an important role in sustainable tourism, and the guide as interpreter of local customs provides one of the most effective means of communication.

The breakdown in host–guest relationships can be largely ascribed to the volume of visitors. Doxey (1975)[6] developed an 'Irridex' model of the relationship between tourism growth and community stress (see Table 6.3). In the early stages of tourism development, the locals are euphoric, pleased to see investment and improved job prospects for local people. The comparatively small numbers, and the fact that most tourists will belong to the 'explorer' category and accept the norms and values of the hosts, mean that tourists are welcomed, and even cultivated as 'friends'. As locals become used to the benefits they receive from tourism, and become aware of the problems which tourism generates as it grows, so they come to accept it, and their meetings with tourists become more common and more commercial. Further growth leads to a general feeling among locals that tourists are an irritant rather than a benefit, as they note how tourism is changing their community and their cultural norms. In the final stages, locals show open antagonism towards the steady stream of visitors, many of whom will have the attitude that locals are there to meet the tourists' needs and will insist on western standards.

Naturally, this is a simplified model of the fairly complex relationships which actually develop between tourists and locals. Other factors that must be taken into account are the length of time a tourist stays in the community (longer-stay tourists will accommodate better and be seen as making a more effective contribution to the local economy), and the cultural gap between locals and tourists (domestic tourists sharing the values of the locals will be less resented).

Examples abound of the antagonism engendered between locals and tourists, even within Britain. An attitude change among locals can be detected by changes in the vocabulary of tourism – for example, in some parts of England, derogatory terms

Table 6.3   Irridex model of stress relative to tourism development

Stages	Characteristics	Symptoms
Stage 1	Euphoria	Visitors welcomed, little formal development
Stage 2	Apathy	Visitors taken for granted, contacts become commercial
Stage 3	Irritation	Locals concerned about tourism, efforts made to improve infrastructure
Stage 4	Antagonism	Open hostility from locals, attempts to limit damage and tourism flows

Source: G V Doxey, A Causation Theory of Visitor–Resident Irritants, 1975[7]

like 'grockles' or 'emmets' are in use, and locals may carry bumper stickers on their cars saying 'I'm not a tourist: I live here'. More open hostility can be detected in Bath, where hoses have been turned on open-top touring coaches in which megaphones are used to provide a commentary. Breaking cultural taboos can produce a backlash: Alassio banned bikinis in the streets, and in the Alto Adige region of the Italian Dolomites in 1993, a local movement erupted spontaneously to prevent the spread of topless bathing in the lakes – while other residents expressed their concern that the publicity accorded this might dissuade some tourists from visiting! In Greece, what has become known as the 'Shirley Valentine factor' – British women escaping a humdrum life at home to find romance in Greece – has led to a reaction from women in Corfu and Crete, who resent the attention paid to foreign females, and feel that Greek women are now undervalued. However, it is also true to say that some Greek women have welcomed the increasing liberation from male dominance which tourism has brought.

A lack of understanding of local cultural traditions is common where these traditions appear to be contrary to what we view as tasteful and appropriate. British tourists in Tokyo may be surprised to see signs outside some nightspots declaring 'Japanese only here', reflecting a nineteenth-century imperialist tradition which has long died out in the Western world.

Example   Ignorance of local cultural tradition

Following the crash of a Pakistani Airlines plane over Nepal in 1992, it was reported that 'British Embassy officials were appalled by the public display of the bodies for relatives of the English victims, which they described as a 'grotesque peepshow'. In Nepal, however, viewing the remains of the dead is an important part of the act of grieving, and the Nepalese were merely extending this courtesy to the foreign mourners.

While a considerable amount of research has now been undertaken into the effect of tourists on locals, rather less is available to tell us how locals in turn influence the tourists. We can undoubtedly ascribe our widening acceptance of foreign food and fashions in Britain to the influence, in part, of overseas travel, and the quality of foreign food, service, transport and hotel facilities have encouraged us to become more demanding in the provision of these in Britain. Research (Gullahorn and Gullahorn,

1963)[8] also suggests that tourists go through three stages in adapting to the local culture of their holiday environment. In the first stage, the tourists are excited by the environment and the novelty of the situation; later, a second stage is reached in which the tourists become disillusioned, and more critical of the environment, as they become accustomed to the situation. Finally, in what may be a slow process, they learn to adapt to the new setting, and in doing so may experience 're-entry crisis', where it becomes difficult to readapt to their home environment when they return.

Other studies have examined the extent to which pre-travel attitudes affect adaptability, and whether travel broadens understanding or reinforces stereotypes (see, for example, Sutton 1967[9]). The evidence suggests that the self-fulfilling prophecy is at work here; that if we travel with the expectation of positive experiences, we will experience them. However, much more work is needed to explore the relationship between the tourist and the host from the former's perspective.

Finally, the phenomenon of second homes abroad is due in large part to the increase in travel, which has led to greater awareness of, and desire for, residences in attractive resorts on the Continent, and around the Mediterranean in particular. One survey (drawing on statistics provided by the office of the Deputy Prime Minister) revealed that 229,186 English households owned second homes outside of the UK in 2004, while other sources have put the figure even higher, suggesting that the total for UK second-home ownership abroad may be as high as half a million. Where expatriates are willing to learn the language and blend in with the culture, little conflict emerges, but where large groups of British (or other nationals) buy homes within a small region and begin to seek products and forms of entertainment with which they are familiar in their own country, this can transform the indigenous culture and undermine traditional lifestyles. Many of these homes are bought with the intention of renting, largely to nationals of the same country as the owners, reinforcing both the cultural gap and the transitional nature of the interaction between locals and tourists.

Of course, the problems arising from second-home ownership are not restricted to homes purchased abroad. In Britain, there has been resentment between locals and 'in-comers' from other parts of the country, and this resentment is compounded where regional rivalries already exist, as is evidenced in the purchase of second homes in attractive areas of Wales by English in-comers, who drive up house prices and may intend only to rent out their properties to tourists. Where these homes are occupied infrequently, this leads to resentment by shopkeepers and others who fail to benefit; if not an all-year-round destination, this can soon result in an apparently 'dead' village in the off-season, with a high percentage of homes owned by outsiders. Over 229,000 properties were identified as second homes in the UK in 2005, and in some regions like South Hams, Devon, prices have been driven up to a point where houses can no longer be purchased by locals. In the popular coastal resort of Salcombe 45 per cent of homes are owned by outsiders, the highest percentage in the country after Central London (see Plate 6).

Staged authenticity

Given the constraints of time and place, the tourist demands *instant culture,* an opportunity to sample, even if superficially, the 'foreignness' of the destination. This gives rise to what Dean MacCannell (1989)[10] has referred to as *staged authenticity*, in which a search by tourists for authentic experiences of another culture leads to locals of that culture either providing those experiences, or staging them to appear as realistic as possible. Culture in this way is in danger of becoming commercialized and trivialized, as when 'authentic' folk dances are staged for the package tourists as a form of cabaret in hotels, or traditional tribal dances are arranged, often in an artificially shortened form, as performances for groups of tourists. Such trivialization is not unknown in Britain, with pastiche 'mediaeval banquets', town criers and ceremonies reminiscent of earlier times. One proposal was made that the traditional ceremony of Changing the Guard should be mounted more frequently each day, in order to give tourists more opportunity to view it. Similarly, a suggestion (considered seriously by the authorities) was made that Stonehenge be replicated in fibreglass near the actual site, to give the tourist an 'authentic' experience of seeing the stones more closely than was now possible.

Tourists will seek out local restaurants not frequented by other tourists in order to enjoy the 'authentic' cuisine and environment of the locals, but the very fact of their discovering such restaurants makes these tourist attractions in their turn, and ultimately the 'tourist traps' tourists sought to avoid. Meantime, the locals move on to find somewhere else to eat.

The downgrading of traditional hospitality towards the tourist in Hawaii is exemplified by the artificial welcome to which tourists are subjected on their arrival in the islands. Traditionally, welcoming natives would place a *lei* of flowers around the neck of each tourist, but the cost of this courtesy and the huge volume of tourists has led to the *lei* being replaced with a plastic garland, reinforcing the impression of a commercial transaction which this has now become.

Tourists seek local artefacts as souvenirs or investments. In cases where genuine works are purchased, this can lead to loss of cultural treasures from a country, and many countries now impose strict bans on exports of such items. However, tourists are often satisfied to purchase what they believe to be an authentic example of local art; this has led to the mass production of poorly crafted works (sometimes referred to as *airport art*), common among African nations and the Pacific islands. Alternately, it encourages the freezing of art styles in pseudo-traditional form, as in the case of the apparently 'mediaeval' painted wooden religious statuary produced in Oberammergau and other villages of southern Germany. In turn, artists and craftsmen are subtly encouraged to change their traditional styles, by making their works in the colours that are found to be most attractive to the tourists, or by reducing the size of their works to make them more readily transportable for tourists.

It is perhaps too easy to take a purist stance in criticizing these developments. One must point to the evident benefits which tourism has brought to the culture of many tourist destinations – indeed, in many cases it has helped to regenerate an awareness and pride in local culture and traditions. But for the advent of tourism, many of these traditions would have died out long ago. It is facile to ascribe cultural decline to the impact of tourism, whereas it is as likely to be the result of mass communication and technological development. Since Western (and specifically American) culture is the dominant influence around the world, it will inevitably undermine other cultures, particularly those of the developing world. However, it is equally clear that tourism from the Western nations has led to a revival of interest in tribal customs in other countries (and not just in developing countries; the revival of morris dancing in English communities is a direct result of the impact of tourism). Traditional local cuisines in Britain have been regenerated, with the support of the national tourist boards, with 'taste of England', 'taste of Wales' and 'taste of Scotland' schemes, a concept regenerated in promotions undertaken by VisitBritain in 2004, emphasizing once again the originality and quality of regional dishes in Britain. Dying local arts and crafts have been revived through cottage industries in rural areas which have benefited economically from the impact of tourism.

Cultural transgressions

Although not exclusively a British problem, other patterns of behaviour among a small but significant minority of Britons while abroad have made such tourists unwelcome in several leading resorts on the Continent. Freed from the normal restraints of their everyday surroundings, many young tourists have been attracted to resorts promising unlimited cheap alcohol, 24-hour entertainment and readily available sex, either with fellow tourists or with locals. Some of the less responsible tour operators have promoted these resorts to niche markets of youngsters, driving away the family market. This in turn has fuelled the growth of bars and discos offering popular music of the day, while resort reps for the operators laid on bar crawls, earning high commissions from favoured bars.

The popularity of these resorts quickly led to their becoming overwhelmed by ill-behaved visitors, soon commonly referred to as 'lager louts'. Bar and street brawls, open drunkenness and impolite behaviour quickly led to conflicts with locals, not infrequently resulting in visitors being hospitalized. One after another, resorts like Benitses and Kavos on Corfu, Ibiza in the Balearics, and Faliraki on Rhodes found their more traditional markets drying up; efforts to change the image of the destinations were often taken too late. As local authorities intervened, imposing curfews, licensing bar crawls by groups, employing undercover police, even attempting to quarantine noisy groups within zones, the revellers simply moved on to other resorts, threatening their decline in turn.

This 'slash and burn' approach to tourism is not easily resolved, although the tour operators responsible for some of the worst excesses have sobered up as a consequence of the bad media publicity they received, and have modified their packages and promotion. The problem for the destinations, in attempting to regain public trust and to reposition their product, is less easily solved.

The exploitation of indigenous populations

Perhaps the most serious accusation that can be made against tourism is the manner in which both members of the industry and destination authorities alike have exploited indigenous populations in their desire to develop tourism in ways that maximize their own interests. There are countless examples of such exploitation, involving child labour, forced labour, sexual exploitation and the wholesale removal of locals from their tribal lands to permit development of tourism. Recent examples of the latter have been the removal of Masai tribespeople from their Ngorongoro crater hunting lands in Tanzania, to allow tourists free movement to photograph wildlife; Botswana has evicted Gana and Gwi Bushmen from their land in the central Kalahari game reserve to open the area to tourism, while international opprobrium followed the removal and forced labour of Burmese to enhance tourist projects in Myanmar. Tourism Concern and other sustainable groups such as Tourism Watch in Germany have been particularly active in recent years in drawing attention to the exploitation of porters engaged in trekking and mountaineering tours in several countries. Publicity about their plight led to the formation of an International Porter Protection Group to oversee conditions on Mt Kilimanjaro, Tanzania (where porters were frequently obliged to carry loads of up to 60 kgs for low wages, dressed in inadequate protective clothing), in the Himalayas, and on the Inca Trail in Peru, where official guidelines are designed to ensure that packs do not exceed 20 kgs, and are weighed by government officials. Sexual exploitation, especially of minors, has also been a cause of considerable concern in several Third World countries, and pressure groups like ECPAT (End Child Prostitution, Pornography and Trafficking) and the World Council of Churches have encouraged the implementation of legislation to protect minors and prosecute offenders within their own countries for offences committed abroad. Britain reacted in 1997 with the passing of the Sex Offenders Act (UK), including a section which for the first time allowed such prosecutions to take place, although the difficulty of gathering evidence in Third World countries has hindered the implementation of the Act.

Managing the social impact of tourism

Sustainable tourism, in terms of the social impact of tourism on indigenous populations, needs to be managed in two ways. First, it is important that good relations are established between locals and guests, so that guests are welcomed to the region or country and social interaction benefits both parties. There are different approaches to ensuring this, and the choice is essentially between two diametrically opposed management methods. Responsible officials can attempt to integrate the guest into the local community, and to control the overall number of visitors so that the local population does not become swamped by tourists. This is really only practical where demand for the destination is limited to comparatively small numbers, and the market attracted shows empathy for, and sensitivity towards, local culture; specialist tourism will allow for this solution to be adopted, but mass tourism will not. Alternatively, officials can aim to concentrate the visitors in particular districts, sometimes referred to as tourist 'ghettos', often some distance away from residential neighbourhoods, so that any damage is limited to the few locals who will have contact with these guests, usually involving commercial transactions. In this way, most locals and visitors will not come into direct contact with each other, though this may also reduce the economic benefit of tourism to the local community. The integrated resort complex offering all-inclusive packages is becoming increasingly common at long-haul destinations, examples being found in Cancun, Mexico, Nusa Dua in Bali, Indonesia, Puerto Plata in the Dominican Republic and the Langkawi development in Malaysia. However, all-inclusive resorts can also be operated sustainably, if locals are employed in skilled as well as lesser skilled jobs within the site, and much of what is consumed on site is produced in the surrounding area.

Government policies to attract large numbers of tourists have given way to policies designed to attract particular tourist markets. While this has in most cases meant trying to attract wealthy, high-spend visitors, it has sometimes led to a move to encourage visits by those who will have the least impact on local populations, i.e. those who will integrate and accept local customs rather than seeking to impose their own standards on locals. Some have gone farther, however. The local authority at Alassio, Italy, took rather extreme action in 1994, in an effort to discourage day trippers and *sacopelisti* (sleeping-baggers), who slept on the beaches and brought little income into the town, by asking the railways to provide fewer trains to the resort on weekends. Tourists were also to be accosted and asked to show that they were carrying at least 50,000 lire as spending money. But these are isolated instances, and for the most part, destination authorities have recognized that their obligation is to grow tourism, while ensuring that, as far as possible, whatever impact tourists have on local populations should be beneficial to the locals.

Bringing economic benefits to locals

One other issue is the need to ensure that locals are involved in all stages of tourism development in a destination. This means that the onus is on developers and authorities to consult with locals at all levels during the process of development, to encourage their participation, and to ensure that indigenous populations benefit economically from incoming tourism, through the provision of employment at all levels, and through ownership of facilities. However, all these activities require a measure of sophistication among the local population, with the provision of essential education and training, as well as assistance in raising finance for investment in local tourist businesses. The solution cannot be achieved merely by putting businesses into the hands of local residents. To illustrate this, the example can be given of a tour operating company in Arnhem Land, Australia, which was originally managed by foreign nationals, but was eventually handed over to local Aboriginal administration. While the new Aboriginal owners were fully capable of handling the operational aspects of the programme, they had little knowledge of, and no contacts with, the overseas markets they existed to serve, and in consequence they found it difficult to attract new business. Other, more recent, schemes, however, have been handled more successfully. One simple example is the recent innovation of employing local Bedouin tribesmen to act as escorts for groups of trekkers across the Sinai Peninsula. Similarly, a sustainable village project in Gomorszolos, Hungary, involves small group tours (a maximum of twelve people) staying in locally owned hotels, using local guides, and with local conservation projects partly funded by the income generated by the tours.

Example Blue Lagoon Cruises

Blue Lagoon Cruises operates in the Yasawa Islands north west of Fiji. The company makes direct and indirect contributions of some £165,000 annually to the islands, whether visited or not. Locals are employed, and care is taken to minimize the impact of tourists on the islands during visits. Expansion plans include calls at some of the more northerly, seldom visited islands such as Rabi and Kioa, where locals have notable basketry skills and the economy can be boosted by craft sales. Funds earned will be channelled into community halls, water tanks and the construction of sea walls against erosion.

The impact of travel on tourist health

Impact is a two-way process, and we have examined both positive and negative effects of tourism in these paragraphs. It is notable how the lifestyles of many tourists have changed as a result of their experiences in travelling abroad; a more adventurous taste in food, higher consumption of wine at the expense of beers and hard spirits, a wider appreciation of foreign cultural activities, even a greater willingness to master the elements of a foreign language (a real breakthrough for the British!) are just some of the changes that tourists bring back with them to enrich their lives in their home countries. Unfortunately, other things they bring back with them can be less welcome.

Severe sunburn is among the most common of the ailments afflicting tourists from the generating countries, the result of a desire to maximize exposure to the sun during the brief period spent abroad on holiday. While sunburn is by no means uncommon among tourists visiting the seaside in northern communities, the increased intensity of the sun's rays nearer the equator, coupled with higher consumption of alcohol abroad leading to carelessness in taking measures to protect against burns on fair skin, has resulted in rather more than the pain and nausea that accompany a bad case of sunburn. The propensity to skin cancer is enhanced as the world's protective ozone layer is reduced by atmospheric pollution. The long-term effect of such exposure to the sun is a substantial rise in skin cancers, anything up to 20 years or more after the sunburn. Although the danger has now been recognized for some years, and governments have mounted campaigns to draw attention to the problem, many tourists either remain ignorant of the problem or choose to ignore it in their desire to cultivate an attractive tan (research indicates over 70 per cent of young people between the ages of 16 and 24 in Britain still want to tan while on holiday). The United States experiences over a million new incidences of skin cancer annually, and the problem has also been well publicized in Britain, where some 40,000 cases occur each year. By the early twenty-first century, incidence among British males was increasing at a rate of 4.2 per cent per annum, with mortality increasing at 2.9 per cent. However, in Australia (where in Queensland as many as one in three of the population is affected) the 'slip, slap, slop' campaign (slip on a T-shirt, slap on a hat, slop on sun cream) has been far more effective in educating a country of sun-lovers, and deaths from all forms of cancer have been reduced to around one thousand a year.

Skin cancer is of two varieties. The more common, carcinoma, occurs as a result of long-term exposure outdoors, common among people such as construction workers and farmers who spend long hours each day in the sun – but also a danger to employees in the tourism industry such as bus and coach drivers, lifeguards or resort representatives, all of whom spend long hours exposed to the sun in their daily work. Melanoma, on the other hand, results from short but intensive exposure to the sun, such as is commonly experienced by tourists on holiday. The danger of malignant melanoma is greatest for fair-complexioned tourists, especially those from Anglo-Saxon races like Britons, Germans and Scandinavians – young children are particularly at risk – although the effects of such exposure may take many years to develop into cancer. There were about 7,000 cases of malignant melanoma in Britain in 2003, resulting in some 1,700 deaths (Cancer Research UK); during the period 1995–2000 a rise of 24 per cent occurred.

The problem with solar rays is that tourists going on holiday, whether to beaches at home or abroad, remain largely unaware of their danger. There are, in fact, two forms of ultra-violet light rays, known as UVA and UVB. The former (which are also those to which people are exposed in the use of sunbeds) have longer wavelengths, and affect the skin throughout the day when exposed to light, even during cloudy periods. These rays have long-term effects on the skin, creating wrinkles and liver spots, and can also lead to carcinomas. There is doubt whether most SPF (sun protection factor) creams offer adequate protection against these rays. UVB rays are shorter in wavelength but stronger, far more damaging than UVA rays, and at their most dangerous when the sun is at its height between the hours of 11 am and 3 pm. While SPF creams prevent burning from these rays, it is now believed they have little effect in reducing the incidence of long-term skin cancer (unless sunblock creams are used).

Attitudes towards sun-tanning are expected to change only gradually over the next few years, with many tourists still choosing to visit seaside resorts for their perceived health and relaxation benefits. The media, with the support of health experts, are encouraging tourists to change their behaviour patterns while at the seaside, by applying high-factor suncreams – or better, sunblocks – while sunbathing, ensuring young children are well covered, and generally reducing outdoor activities when the sun is at its most intense. The seaside resorts are coming to recognize that if they are to survive they must construct more indoor facilities and offer their visitors better protection from the sun (such as parasols, now commonly found on Caribbean beaches) while on the beach.

Exposure to contaminated food results in other common holiday ailments, ranging from simple upset stomachs to hepatitis and dysentery. Incidence is increasing as holidaymakers become more adventurous, visiting areas of the world where poor hygiene and inadequate supervision are widespread. Tropical diseases are similarly becoming more commonplace, with malaria leading the field – several deaths occur each year among British tourists, many of whom disregard recommended precautions. Some forms of malaria are becoming highly resistant to standard prescription drugs, although recent research offers hope of a vaccine within a generation. Outbreaks of SARS (severe acute respiratory syndrome) have also severely impacted on tourist movements, especially to popular Asian countries, while the global spread of

HIV/AIDS, especially but by no means restricted to African and Asian destinations, coupled with lax sexual mores among many travellers, compound the health threats for tourists. The solution to most of these problems lies in better education, of both hosts and guests, with the onus on the travel industry to get the message across to their customers through brochures, websites and on-the-spot resort representatives.

Politico-cultural impacts

Finally, it would be inappropriate to close this chapter without making reference to the growth in global terrorism, which threatens to undermine both travel and understanding between nations. Attacks directed against Westerners, especially in Muslim-oriented countries, can lead to a dramatic reduction in the flow of tourists to those countries, some of whose economies (e.g. Egypt, Bali) are heavily dependent upon tourism. Local civil wars in some popular areas of the globe inhibit tourism (e.g. Kathmandu in Nepal has seen a sharp decline in tourist arrivals following the rise of Maoist revolutionaries in the country). The British foreign office has been frequently accused of ambivalence in the guidance given to tourists, while the industry itself – and travel insurance companies – are obliged to follow their governments' directives in determining whether package programmes should be withdrawn following attacks. The authorities in the leading generating countries are seldom consistent in tackling these issues uniformly. American tourists show greater reluctance to travel to countries where there is a perceived threat, however remote, while European travellers appear more resilient. Indeed, following the events of 11 September 2001, Americans have been slow to travel abroad even to relatively safe countries, slowing the annual global expansion of tourism considerably.

Notes

1 Definition given at forum 'Conservation of the Americas', Indianapolis, 18–20 November 1987

2 www.ecoturism.org

3 Eber, S, *Beyond the Green Horizon: Principles of Sustainable Tourism*, Tourism Concern/WWF, 1992

4 Brundtland Commission, *The Brundtland Report: World Commission on Environment and Development, Our Common Future*, OUP 1987

5 From the 1992 UN Conference on the Environment and Development, Rio de Janeiro

6 Doxey, G V, A Causation Theory of Visitor-Resident Irritants: Methodology and Research Inferences, *Proceedings of the Travel Research Association Sixth Annual Conference*, San Diego, 1975

7 Ibid

8 Gullahorn, J E and Gullahorn, J T, An Extension of the U-Curre Hypothesis, *Journal of Social Sciences*, 19, 1963, pp 33–47

9 Sutton, W A, Travel and Understanding: Notes on the Social Structure of Touring, *International Journal of Comparative Sociology* 8/2, 1967

10 MacCannell, D, *The Tourist: a New Theory of the Leisure Class*, Schocken Books, 2nd edn 1989

Website

International Porter Protection Group   www.ippg.net

Questions and discussion points

1. Some tourist-generating countries appear to set double standards in their expectations of tourist behaviour. Many hold that for tourists visiting their country, the adage, 'when in Rome, do as the Romans do' offers appropriate guidance; yet when travelling abroad themselves, many insist on standards and customs familiar in their own countries, including types of food not readily available and patterns of dress not acceptable in developing countries. In this, they would appear to be applying another adage, 'he who pays the piper calls the tune'. Which is right?

2. Discuss the research findings of the Gullahorns outlined in this chapter. Have any in your group experienced these stages in the manner described? Were they influenced by – length of stay, the culture of the country, or attitudes shown towards you as visitors? What effect did knowledge of, or lack of, a local language inhibit acclimatization?

3. What sociocultural impacts will arise from the growing tendency for Britons to buy properties as second homes, or to rent out, in developing countries?

4. Can all-inclusive holidays be sustainable?

5. In this chapter, a description is given of SAVE's programme to draw tourists away from the coast in favour of inland villages. If these programmes become popular, is there a danger that they, in turn, will become swamped, creating similar problems to those experienced along the coast? How can this be avoided?

Assignment topics

1. Construct a research programme to investigate whether people visiting foreign countries have found their attitudes changed as a result of their visits. Ideally, this should be undertaken using qualitative techniques, but if a questionnaire is to be used, explain how the information you are soliciting could be collected and analyzed quantitatively.

2. There are presently strong arguments against travelling to Myanmar, owing in part to the exploitation of locals by the Government in order to encourage tourism. Pressure groups like Tourism Concern are lobbying against tour operators who organize visits to the country. In the role of an assistant in the planning department of a specialist tour operator, undertake research and produce a report which illustrates the arguments and counter-arguments, and make recommendations to your boss on whether you feel it is justifiable to mount a programme to the country in the present circumstances.

7 The environmental impact of tourism

Objectives

After studying this chapter, you should be able to:

- understand the various ways in which tourism can impact on the environment
- identify and evaluate different approaches to finding solutions to these problems
- understand the importance of sustainable tourism, as it relates to the environment
- recognize that appropriate planning and cooperation between the private and public sectors can help to ensure sustainability.

Introduction

Half our operators are bankrupt. What reward is there for being more environmentally-friendly?
Noel Josephides, MD Sunvil Holidays, quoted in *Tourism*, No. 119 Winter 2004

In Chapter 6 we explored the different ways in which tourism can impact upon people, both travellers and residents in destination countries. In this chapter, we go on to look at tourism's impact upon the environment in which they travel. While the obvious focus will be upon how tourism affects the environment at popular tourism destinations, we need to be aware at the same time that the rise in global tourism has environmental impacts that go far beyond these destinations alone. In fact, it is no exaggeration to say that tourism is a major contributor to despoliation of the environment, notably through transport's contribution to pollution, whether by air, sea or on land.

As tourism expands, so are new destinations put at risk – and twenty-first century tourists are tending to seek out ever more remote areas of the globe.

Example   Antarctica (see Plate 7)

Even the Antarctic continent has become a regular target for mass tourism today, with cruise ships which can carry up to 600 passengers now visiting the peninsula on a regular basis, and passenger-carrying ice-breakers calling as far south as Scott's and Shackleton's bases; there is even a 100-bed hotel on the peninsula, built by the Chilean armed forces based there. Annual visitor figures to Antarctica, a mere 4,800 in 1991, rose to 15,325 in 2001, and the figure is conservatively expected to exceed 26,000 by 2006. Package tourists can now enjoy visits to this least explored continent which, in addition to penguin watching, can include anything from travel by snowmobile to 'adventure flights' to the South Pole itself. The popularity of the huge penguin colonies has meant that some of these colonies are receiving as many as three visits every day, impacting on the birds' behaviour and breeding patterns. One unexpected result of this influx has been the large number of birds contracting diseases found in chickens, thought to be the result of food carelessly discarded by visiting tourists. Such ill-effects have led to members of the International Association of Antarctic Tour Operators adopting a voluntary code of practice to minimize the impacts of visitors, including limiting the number of passengers put ashore at any one time to one hundred, and restricting the closeness of their approach to the penguin colonies. The difficulty, however, is in policing the ruling.

In other ecologically sensitive regions such as the Galapagos Islands, Costa Rica and Belize, tourism development is also controlled, and efforts are made to ensure that all tourism visits are sustainable. However, demand pressures are difficult to resist where the economic benefits to lesser developed countries are significant; while in 1974 the authorities set an original target of 12,000 visits to the Galapagos (later revised to 40,000), visitors now number close to 100,000, and the ceiling has been to all intents and purposes abolished. The authorities have now agreed to allow twelve visits a year by cruise ships carrying up to 500 passengers, far exceeding the previous limit of 100 – although all are escorted and are restricted to just 8 per cent of the total land mass.

The environmental effects of tourism

Transport pollution

Large-scale tourist movement requires the use of mass transportation, particularly by air; and while aircraft are now twice as fuel efficient as they were three decades ago, air travel has quadrupled in this same interval. In 1970, airline passengers travelled some 350 billion air passenger miles (this figure, of course, includes all forms of passengers, not merely tourists); by 2000, APMs had increased to 1,500 billion, and forecasts are for this to double by 2015 and triple by 2050 (given the expansion of the low-cost carriers, these figures may prove conservative). Apart from emissions of nitrous oxides (and the introduction of quieter, more fuel-efficient and cleaner jet engines unfortunately has the side effect of increasing those emissions), these aircraft pump some 600 million tons of carbon dioxide into the upper atmosphere each year. According to the Intergovernmental Panel on Climate Change, this accounts for at least 3.5 per cent of all greenhouse gases; again, this will rise to 15 per cent by 2050, on present estimates. One EU study in 2004 claimed that air travel was responsible for 9 per cent of all global warming. In Britain alone, according to a Government Aviation White Paper in 2003, the number of people flying into and out of the UK would rise from 180 million to over 500 million in 2030, while an environmental audit committee estimated that aviation would have become responsible for two-thirds of all the UK's greenhouse gas emissions by 2050. These figures also do not take into account the costs of congestion, leading to stacking over airports, and resultant fuel waste, a problem likely to grow as air corridors become more crowded. The rapid expansion of the low-cost airlines, operating on short-haul routes, accounts for a sizeable increase in pollution figures, given that one-fifth of a short-haul aircraft's fuel load is burnt in take-off and landing.

Yet in spite of the clear threat to world health, aviation fuel remains largely untaxed. Fuel taxation was ruled out at the 1944 Chicago Convention in order to boost the post-war airline industry, and even VAT has not yet been applied to airline tickets, in spite of protests from the environmentalists. Aviation is specifically exempted from the Kyoto Protocol on climate change. There are growing calls for a carbon tax on fuel, which it is thought would help lead to the conversion of aircraft fuel from high carbon kerosene to low carbon liquid methane and ultimately the development of carbon-free liquid hydrogen fuels (a move likely to be hastened by the current growing fear of world oil shortages), but any such tax, to be truly effective, would have to be globally applied, and would encounter strong resistance from the airlines, and from authorities in countries like the USA which are heavily dependent upon low-price air travel. Alternatively, carbon trading agreements could be extended to airlines, requiring either their reducing emissions or purchasing expensive permits (fees for which would have to be recovered through higher ticket prices). Regionally, taxes have been mooted (in Britain, a government green paper, *The Future of Aviation* (2000) accepted the principle that polluters should pay, and the Royal Commission on Environmental Pollution proposed a green tax on air tickets in 2002), but not implemented.

Example   Taxing to off-set carbon dioxide damage[1]

Climate Care estimates that each passenger flying to Mauritius is responsible for releasing 2.7 tonnes of carbon dioxide. Flyers on this route are to be advised by computer 'aviation calendar' how much pollution their flight is causing.

The organization has also estimated the cost of off-setting carbon dioxide damage on short-haul and longer flights. This would call for payment per passenger travelling from London on return flights, of the following sums:

£5 to Lisbon, Portugal

£16 to Los Angeles, USA

£31 to Sydney, Australia.

Other forms of tourism transport make their own contributions to pollution. Up to 300 passenger ships now ply world cruise routes, carrying in excess of ten million passengers each year. The US-based Ocean Conservancy estimates that, apart from the daily fuel burn, each ship generates some 30,000 gallons of sewage and seven tons of rubbish each day – not all of it properly disposed of; several leading cruise companies have been prosecuted in recent years for pollution of the seas and rigging instruments to deceive inspection. Water-borne vessels of all kinds, whether on the high seas or on inland rivers, lakes and canals, by cleaning out their tanks or dumping waste overboard, significantly contribute to water pollution; and this in turn impacts upon aquatic wildlife. Even without such illicit dumping, the sheer number of cruise vessels plying popular waterways such as the Caribbean poses a threat through leakages and congestion at key ports, and Bermuda is among islands that now impose restrictions on the number of cruise ship visits permitted each year.

Example Alaskan cruises

Alaskans, once overjoyed at the arrival of tourist ships, have become angered by the rapidly increasing numbers of cruise ships visiting the state, fearing contamination of their waters; while the large number of vessels being routed to the area to engage in whale-watching is having the effect of driving these mammals away from the Alaskan shores. The state's Department of Environmental Conservation now levies a charge on all cruise vessels to pay for the clean-up of pollution.

Inland waterways are, if anything, even more fragile and endangered through excessive use by water-borne leisure transport, whether private or public. Apart from the danger of pollution caused by fuel or oil leaks in rivers, lakes and canals, unless strict speed limits are enforced, river banks may be damaged or undermined by the wash from passing boats, causing soil erosion and endangering wildlife. The popularity of the Norfolk Broads in Britain among boaters has led to overuse of these waterways during the past fifty years, with resultant damage to banks.

Example Venice

Venice, with its network of canals, receives up to seven million visitors every year. Most are transported by water during their stay, and gondola trips are an expensive but popular form of excursion. However, the city is slowly sinking, and its paved areas are subject to frequent flooding. Since public transport on the canals is largely motorized, the wash from these vessels is contributing to undermining the foundations of many historic buildings. The Italian government gave Venice the power to limit motorized transport, introduce speed limits and tolls on tourist boats and establish 'blue zones' where transport is limited to gondolas and rowing boats.

Finally, account must also be taken of the impact of the many millions of motorists using private and hire cars for their holidays and short breaks. While congestion is the more visible problem arising out of the expansion of vehicles at popular tourism destinations, pollution resulting from the concentration of exhaust gases in both city and rural tourism destinations can seriously affect the health of tourists and residents alike. Uncontrolled expansion of private vehicles in key cities like Bangkok can so adversely affect the tourist experience that it threatens to discourage visitors either from travelling there, or staying in the city. A proportion of the petrol purchased all over the world is for leisure purposes, whether for touring or day trips; and in some regions the exhaust fumes from these vehicles, when added to local consumption, can damage the clean air which is the prime attraction for tourists. This is particularly true of mountainous destinations, where not only touristic appeal, but also even plant and animal life can be affected.

Example	Mountain resorts

Some popular mountain resorts, such as Zermatt in Switzerland, have banned non-residential private vehicles from the town, requiring tourists to use park-and-ride services, or rack-and-pinion railways into the resort. The latter often provide a picturesque added attraction to visitors' stay.

The popularity of off-roading with SUVs (sports utility vehicles) is also damaging to the environment in sensitive areas of the world. This sport is popular among American tourists, and some wilderness areas are now under threat, particularly in Utah. Moab (scene of Butch Cassidy's adventures) has attracted significant numbers of SUVs, as have sand dunes in several parts of the world, where these vehicles can destroy sparse scrubland and erode the landscape.

Noise pollution by transport

All motorized forms of road, sea and air transport can intrude on the calm of a resort by raising noise levels, whether in rural surroundings or in residential areas, and this, too, must be considered a form of pollution. Aircraft taking off and landing at busy airports severely disturb local residents and tourists alike. Authorities have long recognized the problem of air traffic noise, and action has been taken to reduce it. For example, aircraft are categorized under three classes, known as chapters, according to the noise levels they emit. Under government regulations, especially in the United States, the more recently introduced Chapter 3 aircraft, such as the Airbus, are 85 per cent less noisy than were Chapter 1 aircraft, and are consequently allowed greater freedom to operate. The problem is compounded for night flights, where restrictions are often in force to reduce the problem. While effective lobbying in the UK has largely restricted the problem to Luton and Stansted Airports, in India all airports are still obliged to accept jumbo aircraft throughout the night.

Noise from water-borne vessels is most notable along coasts and in tranquil rural areas where boats using their motors can disturb the peace of the night when travelling along rivers and canals. New water-borne vehicles like jet bikes and water bikes, often used off-shore at popular beach resorts, are noisy, and this (coupled with possible danger to life) has been a factor in attempts to reduce their use off-shore at popular Mediterranean resorts.

Pollution at tourist destinations

The physical pollution of popular destinations poses a growing threat for global tourism. Perhaps the most wide-spread example is seen in coastal resorts, where beach and off-shore water contamination is both visible and in some cases, can be life-threatening to bathers. In this respect, British coastal resorts have in the past fared badly by comparison with their European neighbours, although recent years have witnessed marked improvements, following clean-up drives within the EU. Nevertheless, some popular bathing areas in Britain remain seriously contaminated by raw sewage or other pollutants.

Beaches in Britain are monitored in several ways. Key certification is in the hands of ENCAMS (Environmental Campaigns) which runs the Keep Britain Tidy campaign, awarding yellow and blue flags to beaches and bathing water satisfying certain minimal criteria, including water purity and freedom from litter and other pollutants on the beaches themselves. More criteria are applied to beaches qualifying as resorts rather than rural, but both require the beaches to meet at least the mandatory standards of bathing water applied in the EU. ENCAMS also administers, within Britain, the more stringent Blue Flag campaign on behalf of the international body FEE (Foundation for Environmental Education), which monitors beaches in some 40 countries in Europe, South Africa and the Caribbean. In 2003, 332 beaches in Britain were awarded yellow and blue flag status (compared with only 92 in 1992, the first year of monitoring), while 105 achieved European Blue Flag standard, but by 2005, 98 per cent of beaches were passing the more stringent tests, with just 13 of the 562 failing. Nevertheless, a handful of UK tourist beaches, including such popular resorts as Blackpool, have consistently over the years failed to meet minimum standards – perhaps it is as well that only some 7 per cent of those spending time on beaches in the UK actually have any intention of bathing!

Environmental 'pollution' is as much aesthetic as physical. An area of scenic beauty attracts greater numbers of tourists, so more and more of the natural landscape is lost to tourist development; the countryside retreats before the growth of hotels and other amenities which spring up to cater for the tourists' needs, with the eventual result that the site is no longer seen as 'scenic', and the tourist moves on to find somewhere more tranquil as well as beautiful. Similarly, without careful control, the stately home which tries to meet the needs of its visitors will provide an ever-expanding range of facilities such as larger car parks, cafes, shops, directional signposts and toilet facilities, all of which detract from the appeal of the main attraction. Extreme examples of despoliation of the scenery by signposting are readily found in the United States where, with fewer controls than are exercised in Britain, both countryside and towns can be destroyed by directional signs and advertising hoardings (however, some might argue

Figure 7.1
Visual pollution
resulting from
high-density
caravan siting

(Photographed by the author)

that at night, the forest of illuminated signs in towns like Reno and Las Vegas is very much part of the attraction of the resort). There are fears that a relaxation of regulations in Britain could lead to a similar explosion of countryside billboards.

Noise pollution (to which tourism contributes not only through transport) is a common problem of contemporary life, and not only in towns. At the Treetops Hotel in Kenya's Masai Mara National Park, animals visiting the adjacent water-hole at night are driven from the site by the careless loud talk or laughter of a minority of the visitors waiting to see them. In the seaside resorts of the Mediterranean, building construction in fast-developing resorts can be both visibly and audibly offensive, especially during hours of darkness. The peace of the night is also frequently destroyed by late-night disco bars catering to younger tourists. In some of these resorts, the authorities have perceived the danger of negative publicity driving away the family market, and have authorized the police to undertake night patrols to combat excessive noise. One such example is Magaluf in Majorca, where police act against pubs or nightclubs registering noise levels higher than 65 decibels.

Another aesthetic form of visual pollution is illustrated by the frequent insensitivity in design of tourist buildings. Lack of planning control is often to blame, as developers prefer to build cheaply, resulting in high-rise concrete hotels lacking character and out of keeping with the surrounding architecture. British towns are also losing their local character, as builders have chosen to build in ubiquitous (but cheap) London brick rather than the materials available locally (although planning authorities have taken stricter measures in recent years to control against this practice). In seaside resorts around the world, the concrete skyscraper hotel has become the norm, and from Waikiki in Hawaii to Benidorm in Spain the tourist is confronted with a conformity of architecture which owes nothing to the culture or traditions of the country in which it is built. Some far-seeing authorities have recognized the damage potential, and brought in controls to limit it. In some cases this has led to insistence that hotels must be built in local materials, or conform to 'vernacular' architecture, that is, styles indigenous to the region. Others require buildings not to exceed a certain height – for example, Tunisia requires that new hotel developments in tourism resorts should be no higher than the normal height of the palm trees which will surround them. Mauritius has imposed constraints on both the architectural style and the materials employed in hotel building. While some critics have questioned the rather 'staged' results, with thatched cottages vaguely resembling African kraals, no one questions the appeal which these accommodation units have for tourists. Such legislation clearly must apply to all buildings, not just those for tourism.

Example   Lanzarote

On Lanzarote, in the Canary Islands, all housing, apartments and hotels are required to conform to rigorous building regulations imposed by the Department of Tourism on the island. These control not only the style of the buildings but the colours in which doors and windows may be painted; only white, blue and green paintwork is permitted.

Sometimes, planning controls will have the effect of restricting innovation in architecture, leaving developers to play it safe by falling back on 'pastiche' or bland designs attractive only to the most conservative visitor. The attempt to protect local building styles and materials can sometimes have unexpected results, as in Ireland, where traditional corrugated roofs have now become such a familiar feature of the landscape that they have been designated 'vernacular' building material.

Sometimes, the problem of scale can relate to far smaller buildings than hotels, but the significance of the problem is no less. During the early 1990s, two historic properties were both under threat owing to plans either to build or to expand visitors' centres adjacent to the site. The Haworth Parsonage, home of the Brontë sisters in the Yorkshire Moors, was threatened with a massive expansion of the visitors' centre, which would have greatly exceeded the size of the original house; the project resulted in an outcry from the public, and a rethink of the plans. Similarly, trustees of the birthplace of Sir Edward Elgar, in the Malvern Hills, submitted plans for a new visitors' centre adjacent to, and much larger than, the composer's original cottage. This, too, led to a public outcry in the media, but construction went ahead, with a visitor centre resembling, according to one architectural critic, a Tesco supermarket. The problem of providing sufficient room to accommodate all the visitors, some 10,000 a year, at such a small site is a common one and offers no easy solution – or at least, no cheap solution. One plan proposed at Haworth was to conceal the new visitor centre underground, which although an ideal solution, proved to be too costly for the funds available.

Other common forms of visual pollution by tourists include littering, particularly in areas around picnic sites, and graffiti on buildings. It is a curious fact that even those tourists who come from large cities, where they are so used to seeing litter that they become unconscious of it, immediately become sensitive to litter in a tourist destination. Resorts which have made the effort to improve their image in recent years tend to start by undertaking a drive against both rubbish in the streets and graffiti on buildings. An important point here is that litter bins should not only be readily available, but should also be attractively designed. Unfortunately, at many sites both in Britain and elsewhere the fear of terrorist bombs or vandalism has caused rubbish bins to be sealed or removed, making rubbish disposal more difficult for tourists. In very sensitive areas of the world, such as wilderness regions, littering becomes a critical issue because these areas are too far from any public services which could resolve the problem, and the onus is on tourists themselves to safeguard the environment by taking their rubbish with them. This is a very real issue in the Himalayas, as trekking becomes more popular in the region. Many trekkers and organized trekking parties are failing to carry out their litter, or to dig latrines to hide human waste, with the result that some valleys have become littered with unsightly rubbish, much of which fails to decompose at these altitudes. Environmentalists and enlightened tour operators are encouraging visitors to ensure that their rubbish is either burned or carried out (although local villagers often make use of tins, bags or bottles left behind), and that human waste is buried. The authorities are being encouraged to build more permanent composting toilets in frequented areas, using the 'twin vault' principle – each vault is used in alternative years, to allow waste to decompose. Nutrients from composted waste can then be used to encourage rapid growth of willow trees, providing a much-needed timber source for local villagers.

Graffiti has become a common problem in the Western world, with thoughtless tourists desecrating ancient monuments with spray-painted, scratched and even chiselled, messages. This of course is no new development: the Romans were chiselling their names on Greek monuments two thousand years ago. But the sheer scale of modern tourism has forced authorities to take action. In extreme cases, this had led to denial of access, as in the case of Stonehenge, where visitors are no longer permitted to walk among the stones themselves, but must be content to view them from a distance.

Problems of congestion and erosion

Perhaps the most significant problem created by mass tourism is that of congestion. This is a complex problem, because it exists at both a *psychological* and a *physical* level.

The latter is more easily measured, in terms of the capacity of an area to absorb the tourist; car parks, streets, beaches, ski slopes, cathedrals and similar features all have a finite limit to the number of tourists which they can accommodate at any given time. Theoretically, this is also true of entire regions and countries, although attempts to define the tourist capacity of a city or country have seldom been attempted. National tourist offices continue to develop policies aimed at an ever-expanding influx of tourists year-on-year, without considering the ability of the areas to absorb these numbers – although efforts are made to divert these influxes to off-peak periods, or to less crowded areas of the country. At the urban level, a few cities under extreme pressure, like Florence and Venice, have taken more positive action, as will be seen later in this chapter.

However, it is also necessary to understand the psychological capacity of a site. This is the degree of congestion which the tourists will tolerate before the site starts to lose its appeal. Quantifying this is far more difficult, since the perception of capacity will differ, not only according to the nature of the site itself but also according to the market which is attracted to it. A beach in, say, Fiji will be judged overcrowded much more quickly than, say, Bournemouth, while in a resort such as Blackpool a much higher level of crowding may be tolerated, or even welcomed as part of the 'fun experience'. One attempt to measure the psychological capacity of a beach was carried out at Brittas Bay in Ireland in the early 1970s. Aerial photographs were made of the number of tourists on the beach on a crowded Sunday afternoon, and a questionnaire was circulated to those on the beach to receive their views about the congestion. It was found that most visitors would accept around 1,000 people per hectare (ten square metres per person) without feeling the beach was overcrowded.

Example   Koh Phi Phi Ley, Thailand

Koh Phi Phi Ley (Maya Bay) was until the turn of the millennium a rather isolated beach and natural beauty spot, one of the Phi Phi Island group near Phuket, until a popular film, *The Beach*, starring Leonardo di Caprio, romanticized for millions of young film-goers the idea of 'lotus-eating' holidays in faraway places, resulting in hordes of backpackers descending upon the area to search out the exact location of the film. The subsequent despoliation of the idyll was condemned by tourist officials in the country, although the resulting development of the nearby Ao Ton Sai resort on Koh Phi Phi Don has benefited locals economically. A five-fold increase in tourist fees was implemented in order to control visitor numbers to the site. The Phi Phi group were badly affected by the 2004 Tsunami, and authorities are keen to re-establish the area as a popular venue for tourism.

In so-called *wilderness* areas, of course, the psychological capacity of the region may be very low, and areas sensitive to environmental damage may suffer physically even where there are comparatively few visitors. In the United States, Yellowstone and the Everglades National Parks are both physically under severe threat from tourism, and psychologically they are so remote that any mass tourism will greatly reduce their attractiveness. In Britain, from the psychological viewpoint of the hiker, sites such as the Derbyshire Peak District should not support more than a handful of tourists per square kilometre, although the mass influx to its major centres such as Dovedale on an August Bank Holiday fails to act as a deterrent for the majority of day trippers. Indeed, it has been demonstrated in the case of Cannock Chase, the beauty spot near

Table 7.1 Visitor capacity for selected sites

Site/activity	Visitors per day/hectare
Forest park	15
Suburban nature park	15–70
High-density picnicking	300–600
Low-density picnicking	60–200
Golf	10–15
Fishing/sailing	5–30
Speedboating	5–10
Waterskiing	5–15
Skiing	100 (per hectare of trails)
Nature trail hiking	40 (per kilometre)
Nature trail horseriding	25–80 (per kilometre)

Source: E Inskip (1991)[2]

Birmingham, that this area draws tourists from the Midlands as much for its role as a social meeting place as for its scenic beauty.

The behaviour of tourists at wilderness sites will be a factor in deciding their psychological capacity. Many trippers to an isolated area will tend to stay close to their cars, and hikers who are prepared to walk a mile or so away from the car park will readily find the solitude they seek. This is obviously a key for tourism planners, since by discouraging or forbidding car parking and access by vehicle to the more remote areas they can effectively restrict these areas to those seeking solitude.

Some authorities have tried to set standards for particular types of tourist activity as a guide to planners. Table 7.1 offers one attempt, by the World Tourism Organization (WTO), to lay down guidelines, in terms of visitors per day per hectare.

The ecological capacity to absorb tourists must also be taken into account. While too many tourists in a built-up area such as the narrow shopping lanes of York or Brighton can detract from tourism, the physical wear and tear on the environment is limited – at least, in the short term. However, too many tourists in a rural or otherwise fragile environment can destroy the balance of nature. This can be seen by the increase in tourists visiting African safari parks, where the number of vehicles hunting for the 'big five' at any one time can resemble a car rally in some areas of the parks. Some idea of the effect of erosion can be gained from a report in the *Guardian*[3] which revealed that 400 tons of sand are removed from the beach of Benidorm each year on the soles of holiday-makers' feet!

Some sites are particularly fragile. Many sand dunes have been destroyed or seriously eroded in the United States by the use of beach buggies and, as we noted earlier in respect to other sensitive ecological systems, by SUVs. In the UK similar problems are thrown up by motor-cycle rallying, which can easily uproot the few clumps of dune grass on which the ecosystem depends. The UN Environment Programme has reported that three-quarters of all the sand dunes on the Mediterranean coastline between Spain and Sicily have disappeared as a direct result of tourism development.

Example   The Great Barrier Reef (see Plate 8)

The Great Barrier Reef off the coast of Queensland, Australia, is a World Heritage Site generating some A$1.5 billion per annum from tourism. However, its 1,450 miles of fragile coral reefs can be easily damaged by divers or snorkelers – even touching or standing on live coral can be sufficient to kill it, and some visitors go so far as to break off pieces for souvenirs. Coral can also be damaged by boats anchoring. Compounded by the effects of global warming, this is contributing to the death of large tracts of the reef. In an effort to reduce its destruction, in 2004 the Australian government banned commercial fishing from 44,000 square miles of the reefs. Companies which thrive by running boat trips for tourists to visit the reefs are now aware of the threat to their livelihood, and are taking on the responsibility to educate their passengers. During the boat trip the tourists are given information on the fragility of the site and how it can be preserved by careful use.

Individual buildings attracting very high levels of tourist demand are no less problematic, requiring firm measures to manage and limit access. This can of course lead to disappointment for tourists. In recent years crowds visiting the Uffizi Gallery and Galleria dell'Accademia (the site of Michelangelo's David) in Florence during peak holiday periods have become so great that the local authorities have had to take the unusual step of temporarily closing the buildings. Both Florence and Venice face exceptionally heavy demand from international tourists; the latter welcomes over seven million tourists each year, with 1.5 million seeking admission to the Doge's Palace and St Mark's Square alone, while on some days as many as 40,000 tourists have visited the Baptistry of San Giovanni and the adjoining Duomo in Florence. Such crowds produce high levels of condensation which affect the thirteenth- and fourteenth-century mosaics. The authorities have responded by reducing coaches to the city from 500 to 150 a day, charging them high fees for the privilege and spot-checking on arterial roads out of the city to enforce compliance. Numbers admitted to the Baptistry were reduced to 150 at a time, and for the first time charges were applied for entry. In 2005 Italy's new culture minister proposed a big increase in prices charged at the most popular sites in Italy, in the hope that tourists could be diverted to lesser known museums and attractions, but tourists and officials felt that the suggestion would be impractical.

Example   Macchu Pichu

The long lost Inca city of Macchu Pichu, now a UNESCO World Heritage site, was rediscovered only in 1911. It is now the country's major tourist attraction, with 85 per cent of all visitors to Peru planning a visit there. Public access was enhanced with the building of a railhead nearby, and helicopter flights bring others from Cuzco. As a result, over 400,000 now visit the site annually, and UNESCO has recommended that daily admission should be limited to 2,000 during the high season, and 800 off-season, to avoid irreparable damage. The Peruvian Government countered with a proposal to limit the number to 2,500 daily, which it hoped would be sufficient to avoid the site's being placed on UNESCO's danger list. In 2000, it had also announced plans to build a cable car to replace the buses transferring tourists from the railhead to the top of the mountain, but a public outcry from UNESCO and the environmental lobby forced a retraction of the plan (although the cable car would have eliminated growing concern about the environmental damage caused by buses climbing the present steep access road).

Initially, the site could only be reached via the Inca Trail, a hazardous narrow footpath which appeared to place a natural ceiling on visitor numbers, but the growth in trekking has matched that of visits via public transport. Just 7,000 trekkers arrived by trail in 1988, but a decade later this had risen to 66,000. The Peruvian government were forced to impose new controls to reduce erosion of the path. Walkers unaccompanied by guides or porters were banned in 2001, entry charges to the site itself were tripled, and limits were introduced on the number of tour operators organizing the guided treks. No more than 500 trekkers daily (including porters) are now permitted to use the trail. The fees paid, however, go the central government, and are not used to protect or restore the site.

Another Inca city was recently discovered at Cerro Victoria, and the government hopes that this can be developed to take some of the pressure off Macchu Pichu.

Another tourism site suffering from extreme popularity is the Taj Mahal in India. This building alone attracts some two million visitors a year, and up to 6,000 each day. Since 1995, a price differential was introduced, with higher entry charges for foreign visitors, and the Indian government periodically has attempted to impose further swingeing price increases (although these were reduced after tour operator complaints). However, such unique sites are highly price-inelastic, and only a rationing system is likely to limit demand.

Congestion in Britain's National Parks

Many popular rural sites such as National Parks are at risk from the number of visitors they receive – and in the case of Britain, their proximity to centres of high population. Well over 100 million visitors visit the UK's National Parks each year, the Peak District being the most popular– claimed to be the second most visited National Park in the world, after Mount Fuji in Japan, with over 22 million visitors annually, and 3,000 vehicles on peak days. As a result, footpaths are overused, leading to soil becoming impacted, and grass and plants dying. Under some circumstances, the soil becomes loosened, and is then lost through wind erosion. Derbyshire County Council have proposed barrier charges to reduce traffic entering the National Park at weekends and on bank holidays, in an attempt to reduce this congestion.

Another attempt was made, in the early 1990s, to counteract the erosion of the footpath across the moors near Haworth; some 25,000 visitors had turned parts of the Brontë Way into a quagmire, necessitating flagstones being set into the track. Other running repairs have had to be made to long-distance footpaths such as those on the

Pennine Way and Cleveland Way. Such artificial landscaping, of course, creates a very different visual landscape to the wild moorland it replaces, but it is a solution being used more widely, as such footpaths have to deal with greater numbers of visitors each year. In places, these popular paths in the National Parks have widened to 45 yards.

Climbers, too, will also damage the parks. With the increased interest in activity holidays, climbing is becoming a very popular pastime; some 250,000 people climb Mam Tor in Derbyshire every year, and this has so affected the mountain that the summit had to be restored with an importation of 300 tons of rock and soil.

There is, however, an inevitable trade-off between protection and economic well-being, as is demonstrated by the imposition of recent controls in the English Lake District.

Example Lake District National Park

In 2005 the national park authorities in the Lake District introduced a 10 miles per hour speed limit on Windermere Lake, aiming to reduce noise pollution and erosion, and enhance the sense of peace for which the district is renowned. The decision has had a severe impact on the economy of the region; the TIC received 12,000 fewer enquiries in the first six months of the year, boat registrations and launches fell sharply, and the water-skiers, jet-skiers and powerboat drivers who are traditionally high spenders withdrew, leaving local firms to face business losses which are believed to be costing the local economy over £7 million annually. The local tourist board chairman accused the national park authority of 'ignoring its duty to foster the economic and social well-being of local communities'.

Sustainability and winter sports tourism

One fragile ecosystem in Europe is under particular threat. This is the Alps, and because the system is spread across no fewer than seven countries, collaboration to prevent the worst of the environmental effects of tourism is more difficult. The Alps receive over 50 million international visitors a year, and some 7 million passenger vehicles cross them each year, as they lie at the heart of Europe. To accommodate the huge increase in winter sports tourism that has occurred since World War II, some 41,000 ski runs have been built, capable of handling 1.5 million skiers an hour.

The region suffers in a number of ways. The proliferation of ski-lifts, chalets and concrete villages above 6,000 feet, and the substantial deforestation required to make way for pistes, have led to soil erosion, while the high volumes of traffic crossing the Alps contribute to the acid rain caused largely by factory emissions. These emissions are having a serious impact on the remaining forests, 60 per cent of which are now affected. Artificial snow-making machines have smothered alpine plants, reducing the vegetation, while wildlife has also declined as the animals' territories are reduced. A new danger is posed by the introduction of roller-skiing on grass and four-wheel-drive car-racing in summer. Potential damage, both ecological and economic, to the region is now so great that an organization, Alp Action, has been set up, with the support of the Aga Khan, to help preserve the Alps as a single ecosystem. It has to be added, however, that not all authorities welcome further control in this fashion; some Swiss cantons have expressed concern at the potential slowdown in the economic development of their region which results from this conservation movement.

Some local authorities have taken steps to control overuse. At Lech and Zuers in Austria, skiers are counted by computer through turnstiles which give them access to the pistes. Once 14,000, deemed capacity, have been admitted, tourists are diverted to other sites. Lillehammer in Norway, site of the 1994 Winter Olympic Games, took account of the problems already occurring in the Alps when designing its new facilities. Apart from efforts to minimize tree clearance, the authorities also took steps to avoid visual pollution in an area where comparatively few buildings exist; ski-jump runs were moulded into the mountainside to ensure they did not project above the tree line, and similar efforts were made to conceal bobsleigh and luge runs in the forests. The speed-skating stadium was built 20 yards away from the water's edge to protect waterfowl, and leak-proof cooling systems were embedded underground in concrete containers. Private cars were excluded from the town during the period of the Games.

Not only sports activities threaten snowscapes. Glaciers, whose ecosystems are invariably fragile, attract large numbers of sightseers when located in accessible regions. At the Columbia Icefield in Banff National Park, Canada, giant snowmobiles are employed to bring tourists on to the glacier (see Figure 7.2). The inevitable consequence will be damage to the surface of the site, unless control is exercised over the numbers of trips organized.

Figure 7.2
Snowmobiles at the Columbia Icefield, Alberta, Canada

(Photographed by the author)

Erosion of constructed sites by tourists on foot

Although constructed sites are generally less fragile than natural ones, these too can be affected by erosion in the long term: externally by weather, internally by wear and tear from multiple visitors. Sites exposed to the elements may have to have access restricted, especially if they become so dilapidated that they pose a danger to visitors, as is the case with some historic castles.

The Acropolis in Athens has had to be partially closed to tourists to avoid wear and tear on the floors of ancient buildings, while the wooden floors and staircases of popular attractions such as Shakespeare's birthplace in Stratford-upon-Avon or Beaulieu Palace in Hampshire also suffer from the countless footsteps to which they are subjected each year. Stratford, with a population of only 23,000, receives over 3.8 million visitors every year, a substantial proportion of whom will want to visit Shakespeare's birthplace or Anne Hathaway's cottage. These numbers led major attractions to construct artificial walkways above the level of the floor to preserve the original flooring. Nearly a million people visit Bath's Pump Room and Roman Baths complex each year, and inevitably there will be fears for the original stone flooring in the Baths; but it may put the problem into context when it is revealed that Roman visitors, wearing hob-nailed boots, did even more damage to the original flooring than do contemporary visitors, though they were far fewer in number.

The tourism danger to flora and fauna

Even souvenir-hunting can affect the ecological balance of a region. The removal of plants has long given cause for concern (the Swiss were expressing anxiety about the tourists' habit of picking gentians and other alpine flowers even before the start of the mass tourism movement), and in Arizona, visitors taking home cacti are affecting the ecology of the desert. The removal, either as souvenirs or for commercial sale by tourist enterprises, of coral and rare shells from regions in the Pacific is also a cause for concern.

But perhaps of even greater concern is the threat to endangered animal species from the rise in tourism. There are many examples to cite. While safari big-game hunting is now limited largely to the use of cameras, animals hunted down by tourist vehicles in the game reserves have declined due to lack of privacy to mate; loggerhead turtles in Greece and Turkey, and in the Caribbean, are distracted from laying their eggs by the bright lights of tourist resorts or the use of searchlights to observe their coming ashore to lay their eggs on the beach.

Example   Saving the turtle

Widespread media publicity of the threat facing the turtles' survival has resulted in much greater general awareness of the problem, and both operators and tourists have become more responsible when paying visits to egg-laying sites. The Travel Foundation made a financial award to Tobago which has allowed beaches to be patrolled. Tourists are now made aware of sustainability issues in a video shown at the airport upon their arrival, and both hotel staff and guests are informed about the need to protect nesting turtles. Tourists have restricted access to egg-laying turtles, although small groups are permitted to observe them from a suitable distance. The foundation has also provided funding for demarcation buoys to be positioned near reefs in Tobago (and in Cancun, Mexico), to protect them from anchor damage by tourist boats.

At Philip Island, near Melbourne in Australia, 500,000 people a year come to sit and watch the evening 'penguin parade' of fairy penguins coming ashore to their nests. This event has become highly commercialized, and the large crowds are proving hard to control, even though ropes are in place to prevent people getting too close to the penguins. Flash photography is forbidden, and wardens caution the audiences against noise or even standing up, all of which disturb and alarm the penguins; however, in practice the public frequently ignore these strictures.

Animal behaviour can change as a result of prolonged exposure to tourists. In some countries, food lures are used to attract wildlife to a particular locality; for example, in Samburu National Park, Kenya, goats are slaughtered and hung up for crocodiles or leopards. This modifies hunting behaviour, and may encourage dependency upon human feeding. In some wildlife parks, hyenas are known to watch for assemblies of four-wheel-drive vehicles in order to take the prey from cheetahs' hunts. 'Bearjams' are created in Yellowstone National Park, USA, as bears trade photo opportunities in exchange for offerings of food.

Example Sustainable tourism in Botswana

An excellent example of sustainable tourism at a wildlife park is demonstrated at Xigera Camp, in Botswana's Okavango Delta. A sandpit between the river and camp is raked clean each night, and the following morning the guide provides a short talk for the tourists by identifying the prints of nocturnal animals which have visited the site to drink.

Guests to the area are catered for at the 'chief's camp', situated on land leased by a specialist British tour operator from tribal authorities and employing well-paid locals, some of whom provide trips by mokoro (dugout canoe) through the delta. Furnishing is luxurious but ethnic, and food is sophisticated yet locally grown.

The desire to bring back souvenirs of animals seen abroad poses another form of threat to endangered species. The Convention on International Trade in Endangered Species (CITES) imposes worldwide restrictions on the importation of certain animals and animal products from countries visited by tourists. Around 34,000 endangered species have been identified, and the importation of many of these or their by-products is banned, including ivory, sea turtle products, spotted cat furs, coral, reptile skins and sea shells, as well as certain rare plants. Concern is also expressed about the ill-treatment of animals which are kept in captivity for the amusement of tourists. While performing bears have largely been removed from the streets of some Eastern European countries following EU pressure, these are still a common sight in China. Even within the EU one can still find chimpanzees and monkeys exploited for tourist photographs in countries like Spain, and, of course, bullfighting remains not only legal but also a popular tourist attraction in that country and the South of France. A number of action groups in Britain have been set up to protect and free these animals.

Other environmental consequences of mass tourism

Many popular tourist towns have narrow roads, leading not only to problems of severe traffic congestion, but also to potential damage to buildings as coaches try to navigate through these streets. Increasingly, cars and particularly coaches are restricted from access to the centres of such towns, with park-and-ride schemes or other strategies employed to reduce traffic. However, impeding coaches from picking up and setting down passengers in the centre of towns like Bath or Oxford can make it very difficult for coach companies to operate, as many are on short stopover visits as part of a day trip.

Many developing countries face similar problems of congestion and erosion, as the popularity of long-haul travel expands. Goa in India was hailed by many operators as an 'unspoilt paradise', but its wide appeal since the 1990s has caused environmental lobbyists such as Tourism Concern to draw attention to the dangers the region faces. Water shortages in the area are aggravated by the tourist consumption (one five-star hotel uses as much water as five villages, and locals face water shortages while swimming pools are filled), and sand dunes have been flattened. Apart from the environmental impact, there is also a social cost, with private beaches denying access to the locals, and a 'westernization' of the local carnival which dilutes the traditional identity and culture of the region. The problems of Goa have been well publicized in recent years, but this has had little effect in reducing the number of visitors or ensuring that tourism in the area is sustainable.

Sometimes, well-meaning attempts by tourist officials to 'improve' an attraction can have the opposite effect. Historic rock carvings over 3,000 years old in Scandinavia were painted to make them stand out for visitors. When the paint eventually flakes off, a process that has speeded up with the effect of acid rain, it takes part of the rock surface with it.

Any tourism development will inevitably require the sacrifice of some natural landscape to make way for tourist facilities. An extreme example of this is to be found in the demand for golf courses. It has been estimated[4] that there are some 30,000 golf courses in the world, with a further 500 being built each year. Many of these are constructed in areas where water shortages would normally discourage their construction, such as in Dubai, Tunisia and the Egyptian desert, but the popularity of golfing tourism drives their development. Golf as a holiday activity, especially among Japanese tourists, has led to a huge increase in demand for courses in the Pacific region; for example, the island of Oahu in Hawaii, which had already constructed 27 courses by 1985, received a further 30 applications after the Hawaii legislature agreed to allow them to be built on agricultural land. Apart from the loss of natural scenery, golf courses also require huge amounts of fresh water, which in some areas of low rainfall imposes a severe burden on local resources.

Public-sector planning for control and conservation

We have now seen many examples of the environmental impact of tourism, and a few illustrations of how the problems might be managed. Some argue that it is not enough for individual authorities to tackle the situation; that it should be tackled on a global scale. Unfortunately, few governments so far have appeared willing to tackle the issue on this scale. International designation of an attraction as a World Heritage Site by UNESCO, the United Nations Educational, Scientific and Cultural Organization, undoubtedly helps, but Stonehenge, arguably Britain's greatest heritage attraction, is so designated and yet the site has been called a 'national disgrace' by the Public Accounts Committee of the House of Commons, financial support from the Millennium fund was refused, and arguments continue about how best the site should be developed and protected. Estimated costs for burying the main road in a tunnel have doubled to around £470 million since the proposal was first made, and alternatives involving by-pass routes are now being discussed.

In Chapter 6 we looked at some of the moves across the globe since the early 1980s to embrace tourism sustainability. For the most part, these conferences and resulting papers have focused on making recommendations, leaving the question of mandatory control in the hands of national governments. However, 150 countries signed up to the Agenda 21 proposals arising from the Rio Summit in 1992, and the European Union has taken an active role in recent years in attempting to control the worst effects of environmental pollution, the Blue Flag scheme being typical. Costa Rica can be cited as an outstanding example of a sustainably-aware developing country with a rapidly growing tourism market, issuing Certificates for Sustainable Tourism to tourist companies organizing holidays in the country.

The creation of national parks to preserve tourism sites of scenic beauty is by no means of recent origin. As early as 1872, the United States established its first National Park at Yellowstone, while Europe's Abisco National Park in Sweden dates from 1909. The intention behind the creation of these parks was to ensure that visitors did not destroy the landscapes they had come to see. Sustainability may be a word of recent origin in tourism, but the concept is much older. The World Conservation Union (IUCN) now recognizes more than 68,000 protected areas worldwide, covering an area of 5.7 million square miles, nearly 10 per cent of the globe; and as sustainability becomes a more important issue each year, the volume swells.

Example   Gabon

After an approach by American ecologist and explorer Mike Fay to the Gabon President in 2002, the country's authorities announced at the Rio conference the planned creation of thirteen new national parks, with the aim of becoming Africa's leading destination for eco-travel. The new parks extend to over 11,000 square miles, around 11 per cent of the country's land mass, equivalent to the proportion of land occupied by the national parks created in eco-conscious Costa Rica[5].

Most countries and local authorities are generally well-intentioned, but can also inadvertently become partners in despoliation when putting commercial advantage before aesthetic considerations. Spain, for example, experienced a sudden boom in tourism during the 1960s, but went on to allow massive over-development along its east coast and in the Balearic and Canary Islands, which nearly destroyed its success. Failure to maintain the quality of the environment in other directions can also lead to a massive loss of tourist business, as the popular Spanish resort of Salou found, following a drinking water scare in 1989. However, the widespread fall-off in Western European visitors to Spain in the 1980s and 1990s (mitigated to some extent by a rise in Eastern European and Russian visitors) caused a reversal of policy and much greater control over speculative tourism development. A good example of this can be found in the Balearics, whose parliament passed legislation in 1991 to nominate large tracts of land in Majorca, Ibiza and Formentera as restricted zones for further development. In Majorca, only four- and five-star hotels were permitted to be constructed, with a minimum of 120 square metres of land per bed, in an effort to drive tourism up-market; in order for planning permission to be granted for the construction of new hotels, developers have been required to purchase and knock down an existing and deteriorating hotel of inferior status. Badly run-down resorts like Magaluf were given an injection of capital to widen pavements, introduce traffic-free zones, plant trees and shrubs and install new litter bins and graffiti-free seating. In all, Spain spent over £300 million, in a five-year period ending in the early 1990s, in improving tourism facilities along its coasts. In 2003, the Balearics took a further step in sustainability, by introducing an eco-tax which was designed to fund sustainable improvements to tourism in the islands; unfortunately, insufficient thought went into its implementation (hotels were expected to collect this from guests direct) and the resultant discontent led to the tax being scrapped by the new local government which was elected a year later.

Other countries notable for their failure to provide adequate controls as their tourism industry boomed (and failure to learn the lessons of Spain) include both Greece and Turkey. In developing countries, Goa in India and the Dominican Republic in the Caribbean were both unprepared for the scale of mass tourism generated by tour operators in the 1990s, and failed to control its development adequately. Spain's experience is a cautionary one, and the degree to which it has been successful in turning around its fortunes notable. In general, however, the evidence suggests that once a resort has gone down-market, it can very hard to bring back a higher quality of tourist, and simply constructing new high-price hotels alone will not lead to success in attracting a new market.

Example   Governmental control on entry

Some countries have taken the view that, where tourism has not already have a strong hold, it is better to control entry to reduce the dangers of environmental and cultural despoliation. The Government of Bhutan established a policy to limit the number of foreign visitors to just 15,000 per year. They introduced high charges to reduce demand ($200 per day, with reductions off-season), but provided food, internal transport and lodging within these amounts. Mustang, the kingdom on the border with China which was absorbed into Nepal in 1951, was closed to all tourists until 1992. The Nepalese Government has since introduced a limit of just 1,000 foreign tourists to the region each year, charging $700 for a 10-day permit, of which only about 10 per cent goes back to the region.

At the local level, some form of public control is also essential to ensure good design in each new building, as well as careful preservation and restoration of all existing buildings of quality. Heritage is also a sustainable issue, going beyond the interests of tourism alone. It underpins the very fabric of society, and in a nation with a wealth of heritage buildings, each building lost through failure to protect it or enforce its restoration becomes an irreparable loss to the culture of a nation. Europe owes much of its tourism demand to the attraction of its traditional heritage and landscape, and destinations, whether rural, urban or seaside, which fail to concern themselves with the sustainability of their attractions cannot expect to retain their tourists.

Environmental protection in the UK

In Britain, sensitivity to the impact of tourism on the environment dates back at least as far as the nineteenth century. Concern over possible despoliation of the Lake District, then growing in popularity, led to the formation of a Defence Society in 1883 to protect the region from commercial exploitation. The National Trust was created in 1894 to safeguard places of 'historic interest and natural beauty', and promptly bought four and a half acres of coastal cliff-top in Cardigan Bay.

The National Parks and Access to the Countryside Act 1949 led to the formation of ten National Parks in England and Wales, each administered by a National Park Authority. The Norfolk Broads achieved equivalent National Park status under the Norfolk and Suffolk Broads Act of 1988. The New Forest on the Hampshire/Dorset borders was raised to National Park status in 2004 and the South Downs is likely to follow by 2006, the latter being formed from two existing Areas of Outstanding Natural Beauty. Scotland created its first two designated national parks, Loch Lomond and the Trossachs, and the Cairngorms, in 2002 and 2003 respectively (see Figure 7.3).

The National Parks Act also led to the designation of 37 areas (nearly 8 per cent of the area of England and Wales) as Areas of Outstanding Natural Beauty meriting

Figure 7.3
National Parks of England, Wales and Scotland

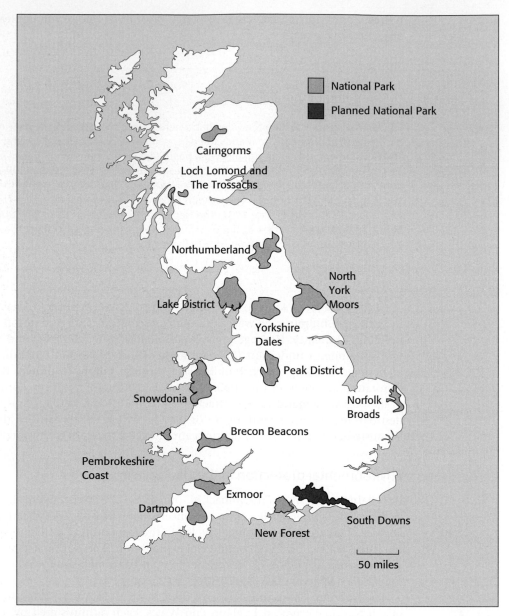

protection against exploitation; the first of these, the Quantock Hills in Somerset, was so designated in 1957, and the last, the Tamar Valley in England's West Country, in 1995. Since this date, there have been numerous moves to protect features of historical or architectural interest, or areas of scenic beauty, from over-development, whether from tourism or other commercial interests. Notable among these are some 150 designated nature reserves and a large number of Sites of Special Scientific Interest (SSSI) which contain rare flora or fauna. An EU Wildlife and Habitats Directive gives stronger

Figure 7.4
Sustainable
tourism: signs
can play a role in
directing tourists
towards good
practice

(Photographed by the author)

protection to some of the most notable SSSIs, which were decreed Special Areas of Conservation in 2000. The UK government recognizes the threat to these sensitive areas caused by the growth in tourism, and by leisure generally, and is attempting to control it, although the countryside remains under threat from the need for more land for the construction of roads and private housing.

The public–private sector interface in sustainable tourism development

Planning controls, whether executed centrally or regionally, are essential to avoid the inevitable conflicts of interest that arise between the public and private sectors. Private enterprise, unrestricted, will seek to maximize profits, often in the short term, and this can more easily be achieved by concentrating marketing effort on popular attractions and destinations, rather than investing in the development of new ones. Airlines will clearly find it more profitable to focus on the routes already generating the most traffic, while hotels in a boom resort will build large and relatively cheap properties, if this proves to be producing the highest margins.

Tour operators, and to a lesser extent travel agents, exercise massive marketing power over destinations through their influence on the decisions of consumers on where to go and what to do. Operators can make or break destinations through their decisions to enter or withdraw from destinations – decisions which often border on the 'slash and burn' techniques outlined earlier in this text. Sustainability means cooperation between carriers, hotel companies and operators which will ensure that development is not for short term gain but in the long term interests of the locals.

This is by no means a condemnation of the industry as a whole. For every large company that seeks to exploit its market position, there are others that recognize their responsibility to their destinations, as well as numerous small companies, both airlines and operators, which are actively seeking market gaps – untapped markets, destinations where the opportunity to develop tourism would be welcomed by locals, or where a focus on superior facilities would be appropriate.

By contrast with the failures in development planning cited earlier, the planning of the Orlando Disney World site reveals a better approach to the protection of a fragile environment. The site chosen, in central Florida, was largely scrubland, and a deprived area in need of economic support. Disney Corporation took due account of the potentially enormous impact which the theme park would have on the State, including new road networks and airport construction. Protected sites well away from the park itself and the emerging town were clearly designated, and arguably the site itself stands as a model of good development. The contrast can be seen in the impact development further south has had on the Everglades National Park, where the wetlands have been significantly affected by engineering to provide water for coastal development, including meeting the needs of tourists.

The UAE coastline in the Middle East can be cited as further evidence of effective development planning for tourism. Dubai in particular has sunk vast resources, including artificial islands off-shore, into attracting tourists to an area which has seen little development to date and where environmental protection is not a key issue. The airlines (including that of Dubai itself) are supporting this growth by massive expansion of their services to the region.

The low-cost airlines have been widely criticized for the air pollution they generate, but on the plus side, by exploiting opportunities at small regional airports, and working in cooperation with specialist tours operators, they have brought prosperity to many regions which previously had only limited access to tourists. Clermont-Ferrand in France, Graz in Austria and Trieste in Italy have all reason to be grateful for their services in making these cities and regions more accessible to tourists. These budget airlines have also been responsible for generating substantial local employment for air crew and ground staff when concentrated at airports like Stansted and Luton.

Example Cox and Kings

Cox and Kings, the oldest British tour operator, has demonstrated a strong commitment to sustainable tourism, promising that for every customer buying one of its 'environmental journey' holidays, it would buy one acre of rainforest in Belize, to be kept in its natural state in perpetuity. The relatively high cost of these package tours allows for some discretionary spending of this sort; the challenge will be to encourage down-market operators to increase their own prices to allow for a more sustainable product to be delivered.

The travel industry is continuing to take sustainability more seriously, with greater cooperation between the public and private sectors. Other notable examples to those cited include the Australian Nature and Ecotourism Accreditation Programme (NEAP) and Cooperative Research Centre (CRC) for Sustainable Tourism, South Africa's Fair Trade in Tourism (FTTSA), and the developing Sustainable Tourism Stewardship Council launched in Latin America in 2003 to explore opportunities for certification within the industry. The World Travel and Tourism Council (WTTC) has worked with the industry since 1994 to develop the Green Globe awards for sustainability (albeit initially with limited success) and to promote guidelines for travellers, disseminated through leaflets. The WTTC has also taken on responsibility for the Tourism for Tomorrow awards, initiated by British Airways, which gain widespread publicity for sustainable tourism enterprises. Finally, in Britain the formation of the Travel Foundation, referred to in the previous chapter, signals cooperation between the public and private sectors, including some of the largest companies in the industry, reflecting for the first time a real commitment by the industry towards the idea of sustainability.

American-owned companies operating globally have been notable in their commitment to sustainability, reflecting a strong environmental movement in that country. Walt Disney Enterprises, to take one example, recycle oils, paints and cleaning materials used on their sites. The Intercontinental Hotels chain undertook a worldwide environmental audit at the beginning of the 1990s, which led to a policy of recycling waste and introducing cruelty-free (not tested on animals) toiletries in the guest rooms.

Other examples include German airline Lufthansa, which introduced snacks at departure gates to avoid wastage resulting from serving in-flight meals (as well as being sustainable, this is also highly cost-efficient!), and UK company Center Parcs, which planned its resorts as car-free zones, offering visitors the use of bicycles during their stay.

The accommodation sector has been a notable leader in introducing sustainable approaches, initially through their desire to save on costs. The now well established policy of reducing laundry bills by limiting the frequency of washing towels has extended to other cost-saving tactics which offer sustainable benefits – for example, some hotels in Hawaii have installed flow regulators on showers and taps to control water wastage. Even small businesses in the accommodation sector have revealed initiatives – Bloomfield House, a bed-and-breakfast establishment in Bath, England, introduced a 10 per cent discount to its guests arriving by public transport.

The concept of the environmental audit is gaining acceptance among tourism companies, British Airways being one notable example to have adopted it. While the publication of environmental reports, as an element of the annual report, has become widespread as policy among other industries in recent years, the travel industry is only gradually coming to terms with this innovation.

There is still scepticism as to the extent to which sustainable activities can be viewed as a genuine response to the threat to our environment, as opposed to a public relations exercise designed to win public favour. Many businesses chose to cut back on their sustainable investment when faced with difficult trading conditions in the post-2001 era, and there is little doubt that a number will continue to pay no more than lip-service to the concept unless it can be shown to be in their financial interest to do so, based on their customers' demand. The fact that some 20 per cent of tourists are now believed to actively include some element of eco-tourism in their travelling[6] suggests that this point may be approaching, although there is still doubt about the majority of the travelling public's willingness to pay more for their holidays if they are designed to be more sustainable.

Nonetheless, what will have started out for many companies as no more than a marketing ploy may later turn to a genuine commitment to improve the environment, as lobbying by environmental interests takes effect and public awareness of the issues spreads.

Notes

1 Also see Green Tax Looms for Airlines, *The Times*, 12 June 2004, p 4
2 Inskip, E, *Tourism Planning: an Integrated and Sustainable Development*, van Nostrand Reinhold, 1991
3 Everyone a Tourist Now!, *Guardian*, 27 January 1990
4 O'Connor, J, Fairway to Tourist Hell, *The Observer*, 8 June 2003
5 Quamman, D, Saving Africa's Eden, *National Geographic*, September 2003, pp 50–74
6 *The Times*, 6 March 2004

Further reading

L Archer, *The Environmental Impact of Aircraft on the Atmosphere*, Oxford Institute for Energy Studies, 1994
Eber, S, *Beyond the Green Horizon: Principles for Sustainable Tourism*, Tourism Concern/WWF, 1992
Kalisch, A, *Corporate Futures: Social Responsibility in the Tourism Industry*, Tourism Concern, 2002

Websites

Keep Britain Tidy Campaign	www.encams.org
Seaside Awards	www.seasideawards.org.uk
Journey Latin America	www.journeylatinamerica.co.uk
Naturetrek wildlife holidays	www.naturetrek.co.uk
Rainforest Alliance	www.rainforest-alliance.org
Derbyshire County Council	www.derbyshire.gov.uk
Certificate for Sustainable Tourism	www.sustainable-tourism.co.cr
Marine Conservation Society	www.goodbeachguide.co.uk
Institute for Sustainable Development in Business	www.greenbusiness.co.uk
Blue Flag Campaign	www.blueflag.org
International Centre for Responsible Tourism	www.icrtourism.org
Centre for Environmentally Responsible Tourism	www.c-e-r-t.org
Responsible Tourism Partnership	www.responsibletourismpartnership.org
Green Globe 21	www.greenglobe21.com
Tourism Concern	www.tourismconcern.org.uk

Questions and discussion topics

1 The eco-tax imposed on tourists visiting Majorca was dropped, largely because of political expediency after complaints by tourists and the industry. Some observers believe that there should be no need for a separate tax of this kind to protect the environment, and that this would best be achieved through general taxation, to which tourists contribute in the form of VAT and sales taxes imposed at the destination. Argue for and against the direct imposition of taxation for sustainability, as it applies both to destinations and air transport.

2 The conflict between preservation and economic benefit is clearly presented in the example given in this chapter of the ban on speeding on Lake Windermere. How can this best be resolved?

3 Taking any tourist destination with which you are familiar, draw up an action plan prioritizing the actions that need to be taken to ensure that the destination is sustainable for long-term tourism.

Assignment topics

1 Undertake a research study which measures the degree of awareness among former holidaymakers about sustainability at their destination (their holidays may have been taken in their own country or abroad). You will need to employ a questionnaire, which includes questions such as:

■ What do you understand by sustainable tourism?

■ What evidence did you find at your destination of sustainability in practice?

■ What evidence is there of the need for controls to ensure sustainability in the future?

Also include a measurement of the level of concern that the holidaymakers have about sustainability when they book their holidays. What common factors have you found in your results?

What is their highest priority for sustainable tourism?

2 By evaluating a cross-section of tour brochures, write a report which reveals how extensively tour operators are aware of the need for sustainability, and the actions they are taking to ensure their holidays are sustainable.

Part II The travel and tourism product

8 The structure and organization of the travel and tourism industry

Objectives

After studying this chapter, you should be able to:

- identify the integral and associated sectors of the travel and tourism industry
- explain the chain of distribution and how this applies within the industry
- understand the relationships, formal and informal, between each industry sector
- be aware of the extent of integration within the industry, and the reasons for this
- identify the factors leading to change within the industry, and predict likely directions in the future.

The tourism chain of distribution

Organizations are set up to achieve goals. . . . These are best met by united action accomplished through a formal structuring of the participants involved.

Independence, small size, market fragmentation and spatial separation are all factors which may lead to a desire for combined action, a willingness to unite to achieve common goals, a need to form tourist organizations.

Pearce, D, *Tourist Organizations*, Longman, 1992, pp 3, 5

When we talk of a tourist product, we are referring to a complex amalgam of different tourism services, each of which must be brought together and presented to customers by the various sectors of the industry. Tourism demand is first created, and then satisfied, by the concentrated marketing efforts of a wide variety of organizers providing tourist products and services. These together form the world's largest and fastest-growing industry. Because some of these services are crucial to the generation and satisfaction of tourists' needs, while others play only a peripheral or supportive role, defining what is meant by a 'tourism industry' is fraught with difficulties. Several services, such as catering and transport, obviously serve the needs of other consumers apart from tourists. Other services, such as banks, retail shops and taxis – or launderettes in a

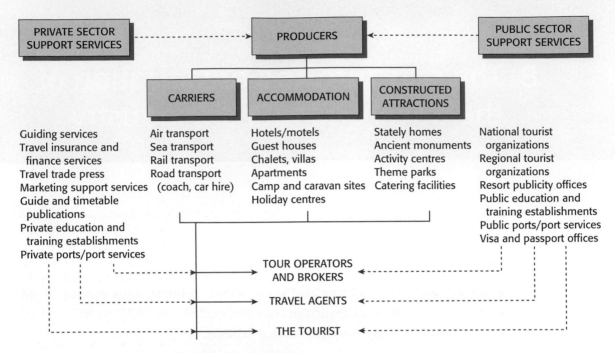

Figure 8.1 The network of sectors in the tourism industry

resort where a significant number of tourists are in self-catering facilities – may only serve tourist needs incidentally along with local residents' needs, although at peak periods of the year the former may provide the bulk of income. Inevitably, what one decides to include under a definition of the tourism industry must be to some extent arbitrary, but Figure 8.1 provides a framework for analysis based on those sectors commonly seen as forming the core of the industry. An examination of these sectors will form the basis for the bulk of this book.

Figure 8.1 is also an illustration of the *chain of distribution* in the travel and tourism business. This term is used to describe the system by which a product or service is distributed from its manufacturing/creative source to the eventual consumers. The alternative term *marketing channel* can also be used to describe this system. Traditionally, products are distributed through the intercession of a number of intermediaries who link producers, or manufacturers, with consumers. These intermediaries are either wholesalers, who buy in large quantities from suppliers and sell in smaller quantities to others further down the chain, or they are retailers, who form the final link in the chain and sell individual products, or a bundled set of products, to the consumer. The structure of the chain of distribution is shown in Figure 8.2.

Producers, of course, are not obliged to sell their products through the chain. They may instead choose to sell direct to consumers, or direct to retailers, thus avoiding some or all of the intermediaries. Wholesalers in turn sometimes sell products direct to the consumer (a common example being 'cash and carry' companies), avoiding the retailer. All these alternatives can be found in Figure 8.1, and all are common forms of distribution within the tourism industry.

Figure 8.2
Marketing
channels, or the
chain of
distribution

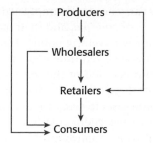

As we have seen earlier, the core tourism product consists essentially of transport, accommodation and attractions, whether constructed or natural. The producers, or 'manufacturers', of these services include air, water-borne, road and rail carriers, hotels or other forms of tourist accommodation, and the various forms of constructed facilities designed to attract the tourist, such as stately homes or heritage sites, amusement parks and other purpose-built activity centres like skiing resorts. These services can be sold to the tourist in a number of ways, either direct, through travel agents (still the principal retailers of the tourism industry) or through tour operators or brokers, who could best be described as wholesalers of tourism.

Tour operators can be accurately viewed as wholesalers because they buy a range of different tourist products, such as airline seats, hotel rooms or coach transfer facilities, in bulk, and bundle or 'package' these for subsequent sale to travel agents or to the tourist direct. By buying an amalgam of individual products and services in this way and presenting them as a single product – the 'package holiday' – they are seen by some theorists as *producers* of a new product rather than wholesalers of an existing product. This is a debatable point, but in the author's view they are best viewed as intermediaries, in the sense that their fundamental role is to bulk-purchase products, organize them into bundles and sell these bundles off individually. The current pattern of trading, in which both tour operators and agents are moving towards *dynamic packaging,* which involves bundling products to meet consumer choice at the point of sale, or 'unbundling the package tour' as some operators express it, is muddying the former rather ill-defined distinction between the roles of operators and agents.

Brokers, who bulk-buy tourist products and sell in smaller quantities, are most frequently found in the distribution system within the air transport sector, although others involve themselves in the bulk purchase of hotel rooms or certain other services. As with tour operators, by purchasing aircraft seats in bulk they are able to negotiate much lower prices, which can be sold on to tour operators or travel agents either individually or in quantity, at net prices, allowing the other intermediaries to determine their own profit level and the selling price for the seats. One of the most common forms of brokering in the travel industry is found in the role of the *consolidator*. These are specialists working in airline brokerage who bulk-purchase unsold charter aircraft seats for sale through intermediaries, thereby helping airlines to clear unsold 'stock'.

Although retailing through the Internet is now becoming a significant threat to travel agents, they remain an important outlet for retailing most travel products within the distribution chain, buying packages and travel services according to client demand. They carry no stock, simply acting as an intermediary between the consumer and the supplier, or *principal*, and their main role is to provide a convenient network of sales outlets for the travelling public. Traditionally, agents did not charge for their services, since they were remunerated in the form of a commission on each sale they negotiated. However, one of the most significant changes in distribution patterns in recent years has been the tendency for suppliers either to reduce commission payments or in some cases to scrap them altogether, forcing agents in many cases to initiate a charge to their clients. Airlines were among the first principals to withdraw commissionable sales, mainly in the belief that they could reach the consumer more cheaply by direct contact via the Internet, rather than depending upon agents who for the most part retain no particular loyalty to any one supplier. Agents are now obliged to add a fee when selling most airline tickets.

Some other transport companies and tour operators are beginning to follow suit, although the large operators are unlikely, at least for the foreseeable future, to adopt such a policy. There appears to be a global trend in travel retailing whereby agents buy many of their principals' products at market price and add a fee for service rendered, but this presupposes an adequate level of agency sales expertise and product knowledge to add value to the process when a customer books through an agent. In fact, pressure on margins seldom allows retail agencies to provide the salaries and conditions which would enable them to recruit sales staff of the right calibre to meet these criteria.

Apart from these core services of producers, wholesalers and retailers, a wide variety of ancillary and support services interact within the distribution system. For convenience, these can be divided between public-sector organizations (those funded, controlled or organized through central or local governments) and those privately owned. The former include national tourism organizations such as tourist offices, publicly owned airports or seaports, passport and visa documentation and other ancillary services such as public education and training institutions offering courses in tourism. The private sector includes privately owned airports and seaports, services offered by freelance guides, travel insurance and financial services (including foreign exchange and credit card facilities), travel trade newspapers and journals, printers of travel literature, publishers of guides and timetables, and a number of specialist marketing services such as travel consultants, advertising agents and brochure design agencies. In addition, there are private visa agencies which will collect customers' documentation, check it and procure any necessary visas for a fee. This is becoming a more typical pattern for visa procurement, since few embassies are willing to mail documents to clients and submission in person is often inconvenient, expensive and time-consuming. Most tour operators now use these intermediaries too as they have a good rapport with the embassies and consulates they use frequently and provide a dependable service.

The distinction between public and private bodies is not always straightforward. Some national and regional tourism organizations (the USA and the city of Berlin are two examples) are run as private consortia, having been delegated the role by the public sector. Others, while nominally public, would collapse without financial support from the private sector. BAA, Britain's leading airport owner, is an example of a former public body, now a plc, which exercises control over three of London's five airports.

Figure 8.3
Card and travel
services
provided by
American
Express

(Courtesy: American Express)

Example   Public ownership of tourism attractions

Sometimes, governments invest in the private sector in ways which will not be immediately apparent, such as through holding companies. One example of this is the Tussauds Group which, in addition to the waxworks museum, also owns a number of other tourist attractions – Chessington World of Adventures, Alton Towers, Thorpe Park and Warwick Castle. The company also owns a share of London's big wheel, the London Eye. In 2005 the company passed into the ownership of Dubai International Capital, an investment firm set up by state-controlled Dubai Holding. The holding company is ultimately controlled by the Crown Prince of Dubai, representing the Dubai Government.

For the most part, the tourism industry depends for its success upon a close working relationship between the private and public sectors. Many tourist attractions, such as heritage sites, are publicly owned, either by the state or by local authorities, while public authorities are also frequently responsible for the promotion and distribution of information about tourism (through, for instance, their tourist information centres). This interdependence between private and public sectors, which is an important element in the dynamics of the industry, will be explored in subsequent chapters.

Common-interest organizations

A feature of the tourism industry is the extent of association, voluntary or otherwise, that has taken place between businesses and/or public-sector bodies that share similar interests or complement one another's interests in some way. Such associations can take a number of forms, but typically fall into one of three categories:

1 *sectoral organizations*, based on the interests of a particular sector of industry (or link in the chain of distribution);
2 *destination organizations*, concerned with a specific tourist destination, whether country, region or resort;
3 *tourism organizations*, based on a concern with travel or tourism activity as a whole.

Each of these can in turn be subdivided according to whether they are trade or professional organizations. The latter are normally composed of individuals whose common interest is likely to be based on objectives which include establishing educational or training qualifications for the industry or the sector, devising codes of conduct to guide members' behaviour, and limiting or controlling entry to the industry or sector. Membership of such bodies is often associated with a personal drive to enhance status and prestige. Trade bodies, by contrast, are groupings of independent firms whose common purpose will include such aims as the opportunity to exchange views, co-operation (especially in the functions of marketing), representation and negotiation with other organizations, and the provision of identifiable services to their members. In some circumstances, these trade bodies may also take on activities more generally associated with professional bodies, such as restricting entry to the industry or sector, and providing or recognizing appropriate qualifications.

Example   Marketing consortia

Many sectoral organizations come together in order to benefit from opportunities to bulk-buy at discount prices from their suppliers, or to sell themselves more effectively and at lower cost. Websites which offer a range of products rather than a single one, for example, will be more effective in reaching the public.

Treasure Houses of Britain is one such example in the attractions sector of the industry. Composed of ten of the leading stately homes in Britain, the consortium has its own website (www.treasurehouses.co.uk), produces a joint brochure and offers discounts at partner properties.

The structure of these bodies may vary considerably. In some cases, particularly in the case of the larger organizations, there will be a paid administrative staff to carry out administrative functions, while in the case of smaller bodies (such as local marketing consortia) there may be no full-time staff, and administration is often carried out by volunteer staff seconded from member companies. A key characteristic of trade bodies, however, is that their membership is made up of autonomous companies or other organizations subscribing to the common purpose of the body concerned.

Sectoral organizations

Probably the most numerous organizations are those which reflect sectoral interests. As we have seen, there is a wide range of sectors making up the tourism industry, and each of these can be expected to have at least one common-interest association. Professional bodies catering for sectoral interests include the Chartered Institute of Transport (CIT) and the Hotel, Catering and International Management Association (HCIMA). The Chartered Institute of Marketing (CIM) has a section devoted to travel industry members, known as the Chartered Institute of Marketing Travel Industry Group (CIMTIG), while tourism educationalists and consultants each have their own professional body – the Association of Tourism Teachers and Trainers and the Tourism Society Consultants' Group (both autonomous divisions of the Tourism Society). Some bodies provide their own training for the industry (e.g. CIT), while others rely on training organizations set up separately for this purpose (e.g. the UK's sector-skills organization People 1st).

Sectoral trade bodies may be regional, national or international in scope. Some international bodies retain significant influence over the activities of their members, an example being the International Air Transport Association (IATA) which continues its role in negotiating with international airlines worldwide, even though some of its erstwhile power has diminished under the impetus to liberalization in this sector of the industry. The International Federation of Tour Operators draws its members from European national tour operating bodies, including the British Federation of Tour Operators (FTO), an influential consultative body made up of around ten leading UK operators.

Apart from the FTO, other examples of UK national bodies include the Association of British Travel Agents (ABTA), which represents both tour operators and travel agents, the Meetings Industry Association (MIA) and the British Resorts Association (BRA). Similar bodies are to be found in all countries with a developed tourism industry. The American Society of Travel Agents (ASTA), for example, fulfils a similar role in the USA as ABTA does in the UK, but also draws on members from other sectors of industry, as well as overseas members, due to the importance and influence of the USA as a tourist-generating country.

Regional bodies will comprise groups such as local hoteliers or tourist attractions. These will often act as pressure groups in their relations with local tourist authorities, but also provide arenas for discussion on issues of mutual interest among members.

The role of ABTA

ABTA has played a key role as a sectoral trade body in the British travel industry, and for this reason it will be useful to examine this organization's role here, and to consider its relationship with other sectors of industry. Its role with respect to its own members, whether tour operators or travel agents, will be dealt with in forthcoming chapters. However, as a result of legislation within the European Union which has had the effect of reducing the monopoly position enjoyed by ABTA in the past, it lost some of its influence in the latter half of the 1990s, with other organizations coming into being to meet the needs of tour operator and travel agency groupings. ABTA nevertheless

Figure 8.4
The ABTA logo

ABTA
Association of British Travel Agents

(Courtesy: ABTA)

remains the principal trade body in the UK; the vast majority of package holidays sold in the UK are still sold through its members, and the financial safety net it provides remains a key reason for this.

ABTA was founded in 1950, initially to represent the interests of travel agents, and later, as operating developed discretely from the retail sector, those of tour operators. It acts as a mouthpiece for these two sectors of industry and is consulted by government and by other bodies on issues of national concern and on legislation affecting the industry. Formerly administering policy through two distinct councils, the Tour Operators' Council (TOC) and Travel Agents' Council (TAC), since 2000 the organization has reverted to a single class of membership for both agents and operators, governed by a Board of Directors. ABTA works closely with the Travel Training Company (TTC), which is responsible for approving vocational qualifications for the industry. The TTC in turn works closely with the City and Guilds of London Institute (CGLI), the educational validating body.

From 1965 until 1992, ABTA was legally permitted to operate a 'closed shop', whereby tour-operating members were required to sell their products exclusively through ABTA member travel agents, who in turn could only sell packages organized by tour-operating members. This process, known as 'Operation Stabiliser', allowed ABTA to exercise a quite astonishing degree of control over its members. It set fees for obtaining passports and visas, for making long-distance telephone calls on behalf of its members' customers, even going as far on one occasion as to reprimand a chain of agents for providing its clients with free transfers to their local airport. Stabiliser was finally overturned by an EU Directive which, in common with broader EU policy, required tourism products to be available to consumers without constraint on channels of distribution. As a result, ABTA had fundamentally to rethink its role as other trade bodies formed and membership of all bodies became voluntary for operators and agents. Many felt that such a re-evaluation of its role was long overdue, given that the interests of ABTA members have often been in conflict. The interests of tour operators, for example, will inevitably conflict with those of travel agents, and it becomes difficult for the trade body to represent both these sectors' interests equally. Conflicts also emerged between the larger tour operators and the smaller independents, as well as between the large agency chains, with their ties to tour operators, and the smaller independent travel agencies.

Emerging from this reorganization, a new tour-operating body, the Association of Independent Tour Operators (AITO), was established to represent the interests of independent specialist operators. In the case of retailing, the widening gap in interests between the so-called multiples (travel agency chains vertically integrated with tour operators) and the independent agents made a reassessment of the ABTA role inevitable. Since the demise of Operation Stabiliser, a number of consortia of independent retailers have been established, the best known of which include WorldChoice, Advantage, Midconsort and the Global Travel Group.

ABTA claims to serve the interests of travel consumers, although conflicts of interest must inevitably arise from time to time with its role in serving the needs of its members. However, in one respect, ABTA has served the travelling public exceptionally well. Apart from ABTA's Stabiliser role, it has undertaken the responsibility of protecting the consumer through a system of bonding, so that consumers booked through ABTA members have had their holidays protected, in the event of the collapse of either the agent or the operator concerned before or during the holiday. This insurance, which has worked so effectively in the British package tour market, was extended by the government, as part of the requirements contained in the European Union's Package Holiday Directive, to other forms of travel, and bonding has enabled other organizations to offer similar guarantees to their members. With the growth of dynamic packaging, where customers are buying elements of the package tour separately, grey areas are emerging in the extent of protection offered to the public, but the obligation to bond all packages sold as an entity through a single source is providing a risk-avoidance guarantee that is expected to attract customers back to travel agents, rather than risking booking hotels and flights separately and directly with suppliers over the Internet.

ABTA's bonding scheme remains a leading means of consumer protection in the industry, and the organization's logo is widely recognized by members of the public – more so, for example, than the CAA's ATOL logo. ABTA is invaluable in helping smaller companies to keep abreast of changing legislation, in advising and being advised by the Foreign and Commonwealth Office (in matters of safety, for instance), in acting as a financial clearing house for members and for interceding between customers and members where arbitration is required – most cases are resolved in the client's favour, and the Association has shown itself to be impartial in its dealings with clients vis-à-vis its members. Where travel issues of national importance arise, it is to ABTA that the media turn first for advice and consultation. ABTA's role will be further examined in Chapters 16 and 17.

Destination organizations

A destination organization is one drawing its membership from both public and private sector tourism bodies sharing a common interest in the development or marketing of a specific tourism destination. That destination may be a resort, a state or region, a country or even an area of the globe. Membership of such bodies is open to firms or public-sector organizations rather than individuals. These bodies generally share two common objectives:

1 to foster cooperation and coordination between the various bodies that provide, or are responsible for, the facilities or amenities making up the tourism product;

2 to act in concert to promote the destination to the travel trade and to tourists.

Consequently, these organizations are trade, rather than professional, bodies. Examples range from such globally important regional marketing bodies as the Pacific Area Travel Association (PATA) and the European Travel Commission (ETC), to local marketing consortia made up of groups of hotels or tourist attractions within a particular region or resort. A marketing consortium currently comprising public-sector tourism interests in Germany, Austria, Hungary, the Czech Republic, Slovakia and Poland was formed in 1999 as the Central European Countries Travel Association (CECTA) in order to market more effectively this large European region, to stress its geographically central, rather than eastern European, roots and to take advantage of opportunities for growth following the advent of four of these nations into the European Union. At the other end of the scale, the Bournemouth Hotels and Restaurants Association, the Devon Association of Tourist Attractions, and the Association of Bath and District Leisure Enterprises are all typical examples in Britain of localized groupings within a single country.

Tourism organizations

The activities of some bodies transcend sectoral boundaries within the industry. These organizations may have as their aim the compilation of national or international statistics on tourism, or the furtherance of research into the tourism phenomenon.

The United Nations World Tourism Organization (UNWTO) plays a dominant role in collecting and collating statistical information on international tourism. This organization represents public-sector tourism bodies from most countries in the world, and the publication of its data enables comparisons of the flow and growth of tourism on a global scale.

Similarly, the Organization for Economic Cooperation and Development (OECD) also has a tourism committee composed of tourism officials drawn from its member countries, which provides regular reports comprising comparative data on tourism developments to and within these countries. Other, privately sponsored, bodies have been set up to produce supporting statistics, such as the World Travel and Tourism Council (WTTC), whose members are drawn from over 30 leading airlines and tourist organizations. This body also regularly commissions and publishes research data. An equivalent body exists within the UK, known as the Council for Travel and Tourism (CTT).

Within countries, bodies are set up to bring together public and private tourism interests, as a means of influencing legislation, encouraging political action or sometimes to overcome crises affecting the industry. One such body in the UK is the Tourism Review and Implementation Group, chaired by the Minister for Tourism, while another, the Tourism Industry Emergency Response Group, was established to take action on problems facing the UK tourism industry, comprising representatives of the DCMS and directors of principal tourism bodies. Wider aims are designed to be achieved by the Tourism Alliance.

Example   The Tourism Alliance

In 2001, the travel industry in Britain was severely affected by foot-and-mouth disease in cattle, which restricted travel to the countryside and inhibited visitors from abroad, especially North America. Travel organizations recognized that they needed a common mouthpiece to lobby government and to handle future problems affecting the industry, feeling that the existing bodies were inadequate for this purpose. The Tourism Alliance was formed, bringing together a mix of public and private organizations, including ABTA, the Association of Leading Visitor Attractions, the British Hospitality Association, BITOA (now UKInbound), the Association of Recognized English Language Services, the British Beer and Pub Association, the British Holiday and Home Parks Association, together with the Local Government Association, and national and regional tourist boards (excluding Wales and Scotland, which have their own tourism forums). The organization has come to form a strong pressure group and debating forum.

Many countries with a strongly developed tourism industry will establish professional bodies composed of individual members drawn from several or all sectors of the industry. The purpose of these bodies is to promote the cause of the tourism industry generally, while simultaneously encouraging the spread of knowledge and understanding of the industry among members. In Britain, there are two professional bodies devoted to the tourism industry generally, although they tend to draw their membership from different sectors of industry. The Institute of Travel and Tourism (ITT) originated as an institute designed to serve the needs of travel agents and tour operators, and still draws its membership largely from these sectors, while the Tourism Society, a more recently formed professional body, attracts its membership particularly from the public sector, tourist attractions and the incoming tourism industry. As has been pointed out earlier, this body also draws its members from the fields of tourism consultancy and vocational education.

Occasionally, relevant organizations are set up by non-tourism interests, if tourism comes within their provenance. Such a body is the Confederation of British Industry's Tourism Action Group, established in 1993 to help advance the interests of tourism as one area of business. This body has concerned itself principally with improving tourism career appeal and the quality of training on offer to new recruits to the industry, improving the marketing of tourism overseas to the UK, ensuring tourist attractions come up to expectations in their quality, and improving accessibility for tourism through an integrated transport system within the UK. In this work, the CBI complements many of the concerns of sectoral organizations within tourism.

Integration in the tourism industry

A notable feature of the industry over recent years has been the steady process of integration that has taken place between sectors of the tourism industry. If we refer to our earlier model of the chain of distribution (Figure 8.2) we can identify this integration as being either *horizontal* or *vertical* in character. Horizontal integration is that taking place at any one level in the chain, while vertical integration describes the process of linking together organizations at different levels of the chain (some writers refer to *diagonal* integration, a term used to describe links between complementary businesses within each level in the chain).

All business is highly competitive, and the tourism industry is no exception to this rule. Such competition, often encouraged by government policy, has been evident within the British tourism industry ever since the development of the mass market in travel, which began in the 1960s. Following policies of deregulation, particularly those in the transport sector affecting air, rail and coach companies, competition has become steadily fiercer throughout the latter part of the twentieth century and the early years of the new century. Competition forces companies to seek ways of becoming more efficient in order to cut costs. Integration makes this possible. Horizontal integration enables companies to benefit from economies of scale by producing and selling more of a product, thus reducing the unit cost of each product, since the fixed costs incurred are spread over a larger number of units, whether these are hotel bedrooms, aircraft seats or package tours. Equally, buyers of these products, such as tour operators, can obtain lower net prices if they buy in larger quantities, just as airlines can negotiate lower prices if they order more aircraft from the manufacturers. The savings achieved through both these economies of scale can be passed on to clients in the form of lower prices, making the product more attractive to the consumer. Vertical integration offers economies of scale through the integration of executive and administrative functions, as well as increasing leverage on the market through advertising and promotion.

The World Wide Web is undermining some of the former purposes of integration, by speeding up distribution and reducing the necessity to depend upon so many links in the chain. Today, no hotelier need any longer depend upon granting an allocation of beds to a local ground handler, who would sell them on to a tour operator, who in turn would make them available to customers via a travel agent. Beds can be sold direct via a website, and in any number of foreign languages to meet the world market needs. In so doing, distribution prices can be held down to a level where they may well undercut traditional distribution techniques.

The benefits of size

Large companies offer benefits to both the supplier and the tourist. Suppliers, knowing the reputation of the major companies in the field, are anxious to do business with them, in the belief that such corporations are less likely to collapse in the face of competition (a belief that is not always well founded, as shown by the collapse of the International Leisure Group, Britain's second largest operator, at the beginning of the 1990s). The tour operator's operational risks are minimized, because suppliers, faced with an overbooking situation, will be less likely to turn away the clients of their best supporting companies. Similarly, hotels uniting into larger groups will be able to negotiate better deals through their own suppliers for the bulk purchase of such items as food and drink, while airlines will bring greater bargaining strength to the negotiating table in their dealings with foreign governments for landing rights or new routes.

Most companies, asked to identify their organizational goals, would cite market expansion as a major objective. Growth in a competitive environment is a means of survival, and history testifies to the fact that few companies survive by standing still. Integration is a means of growth, enabling a company to increase its market share and simultaneously reduce the level of competition it faces, by forcing less efficient companies out of business.

Greater sales mean more revenue, and therefore potentially more funds to reinvest in the company to assist expansion. This in turn enables the company to employ or expand its specialist personnel. Nowhere is this truer than in those companies whose branches are individually quite small. A small chain of travel agents, for instance, or of hotels, may for the first time become able to employ specialist sales or marketing staff, or recruit its own legal or financial advisers. Higher revenue also releases more money for the marketing effort – a programme of national advertising in the mass media may become a real possibility for the first time. Few readers will have missed the frequent – and highly effective – post-Christmas TV advertising campaigns of the multiple travel agents, which have enabled the market leaders to extend still further their share of the travel market at the expense of the independents.

In addition to these broad benefits offered by integration generally, there are other advantages specific to horizontal or vertical integration, and these will be examined in turn.

Horizontal integration

Horizontal integration can take several forms. One form is the integration between two companies offering similar (i.e. potentially competing) products. Two hotels within the same seaside resort may merge, for example, or two airlines operating on similar routes may unite. Such mergers may result from the takeover of one company by another, or they may simply result from a voluntary agreement between the two to merge and obtain the benefits, identified above, of a much larger organization. Voluntary unions, however, can be established which allow the companies concerned to maintain their autonomy while still obtaining the benefits of an integrated organization. This is the case of a consortium – an affiliation of independent companies working together to achieve a common aim or benefit. One example of this affiliation is the marketing consortium, which allows independent companies to gain economies of scale in, for example, mass advertising or the publication of a joint brochure. Alternatively, the consortium may have its prime benefit in the purchase of supplies at bulk prices for its members – a feature of certain hotel consortia, and of groupings of independent travel agents like Advantage, which in this way can negotiate higher commission levels from tour operators and other principals.

A second form of integration occurs between companies offering complementary rather than competing products. Tourism, as we have seen, is defined as the travel and stay of people. Close links therefore form between the accommodation and transport sectors, which are interdependent for their customers. Without hotel bedrooms available at their destinations, airline passengers may be unwilling to book seats, and vice versa. Recognition of this dual need led many airlines to buy into or form their own hotel divisions, especially in regions of high tourist demand, where bed shortages are common. This trend was common in the early years of the jumbo jet, when airlines woke up to the consequences of operating aircraft with 350 or more passengers aboard, each requiring accommodation over which the airline had little or no control. This led to the integration of several major airlines and hotel chains. However, rising competition between airlines, which led to huge losses and massive investment in new aircraft, obliged many airlines to sell their hotel investments to raise capital, in order to survive. Since those days, the more common relationship has been through closely linked computer reservations systems (CRSs), which allow the airlines a measure of control over hotel bedrooms without major capital investment in the accommodation sector. The growth of dynamic packaging in the early 2000s reinforced the need for airlines to have access to accommodation, many developing their own websites to include hotel accommodation at prices competitive with specialist hotel websites.

Airlines are increasingly seeking to benefit from liaisons which do not involve competition on the same routes. Interlining agreements allow airlines to benefit from connections globally, and such agreements have been extended to code-sharing and similar close links, including the global airline alliances which have formed in recent years, such as Star Alliance. Transatlantic routes, for example, provide 'feeder' opportunities into the US network of domestic routes, and through code-sharing and other alliances allow foreign airlines to compete with US airlines which have cabotage rights to carry passengers between two US domestic airports. Such agreements overcome the problems faced by merging airlines, which are often seen as anti-competitive and challenged by monopolies commissions which favour open competition.

The changing nature of tourism demand may also cause companies to diversify their interests horizontally. In the previous century, shipping companies woke up far too late to the realization that the future of long-haul travel lay in air travel, and by the time they began investing in airlines the sums involved were too great for the loss-making shipping companies to absorb.

At the retailing level, integration is also common, but because the traditional development of travel agencies has led in many cases to regional strengths, integration has tended to be regionally based, leading to the development of so-called 'miniples' – agencies with a significant number of branches within one region of the country only, which may well, within that region, outperform the multiple agents. The massive growth in the number of branches of the big multiples has tapered off and is even reversing in the opening years of the new century, while performance of miniples like Let's Go Travel and Global Independent Travel has actually improved. Initially, this had led to some large travel companies taking over a miniple as a means of building or strengthening their profile in a particular region, but as competition increased and the profits of large companies were squeezed, the process is reversing and miniples are regaining their autonomy.

Example   Travel House

Large chains are constantly rethinking their strategies. In the UK, the thinking within the multiple agencies was in the direction of expansion to compete with rivals. More recently, the move to direct selling and the contraction in agency numbers has encouraged the Big Four to reduce their investment in branches. In 2004, TUI, the world's leading travel agency chain, sold twenty-one of its Travel House branches back to the original owner, having purchased them only a year or two earlier.

Tour operating has also experienced growth through integration in the past decade, first between large companies in Britain, and later internationally. Two of Britain's leading companies, Thomas Cook and Thomson Holidays, are now both in German hands (the latter, part of world leader TUI). While integration in the principal travel sectors is likely to continue, it is unlikely to be as frenetic as in recent years, given the instability of the industry, and most companies are keen to see a return to stable profits rather than chasing expansion. Some major ventures, such as expansion by European companies into North America, have in fact been reversed as the companies consolidate their positions.

Vertical integration

Vertical integration is said to take place when an organization at one level in the chain of distribution unites with one at another level. This integration can be forward (or downward in the direction of the chain), such as in the case where a tour operator buys its own chain of travel agents, or it can be backward (or upward against the direction of the chain), such as in the case where the tour operator buys its own airline.

Example   Libra Holidays Group

In 2004, Libra Holidays bought Helios Airways, a largely scheduled airline, in a move to expand its Cyprus tour operating programme. Formerly, the company had held a stake in Excel Airways, reducing this investment in order to invest in its own carrier.

Such backward integration through takeover is fairly uncommon. More frequently, in the past operators have set up their own airlines internally. Forward integration is more typical, since organizations are more likely to have the necessary capital to buy businesses further down the chain of distribution, which require less capital investment. For example, even the largest independent travel agency chain would be unlikely to have the capital needed to form its own airline. Generally speaking, the higher in the chain of distribution, the greater the investment required.

As with horizontal integration, organizations can achieve significant economies of scale by expanding vertically. Where total profits in individual sectors may be slight, a reasonable profit overall across the sectors may still be made by an integrated business which controls all levels in the chain. Even in a year of intense competition, tour operating companies owning their own airlines and retail sales outlets (neither of which may be committed to the exclusive sale of the operator's products) may still remain profitable.

As with the linking of complementary services in horizontal integration, many companies are concerned to ensure the continuation of their supplies. A tour operator depending upon a continuous supply of aircraft seats and hotel beds, and facing international competition for such supplies, can best ensure adequate and regular supplies by directly controlling them, i.e. by 'buying backwards' into the airline and hotel businesses.

Large multinational corporations are well equipped financially to diversify their interests into new products when they see opportunities arise. All the leading British tour operators, several of which are now owned by Continental European multinationals, have integrated airlines. These vertical links between airlines and tour operators are examined fully in Chapter 16.

Integration leads to control

Several of the leading operators have in recent years sought to own and operate their own hotels in key resorts abroad to ensure the availability of rooms and their price. Integration here can be achieved either by direct purchase, or by setting up joint-venture companies with partners in the hotel industry, or other sectors of the industry. Such integration offers the added advantage of improved control over the quality of the product. This is frequently difficult to achieve in the case of foreign hotels, and, indeed, ensuring that standards are uniform, consistent and of the required quality is no easy matter in the case of a business composed of such diverse and disparate services. Although operators do own hotels, this has up to now been on a limited scale only, with many preferring to exercise control through a franchising scheme or branding, which allows control of standards while management remains in the hands of the hotel company.

Equally, the production sector will attempt to exercise control over the merchandising of its products. Airlines, shipping services and hotels are all multi-million pound investments, yet, curiously, in the recent past they had to rely to a considerable extent on a fragmented, independent and frequently inexpert retailing sector for the sale of their products. Travel agents carry no stock, and therefore have little brand loyalty to a particular travel company. It was logical for principals to seek to influence distribution by buying into retail agencies. British Airways has a handful of retail shops in the UK, for instance, and many domestic US airlines' shops compete with agents in the sale of flight tickets, although these shops are being cut back as the airlines encourage sales through their websites and those of on-line distributors like Expedia and Opodo. The leading British tour operators have their own retail agency chains, and engage in the practice of *directional selling*, in which counter staff are expected to give priority to the sale of the parent products.

This forward integration is now becoming unnecessary with the growth of the World Wide Web. Distribution can be made direct rather than through retailing or wholesaling divisions further down the ladder. The no-frills carriers have depended least upon this form of distribution; easyJet has never used retail agents, and Ryanair has now abandoned them. Both depend to such an extent upon the Web that they even penalise with a higher charge any direct bookings taken via telephone from their clients.

In Britain, and within the European Union, vertical integration has drawn far less criticism from bodies such as the Competition Commission than has horizontal integration. The Monopolies and Mergers Commission, as it then was, investigated the growing control of travel agency chains by tour operators in the UK, and ruled that the links between operators and agents must be spelled out clearly at the point of sale (the travel agent). There are, however, some curious anomalies regarding the Commission's ruling, which exempts certain large operators and has failed to rule on sales via the Internet. Tourism organizations seeking to grow their operations may be expected to continue expansion across several sectors of the industry, both domestically and overseas, providing they are confident this will not open them to investigation by the monopolies bodies.

Vertical integration clearly poses a threat to independents in the retailing sector. Airlines or tour operators opening their own retail outlets are likely to attract the market away from the independents by competitive pricing or other marketing tactics. Many independents have combated this threat by forming consortia which allow them to negotiate better returns from their principals. This may in time lead to the creation of 'own brand' labels for tour operating, already tested on a limited scale, if this is judged the best means of competing with the multiples.

Conglomerates and international integration

No discussion about the changing structure of ownership within the tourism industry would be complete without examining the growing role of the conglomerates. These are organizations whose interests extend across a variety of different industries in order to spread the risks incurred by operating within a specific industry such as tourism. Although tourism has the reputation of being a highly volatile industry, the long-term growth prospects for leisure generally have attracted many businesses from outside the tourism industry itself. Breweries, for example, have expanded into hotels and holiday centres. Abroad, conglomeration is well established in numerous countries; Germany invested heavily in travel and tourism businesses through department stores and leading banks, although recently these have been divesting their interests as the German economy faltered.

Example   Cendant

US conglomerate Cendant was created by the merger of two franchising businesses, HFS International and CUC International. It has actively been pursuing purchases in the travel industry since its formation. Apart from real estate company Century 21, it owns Avis and Budget Rentacar in the car rental field, Ramada, Days Inn and Howard Johnson in the accommodation sector, RCI in holiday timeshare, Orbitz and EBookers in on-line agencies and wholesalers Gullivers Travel and Octopus Travel. It has now become the world's largest on-line travel company after Expedia.

Paralleling this diversification, as we have seen, the travel industry is also experiencing rapid internationalization in ownership. This is a process which has been hastened within Europe by the harmonization among member countries. Travel businesses are actively expanding their interests in each other's countries. While it is tempting to offer some examples of the current spate in such expansion, the pace of change is now so fast that any examples are likely to date very quickly. Readers are encouraged to keep in touch with the trade press in order to update their knowledge of this process. Suffice it to say that, increasingly, British travel companies must look beyond their own borders to understand the nature of the competition they face.

Questions and discussion points

1   Does the advent of the World Wide Web herald the decline of large corporations in the travel industry?

2   A notable feature of UK organizations is their tendency to splinter among different organizations representing broadly similar interests (e.g. ABTA and the FTO; The Institute of Travel Managers and the Association of Corporate Travel Executives; The Tourism Society and The Institute of Travel and Tourism). In recent years all of these bodies have at one time or another discussed integration, recognizing that they could achieve more by speaking with a common voice, but for political or other reasons merger talks have been broken off, often ending with promises of closer cooperation. Taking any one sector, outline the advantages and disadvantages of full integration, and give your own views on how best the organizations could operate in future.

3   One problem in promoting destinations through organizations is their often ill-defined boundaries (e.g. the Cotswolds, or Wessex, in England) which overlap into territories controlled by differing authorities. Is the promotion of such regions better served by tourist boards or other organizations operating within the context of more clearly defined regional (e.g. county) borders?

4   Given the importance outlined in this chapter of bodies like airlines and tour operators having access to beds, why has ownership of hotels by these principals actually declined in recent years?

Assignment topics

1   The reaction to crisis in the UK tourism industry appears frequently to be establishing yet another body to collaborate between the public and private sectors. Such bodies frequently change, and are often criticized for their failure to achieve their aims. Undertake research into the existence of these various bodies, their component membership, their aims and structure. How much overlap is there between the various bodies? Could their aims be better achieved through the formation of a single body representing both public and private interests and speaking with a common voice?

    Prepare a paper to be given to a meeting of senior members of the industry proposing how this issue can be resolved.

2   Organizations change rapidly, and since the publication of this book, there will doubtless be numerous changes in terms of the composition and structure of the industry in your own country. Present a report which outlines the key changes in the various sectors over the previous twelve months, and the reasons these have occurred.

9 Tourist destinations

Objectives

After studying this chapter, you should be able to:

- understand the complexity of the destination as a tourism product
- recognize the importance of the image and the brand in marketing destinations
- distinguish between different categories of destination
- understand the appeal of each form of destination
- explain why destinations are subject to changing fortunes.

Introduction: what defines a destination?

In the first chapter, we briefly outlined what is meant by a tourist destination. This chapter will be devoted to expanding on that definition, so that we can learn to understand the appeal which different types of destination have for the tourist.

Describing all the characteristics which go to make up a destination is probably one of the most difficult tasks in the study of tourism. It would be easy to say that the destination is the principal purpose of all tourism, but in some instances this is far from the case. The destination may be only one element in the appeal of the trip, and sometimes a very minor one. When Concorde was flying, many tourists made it their lifetime ambition to travel on the world's only supersonic aircraft; where it was flying to was only of minor interest to the enthusiasts. Equally, impressive cruise liners like the *Queen Mary 2* may represent the destination for aficionados of cruising, and the ship's port of call may be of only passing interest (some enthusiasts of cruising do not even bother to disembark at ports of call en route). Anniversaries are often enjoyed on the Orient Express, the nostalgic rail journey offered by this distinguished train becoming the prime purpose of the trip, and the attraction of the long rail journey across Russia from Moscow to Vladivostok owes little to the brief stops which the train makes during its epic journey. Sometimes the ambition to drive along a historic route, such as the silk route across Asia or Route 66 across the United States, outweighs the destinations visited en route during the drive.

In other examples, the attraction has become the destination. This is true of many theme parks; Orlando in Florida did not exist as a tourist destination thirty years ago, before the Disney Corporation decided to make it the site of its second development, just as Alton Towers had little to interest the visitor before the construction of a major theme park on the site in Northamptonshire.

In discussing destinations, we must always bear in mind two important considerations. First, they have both physical and psychological characteristics: that is to say, the image of a destination consists of a number of physical attributes – attractions and amenities, buildings, landscapes and so on – together with perceptions allied to the destination, which will include less tangible attributes such as the hospitality of the locals, the atmosphere generated by being there, the sense of awe, alienation, *Gemütlichkeit*, or other emotions generated by the place. The feelings one experiences standing on the rim of the Grand Canyon in Arizona will be different to those experienced when passing through Glencoe in Scotland, the sombre location of the massacre of the MacDonalds by the Campbells in 1692, or shock and revulsion felt when visiting the former concentration camp at Auschwitz-Birkenau in Poland; while at the other end of the scale, the emotions generated by a visit to the Japanese formal gardens in the Royal Palace in Tokyo will be dissimilar to those experienced by the tourist coming across a charming village like Castle Combe in Wiltshire or Rothenburg ob der Tauber in Germany and admiring the residents' gardens and floral displays, although all three sites could be marketed as appealing to gardeners, and all could equally be described by the viewer as beautiful.

Second, destinations have very different appeals to different markets. Some people love crowds, others love isolation and find crowded beaches unbearable. Holidays in the mountains, for some, will awaken the concept of majestic landscapes, with few visitors apart from the occasional hiker, such as might be found in Tierra del Fuego National Park in Argentina; for others, the concept may immediately trigger thoughts of expensive resorts like Gstaad in Switzerland or Courchevel in France, with their busy ski-slopes and lively social life in the bars and restaurants. It is fortunate that the appeal of destinations is so varied, allowing opportunities for tourism to be developed in almost any country, and to almost any region, providing that it is aimed at the appropriate market.

Destinations depend on their image for their success in attracting tourists, even if that image is frozen in time and no longer represents a true picture of the place. Most well-known tourist countries and destinations like cities and beach resorts rely on the stereotypes which have been built up over the years and, as long as these remain positive, promotional bodies will seek to support these images in their advertising. Thus, the prevailing image of London for the foreigner is of guardsmen riding on horseback through the city, past Big Ben and the Houses of Parliament; whilst Paris remains for ever the city of lovers, with couples embracing on the banks of the Seine with the Eiffel Tower or Notre Dame in the background. No matter that these images are stale icons bearing little resemblance to real life in these modern cities; the power of the image is the branding iron that drives tourism, and to jettison it in favour of a more modern, but less graphic, image is a far more difficult – and risky – task for marketing.

Example East of England

In 2003, the East of England Development Agency launched an international competition to find a 'visionary plan for a landmark, or series of landmarks – an icon that will foster a sense of identity for the region as a whole'. Clearly, the image of any one attraction, or group of attractions, within the region is thought insufficiently strong to be self-evident without further research[1].

It is convenient to divide destinations into five distinct groupings.

The first, and most common, would be the traditional form of holiday arrangement in which a tourist travels to a destination, whether urban or rural, where they expect to spend the majority of their time, with perhaps occasional excursions away to visit nearby attractions. The classic seaside holiday, winter sports resort or short city break, represent the most common types in this grouping.

A second grouping is composed of destinations which form a base from which the surrounding region can be explored. Some British seaside resorts have successfully reformulated their marketing strategy to sell themselves as bases to explore the nearby countryside. Resorts in Devon and Cornwall, for instance, have drawn attention to their proximity to the national parks of Exmoor and Dartmoor, while Cirencester and Cheltenham have both promoted themselves as gateways to the nearby Cotswolds, one of the most popular tourist regions in England. Interlaken has successfully promoted itself for many years as the base for the exploration of the scenic Vierwaldstättersee region in Switzerland, while Gatlinburg in Tennessee promoted the town as a base for the exploration of the Great Smoky Mountains region.

A third group comprises holidays in which two or more destinations are of equal importance in the itinerary. A good example would be the relatively unsophisticated tourist with an interest in exploring the new central European countries of the Baltic, who buys a package comprising the three capitals of Tallinn, Riga and Vilnius, fearing that a short break in just one of these would not represent good value for money.

Touring destinations form a fourth group. A linear itinerary will include stops at a number of points; a Caribbean cruise, for instance, will call at several ports en route, while a tour of the American Midwest or Far West, or a rail journey across Canada, will make stopovers a key element in the itinerary.

Finally, the destination which merely provides an overnight stop en route to a destination gives us a fifth grouping. Such stopovers may or may not be pre-planned, but occur at convenient points particularly for drivers contemplating long journeys by car. Typical examples would be the tourists driving by car from Britain, Scandinavia or northern Germany whose destination is the south of France or the east coast of Spain, who will identify useful points at which to stop over en route through France when they become tired – this may be a destination which offers touristic opportunities also, but this is not necessarily the case; the principal aim is to break the journey.

Once again, it is important to stress the importance of the no-frills airlines in growing tourism to both existing and new destinations, by offering cheap fares and in many cases developing new provincial hubs. Many of these are sited in areas about which tourists had only limited knowledge previously. Among destinations to have benefited from the no-frills airlines are Turkey, Austria and the regions of the former Yugoslavia, particularly Croatia and Slovenia.

Coastal tourism

When we think of coastal destinations, most of us will immediately conjure up the image of a typical *seaside resort*, this being the destination with most popular appeal along any coastline (see, for instance, Plate 4). The attractiveness of the seaside resort is the combination of sun, sand and sea, which still appeals to the largest segment of the tourist market, either as a form of passive recreation – lying in a deckchair or on the sand and watching the sea – or a more active pastime, including swimming and other water sports, beach games, and the like. This form of tourism remains popular in Britain, even if less so than in former years – some 33 million Britons still take trips to English seaside resorts every year. Many seaside resorts in Britain, however, have moved on from their nineteenth century image and now cater to a variety of different markets, seeking very different benefits. The concept of a seaside resort can now embrace everything from the traditional workers' paradise to the village centred around a harbour catering to the yachting fraternity, and the cultural town with its art galleries, museums and concert halls. The traditional resort has been hardest hit by the change in demand, above all because these have been slowest to invest in new facilities and renovate their heritage buildings. Many one-time popular resorts like Clacton, Cleethorpes, Llandudno, New Brighton, Skegness and Southport have remained frozen in time, with their sweet shops selling candy floss and rock, their amusement arcades and funfairs, 'kiss me quick' hats and fish-and-chip takeaways. The market for these resorts has dwindled as older, loyal regular visitors (many of whom came only because their parents had brought them there as children) died off and their own children chose instead to holiday overseas. A handful of resorts accepted the challenge, and invested. Blackpool remains popular simply by dint of its huge investment in the tourism paraphernalia of funfair rides, nightlife amenities and – increasingly – gambling casinos. Modest investment by towns like Scarborough have enabled the towns to survive, if not prosper, while some have striven to change their image by focusing on a single attraction; Bexhill-on-Sea, for example, has the de la Warr Pavilion, perhaps the greatest example of mid-twentieth century architecture in the country, which was narrowly saved from destruction, and, with the aid of heritage funding, has been restored to its former glory; while Margate, trading on its earlier links with the painter J M W Turner, has decided to construct an eponymous modern art gallery in the form of a giant abstract sculpture, with no concessions to the town's traditional architecture, in the hope of attracting a new, more cultured market. A few genteel resorts like Eastbourne, Worthing and Deal have largely resigned themselves to the role of retirement resort, while a handful of larger resorts have diversified sufficiently to be no longer entirely dependent upon tourism. Bournemouth, for example, while retaining its tourist market by new investment in attractions and the restoration of its Victorian heritage buildings, is also large enough to have attracted industry, particularly banking and financial services, and education, with its language schools and new university, which now boost its economy. The town also remains one of the closest to the heavy population centres of the South East with good sandy beaches and gently sloping shores, making it an ideal swimming base. Brighton, while not sharing the same quality of beach (like much of the Sussex coastline, its beaches are pebbled), has built on its proximity to London and its cultural facilities to remain an important short-break destination, and has also developed a major new marina to attract yachtspeople, whilst also growing other non-leisure industries.

However, the big beneficiaries of changing tourist taste have been the myriad small fishing ports and seaside villages which have largely retained their character, and resisted expansion, through strict planning controls. The scenic beauty of the many resorts in Devon and Cornwall (and notably those based around an estuary, like Salcombe or Falmouth) have made these highly desirable for second-home owners and the self-catering market. Shops and restaurants have moved upmarket, and where there is a strong cultural tradition, like the art colony of St Ives, this has led to a focus on the arts, attracting many galleries, including a notable extension of London's Tate Gallery which is attracting over 200,000 visitors a year, three times the number

Figure 9.1
Everyone's ideal beach: uncrowded, acres of sand gently sloping into the sea, acres of fine sand, blissful weather. The beach at le Touquet, France

(Photographed by the author)

envisaged when it was constructed. Those with the best marina facilities appeal to the wealthiest members of the yachting fraternity, ensuring that the markets attracted remain high-spend. Being essentially rural as well as on the coast, these resorts provide a good base for exploration of the surrounding countryside. The extent to which demand will inevitably continue to outstrip supply in destinations like these will ensure their long-term success, providing they can resist the temptation to expand exponentially, thus threatening their appeal as small, quaint resorts.

Example   Provincetown, Cape Cod

Provincetown is at the tip of Cape Cod, in Massachusetts, USA. A popular seaside resort, it experiences wide fluctuations in visitors between seasons, from as low as 4,000 in winter to some 30,000 in summer. Long a resort of choice for artists, the town is transforming itself into a destination for 'intellectual tourism', under the direction of Campus Provincetown, a public–private partnership, offering educational courses leading to credits towards academic qualifications or certification. Art courses are proliferating, and the Provincetown Theatre Company runs a full-season programme for visitors. The result has been a significant improvement in the number of out-of-season visitors.

Many former UK tourist resorts, however, cannot expect to regain their lost markets, given the significant movement of popular seaside tourism, over the past five decades, away from the colder, Northern European beaches in favour of those of the Mediterranean, as prices for air transport fell and the tourists could be assured of sunshine and warm water – something that was always a gamble when holidaying in Northern Europe. Similarly, lower fares have enabled the Americans to fly to their warmer beaches in Florida or California, or even further afield to Mexico, the Bahamas and the Caribbean, abandoning the traditional northern beaches of resorts like Atlantic City, New Jersey, or the Long Island beaches of New York State. Atlantic City fought back by renovating its beachfront and developing mega-casinos to attract the high-spend gamblers, but while this has restored the fortunes of the beachfront itself, it has done little in terms of investment behind the foreshore. Miami itself has successfully rebuilt its market, following a decline in fashion as domestic visitors became more adventurous and sought beaches further afield. By investing massively in the restoration of its art-deco hotels and apartments along Miami Beach, the destination spearheaded a tourism regeneration which has boosted the town economically.

The fall in long-haul air fares has now meant that European sun-sea-sand tourism has now extended to distant destinations like Phuket and Pattaya Beach in Thailand, as well as medium-haul resorts like Sharm el-Sheikh in Egypt and Monastir in Tunis. Both these Middle-East resorts offer the opportunity for combining cultural visits with a traditional beach holiday – the monastery of St Catherine and the landscape around Mount Sinai becoming major attractions in Egypt, while the Roman amphitheatre at el

Djem and the opportunity to explore the fringes of the Sahara Desert both have great appeal to tourists visiting the many resorts of the Tunisian coastline.

A question mark hangs over the long-term future of seaside resorts, in the face of the threat of global warming. Most tourists are tending to ignore for the present the warnings they are receiving from the medical profession about the dangers from skin cancer, but over time these warnings, and the escalating figures for melanoma operations and fatalities, must start to influence demand. The challenge for the resorts will be to amend their facilities, and their marketing, dramatically enough to ensure that tourism can continue to survive even without the current appeal of sun, sea and sand. One alternative is to provide facilities similar to those found at the beach but constructed indoors.

Example   The indoor beach Ocean Dome, Miyazaki, Japan

One possible solution to the problem of exposure to the sun can be found in the development of 'indoor beaches' such as the Ocean Dome at Miyazaki in Japan. The world's largest indoor beach, complete with plastic palm trees, artificial breeze, a surf machine and opening roof, it initially proved immensely popular with Japanese visitors as an alternative to the traditional beach holiday. However, the huge capital investment in the high technology project proved too great to allow the company to break even, and it collapsed in 2001.

Just south of Berlin, in Germany, a hangar has been modified to provide a similar dome covering 66,000 square metres, making it one of the largest buildings of its kind in the world. The Tropical Islands Resort contains a lagoon swimming pool, beach with palm trees and waterfalls, and can accommodate up to 7,000 visitors at a time (www.my-tropical-islands.com).

The development of the indoor 'tropical' pools at the Center Parcs sites in Britain and Northern Europe, while less ambitious in scope, have proved highly profitable. In countries where the appeal of outdoor pools is restricted by poor weather, such domed attractions offer an attractive alternative for swimmers and leisure-seekers alike.

Quite apart from resorts themselves, coastlines are an obvious attraction for tourists, whether seen from the land (via coastal footpaths or cycleways) or from the sea (coastal excursion boats are still popular with tourists, even where no landing is included). England's longest coastal path, from Minehead to Poole in the South West, can take up to eight weeks to complete, tempting walkers who may not usually be attracted to the seaside to return time and again in order to undertake the walk in sections. In summer, excursion boats sail from Bristol, and the Somerset and Devon coasts, circling the islands of Steep Holm, Flat Holm and Lundy. More ambitious visits are made by cruise ships to islands in the Pacific, or in Arctic waters, where conditions often do not favour landing, not even by Zodiac inflatable craft; yet the bird and other wildlife along these coasts, coupled with the geological formations of the shoreline, will frequently provide sufficient appeal merely to observe the islands from the ship.

Example   Thailand

The limestone karst formations around Phang Nga Bay, a marine national park in Thailand, have become popular for visits by excursion boats, especially since filming took place at some of the sites. Koh Phing Kan featured in the feature film *The Man with the Golden Gun*, and has now become more popularly known as James Bond Island. The Phi Phi Island group east of Phuket includes Koh Phi Phi Ley (Maya Bay), the main location for the film *The Beach*, starring Leonardo di Caprio. This has not only led to a dramatic upsurge in excursion boat visits, but also increased the popularity of nearby Ao Ton Sai resort (sadly severely damaged by the Tsunami disaster in 2004). Similar karsts are found in Vietnam, and they, and the caves which they frequently contain, have become popular attractions for the growing numbers of tourists visiting that country.

Urban tourism

The Grand Tour of the 18th century has been democratised for the age of easyJet. We travel the world to get our fix of architecture, and cities respond with ever-glitzier buildings.

Tom Dyckhoff, *The Times*, 15 June 2004, p 17

A second category of destination is the *town* or *city*. While seaside tourism has struggled to maintain its earlier attraction for visitors, urban tourism has prospered in recent years, fuelled by a growing interest in cultural activities such as visits to theatres, museums and art galleries, as well as interest in historical architecture and in the appeal of shopping as a leisure activity. This can be exemplified by comparing figures from Germany on top tourist attractions (see Table 9.1).

More than half of these attractions are located in major cities, and all, with the exception of Neuschwanstein, are urbanized.

Britain is well placed to attract large numbers of tourists, both domestic and overseas, to urban destinations: it has a plentiful stock of towns of both architectural and

Table 9.1   Top ten attractions in Germany (annual visitors in millions)

Cologne cathedral	6.0+
Rudesheimer Drosselgasse	3.0
Reichstag, Berlin	2.7
Bonner Museumsmeile	2.5
Rothenburg ob der Tauber	2.5
Bad Münstereifel	2.4
German Museum, Munich	2.0
Heidelberg Castle	1.3
Neuschwanstein Castle	1.25
Zwinger Palace, Dresden	1.2

Source: *The Times*, 20 July 2004

historic importance. Capital cities, including of course London, have long exercised a particular draw for the tourist, and the low fares on no-frills airlines have attracted new markets not just to major cities, but also to smaller provincial towns throughout Europe, growing the short-break holiday market of one to three nights. Formerly popular cities like Amsterdam, London, Rome, Vienna and Paris have been joined by cities like Lille, Copenhagen, Stockholm, Dublin, Prague and Barcelona, the latter now a leading city for short-break holidays, combining all the benefits the short-stay visitor requires: good shops and restaurants, outstanding architecture (notably by Antonio Gaudi), quality hotels, fine museums and substantial investment in the local infrastructure in the past few years. It also benefits from competitive prices compared with similar cities elsewhere in Europe. Prague alone now attracts over seven million visitors every year, including 1,500 stag-party groups.

Low transatlantic prices have made cities like New York and Boston popular as short-break destinations for Europeans, especially for shopping, as the dollar dropped in value against the pound and euro in 2004–05. Even Reykjavik, capital of Iceland, has become a popular short-break destination for Europeans due to its lively nightlife and the curiosity of its surrounding landscape, with a visit to a hot geyser an obligatory add-on.

Britain is fortunate in that most incoming visitors have as their motivation the desire to see the country's heritage, much of which is found in the urban areas. Apart

Figure 9.2
Lille has become a popular short break destination, fuelled by the Eurostar train from London and budget flights

(Photographed by the author)

Figure 9.3
A popular destination for outings from London and on the UK milk run: Blenheim Palace, Oxfordshire

(Photographed by the author)

from London and its myriad attractions, architecturally, historically and culturally, all the leading destinations in Britain are dependent upon their heritage to attract the overseas tourist. The university towns of Oxford and Cambridge, the Shakespeare connection with Stratford-upon-Avon, Windsor with its royal castle, the cities of Bath, York, Edinburgh and Chester, all feature on the standard 'milk-run' tours sold to the package-tour market abroad. Apart from their beauty, all these cities benefit from having a clear-cut image in the public eye, and strong associations which are easy to market as products composed of a complex of benefits.

While large cities like Paris, New York and London have the capacity to absorb substantial numbers of tourists, smaller, very popular cities like Oxford suffer from severe congestion in summer, as thousands of foreign tourists visit by coach and car during the peak months, creating major problems in tourist management for the local authority. Marketing of these destinations has to focus on tight planning and control, coupled with efforts to extend the holiday season, so that tourists can be managed more easily. In towns such as these where demand exceeds supply, compulsory park-and-ride is becoming the norm.

The urgent need for urban renewal in decaying cities, coupled with rising interest in industrial heritage, has led many governments to invest public funds to restore run-down buildings as tourist attractions. Former warehouses, woollen mills in the north of England, and other important centres of industry during the eighteenth and nineteenth centuries have been converted into museums or other buildings to attract tourism and leisure. In some cases this has extended to entire areas of a city, such as the jewellery centre of Birmingham (now firmly on the tourist trail) where tourism has become an economic saviour, attracting residents back into the city centre. Other notable successes include the cities of Bradford and Glasgow, both of which suffered severe decline in the 1980s. They nevertheless contain some fine examples of Victorian architecture, which has now become fashionable again after a long period out of favour. Bradford benefits from its location close to the Yorkshire Moors and Haworth, home of the Brontës, and now promotes itself as a base from which to tour, with good shopping and entertainment.

As with all resorts, the urban destination with an established reputation and image attracts the tourist more readily than those towns which have no such image. Cities like London, Paris, Rome, Venice and Amsterdam all have clear and immediately recognizable images – although it is interesting to note that in the 1990s the London Tourist Board expressed concern that Japanese tourists were diverting to Paris rather than London. The explanation given was that among Japanese visitors female tourists are in the majority, and they perceived Paris as being gentler and more feminine than London. Such is the power of the image to influence tourist choice. However, recent reports suggest that the Japanese are beginning to become disenchanted with Paris, finding it less friendly and romantic than the dream that inspired the visit.

Cityscapes are an important element in the appeal to tourists, not least for their possessing a clearly defined centre, well established shopping and entertaining districts, attractive enclaves and parkland. English towns are noted for their many green swards and floral displays; Milan for cutting-edge clothes and furnishing shops; Stockholm has its Gamle Stan, or Old Town, for historical appeal as well as an attractive waterfront. Some cities, however, suffer from a lack of a clearly defined centre to provide the focus for a visit. Los Angeles, Moscow and Tokyo all have this disadvantage, which reduces their appeal to the independent traveller.

Stockholm is not alone in benefiting from being a city on the water. Cities which had formerly been important seaports, and which had suffered from the decline in shipping in recent years, were slow at first to catch on to the value of their waterfront sites for leisure purposes. Today, many cities have transformed what was formerly a decaying port into an area of recreation for residents and visitors alike. One of the first, and an outstandingly successful example, is the Inner Harbour at Baltimore, USA which, through a combination of private and public investment, was one of the first to become a magnet for tourists due to the wide variety of attractions it introduced along the restored harbourfront. In Australia, Sydney's Darling Harbour has similarly benefited from renewal as a leisure and marine site, while in the UK more than a dozen waterfronts have been renovated, while retaining the many attractive warehouses and other features of their former port status. London's Docklands, the Albert Dock area of Liverpool (the site of the Tate Gallery's first provincial art gallery), and docklands at Southampton, Bristol, Salford, Manchester, Swansea, Cardiff, Portsmouth, Plymouth, Newcastle, Gloucester, Glasgow and Dundee, have all expanded their tourist markets as areas of leisure as well as commercial activity. Other cities around the world to have landscaped their water frontages to attract tourists include Boston, San Francisco, Fremantle (the port for Perth, Western Australia), Cape Town and Toronto.

Rivers and canals flowing through city centres can likewise add appeal when landscaped attractively. Major capitals like Rome, London and Paris have long traded on

Figure 9.4
Excursion boats
at Bruges

(Photographed by Jan Walker)

the appeal of their Rivers Tiber, Thames and Seine, but more recently disused water-ways have been resurrected for tourist appeal. A noted example is Birmingham's net-work of city centre canals, which have become a focal point for locals and visitors alike, with their outdoor canal-side cafes and pubs, and narrowboat tours. Similarly Bruges in Belgium successfully restored its canal network to make this a major feature of one of Europe's most attractive mediaeval cities (see Figure 9.4).

The EU gives a boost to cities with high levels of cultural activity by awarding the title European Capital of Culture to one city (two cities from 2007) in different member countries each year. The impact of this award on tourism is a major benefit for the named city, leading first to significant investment in infrastructure and superstructure to cater for the anticipated demand, and then a huge economic boost in the year of the award and in the years following. In 2004, Lille in France was City of Culture, followed by Cork in 2005; nominees for future years are shown in Table 9.2.

This list will doubtless be modified by including cities based in the recently admit-ted Eastern nations, just as Sibiu has been selected for 2007 even prior to Romania's formal admission.

Britain last received the award in 1990, when Glasgow gained the title. It was esti-mated that the award brought in some £2.5 billion in extra investment, a significant rise in hotel rooms and an increase in the number of tourism-related jobs to some 55,000. Above all, it changed the perception of Glasgow as a dirty, economically depressed city for all time. Cork, hoping for a similar economic boost, transformed its

Table 9.2   Nominees for European Capitals of Culture, 2006–2019

2006 Patras, Greece
2007 Luxembourg and Sibiu, Romania
2008 Liverpool, England and Stavanger, Norway
2009 Linz, Austria and Vilnius, Lithuania

The countries selected beyond 2009, whose cities are still to be determined, are:

2010 Germany
2011 Finland
2012 Portugal
2013 France
2014 Sweden
2015 Belgium
2016 Spain
2017 Denmark
2018 Netherlands
2019 Italy

main street, St Patrick's Street, constructed a new art gallery and traded on its literary heritage with the construction of a 50-foot centrepiece sculpture, The Quill.

The EU has also granted the status of European Region to parts of the Community, as a means of enhancing the profile of the regions and aiding its marketing. In 2003, this title was awarded to the Balearic Islands, and in 2004, to Madeira.

Efforts to emulate the concept in the Americas, supported by the Organization of American States, have been frustrated by the financial basis for awards, in which regions are expected to put up funds in advance. Santiago in Chile (2004) and Guadalajara, Mexico (2005) were nominated, but Austin, Texas and Saskatchewan, Canada both rejected the offer on grounds of expense.

Medical tourism

Finally, reference should be made at this point to medical tourism, which generally takes place in cities. While health tourism has a long history, and is linked to spa tourism, about which more will be found towards the end of this chapter, the term *medical tourism* is now being used to refer to tourists who travel to another country specifically to consult specialists or undergo operations. British patients have sometimes been referred by the National Health Service for treatment in other EU countries, but others are seeking medical attention privately, and often further afield. Private hospitals in Eastern Europe are planning to target patients in Britain who could not afford private treatment in their own country, but could be persuaded to pay the lower fees charged abroad. In the same way, Austrians now travel to Sopron in Hungary for dental treatment, and the Finns are visiting Tallinn for eye tests and dental work.

Good medical treatment delivered promptly, cheaply and efficiently is appealing in cases where here lengthy waitlists for operations exist, such as for hip operations. Thailand offers private health care to medical tourists in Bangkok, Chiang Mai and

Phuket, while South Africa has attracted tourists for specialist cosmetic surgery. India has gone further, taking a stand at the World Travel Market in London to promote medical tourism: it offers specialist treatment at reasonable prices for dentistry, cosmetic surgery and alternative medicine such as Ayurveda. Some organizations are even arranging package tours around such treatment, with accommodation at four-star hotels included.

There is some evidence that this traffic is not all one-way. Many well-off visitors – reports place the number as high as 100,000 annually – are coming to Britain to exploit inadequate checks on NHS eligibility in order to receive treatment while on holiday in the UK. Exact figures on the numbers involved are hard to verify, but the government has taken steps to plug this loophole.

Rural tourism

Our third category of tourism, the *countryside*, offers a very different holiday experience to our first two. Widespread appeal of the countryside is of relatively recent origin; appreciation of nature dates back in Britain only as far as the nineteenth century – and even more recently in the case of other European countries. Initially limited to those in the higher socio-economic groups, led by gentlefolk in aristocratic circles who enjoyed a 'seat in the country', its extension to the merchant, and later, labouring classes, emerged only as congestion and pollution made life unbearable in the big cities and escape to the countryside a necessity for health and tranquillity. Early appreciation of scenery, however, was somewhat artificial; travellers to the countryside were accustomed to base their expectations of the landscape on memories of the highly imaginative and frequently hyperbolic paintings by popular artists of the Romantic Movement; in some cases even going so far as to observe the scenery by use of a 'Claude' glass – an elegantly framed mirror, named after the French painter Claude Lorraine, which observers were encouraged to use by standing with their backs to the scene and viewing its framed reflection.

Developing countries, even those with little appeal for the traditional tourist seeking attractive cities or beach resorts, are gaining from increasing demand by more adventure-minded tourists for holidays 'off the beaten track'. In recent years travellers have discovered such diverse rural gems as the Cameron Highlands in Malaysia, the northern hills of Thailand around Chiang Mai and the tropical heartland of Costa Rica, as well as attractive landscapes in more developed countries, such as the Cape York peninsula in Australia and Canada's North West Territories, to say nothing of regions closer to home for Europeans, like Tuscany in Italy and the Ardèche in France (both now popular as second-home destinations for Northern Europeans).

One of the principal draws of rural tourism is lakes and mountains – preferably a combination of the two; and areas blessed with both have been attracting visitors from the very beginnings of the tourism movement. The Alps and Dolomites in central Europe, stretching through France, Switzerland, Germany and Italy, were catering to British and other holidaymakers as early as the nineteenth century, and in each of these countries, nearby lakes are plentiful. On a more modest scale, England's Lake

Figure 9.5
Mountain
trekking
in the Alps:
Switzerland

(Photographed by the author)

District, with its combinations of mountains and lakes, has special protection as a National Park and ranks as one of the most popular tourist destinations in the British Isles.

The combination attracts distinct markets. Leisure visitors of all ages enjoy the scenery either passively or on hikes, while more active visitors enjoy climbing and mountaineering in summer, and, where circumstances allow, winter sports at other times. However, the enormous expansion in winter sports holidays has also put huge pressures on the Alps, which have a fragile environment easily damaged by overuse. Global warming is apparently affecting Alpine and other mountainous regions, with the snow line receding further up the mountainsides, leaving resorts at lower altitudes bereft of snow for much of the season. This is causing alpine regions to reinvest to focus their winter sports construction at higher altitudes. Snow lifts, gondolas and cable cars are under construction, with France alone investing more than one billion euros over a three-year period to retain their winter tourism markets.

The challenge of climbing major peaks in mountain ranges has moved on from the Alps to more adventurous locations like the Rockies, Andes and Himalayas, while for those not induced to climb, trekking to base camps along trails below the peaks has proved a challenge sought by fit tourists of all ages. Specialist tour companies now organize both climbing and trekking expeditions even to Everest, forcing the Nepalese government to impose swingeing charges for climbing rights in an effort to control numbers. Even packages costing in excess of £20,000 seem to have little effect in stemming demand. Equally, simple rambling holidays are now enjoyed by countless independent travellers to beauty spots all over the world, and also packaged for the inclusive tourist.

Although British, and Irish, climate has proved a deterrent to the enjoyment of seaside holidays, it accounts for much of the demand for rural tourism. A temperate climate, with frequent precipitation, provides us with the richness of green fields and abundant woodland which, coupled with rolling hills and stretches of water, make up the idyll that is the quintessential rural scenery of the British Isles. In spite of its small land mass, the British Isles offer considerable diversity in their countryside, from the meadows and tightly hedged fields in the south and west of England to the dry-stone walls and bleak moors of the north; from the flatlands and waterways of East Anglia and Lincolnshire to the lakes and mountains of Cumbria and the wild beauty of the Welsh mountains and the Highlands and Islands of Scotland; from the gentle Irish landscape surrounding the lakes of Killarney to the barren wilderness of the adjacent Dingle Peninsula.

As modern living forces more and more of us to live in built-up areas, so the attraction of the countryside grows, whether merely to take a day out on the weekend or to spend a longer holiday touring, or perhaps holidaying on a farm. Rural tourism attracts international tourists too, with a growing number of Continental visitors coming to tour Britain by car, while in turn Britons take their cars to France or Germany to tour. The attraction of contrasts is important here; the Dutch, Danes and Swedes, whose countryside is limited to flatland and waterways, find great appeal in the undulating hills and mountains of their European neighbours.

To protect the vulnerable countryside from development and to cater for the demand for rural recreation, Britain created a network of National Parks in England and Wales (see Figure 7.3) as we discussed in Chapter 7. Following the passing of the National Parks and Access to the Countryside Act (1949) the Peak District National Park was the first created, in 1952, soon followed by nine others. The Norfolk and Suffolk Broads were given similar protected status in 1988, and the New Forest was designated in 2004 (with the new authority due to take up its responsibility in 2006). There are currently fourteen parks (including three in Wales and two in Scotland) with National Park status or equivalent, and a fifteenth is expected to join them in 2006 with the creation of the South Downs in Sussex, which already receives more than 39 million visitors a year. The Cairngorms National Park became the largest in the UK when it was designated in 2003, totalling 1,466 square miles, although the exclusion of the highland area of Perthshire adjoining the site was controversial.

Hiking, or rambling, has become a popular pastime for tourists in recent years and Britain is fortunate to possess many country footpaths with public rights of way which the Ramblers' Association is anxious to protect, as pressures on the countryside grow. The Countryside and Rights of Way Act (2000) opened up large areas of the country, giving ramblers the statutory right to ramble on 'access land' in England and Wales in 2005, extended in 2006 to beaches and coastlines. The Land Reform (Scotland) Act 2003 offers similar rights in the north. The National Parks and Access to the Countryside Act (1949) which established Britain's National Parks also created a network of long-distance footpaths which is enjoying growing popularity with hikers.

Figure 9.6
Major national
trails in Great
Britain

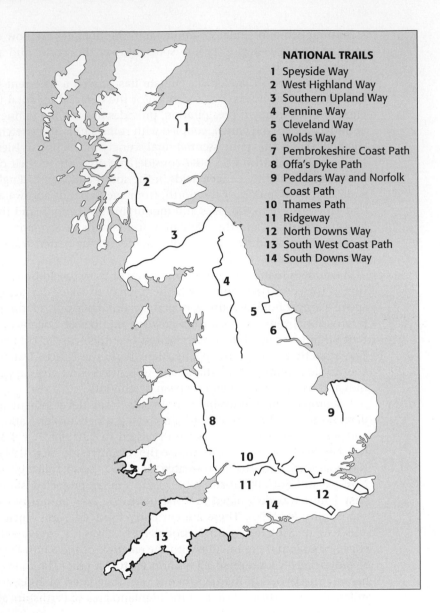

NATIONAL TRAILS
1 Speyside Way
2 West Highland Way
3 Southern Upland Way
4 Pennine Way
5 Cleveland Way
6 Wolds Way
7 Pembrokeshire Coast Path
8 Offa's Dyke Path
9 Peddars Way and Norfolk
  Coast Path
10 Thames Path
11 Ridgeway
12 North Downs Way
13 South West Coast Path
14 South Downs Way

These national trails are illustrated in Figure 9.6. Among the most popular is the South West Coast Path, which extends for a total of 630 miles between Minehead in Somerset and Poole Harbour in Dorset.

Trails are also popular in the United States, where wilderness areas give maximum scope for challenging, long-distance footpaths, as well as a plethora of shorter trails in urban areas.

Example   Trails in the United States

Although one associates trails commonly with rural areas, they are also frequently created in towns to allow people to guide themselves around sites to which they are attracted. The USA is best known for its wilderness trails, often taking weeks to complete, such as the Appalachian Trail. However, the variety available can be exemplified by Maine, which in addition to many rural trails (and the completion point of the Appalachian Trail) also offers a Garden and Landscape Trail, visiting more than 50 gardens and arboreta, a Maritime and Heritage Trail, visiting 30 different sites, and a Maine Art Museum Trail, taking in seven different museums.

Cycling, too, has experienced a regeneration of interest, as we will see in Chapter 14. This is a sport which is largely dependent upon rural scenery (preferably flat land, although more active cyclists will also opt for hill touring or mountain-bike holidays). Both independent and package-tour cyclists are attracted to these programmes, with operators offering inclusive tours by bike to a growing number of countries. Most of these forms of tourism are encouraged as examples of environmentally friendly tourism.

Demand for leisure and recreation using boats has always been popular among the British, and the rural waterways of Britain provide ideal opportunities for water-based tourist activities. The Norfolk and Suffolk Broads are a paradise for both yacht and motor-boat enthusiasts. On the Continent, the canals and waterways of the Netherlands, France and Ireland, to name but three countries, all attract growing numbers of tourists seeking the pleasure of 'messing about in boats', and the countless lakes of Finland and Sweden are popular, particularly with domestic tourists and second-home owners, during the short Nordic summer. The appeal of water-dependent holidays will be fully explored in Chapter 13.

Sites which include major waterfalls can also attract the international tourist. Those that are readily accessible, such as Niagara Falls on the Canadian/US border, and Victoria Falls on the Zambia/Zimbabwe border, enjoy considerable popularity, and have been built up as key destinations by their countries' tourism authorities. More inaccessible falls, including the world's highest, Angel Falls in Venezuela, do not yet attract the number of tourists that could be anticipated at such a unique scenic attraction, were adequate transport and other infrastructure available.

Areas of woodland and dense foliage provide yet another appeal for tourism. In the USA, the New England states of Vermont, New Hampshire and Maine and the Canadian eastern provinces attract large numbers of domestic and international tourists to witness the famous 'fall foliage' colours in the autumn. For those demanding more strenuous activities in woodland, the US has designated national trails, of which the best known and most challenging is the Appalachian Trail, from Georgia to Maine, taking several weeks to cover on foot.

More exotic foliage is available to tourists in the form of jungle, and in South America, the Amazon has become a popular supplementary tour for those travelling to

Ecuador and Peru. Pristine jungle still exists in West Africa, which to date has been little exploited, although small group tours are organized to see the gorillas in Rwanda and the Congo, but tourism is limited by political instability in these areas of the world. Smaller but more accessible jungles are still accessible in developed countries, notably El Yunque Rainforest in Puerto Rico and in the Cape York area of northern Queensland, Australia. Countries like Borneo and Papua New Guinea offer great potential for exploration of dense tropical forest, if political and potential health problems can be overcome.

In Britain, there are over fifty historic forests, and many further areas of woodland that attract the day tripper or walking tourist. Burnham Beeches, near London, is noted for the superb foliage of its beech trees, while forests such as the New Forest (a royal forest, now a National Park, with its memorial commemorating the spot where King William Rufus met his death in a hunting accident) and Sherwood Forest, associated with Robin Hood, have close links with history, myth and literature. Apart from its National Parks, the UK also introduced the concept of National Forest Parks, the Royal Forest of Dean becoming England's first National Forest Park in 1938. In the 1990s the government announced the formation of a new National Forest, covering some 200 square miles, in the English Midlands. Some limited protection, at least in theory, is also afforded through designation of Areas of Outstanding Natural Beauty (AONB) and Sites of Special Scientific Interest (SSSI). There are 41 AONBs in England and Wales, and the North Pennines (covering 2,000 sq. km), in recognition of its world-class geological heritage, became the first European Geopark in 2003. This designation by UNESCO is expected to lead to greater nature-based tourism interest and better protection for the environment.

The association of a particular rural area with literary or media connections can provide a powerful draw for tourism, and regional tourist authorities have not been slow to take advantage of this. In England's West Country, Doone Country, based on the North Devon setting of R D Blackamore's Lorna Doone, led the way for many other regions to promote their links with literature, including Catherine Cookson Country, the South Tyneside setting for many of that author's books, and the Tarka Trail in Devon, mythical home of Tarka the Otter. Several sites in England have promoted the association of their district with the mythical King Arthur, most notably the area around Tintagel in Cornwall, and a Dylan Thomas Trail has recently been established in Wales which emphasizes the use of the Celtic Trail cycle route.

One other form of tourism destination which we should include under this grouping is the appeal of islands. Initially, off-shore islands, easily accessible by boat or aircraft from the mainland, proved a draw – Helgoland north of Germany was a popular destination for German tourists between the two world wars (before being saturation-bombed by the Allies in World War II), and islands like the Danish Bornholm and the Swedish Gotland attracted first the domestic tourist, and more recently, the international-cruise passenger sailing around the Baltic. In the Atlantic, the Canaries and Madeira have, of course, attracted tourists for many years but more recently operators have developed tours to more remote destinations like the Azores and Cape Verde Island. Often, their appeal is due to their isolation, and those least accessible represent a challenge to the adventurous tourist. These are predominantly rural in character, and planning controls are often rigidly exercised to ensure they remain unspoilt. More recently, relatively inaccessible islands have become the challenge, especially those without air connections, with the most isolated becoming a quest for the specialist traveller. Examples include Pitcairn, St Helena, Tristan da Cunha, Easter Island and the Marquesas. Lesser known but less remote islands are also growing in appeal. Australia is a jumping-off base for many island paradises, and these are now being actively promoted, to a greater or lesser extent, by the tourism authorities. Islands with which we are likely to become more familiar include Norfolk Island, Whitsunday Island, King Island, Flinders Island, Three Hummock Island – and Cato Island, promoted as the gay and lesbian kingdom of the Coral Sea Islands.

Agritourism

Rural tourism has long been popular with the independent traveller, and its importance to the economy of the countryside has been widely recognized in recent years. The concept of agritourism, which emphasizes sustainable tourism in agricultural areas of the countryside, has become highly significant in tourism planning, following the success of the *gîte* development in France. French government grants were awarded in the post-war years to help convert crumbling farm buildings into rural cottages for tourist sojourns, and the gîte holiday became popular, particularly with the independent British tourist. The Portuguese *quintas*, or rural estates, also attracted a strong following from tourists eager to experience something a little different from the standard forms of holiday accommodation. There is now a programme of strong financial support from the EU, with grants that are allowing rural tourism provision to become increasingly luxurious. Recent development also takes account of the interest in adventure sports, many of which are best enjoyed in the rural community, and outdoor sports such as ballooning, horse riding and mountain biking are now catered for. Spain, Portugal, Cyprus and Italy have all invested heavily in agritourism. Notable developments include those in the Epirus province in north-western Greece and at Sierra Aracena, province of Seville.

Example Cyprus agritourism

The Cyprus villages' agritourism programme was launched in 1987, in an attempt to draw tourists away from the coastal resorts and give the inland villages some benefits from the inflow of tourists. From a base of just 100 visitors, the villages now draw in excess of 7,000 a year, reaching a point where the programme is now actively promoted in the UK by the Travel Foundation as an excellent example of sustainable tourism.

Britain has also actively promoted its farming and rural holidays, which for farmers have become increasingly important as a source of revenue as traditional farming revenues dry up. Tourist boards and local authorities have helped the private sector to develop new ideas in rural tourism. One example is that of the Heart of England Tourist Board, which has piloted short breaks involving culinary trails – a cider trail in

Herefordshire, a pork pie trail at Melton Mowbray, famous for its pies – designed to link farmers, food producers and the tourism industry under the banner 'farms, food and peaceful surroundings'. DEFRA (the Department of the Environment, Food and Rural Affairs), which allocates around £34 million to farmers in grants to diversify their activities, reports that around 48 per cent of Britain's farmers – mainly those in the south of England – have initiated some form of enterprise, bringing in extra income averaging £5,000 per annum. Activities range from B&Bs to holiday cottages and equestrian centres.

The growth of tourism in rural areas has encouraged an equivalent growth in small-scale economic ventures dependent upon tourism. Crafts are a notable example of this, with potters, glassmakers, woodworkers, basket weavers and countless other forms of craftspeople opening up outlets in the country to make and sell their wares. In Britain, the Countryside Agency reported in 2004 that some 300,000 people now earned their living from rural crafts, earning in excess of £1 billion. The Agency anticipates that crafts are likely to eclipse farming within fifteen years.

Finally, mention should be made of summer camps for children, long popular in North America and likely to be adopted in the UK on a larger scale in the future. Over six million children attend summer camp each year in the USA, bringing prosperity to the areas in which they are sited (notably New England), and UK authorities reckon that up to 600,000 children would be attracted to similar facilities in Britain. These would not necessarily have to be sited within areas of highest touristic appeal, helping to spread the benefits of rural tourism and avoiding congestion at popular destinations.

Figure 9.7
The Bovey Tracey craft fair in Devon has become an important annual event in tourism

(Photographed by the author)

Wilderness areas

As open countryside becomes rarer in the developed countries, measures are introduced to protect what remains, especially where this has been largely untouched until recent years. We have seen how Britain established its National Parks, but this country was merely following the lead set by the United States (see Figure 9.8), which designated the world's first national park at Yellowstone in 1872. This huge park, containing the

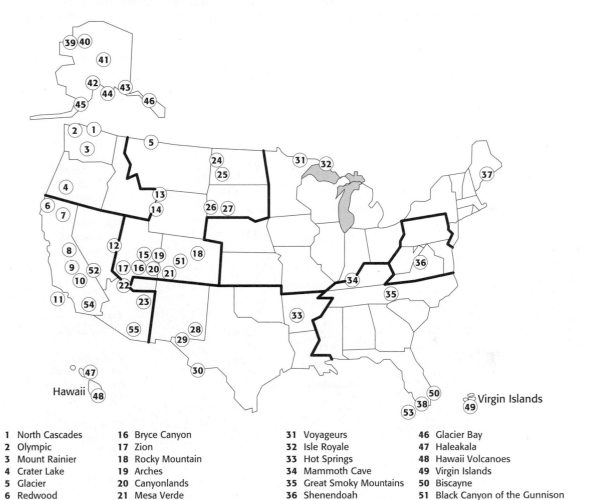

1	North Cascades	16	Bryce Canyon	31	Voyageurs	46	Glacier Bay
2	Olympic	17	Zion	32	Isle Royale	47	Haleakala
3	Mount Rainier	18	Rocky Mountain	33	Hot Springs	48	Hawaii Volcanoes
4	Crater Lake	19	Canyonlands	34	Mammoth Cave	49	Virgin Islands
5	Glacier	20	Canyonlands	35	Great Smoky Mountains	50	Biscayne
6	Redwood	21	Mesa Verde	36	Shenendoah	51	Black Canyon of the Gunnison
7	Lassen Volcanic	22	Grand Canyon	37	Acadia	52	Death Valley
8	Yosemite	23	Petrified Forest	38	Everglades	53	Dry Tortugas
9	Kings Canyon	24	Theodore Roosevelt (north unit)	39	Kobuk Valley	54	Joshua Tree
10	Sequoia	25	Theodore Roosevelt (south unit)	40	Gates of the Arctic	55	Saguaro
11	Channel Islands	26	Wind Cave	41	Denali		
12	Great Basin	27	Badlands	42	Lake Clark		**Not shown**
13	Yellowstone	28	Carlsbad Caverns	43	Wrangell-St. Elias	56	National Park of American Samoa
14	Grand Teton	29	Guadalupe Mountains	44	Kenai Fjords		
15	Capitol Reef	30	Big Bend	45	Katmai		

Figure 9.8   National Parks in the USA and territories

famed Old Faithful geyser, covers an area of some two and a quarter million acres on the borders between Wyoming, Montana and Idaho. Since then, numerous National Parks have been created in the US and elsewhere throughout the world. The largest is North East Greenland National Park, covering an area of 373,300 square miles, but one of the most significant moves was the formation in 2002 of thirteen new parks, covering 11,294 square miles, created out of virgin forest in Gabon, a move described earlier in Chapter 7. This country currently has only a very small base of tourism, but hopes to attract a flow of tourists to replace the logging industry, which in time would threaten the destruction of the forest, the country's prime resource. Even these parks,

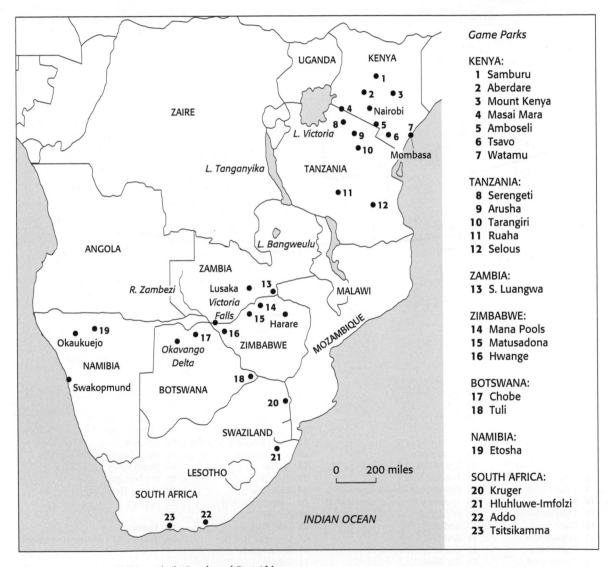

Figure 9.9 Major wildlife parks in South and East Africa

representing 11 per cent of the country, are tiny when seen against the total protected territory in Africa, amounting to some 850,000 square miles.

Many wilderness areas contain spectacular scenery, draw huge tourist crowds in their peak seasons who have to be monitored and managed. Examples include the Grand Canyon, Bryce and Zion Canyons and Monument Valley, where the appeal of solitude and communing with nature, the original concept of the US National Parks, is soon lost.

Another form taken in designating land masses is the safari park, most commonly found in South and East Africa. The Sabi Sabi Game Reserve in South Africa was the world's first designated wildlife park, but as other African nations started to become aware of the threat to their wildlife resources and the appeal of wild animals to tourists, the number of parks quickly expanded, and rangers introduced to reduce poaching.

Spa tourism

'Spa' is said to have originated from the town of that name in Belgium (although some claim *Sanitas Per Aqua* to be the true derivation of the term). Although this large spa and others like it at Vichy in France and Baden Baden in Germany have developed into urban areas, often becoming popular destinations in their own right (Bath, Cheltenham, Harrogate and Buxton being good examples in the UK), most spas are still small enough to be considered for the purpose of this book as rural destinations. They form an important element in international tourism, and one too readily over-looked by students of tourism in the UK, where they have fallen out of favour to some extent. However, Britain itself could boast of more than 250 active spas in the seventeenth century. Some were surprisingly urban; Streatham Vale, now in the London suburbs, was a popular watering hole as early as 1659. By the twentieth century their appeal had waned to a point where the final ten, then under the control of hospitals, were taken over on the formation of the National Health Service in 1948, but had their financial support withdrawn in 1976. The last publicly funded spa, Bath, closed in 1978 (although at the time of writing they are due, at great expense, to reopen one), while Droitwich Spa lingered on, providing medical treatment in a private hospital with a small indoor brine bath.

On the Continent, though, spa tourism (and its study as a subject in tourism studies) remains popular, with an estimated 1,200 active spas, and the industry makes a valuable economic contribution to the GDP of several countries. In Germany, Hungary and the Czech and Slovak Republics thermal treatment, in mud or mineral water baths, still plays an important part in health care. Italy's spas are also notable, with a large concentration around the Euganean Hills south of Padua, notably at Albano Terme and Battaglia Terme: some 200 hotels in the area are dedicated to the accommodation of spa visitors. North of Vicenza in the Dolomites the spa town of Recoaro Terme has been noted since the eighteenth century for its mountain spring waters. Typical treatments at all these resorts include mud baths, hydrotherapy, saunas, mineral baths, steam baths and beauty treatment. The popularity of spas in other areas of the globe is also well established. Around 21 per cent of the American tourist market visits spas each year, while in Japan, onsen (hot springs) like Ikaho and Shirahone thrive on tourism (although scandals in the early 2000s in which it was revealed that tap water was in some cases being provided in place of traditional water sources severely undermined public confidence).

In the past, European spa treatment was often supported by the State health services, although escalating costs have led to cutbacks; Germany, in 1996, reduced the amount of time State-funded health claimants were permitted to stay. Nevertheless, some 15 million Europeans daily immerse themselves in thermal waters in the belief that 'the cure' will alleviate their ailments, and the spas of Europe continue to benefit from this belief. In Britain, which formerly attracted many domestic tourists to its spa towns, as we saw in Chapter 2, medical experts became more sceptical about the health benefits of spas in the twentieth century. Recent evidence concerning sufferers from osteoarthritis and osteoporosis, and a growing interest in alternative medicine generally, is causing some medical experts to re-evaluate their former views, and this is encouraging some former spas to reopen. National Lottery funding has been made available at Buxton, Malvern, Leamington Spa, Harrogate, Tunbridge Wells and Bath. Others may choose to follow suit if demand is evident, although not all funding will necessarily go towards recreating the medical facilities of these famous spas.

Meanwhile, the ETC estimated in 2002 that some 13 million Britons made visits to spas abroad, whether to stay at the resort or hotel purely for leisure purposes or to

Figure 9.10
The Casino at Spa, Belgium, helps to keep this early spa economically active

(Photographed by the author)

enjoy the facilities. In spite of the lack of medical facilities at British spas, a number of tour operators in the UK are featuring spa treatment abroad in their promotions, and over 300,000 British tourists continue to travel abroad specifically for treatment each year. The response to this demand is being met by the growth of purpose-built facilities supplied within the accommodation sector (see Figure 9.10).

Example   Hotel-based spas

Many town and country house hotels have turned to constructing spas for their guests. The international chain Hyatt International announced in 2004 their intention to build seventy-four spas by 2008, and the holiday-centre operator Warners have opened an important spa in their centre at Thoresby Hall, Nottingham.

The successful destination

Three important points should be highlighted in relation to tourist destinations. First, the chances of their long-term success will be significantly enhanced if the benefits they offer are unique. There is only one Oberammergau Passion Play, just as there is only one Eiffel Tower, Grand Canyon or Big Ben, and these attractions can provide the focus for a destination's marketing campaign. Because of the singular properties of 'heritage' tourism, these types of destination retain their attraction even if their prices may become less competitive with other destinations, providing the increase is not exorbitant by comparison.

However, it is true to say that the majority of the mass tourism movement is directed at sun-sea-sand destinations, which the Mediterranean and Caribbean countries provide so effectively. Such destinations are seldom unique, and their customers do not require them to be so. The tourists will be satisfied as long as the amenities are adequate, the resort remains accessible and prices are competitive. Indeed, the similarities in attraction and amenity, as well as the way these destinations are marketed, gives rise to the concept of the 'identikit' destination, which results from the evidence produced by market research studies designed to find common denominators among the various international markets in order to develop a product with guaranteed mass demand. These identikit destinations have been developed through the activities of multinational tourism organizations. In the development of such destinations, the emphasis changes from an attempt to distinguish the product to one which concentrates on maintaining or improving its image, by offering good standards which reflect value for money and ensuring that the destination remains competitive with other, similar destinations. The characteristics of identikit destinations are discussed in greater detail in Chapter 3.

The second point to stress is that the more benefits a destination can offer, the greater the attraction of the destination. Multiple attractions provide added value, and the concentration within a specific geographical area of a number of different products appealing to different markets (such as the City of Bath, and the region surrounding Bournemouth) will improve the chance of success.

Finally, it should be clear that resorts cannot rest on their laurels. Most destinations depend at least to some extent on the return visitor, and will need continually to update and augment their range of attractions to encourage repeat visits. This means constant investment. Destinations, like all products which depend upon consumer demand, have 'life cycles', in which they experience periods of growth, expansion and, eventually, decline. If we examine the history of any well-known resort we can see the truth of this. Along the French Riviera, Nice, Cannes, Antibes, Juan les Pins and St Tropez have all in turn enjoyed their periods as fashionable resorts, but ultimately, their visitors moved on to more fashionable resorts, often to be replaced by less fashion-conscious, less free-spending tourists.

A decline into decay, all too evident in many British seaside resorts today, can only be arrested through redevelopment and innovation. In some cases, resorts have been allowed to run down to an extent where the cost of renovation may be beyond the scope of the council, and decay becomes inevitable.

Notes

1 Landmarks of Hope and Glory, *The Observer Review*, 26 October 2003

Websites

The Travel Foundation

www. my-tropical-islands. com
www.thetravelfoundation.org.uk

Questions and discussion points

1 Are any forms of transport so appealing to you that their actual destination in irrelevant? If so, what is it that appeals? Could other forms of transport exert a similar fascination for the tourist? Identify some that already do.

2 As is made clear in this chapter, some destinations are hard to sell to tourists because they have no clear image (Belgium is often cited as an example, while Canada is also said to suffer from this lack of image) – yet individual towns in the countries have strong appeal (Toronto, Vancouver; Bruges, Antwerp). Of what other countries can this be said to be true? How can the tourism authorities create a clearer and more positive image of their country?

3 Rises of between one and three degrees in temperature by the end of this century have been ascribed to a general increase in global warming. How are traditional tourism destinations in the UK likely to be affected by this rise in global warming? Are there potential benefits as well as disadvantages?

4 How are traditional touring destinations likely to be affected by a continuing rise in the price of oil, and hence of petrol?

Assignment topics

1 Taking any destination (region, town, village) known to you as having little obvious appeal in attracting tourists, undertake some research which will provide ammunition to mount a campaign to draw tourists to the area. This could involve historical figures born, living or dying in the area, or something in the geography or history of the region which could be developed to appeal to visitors (a visit to the regional museum and library can help in gathering such data).

Devise a scheme to develop tourism and prepare a report for the area tourist board, with a suggested plan of action.

2 Ryanair was obliged to withdraw from Charleroi Airport after having been found to have been subsidized by the airport to encourage the growth of tourism to the region, a breach of European Union regulations.

Since this date, the EU has relented and accepts the case for some subsidization, the amount depending upon the economic circumstances of the region in which the airport is situated. However, it took the view that a subsidy of 90 per cent over fifteen years was too great an allowance.

Prepare a set of notes which will enable you to speak at a meeting of EU officials supporting an increase in the proposed subsidies in order to benefit small regional airports.

10 Visitor attractions

Objectives

After studying this chapter, you should be able to:

- distinguish between a destination and an attraction, and define each
- understand what it is that attracts tourists, and which attractions appeal to each market
- appreciate the problem for attractions of changing taste and fashion, and propose solutions to overcome this
- recognize the potential for new attractions, and how these can be developed.

Introduction: defining the attraction

> Tourism is also about activity and special interest – from fell walking to cathedrals, from international rugby to surfing, from golf to gardens, and from film locations to battlefields.
>
> Tessa Jowell, Secretary of State for Culture, Media and Sport,
> DCMS, May 2004 Prospectus

What exactly do we mean by a tourist attraction? Trying to define it is no easy matter, but to understand the sector and how it operates we have to start with a definition. After all, it is generally the attraction which prompts the tourist to travel in the first place; but the concept of an 'attraction' is a very broad one, encompassing a great many different sights – and sites. Often we use the term synonymously with 'destination', the attraction in this case being the benefits *inherent* in the destination, rather than any *purpose-built* facility specifically designed to appeal to the tourist. The medieval town centre of Dinant, Southern Germany's Black Forest and Luquillo Beach in Puerto Rico are all 'attractions', but do not exist either primarily or necessarily to serve tourists' needs. A trip to the seaside may be taken principally for the opportunity to enjoy a swim in the sea at a good beach in warm weather, another trip may consist of a drive through the countryside to take in the scenery. In both trips, the attraction is the destination (in the first case, nodal, in the second case, linear), but in neither case is the attraction purpose-built to serve the interests of tourism, even if it may have been modified to do so (e.g. the beach may have been spruced up, deck chairs and wind-breaks provided for hire; the appeal of the drive will be heightened by look-out points, or picnic areas may be provided by the local authority at which tourists are invited to stop off and enjoy their packed lunch). Old buildings in town centres were not built to bring in tourists, but over time many have become architectural or historical sites which have tourist appeal. All three of these 'destinations', seaside resort, countryside or town, serve the needs of the local residents as well as tourists, and indeed, many residents may have chosen to live in that particular part of the world because of its attractiveness – German speakers have a useful term, *Freizeitswert*, implying the possession of enhanced leisure as a result of one's residence, which could usefully be incorporated into the English language. On the other hand, some attractions will have been constructed for the prime purpose of appealing to tourists, as would be the case of an art gallery like the Kröller-Müller Museum in the countryside near Otterloo in the Netherlands, or – on a much larger scale – the many Disney theme parks now constructed around the world.

So we must accept that no clear definition exists for the term. It is easiest just to accept that any site that appeals to people sufficiently to encourage them to travel there in order to visit it should be judged a 'visitor attraction'.

It will be helpful, however, to make some effort to categorize attractions. Swarbrooke[1], who has considered a number of attempts at definition, splits attractions into four categories (modified here):

1 Features within the natural environment.
2 Purpose-built structures and sites designed for purposes other than attracting visitors.
3 Purpose-built structures and sites designed to attract visitors.
4 Special events.

Fyall *et al*[2] similarly distinguish between built and natural attractions, and whether or not purpose-built. They also categorize on the basis of whether the attraction is paid for or free, privately or publicly owned, and a simple or complex product.

For simplicity's sake, we can conclude that attractions may be defined as natural or constructed, purpose-built for tourism and, if constructed, they may be to a greater or lesser extent 'managed', or left entirely in their natural state.

Some sites attract tourists because of events that occur there, or have occurred there in the past. In either case they will then be known as *event* attractions, and these can be either temporary or permanent. Temporary events may be one-off events at different sites on each occasion they occur (such as garden festivals on the Continent of Europe, which are arranged at intervals in different cities), while others (like the Ludlow Food Festival) reoccur at the same site. Some events are of very short duration – one day, or even a matter of hours.

Events are also either 'artificial' (constructed) or natural: the Changing of the Guard is a ceremony that attracts many overseas tourists visiting London; while the spring high tides which create the famous Severn Bore along the River Severn, the annual migration of wildebeest across the Serengeti Park in East Africa, and the regular eruptions of Old Faithful, the geyser in Yellowstone National Park in the USA, are all examples of natural events that attract the tourist. Many sites owe their continuing attraction to some event in the past: Liverpool became a place of pilgrimage for many visitors due to its links with the Beatles in the 1960s (both John Lennon's home at 251 Menlove Avenue, Woolton, and Sir Paul McCartney's home at 20 Forthlin Road have been bought by the National Trust and are open to the public); Gettysburg, created a National Military Park in 1895, attracts millions of domestic tourists as the key battlefield site of the US Civil War in 1863; while Lourdes, a place of religious pilgrimage, owes its appeal entirely to a single event occurring in 1858, when 14-year-old Bernadette Soubirous was said to have experienced a vision of the Virgin Mary.

One useful listing of different attractions was undertaken by the former English Tourism Council. While not totally comprehensive (its final category is something of a catch-all, while 'leisure attractions' might encompass anything from swimming pools and gymnasia to theme parks like Disney World), it does give us some direction for analysis of this sector of the industry:

- historic properties
- museums and art galleries
- wildlife parks
- gardens
- country parks
- workplaces
- steam railways
- leisure attractions
- other attractions.

In all, there are well over 6,000 such attractions in the UK for which entrance figures are maintained, a quarter of these being historic properties and a similar number, museums. To this number must be added the numerous buildings open to the public for which no attendance records are kept. There are, for instance, nearly 3,000 Grade I listed churches in England alone. The total number of attractions continues to increase every year, boosted by the additions of heritage and lottery funding (the Millennium Fund at the turn of the century accelerating the process). A few of these proved almost instant successes; Our Dynamic Earth in Edinburgh estimated, and budgeted for, 430,000 visitors a year, but actually received 500,000 in the first four months. Many others, however, were hopelessly over-optimistic in their attendance estimates, and have either struggled to survive or collapsed, the notorious Millennium Dome perhaps being the outstanding example, running up debts in excess of £1 billion (in spite of drawing the largest audiences in the country during the millennium year itself). The National Centre for Popular Music in Sheffield, opened in 1999, was effectively bankrupt within seven months, having estimated 400,000 visitors a year but achieving only a quarter of this figure. The performance of the Earth Centre in Doncaster was even poorer. Forecasting 500,000 visitors when it opened in 1999, it attracted only 80,000 and collapsed financially in 2004.

Most attractions in the UK, however, do not anticipate hosting anything approaching these figures. Over 90 per cent are geared to receiving less than 200,000 visitors annually[3], and some of the smallest admit fewer than 10,000 (Case Study 1 at the end of this text being one example). However, these are not necessarily to be thought of as failing, if sponsored funding is available, or costs are kept low and business plans carefully managed.

It is important to recognize that many destinations owe their appeal to the fact that they offer a cluster of attractions within the immediate locality. Urban destinations are far less dependent upon climate than are rural or coastal sites, and Britain (and other temperate cities in Northern Europe, North America and Southern Australia) is fortunate in being able to attract to its cities year-round visitors to theatres, galleries and other indoor entertainments. The attraction of the seaside is also heightened – particularly in Britain, with its uncertain climate – by its being able to offer, either in the resort itself or within a short drive, a number of sites which are not weather-dependent, such as museums, amusement arcades, retail shopping malls, theatres and industrial heritage sites. In Britain, the need for a focal point even in seaside resorts had already been widely recognized by the nineteenth century, the great era for the construction of piers.

The focal point, or icon

Contemporary tourism marketing implicitly or explicitly recognizes the importance of the focal point – or a synthesis of focal points – at a site, which acts as a magnet to attract the tourist. The focal point may be a historic building, such as a castle or monument, or it may be a construction owing its success to its architectural features, such as a tower, bridge or pier. The supreme focal point becomes a cultural icon, and the more popular tourist destinations are those blessed with this attraction. The fame of the cultural icon often extends far beyond the region itself, with the result that the images of the icon and destination are inseparable in the mind of the prospective visitor. This powerful image has led to some locations setting out deliberately to create a cultural icon with which their region will be associated in the public mind – not always successfully. A few examples of the most successful will reveal the significance of the icon in tourism promotion (Table 10.1).

Table 10.1   Locations and their touristic icons

Location	Cultural icons
London	Big Ben and Houses of Parliament, Buckingham Palace
Paris	Eiffel Tower, Notre Dame
New York	Empire State Building, Statue of Liberty
San Francisco	Golden Gate Bridge
Sydney	Sydney Harbour Bridge, Opera House
Kuala Lumpur	Petronas Towers
Copenhagen	Little Mermaid statue
Bilbao	Guggenheim Museum

With the possible exception of the last in this list, none of these buildings were created with the deliberate intention of attracting tourists – yet over time, their appeal has widened to a point where tourism flourishes because they exist. In the case of more recent construction (and no doubt boosted by the success of Bilbao, which prior to the construction of the Guggenheim had little to attract tourists) developers and architects have designed with one eye on the potential for tourism – and in some cases, of course, have built with tourism in mind. It is not without significance that 80 per cent of visitors to the Guggenheim don't enter the building – its attraction is not the artistic contents, but the building itself. Frank Gehry's innovative museum has influenced the design of countless more recent constructions straining for recognition as cultural icons within their community, including the Kunsthaus in Graz, Austria, and the new Imperial War Museum in Manchester. Recruiting an architectural practice of international standing such as Foster and Partners (responsible *inter alia* for the renovated Reichstag in Berlin, the Millennium Footbridge in London and the Sage Concert Hall in Gateshead) is now seen as the first step in establishing a landmark building. The London Eye, the big wheel sponsored by British Airways to provide aerial views over the city, has proved both culturally and commercially successful, having rapidly become an integral component of the Central London townscape (and its success has led Singapore to build a 150-metre big wheel, to be known as the Singapore Flyer, due to be open by the time this text appears. They anticipate 2.5 million visitors in the first year. Not to be outdone, China has already announced plans to build an even larger one, of around 200 metres, in Shanghai).

It is worth stressing that while cultural icons such as these are crucial in attracting the first-time visitor, all important tourist cities will also need to replenish and complement their stock of tourist attractions from time to time to attract the repeat visitor. The appeal of cities like London and Paris is that they can attract so many visitors back again and again because of the wealth of attractions they offer – smaller, less well-known museums and newly constructed attractions alike.

Example   The Angel of the North

Officials in Gateshead, in the North East of England, sought the help of a sculptor, Anthony Gormley, to construct a landmark work of art to represent the Tyneside region, with the intention of creating an image which up to that point had had little sense of identity, either among the local population or throughout the country as a whole. Gormley devised a 20-metre-high steel and copper sculpture – the largest in Britain – to surmount a hill outside the city, with its arms extending 54 metres (almost the width of a jumbo jet) in a sheltering embrace of the surrounding countryside (Figure 10.1). The sculpture rapidly became an icon, gaining massive media publicity; its siting ensured that it would be seen by an average 90,000 motorists a day passing on the A1, as well as countless rail travellers approaching Newcastle on the East Coast main line. Gateshead Council anticipated some 150,000 visitors a year would divert their trips to see it. Initially, there had been fear that the image would be seen as too modern for a traditionally minded local population and inappropriate to the site; but the overwhelming success and publicity which followed its erection soon won over the locals, who now take great pride in their new icon.

Figure 10.1
The Angel of the
North

(Photographed by Colin Cuthbert. Courtesy: Gateshead Council)

Arguably, the 'B of the Bang' landmark recently erected in Manchester by sculptor Thomas Heatherwick will do for that city what the Gormley sculpture has done for Tyneside.

The truly outstanding sites of architectural, cultural or historic importance around the world are those recognized as UNESCO World Heritage Sites. In 2004, 788 such sites were listed in 134 countries, including 611 cultural sites, 154 natural sites and 23 of mixed composition. Britain has almost 3 per cent, a favourable share, of this total, as Table 10.2 reveals.

Historic buildings and architectural features

Probably what most of us think of first, when considering the touristic appeal of an urban location, are its historical and architectural features. Often these features are subsumed into a general 'feel' about the destination, rather than an appreciation of

Table 10.2 UNESCO World Heritage Sites in the UK

Giant's Causeway and Coast
Durham Cathedral and Castle
Ironbridge Gorge
Studley Royal Park and ruins of Fountains Abbey
Stonehenge, Avebury and associated sites
Castles and town walls of King Edward I in Gwynedd
St Kilda Island
Blenheim Palace
Westminster Palace, Westminster Abbey and St Margaret's Church
City of Bath
Hadrian's Wall (Frontiers of the Roman Empire)
Tower of London
Canterbury Cathedral, St Augustine's Abbey and St Martin's Church
Old and New Towns of Edinburgh
Maritime Greenwich
Heart of Neolithic Orkney
Blaenavon Industrial Landscape
Saltaire
Dorset and East Devon Coast
Derwent Valley Mills
New Lanark
Royal Botanic Gardens, Kew
Liverpool Maritime Mercantile City

Note: The UK listing also includes the historic town of St George and related fortifications in Bermuda, and Henderson, Gough and Inaccessible Islands in the Pacific, which are dependent territories.

any individual building; the sense that the town is old and beautiful, its buildings having mellowed over time and their architecture quintessentially representative of the region or nation and its people. Thus, old cobbled streets lined with protected shop fronts, with their gabled roofs and ornamental features, such as those to be found in towns like York and Chester, Dinant and Tours, Rothenburg and Rüdesheim, Aarhus and Odense, Bruges and Ghent, all convey an overall impression of attractiveness and warmth, inviting us to shop there and enjoy the local food and lodging (over 2,500 hotels in Britain enjoy listed status as being of historic or architectural interest). These features are the supreme attraction of the 'old' countries of Europe, to which American, Arab and Japanese tourists alike are drawn when they first visit the country. In spite of an earlier disdain for older properties, the damage wrought by two world wars and the poor quality of architectural construction in their aftermath, most nations of Europe have retained major elements of their old city centres, even in some cases (as in Warsaw and Dresden) building entire replicas of the pre-war city centre in an attempt to regain their original character and heighten their appeal for visitors and residents alike.

This type of attraction is not limited to the Old World. Quebec City is among a number of New World towns and cities marketing themselves as winter (and not purely winter sport) destinations to Europeans as well as North Americans, selling the charm of its old town under snow.

Figure 10.2
Castles are a big attraction for tourists. Conwy Castle, North Wales

(Photographed by the author)

Britain has been more sensitive than some other European nations in retaining and restoring its buildings, having introduced a policy of listing historic buildings from 1950 (although the French had in fact introduced a similar policy at least a hundred years earlier). Today, the nation boasts over 500,000 buildings listed as of special historic or architectural interest. In England and Wales, truly outstanding buildings fall into Grade I category, as of 'exceptional interest', and these number about 2 per cent of the total, with a further 4 per cent falling into the second category of Grade II*, rated of 'special interest'. Most others are listed as Grade II (in Scotland and Northern Ireland, similar buildings are categorized as A, B or C). Today, all buildings in reasonable repair dating from before 1700, and most between 1700 and 1840, are listed, with strict controls over any cosmetic change to their exteriors. Among these, a handful (together with some of those scheduled as Ancient Monuments, but not necessarily all Grade I listed buildings) will stand out as icons sufficiently powerful to draw visitors from all over the world. Castles and cathedrals, palaces and historic manor houses will head this list, as will key sites of archaeological interest protected under the Ancient Monuments and Archaeological Areas Act (1979). The Tower of London alone receives over two million visitors annually, attracted not just by the building itself but also by the added attraction of the Crown Jewels which are on permanent display there.

At the other end of the scale, 'listed buildings' include post-war prefabricated houses, garden sheds, army camps, pigsties, lamp-posts, even toilet blocks. The National Trust, with the aid of Heritage Lottery Funding, has even saved some of the last survivors of the back-to-back slums built in Birmingham between 1802 and 1831, some of which have been renovated and are now being rented out as visitor accommodation. The importance of all of these structures as key ingredients of our national heritage has been recognized by successive British governments.

Most heritage buildings in England are in the care of English Heritage, while those in Wales are cared for by the Welsh equivalent, Cadw, and those in Scotland by Historic Scotland. The Church Commissioners are responsible for most of the great cathedrals and historic churches, the focal points for tourism in so many cities in the UK, and they part-fund, with government help, the Churches Conservation Trust, which cares for more than 300 redundant churches earmarked as historic or of architectural merit.

Apart from key sites, many other important buildings are open to tourist visits. There are believed to be well over 6,000 historic houses, commonly referred to as 'Stately Homes', of which over 800 are open to the public. Others are under the care of the National Trust (National Trust for Scotland, in that country), while still others are in private hands. The Historic Houses Association comprises around 1,500 owners of private houses, of whom some 300 regularly open their houses to the public for at least 28 days a year (the minimum required to reduce inheritance tax). Some will only open by appointment, and to small escorted groups, due to limitations of space. The particular value of all of these properties is their location, generally in the heart of the countryside, so they become a major support for rural tourism and the coaching industry.

On the European Continent, historic buildings play an equally important role in tourism for many countries. Notable among these are the chateaux of the Loire in France, Bavarian castles like Neuschwanstein in Germany and medieval cities like Florence and Venice in Italy. In Spain and Portugal, former stately homes, known respectively as *paradores* and *pousadas* and operated by the state, have been converted into luxury hotels attracting up-market touring visitors.

Figure 10.3
Early vernacular buildings are a popular draw for domestic tourists in Germany. Worpswede is an artists' colony near Bremen with a well-maintained stock of such buildings

(Photographed by the author)

Sadly, many hundreds of colonial buildings built by the British abroad are now in ruins, in India, Malaysia and the West Indies, due to lack of resources to maintain them, and even Lutyens' famed government buildings in New Delhi are deteriorating rapidly in the harsh climate. Others needing urgent restoration and with tourism potential include Clive of India's house in Calcutta, Georgetown trading post in Penang Island, Levuka in Fiji and Falmouth in Jamaica. English Heritage has made moves to contribute to their restoration before many such buildings are lost for ever. Although history is shorter in the new world, funding is more readily available, and early buildings which have survived are treasured. Americans take great pride in their prominent historic buildings like Monticello in Virginia, home of Thomas Jefferson, third president of the United States; while the town of Williamsburg in the same State has been preserved as a living museum of the colonial period. Buildings from the Spanish colonial period are preserved, including the missions of San Luis Rey in California, dating from 1789, and what is believed to be the nation's oldest house, in St Augustine, Florida.

Modernism and tourism

In the earlier discussion of the search for a cultural icon, it will be readily apparent to the reader that modern constructions are becoming almost as important as historic buildings in their ability to attract tourists. Commercial offices, private houses, bridges, monuments and memorials, towers and many other constructions which represent a fusion of artistic creativity and high technology are all becoming important as attractions appealing to tourists, when sufficiently spectacular. The recent proliferation of holocaust museums in Europe and North America were not specifically designed with the intention of boosting tourism, but the outstanding quality and originality of their designs (and the widespread media publicity which followed their construction) are ensuring that they will become popular places to visit. This might be defined as one form of cultural tourism, were it not for the fact that the majority of sightseers are concerned less with aesthetics as with the appeal of a 'wow' factor, the adrenalin rush which accompanies viewing of many new spectacles like the towering 'seven star' Burj al-Arab Hotel in Dubai, or the extraordinary 'art gallery' lobby of the renovated Cumberland Hotel in London.

Nothing defines a city better than a prominent landmark, and the higher the landmark, the greater the impression upon visitors – hence the popularity of tower and skyscraper construction at key sites around the globe. The search for status among developers and their clients has led to a scramble to build the highest building in the world – an honour held, at the time of writing, by Tower 101 in Taipei, which, at 1,667 feet, exceeds the former record holder, the Petronas Towers in Kuala Lumpur, Malaysia, at 1,483 feet (the CN Tower, at 1,815, is presently the world's tallest structure, but is not considered a 'building' by all observers). This may be superseded by the planned Freedom Tower on the site of the World Trade Centre in New York, which was planned to rise to a symbolic 1,776 feet, but there are fears that this will become too easy a target for terrorists, and plans are on hold at the time of writing. However, the Burj Dubai is expected to become the world leader when construction in Dubai is completed in 2008. At around 2,624 feet and 160 storeys high, this will be both the world's tallest building and the tallest structure. The building will also contain the world's largest shopping mall, and with other developments planned in Dubai, it puts that country firmly on the map as a market leader in tourism development; Dubai is expected to attract some 15 million tourists a year by 2010, at which point tourism to Dubai alone will contribute around 20 per cent of the UAE's entire GDP.

As was the case with the Guggenheim in Bilbao, the significance of modern architecture's appeal is that many of the great buildings are constructed in sites that are not traditional tourism venues. The following ten buildings were recently cited as 'worth a visit from the international tourist'[4]:

■ The Museum of Fantasy, Bernried, Germany

■ Bao Canal Village, China

■ The concert hall at Leon, Spain

■ Bodegas Ysios, Rioja, Spain (designed by leading architect Antonio Calatrava)

■ Parliamentary Library at New Delhi, India

■ UFA Cinema, Dresden, Germany

■ The 'Aluminium Forest' Visitor Centre, Utrecht

■ Tango Ecological Housing, Malmö, Sweden

■ Art Museum, Milwaukee, USA (also by Calatrava)

■ Modern Art Museum, Forth Worth, USA.

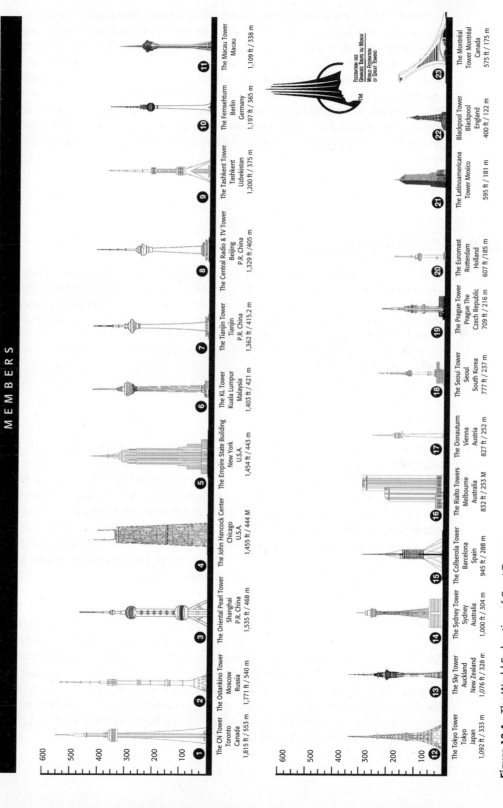

Figure 10.4 The World Federation of Great Towers
(Courtesy: World Federation of Great Towers)

These are hardly mainstream tourist destinations, but several could be described as actively striving to build their tourism markets, and are using contemporary architecture as one weapon in their armament to achieve this. The growing influence of Bauhaus-style architecture in modern townscape development has generated interest in all forms of modern design, especially in housing (see, for example Plate 10); cultural tours to the Frank Lloyd Wright and Richard Neutra houses in the United States and those designed by prominent Nordic architects like Alvar Aalto in Denmark, Sweden and Finland, are now popular. However, many of these properties are still in private hands, and can only be viewed externally, while others limit admissions due to demand and size.

Example	The Rietveld-Schröder House

Influenced by the works of Piet Mondrian and the de Stijl art movement, Gerrit Rietveld designed this versatile open-plan home, with its sharp angles and blocks of colour, for the Schröder family in 1924. It is now seen as a landmark in the history of modern house design. Located in a suburb of Utrecht, in the Netherlands, the house contrasts vividly with its conservative neighbours, and since its opening to the public, has drawn architects, and those with an interest in house design, from all over the world. Latent demand and space restrictions usually require advance booking.

The fickleness of public taste in modern buildings is problematic, both in terms of whether such buildings deserve to be listed and/or protected, and whether they are seen by tourists as worthwhile visiting. The numerous Art Deco period buildings in Miami Beach present us with a good example of this fickleness; for years spurned by the public and threatened with replacement by more modern hotels, their value was not recognized until the 1990s, when a systematic campaign was carried out to restore them to their former glory. Listed buildings in Britain must normally have been built at least 20 years before they can obtain listed status, but experience would suggest that attitudes towards Britain's modern buildings, and the decision whether they are of sufficient merit for sightseeing on historical or aesthetic grounds, may take much longer to mature. Coventry Cathedral, severely damaged during World War II and replaced by an unashamedly modern building after the war by the architect Basil Spence, was vilified for decades, but a poll conducted by English Heritage in 1999 found that it had become the country's favourite twentieth-century building. Other formerly despised modernist buildings now popular with the public include Liverpool's Roman Catholic cathedral, the De la Warr Pavilion in Bexhill-on-Sea (saved, by the local authority's last-minute rethink, from the desecration of conversion to a pub, and now restored to its former glory), and the 1951 Royal Festival Hall in London (also listed, and the subject of a recent face-lift).

Example The Midland Hotel, Morecambe

The Midland Hotel in Morecambe is a building of equal worth to the Art Deco hotels of Miami Beach, but its architectural value has still to be fully appreciated by the public at large. Of roughly the same period (1933) as the Miami Beach hotels, the hotel is a Grade II* listed building which has lain vacant for several years with its fabric steadily deteriorating while the local authority tries to find a use for what is undoubtedly the best building in this erstwhile popular seaside resort in Lancashire. While of exceptional merit, it still faces the threat of destruction, and typifies a problem faced by many buildings of architectural worth in formerly popular seaside resorts.

The bridge is another type of structure which has always found favour with tourists (American enthusiasts actually purchased and transported the former London Bridge to be re-erected on Lake Havasu in Arizona); and Tower Bridge in London, the Pont du Gard in France, the Golden Gate in San Francisco and the Sydney Harbour Bridge are all well-established tourism attractions in their own right. Advances in technology are making the construction of modern bridges ever more awe-inspiring. The opening in 2004 of the world's highest bridge, the Millau Viaduct bridge across the Tarn Valley (another Foster design) is likely to attract many sightseers to the Massif Central region of France, quite apart from the 10–25 thousand motorists expected to drive across it each day; it is estimated that half a million sightseers had already come to watch during its construction. The tallest of the bridge's seven piers is 343 metres, higher than the Eiffel Tower, while vehicles will cross at a height of 270 metres. Again, local residents who first complained of the construction are now relishing the inflow of tourism which the bridge has generated.

Seaside piers

The idea of a pier is a particularly British phenomenon; very few are to be found abroad, while at one time Britain boasted more than a hundred. These soon proved to be an attraction in their own right at many of Britain's most popular seaside resorts. The first pier was constructed at Weymouth in 1812, soon followed by that at Ryde, Isle of Wight, in 1813. Their heyday, however, occurred between the mid-1800s and early 1900s, with 78 constructed between 1860 and 1910. They were first constructed to serve as walkways to reach the numerous paddle steamers moored off-shore to provide excursions for holidaymakers, but were soon used for 'promenading', a popular Victorian pastime; Margate Pier, built in 1853, became the first pier built purely for pleasure. They have now become nostalgic accoutrements to seaside holidays at Victorian resorts, and those that remain (some 55 in the UK in varying states of preservation) are currently enjoying something of a revival, with the formation of a National Piers Society to further public interest in their regeneration; although sadly too late to save the dilapidated West Pier in Brighton, a Grade I listed pier, which collapsed during a storm while efforts were still being made to raise funds for its restoration.

Figure 10.5
Now Britain's only Grade I listed pier, Clevedon still serves as an embarkation point for excursion steamers

(Photographed by the author)

Archaeological sites

Archaeology is the study of human antiquities, usually through excavation, and is generally thought to be concerned with pre- or early history – although the term is now also used to refer to industrial archaeology, relating to study of the industrial relics of the eighteenth and later centuries. Areas where early civilizations arose, such as the countries of the Middle East, are rich in archaeological sites, and Egypt in particular attracts visitors from around the world to sites such as the Pyramids at Giza, the burial sites at the Valley of the Kings, and the temples at Luxor. Great Britain is also rich in early historical sites such as those at Chysauster prehistoric village in Cornwall, the Roman remains at Fishbourne in Sussex, with some of the richest mosaic flooring in the country, and the Skara Brae Neolithic site in the Orkney Islands. Myth and history are closely interwoven in our heritage, and the legend of King Arthur, which locates his castle of Camelot at Tintagel, and the association of this mythical king with the archaeological digs at Cadbury Camp in Wiltshire, exercise a fascination for young tourists in particular.

In the early 1990s, the world's largest collection of paleolithic art, embracing hundreds of ice-age drawings of animals, was discovered in a remote area of northern Portugal. A fierce battle then developed between those seeking to dam the area as a reservoir and others seeking to conserve the site for tourism. The latter won the day, and the Côa Valley Archaeological Park was opened to the public in 1996.

Industrial heritage

Britain became the seat of the industrial revolution in the eighteenth century, and over the past half century interest has been awakened in the many redundant buildings and obsolete machinery dating back to this period. The fact that so many of the early factories and warehouses were also architectural gems in their own way gave impetus to the drive to preserve these building and restore them for tourism. Other European countries, and the USA and Australia, have also recognized the potential of redundant buildings. Lowell, in Massachusetts, where a number of early mills had survived intact, received massive federal government funding to be restored as an Urban Heritage Park, and since the conversion of its buildings into museums, offices and shops, it has enjoyed considerable commercial success as an out-of-the-ordinary tourist destination. A similar success has been recorded in Britain for Ironbridge, where the industrial revolution is claimed to have originated in 1709. Now a UNESCO World Heritage site, it has enjoyed the benefit of substantial tourism investment on its seven sites spread over some six square miles.

The variety of industrial sites is astonishing. Early mining sites such as the coal and slate mines of South Wales or the copper mines of Cornwall have been converted into tourist attractions, as have former docks and manufacturing sites. Derelict textile mills of the north of England, driven out of existence by the import of cheap textiles from developing countries following World War II, have taken on new life as museums – or in some cases have been converted to attractive new homes. The open-air museums which are based on a combination of industrial archaeology and industrial heritage provide settings which, to be properly appreciated, will require many hours, if not days, of viewing, and have helped to turn former areas of urban decay into major tourist attractions. Apart from Ironbridge, other significant developments in Britain include Beamish open-air museum in the north of England, and the Black Country Museum near Dudley, in the Midlands. The Big Pit Mining Museum at Blaenavon in South Wales, and the Llechwedd Slate Caverns near Blaenau Ffestiniog in North Wales have both made important contributions to the local economy of their region, with tourism helping to replace the former dependency upon mining.

Other countries have emulated Britain, in recognizing that their recent industrial heritage can play a part in attracting tourists. Countries with shorter histories, like the United States and Australia, are fervent protectors of their earliest sites, both indigenous and of European origin. Former mining sites provide plenty of interest for tourists, not just for their history but also sometimes for the opportunity for them to do a spot of mining themselves. Bodie, California, was the site of early gold mining, and is now protected as Bodie State Historic Park. Tip Top, Arizona was a silver mining area, which is now attracting tourists, as is Macetown, New Zealand, an early gold mining site. Tourists in Australia are invited to pan for gold at former industrial sites (this author struck lucky, and still retains his minute gold nugget!). Kolmanskop in Namibia, an abandoned diamond-mining town, is aiming to attract tourists not only for its industrial heritage but the lunar landscape which surrounds the site.

Transport attractions

Early transport has provided another focus for tourist interest. In some cases, the equipment can be restored and brought back into service for pleasure trips; this is particularly notable with the many steam railways which are either in private hands or managed by trusts in Britain. Many of these railways run through very scenic countryside, especially those in Wales. The continuing role of classic modes of transport as tourist attractions will be examined more thoroughly in Chapters 13 and 14.

Transport museums are popular attractions in many countries; there are eight significant museums of transport, and numerous smaller ones, in Britain alone; these encompass a mix of aircraft, maritime vessels and public and private road transport. Historic ships provide unique attractions in local museums. Some of the earliest are the Viking ships which have been found in Scandinavia, and some splendid museums have been created to display them, notably that at Roskilde in Denmark. The only seventeenth-century warship to survive is the Swedish *Vasa* which capsized and sank in Stockholm harbour soon after its launch in 1628. Raised in almost perfect condition, it is now a major museum attraction in Stockholm. Still in Scandinavia, Oslo in Norway provides the setting for the *Fram*, the vessel in which Roald Amundsen sailed in 1910, on his way to become the first person to reach the South Pole. Similarly, Captain Scott's vessel, the research ship *Discovery*, has now returned to Dundee where it was built in 1901, and serves as a museum.

In Britain, the oldest surviving vessel built in Bristol's former shipping yards, the tug *Mayflower*, is still in working order and a key attraction at the industrial museum, offering frequent trips along the floating harbour for visitors in summer. Bristol is also the setting for Isambard Kingdom Brunel's *SS Great Britain*, the first iron-hulled screw-driven vessel, launched in 1843, brought back from the Falklands as a rusting wreck in 1970 and now being extensively restored with the aid of Heritage Lottery Funding. Together with the city's famous suspension bridge, this early ship has helped to create a new identity for the city.

The cost of preserving more recent passenger vessels, due to their size, militates against their preservation. Perhaps the best known of all twentieth-century ships, the *RMS Queen Mary*, was saved from the breaker's yard and converted into a dry-dock hotel near Long Beach, California, but only at considerable cost to its developers. Britain, formerly a leading maritime nation, has sadly no examples of its great passenger vessels of the last century on display, although there are numerous examples of fighting vessels from that and earlier centuries preserved and open to the public. *HMS Belfast*, a World War II cruiser, is moored near Tower Bridge in London, and attracts some 200,000 visitors each year. Portsmouth is particularly lucky to have three great examples of our maritime history, including Nelson's flagship *HMS Victory*, the nineteenth-century *HMS Warrior* and the Tudor warship *Mary Rose*, raised from the sea in 1982 and still undergoing conservation. The combination of three vessels of historic value located close together in the same city acts as a powerful magnet for the day excursionist and helps to account for a high number of visitors.

There are numerous vintage-car museums throughout Britain, although that at Beaulieu is probably the best known. Vintage aircraft are preserved at Yeovilton, among other sites, while elsewhere, museums have been devoted to early carriages, bicycles and canal-boats. Where artefacts are too large to house indoors, the costs of preservation are very high, adding to the difficulties faced by museums that wish to focus on such attractions. This was a factor in the collapse of the Exeter Maritime Museum in 1996.

Modern industrial tourism

Interest in our industrial heritage has now spread further to include an interest in modern industry. A number of companies have recognized the possibilities of achieving good public relations by opening their doors to the public, either to see work in progress in the factory, or to maintain a workshop or museum of some kind on site. American businesses were the first to recognize the public-relations value of this, and car companies in particular were soon arranging visits to manufacturing plants where prospective purchasers could watch cars being built. Today, this practice is widespread in the USA, and is particularly beneficial for tourism in the sense that most automobile plants are not sited in areas which would normally attract tourists. Among those opened to the public are General Motors' Chevrolet Corvette factory in Bowling Green, Kentucky (one of that state's major tourist attractions); the Toyota Assembly Plant at Georgetown, Kentucky; GM's Saturn plant at Spring Hill, Tennessee; the Nissan plant in the same state at Smyrna; BMW's plant at Spartanburg, South Carolina; and Ford's Lincoln plant at Wixom, Michigan, now the nearest such plant to Detroit, the traditional home of automobile manufacturing, which still remains open to the public. Some visits to these plants are booked months in advance, such is their popularity. German-based car plants have also developed their own themed attractions, with Opel Live at Rüsselsheim and Volkswagen's Autostadt.

There are other commercial benefits apart from public relations. Watching the production processes of, for example, modern china and glass will stimulate an interest in purchasing, and people can be encouraged to purchase direct at the factory shop. At Cadbury's, the chocolate confectioners located at Bourneville, England, chocolates have been made by hand and are sold to members of the public individually by members of staff in traditional costumes. Other museums based on publicizing internationally popular products include Guinness in Ireland, Swarovski Crystal in Austria, and Hershey Chocolate, Kelloggs and Coca-Cola in the USA.

China is probably the supreme example of a country where factory visits have been launched to encourage visitor-spend in the shops. What is often a minimal tour of the 'factory' itself is followed by an extended visit to the shop, fuelled with liquid refreshment, to encourage visitors to linger and purchase.

In 1980, the Sellafield nuclear fuel plant was opened to visitors to help counteract much negative publicity about nuclear energy appearing in the media. This quickly became a major, and quite unexpected, draw for tourists in the area, since when other nuclear processing plants have also opened their doors for guided tours of the site. The variety of factories and workplaces open to the public is now considerable, from leading companies such as the car manufacturers to small individual workshops like Langham Glass in Norfolk, which makes lead-crystal glassware by hand and received an industrial award in 1993 for the numbers of tourists it was attracting. Another popular innovation has been access to the Scotch whisky distilleries in Scotland; of more than 100 distilleries, over 40 admit members of the public, and a distillery trail has been established for aficionados of single malt. French vineyards have been equally enterprising in opening their *caves* for a *dégustation* of their fine wines. Vineyards in South Africa, Chile and Australia have followed suit.

Many craftspeople depend upon tourists visiting their studios in order to sell their products, and as these studios are frequently set in the countryside, they will stimulate tourism to the area. For this reason, the Countryside Agency, formed in 1999 by the merger of the Rural Development Commission and the Countryside Commission, will sometimes provide financial aid to companies willing to open to the public, as they did in the case of Langham Glass.

Example   Open Doors

In Britain, businesses and other public institutions open their doors to the public annually on a weekend in September, in order to encourage locals and tourists to visit. This has both a promotional and political purpose. Access to government departments, for example, acts as an opportunity to recruit, and – in the case of the Foreign Office particularly – to reassure the public that careers in government are open to all. At the same time, it offers to departments an opportunity to publicize a political issue through exhibitions on site. Germany has emulated this occasion, giving access *inter alia* to the Chancellery in Berlin which, with its cutting edge design, appeals to those with an architectural as well as political interest.

Safety issues, following the bombing in London on 7 July 2005, are paramount, and an inevitable conflict emerges between the desire to give the public access to their democratic institutions and the need to ensure their security.

Battlefields

Historic battlefield sites are also important tourist attractions, not least because many are situated in rural areas and encourage tourism to what may be otherwise unappealing countryside. A growing enthusiasm for knowledge of military encounters on the field of battle has been encouraged by the popularity of historical documentaries on television, bringing awareness of these sites to a wider audience. In fact, many battlefield sites have offered little for the tourist to see, the authorities feeling that the events taking place at the sites are best left to the visitors' imaginations. As a result, they have remained relatively undisturbed, but this also means that they are often under threat from development, or construction of access roads. Local authorities are now making greater efforts to provide interpretation at these sites, using audio-visual displays and, in some cases, restaging battles in the field on the anniversary of the event.

In Britain, English Heritage has listed 43 sites in England as of historical importance (Figure 10.6). On the Continent, sites of major battles from the field of Waterloo to World War I and, increasingly, World War II, are attracting tourists in large numbers. War graves, equally, draw tourists; and the museum at Ypres, the site of one of the major battles of World War I, receives over 200,000 visitors each year, half of them British. Similarly, the US preserves and commemorates its battle sites from both the War of Independence and the Civil War. A number of specialist tour operators focus on battle sites in their tour programmes, the best known in Britain being Holts and

Figure 10.6
English battle
sites listed by
English Heritage

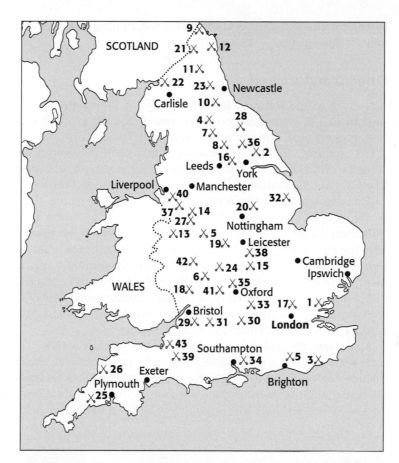

LISTED SITES

English Heritage has listed 43 battle sites:
1 Maldon, Essex, 991; **2** Stamford Bridge, North Yorks, 1066; **3** Hastings, E. Sussex, 1066;
4 Northallerton, North Yorks, 1138; **5** Lewes, E. Sussex, 1264; **6** Evesham, Hereford &
Worcester, 1265; **7** Myton, North Yorks, 1319; **8** Boroughbridge, North Yorks, 1322;
9 Halidon Hill, Northumberland, 1333; **10** Neville's Cross, Co. Durham, 1346;
11 Otterburn, Northumberland, 1388; **12** Homildon Hill, Northumberland, 1402;
13 Shrewsbury, Shropshire, 1403; **14** Blore Heath, Staffs, 1459; **15** Northampton, 1460;
16 Towton, North Yorks, 1461; **17** Barnet, N. London, 1471; **18** Tewkesbury, Glos, 1471;
19 Bosworth, Leics, 1485; **20** Stoke Field, Notts, 1487; **21** Flodden, Northumberland, 1513;
22 Solway Moss, Cumbria, 1542; **23** Newburn Ford, Tyne and Wear, 1640; **24** Edgehill,
Warwicks, 1642; **25** Braddock Down, Cornwall, 1642; **26** Stratton, Cornwall, 1643; **27** Hopton
Heath, Staffs, 1643; **28** Adwalton Moor, West Yorks, 1643; **29** Lansdown Hill, Avon, 1643;
30 Newbury, Berks, 1643; **31** Roundway Down, Wilts, 1643; **32** Winceby, Lincs, 1643;
33 Chalgrove, Oxon, 1643; **34** Cheriton, Hants, 1644; **35** Cropredy Bridge, Oxon, 1644;
36 Marston Moor, North Yorks, 1644; **37** Nantwich, Cheshire, 1644; **38** Naseby, Northants,
1645; **39** Langport, Somerset, 1645; **40** Rowton Heath, Cheshire, 1645; **41** Stow-on-the-Wold,
Glos, 1646; **42** Worcester, 1651; **43** Sedgemoor, Somerset, 1685.

Bartletts Battlefield Journeys. They have a high level of repeat business from amateur military strategists.

Gardens and arboreta

According to the National Botanic Garden of Wales, there are some 1,846 botanic gardens in 148 countries around the world, and these admit more than 150 million visitors every year. The cultivation of gardens has an enthusiastic following in the UK, a fact not lost on those organizing visits; both private and public gardens, and arboreta, which are essentially museums for living trees and shrubs, are popular. The Royal Botanic Gardens at Kew attract in excess of two million visitors every year.

Many gardens popular with visitors are in the care of the National Trust, generally as adjuncts to stately homes, and in some cases (as is the case with Stourhead in Wiltshire) the gardens may prove a stronger draw than the house itself (and in others, only the gardens are open to the public). Great landscape architects of the eighteenth century like Capability Brown and Humphrey Repton built splendid parks to complement these buildings, and as recently as the twentieth century famous gardens were still being constructed, notably by the great landscape gardener Gertrude Jekyll, whose work was often used to complement that popular architect of great houses of the early part of the twentieth century, Sir Edwin Lutyens.

Apart from the gardens at Kew (a World Heritage site with well over a million visitors each year) and the arboretum at Westonbirt (see Example), other popular attractions include Kew's off-shoot, a 500-acre site at Wakehurst Place, Haywards Heath (one of the National Trust's most popular attractions), the grounds of Hampton Court, and the famous Wisley Gardens. The proximity of all these to London helps to ensure their success for day visits.

Example   Westonbirt Arboretum

Westonbirt, in Gloucestershire, is one of the most important arboreta in Britain, registered with English Heritage as a Grade I listed landscape in their Register of Parks and Gardens of Special Historical Interest. Managed by the Forestry Commission, its site on the fringe of the Cotswolds makes it easily accessible to tourists, and it receives more than 300,000 visitors a year – partly due to the pattern of regular events mounted year-round at the site. In addition to summer concerts, it stages an annual Festival of Wood (in which dead trees are turned into sculptures), open-air plays, and, between June and September, a Festival of the Garden, featuring installation art which is then sold to raise money for Tree Aid, a charity planting trees in Africa. In midwinter evenings it offers an illuminated trail, the trees emblazoned tastefully with white lights, which attracts many tourists who might otherwise have never visited the site.

Another highly successful attraction in Britain is the Eden Project in Cornwall, which received 1,285,000 visitors between April and September in its first year. Early research indicated that 92 per cent of all visitors were staying in holiday accommodation nearby when visiting, and the Cornish economy has been forecast to benefit by some £1.8 billion over the site's first decade of operation between 2001–2011. Its appeal is boosted by its proximity to another garden attraction, the Lost Gardens of Heligan, making it a popular coaching excursion for a short-break holiday for garden enthusiasts.

Public and private sectors are now uniting to further this interest in all things horticultural. In Wales, a joint marketing initiative brought together seven leading gardens under the promotional theme Premier Gardens Wales. The bicentenary year of the Royal Horticultural Society, 2004, was declared the Year of Gardening in the UK, leading to the promotion of 200 prominent gardens around the country. Smaller private gardens are also regularly opened to the public throughout the summer each year under the National Gardens Scheme to benefit charity. While primarily aiming to attract locals, enthusiasts, in practice, will travel considerable distances to visit some of these gardens, and must certainly be counted among day-visitor figures for the region, and a number of visitors will even have travelled from abroad to visit these sites.

Example   The National Wildflower Centre

The National Wildflower Centre opened in Knowsley, on Merseyside, in 2004. On a 35-acre site, the Centre's objectives are to promote the creation of new wildflower landscapes, to encourage sustainability in the landscape and to encourage visitors to learn informally about wildflowers. The visitor centre has already received a RIBA award for its architectural design. Funding to establish the centre was raised through a number of sources:

	£
Millennium Commission	2,000,000
NWE Regional Development Agency	600,000
European Regional Development Fund (Objective 1 programme)	450,000
Other sources	1,300,000
Total:	4,350,000

The initial visitor target was 25,000 visitors annually, at an entrance fee of £3.00.

Website: www.nwc.org.uk

The interest of British garden enthusiasts is such that they are willing to travel far to see unusual plants in beautiful settings. This has led to the development of specialist tours, and even cruises, by the travel operators to meet this demand. Already in the 1970s, the famed garden expert Percy Thrower had launched garden breaks at the Imperial Hotel in Torquay, a base from which a number of striking gardens can be visited in Devon and Cornwall. Today, garden tours are organized by a number of leading operators, including Gardeners' Delight Holidays, Saga Holidays and Page & Moy. Popular destinations include gardens in the Azores, the Indian Ocean, South Africa and New Zealand; while tours of Arab-influenced gardens in Andalucia, Spain, are also becoming popular. British gardening enthusiasts' growing awareness of Bonsai and Japanese landscape design is leading to small groups travelling to visit the gardens of Japan.

Garden festivals (strictly speaking, event attractions) are also popular tourist attractions in Germany, France and the Netherlands. A national garden festival is held in Germany every two years, and the 2005 event, the Munich Flower Festival, forecast in excess of four million visitors to its 190-hectare site. France, too, benefits significantly from garden tourism, from their formal gardens attached to chateaux in the Loire valley to Monet's garden at Giverny, which has become a major international tourist attraction since its restoration (see Plate 11). North America also has its share of notable garden attractions; perhaps the most famous are the Butchart Gardens on Victoria Island, British Columbia in Canada; but popular and much-visited botanic gardens in the US include the Denver Botanic Gardens in Colorado and Longwood Gardens, a thousand-acre site founded by the du Pont family at Kennett Square, Pennsylvania, which attracts over 900,000 visitors a year.

Britain itself mounted a succession of garden festivals over an eight-year period at the following sites:

Liverpool	1984
Stoke on Trent	1986
Glasgow	1988
Gateshead	1990
Ebbw Vale	1992

Although highly successful, they offered little long-term benefit to their communities, as for the most part they failed to attract visitors to the surrounding areas, and at the end of the year the sites were landscaped or developed, unlike the Dutch Garden Festivals, in which the entire gardens are donated as regional parks to the communities in which they are constructed.

Theme and amusement parks

Purpose-built leisure parks are, not surprisingly, major attractions for tourism, receiving the greatest number of visitors. The appetite for leisure parks to entertain the public seems never-ending, and in Europe these have a very long history. Bakken, near Copenhagen, lays claim to being the oldest amusement park in the world, having opened in 1583. London's Vauxhall Gardens opened in 1661, followed in the eighteenth century by Ranelagh Gardens and the Tivoli Gardens in Paris. By the nineteenth century, entertainment parks were firmly established, with the Tivoli Gardens in Copenhagen, which first opened in 1843, soon becoming one of the world's leading centres of entertainment. This park continues to attract over four million visitors annually. Blackpool Pleasure Beach, Britain's first seaside entertainment centre, opened in 1896 and is still the most visited tourist site in the country.

The world's biggest amusement park became established at around the same time at Coney Island, in the Brooklyn borough of New York City. The world's first roller coaster had been built here in 1884, and by 1895 an indoor amusement park, Sea Lion Park, had been added. Eventually, three separate parks, Luna Park, Steeplechase Park and Dreamland, opened on this seaside site between 1897 and 1904, with up to 250,000 visitors a day. A succession of fires destroyed two of these parks, but Luna Park remained popular until its decline after the Wall Street crash in 1929, after which it struggled to survive until finally closing in 1944. In Australia, a Luna Park was built in Melbourne in 1912, followed by one in Sydney in 1935.

The 1920s were the heyday of these amusement parks. The Great Depression caused attendances to decline until a new generation of theme parks arrived in the 1950s.

Although de Efteling was opened in Europe as early as 1951 with a 'fairy tales' theme, and Bellewaerde Park followed in 1954, it was the Walt Disney Corporation which popularized the concept of the theme park in their development at Anaheim, California in 1955, which was to invigorate the market. This was followed by a major Disney development near Orlando in Florida, opened in 1971, which attracted tourists from all over the world.

Today, the modern amusement parks fall into two distinct groups, theme parks and amusement parks, and can be classified according to size, into three distinct categories:

1 local parks, catering largely to the day-tripper market;

2 flagship attractions, such as the Tivoli or Prater, Vienna, which draw on national markets and a significant number of foreign visitors;

3 icons, or destination parks, such as those of the Disney empire, which have become destinations in their own right and attract a worldwide market.

Among the latter, the four Disney parks in Florida, together with those near Tokyo and Paris, were attracting well over 80 million visitors by the end of the 1990s. Disney has since opened a further park adjacent to its Anaheim site in California, entitled California Adventure, to enhance the appeal of its first Disneyland complex. Disneyland Resort Paris, first opened in 1992, has similarly expanded, and now includes Walt Disney Studio Park and Disney Village. Tokyo Disney opened in 1993, and a further site opened in Hong Kong in 2005; there are discussions under way which may lead to another being built in mainland China (probably Shanghai) by 2010.

The USA alone boasts over 750 leisure parks, attracting over 300 million visitors a year. The clustering and scale of several of these attractions in one region of Florida, around Orlando, has given the European tourism industry the scope to develop package holidays focused on this region; visitors tend to spend several days in visiting the parks, allowing the construction of a huge bed stock approaching 100,000 rooms.

Example The Disney Resort, Paris

The initial problems Disney faced when expanding its concept into Europe make for an interesting case history in theme park management. Disney decided to build at a site near Paris, accessible to the largest European market – some 17 million people reside within two hours' drive of the site – rather than near Barcelona in Spain, partly due to subsidies promised by the French government. However, this decision ignored the inclement weather of northern Europe, which made it far more difficult to attract a market in the winter months. Disney also misjudged its market; the French resented the encroachment of American culture and initially proved more resistant to the attraction than the British and German markets, particularly as French tastes were not catered for (Disney failed to serve alcohol in its restaurants, in common with its practice in the USA, although the French traditionally enjoy a glass of wine with their meals). By adding more all-weather attractions and applying for licences to serve alcoholic beverages, Disney was able to improve its appeal to the French, who now make up about half of all visitors. However, additional investment in the site has not produced the turnover forecast, and the park is struggling to prove its long-term viability.

In Europe there are some 225 parks represented by Europarks, the Federation of National Associations of Leisure Parks and Attractions in Europe, which together attract around 180 million visitors annually. European parks tend to be smaller, and have lower investment in both development and marketing than do the Disney parks, but do not attempt to compete directly with them. Rather, they draw on mainly national markets, but the handful of major parks do compete for international visitors.

Figure 10.7 identifies the major Continental sites and the larger UK sites. A number of the leading British theme parks attract over a million visitors every year, with Alton Towers in Staffordshire by far the biggest crowd-puller with over 2.6 million visitors. Other notable attractions include the Chessington World of Adventures; Flamingoland in North Yorkshire; American Adventure World near Ilkeston in Derbyshire; Lightwater Valley near Ripon, North Yorkshire; Frontierland in Morecambe, Lancashire; Thorpe Park in Surrey; and Pleasurewood Hills, near Lowestoft in Suffolk. Entry numbers for several of these exceed a million people each year, but it is questionable how many more such major attractions can be built and become viable. Several big planned projects in recent years, including the massive Wonderland theme park planned as part of the redevelopment of the Corby steel mills site, have been abandoned or have not yet proceeded because of difficulty in raising capital. Britain also suffers from a poor winter for outside events, and many attractions do not attempt to remain open year-round.

The distinction between a theme park and an amusement park is not always a clear one, although the former is rather loosely based on some theme, whether geographical, historical or based on some other concept. The future is a popular theme, as it can allow the development to focus on advanced technology to attract the public. One of the most recent examples in Europe is that of Planete Futuroscope, near Poitiers in France, where imaginative architecture of the future is combined with advanced technology; to cite one example, theatre seats are fitted with hydraulic jacks which move in sympathy with what is showing on the screen, so that sporting events such as whitewater rafting can be experienced as well as observed. The park attracted over a million visitors in its first year, 95 per cent of whom were French.

European theme park operators are searching constantly for new themes that will draw the crowds. Germany, which has long enjoyed a love affair with America's Wild West (largely through the popular western novels of Karl May) opened a new park, Silver Lake City in 2004 near Berlin, based on images projected by Hollywood films over the past century. Spyland, which is to open in 2007 south of Lyons in France, will include a history of espionage, and accounts of the exploits of the intelligence services. There are plans for an annual espionage film festival.

Before the development of new theming concepts, the predominant aim of the leisure park was to entertain by means of the traditional funfair, with stalls, helter-skelters, candy floss and other trappings familiar for many decades to the funfair market. Later, parks began vying with one another to devise new rides, and to challenge younger visitors by incorporating ever more frightening 'white-knuckle' experiences in the major centrepieces. With the introduction of the new theme parks, while amusement rides remained an important element, the ability to theme these (such as by associating the park with popular cartoon characters like those at Parc Asterix and Disney) heightens the attraction for many. Building on the popularity of film and TV characters among younger visitors is important for a market that is composed chiefly of family groups.

Figure 10.7 Major theme parks in Europe

Table 10.3 Some leading rides in Britain and the rest of the world

Apocalypse, Maelstrom and Shockwave	Drayton Manor, Staffordshire
Nemesis, Oblivion and Rita – Queen of Speed	Alton Towers, Staffordshire
Magnum Force	Flamingoland, Kirby Misperton, North Yorkshire
G Force and Jubilee Odyssey	Fantasyland, Skegness, Lincs
MegaFobia	Oakwood Park, Pembrokeshire
Pepsi Max Big One and Grand National	Blackpool Pleasure Beach, Lancs
Colossus, Tidal Wave and Nemesis Inferno, Rush and Slammer	Thorpe Park, Surrey
Space Shot	Pleasureland, Southport, Lancs
Silver Star	Europark, near Rust, Germany
Dodonpa roller coaster	Fujikyu Highland Park, Fuji-Yoshida-shi, Japan
Steel Dragon 2000	Nagashima Spaland, Mie, Japan
Superman the Escape	Six Flags Magic Mountain, Valencia, California, USA
Top Thrill Dragster	Cedar Point Amusement Park, Sandusky, Ohio, USA
Big Shot Stratosphere Tower	Las Vegas, Nevada, USA
SheiKra	Busch Gardens, Florida, USA
Perilous Plunge	Knotts Berry Farm, Buena Park, Los Angeles, California, USA
Adventures of Spiderman	Islands of Adventure, Orlando, Florida, USA
Tonnerre de Zeus	Parc Asterix, near Paris, France
Thunder Coaster	Tusanfryd, Norway

'Crowd pullers' are now a principal ingredient in the promotion of all major parks today, and this means ever more capital investment (of the order of 5–10 per cent per annum), particularly in gravity-defying rides. Some indication of their popularity will be seen from Table 10.3 identifying some of the important rides in major theme parks. This list is unlikely to be comprehensive: new rides are constantly being invented and introduced to better the 'tallest', 'longest' and 'fastest' that currently exist.

Mention should also be made of the success of Lego in developing its own form of theme park in Europe. The global appeal of this children's 'building brick' toy enabled the company to expand the brand to Legoland parks first in its country of origin, at Billund in Denmark, and later to England (at Windsor), Günzburg, Germany and Carlsbad, California. The sheer scale of these developments is on a level with the major theme parks and in terms of visitor numbers they count among the more important tourism attractions in their countries.

On a much smaller scale, there are innumerable other 'model village' type attractions scattered around Britain, usually based in popular tourist destinations to appeal to visitors as impulse purchases. These form just one group of small attractions which generally receive little attention from academics, or support from public-sector bodies, and include other forms of tourist entertainment like amusement arcades, model railways, waxworks (including increasingly popular 'dungeon' settings) and similar small commercial exhibitions. They may be indoor or outdoor attractions, and together they make up the largest proportion of the attractions business; it would therefore be wrong to ignore their importance within the organizational structure of the industry, even though, for many, income may be only a tiny fraction of that of the major amusement parks. Like the smallest museums, their very existence is tenuous, often depending upon the commitment of owner-managers and their families, and a voluntary labour force.

Wildlife attractions

Wildlife is a growing attraction for tourists, and the industry has responded in different ways to meet this interest. At one time, the most common way for tourists to see wild animals would be in the numerous zoos which exist in most countries around the world. The keeping of collections of animals goes back at least two thousand years, but the present-day concept of a zoo dates back only to the eighteenth century. In Britain, although zoos are known to predate the turn of the nineteenth century, the founding of the Zoological Society in London by Sir Stamford Raffles at the beginning of that century led to the interest which Victorian England took in caged animals.

Today there are some nine hundred established zoos around the world, but attitudes to zoos have changed, as people in Western countries have come to consider it cruel to keep animals in captivity. Nevertheless, zoos still enjoy high attendance figures, although not at the peaks to be found 30 years ago, and they are adapting to the new perspective by stressing their curatorial role in preserving rare species of wildlife, rather than the former emphasis on displaying animals for the purpose of entertainment. There was a fear at the end of the 1980s, as attendances fell, that London's famous zoo in Regent's Park might be forced to close. Although that fear receded with a massive private investment of capital, this sharpened awareness of zoos as a whole in Britain, renewing interest in visiting them, and encouraging the construction of better facilities to keep the animals in settings of less constraint.

With the growth of long-haul travel, more tourists are taking advantage of the opportunity to see these animals in the wild, usually in safari parks, of which the best known are situated in South and East Africa, and can be seen in Figure 9.9 in the previous chapter. Some of these big-game parks have become world famous, including Kenya's Masai Mara, Tsavo, Amboseli and Samburu Parks, Tanzania's Serengeti National Park and South Africa's Kruger National Park. The attraction of these parks lies in the opportunity to see big game such as lion, elephant, leopard, buffalo and rhino, the so-called 'big five' (although poaching is rapidly diminishing the last of these). All of these parks feature in tour operators' long-haul programmes, although political uncertainty in many African countries, and the lack of tourism investment in Tanzania, has hindered the expansion of tourism to the safaris parks in recent years. This has, however, benefited some lesser-known parks in countries like Botswana.

With the decline in zoo attendance, there have been some efforts to introduce the atmosphere of the safari park in Britain, notably at the Marquess of Bath's property at Longleat in Wiltshire. Running costs for such projects are high, taking into account the need for maximum security to protect visitors; another safari park at Windsor was attracting close to a million visitors a year, but still proved a financial failure, closing in 1992.

Another form of wildlife park is the wildfowl reserve. Ornithology is a popular pastime in Britain, and the Wildfowl Trust at Slimbridge in Gloucestershire has been a model for other sites around the country, where birds can be viewed in their natural setting. Other attractions, for which tourism is a secondary consideration in some cases, include falconry centres and owl sanctuaries; while sanctuaries for other specific animals have been built in a number of places in Britain, an example being the seal sanctuary at Gweek in Cornwall. Sanctuaries, of course, exist to protect animals and to tend to wounded animals, but most are open to visitors, who make a useful contribution, through admission fees, to the running costs of the project.

Bird-watching in particular is attracting the specialist long-haul market, with tour operators such as Naturtrek and Birdquest among a number offering specialist holidays for the study of bird life, frequently accompanied by well-known ornithological experts who will lecture to clients en route.

Finally, reference should be made in this section to the popularity of aquaria (now more commonly known as sealife centres), both in Britain and elsewhere. The popular revulsion against keeping animals in cages has not yet generally extended to fish (and although there are movements to close down entertainments incorporating captive sea-water mammals like porpoises and dolphins, these remain popular in the USA). Some notable sea-life centres have been constructed in Britain, such as the London Aquarium, The Deep in Hull, the National Maritime Aquarium in Plymouth and the National Sealife Centre in Birmingham – and plans have been revealed by the National Institution for Research into Aquatic Habitats to build the world's largest aquarium near Stewartby, Bedfordshire. This 40-acre site will be eight times larger than the current world leader in Osaka, Japan. On the Continent, the Sea Life Centre in Paris and Nausicaa, le Centre Nationale de la Mer, in Boulogne are two popular recent additions to the theme. Many such centres have been constructed in the USA – that at Monterey in California is of particular note, both for the size of the tanks (one of which includes a full-scale kelp forest) and for a unique pen with direct access to the Pacific Ocean, which allows sea otters to swim into and out of the setting at will.

Cultural tourism

Cultural tourism – however that is defined – is one of the fastest growing areas of tourism. In its widest definition, it encompasses both 'high' and 'low' culture. The so-called 'high arts' in all their forms – fine arts, decorative arts, architecture. classical forms of music, theatre and literature – are matched by 'popular culture' attractions which will include sports and popular music, along with traditional forms of entertainment like folk-dancing, gastronomy and handicraft. In post-modern societies, these former divisions between 'high' and 'low' culture have become increasingly artificial, and certainly will have little relevance to the study of tourism, where the industry has become adept at packaging and popularizing culture in all its forms.

Example   The theatre and tourism in Britain

In 2004, the Arts Council estimated that theatres contributed some £2.6 billion to the UK economy, of which £1.5 billion accrued in London's West End alone. Against this, public subsidy for the theatre amounted to only £121.3 million, representing an outstanding return on the investment of public money. Tourists make up a substantial proportion of the audience for theatres in Britain, especially in London, which specifically attracts out-of-season tourists to its cornucopia of theatrical performances.

France, noted for its predominance in the fine-art field, has packaged art trails covering Cézanne's sites at Aix-en-Provence, Monet's garden at Giverny (Plate 11), and areas associated with Gauguin, Manet, Renoir, Dégas, Pissaro and Sisley. Embracing wider tours, the 'circuit Pissaro–Cézanne' and 'circuit Toulouse-Lautrec' have proved popular for cultural tourists. Where a place is popularly identified with an author or artist, tourist interest follows automatically; where the link is less well established, it can still be built upon. The poet Dylan Thomas's disparaging comments about the town and people of Laugharne have not stopped a steady flow of 25,000 visitors annually to the Boathouse where he lived between 1949 and 1953, in spite of the locals' preference to play down this link, while by contrast the towns of Rochester and Broadstairs in Kent have both traded on their links with Victorian author Charles Dickens. Elsewhere in Britain, numerous other associations exist between literary settings and tourist destinations with clearly defined 'trails', for example those between Thomas Hardy and Wessex, and Laurie Lee and Gloucestershire. Brontë country in Yorkshire offers 'Great British Literary Tours', while the popularity of Jane Austen's books, and subsequent visits to associated sites following their translation to film, is noteworthy. South West Tourism promptly published a map covering eighty-nine film and TV locations in six counties.

A discussion of all the different forms of cultural attraction, ranging from 'high' to 'low' culture, would be far too extensive to be examined in any detail in this text, and the reader is directed to the many recent publications which focus on this sector to gain greater knowledge of the many forms which this takes, and the issues arising from each[5]. This chapter will serve as an introduction to the topic by highlighting some of the variety of cultural activities available which have become important for tourism.

Museums and art galleries

Both museums and art galleries are visited by huge numbers of tourists each year. Many are established primarily to serve the needs of the local inhabitants, at least initially, but others quickly gained international reputations. Examples of the latter include the British Museum in London, the Ashmolean Museum in Oxford, the Louvre in Paris, the Smithsonian Museum in Washington DC and the Museum of Modern Art (MoMA) in New York. The significance of these for tourism is that they can act as a catalyst for a destination, and in some cases become the major reason for a visit to the destination, especially in cases where outstanding exhibitions are on show.

Museums have a very long history, and in Britain date back to at least the seventeenth century, when some private collectors opened their exhibitions for a fee. John Tradescant's Cabinet of Curiosities provided the foundation for the Ashmolean Museum at Oxford University in 1683. The equally famous Fitzwilliam Museum art collection at Cambridge did not follow until 1816. In Britain now, there are well over 3,000 museums, and of the 1,300 listed in the *Cambridge Guide to Museums*, there are 180 in London alone.

There are six categories of museum in Britain:

1 *National museums*, which are usually funded directly by the Department for Culture, Media and Sport (DCMS) and include such famous museums as the British Museum, the National Gallery, the Tate Britain and Tate Modern art galleries, the Victoria and Albert Museum, the Imperial War Museum and the Royal Armouries, Leeds. Certain national museums are funded by the Ministry of Defence, such as the RAF Museum in Hendon, and the National Army Museum, both in London.

2 *Independent (charitable trust) museums*, financed by turnover; the National Motor Museum at Beaulieu is an example.

3 *Independent non-charity museums*, such as Flambards Museum in Helston, Cornwall. Some university collections are funded indirectly by the Department for Education and Skills.

4 *Regional museums*, which are funded publicly, or by a mix of public and private funding. The DCMS also funds museums such as the Geffrye and Horniman Museums in London and the Museum of Science and Industry in Manchester.

5 *Local authority museums*, such as the Cotswold Countryside Museum in Gloucester, and the Georgian House and Red Lodge Museums, owned by Bristol City Council.

6 *Small, private museums*, which depend entirely upon private funding.

Museums have experienced two boom periods in recent history, first during the period between 1970 and the mid-1980s, when many of them were able to take advantage of government-grant aid, coupled with charitable status which avoided taxation, and later, in the lead up to the millennium celebrations, through Millennium Commission funding or Lottery grants. In the initial stage, a large number of redundant buildings, ideal for conversion into museums, became available, and the nostalgia boom and a generally positive view towards urban renewal and heritage all encouraged new museums to open. In the second stage, funding tended to favour larger projects.

The problem for those who manage museums is that the initial capital investment is not the only financial consideration. Indeed, many collections are donated, or gifts of money are made to establish a museum, but steadily rising operating costs are seldom met by increases in revenue, and after the first two or three years, during which time the museum has novelty value, attendance figures slump. As new museums are opened, so the available market to visit them is more thinly spread. Museums have also been badly hit in recent years by the consequences of the Education Reform Act, which has made the financing of educational visits – the core business for many museums – more difficult.

Figure 10.8
Barlach Haus
Museum in
Hamburg,
Germany,
displays works
of the renowned
twentieth-
century sculptor

(Photographed by the author)

Many museum curators argue in favour of subsidies, on the grounds that their museums help to bring tourists into an area, where they can be encouraged to spend. Certainly, clusters of museums and other complementary attractions such as shops do give rise to greater tourism demand. The Castlefield site at Manchester is a good example of a 'critical mass' of attractions sited close together which makes the destination an attractive day out. Conference and exhibition halls have long been underwritten by local authorities on just these grounds, but local authorities are today much more constrained financially, and in some cases have been forced to reduce the support they formerly provided to the museums in their territory. This has led to winter closures in some cases, or more restricted times of opening. Museums have become increasingly self-sufficient, and their curatorial role is now less significant than their marketing one. The national museums in London were briefly obliged to introduce charges, or at very least 'suggested contributions', in the 1990s, resulting in a very sharp drop in attendance, while those that did not introduce charges benefited. However, those deciding to charge were able to invest in refurbishing which, with government subsidies alone, would not have been possible. Since the obligation to charge was removed, these galleries have experienced an upsurge in attendance, and it is notable that seven of the top ten most visited attractions in Britain are museums or art galleries (see Table 10.4).

As a result of the reduction or withdrawal of public funding, museums have been obliged to become increasingly commercial in their approach. Buildings are redesigned

Table 10.4 ALVA attractions with over 1 million admissions in 2004

Blackpool Pleasure Beach	6,200,000
National Gallery, London	4,959,946
British Museum	4,868,176
Tate Modern	4,441,225
Natural History Museum	3,250,376
British Airways London Eye	3,700,000 (c)
Science Museum	2,154,366
Tower of London	2,135,204 (c)
Victoria and Albert Museum	2,010,825
National Portrait Gallery	1,516,402 (pt c)
National Maritime Museum	1,507,950
Legoland Windsor	1,369,308 (c)
Edinburgh Castle	1,243,304 (c)
Eden Project	1,223,959 (c)
Chester Zoo	1,161,684 (pt c)
Canterbury Cathedral	1,091,684 (pt c)
Royal Botanical Gardens, Kew	1,090,445 (c)
Westminster Abbey	1,036,918 (pt c)
Roman Baths and Pump Room, Bath	1,010,769 (c)

(c) charge for entry   (pt c) charge for entry to some areas or exhibitions
Source: Association of Leading Visitor Attractions www.alva.org.uk/visitor_statistics

to ensure that all visitors exit via the shop, and investigations are made into what sells or fails to sell, and into price-sensitivity. Galleries are hired for private functions, sponsorship is sought to finance exhibitions – and sometimes even whole galleries (such as the Annenberg and Hutong Galleries at the British Museum). Catering also has become an important money-raiser, with increasing emphasis placed on the location and design of cafés and restaurants. All principal museums in Britain are now expected to engage in fund-raising, both publicly and through their memberships and friends' associations.

Museums not sited close to major centres of population, or with poor accessibility, generally find it difficult to attract tourists in large numbers. One notable exception, to which repeated references have been made in this text, has been the Guggenheim in Bilbao, which rapidly became an authentic cultural icon soon after its construction.

Example   The Guggenheim, Bilbao

It is interesting to compare the success of the Guggenheim Museum in Bilbao with the picture in Britain. The Guggenheim received very strong public-sector support and significant financial aid from the Guggenheim Foundation, and had the foresight to contract an outstanding architect, Frank Gehry, to design the unconventional building. The result was that tourists beat a path to its door, even though Bilbao was not a traditional tourist destination and had, at least at that point, little else to attract the tourist. Bilbao now enjoys success as a strong short-break destination.

To attract new audiences, and bring back former visitors, many museums are moving away from the concept of 'objects in glass cases' in favour of better interpretation and more active participation by the visitors. New techniques include guides dressed in period costume, audio-visual displays, self-guided trails using cassette tapes, reconstructions of the past, and interactive programmes which provide opportunities for hands-on experience. In the kitchen of the oldest house in Toronto, to take one example, the guide demonstrates the making of soap, provides souvenirs of the finished product to the visitors, and reveals that the soap can be eaten, too! Some museums are fully interactive, such as the new Explore at Bristol Museum, which is designed to explain science to the lay visitor by giving them the opportunity to become involved in practical experiments. At the Big Pit Mining Museum in Blaenavon, a former colliery transformed into a mining museum in 1980 and now a World Heritage Site, former miners act as guides, providing vividly illustrated tours which draw on their own former experiences in the mines. In a similar manner, former inmates interned by the KGB at their headquarters in Vilnius, Lithuania, now act as guides at the site, which has become a KGB museum. An example of a 'living history' museum can be found at Llancaiach Fawr Manor, a sixteenth-century fortified house in the South Wales valleys. Here, actor/interpreters (more correctly referred to on the Continent as 'animateurs') dressed in costumes of the period, guide visitors around the site, using the language and speech patterns of the time and authentically recreating the year 1645.

It is debatable what distinguishes a 'museum' from an 'attraction'. Many museums, for example, are the former homes of famous people, and the trustees have a curatorial and research role in safeguarding and investigating documents of the previous owner, as well as encouraging tourist trade for commercial reasons. A good example of this is Graceland, the former home of Elvis Presley in Memphis, Tennessee which, long after the star's death, continues to attract huge crowds of fans to see his house, his former possessions and his grave – especially in the year 2005, the seventieth anniversary of his birth (see Figure 10.9). Graceland has become one of the major tourist attractions in the United States, and is listed in the National Register of Historic Places; with over 700,000 visitors annually, it is now second only to the White House itself in terms of annual visits. It cannot be purely coincidental that the murder of French actress Marie de Trintignant, murdered in Vilnius by her lover while filming *Colette* in 2003 (an episode widely reported in the French media, along with some helpful travel background to the country) was followed by a sudden and rapid rise in French visitors to the Lithuanian capital.

Culture, the media and tourism

The growing interplay between culture, the media and tourism deserves specific mention, given the extent to which the tourism industry is now exploiting for its own ends consumer interest in sites associated with 'celebrities'.

A noteworthy aspect of post-modern culture is the fascination which fame, however transient, holds for the masses, as witnessed by the appeal of reality shows on television which guarantee minor celebrities instant fame. Tourism destinations have not been slow to exploit opportunities for publicity in the media, especially cinema and television, either by promoting the sites associated with these celebrities, or offering

(Photographed by the author)

inducements to film within their territory – and in many cases, governments have col-luded with local authorities and the private sector by directly subsidizing the media's production costs, well aware that the publicity engendered by global distribution of a film or television programme will generate tourist interest. In Britain, the National Trust now actively solicits film companies for its sites, following the success of their heritage buildings when used as sites for costume dramas: Lyme Park, near Stockport, the setting for the popular BBC film of Jane Austen's *Pride and Prejudice*, experienced a 178 per cent increase in visitors following the drama's showing on British TV.

Tourist offices all over the world are producing 'film maps' listing sites which appear in popular films – among them, 24 London locations for the film *Love Actually*. New York City has *Sex and the City* and *Seinfeld* tours. *Master and Commander*, featuring Russell Crowe, is the focus for a map listing 20 locations, including Portsmouth, Hartlepool and Whitby – conveniently linked to the maritime heritage theme of 2005. The film *The Italian Job* has a cult following, to the extent that bespoke tours to the sites in Turin where it was filmed are now organized (www.italianjob-tour.com).

The enormous popularity of the Harry Potter films has vastly expanded travel to sites associated with the films in England, including Gloucester Cathedral, Goathland Station (Hogsmeade) and Alnwick Castle (Hogwarts School of Witchcraft). Again, the tourist office stepped in, with 'Discover the Magic of Britain' maps and themed tours. Domestic tourism to the North East was boosted by the television series *Last of the Summer Wine* and *Heartbeat*, both filmed on the Yorkshire Moors, while Turville in

Bucks, the setting for the popular TV series *The Vicar of Dibley*, quickly became a featured destination on the tourist trail.

The popularity of certain cult films will guarantee a steady audience of aficionados to the locations where the films were shot. The enduring 1945 film *Brief Encounter*, shot at Carnforth railway station in Lancashire, has enticed so many tourists (more than 100,000 annually), some from as far afield as Japan, that Railtrack (now Network Rail) considered the possibility of creating a theme park at the fast-deteriorating site. The long-standing popularity of the film *The Railway Children* (remade as a BBC-TV film in 2000), which featured the Keighley and Worth Valley Steam Railway in West Yorkshire, led to that company promoting its 'Railway Children' connections through leaflets, advertising and special events. In France, Provence tourist authorities have established a 'Marcel Pagnol route' to popularize the locations at which the French film *Manon des Sources* was filmed.

The power of Hollywood is of course most noted in its own territory, and tourists both domestic and foreign flock to scenes filmed in the United States. To cite recent examples of areas that formerly drew few tourists and now, as a result of popular films, attract many: the general store in Juliette, Georgia, was the setting for the Whistlestop Café in *Fried Green Tomatoes*, and has now become a tourist attraction in its own right. North Carolina, and especially the area around Asheville, has been blessed as the setting for numerous films in recent years, including *Cold Mountain, The Last of the Mohicans, Forrest Gump and Hannibal*, and the State has actively promoted these settings in their marketing campaigns. The US tourism authorities ran a TV promotion in Britain during the winter of 2004/5 with the strapline 'You've seen the films, now visit the sets', backed by scenes from famous films like *Thelma and Louise*.

Entire regions and countries can be similarly boosted by media exposure. Notable in recent years has been the New Zealand Government's exploitation of the *Lord of the Rings* cycle, with advertising directed to film locations like Matamata (Tolkien's Plains of Gorgoroth), Tongariro National Park and Nelson (the fact that Tolkien actually based Gorgoroth on the Ribble Valley area in England is conveniently overlooked!). Tunisia, where *Star Wars*, *Raiders of the Lost Ark* and *The English Patient* were filmed, has actively solicited film work and their tourism authority helped to develop an 'English Patient Route' for tourists. This phenomenon is not limited to Western settings and audiences. Bae Yong Joon, now known to fans as Prince Yong and the hero of the South Korean TV drama *Winter Sonata*, which has a huge following in Japan, made the country an acceptable destination for Japanese mass tourism, with a 10 per cent increase in visitors in 2003. Packages which included visits to locations in the star's films sold well.

These are just a handful of examples to demonstrate the power of the media in influencing tourism, a factor that is, for the most part, fully taken into account and built upon by tourism authorities today in their efforts to promote 'cultural tourism'. There are worries, however, when these films are made in remote beauty spots which subsequently attract large numbers of tourists. Khao Phingkan in Thailand was the setting for the James Bond film *The Man with the Golden Gun*. This ideal setting was rapidly destroyed by unplanned tourism development. As we have seen earlier, a similar fate befell Maya Bay on Phi Phi Ley Island, following the popularity of *The Beach*, which starred Leonardo di Caprio (and arguably, as much damage is done by the film crew at these locations as by subsequent tourism).

Religious tourism

Travel for religious purposes tends to be grouped among the 'miscellaneous' forms of tourism, falling outside the central purposes of leisure or business. It would be unfair to dismiss it lightly, however; it represents a most important feature in the worldwide movement of tourists, not least the millions who follow the faith of Islam and make the obligatory once-in-a-lifetime pilgrimage to Mecca, the birthplace of Mohammed in Saudi Arabia. If taken at the time of Ramadan, this is known as the Great Pilgrimage, or Hadj; at other times, Umrah, or the Lesser Pilgrimage, attracts tourists through eleven months of the year. While the hundreds of thousands who visit Mecca every year can be said to be visiting an attraction, the Kaaba or temple, the trip itself is viewed as an obligation arising out of the faith, rather than a pleasure trip. However, it brings substantial financial and commercial benefits to the country which caters to these tourists. Medina, the second city of the Islamic faith, also attracts religious tourists, while Christians, Jews and Muslims alike are drawn to Jerusalem for its historical importance to all three religions. Other prominent religious destinations include the Vatican, St Katherine's monastery (often linked with visits to Petra in Jordan for package tours), Assisi, Lourdes, Amritsar and Varanasi in India. Each will have its own attractions associated with the religion, but the purpose of the visit is in the sense of place, and perhaps the opportunity to touch a holy site like the Wailing Wall or the tomb of a religious leader. Many observers believe that popular culture gives expression to emotions formerly reserved for faith, as secular mass tourists visit the grave sites of their idols, or sites with which they are associated or met their death.

Figure 10.10
Kevelaer, Germany, is a site of pilgrimage for Catholics, predominantly from India and the Far East

(Photographed by the author)

Specialist operators exist to provide for religious tourism. Tours are often accompanied by spiritual leaders, and in one sense can be defined as educational tourism, while in other instances (such as pilgrimages to Lourdes, to seek intercession for a cure) the motive comes closer to health tourism.

It is debatable in which category to include the religious theme parks which are now appearing. First introduced in the United States, their appeal is now spreading, and plans to construct a Christian theme park in Yorkshire, to be known as Ark Alive, were announced in 2005, subject to funds becoming available – cost is estimated to be around £144 million. Part educational, part missionary, part entertainment and quasi-history, these parks appear to be finding a new market for the curious and the committed alike.

Retail shopping

Shopping plays an important role in tourism. While retailing is not normally considered a sector of the industry, tourist purchases make up a considerable part of the revenue of many shops, and in resorts shops may be entirely or very largely dependent upon the tourist trade. Shops selling postcards, souvenirs or local craft are often geared specifically to the needs of visitors, and out of season may close down for lack of demand.

Cross-border tourism is fuelled by shopping expeditions, and where large discrepancies in prices are noted on each side of the border, authorities often impose limits on purchases that can be transported back into the home country. For several years, the German and Austrian governments were concerned about cross-border shopping into Poland, the Czech and Slovak Republics and Hungary; now these countries have joined the EU, the concern has shifted to governments in those countries concerned about shopping expeditions into the Ukraine, Russia and Romania (although an obligation to obtain visas for entry into Russia acts as a hindrance). The EU limit on importations of goods from non-EU countries has remained at £145 since 1994 in an effort to restrain this shopping – although with a weakening dollar, goods bought in the USA are still cheap even after paying duty. However, with virtually no limit on the transfer of goods between EU countries, shopping expeditions cross-Channel from England to Calais, across the Baltic from Helsinki to Tallinn and across the Oder from Germany into Poland are a major factor contributing to statistical growth in tourism between these countries.

Tourist cities like London, Paris, Rome and New York owe much of their popularity to the quality of their shops, greatly benefiting from the flood of visitors they receive from overseas, many of whom come to take advantage of sales periods or beneficial rates of exchange. To take one recent example, the relative value of the pound against the dollar was responsible for a substantial increase in shopping expeditions from Britain to New York in the run-up to Christmas 2004. Similarly, many Britons make their way to the French supermarkets to stock up on alcohol and cigarettes, as well as cheaper food. Large department stores like Saks Fifth Avenue and Bloomingdales in New York, Kaufhaus des Westens (KaDeWe) in Berlin (claiming to be the largest store in the world) and Harrods in London are heavily dependent on visitor spend, and of course expenditure on shopping is an important feature in the tourism balance of payments.

The downside in small towns popular with tourism is that shops with products appealing to tourists can squeeze out those serving the more basic needs of residents, simply because they can afford spiralling rates and rents.

Increasingly, shopping is being combined with other forms of leisure in the development of shopping malls, which have become virtual mini-towns attracting huge numbers of visitors prepared to pass several hours enjoying themselves in an environment that encourages people to spend. Apart from shopping, amenities include restaurants, family entertainment and performance venues, all under cover (and often underground) to allow year-round visits – important in northern cities during the winter. Perhaps the outstanding example of this development is the Mall of America, built in 1992 at Bloomington, Minneapolis and claiming to be the second most visited site in the USA, with some 40 million visitors a year. At 4.2 million square feet, and offering 400 stores, 45 restaurants, 14 cinemas, a 7-acre amusement park and a miniature golf course, the site provides everything that the leisure shopper could hope for. It attracts a global market, and most notably brings in shoppers from both European and Asian cities. The enormous West Edmonton Mall in Canada, covering an area of 48 city blocks in downtown Edmonton, vies with this mall to draw consumers from all over the world, boasting more than 800 shops, 110 eating establishments and seven themed attractions. There are on-site hotels and events are mounted throughout the year. These are merely examples of the largest in a huge variety of 'leisure malls' designed to attract visitors. In all, America boasts some 228 malls attracting 55 million visitors annually, with a spend exceeding £8 billion. Some of these malls have more than 200 stores. Notably, eight of these malls have been built within easy reach of the theme park attractions at Orlando, Florida, and are clearly aimed to attract the tourist market.

In Britain, some towns have copied the American concept, and in recent instances have even gone as far as emulating the architecture of that continent, with 'New England' style themes such as that found at the Bicester Village shopping centre near Oxford. Bicester, and similar malls in Swindon, Wiltshire, and Ellesmere Port, South Wirral, have focused on the concept of 'designer outlets' selling up-market products which bring high-spend shoppers from some distances away. Others focus on size and choice, including such well-established sites as the Lakeside Shopping Centre at Thurrock, Essex, the Bluewater mall in Kent (with over 330 shops, see Figure 10.11) and Merry Hill Centre in Birmingham. 'Factory outlet' malls like those at Street in Somerset and Festival Park, Ebbw Vale in Wales offer direct sales to the public from manufacturers at discounts attractive enough to bring in tourists up to two hours' or more driving-distance away. The Gateshead Metro Centre is the largest in the UK, while Covent Garden in London, transformed from the site of a former fruit, flower and vegetable market, has been able to combine the appeal of a first-class tastefully restored set of nineteenth-century buildings with a shopping mall in the heart of London. The added attraction of round-the-clock events such as buskers has made this shopping facility an important addition to the visitor attractions in Britain's capital.

Some towns have established a reputation for their book shops, and building on this, they have marketed the town as a 'booktown' to avid book collectors and browsers. Hay-on-Wye was among the first to build on this reputation, in 1961, but

Figure 10.11
The Bluewater shopping mall near London, one of the largest in Britain

(Photographed by the author)

there are now around 20 such towns in existence, in the USA, Japan, Malaysia, across the Continent and at Wigtown in Scotland. Two purpose-built booktowns are Fjaerland in Norway and Blaenavon in Wales, the latter already possessing World Heritage status for its Big Pit mine.

Souvenirs

No study of tourist shopping would be complete without consideration of the role of souvenirs, an essential item in most visitors' purchasing. The collection of souvenirs as mementos of one's visit has a long history; certainly, both Greek and Roman tourists were noted for their collection of memorabilia from their journeys, and later, during the period of the Grand Tours, prestigious souvenirs collected by aristocratic travellers would invariably include Italian landscape paintings and archaeological 'finds'. Historians have commented on the collection of souvenirs from the earliest days of travel in North America, when 'items cut from local rock or wood, beaded moccasins, baskets and . . . miniature canoes' featured prominently among items taken home as mementos[6].

Today, we can divide souvenirs between those mementos picked up by tourists, often of little value in themselves but representative of the sites visited, and those which are bought commercially from shops or local traders. The former will include items like stones and shells collected on the beach, pressed flowers or leaves from jungles and parks, lava from volcanic eruptions, or small shards of broken pottery which abound on sites like those surrounding former Chinese emperors' tombs. For the most part, the collection of these items is harmless, although removing plants, flowers or seeds from parks and gardens is not an act to be encouraged, and is actively banned in areas where plants are under threat. Edelweiss in Switzerland, and cacti in Arizona have been protected by laws in this way. Similar laws prevent the collection of rare stones or fossilized trees, like those found in the Petrified Forest in Arizona. It was not uncommon in earlier centuries for travellers to chisel off small chunks of stone from monuments like Roman amphitheatres and the Egyptian Sphinx – or at very least, to deface them with graffiti – but in more enlightened times this practice is frowned on, and diminishing.

Commercial souvenirs are not only essential items of shopping for many tourists; for some, such as the Japanese, gifts are culturally obligatory, tourists buying mementos for their own use as well as numerous mementos of the trip for friends and relatives. This is one explanation for the relatively high spend of Japanese tourists abroad. Some commercial souvenirs are bestowed on visitors without charge, such as the Leis, garlands of flower, placed around the necks of visitors arriving in Hawaii. Visitors to China are often given small souvenirs of their visit, both while travelling within the country and when visiting sites like the Great Wall, Republic of China.

Example   The Dala Horse (*Dalahäst*)

Carving horses has been a traditional folk art in Sweden since at least 1624. The Dalecarlian horse, in its present form, has been hand-carved by the farmers of the Dalarna district in Sweden for over 200 years, painted in colours that are associated with traditional 'curbits' patterns. In 1928 two brothers, Nils and Janne Olsson, began producing colourful copies of the horse in their shed at Hemslöjd on the edge of Lake Siljan, near the village of Nusnäs. A giant model displayed at the New York World's Fair in 1939 popularized the design abroad, leading to a strong export market. It was not long before the horses, which have become a symbol of Sweden, were by far the most popular souvenirs for tourists to bring home. Their importance to the Swedish economy is such that production and design are now carefully controlled by the authorities. Most popular colour is the red traditionally associated with the Faluröd red paint used on houses in the region. The horses are sold at prices ranging from SEK54 for a miniature just 3 cms high to as much as SEK8250 for the biggest model, at 75 cms high.

Website: www.nohenslojd.se

The transmogrification of cheap baubles into indigenous craft purchased by tourists as souvenirs is characteristic of recent tourism, exemplified by such items as straw donkeys and flamenco dolls from Spain, brass Eiffel Towers from Paris, straw hats from the Caribbean Islands or Bali and bamboo models of cormorant fishers from China. While widely derided, these mementos still have a place in many tourists' homes, and in the minds and emotions of their purchasers they retain their association with the sites from which they originated. The name 'airport art' is frequently given to such debased craft on sale to tourists at airports, but the popularity of these items cannot be denied, and they make a valuable contribution to the economy of the countries where they are purchased.

Finally, the significance of postcards as essential purchases while abroad should not be overlooked. Since the advent of photography, the desire to send home to family, friends and neighbours pictures of destinations visited, has become a well-established ritual, the motives for which have frequently been questioned. Whether for social contact, out of a sense of obligation to those less fortunate, to demonstrate one-upmanship or simply to inform, the drive to send cards is universal, and, particularly among the developing countries, the cards are cherished equally by those receiving them, being pinned up on the walls of homes, offices and bars, signifying to others possession of a wide circle of well-travelled friends. Although modern technology now allows us to send home snaps taken on the mobile phone, there is something reassuring about the continuing popularity of the old-fashioned postcard, and its permanence is part of its attraction.

Gastronomic tourism

VisitBritain research has shown that half of all visitors to the UK cite food and drink as important to their holiday experience. Of course, eating and drinking has always been part of the enjoyment of a holiday, enhanced where the food and drink in question is exceptional and/or exotic, as is often the case on holidays abroad. The extent to which Britons have become more adventurous in their eating and drinking habits in their own country can be directly attributed to their experiences as tourists abroad. However, there are instances where the food and drink become the principal purpose of the trip, whether a short break or longer holiday. The reputation of French food and drink, to take one example, has led to this becoming a key attraction for many tourists to that country, and the importance of good – or at least reliable – cuisine abroad is often a priority concern, not least as a measure of health and safety.

Countries with well-established reputations for their food or drink have ensured that these attractions are promoted prominently in their tourism campaigns, whether informally or in the form of package tours. *Dégustation* in France is a widely recognized element in any tour of French vineyard regions, while distilleries in Scotland, breweries in Belgium, Germany and Denmark and bodegas in southern Spain have welcomed the tourist with opportunities for sampling and purchasing. Enhanced awareness of good food has led to more flexibility in packages, allowing tourists to 'eat around' either in partner hotels or in associated restaurants.

There is also a strong association between food and tourism within the UK, and the days when 'seaside rock' and fish and chips were the best known food products, and the quality of food served in hotels and restaurants was actually a disincentive to visit the country, are long gone. Starred restaurants, gastro-pubs, farmers' markets, even English wines are now gaining a reputation among overseas visitors, and regional tourism bodies have not been slow to adopt food as an attraction in its own right. At various points in the recent history of tourism, authorities have promoted 'Taste of

England/Wales/Scotland' campaigns, culminating in a recent 'Enjoy England, Taste England' promotion by VisitBritain, prominently featuring famous British chefs. No museum or heritage attraction of any size is today without its restaurant and shop, many of the latter selling food products grown or manufactured locally, such as Pontefract cakes, Kendal mint cakes and local ice-creams.

Example   Ludlow (see Case Study 7)

Ludlow in Shropshire has a population of just 10,000, but has succeeded in establishing an international reputation for the quality of its food, with several outstanding restaurants (two with Michelin stars) and many fine local shops, including no fewer than six butchers selling organic locally-produced meats. In 1995 a three-day Food and Drink Festival was launched, which includes an ale trail, festival loaves, cooking demonstrations and a popular regular feature, the 'sausage trail'. Food quality is monitored carefully to ensure consistency, and the event has become an important annual event in the tourism calendar, attracting around 17,000 visitors. There is now some danger of the event becoming a victim of its own success, as it draws many thousands of visitors into an already popular country town within easy reach of the heavily populated Midlands; the introduction of park-and-ride schemes during the event have helped to reduce the worst of the transport problems.

Interest in gastronomic tourism has been recently boosted by the development of the 'slow food' movement. This was initiated by an Italian journalist in 1986 who, distressed by the invasion of fast food in that country, determined to reinstate a concern for good traditional regional food. The slow food movement has spread rapidly through Europe, and now organizes tastings, themed dinners and visits, collecting and disseminating information about food and drink. Membership had already reached 80,000 at the time of writing, with 104 convivia (branches), including 13 in Britain.

Other site attractions

The scope for providing new attractions to feed the insatiable appetite of the tourist is never-ending, and would be quite impossible to cover fully in a single chapter. Sometimes attractions are unique within their destination, but share some common features with those in other areas or countries, thus offering scope for joint marketing schemes or twinning. An example of this is the Walled Towns Friendship Circle, established as a marketing association in 1992 by a group of European towns which benefit from one characteristic tourism attraction: an encircling fortification wall. Others depend upon a unique feature of the district, coupled with an imaginative initiative in marketing. For example, after the recent discovery of Cleopatra's sunken city adjacent to Alexandria Harbour, packages were organized to the site to allow tourists to dive and explore the ruins.

In general, the attractions we have been examining in this chapter up to this point have been permanent sites, available to the visitor at any time of the year. We will now turn to examine attractions of a more temporary nature, either arranged specifically to encourage tourism or sufficiently attractive to encourage tourists as well as locals to visit the site.

Events

Tourists will also visit a place in order to participate in, or observe, an event. In some cases, these events occur regularly and with some frequency (for example, the Changing of the Guard in London); in others, the events are intermittent, perhaps annually or even less frequently (e.g. arts festivals such as the Venice Bienniale, held every two years, the four-yearly Olympic Games, or the Floriade flower festival which takes place in a different Dutch city every decade). In other cases, they may be ad hoc arrangements to take advantage of a particular occasion. Such arrangements can last for as little as a few hours (e.g. a Christmas pageant or street festival), or many months (events associated with the Cities of Culture award, or those organized around a historic anniversary, e.g. Maritime Britain, commemorating the bicentennial anniversary of the Battle of Trafalgar in 1805). Anniversaries are crucial in this respect, whether of past events, as in Trafalgar, or of dates commemorating the birth or death of famous figures from the past. Tourist authorities will invariably look towards the fiftieth, sixtieth anniversaries or beyond and plan suitable events up to five years in advance; the sixtieth anniversary of the ending of World War II in 2005 is a case in point, and this was both commercially and politically exploited to the full. If a centenary or even longer anniversary is involved, and the individual concerned is internationally famous, this provides an excuse for a major festival in the home town or country to attract the foreign tourist. The 250th anniversary of Mozart's death in 2006 offered scope for a worldwide celebration, not least in his home town, Salzburg.

Example   Kaliningrad, Russia

The Russian enclave of Kaliningrad provided a curious opportunity for joint festivities in 2005, when the Germans celebrated the 750th anniversary of the founding of 'their' town, Konigsberg (the former name for the town), while the Russians celebrated the sixtieth anniversary of its fall to the Soviet army. Political compromise allowed the two countries separately to mark the occasion with renovation work, with the Germans paying for renovation of the cathedral, while the Russians built a new orthodox church and opened a space gallery to celebrate the number of cosmonauts who grew up in the area.

Events will draw people to an area which otherwise may have little to attract the tourist. They may also be mounted to increase the number of visitors to a destination, or to help spread tourism demand to the shoulder seasons. One interesting example of this is the costume events mounted by the Sealed Knot Society in England, a voluntary body with an interest in English history of the Civil War period, which, *inter alia*, recreates battle scenes on the original sites, drawing very large audiences. Certain forms of event will be more likely to attract a market consisting of older or wealthier people; these groups are more likely to have the freedom to choose the time of their travel and, indeed, may even wish to avoid the crowds that are common in the peak seasons. Some off-peak events have been so successful that the destination has managed to turn a low winter season into a peak attraction; the Quebec City Winter Carnival is a case in point.

There is, of course, a direct relationship between the degree of attractiveness of the event and the distance visitors are willing to travel to visit it. Some events, such as sports, will have global appeal, while the appearance of top pop singers at stadiums holding many thousands of fans will be marketed internationally as a package to include travel and hotel accommodation. In 2004, 28 major pop festivals were listed between the end of May and end of August in the UK, while top events like Glastonbury, WOMAD, Creamfields, V2004 and other outdoor events such as those held at Reading and the Isle of Wight will draw tens of thousands of admissions.

The variety of festivals and events around the world is enormous. As examples of how these are reaching the international traveller, in 2004 packages were organized from Britain to such disparate events as the Sundance Film Festival at Park City in Utah, the Inti Raymi Festival at Cusco, Peru, held to welcome the winter solstice, and the mediaeval Kandy Esala Perahera Festival in Sri Lanka.

Example   Festival of the Senses, Tasmania

Food and drink are the themes of this Australian festival, held in February in the Tamar Valley wine-making region of Tasmania. It includes a table seating 1,000 people in Launceston's City Park, serving brunch, as well as concerts, parades, tastings and sporting events.

Even sites as inhospitable as the Arctic in winter can attract visitors with appropriate events. In Kemi and Rovaniemi, Finland (both close to the Arctic Circle), an annual Snow Show includes art installations created by leading sculptors, snowmobile and husky-riding. Visitors can stay at the Snow Castle, an ice-hotel. Events in winter to bring in the off-season market are increasingly apparent. Throughout Europe, the Christmas market, a concept originating in Germany and still immensely popular there, has spread, to a point where numerous similar markets are now organized in British towns and cities; that at Lincoln, the largest in the UK, draws 300,000 visitors annually.

International Expo exhibitions, such as that held at Seville in 1992, are major but infrequent events, often used as a showcase to promote the country as well as attracting the international tourist willing to pay the high gate fees that are charged for entry.

However, the success of even the most popular events can be jeopardized by greed, and overcharging by hotels is widespread at these events, discouraging many visitors. Their popularity is thought to be diminishing now, and the high cost associated with launching these events is discouraging other cities from following Hanover's costly exercise, the most recent international Expo event.

Smaller, but still significant, events capable of boosting the local economy are prominent features of many towns and villages around the world. Some have very long traditions. In Britain, ancient fairs continue to play a role in attracting visitors. Many trace their origins to the Middle Ages, often linked to the horse fairs organized by gypsies, and a strong element of Romany culture survives at these sites. Notable examples include the Ballymena Fair in Northern Ireland, the Appleby Fair in Cumbria, the Stow Fair in Gloucestershire and the Nottingham Goose Fair.

In all countries where tourism is efficiently organized, events are mounted throughout the year to increase tourism flows. One supplement in Britain's national Sunday press carried details of no fewer than 175 festivals in France for the year 2004/5, including festivals of art, film, jazz, classical music, literature, kites and gastronomy; the last-named events included such exotica as a soup festival in Lille, a scallop festival in Paimpol, Mirabelles in Metz, oil and truffles in Aix-en-Provence and violets in Toulouse.

Figure 10.12
Many villages and towns in Britain have annual festivals to attract both locals and visitors. The Medieval Fair at Machynlleth, Wales, includes street performers

(Photographed by the author)

Arts festivals

Arts festivals, an important aspect of cultural tourism, have a long history in many countries, arising out of cultural and traditional festivals which often have local associations. In Britain alone, well over 500 arts festivals are held every year, lasting from two days to several weeks in duration. More than half of these have been founded since 1980, and over 60 per cent are professionally managed. Most depend upon sponsorship and financial support from their local authority. The leading events in the UK, in terms of revenue achieved, include the Edinburgh Festival and Fringe Festival, and the BBC Promenade Concerts.

Major exhibitions draw an international audience of mass tourists; 1.1 million visitors attended the Barnes Foundation's exhibition 'A Century of Impressionism' held at the Musée d'Orsay in Paris in 1993, while a later showing of the Barnes Foundation's collection in Germany drew such crowds that the museum exhibiting the collection stayed open all night (a practice which has led to longer opening hours in Germany. Berlin has 'Die lange Nacht der Museen' twice a year, when all museums are open until at least midnight). Britain's Royal Academy has followed suit, with 24-hour opening for its popular Monet exhibition in 1999, which helped to push visitor numbers to the Academy up to 1.4 million, making it the eighth most popular admission-charging visitor attraction in Britain that year. Increasingly, these blockbuster exhibitions have as much to do with raising the social profile of the institution and encouraging the public to perceive it as a leader in its field, as in directly raising revenue through entry tickets.

Several music festivals in Europe have achieved international recognition, and visitors make significant contributions to the economies of the cities where they are held. In addition to these leading European music festivals there are countless smaller festivals in these countries, each of which makes an important contribution to local revenues through tourist visits. While the largest festivals tend to run during the tourist season, many smaller events are held outside the peak summer periods, especially in cases where sites are subject to heavy congestion during the season. Lengths of music festivals vary greatly, from two or three days up to, in the case of the Drottningholm (Sweden) summer season, more than three months.

Ad hoc events can always be built around a commemorative date. Of course, if the festivals are capable of drawing people from greater distances, and keeping them on site for longer periods of time, the average spend increases; visitors will need overnight accommodation and food, and will be tempted to spend money on other activities during their stay. Apart from music and fine arts, crafts, drama, dance, literature and poetry festivals are popular. Some will commemorate historical occasions, and may be highlighted with parades, pageants and *son et lumière* events. Most provide an opportunity for hosts and guests to meet and get to know one another. As well as meeting a wide variety of tourist needs, they also fulfil an essential requirement of contemporary tourism, that of sustainable development.

Sports tourism

The relationship between tourism and sports events is now so well established that sports tourism is recognized as a field of study in its own right, and several texts are devoted to its study[7]. At its most successful, sports tourism will draw the greatest number of tourists to any one site on the planet: tickets to the Olympic Games are in such high demand that sports enthusiasts will be attracted from all over the world. Similarly, Football's World Cup, with matches staged throughout Europe, will also draw huge crowds. World-class events in golf and tennis witness demand for tickets well beyond available supply. The economic benefits of these events to the destinations where they are staged can be enormous.

| **Example** | Barcelona Olympics |

The 1992 Olympic Games held at Barcelona boosted much-needed investment, and the city undertook a huge urban renewal programme in the run-up to the event, which has since made it one of the most important cities in Europe for short breaks. Tourism accounted for less than two per cent of GDP in the region before the Olympics: ten years after they were held, it accounted for 12.5 per cent.

Similar success was recorded by Atlanta in 1996 and Sydney in 2000, but in both cases huge initial investments were required (Atlanta spent over $2 billion). Montreal, however, lost more than this amount when it staged the Games in 1976, and is still paying off its debts, while Athens in 2004 experienced some disappointing turnouts (believed to be partly due to the high prices set by hotels in the city during the event) and is unlikely to have broken even, given the huge investment in infrastructure to support the games, in spite of having mounted a notably successful games. The euphoria which followed the announcement that the games would come to London in 2012 was soon tempered by the sober realization of the enormous public and private investment that will be necessary to make the event a success, although the construction of the associated infrastructure and superstructure will have long-term benefits for the residents of East London.

The growth and promotion of 'dark tourism'

The beauty of tourism is that the number of products that can be devised to interest the tourist is virtually unlimited. One reads regularly in the press of new ideas that have been promoted, of new – and frequently bizarre – reasons tourists advance for visiting a site. Perhaps our ideas of what is appropriate to view have changed a little since the nineteenth century, when in England people would travel considerable distances to view public hangings, while in the United States, Coney Island amusement park displayed 300 dwarfs in 'Midget City' and publicly electrocuted Topsy, a performing elephant, as a tourist event. There remains, nonetheless, a fascination at times bordering on the macabre to observe scenes such as those exploiting sudden and violent death, sites which Chris Rojek[8] has termed 'black spots'. Rojek describes the flood of tourists to Scotland to see the scene of the Pan Am crash at Lockerbie in 1988. Similarly, following the earthquake which rocked the city of San Francisco at the end of 1989, visitors to the city were asking to be accommodated in hotels that 'overlooked the collapsed freeway'. The BBC reported in 1995[9] that visitors to Blackpool were clamouring to 'ride the Alan Bradley Death Tram' after a character of this name was killed in front of the tram in the popular soap opera *Coronation Street.*

The term *thanatourism*[10], or 'dark tourism' has been used to describe the tourist fascination with death and the macabre. Motives for such tourism may be thought questionable, although travel to 'dark' sites cannot necessarily be ascribed to gratuitous pleasure – visits to World War II concentration camps are popular, for instance, but these, especially by Israeli parties, can often take the form of a pilgrimage, while for others the visit is tied in with historical interest. Major death sites associated with 'celebrities', however, do attract more than their fair share of curious observers (see Plate 12). Jim Morison's tomb at Père-Lachaise cemetery in Paris is said to be the most visited grave in the cemetery, while those of Oscar Wilde, Edith Piaf, Marcel Proust and other representatives of 'high culture' draw far fewer visitors; the outbuilding in Seattle where Kurt Cobain of pop group Nirvana fame committed suicide in 1994 was torn down, but the site is still visited by hundreds of admirers, just as hundreds still seek out the underground road tunnel in Paris where Diana, Princess of Wales, met her death in a car crash.

Whatever the merits of thanatourism, the quest for the bizarre features ever more prominently in tourist motivation. Sometimes this is a reflection of the desire for ever more dangerous activities, whether sporting or otherwise, particularly among the younger tourist. A press listing of the most dangerous streets in the world led to a flurry of interest in visiting those at Snake Alley, Taipei, Khao San Road, Bangkok, Tverskaya Ulitsa, Moscow and King's Cross, Sydney. The *Sunday Times*[11] coined the term 'terror tourism' to describe the growing trend for tourists to plan visits to countries beset by political disturbances or even civil wars. Noting the demand for trips to Afghanistan and Iraq after the recent wars in those countries (visits to Afghanistan were organized soon after the end of the war there, both operators and clients ignoring government warnings of the potential dangers), and the fact that the site of the Twin Towers disaster became the biggest tourist magnet in New York after 11 September 2001 (with over one million visitors within the year), one can only conclude that dark tourism is flourishing.

The problem for the industry is to judge whether such tourist attractions are educationally valuable or merely satisfying the prurient interest of the spectator. Indeed, the very term 'visitor attraction', when applied to sites such as these, raises questions. Are visitors expecting to be entertained, or does the explanation arise from some deeper psychosis in modern societies?

Whether prurient or otherwise, there is no doubt that countries with a dark history are not slow to cash in on its evident commercial value. In recent years the world has seen:

1   Croatia preparing to reopen its prison on the island of Goli Otok, formerly designed to hold 'enemies of Communism', for visitors to experience what life was like there as a prisoner. Similarly, the former Nazi and Communist prison camp at Liepaja, Latvia, now accommodates overnight visitors.

2   A Lithuanian entrepreneur, Viliunas Malinauskas has preserved 65 bronze and granite statues of former Soviet leaders at Grutas Park, south west of Vilnius, where loudspeakers relay marching music and Stalin's speeches. Plans to construct a railway between the theme park and the capital by which visitors would be transported by cattle wagons, then monitored by guards in machine-gun towers and restricted within the site by barbed wire fencing, were greeted with outrage by Lithuanians who had suffered under the Soviet regime, and the park has been dubbed 'Stalinworld' by its critics. Nevertheless, 200,000 visitors were admitted to the site in its first year. Vilnius itself also boasts a genocide and resistance centre, opened in 1992.

3   The Cambodian Government has turned Pol Pot's Khmer Rouge complex of huts and bunkers at Anlong Veng into a tourist resort.

4   The construction of Ossi World, a theme park commemorating the former East German regime on the outskirts of Berlin, was aimed to appeal to *Ostalgie*, the nostalgia among East Germans for the old regime, in the face of rising economic problems since unification. Plans for the park had the support of the Berlin tourism Marketing Board. Stasi (former DDR security service) buildings in Leipzig, Halle and near Berlin are also popular venues for tourists. The holocaust site at Dachau and Hitler's retreat at Berchtesgaden are among many 'dark tourism' sites in Germany dating from the Nazi period.

5   Visitors to Rwanda can tour genocide sites where a million Tutsis were massacred in 1994. The war crimes tribunals in Kigali were also open to tourists, who could include a visit to the bunker hideouts of the Rwandan Patriotic Front Army.

6   In 2004, Israel's tourism minister urged tour operators to include its 425-mile 'terror prevention fence', topped with razor wire and electronic sensors, which separate Israelis and Palestinians, in itineraries organized for foreign tourists.

Britain has not been slow to trade on the attraction of dark tourism sites, either. Among World War II sites open to tourists or groomed as future sites for tourists, one can include the Eden Prisoner-of-War camp at Malton, North Yorkshire, where some 30 huts from the World War II period house displays commemorating events during the war; air raid shelters in Stockport; the former secret bunker at Kelvedon Hatch in Essex (receiving 60,000 visitors a year); Hack Green nuclear bunker near Nantwich; and the bunker built during the 1950s near St Andrews, Scotland to house the regional government in the event of a nuclear war. National Park rangers regularly lead guided walks to the sites of 60 crashed World War II planes in the Peak District. In Belfast, tours are operated to former Northern Ireland troublespots, including Falls Road, Shankill Road and the Peace Wall.

Certainly visits to sites of this nature can be illuminating and instructive, if not entertaining in the traditional sense of the word. Some sites however, are heavily restored – perhaps over-restored (as at Auschwitz-Birkenau death camp, where the original gate and ovens have been replaced with replicas). Objectivity of interpretation at such sites is always open to question, depending as it does on the political colour and viewpoint of the day, and of those presenting the data. At another death camp, in Buchenwald, Bauhaus university students were recently recruited to design souvenirs

Figure 10.13
Even major
tragedies
become
opportunities
for commercial
promotion.
Organized
tours to the
concentration
camps at
Auschwitz,
Poland

(Photographed by the author)

and memorabilia to be sold at the site to raise money for its preservation. The intentions were doubtless good, but many critics described the move as 'disrespectful'.

The scope for innovative tourism

Some of the more curious tourist attractions in recent years, as well as efforts to develop tourist interest in the banal or bizarre, are listed below:

1 Corpses displayed as tourist attractions. Perfectly preserved bodies retrieved from bogs in Denmark are on display in museums at Silkeborg and Moesgaard. The exhibition of corpses in this manner, however, raises serious ethical questions.

2 Deep Ocean Expeditions operates three-seat submersibles to descend 4,000 metres to the ocean floor off Newfoundland to see the Titanic, at a cost in excess of £20,000.

3 SATOUR, the South African Tourist Office, has introduced visits to Soweto Township, an impoverished suburb in which Nelson Mandela's former home is based. Visitors also glimpse Winnie Mandela's palatial house. Visits can also be made to Robben Island, the scene of Mandela's imprisonment (and now a World Heritage site), where his cell features prominently.

4 China has opened the site of a hitherto secret armaments factory, to allow tourists to practise on the firing range with rocket launchers and anti-aircraft guns. The tour is particularly popular with Americans and Japanese.

5   The world's first dung museum opened at Machaba safari camp in Botswana. Necklaces of dried polished dung can be bought in the shop.

6   In Sweden, moose droppings are sold as souvenirs to tourists visiting Lapland, and have been given as gifts to conference delegates. The reaction of the delegates was not recorded.

7   Lignite pits near Hamburg attract tourists because of their resemblance to the lunar landscape.

8   Two-hour guided tours are available around the municipal rubbish dump at Fresh Kills, Staten Island, New York. Visits to urban sewers have also proved popular in some cities.

9   Special tours and cruises are arranged for visitors to approach active or recently active volcanoes. These include sites in Ecuador, Sicily, Crete, Nicaragua, Iceland and the Azores.

10 Walking tours across the arches of Sydney Harbour Bridge have proved immensely popular. A jumpsuit and safety cable are obligatory accompaniments.

11 Two-hour guided tours are on offer in Berlin's red light district, with off-duty prostitutes acting as tour guides. They will answer clients' questions on all aspects of the city, including their own activities.

12 At Bovington Camp in Dorset, the army medical team put on realistic displays of amputations for visitors.

13 In Palermo, Sicily, tourists can be taken on tours to sites associated with the local Mafia, including a visit to a former Godfather's torture chamber.

14 Many domestic tourists in the Philippines are attracted to the annual rite of Catholic fanaticism at San Pedro Cutud, where volunteers undergo crucifixion.

15 Omanis visit Salalah, on the southern tip of Oman, between June and September each year because of the unusual rainfall in the monsoon season – this is the only area of the Arabian Gulf so affected. Perhaps the only example of rain attracting tourists?

Hoteliers are noted entrepreneurs, and many have introduced special events to attract out-of-season tourists, or fill rooms during the recent recession. 'Murder weekends' have been popular, while one hotel offered heavy discounts for people whose surname was Smith. Perhaps the prize for originality should be awarded to the group of hotels situated near the M25, London's notoriously crowded orbital motorway. These developed a series of 'M25 theme nights', with a 'motorway madness' banquet.

Other hotels attract tourists because of the bizarre form of their accommodation. In the USA, tourists can stay at a former research laboratory and the world's first underwater hotel, Jules' Undersea Lodge at John Pennecamp Coral Reef State Park in Key Largo, Florida (swimmers only – this requires a 21-foot dive to the entrance!); they can bed down in railway cabooses at the Featherbed Railroad Company in Nice, California; spend a night in the cellblock at the Jailhouse Inn in Preston, Minnesota; or sleep underground in the Honeycombs at the Inn at Honey Run, Millersburg, Ohio. Lower

Saxony in Germany offers 'Hay Hotels' where sleeping bags in hay are provided for visitors. The hotels are said to be popular with cycling tourists, and others have been opened in Poland, Denmark, Italy and the Czech Republic.

Effectively marketed, bizarre sites and events can draw tourists. However, one tourism entrepreneur has gone further by devising a totally new approach to tourism, as seen in the example below.

Example The Laboratory of Experimental Tourism

Joel Henry founded the Laboratory of Experimental Tourism (Latourex) in France in 1990. Its object is to find new ways of taking original holidays, for jaded tourists who have 'done everything'. His idea of experimental travel was initially centred on Ariadne's Thread, the mythical ball of yarn leading Theseus through the labyrinth. From this, he dreamed up different ways of taking trips, including getting a friend to pinpoint 20 places on a map which had some personal meaning, and visiting them. Other ideas advanced have included:

Anachrotourism:	using old-fashioned vehicles as transport, or following an ancient guidebook
Antipoddysey:	visiting a point on the globe exactly opposite to where you live
Bi-tourism:	taking alternative left and right turns on a trip until encountering a dead end
Countertourism:	photographing sites which stand opposite a landmark
Cuneitourism:	visiting only sites recommended by locals
Melanotourism:	visiting sites connected to the word 'black' (eg Blackpool, the Black Mountains, Montenegro)
Monopoly tourism	determine where to travel by throwing dice, using a local map, or visiting a randomly selected grid reference on a map
Retourism	travelling to a distant destination as quickly as possible, returning by the slowest possible route
Retro tourism	using a century-old Baedeker guide to visit a destination and see the sights

Some 40 ideas in all are designed to give tourists a new perspective on towns they visit, a process of serendipity and an attempt to look at everyday sites and objects in a new light.

Henry's experiments are one of several new approaches to tourism. Others have suggested couples split up and endeavour to find each other within a town without any guidelines or defined meeting places. An imaginative alternative was devised by the owner of the Blinde Kuh (blind cow) restaurant in Zürich, which will be described in the following chapter.

Notes

1 Swarbrooke, J, *The Development and Management of Visitor Attractions* Oxford, Butterworth-Heinemann, 1995, pp 1–3
2 Fyall, A, Garrod, B and Leask, A, (eds), *Managing Visitor Attractions: New Directions*, Oxford, Butterworth-Heinemann, 2003, pp 6–9
3 Ibid, p 30
4 Phaidon Atlas of Contemporary World Architecture, cited by Marcus Binney, *The Times*, 10 May 2004, *A Guide to Wonders of the Modern World Worth Visiting*, p 31
5 A good starting point for an overview of cultural tourism is the series of four books produced following the 1996 International Tourism and Culture Conference organized by the Centre for Travel and Tourism at the University of Northumbria, edited by Robinson M, Evans, N and Callaghan P (eds) and published by the Centre and Business Education Publishers, Sunderland:

   I *Culture as the Tourist Product*
   II *Managing Cultural Resources for the Tourist*
   III *Tourism and Cultural Change*
   IV *Tourism and Culture: Image, Identity and Marketing*

6 Löfgren, O, *On Holiday: a History of Vacationing*, Berkeley, University of California Press, 1999
7 See, for example, Weed, M and Bull, C, *Sports Tourism: Participants, Policy and Providers*, Elsevier/Butterworth-Heinemann 2004, and Higham, J, (ed), *Sports Tourism Destinations: Issues, Opportunities and Analysis*, Elsevier, 2005
8 Rojek, C, *Ways of Escape: Modern Transformation in Leisure and Travel*, Basingstoke, Macmillan, 1993
9 Technology Season, BBC2, 7 November 1995
10 See, for example, Foley, M and Lennon, J, *Dark Tourism*, Continuum, 2000. Also Seaton, A V, Guided by the Dark: From Thanatopsis to Thanatourism, *International Journal of Heritage Studies*, 2, 1996, 234–44
11 *Sunday Times*, 16 March 1997

Further reading

Anthony, R and Henry J, *The Lonely Planet Guide to Experimental Travel*, Lonely Planet Publications, 2005
Jencks, C, *The Iconic Building: the Power of Enigma*, Frances Lincoln, 2005
Stewart, S, *On Longing: Narratives of the Miniature, the Gigantic, the Souvenir, the Collection*, Baltimore, Johns Hopkins University Press 1984, p 86

Websites

Historic Houses Association	www.hha.org.uk
Visit England (Taste of England campaign)	www.visitengland.com/taste
Regaldive tours to visit Cleopatra's sunken city	www.regaldive.co.uk
Eden Camp Prisoner of War Camp	www.edencamp.co.uk
Year of the Garden	www.visitbritain.com/gardens

The National Wildflower Centre   www.nwc.org.uk
Industrial tourism   www.visitbritain.com/ukindustry
The Dala Horse   www.nohenslojd.se
Slow food movement   www.slowfood.com
Hinterland Travel (tours to Iraq and Afghanistan)   www.hinterlandtravel.com
Italian Job tours in Turin   www.italianjob-tour.com

Questions and discussion points

1   You cannot make a tourist attraction out of an instrument of torture.

> Walter Momper, Former Social Democrat mayor of Berlin,
> reacting to the news that plans were being drafted to rebuild a
> 200-yard section of the Berlin Wall. (*The Times*, 12 December 04)

Do you agree? On what grounds do you believe dark tourism attractions may be justified, and where do you draw the line?

It is interesting to note that, while Nazism and its sites are readily identified in Germany, individual reference in tourist literature to Hitler and his henchmen is rare. Why do you think this is, and should the individual personalities be separated from the events of the past in this way? How should 'dark tourism' at sites such as Auschwitz be presented to serve the needs of the diverse interests of visitors?

2   This chapter finishes with some innovative ideas for tourism. Here's a contribution from the author – to find the incorporated township with the smallest population in any country you travel to, and pay it a visit. For example, the smallest township in the United States is Monowi, Nebraska, with a population of just one person. Nebraska is off the beaten track for tourism – could the State encourage visitors by promoting this? Would the result simply be to increase the population in providing facilities for tourists to eat and stay over, thus undermining the original appeal? How might this be overcome?

3   Locals at Chucuito, a village on Lake Titicaca near Puno, have been condemned for building a fake 'ancient Inca fertility site' to entice tourists. They were successful in this, until an archeologist visited the site and denounced the deception. Would the construction of this attraction have been acceptable if the locals had not attempted to pass it off as genuine, but merely as a 'replica'? How concerned are tourists, when they visit ancient sites, to know the extent to which it is genuine, or restored? How does the construction differ from similar tourist sites which are restored pastiches of the original, or 'authentic' reproductions of earlier constructions? (Examples in Britain include Vindolanda on Hadrian's Wall and the mediaeval pastiche Castle Drogo, completed in 1930).

4   Discuss whether you would plan to send postcards to friends and family when you travel abroad, or prefer to rely on pictures on your mobiles and communications by e-mail while away.

Assignment topics

1   At the time of writing, the British Government was planning to push through legislation in two areas which would (a) allow a considerable expansion of legal gambling casinos in the UK, and (b) permit the extension of drinking hours in licensed premises. As a research assistant employed by your local authority, you have been asked to undertake research to determine the

local population's attitudes to both of these moves. Devise a research exercise which will include the use of a questionnaire to solicit answers. You line of questioning should be in two directions; first, as to what benefits and disadvantages these moves might have for the neighbourhood, and second, whether they, personally, have a moral objection to the moves. On balance, are locals for or against the proposals? Your results should break down your findings by gender and age. Ideally, the research should be carried out within an area which attracts tourists, in which case tourists may be included in your research framework, with whatever additional questions you think appropriate to direct to this group.

2   Today, many attractions seek to attract their audiences through the Internet. As a museum employee, your job is to develop a new website for the museum which will be designed to make browsers aware of the product, to encourage them to visit, and to alert them to any temporary exhibitions that are due to be mounted in the coming year.

   Search the Web to gather data on 20 existing museums, and produce a report for your boss which spells out the best and poorest features of each, summarizes how effective the site is in its aims, how easy to use and how clearly set out is the material and whether viewers are encouraged to take action as a result of their browsing. Complete your report with recommendations on the design of your own website (accompanied if desired with illustrations depicting the proposed layout).

11 The hospitality sector: accommodation and catering services

Objectives

After studying this chapter, you should be able to:

- explain the structure and nature of the hospitality sector, distinguishing between the various categories of tourist accommodation and catering services
- describe how accommodation is classified and be aware of the problems involved in classification
- understand the nature of demand for accommodation and catering, and how the sector has responded to changing patterns of demand over time
- understand the relationship between the hospitality sector and other sectors of the tourism industry.

Introduction

The customers in package tour hotels are known as 'geese'. This is a misnomer. Geese tend to hiss if they are too rigorously disciplined and kept in line. 'Sheep' would be more accurate, for the ambition of every package hotel is to have uncomplaining guests who fall in with its plans.

Brian Moynahan, *The Tourist Trap*,
Pan Books, 1985, p 142

In this chapter, we are principally concerned with examining the commercial accommodation and catering sector. It must not be forgotten, however, that this sector must compete with a large non-commercial hospitality supply which is equally important to tourism; the VFR (visiting friends and relations) market is substantial, and in addition there is a wide variety of other forms of accommodation used by tourists, including the tourists' own camping and caravanning equipment, privately owned boats and even second homes, both in the home country and abroad. There is also a growing market for home exchanges, and the swapping of time-share accommodation, which the industry has encouraged through the establishment of time-share exchange companies.

It is, in fact, difficult to distinguish between the strictly commercial and non-commercial aspects of the hospitality business. Youth hostels and YMCAs, for example, are not necessarily attempting to make a profit, but merely to recover their operating costs, while it is increasingly common to find educational institutions such as universities and schools hiring out their student accommodation to tourists outside the academic terms, in order to make some contribution to the running costs of the institutions. One result of this has been a marked increase in the quality of student accommodation, with en suite bathrooms now the norm in new building.

Other forms of tourism which by their nature embrace accommodation would include privately hired yachts, or bookings on a cruise ship. Operators in some countries provide coaches which include sleeping berths, while in others packages are available using specially chartered trains which serve as the travellers' hotel throughout the trip. Independent travellers can also book sleeping accommodation on rail services in many popular tourism destinations. To what extent should all these services be counted as elements of the commercial accommodation available to tourists? Certainly, any study of tourism must take account of these overnight alternatives, and the expansion or contraction in demand for sleeping arrangements which compete with the traditional accommodation sector. The rapid rise in cruise holidays over the past few years, to take one instance, will have affected demand for more traditional forms of holiday in which travel and stay is the norm.

Tourists staying in private accommodation away from their homes, whether with friends and relatives or in second homes owned by themselves or their friends, are engaging in tourism, and will almost certainly be contributing to tourist spend in the region, as they tend to use local commercial transport, restaurants and entertainment. Their spend must therefore be included in tourism statistics for the region. Apart from the economic benefits at the destination, there are frequently commercial transactions in the home country associated with their trips. Tour operators and budget airlines sell flights to airports near second homes (the expanding second-home ownership among Britons in France, Italy and Spain has been a big contributing factor to the strength of the budget carriers), and many tourists will hire cars during the period of their stay, for which in some cases payment will be made through agents in the home country before departure. Airlines, recognizing that home exchanges can represent a healthy source of flight revenue, have developed and commercialized the home-exchange business by establishing directories to assist people in arranging exchanges. Some national or regional tourist offices keep directories of home owners who are prepared to make exchanges, and others maintain lists of local householders willing to invite guests from overseas into their homes for a meal (a particular feature of US hospitality).

The structure of the accommodation sector

The accommodation sector comprises widely differing forms of sleeping and hospitality facilities which can be conveniently categorized as either serviced (in which catering is included) or self-catering. These are not watertight categories, as some forms of accommodation, such as holiday camps or educational institutions, may offer

Figure 11.1
The structure
of tourist
accommodation

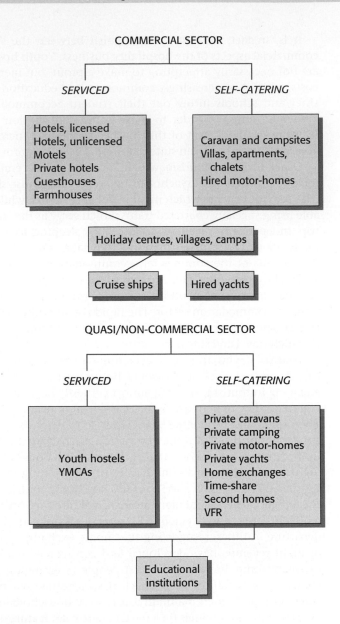

COMMERCIAL SECTOR

SERVICED

Hotels, licensed
Hotels, unlicensed
Motels
Private hotels
Guesthouses
Farmhouses

SELF-CATERING

Caravan and campsites
Villas, apartments,
  chalets
Hired motor-homes

Holiday centres, villages, camps

Cruise ships

Hired yachts

QUASI/NON-COMMERCIAL SECTOR

SERVICED

Youth hostels
YMCAs

SELF-CATERING

Private caravans
Private camping
Private motor-homes
Private yachts
Home exchanges
Time-share
Second homes
VFR

Educational
institutions

serviced, self-service or self-catering facilities, but they will help in drawing distinctions between the characteristics of the two categories. Figure 11.1 provides an at-a-glance guide to the range of accommodation which a tourist might occupy.

Hotels are the most significant and widely recognized form of overnight accommodation for tourists. They also form one of the key elements of most package holidays. However, what constitutes a hotel and distinguishes it from other forms of accommodation is not always clear. The English Hotel Occupancy Survey defines it as an establishment having five or more bedrooms, not identified as a guesthouse or boarding house and not listed as providing bed-and-breakfast accommodation only.

The corporate chains

A feature of the industry is that, as mass tourism has developed, so have the large chains and corporations in the accommodation sector. The hotel and motel business has reached a stage of maturity in which a few major companies have come to dominate the international market. This process has been boosted by the development of website marketing, rapidly growing as a key form of accommodation distribution and frequently offering prices to consumers well below those available through more traditional outlets. This expansion has also been aided by franchising, whereby hotels and motels are operated by individual franchisees paying royalties to the parent company for the privilege of operating under a brand name. This form of expansion has been used with great success around the world by companies such as Holiday Inns, while the Friendly Hotel group holds European franchises for such well-established brand names as Quality Hotels, Comfort Hotels and Sleep Inns.

Example   InterContinental Hotels Group

InterContinental Hotels (IHG) now own, lease or manage over 3,500 individual properties, spread over one hundred countries. The largest hotel company in the world by number of rooms, its 537,000 rooms receive well over 120 million visits annually. Once an offshoot of Bass Breweries, the hotel group is now independent, and in recent years has been active in adding properties to its portfolio. It now offers a range of branded products including top of the range Crowne Plaza Hotels, mid-scale Holiday Inn brands and, coming in a little above budget prices, the Express by Holiday Inn/Holiday Inn Express chain. A recent innovation has been to develop a specialized brand for a select range of Holiday Inns, now known as Holiday Inn Select. It has also bought into the corporate hospitality market for extended stays, owning, franchising or operating the US brands Staybridge Suites by Holiday Inn and Candlewood Suites. In 2000 the group extended its strength overseas by purchasing Southern Pacific Hotels, operating the Park Royal and Centra brands in Australasia. Its most recent venture has been the launch of a new hotel concept in 2004 to take advantage of the trend to themed properties. Hotel Indigo is described as 'a refreshing hotel experience, not just a hotel room'.

The company's policy is currently to divest itself of its own hotels in favour of franchises and management contracts, where it plans to add 50,000–60,000 rooms each year. It also seeks to expand its range of brands with a premium economy brand fractionally below the Express range. As Chief Executive Andrew Cosslett says, 'We are the biggest in the world by number of rooms, yet we have just three per cent of all beds'.

Since these chains market their products more aggressively, advertise extensively, work closely with large tour-operating organizations globally and, in addition to their own websites, provide an effective distribution network linked to the airline CRSs, they tend to have a higher presence in the industry than their market share would suggest. In total bed terms, their total bed stock is small compared with the multitude of small independently owned facilities, but these, until recently, have had less ready access both to the market and to the other sectors of the industry. With the growth of commercial websites, smaller units now have greater opportunities to reach their customers directly, even if not on the scale of the large corporations.

Leading chains around the world have tended to diversify their brands by price and image to appeal to a wide variety of markets. American, British and French chains in particular retain a strong hold on the global accommodation market, including, apart from the InterContinental brand, Marriott International and the two major French groups, Accor and Groupe Envergure, both European leaders in the accommodation sector. The policy of these groups is to create an international and uniform marketing image to assist sales around the world.

The expansion internationally of the two French groups is particularly interesting, given that generally the French have been slower to exploit the global market in other sectors, with the possible exception of the Club Méditerranée tour operation (in which Accor took a 30 per cent interest in 2004). Again, policy has been to satisfy a variety of market niches through brand imagery. Accor offers accommodation from luxury to budget, and includes numerous brand names, among them the international chains Sofitel Demeure, Novotel, Dorint, Suitehotel, Mercure, Coralia, Etap, Ibis and Formule 1. In North America, the group operates under the brand names Sofitel and Novotel, along with budget brands Redroof Inns, Motel 6 and Studio 6 (extended-stay hotels). The Envergure group owns the two-star Campanile Hotels along with Bleu Marine, Kyriad Prestige, Kyriad, Climat de France, Première Classe and Nuit d'Hotel. Both companies have successfully sought in recent years to penetrate the UK market. Further afield, other notable chains include the Mandarin group, concentrated in the Pacific Rim area, while Indian-owned Oberoi Hotels have expanded into Egypt, the Far East and Australia. As with other sectors of the tourism industry, there is a growing belief that a handful of mega-chains such as these will in time come to dominate the global tourism market, with independents focusing on niche-market opportunities.

A recent trend within the large chains has been concentration on the development of budget-price properties, long left to the independent sector. In Britain, well-established leisure corporations such as Granada or catering subsidiaries of the big brewers were leaders in the development of what they now prefer to term 'limited service' hotels, to distinguish them from the type of accommodation sought by the backpacker market. Brands new to Britain, such as Days Inn and Sleep Inn, are joining more familiar brands Travelodge and Whitbread-owned Premier Travel Inns to capture a share of this fast-growing market, especially in city-centre properties which attract growing numbers of short-break tourists.

In mainland Europe, Accor Hotels has exploited the deficiency in this sector by introducing the super-budget chains Formule 1 and Etap, while others on the Continent have popularized low-budget brands such as B&B Hotels, Mister Bed, Villages Hotels, Unhotel and Fimotel. These very low-priced hotels have managed to reduce costs by developing a unitary design and automating many of the services provided; reception desks are only manned for short periods of the day, and at other times

Figure 11.2
The international brand: a Radisson SAS hotel in Belgium

(Photographed by the author)

entry is by the insertion of credit cards into a machine on the external wall. Similarly, breakfasts are self-service and highly automated. The introduction of this style of hotel into the UK has not been simple. Land costs push up prices in Britain, while restricted furnishings and service appeared too basic for the British market: for example, carpet soon replaced the linoleum which French hotel guests had seemed more willing to accept (undoubtedly, differing climates are also a factor in this choice).

A different approach has been taken by Stelios Hadji-Ioannou, founder of easyJet.

Example   easyHotels

A new generation of 'super-budget' hotels, easyHotels, was announced by Stelios Hadji-Ioannou in 2005. The first two have opened in Kensington, London, and in Basel, Switzerland. Costs are ultra-low, with a lead-in price as little as £20 a night for advance booking, but rooms are basic; many are windowless, and while overall size varies, some are as small as just 60 square feet. Rooms do have TVs (at a premium) and minuscule shower and toilet cabinets, but are without wardrobes or even bedside lights. There are no communal areas or bars, and housekeeping charges are extra. Sales are exclusively on-line, no advertising

▶

is undertaken and no discounts are offered to distributors such as travel agents. Stelios believes firmly that these ultra-low-priced hotels will be the growth area of the future, in line with the growth of low-cost air travel, and points to budget chains like Motel 6 as adopting a similar strategy in North America. However, they may be judged roomy contrasted with Japan's 'pod' capsule hotels. Whether budget-conscious Western guests will eventually be reduced to, or be willing to accept, these coffin-like stacked bedroom boxes, which have found favour in Japanese cities, is another matter.

The character property

The competition between luxury hotels has led to new forms of market segmentation, based on product differentiation. Country house hotels or town house hotels place emphasis on more personal service, while boutique hotels and designer hotels, especially those taking advantage of the fashion for cutting-edge design, have attracted

Figure 11.3
One of the expanding low-budget chains on the European Continent: a Mr Bed City Hotel in France

(Photographed by the author)

Figure 11.4
The new budget
hotels in Britain:
the City Inn,
Bristol

(Photographed by the author)

widespread publicity (a glance in any bookstore at the range of books devoted to cutting-edge hotel design and 'hip' hotels will confirm this), given additional impetus by their tendency to attract celebrities and celebrity-hunters. Hotels in this category in London include The Halkin, Blakes, Great Eastern Metropolitan, One Aldwych, St Martin's Lane, the Sanderson and the Trafalgar Hilton, while in the USA similar appeal is to be found at the Hudson and Mercer Hotels in New York, the Avalon in Los Angeles and the Delano in Miami. The Hotel Vittoria in Florence (one of the Una Hotel chain) has staked a claim to be the most fashionable in the world, with mural portraits on each door and surrealistic decor.

Other recently constructed hotels have opted for the 'wow' factor, either by reason of their architecture or their sheer size: for example, the hotel Puerto America in Madrid, operated by Silken Hotels in 2005, has chosen to have each floor designed by a different famous architect. Size alone had little appeal in the past, as those mega-hotels in the former Soviet Union proved only too clearly, but if sold as luxury resorts in their own right, virtually cities within a city, they will find a market as readily as the giant cruise ships carrying over 2,000 passengers have done. Las Vegas boasts ten mega-hotels with over 3,000 rooms. The Burj al-Arab Hotel in Dubai is famed not only as the tallest hotel in the world, but also for its self-claimed classification of seven-star status, defining ultra luxury. Within Europe, the Gran Hotel Benidorm, at 186 metres and 43 stories high, offers its own unique appeal. Central atriums with glass lifts, spectacular indoor and outdoor gardens or other eye-catching features all help to reinforce the hotel experience as being something more than 'a room and a bed'.

Figure 11.5
The designer
hotel: minimalist
St Martin's Lane
Hotel, London

(Photographed by the author)

The Conrad chain, like many up-market hotel operators, targets the corporate market, offering all-suite hotels as a principal feature in their luxury product; while hotels which have been converted from buildings formerly used for other purposes have deliberately retained their original character, and have therefore appealed strongly to a business market of frequent users jaded by standardization and uniformity. A good example is the small chain known as the Hotel du Vin & Bistro (part of the Malmaison Group), which purchases redundant property in city centres such as former warehouses and industrial buildings, redeveloping these as lodgings while retaining their original character. Emphasizing their catering strengths, they have succeeded in simultaneously creating some highly praised restaurants. On the Continent, similar aims are shared by Malmaison's Continental hotels and by Germany's Sorat chain, Spain's Melia Boutique and Derby Hotels.

Individual hotels have also succeeded in establishing unique personalities which attract the niche market. Examples in the UK include the Lace Market in Nottingham and the Scotsman in Edinburgh. Such developments reveal alternative ways forward for hotel design; the days of the faceless and monolithic concrete block, favoured in the development of new resorts in the Mediterranean and elsewhere in order to permit rapid construction and cheap operation, are ending, as the sophisticated travel market seeks better service and more character in its lodgings.

Hotels that can offer attributes that are unique to the country visited are always popular with tourists. The *paradores* in Spain, or the *pousadas* of Portugal, national

Figure 11.6
The independent character hotel: Hotel Egmond, Bruges

(Photographed by the author)

chains of state-operated inns located in historic properties, are proving highly successful in spite of their premium prices, while traditional *haciendas* in Mexico and the *ryokans* of Japan, which offer an authentic flavour of the country's culture, greatly appeal to the independent travel market. In Britain, individual character properties owned by the National Trust, the Landmark Trust and similar organizations are greatly in demand: one of the National Trust's most popular properties is Peel Bothy, a tiny former shepherd's home at Steel Rigg, Northumberland offering only very basic facilities – but seen as full of character.

Hotels of character appeal as strongly to leisure travellers as they do to the business traveller. In recent years the 'country cottage' style of accommodation has been popular, and these have been dutifully incorporated into specialist programmes by the tour operators. Association of these properties with a former celebrity owner enhances their appeal: among cottages available for rent in the UK are those formerly owned by the poet Shelley, as well as writers R L Stevenson, D H Lawrence and Thomas Hardy. The appeal of cottage accommodation may have been triggered off by interest in the French *gîtes* which developed in the 1980s. At the other end of the scale, the 'Mansions and Manors' brand consists of around 200 manor house owners who will offer bed-and-breakfast accommodation on a selective basis to the 'right kind of clients' but have no wish to commercialize their product or advertise it directly to the public. This group of products is therefore marketed directly through tour operators overseas. In the USA, the consortium Historic Hotels of America, established with the support of the US

Figure 11.7
Colonial style
clapboard
properties make
popular bed-
and-breakfast
facilities in North
America. The Inn
at the Bay, St
Petersburg,
Florida

(Photographed by the author)

National Trust for Historic Preservations, recruits only hotels at least 50 years old. Among members are the 1773 Red Lion Inn at Stockbridge, Massachusetts and a former Carmelite convent in Puerto Rico which dates from 1651.

Consortia

In an effort to counteract the distribution strengths of the large chains, independent hotels around the world have frequently banded together to form loosely knit consortia. While this allows the group to obtain some of the economies of scale achieved by the large chains, such as benefits of mass purchasing, more critically it reinforces their marketing strength, enabling them to improve distribution through a united website and the websites of other leading suppliers. Many of the larger consortia, such as Best Western Hotels and Inter Hotels, operate on a global scale; others operate on a national scale, as does Flag Hotels of Australia, now established as a strong national brand in overseas marketing. Similarly, some smaller, privately owned hotels have united within a themed consortium in order to market themselves more effectively at home and abroad. This is a highly appropriate strategy when developing a niche approach; for example, 'Small Luxury Hotels of the World' with nearly 300 hotels in 50 countries focuses on building an image of high-standard but personal hotels, while Grand Heritage Hotels, an American-owned consortium which is now drawing membership from high-graded UK hotels, emphasizes luxury and status. Other specialist consortia operating in the UK include Pride of Britain Hotels, Scotland's Personal Hotels and Great Inns of Britain.

Classifying and grading accommodation

Classifying accommodation units of differing types and standards is no simple matter. The process of classification, either for the purpose of legislation or for the systematic examination of business activity, has been attempted on several occasions in Britain in the past (for example, under the Standard Industrial Classification System). However, these attempts were mainly designed to distinguish hotels and other residential establishments from sundry catering activities. Statistics seldom distinguish, for example, between guests staying at hotels and motels. Within the small independent sector, the problem is even greater. There is a broad spectrum of private accommodation which ranges from the 'private hotel', through boarding-house and guesthouse accommodation to bed-and-breakfast establishments, and in Britain under law there is no clear distinction between the private hotel and the boarding house. The only distinction between these two and the guesthouse is that the latter will not have more than four bedrooms or more than eight guests. This distinction is important for legislative purposes, but need not concern us further here. However, tourists are interested not only in what different grades of hotel offer in the way of facilities, but also in the *quality* of the accommodation and catering they are being offered. To clarify these features, we need to distinguish between three terms: categorization, classification and grading. Although these terms are often used interchangeably, the following are their widely accepted definitions:

- *categorization* refers to the separation of accommodation by type, that is, distinguishing between hotels, motels, boarding houses, guesthouses etc.
- *classification* distinguishes accommodation on the basis of certain physical features, such as the number of rooms with private bath or shower etc.
- *grading* identifies accommodation according to certain verifiable objective features of the service offered, such as the number of courses served at meals, whether 24-hour service is provided etc.

Readers will note, however, that none of these refers to the assessment of quality, which calls for subjective evaluation, and is therefore far more difficult – and more costly – to validate, especially when standards, particularly in catering, can change so rapidly over time.

Provision was made under the Development of Tourism Act 1969 for the compulsory classification and grading of hotel accommodation in Britain, but this was widely resisted by the industry itself, and the British Tourist Authority made no attempt to impose it at the time, instead relying upon a system of voluntary registration first introduced in 1975. The separate National Tourist Boards of England, Scotland and Wales were left to devise their own individual schemes. However, urged on by the Scottish Tourist Board in particular, the three boards in 1987 agreed a common scheme which graded hotels into six categories: either 'listed', for the most basic property, or from one to five 'crowns', depending upon the facilities offered. The system remained a voluntary one, but hotels taking part received regular checks from inspectors, and could only display their blue and white signboard or advertise in Regional Tourist Board publications after they had been approved. The hotels were charged an annual fee. While the system was clearly an improvement on the previous form of classification, in which the hotels themselves were responsible for advising the tourist boards of the facilities they provided, because it remained voluntary only a very small proportion of the total accommodation sector in Britain became registered.

Two years later, the boards agreed a unified system of grading quality, additionally awarding the symbols 'Approved', 'Commended', 'Highly Commended' or 'Deluxe' in ascending order of quality. This was planned to take into account such subjective issues as hospitality, service, food and decor. These awards take no account of the facilities or status of the unit, which allows even a humble 'listed' unit to be rated as 'Deluxe', if it meets the quality criterion. Other types of accommodation subsequently received symbols too; moons were awarded to lodges, keys to self-catering accommodation, and 'Qs' to holiday centres. Wales, however, chose to develop its own scheme separately from England and Scotland. The self-catering scheme was applied to a range of different units, including cottages, flats, bungalows, houseboats and chalets, and quality was assessed using the same form of assessment as was used for the hotels. Grading became based on such features as the appearance of the building, the decor and lighting, heating and furnishing, floor coverings, and the crockery and utensils provided.

This system also proved far from satisfactory, given that the private sector had devised its own schemes for grading hotels, some national, some international in scope, and these were often more widely recognized by members of the public than were the public-sector designations. Of the private-sector schemes, the best known in Britain were those offered by the two motoring associations, the AA and RAC, both of which provided a star rating. In addition to these schemes, there were a number of guides on the market which provided subjective assessment of catering in hotels and other establishments, the best known being the *Michelin Guide, Egon Ronay's Guide* and the *Good Food Guide*.

Example   The AA's star ratings

*   Staff are polite and provide informal yet competent service. Most rooms are en suite and there is a designated eating area with a reasonable choice of food and wines.

**   Staff are smartly presented and provide competent service. All rooms are en suite and have a TV. There is at least one restaurant with a substantial choice of food and wines.

***   Staff will be skilled in responding to guests' needs, and there will be a dedicated receptionist on duty. All rooms are en suite and have remote-control TV and direct-dial telephone. There is a restaurant and a bar or lounge.

****   A formal service where staff anticipate and respond to guests' needs. A 24-hour manned reception, porters available on request. Bedrooms offer superior quality than in three-star hotels. Services such as porterage, 24-hour room service and laundry are included, and the restaurant demonstrates a serious approach to cuisine.

*****   Flawless guest services. Luxurious accommodation, with impressive decor and furnishings. En suite rooms offer extras such as bath sheets and robes and an evening turn-down service. Gourmet cuisine served in the restaurant complemented by superior wines.

Source: *Travel Weekly*, 16 May 2003, from the AA

Over the years, further attempts were made to introduce legislation for a common grading scheme for hotels. The harmonization process within the EU gave an additional boost to these initiatives. Although some member countries do impose compulsory registration within their own borders, different grading schemes have been in use throughout the EU, each involving varying criteria, so the problems of standardizing within Europe remain. Clearly, however, no attempt to standardize throughout the EU could be considered unless the UK could itself put forward an agreed standard within its own boundaries. Consequently, talks were held in 1996 between the tourist board representatives and the two motoring organizations in order to try to achieve a commonly recognized system throughout the UK. The outcome of these talks was only a partial success. The English Tourist Board and the two motoring organizations agreed to adopt a common scheme from the year 2000, based on hotel ratings of one to five stars; the Scottish Tourist Board rejected the scheme on the principle that they wished to lay greater emphasis on quality rather than facilities, and therefore adopted a parallel scheme in 1997, while Wales introduced its own scheme in 1999. Agreement was reached between the three boards and the motoring organizations to adopt a common classification scheme for bed and breakfast establishments from the year 2000.

In 2004 the three mainland tourist boards and two motoring organizations met to attempt once again to thrash out an agreement on hotel classification that would be satisfactory to all parties. Agreement was reached on a common star rating (one to five stars) which will gradually be introduced over an 18-month period beginning in 2006. Properties will be categorised by type, such as Country House Hotel, Small Hotel, Town House Hotel, Metro Hotel. The committee took the view that they would not include budget hotels, as these were not subject to common standards and as many were already trading under well-known brands, the public were generally aware of the standards of these. However, others could optionally adopt the new scheme and request inspection. Similar star ratings will apply to inns and guesthouses, farmhouses, B&Bs and self-catering facilities.

As far as common systems across Europe are concerned, the British Hospitality Association feels that comparisons between hotels of similar status in different countries are virtually impossible to make. There are further complications, for example in the fact that some countries impose higher rates of sales tax on their five-star properties, making it unattractive for hotels in those nations to upgrade their property even if standards are comparable with a five-star property in Britain. In the meantime, tour operators have devised their own systems for assessing those properties used on package tours abroad, to meet the needs of their own clients, leading to additional confusion among the travelling public. Thomson Holidays, for example, uses its 'T-rating', based in part on its own customers' assessment of the accommodation.

Within the sector, concern is focusing on the provision of adequate training and achievement of professional service standards. The long hours, poor salaries at lower levels and generally unattractive conditions of work within the hospitality sector, coupled with an unusually high staff turnover rate, even by the standards of the tourism business, have made it difficult to raise standards of professional service to acceptable levels. Employers and associations are concerned to ensure that 'hospitality assured' standards, as laid down by the European Foundation for Quality Management's

Business Excellence model and based on a worldwide model of best practice, can be applied within their own institutions.

The nature of demand for accommodation facilities

The hotel product is made up of five characteristics: its location, its mix of facilities (which will include bedrooms, restaurants, other public rooms, functions rooms and leisure facilities), its image, the services it provides (including such indefinable features as the level of formality, personal attention, speed and efficiency of its staff), and the price which it is prepared to charge.

The location of a hotel will invariably be the first consideration when the tourist is selecting a hotel. Location implies both the destination (resort for the holidaymaker, convenient stopover point for the traveller, city for the business traveller) and the location within that destination. Thus, business people will want to be accommodated in a city-centre site close to the company they are visiting, while the seaside holidaymaker will seek a hotel as close as possible to the beach, and transit travellers will want to be accommodated at a hotel convenient to the airport from which they are leaving, or a motel close to a major highway on which they plan to travel the following day. In economic terms, a trade-off will occur between location and price, as the leisure traveller looks for the hotel closest to the beach which still fits the budget, or the transit traveller opts for a more distant hotel which is prepared to offer a free transfer to the airport. Location is, of course, fixed for all time; if the resort itself loses its attraction for its visitors, the hotel will suffer an equivalent decline in its fortunes.

The fact that high fixed costs are incurred in both building and operating hotels compounds the risk of hotel operating. City-centre sites are extremely expensive to purchase and operate, requiring high room prices. The market may resist such prices, but is nevertheless reluctant to be based at any distance from the centres of activity, even when good transportation is available. This has been evidenced in the problems faced by incoming tour operators in accommodating American visitors on budget tours to central London at prices competitive with other city centres. The reluctance of many overseas tour operators to accept accommodation on the outskirts of the city for their clients has in the past led to loss of business in favour of other European capital cities.

Again, the demand for central London hotels, leading to high capacity and profits, has caused those in the hotel business to maximize profits by upgrading their accommodation and appealing to the business client, rather than catering for the leisure tourist's demand for budget accommodation. Special services were introduced to attract niche customers; London Hilton, for instance, was among several of the corporations to introduce a woman-only floor, in deference to the increasing numbers of women travelling alone on business. This included a private check-in facility, increased security cameras and double locks on bedroom doors. Meanwhile, the French Accor Group was among the first to identify the market gap for low-priced accommodation in big cities as the established hotel chains went up-market and, as we have seen, launched its Formule 1 and Etap brands to tap into these markets.

Hotels will seek to maximize their revenue by offering a wide range of different tariffs to the different market segments they serve. By way of example, one city hotel provides, apart from the normal rack rate, at least nine other rates, including special concessions to corporate bookings, conference rates, air crew, weekender traffic and tour bookings. In the climate of recession experienced by hotels in recent years, it has also been possible for clients to negotiate substantial discounts if they book late in the day; the hotel management, recognizing that any sale is better than none, allows the desk clerks to come to an agreement against any realistic offer, which may be as much as 50 per cent lower than rack rate.

Hotel companies may be further constrained by the need to meet building codes present in the location where they are building. Increasingly, concern about the environment and widespread recognition of the damage done to the architectural styles of resorts swamped by high-rise hotel building have led local authorities to impose stringent regulations on new buildings. This may mean using local (often more expensive) materials in place of concrete, using vernacular style in the design of the building, limiting the height of hotels to four or five floors (some tropical destinations restrict hotel building to the height of the local palm trees), or restricting the total size of the building to ensure it is in keeping with surrounding buildings.

Some characteristics of the hotel product

The demand for hotel bedrooms will come from a widely distributed market, nationally or internationally, whereas the market for other facilities which the hotel offers will often be highly localized. In addition to providing food and drink for its own residents, the hotel will be marketing these services (and sometimes additional services such as a leisure club with swimming pool) to other tourists or members of the local population at a short distance from the site. Clearly, the hotel will be catering for two quite different market segments, and this will call for different approaches to advertising, promotion and distribution.

Another characteristic of the hotel product is that demand is seldom uniform throughout the year, or even throughout the week. Tourist hotels suffer from seasonality, involving high demand during summer peaks and little or no demand during the winter troughs, while hotels catering chiefly to business people may find demand drops during the summer. Care has to be exercised in pricing leisure market hotels; while a differential is expected between peak and low seasons, if too extreme, competitive destinations will attract visitors away from the site – or they will simply not come.

Example   The Athens Olympics

The dangers of over-pricing are nowhere better illustrated than in the example of the 2004 Athens Olympics. Hotels in Athens, envisaging a bonanza during the event, raised their prices by a factor of five to twelve times above regular rack rates. This resulted in a drop of 30 per cent in bookings compared with the previous year, and many later struggled to raise occupancy levels.

Business hotels also suffer from periodicity, in which demand is centred on Monday to Thursday nights, while there is little demand from Friday to Sunday night. The lack of flexibility in room supply, coupled with the perishable nature of the product (if rooms are unsold there is no opportunity to 'store' them and sell them later) mean that greater efforts must be made to unload unsold accommodation by attracting the off-peak customer to hotels in holiday destinations, and the leisure and family markets to business hotels at weekends.

Even with creative marketing and high discounting, many tourist hotels in highly seasonal resorts will find their occupancy levels falling alarmingly in the winter, and must then face the decision whether it is better to stay open in the winter, in the hope of attracting enough customers to make some contribution to overheads, or to close completely for several months of the year. The problem with the latter course of action is that a number of hotel costs, such as rates, depreciation and salaries for management staff, will continue whether or not the hotel remains open. Temporary closure may also result in difficulties in recruiting good staff, if jobs are known to be only seasonal. In recent years more hotels, especially the larger chain hotels, have opted to remain open, and to offer enhanced packages for those willing to travel off-season. The increase in second holidays and off-season short breaks in Britain has helped to make more hotels viable year-round, although room occupancy remains low out of season in many of the more traditional resorts. Here, the hotel sector is also heavily dependent on the extent to which the public sector is willing to invest in order to make the resort attractive out of season. Popular tourist destinations like Bournemouth, through a process of continuous investment and a deliberate attempt to attract the conference and non-seasonal market, have been able to draw in high numbers of winter tourists, making it economic for many more hotels to remain open year-round. This in turn stimulates further business, as local attractions and events are also encouraged to stay open throughout the year.

While we have talked chiefly in terms of the physical characteristics of the hotel, the psychological factors which attract the visitor are no less important. Service, 'atmosphere', even the other guests with whom the customer will come into contact, all play a role when the choice of hotel is made. Only about 22 per cent of British holidaymakers choose to stay at hotels or guesthouses when holidaying in the UK, compared with some 47 per cent who do so when abroad. The difference is accounted for by the large VFR market in the UK, while demand for camping, caravanning and self-catering holidays, and the rising ownership of second homes, provide alternative opportunities both at home and abroad. According to the Overseas Visitors' Survey, 59 per cent of overseas visitors stay at hotels at some point when visiting the UK, although the pattern varies, and many will choose a variety of different forms of accommodation during their tour. Some 20 per cent choose to stay in bed and breakfast accommodation, with 14 per cent staying in unlicensed hotels or guesthouses. Factors such as class, age and lifestyle will also have a bearing on the choice of sleeping accommodation. In particular, the nature of, and consequent demand for, large hotels will be quite different from that of the small guesthouse or bed and breakfast unit. A large hotel may well provide attractions of its own, distinct from the location in which it is situated; indeed, in some cases the hotel may be a more significant influence on choice than the destination. This is often true of the large hotel/leisure complex providing a range of in-house entertainment as is the case with a number of North American and, increasingly, European hotels. Similarly, some hotels are so closely linked with the destination they serve that the combination of stay at hotel/destination becomes the established pattern. This is seen in Canada, where resorts such as Lake Louise and the Chateau Lake Louise Hotel are inextricably linked (see Figure 11.8). This type of hotel and resort combination is rarer in Britain, although Gleneagles Hotel in Perthshire, Scotland, with its golfing links, provides one such example. It is, however, increasingly a characteristic of package holiday hotels, and has been taken a stage further with the growth of the all-inclusive packaged holiday in which all food, drink and entertainment are included in the price. The Sandals Hotel chain based in the Bahamas and Caribbean was a major initiator in this development.

By way of contrast, a noticeable trend in recent years has been the fall-off among guests staying at non-licensed accommodation in the UK, although licensed hotels have been able to retain their overall share of the accommodation market.

The provision of a good range of attractions, as well as a drinks licence, can help to offset the disadvantages which result from the unavoidable impersonality of the large hotels. As the chains increase their hold on the total pool of hotel beds, an increase in the average number of rooms in each hotel tends to follow, since larger hotels benefit from economies of scale. However, hotels with more than a hundred rooms remain the exception, and smaller properties emphasize the personal nature of their service as a feature in their marketing. Refurbishment of the larger, less attractive hotels is seldom

Figure 11.8
The hotel–resort complex: Chateau Lake Louise, Banff National Park, Canada

(Photographed by the author)

a viable option, and the alternative is to pull them down and construct hotels more in keeping with popular taste. In Majorca, local authorities introduced legislation requiring unattractive mid-twentieth century hotels to be pulled down before new, higher quality buildings could be constructed, and this led to the removal of many 1960s concrete eyesores in ageing resorts like Magaluf, in favour of hotels with greater character. In countries where change and novelty is a feature of market demand, hotel companies now 'theme' their properties to distinguish them from others, either through the style of their architecture or their interior decoration. This, as was pointed out earlier in the chapter, is now becoming a common approach in expensive hotels around the world. Flamboyant architecture, often reminiscent of gothic fortresses, is springing up in the most unlikely places, from Sun City in Southern Africa, where a purpose-built resort complex is designed to provide a simulacrum of 'African culture', to the extravagant Royal Towers of Atlantis, on Paradise Island in the Bahamas, where 'exotic' describes both the architecture and the prices. Chain hotels provide in their budget for regular changes of decor to update their properties, while older hotels emphasize their traditional values and style. With the current boom in nostalgia, hotels which can retain the style of yesteryear, while nevertheless offering modern features like modern bathrooms with good plumbing, can find a ready market for their product. A good example here is the restored Raffles Hotel in Singapore, which after an extensive facelift successfully blended modern comforts with the traditional architecture of the colonial era.

Increasingly, holidaymakers search for something different and unusual in their places of stay as part of their experience of travel. Specialist operators and independent hoteliers are catering to this need. Long-haul travellers can book into an authentic and traditional native 'long house' in Skrang, Sarawak, while tourists to Canada are offered the choice of staying in a North American Indian tepee in Manitoba or an Inuit igloo in the Hudson Bay area. At Oak Alley, Georgia, former slave quarters have been refurbished to accommodate tourists, while Bandera, Texas, offers dude ranches. European hoteliers, too, have created hotels of character out of often unprepossessing sites and materials. In Prague, the former secret-police detention centre has become one of the most popular youth hostels in Europe, while the popularity of an ice-hotel at Jukkasjärvi in Swedish Lappland proved such a draw that others quickly emulated it, not only in Scandinavia but in Chena Hot Springs, near Fairbanks in Alaska, at Kangerlussuaq in Greenland, in Canada near Quebec City (where a night-club accommodating 400 was a feature), and even in Bruges, where Belgian winter temperatures are scarcely conducive to the construction of hotels carved out of ice[1]. In 2005, it was announced that an Ice Palace Hotel would be built at Sun Peaks in British Columbia, Canada. All of these have to be freshly reconstructed after winter thaws each year, and are generally open only between January and April – but they have proved a popular way to attract off-season tourists. For those seeking a similar experience in greater comfort, a heated glass igloo in Finland provides one alternative. Other original approaches to accommodation include lighthouses along the Croatian coast, a windmill in Majorca, a police station in Lynton, Devon, a cider press in Abbeville, France, a signal box in Co Kerry, Ireland and converted pigsties in Garstang, Lancashire ('The Piggeries') and at Monteriggioni, Italy. The Hotel Pastura at Postira on Brac Island, Croatia, was designed in its interior to resemble a 1930s ocean liner, while in Svalbard the Norwegians have converted an ice-bound two masted schooner, the *mv Noorderlicht*, into sleeping accommodation for the adventurous – the ship is a three-hour snowmobile ride from the nearest civilization.

The impulse to do something different, and to sleep in something unique, appears to be growing: the more far-fetched, the better. The proprietor of the Dog Bark Inn at Cottonwood, Idaho, promotes his accommodation as the world's biggest beagle, and the sleeping accommodation is constructed within a giant carved sculpture of a dog. The next fashion is likely to be underwater hotels. A modest and rather basic prototype, the Otter Inn on Lake Mäleran at Västerås in Sweden, has already been constructed; more are planned in Dubai and other Middle East countries seeking to expand tourism.

Example   Undersea hotels

Poseidon Undersea Resorts plans to create an underwater hotel off the coast of the Bahamanian island of Eleuthera. The 20 rooms and two suites will have transparent acrylic ceilings and seaward walls, and guests will be able to operate exterior underwater lighting and feed fish automatically from controls in their rooms.

Hotel modules are to be built in Florida and transported to the site. The hotel is expected to open in 2007.

These are all attempts to offer more than simply a 'room to sleep in'. Today, adventurous tourists, whether travelling for business or pleasure, seek a package of physical and emotional experiences which together will make up the total trip experience, and hoteliers are seeking to satisfy that need.

In the same way, tourists are seeking new experiences in eating out. No longer satisfied with full-board or half-board reservations which lock them into eating in their hotel, they seek different meal experiences each day. Some tourist hotels have tried to accommodate to this need by allowing their guests to eat at other hotels in the area with which they have links, but the appeal of small, comfortable restaurants where they can eat well-cooked authentic local food is luring many tourists away from the all-inclusive package. In catering, too, the desire to experiment with new taste sensations is leading to much more adventurous eating out. Heston Blumenthal, who has introduced highly unconventional food at his now world-famous restaurant the Fat Duck in Bray, Berkshire, has become renowned for such delicacies as snail porridge and mousse poached in liquid nitrogen. Another innovation has been dining in the dark, an idea initiated in 1999 by a restaurateur at Die Blinde Kuh in Zürich. His patrons, having selected their meals, are invited to eat in completely darkened rooms, served by blind waiters. The experience in which a key sense is removed allows the diner to concentrate purely on smell and taste, and this is said to enhance the meal experience. The restaurant has proved immensely popular, and is fully booked at weekends for several months in advance. A Parisian restaurant, Dans le Noir, soon followed suit, blindfolding the patrons, and the restaurant has been so successful that the opening of a second was announced in London in 2005. Similar novelty meal experiences will undoubtedly follow.

Figures 11.9 (a), (b) and (c) Contrasts in accommodation in India. (a) The Umaid Bhawan Palace, luxury hotel in Jodhpur and home of the Maharajah. (b) Basic overnight accommodation at Sam Dunes, near Jaisalmer. (c) Rotel Tours of Germany offer 'sleeping buses' on Indian tours

(a)

(b)

(c)

(Photographed by the author)

The British holiday hotel

The traditional British domestic holiday, 14 nights in a small seaside guest house or unlicensed private hotel, represents an experience that is all but dead, many of these types of accommodation unit having been forced out of business through an inability to respond to modern tourists' needs. This has come about largely due to the appeal of holidays abroad, with packages no more expensive than those in the UK, but which provide much better value for money and, of course, guaranteed sunshine. As a result of their experiences in hotels abroad, British holidaymakers now expect the same facilities in their home country, including improved standards of cuisine, choice of entertainment, and en suite facilities. To survive, hotel proprietors had to invest to meet these standards; not all were able to do so. The Section 4 grants available for hotel construction and improvement under the 1969 Development of Tourism Act were withdrawn in England in 1989 (and more recently in Scotland and Wales), and hotel rates were increasing even as recession reduced incomes. The trend for domestic holidays to be of shorter duration posed both a threat and an opportunity. While short breaks help to extend the season, they also raise room costs, which cannot easily be recovered by higher prices, particularly during periods when the market is price sensitive. On the other hand, these guests often provide a greater opportunity for profits than do long-stay summer guests, who spend little time within the hotel itself. Short-stay guests have less time or inclination to shop around, and the shrewd hotelier can sell them tours, taxi rides, special meals or other extras such as cards and souvenirs. Off-season, inclement weather will keep them in the hotel, where they are more likely to take their meals or spend money in the bars.

Liberalization of the licensing laws in 1988, permitting alcoholic drinks to be served on weekday afternoons, was one of the few rays of sunshine in an otherwise difficult period for the industry. This helped to boost sales in pubs and inns catering to the tourist, enabling the industry to compete more equally with their European neighbours. Traditional accommodation units also face the challenge of a shift to self-catering, both in Britain and abroad. This has come about partly in an effort to hold down holiday prices, but of at least equal importance is the demand from tourists for more flexible types of accommodation and catering than have been available in the small hotels and boarding houses. The once-popular fully inclusive holiday comprising three meals a day, taken at fixed times of the day in the hotel, no longer meets the requirements of the modern tourist, who may wish to tour the surrounding area by car during the day, and will therefore want to eat irregularly, or even forgo a midday meal. Self-catering accommodation meets these needs effectively, and its popularity abroad with British tourists has led to the rapid expansion of similar facilities in the UK, at the expense of the boarding houses. Many smaller hotels have adapted their premises to provide self-catering units in order to survive. Motels have also expanded in number to meet the need for flexibility in touring holidays, but these units are really better suited to larger countries, where they serve the needs of the long-distance motorist using motorway networks.

The B&B unit

The increasing desire of many tourists, particularly overseas visitors to Britain, to 'meet the people' and enjoy a more intimate relationship with the culture of the country they are visiting has benefited the smallest forms of accommodation unit, such as the guesthouse or bed-and-breakfast establishment. These are generally family run, catering to business tourists in the towns and to leisure tourists in country towns, rural areas and the seaside. B&Bs in particular provide a very valuable service to the industry, in that they can offer the informality and friendliness sought by many tourists (many have no more than three bedrooms), cater for the impulse demand that results from holidaymakers touring by car or bicycle, and conveniently expand the supply of beds during peak periods of the year in areas which are highly seasonal, and where hotels

(a)

(b)

(c)

Figures 11.10 (a), (b) and (c) Bed and breakfast accommodation in popular tourist villages: (a) Plockton, Scotland, (b) Betws y Coed, North Wales and (c) Windermere, Lake District, England
(Photographed by the author)

would not be viable. There are estimated to be about 11,500 B&Bs in the UK, of which more than one-third have been certified under the tourist boards' grading systems. Most have six or fewer guests, since this obviates payment of business rates, and neither a fire certificate nor public liability insurance is required to operate.

This form of accommodation was virtually unknown in North America until relatively recently, but has boomed since the 1980s, as the Americans and Canadians brought back with them the experiences they had gained in Europe. However, in general these North American properties have moved up-market to provide much more luxurious accommodation and facilities than would normally be found in their European equivalent.

Farmhouse holiday accommodation

Farmhouse holidays have also enjoyed considerable success in recent years, both in the UK and on the Continent. European countries with strong agricultural traditions, such as Britain and Denmark, have catered for tourists in farmhouse accommodation for many years, and as farmers have found greater difficulty in paying their way through farming alone, owing to the reduction in agricultural subsidies within the EU, they have turned increasingly to tourism as a means of boosting revenue, particularly in the off-season. A study of farm tourism carried out in 1991 revealed that 15 per cent of all farms in England (and 24 per cent in the West Country) have some form of tourism project on their land. The simultaneous trend to healthier lifestyles and the appeal of natural food and the outdoor life have also helped to make farm tourism popular. Within rural areas tourist boards have provided assistance and training for farmers interested in expanding their accommodation for tourism. Both Ireland and Denmark have been notably successful in packaging modestly priced farm holidays for the international market, in association with tour operators and the ferry companies. In the case of Denmark, this has been a logical development to attract tourists to what is generally recognized as an expensive country for holidays based on hotel accommodation.

Camping and caravanning

The market for camping and caravanning holidays in the UK is substantial; according to Mintel research, around 20 per cent of all holidays in Britain were taken in caravans in 2004. Bourne Leisure, the leading firms in the leisure park business, attracts about four million holidaymakers a year to its 55 holiday parks, hotels and resorts in the UK, operating under the British Holidays, Haven, Butlins and Warner brands. While many holidays are, of course, taken in private touring caravans (of which there are around 480,000 in Britain), motor-home holidays are also becoming ever more popular, with 112,000 privately owned vehicles in the UK. Static-caravan and mobile-home sites number 335,000, located in over 4,000 UK holiday parks (of which 1,661 were star rated in 2004). Holiday parks entered the tourist boards' grading schemes in 1987, with the introduction of agreed codes of practice for operators, and a trade body, the British Holiday and Home Parks Association (BH&HPA) has been formed to represent the interests of operators.

Holiday centres

Although the Americans were running summer camps for children some years earlier, adult holiday camps as we know them today were very much a British innovation, introduced on a major scale in the 1930s and 1940s by three noted entrepreneurs, Billy Butlin, Fred Pontin and Harry Warner. Their aim was to provide all-in entertainment at a low price in chalet-style accommodation which would be largely unaffected by inclement weather. The Butlin–Pontin–Warner style of holiday camp became enormously successful in the years prior to World War II and the early post-war era, but none are now family-owned; Butlins and Warners are now part of Bourne Leisure, the largest domestic holiday corporation, which, with its other brands Haven and British Holidays, operates on some 50 sites in Britain, and accommodates more than four million holidaymakers. Pontins operates eight sites in the UK. While Butlins and Pontins continue to focus on family entertainment, Warner holidays are now marketed to adults only. Haven's appeal is to three different markets, described as 'lively, all-action', 'leisurely' and 'relaxing'.

For the most part, the balance of the market is split between large numbers of independent companies, each operating a small number of sites. Some of these operate under franchise agreements to improve their marketing; Hoseasons, to take one example, is a leading holiday site franchisor, and operates around 330 franchise sites. The market for holiday centres remains highly seasonal, falling almost entirely between May and September. It had been customary for centres to close during the winter months, but improved marketing, including mini-breaks and themed events, has helped to extend sales into the 'shoulder' months of spring and autumn. As a percentage of the total accommodation used in domestic tourism, though, holiday centres remain relatively small.

Holiday centres have been affected as much as any other accommodation facilities by changes in public taste. Before the war, they attracted a largely lower-middle-class clientele, but in the post-war period their market became significantly more working class, and the canteen-style catering service and entertainment provided reflected the needs of this market segment. Bookings were made invariably from Saturday to Saturday, and most clients booked direct with the companies. Each company had a quite distinct image for its clientele, who were strongly brand-loyal and booked regularly with their favourite company.

More recently, these camps have attempted to move up-market, a process heralded by a change in their names from camps to holiday centres, villages or parks. The former working-class orientation has been modified to cater for wider social tastes. Large chalet blocks have given way to smaller units with self-catering facilities. A choice of catering styles has been introduced, ranging from fully serviced through self-service to self-catering, the latter enjoying the greatest rates of growth. Butlins in particular has invested huge sums of money to redevelop its remaining three centres and give them a more up-market image. Additionally, the company has recently moved into the hotel business, constructing its first hotel adjacent to its Bognor Regis centre. Guests will enjoy superior accommodation, but must then purchase passes in order to enter the Butlin resort. However, these traditional centres face strong competition from the new wave of holiday villages.

The new holiday villages

Holiday villages offer a new concept in resort marketing. In their present form, they owe their development to a Dutch innovator who opened the first of a chain of Center Parcs in the Netherlands in 1967, rapidly expanding to Belgium, France and the UK. These offered a very different holiday experience to that offered by traditional holiday centres. First launched in Britain in 1987, these up-market holiday villages have now grown to four: Sherwood Forest in Nottinghamshire, Longleat Forest in Wiltshire, Elveden Forest in Suffolk, and Oasis Whinfell Forest in Cumbria. There are plans for a fifth to be built on the Duke of Bedford's estate near Woburn by 2009. Offering a wide choice of all-weather facilities (most notably a vast indoor pool designed to resemble a tropical beach), the villages had an extraordinary measure of success in their early years, with an average 96 per cent occupancy year-round. Ownership is now split between those on the Continent and those in the UK. Another company with seven properties in the Netherlands, Gran Dorado, offers a similar product to that of Center Parcs.

Billy Butlin's early attempts to introduce his holiday camp concept to the Continent were unsuccessful, but the more up-market holiday village has been highly successful. The market leader is Club Méditerranée, French-owned and with a world-wide spread of holiday villages, from France to Tahiti. The success of this organization, which in 1950 was among the first to enter the package holiday business, has been attributed to its unique approach to its clients, who are referred to as *gentils membres*. It has been the practice for beads to be used instead of hard currency to purchase drinks on site; this has heightened the feeling for the holidaymakers of being 'divorced from the commercial world' while on holiday. However, this organization also experienced a decline in profits after failing to keep pace with holiday centre development at the end of the 1990s, and was forced into an expensive programme of renovation to restore its position in the market.

Second-home and time-share ownership

Some words are also appropriate here about the growth of second-home ownership, and the effect which this is having on the tourism industry. Owning a second home in the country or by the sea is no new phenomenon; since the age of the Grand Tour, the British aristocracy, and, later, wealthy merchants, invariably had a country seat to retreat to at weekends and through the summer to escape the heat and dirt of the big cities, and wealthy Parisians similarly owned a second property readily accessible to the French capital. Americans have been buying homes along the north-eastern shores of the United States since the nineteenth century, culminating in the ostentatious residences built as summer homes for the very wealthy along the shores of Newport, Rhode Island, in the 1890s (The Breakers at Newport being the most famous of these). Later, holiday homes were built on the West Coast and in Florida. Today, many wealthy Americans have two holiday homes: a summer home along the Cape and a winter home in Florida. In Europe, Nordic residents have a long tradition of owning second homes by the sea, even if many are of very simple cottage construction; Löfgren[2] claims that there were 500,000 such homes in Sweden by the 1970s, owned by a population totalling only some eight million. A high proportion of these were built for Stockholm residents along the popular west coast of the country, some six hours' drive away. He estimates that 25 per cent of Swedes, and a similar number of other Nordic residents owned second homes by the close of the twentieth century, in comparison with 16 per cent of the French and just 4 per cent of Americans. However, earlier second homes were almost invariably constructed as summer homes for the owners and their friends. What has marked the big change in more recent times has been the commercialization of the second homes market. Owners now buy to let, frequently renting out their property, when not for their own use, through commercial rental agencies who manage the properties for a commission. The holiday homes rental market has soared in recent years, as owners moved into property as a principal investment when the share market collapsed.

British residents were rather later in getting into property, but have more than made up for their tardiness in a frenzy of buying since the 1990s. At first this was confined mainly to Britain, but as prices soared and restrictions began to be imposed on property construction in the more popular areas of the countryside like the Lake District, South Devon and the Cotswolds, Britons began to turn to cheaper accommodation in Italy, France, Spain (especially the Canary and Balearic Islands) and Greece. More recently, homes in Florida and the newly admitted countries of the European Union, especially Malta, Cyprus and Slovenia, have been in demand. Investment in second homes has been fuelled both by an increase in disposable income among the better-off sections of British society, and the fall in air transport prices. In the post 9/11 world, transatlantic fares dropped to an all-time low, while the growth of no-frills airlines to smaller regional airports on the Continent has attracted investors to Romania, Bulgaria and Turkey (all with longer-term hopes of entering the EU).

Example   Buy-to-let hotel rooms

The concept of buy to let has moved on to the hotel sector recently, with guest rooms available for purchase on 99-year leases in commercial hotels. In one such transaction in a London property, owners are permitted to spend up to 52 nights per year in their room, at a nominal charge, while on bookings for the rest of the year owners will receive 45–50 per cent of all rental income. This, it is claimed, will produce net income of up to 7 per cent per annum. Organized as a partnership between Guestinvest and Alias Hotels, the company plans to extend the scheme to 30 hotels in larger UK cities.

Website: www.guestinvest.com

The exact number of second homes owned by British residents abroad is hard to establish; the Office of the Deputy Prime Minister indicates that around 500,000 English households own such properties, of which 295,000 are in England, 25,000 in other parts of the UK and 177,000 abroad, mainly in France and Spain. This would suggest that a further 100,000 households from other parts of the UK also have properties

Figure 11.11
Second homes
are also rented
out as holiday
accommodation
at the
Watermark Club,
Cotswold Water
Park

(Photographed by the author)

abroad. Others put the figure much higher, some as high as two million[3]. Certainly the number is sufficiently large to account for a fall in standard package holiday bookings, as owners (and renters) switch to the net to buy their no-frills flights. The search for properties abroad has led to the use of the term 'propotourism', defining those taking holidays abroad to seek out their new properties.

Where an outright purchase is beyond people's means, the concept of time-share offers an alternative means of enjoying a holiday in one's second home, whether in the UK or abroad. Statistics on time-share ownership are notoriously inaccurate and out of date, although an ARDA report[4] estimated that in 2002 around 6.7 million time-shares were owned around the world, in 5,425 sites. Nearly half of all owners are Americans. In Britain, the Timeshare Consumers Association estimated that there were 405,000 owners in 2001, of which about a quarter owned properties in the UK. At that point it was estimated that there were 131 time-share resorts in the UK. Most of those owned abroad are in Spain (especially the Canaries) and Portugal. European ownership has triggered substantial demand for budget air tickets, while undermining the traditional accommodation sector – indeed, there are hotels in Britain which have responded to the challenge by converting some or all of their accommodation to time-share ownership.

Time-share is a scheme whereby an apartment or villa is sold to several co-owners, each of whom purchases the right to use the accommodation for a given period of the year, which may range from one week to several weeks. The initial cost of the accommodation will vary not only according to the length of time for which it is purchased, but also depending on the period of the year, so that a week in July or August, for example, may be three or four times the cost of the same accommodation in winter.

The scheme is reported to have been initiated at a ski resort in the French Alps in 1965, although the Ring Hotel chain in Switzerland was developing along similar lines some years before this. By the early 1970s, time-share had been introduced in the USA, and the concept had also arrived in Britain by the mid-1970s. Since then it has enjoyed enormous success, boosted by schemes allowing owners to exchange their properties for others around the world during their period of ownership. A number of time-share exchange organizations have been established, of which the largest and best known are RCI (Resort Condominiums International), with 2.4 million members registered worldwide in 2003, and II (Interval International). These companies keep a register of owners, and, for a fee, will facilitate home exchanges around the world, and organize flights.

Unfortunately, the sheer popularity of time-share has led to high-pressure sales techniques by less reputable organizations using 'street touts' to approach tourists visiting resorts abroad, and this led initially to some poor publicity for the scheme in the press. The Timeshare Developers' Association was formed to give the industry credibility, and to draw up a code of conduct for members, and since 1991 a Timeshare Council has overseen the regulation of time-share within the UK. The Office of Fair Trading keeps a watching brief on development within the UK, while the Organization for Timeshare in Europe (OTE) has developed a code of conduct for its members, oversees quality and offers a free conciliation service for consumers dealing with the members.

Time-share is not without its problems. It has been found to be difficult to resell property due to the amount of new time-share property coming on to the market, and in some cases management and maintenance fees have been high. There can be a problem in getting widely dispersed owners together to take decisions on the management of the property.

Notwithstanding these difficulties, time-share remains popular, and is likely to grow as an alternative to the traditional package holiday. A recent innovation has been the growth of time-share operated by the leading hotel chains such as Marriott, with its Vacation Club International brand. Hotel ownership has expanded the product, by introducing spas and other activities along with the basic time-share holiday.

Educational accommodation

The significance of the educational accommodation sector must also be recognized. Universities and other institutions of higher education, seeking to increase contributions to their revenue through the rental of student accommodation during the academic holidays, have marketed this accommodation for budget holidays to tour operators and others. Often situated in green-field sites near major tourist destinations, such as Stirling or York, the universities have experienced considerable success in this venture, and have further expanded their involvement with the leisure market by providing other facilities such as activity centres and public rooms for themed holidays.

University standards of accommodation have greatly improved in recent years to meet the expectations of students themselves, whose accommodation standards at home are also rising. En suite facilities are now the norm, bringing the standards up to the levels which budget holidaymakers have come to expect, and making facilities comparable to other accommodation for budget conferences and business meetings – a profitable source of revenue for the institutions during the academic holidays.

The distribution of accommodation

Large hotel chains have in the past enjoyed advantages in gaining access to their markets through their links with the airline sector. This close relationship dates back to the early 1970s when airlines, introducing their new jumbo jets, hastily set about establishing connections with hotels to accommodate their increasing passenger numbers. As a result, hotel chains gained access to the airlines' global distribution systems (GDS), computerized reservations networks which were a key factor in selling rooms to the international market. While this link remains important, the development of the Internet has changed the nature of distribution, making the large hotel groups far more independent in their interface with customers. Apart from hotel representation on airline-owned (or formerly owned) websites like Opodo and Orbitz, on-line agencies like Expedia and Travelocity, which offer a range of travel products, feature hotels prominently and have become a powerful force in the distribution chain. Websites devoted to accommodation only are also springing up as alternatives to sites affiliated to carriers or other principals and intermediaries, with rooms at highly competitive prices. The larger hotel groups are increasingly relying on their own websites to reach their customers, in an effort to cut costs by avoiding payment of commission to intermediaries.

Large hotels depend upon group as well as individual business, so they must maintain contact with tour operators, conference organizers and others who bulk-buy hotel bedrooms. The tourist boards can play a part in helping such negotiations by organizing workshops abroad to which the buyers of accommodation and other facilities will be invited.

All large hotel chains, and many smaller hotel companies, now have their own computer systems to cope with back-of-office and management information as well as providing access worldwide to their reservations system. Some chains maintain their own offices in key generating countries (and of course each hotel will recommend business and take reservations for others in the chain), while independent hotels reach the overseas markets through membership of marketing consortia. The former role of hotel representative agencies has dwindled as on-line booking agencies took over their role, and the few that survive, such as Utell International, are now substantially electronic agencies. Even the smallest hoteliers today operate interactive CRSs via the Internet, although their prospects of reaching the customer are enhanced when in association with other accommodation units.

Some will think of travel agents as obvious distributive outlets. However, few agents, apart from those dealing regularly with business travellers, are keen to handle hotel bookings as distinct from comprehensive travel services, and increasingly travellers are independently prepared to search the World Wide Web for their cheap airline seats and hotel rooms. Domestic bookings are traditionally made direct with the hotel, and for reservations abroad agents are unwilling to get involved unless they hold agreements with the hotels on the payment of commission. Some hotels will pay a standard 10 per cent, while others allow only a lesser rate, or restrict commissions to room sales outside peak periods. Many agents are also unwilling to deal with overseas hotels without making a charge for the service. However, where hotels package their product in the form of short breaks or longer holidays, these may be sold like any other package through the agent. Here, the agent is clear about the commission accruing, but may still be reluctant to stock brochures describing the product due to the limited rack space. The growth of dynamic packaging, essentially tailor-made programmes put together by an intermediary such as an operator or agent by a search of websites, may provide agents with scope to retain their customers' loyalty, if they can show that they are offering expertise beyond what travellers can find for themselves.

Traditionally, clients for UK holiday centres have also booked direct, but the centres are now more supportive of sales through the travel agents, and leading companies like Butlins anticipate a substantial percentage of their sales will be handled in this way.

Finally, mention should be made of the sale of accommodation through public-sector tourism outlets. This is commonly found on the Continent – the Dutch tourist offices (VVVs) provide a reservation service for tourists, and have done so for many years – and today tourist information centres (TICs) in the UK also offer a booking service, as one reflection of their increasingly commercial role. The 'Book a bed ahead' (BABA) system allows visitors to book either hotel or farmhouse accommodation through local TICs, for which a fee is charged and for which the TIC receives a commission from the principal. Increasingly, such bookings can be undertaken using a local computer reservations system, which improves the service which the TICs provide.

Environmental issues

All sectors of the tourism industry are becoming sensitized to the issue of eco-tourism, or ecologically sound tourism which can be sustained as tourist numbers continue to grow. Hotels are in a position to take a lead on this issue. They are also frequently the recipients of complaints by the eco-tourism lobby as a result of their practices; for example, hotels in Goa, in India, have been strongly criticized because of their profligate use of water for showers, swimming pools etc. in a region where the local inhabitants suffer from water shortages due to drought.

Where there are shortages of water, as for example in the Channel Islands in Britain, many hotels will encourage their guests to use water sparingly – to shower rather than bath, to ensure taps are turned off and to take other measures which reduce waste. Hotel proprietors have recognized, for instance, that many guests would prefer not to have their towels and sheets replaced daily, and savings can be effected by offering guests the choice of fresh linen (which they may indicate by leaving towels on the floor in the morning) or reuse of their linen (indicated by hanging towels up). One example of an eco-friendly approach in the industry is the launch of the International Hotels Environment Initiative, referred to in Chapter 7, which now enjoys the support of many large chains. The initiative sets out to monitor environmental performance of

Plate 1
Climbers at the top of Mount Snowdon, Wales

(Photographed by the author)

Plate 2
Awsiters (later Creaks) saltwater immersion treatment baths, first opened at Brighton in 1769

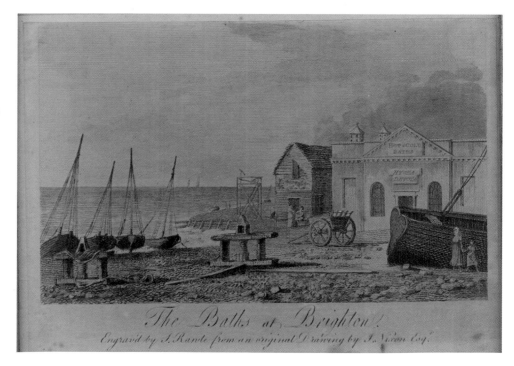

(Private archive)

Plate 3
The early years of the seaside spa: bathing machines at Brighton in the late eighteenth century

(Source: Rowlandson print in Wigstead, H and Rowlandson, T, *An Excursion to Brighthelmstone*, London, 1790. Private archive)

Plate 4
The ever-popular beach holiday: Grömitz, on the Baltic Sea in North Germany

(Photographed by the author)

Plate 5
Sandals Resorts
are leaders in
the all-inclusive
holiday market:
the Regency St
Lucia Golf Resort
and Spa

(Courtesy Sandals)

Plate 6
Salcombe, in Devon, where nearly half the homes are owned by outsiders

(Photographed by the author)

Plate 7
A landing party at Deception Island, Antarctica, from the Marco Polo, largest passenger ship calling regularly at the Antarctic Peninsula

(Photographed by the author)

Plate 8
Scuba divers at coral reef, Tropical North Queensland, Australia

(Courtesy: Tourism Queensland)

Plate 9
Bristol has not been slow to benefit from its restored Harbourside: the scene at the annual Harbour Festival

(Photographed by the author)

Plate 10
An outstanding modernist building: the Villa Savoye, near Paris, designed by le Corbusier, is now a museum open to the public

(Photographed by the author)

Plate 11
Monet's Garden at Giverny, France

(Photographed by the author)

**Plate 12
(a) and (b)**
Graves of the famous are a popular attraction for tourists. The burial sites of (a) Winston Churchill at Blenheim, Oxfordshire and of (b) Vincent van Gogh at Auvers-sur-Oise

(a)

(b)

(Photographed by the author)

**Plate 13
(a) and (b)**
The character hotel: Morgan's Hotel in Swansea, South Wales

(a)

(b)
(Photographed by the author)

Plate 14
P&O's *Oceana* at anchor in the Caribbean

(Courtesy: P&O Cruises)

Plate 15
A narrow boat enters a lock at Bingley, Yorkshire

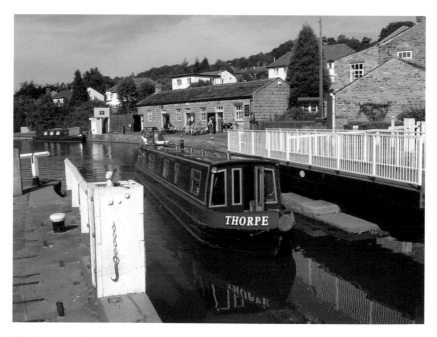

(Photographed by the author)

Plate 16 Many TICs are either in buildings of historical or architectural interest, or have other charms that will appeal to the visitor:

(a) TIC at Lille, France
(Photographed by the author)

(b) TIC in Bourton on the Water, in the Cotswolds
(Photographed by the author)

Plate 16
(*continued*)

(c) TIC in Cordoba, Spain
(Photographed by the author)

(d) TIC in Blackheads House, Old Town, Riga, Latvia
(Courtesy: Riga Tourist Office)

Plate 16
(*continued*)

(e) TIC in Ebeltoft, Denmark, pays tribute to Danish modern design
(Photographed by the author)

(f) TIC in Valga, Estonia, a nineteenth-century former town hall
(Courtesy: Valga Tourist Office)

the participating hotels, and to offer practical advice, especially to small independent hoteliers, on how they can manage their hotels in a more environmentally sensitive manner. This includes encouragement to reuse linen, the efficient use of energy in the hotel, consideration of methods of rubbish disposal and even the replacement of throw-away shampoo containers with shampoo dispensers in the bathroom. Such measures can provide substantial savings on costs for the hotels themselves, as well as helping to improve the environment as a whole and ensuring that as far as possible tourism in hotels is environmentally sustainable.

Notes

1 Escape, special section in *The Observer*, 7 December 2003, pp 2–3
2 Löfgren, O, *On Holiday: a History of Vacationing*, Berkeley, University of California Press, 1999, p 131
3 Keenan, S, Deputy Travel Editor, *The Times*, gives a figure of two million. See No Wonder Sales of Package Holidays are Down, *The Times*, 3 July 2004
4 www.arda.org 2005 website

Websites

Great Inns of Britain	www.greatinns.co.uk
Pride of Britain Hotels	www.prideofbritainhotels.com
Scotland's Personal Hotels	www.scotland-hotels.com
Underwater hotel and bizarre accommodation	www.distinctlydifferent.co.uk
Ice hotels	www.icehotel-canada.com,
	www.icepalacehotel.com,
	www.ijs-sculptuur.com
Gran Hotel Bali, Benidorm	www.grupobali.com
Hotel buy-to-let	www.guestinvest.com
Global Hotel Alliance	www.globalhotelalliance.com
Organisation for Timeshare in Europe	www.ote-info.com

Questions and discussion points

1 Without the Poles and Slovaks, the hospitality industry would have collapsed long ago.
Head Chef at an up-market country hotel, 2005

Since the advent of the new Eastern European nations into the EU, the influx of workers from these countries has been a godsend for the hospitality industry. Does it mean we need no longer increase our efforts to attract British workers into the industry? What potential problems can arise, and do arise, with this reliance upon foreign workers?

2 In 2005, plans were announced to create a holiday village extending over 450 acres within the Pembrokeshire Coast National Park. Approval was granted for the development by the Court of Appeal, in the face of opposition from the Council for National Parks, who fear that this protected area will now be threatened with large-scale tourism development which will threaten

the tranquillity of the area. However, Court took the view that the park had an obligation 'to foster the economic and social well-being of local communities'. Development plans include the construction of 340 timber lodges and a sports club, and are backed by the park on the grounds that it will encourage jobs and tourism growth in south-west Wales.

An appeal to the House of Lords was considered. How would you rule on this issue, if judging the appeal? Could the decision open the floodgates to similar applications in other parks? Should all such development be refused, or should each case be judged on its merits?

3   How do variations in price affect the type of guest at a hotel? How do hoteliers manipulate prices to maximize yield?

4   How do food fashions affect the demand by tourists for food in accommodation and restaurants? How well does the industry respond in your country to these changing patterns of demand?

5   Is the new grading scheme a good solution to the problem of grading hotels and other accommodation in Britain? What suggestions could you make that would improve on this, and can the scheme be brought into line with schemes operated in other countries?

Assignment topics

1   As a trainee manager in a large, but rather tired character hotel in need of thorough renovation and up-grading, you have been asked by your General Manager to identify the revenue-producing resources of your hotel and produce a report for him which will indicate how each can contribute to the overall profitability of the hotel, and how revenues can be maximized. Develop a hypothetical plan which will enable you to produce a suitable report for your boss.

2   Prepare a campaign to increase awareness of opportunities for tourists visiting your town to eat out by developing a 'food event'. Suggest what advertising and promotion you would undertake, establishing a realistic budget, based on funding which will be supported by the local authority and the local restaurants association. The campaign should include a specialized theme.

3   Research among B&B proprietors in some areas of the UK reveals that reservations fraud by guests is becoming a serious problem. A common practice is to book two or more B&Bs, using randomly selected 16-digit credit card numbers and false telephone numbers, failing to cancel rooms not used and sometimes failing to take up any of the bookings made. Interview proprietors in your nearest tourist town or resort, using tape recorders to record their experiences, and find out how extensive the problem is, and what actions they take to avoid loss of revenue. Complete a report with recommendations to be put to the local hotel and restaurant association indicating a programme of action to reduce the impact of this fraud.

12 Tourist transport by air

Objectives

After studying this chapter, you should be able to:

- understand the role that airlines and airports play in the development of tourism
- explain how air transport is organized, and distinguish between different categories of airline operation
- understand the reasons for air regulation, and the systems of regulation in force, both in the UK and internationally
- be aware of the dynamic nature of the airline business, and the changes that have taken place in recent years
- analyze the reasons for success and failure of airlines' policies.

Introduction

However safe the airliners, the travel angst is still visible in the faces in every transit lounge – the white knuckles, finger-biting and strained cheekbones which have deeper causes than the simple fear of the air. Air travel can still provide a unique and devastating combination – of boredom and terror.

Anthony Sampson, *Empires of the Sky*,
Hodder and Stoughton, 1984, p 226

Tourism is the outcome of the travel and stay of people, and, as we have seen, the development of transport is a key factor in the growth and direction of tourism development. The provision of adequate, safe, comfortable, fast, convenient and cheap public transport is a prerequisite for mass-market tourism. A tourist resort's accessibility is the outcome of, above all else, two factors: price (in absolute terms, as well as in comparison with competitive resorts) and time (the actual or perceived time taken to travel from one's originating point to one's destination). Air travel, in particular, over the past four decades has made medium- and long-range destinations accessible on both these counts, to an extent not previously imaginable. In doing so, it has substantially contributed to the phenomenon of mass-market international tourism, with all the economic and social benefits and drawbacks that that has entailed.

Public transport, while an integral sector of the tourism industry, must also provide services which are not solely dependent upon tourist demand. Road, rail and air services all owe their origins to government mail contracts, and the carriage of freight, whether separate from or together with passengers, makes a significant (and sometimes crucial) contribution to a carrier's revenue. It should also be recognized that many carriers provide a commercial or social service which owes little to demand by tourists. Road and rail carriers, for example, provide essential commuter services for workers travelling between their places of residence and work. These carriers (and sometimes airlines, as in remoter districts of Scotland) provide an essential social and economic service by linking outlying rural areas with centres of industry and commerce, thus ensuring a communications lifeline for residents. The extent to which carriers can or should be commercially oriented while simultaneously being required to provide a network of unprofitable social routes is a constantly recurring issue in government transport policy.

Most forms of transport are highly capital-intensive. The cost of building and maintaining track in the case of railways, and of regularly re-equipping airlines with new aircraft embodying the latest technical advances, requires massive investments of capital. This level of investment is available only to the largest corporations, and in some cases subsidies from the public sector may be necessary for political or social reasons such as those outlined above. At the same time, transport offers great opportunities for economies of scale, whereby unit prices can be dramatically reduced. There is a high element of fixed costs, for example, for an airline operating out of a particular airport, whether that airline operates flights four times a day or once a week. If these overheads can be distributed over a greater number of flights, the costs of an individual seat on a flight will fall.

The question of economies of scale is one for caution, however. There comes a point where the growth of organizations can result in diseconomies of scale, which can well offset any benefits of size. The difficulties faced by larger traditional airlines in competing with the leaner, more efficient budget airlines are a case in point. Major airlines, for reasons of prestige, have in the past tended to opt for expensively furnished high-rent city centre offices, imposing added burdens on overheads; today, these have generally opted to move out to airport locations, and it is the subsidized airlines from the Third World which retain their high-rent offices in city centres.

The airline business

In Chapter 3 we explored the way in which the development of air transport in the second half of the twentieth century contributed to the growth of tourism, whether for business or pleasure. Travel by air has become safe, comfortable, rapid and, above all, cheap, for two reasons.

The first reason was the enormous growth of aviation technology during this period, especially following the development of the jet airliner after World War II. The first commercial jet (the De Havilland Comet, operated by BOAC) came into service on the London–Johannesburg route in 1952. Problems with metal fatigue resulted in the early withdrawal from service of this aircraft, but the introduction of the hugely successful Boeing 707, in service first with Pan American Airways in 1958, and later the first jumbo jet, the Boeing 747, which went into service in 1970, led to rapid falls in seat cost per passenger kilometre (a common measure of revenue yield). These costs fell both in absolute terms and relative to costs of other forms of transport, particularly shipping, which up to the mid-1950s had dominated the long-haul travel business. Both engines and aircraft design have since been continuously refined and improved; wings, fuselage and engines have been designed to reduce drag, and engines have become more efficient and less fuel-hungry. Increases in carrying capacity for passengers and freight have steadily reduced average seat costs, with jumbo jets accommodating up to 500 passengers. The next phase in this development arrives in 2006, when the Airbus 'superjumbo' A380, a double-decker aircraft seating between 550 and 800 passengers, enters service with the promise of further economies of scale. However, prices to passengers can only fall if a high proportion of these seats are filled; in the past, sudden jumps in capacity have posed problems for airlines on some routes until seat demand caught up with supply. Of course, the introduction of these huge new aircraft will pose additional problems, in their need for longer runways and new methods of ground handling. The prospect of loading and unloading up to 1,600 passengers for one aircraft within a short space of time is daunting, and will require extensively redesigned terminals – but there are precedents in the loading and unloading of cruise ships, which are now being designed to take up to 3,500 passengers, all of whom have to be disgorged in a short space of time for excursions at ports of call. The motivation behind such large aircraft is not simply efficiency; it also helps to overcome problems caused by growing congestion at airports throughout the world. This is becoming critical at leading hub airports, where there are already acute shortages of take-off and landing slots.

The supersonic Concorde was perhaps the only aircraft whose design ran counter to this drive for economies of scale. Introduced into service in 1976, Concorde carried 100 passengers at speeds in excess of 1,400 miles per hour. Quite apart from the technical problems that have to be overcome when designing an aircraft for supersonic flight, speeds above Mach 1 substantially increase fuel burn, and most current airliners fly at around Mach 0.85, just sub-sonic. However, on some key global routes, speed is more important than cost, and business travellers, celebrities and other wealthy air travellers were prepared to pay highly for the privilege of cutting their travelling time. In spite of this, the high cost of operation, restriction in numbers carried, comparatively short range and excessive noise limited Concorde's use largely to routes over oceans rather than over land. The initial high development costs were written off by the British and French governments, and services were limited to flights between New York (and initially Washington) and London or Paris. The crash of a chartered Concorde in France in 2000 led to the grounding of all these aircraft and the termination of any form of supersonic travel for the foreseeable future. Research is currently taking place into the feasibility of building supersonic executive aircraft with very limited passenger capacity (and smaller sonic booms) to satisfy the latent demand for high-speed corporate travel (French company Dassault, to quote one example, has tentative plans for an eight-seat business jet with a range of 4,000 miles, travelling at mach 1.8) but these are unlikely to materialize before 2020. However, the Cessna Citation X executive aircraft already is capable of reaching mach 0.92, very close to the speed of sound, and for the most part the industry is putting its faith in demand for just-subsonic aircraft to satisfy the executive market for the next decade.

Periodically, crises have occurred in world oil supplies, resulting in escalating fuel costs. This had a huge impact on aircraft costs in 1973–74, and again following the Gulf War in 1991, the 9/11 crisis in 2001, the subsequent war in Iraq and its aftermath. Although these have proved to be generally of short duration, oil supply is not infinite, while demand is growing sharply, and will outstrip supplies within 20 to 40 years, even after allowing for new finds. Moreover, oil prices are unstable and can fluctuate rapidly; in the mid-1990s, the price fell to as low as $10 a barrel, while since the end of 2004 it has tended to exceed $55. World shortages of oil in 2005 again drove prices up to $70 a barrel, and a figure of $100 now seems not outside the realms of possibility. Prices are thought unlikely to drop in the future, given the demand from new economic powerhouses like China and the world political climate; consequently, the aircraft industry is searching in the short term for new ways of improving fuel economy, while in the longer term it will be imperative to discover new means of powering aircraft, unless the industry is willing to embrace a sharp drop in the overall number of passengers carried.

In the past, economies have been achieved through a combination of improved engine efficiency and reduced weight. To achieve weight reduction, some airlines have reduced the number of beverages carried, withdrawn seat phones, replaced division between classes with curtains, and even withdrawn, or reduced the number of pages in, their in-flight magazines. Airlines are obliged to carry some reserves of fuel for emergencies, but they will also often carry excess fuel in order to avoid refuelling in expensive areas of the globe. Airlines facing low profits from competition have to weigh up the advantages of introducing the latest fuel-efficient aircraft against the high capital costs of buying them – a problem which will be discussed later in this chapter.

Example Painting aircraft

Airlines have to determine whether to paint their airframes as well as in what colours. This is not just an aesthetic issue. Boeing's 747-400 has an overall area equivalent in size to 14 tennis courts, and painting this results in a penalty of 252 kg, or the weight of three passengers. White and lighter colours require more coats, pushing the weight penalty up to 454 kg. American Airlines save more than $2 million each year by polishing rather than painting their aircraft.

Source: *Airways*, January 2005, pp 35–42

Many experts believe that the jet engine has now reached a stage of evolutionary sophistication which will make it increasingly difficult to produce further economies, and cost-cutting exercises have replaced technological innovation as a means of reducing prices to the public. However, the search for more economy goes on; there are promising developments in recent research which suggest that the problems of carrying liquefied hydrogen rather than kerosene as fuel have been largely overcome. This would provide three times the energy per unit, and allow aircraft to increase their range substantially.

During the 1980s, the technological focus changed to the development of quieter aircraft, and aircraft capable of taking off from, and landing on, shorter runways. The emphasis on quieter engines originated in the United States, where controls on noise pollution forced airlines to re-equip their fleets, or to fit expensive modifications to existing aircraft. In turn, the airlines press their governments to relax controls over night flying, which would enable them to operate around the clock, easing congestion and increasing their productivity. The British government has shown itself reluctant to permit more than a token increase in night flying, especially from the congested London airports.

Short take-off and landing (STOL) aircraft built by companies such as Fokker, Short and Saab for commuter services, seating 30–50 passengers, and slightly larger aircraft built for regional services, and typically carrying 70–110 passengers, such as BAe Systems' RJX, Fairchild Dornier's 728 and 928JET and the Bombardier and Embraer CRJ and ERJ families, have all helped to revolutionize business travel, allowing airports to be sited much closer to city centres.

Example   London City Airport

London City Airport, situated in the Docklands area (see Figure 12.1), is an example of such a development which has been partly dependent upon STOL technology for success. The airport was initially hampered by the lack of good connections to central London, and by a short-sighted marketing decision to promote the airport exclusively as a business airport, with the expectation that passengers would arrive by taxi. The weakness in this strategy quickly became evident, and public transport connections were encouraged. The airport now operates profitably, with its prospects further enhanced by the construction and opening in 2005 of a Docklands Light Railway station within the grounds to provide connections with the London Underground service.

Another factor in the development of mass travel by air was the enterprise and creativity demonstrated by both air transport management and other entrepreneurs in the tourism industry. At a time of strictly regulated prices, the introduction of net inclusive tour-basing fares for tour operators, variable pricing techniques such as Advance Purchase Excursion (APEX) tickets and stand-by fares helped to stimulate demand and fill aircraft seats. Later, innovative carriers introduced frequent-flyer programmes, in which passengers collect additional free miles based on the mileage they accumulate with a carrier, or one of its partners.

However, by far the most important development in recent years has been the growth of low-cost, no-frills airlines. Prompted by the deregulation of the airline

Figure 12.1
The RJ-85, ideally equipped for short take-offs and landings at London City Airport

(Permission of London City Airport Ltd)

industry in America, many small regional carriers came into being to fight for a share of the potentially lucrative domestic airline market. Many, like People's Express, faded quickly; others, like Southwest Airlines (formed as the first low-cost airline in 1971) maximized new opportunities and went from strength to strength. With the liberalization of air transport in the European Community a few years later, an explosion of no-frills carriers emerged, led by Ryanair, which sought initially to challenge the hold over the Irish market held by Aer Lingus. The entrepreneur Stelios Haji-Ioannou followed with the launch of easyJet. These and other small carriers, together with rising seat-only sales on the charter carriers' aircraft, were soon impacting on the profitability of major airlines[1], forcing these to develop their own low-cost offshoots, with mixed success. British Airways introduced budget airline Go in 1998, but after a management buyout this eventually became part of the easyJet empire in 2002, while KLM's offshoot Buzz was sold to Ryanair in 2003. BMI's offshoot BMIbaby and Virgin Express were more fortunate, continuing to trade successfully up to the present.

The organization of air transport

It is convenient to think of the civil aviation business as composed of a number of elements, namely:

- equipment manufacturers
- airports
- air navigation and traffic control services
- airlines.

As was mentioned earlier, however, each of these is not dependent only on tourists for its livelihood. Apart from non-tourist civilian passengers, they also serve the needs of the military, as well as those of freight and mail clientele. However, the tourist market is important for each of these elements, and they must be included as components within the tourism industry.

Equipment manufacturers

Equipment manufacturers are made up of companies manufacturing commercial airframes and engines. The demand for airframes (fuselages and wings) can be conveniently divided between those for large jet aircraft, typically carrying between 130 and 500 passengers, which provide the bulk of passenger services throughout the world, and those for smaller aircraft seating as few as 18 passengers, which are employed chiefly on business routes or provide feeder services from rural airports. Separately classified are those companies manufacturing private jets such as the Learjet, typically seating four to nine passengers. These also have a role to play in business tourism, as they are extensively employed in air taxi services.

The world demand for airframes is dominated by just two manufacturers, each of which has a roughly equal share of the market: the US-owned Boeing Aircraft Company (which swallowed what was then the second largest airframe manufacturer, McDonnell Douglas, in 1996) and Airbus Integrated Company (AIC), the consortium responsible for building the European Airbus, 80 per cent of which is built in mainland Europe and 20 per cent (the wings) by BAe Systems in the UK. The majority share in the Airbus consortium is held by the European Aeronautic Defence and Space Company (EADS), which comprises French-owned Aerospatiale Matra, German-owned DaimlerChrysler Aerospace AG (DASA) and Spanish-owned Construcciones Aeronáuticas SA (CASA). BAe also cooperates with other companies in the construction of smaller aircraft, to compete more effectively in the global market. A handful of smaller companies build airframes for smaller aircraft, mainly for regional routes, the most important being Embraer of Brazil and Bombadier of Canada, but many others have failed in recent years, including Fairchild, Dornier, de Havilland, Fokker, Shorts and Saab. Even BAe ceased manufacturing regional jets in 2001.

Aircraft engines are manufactured quite separately, and three companies dominate this market: GE Aircraft Engines (USA), Pratt & Whitney (USA) and Rolls-Royce (UK). Due to the intense competition for contracts to supply engines to new airliners as they come on-stream, these manufacturers, and other smaller companies, often cooperate in engine design and construction. One consortium set up for this purpose is International Aero Engines (IAE), comprising Pratt & Whitney, Rolls Royce, MTU Aero Engines of Germany, Snecma Moteurs of France and Aero Engines Corporation of Japan. General Electric and Snecma also cooperate under the banner of CFM

International Aero Engines, and Europrop International comprises Rolls Royce, Snecma, MTU Aeroengines and ITP (Industria de Turbo Propulsores). Pratt & Whitney and GE Aircraft Engines have worked together in the USA on the production of aero engines for the new superjumbo, in competition with Rolls-Royce. As with airframes, we can see that this market too is effectively controlled by an oligopoly, and that the cost of aircraft development and production is now so high that international cooperation between the leading companies is essential.

The world fleet of civil aircraft was estimated at some 10,900 aircraft in 2000. Manufacturers' estimates three years later put the demand for aircraft at 20,000 by 2020. A cumulative rise of about 5 per cent per annum in passenger numbers is expected over the next 15 years, with average seat capacity also rising sharply as economies of scale encourage the purchase of larger aircraft. A single Airbus A319 costs around $50 million before discounts, a Boeing 747-400 around $200 million, and estimates for the price of the new generation of A380 aircraft range between $225–285 million each (although a report funded by Boeing has claimed that initial prices have been as low as $130–145 million, well below the estimated building cost of $199 million). One can clearly see the importance of this industry to the countries and, particularly, regions in which aircraft frames and engines are constructed; aviation represents some 10 per cent of the US economy, with a million employees. The economic health of Seattle, headquarters of Boeing, is substantially dependent on the aviation industry. Toulouse in France, and towns like Broughton (North Wales, where Airbus A380 wings are built), Derby and Filton, near Bristol are key centres of aircraft manufacture in the UK, and the economy of these towns depends to a large extent on demand for new aircraft. However, aircraft demand is subject to global political and economic changes, and hence extremely volatile. In September, 2001, in the aftermath of 9/11, there was a fall of 17 per cent in international scheduled flights (and a 30 per cent fall in North America); the combined losses in 2001–02 wiped out the profits made by all IATA airlines in the previous 45 years, according to that organization's Director-General (later, a loss of $23 billion was reported for the period 2001–04). Nevertheless, the potential long-term economic benefits of aircraft manufacture are such that other fast-developing low-cost countries are keen to enter the field, often with the backing of Western aircraft companies: the world's fourth largest airframe manufacturer, Embraer, for example, is partly owned by a consortium of European aircraft manufacturers. One further point to note is that aircraft, wherever they are manufactured in the world, are priced in US dollars, so currency shifts between the dollar and the euro are critical. Airbus costs are mainly in euros, so a hardening of this currency against the dollar, as occurred through 2004, is detrimental to Airbus profitability, making it harder to sell aircraft on the world market. However, cheaper dollars would make it attractive for Airbus to buy more parts from US sources.

The introduction of the new super jumbo represents a significant gamble for the aircraft industry, as to whether the future success of airlines will depend on high-frequency, low-volume routes, or low-frequency, high-volume routes. The A380 will accommodate up to 550 passengers (but a possible stretched version carrying up to 850–1000 passengers may be marketed for high-density routes like short domestic flights in Japan, where existing Boeing 747s are already operating with 569 seats). Airbus Industrie is convinced that there is a market for these giant aircraft, because the decreasing availability of take-off and landing slots at major airports and the growth of international air traffic favours large jets. It believes that around 35–40 city pairs have reached saturation point, and expansion can only be achieved by increasing the passenger capacity of each aircraft. To take one example, it is estimated that the advent of the A380 would allow London Heathrow to handle an additional 10 million passengers each year. It has forecasted demand for the A380 from launch date to 2023 as 1,650 (plus a further 300 for freight operations), although other estimates have ranged between 320 and 1,500. The break-even point has been placed at 250 aircraft, and 149 had been ordered by the beginning of 2004. First deliveries will take place probably in 2007.

Boeing, on the other hand, is convinced that future demand is for fewer trunk routes and more point-to-point services requiring small to medium-sized jets. Its own forecast is for fewer than 500 superjumbos, and it claims only some 15 routes could support these giants. If proved correct, Airbus will be unlikely to break even on the huge investment necessary to build these aircraft. Boeing has cancelled proposals to build a competing superjumbo aircraft, the so-called Sonic Cruiser (although there have been a number of possible 'rethinks' about this strategy – Boeing would be severely disadvantaged if the superjumbo is a success). It is also known to have considered the feasibility of building a blended-wing delta-shaped aircraft with an 800-seat capacity which would require a fuel load less than three-quarters that of a traditional jumbo, and be far quieter in operation. In the meantime, its strategy is to develop the new 787 Dreamliner, a 200–300 seat passenger aircraft with a range of 7,600 miles, as a replacement for the current generation 757 and 767 aircraft. It claims this will be 20 per cent more fuel-efficient than the current 767 – and based on present industry estimates, it is also likely to be more fuel-efficient than the superjumbo, at 2.6 litres per passenger per 100 km, compared with estimates of 2.9 litres in the A380. This is largely due to lightweight materials used in the fuselage, which will be constructed of carbon fibre reinforced plastic (CFRP) rather than aluminium, while the A380's fuselage is composed of a mix of CFRP and GLARE, a similarly lightweight laminate of aluminium and glass-fibre reinforced glue.

The Boeing 787 Dreamliner is expected to be in service by 2008, and Boeing is predicting sales of 3,100 aircraft (while some 2,000 757/767 aircraft are expected to be withdrawn from service over the next 20 years). Meanwhile Boeing will concentrate on extending sales of its 747-400ER (extended range) jumbo and the smaller, reliable and cost-efficient 737-900 'workhorse' for the cheaper end of the industry. It has also announced plans to build two further aircraft. Firstly, a stretched version of the 777 is to be introduced, to be called the 777-200LR, which will have a range of 10,847 miles. This will provide airlines with by far the longest range aircraft in the world, theoretically capable of non-stop flights between London and Australia (although the popular route to Sydney would be questionable, being against the prevailing winds). The longest flight in the world at present is the New York to Singapore route, an eighteen and a half hour flight using Airbus 340-500s, a distance of nearly 10,000 miles. Whether passengers would be willing to travel even further than this without a stopover is open to question. A second proposal was announced in 2005, to construct a new version of the 747-400, to be termed the 747 Advanced. This is to carry 450 passengers with a range of 15,000 km (similar to the Airbus A380), and the company sees this as filling a gap (in passenger capacity) between the 777 and the A380.

Not to be outdone, and to the chagrin of Boeing, Airbus have plans to compete with the Dreamliner, too. Their A350, similar to the existing A330 but with a longer range, will carry between 245 and 285 passengers depending upon range, and is likely to be in service two years after their rival's Dreamliner. Two models are proposed: the A350-800 and the longer range A350-900, which will carry 285 passengers.

After the advent of deregulation in the USA and Europe, there was a demand for smaller aircraft to provide feeder services from rural airports into hub airports, where connections would be made for long-haul or intercontinental flights. This demand was met by small aircraft, either twin turboprops or, seating 50 or more, pure jets. Later, passengers demonstrated a preference for direct flights between regional airports, even if at slightly higher fares, with a resultant increase in passenger-carrying capacity of aircraft, and the demise of several manufacturers of smaller aircraft.

Airports

Airport ownership varies from country to country. Sometimes they are publicly owned (often by local authorities) but elsewhere they may be in private ownership, or ownership will be split between the public and private sectors. In many German airports, for example, local and state governments may share the responsibility for running the airport, while in Milan control is exercised by a combination of local government and private enterprise. In Spain, all 47 airports (and some outside the country) are operated by the Spanish National Airport Authority AENA. In Britain, many regional airports are in local authority hands, including Leeds-Bradford, Norwich and Durham Tees Valley, while others, such as Manchester, Belfast, Cardiff, Glasgow, Edinburgh and the London airports, are privately operated. Seven of the major international UK airports, including the four London Airports Heathrow, Gatwick, Stansted and Luton, are owned and operated by BAA, a private corporation formed by the denationalization of the former state-run British Airports Authority, under the terms of the Airports Bill (1985). These seven airports had a throughput of 140 million passengers in 2004. Heathrow is the busiest airport in the world, in terms of international passengers; however, both Atlanta and Chicago Airports exceed these numbers when domestic passengers are included. BAA also owns and operates some airports overseas.

The significance of public ownership is that overheads and direct costs are more easily concealed, enhancing the airport's performance figures – on paper, at least. Under private ownership, however, it is easier to raise money for expansion or new ventures. Airports require a good balance of passengers and freight to maximize their profitability, but they also boost their revenue and profits through other commercial activities, such as shops, catering services and franchises for supplementary services such as foreign exchange and car rental companies. The sale of duty-free goods to passengers booked to travel on international flights is particularly profitable. The abolition of duty-free sales within the European Union in 1999 impacted on airline and airport profitability, but in the latter case was offset as the leading airports directed their marketing effort into expanding shopping facilities generally, including duty-paid goods.

BAA took over the largest company in the USA dealing with duty-free goods, to protect profit margins. Evidence suggests that many travellers are willing to spend time and money on the purchase of goods at airports; one 1997 study found that airport profits rise by 20 per cent for every ten minutes passengers are kept waiting by delayed aircraft – so it is not in an airport's interest to reduce congestion! In the mid-1990s, average 'dwell' time at European airports was 94 minutes, and this figure will doubtless increase as congestion worsens, and check-in times are extended to devote more time to screening passengers and baggage in a world beset by terrorism.

Earnings from the airlines using the airport are based on a complex set of landing charges, which are designed to cover parking charges, landing fees and a per capita fee for passengers carried – thus a jumbo aircraft will be charged a considerably higher landing fee than a small aircraft. In cases where civil aviation authorities pass on the cost of air traffic control to the airports, or where the airport itself is responsible for this (as at Jersey Airport), a share of these costs will also be charged to landing aircraft.

Congestion at major international airports is becoming so acute that new technology is being pressed into service to improve ground handling. This will become even more urgent as the new generation of superjumbos is phased in. Increased automation is helping to speed up the throughput of passengers, and 'e-tickets', or electronic tickets issued at the airport against a confirmed reservation and first used widely by the no-frills airlines, are rapidly being introduced by all the major airlines to reduce costs while simultaneously speeding up the check-in process.

Regardless of new technology, there are finite limits to the number of passengers which an airport can handle in a given time, and those such as Heathrow are already close to their capacity. The addition of a further runway and new terminals may postpone the inevitable point where capacity is reached, but air corridors are already overcrowded in many parts of the world, and increasingly aircraft are forced to 'stack' at busy periods, wasting fuel; this creates a knock-on effect delaying later take-offs, and the combined effects of poor weather, lightning air-traffic control strikes and the need for increased security in checking baggage at times of terrorist activity have all led to serious problems of congestion at busy airports all over the world.

In Britain, the pressures on London airports have encouraged the government to seek to disperse traffic to regional airports. However, the importance of major hubs for interline passengers making connections means that delays in expanding Heathrow's capacity has inhibited economic growth. Protests against a fifth terminal at Heathrow, and long drawn out hearings prior to granting approval, have delayed construction which would allow a substantial increase in passenger throughput. The fifth terminal was finally approved in 2001 after many years of consultation and lobbying, and will become British Airways' base at Heathrow, but will not be in service until 2008, increasing capacity by 50 per cent. However, present runways would be unable to cope with an increase of this magnitude. The need for a third runway is evident, but any plans for this development would contravene EU environment rules, and are in abeyance. A legal ruling, based on agreements at the time the airport came into operation, prohibits any new runway at London Gatwick until 2019. Meanwhile, Schiphol Airport, Amsterdam (which is planning to expand to seven runways by 2020, effectively doubling flight capacity) has benefited from London's congestion by employing the hub-and-spoke system, picking up British regional passengers bound for intercontinental connections. Paris Charles de Gaulle is another major competitor seeking to become a leading European hub, with an expansion to seven terminals and capacity for 80 million passengers.

The UK regional airports have shown their enthusiasm for expansion, but have not always had the support promised by the British government, which has been slow to grant approval for American carriers to fly into regional airports. Some also face difficulty due to local authorities' unwillingness to expand facilities in the face of opposition from local residents. By contrast, continental airports have actively sought expansion with the blessing of their governments, and sometimes with financial incentives for the new carriers developing routes. Such subsidies were considered illegal by the EU, but it has since modified its stand, deciding to allow subsidies which will typically range between 30 and 40 per cent, depending upon the economic circumstances of the region. Ryanair and easyJet are two of many no-frills airlines which have taken advantage of the relatively low costs associated with regional airports to expand their services. Ryanair was obliged to pull out of Strasbourg and Charleroi (Brussels South) after the EU ruled its high subsidies illegal.

At popular and congested airports, gaining take-off and landing slots for new services is extremely difficult. Slots are awarded to airlines through processes of negotiation, which usually take place in November each year, to cover flights in the following year. Scheduled services receive priority over charter, and the so-called 'grandfather' rights of existing carriers (a concept challenged by the European Union) tend to take precedence over new carriers – so much so that at airports such as Heathrow, a new airline which seeks to gain slots may find it necessary to take over an existing airline in order to do so. This can give even financially troubled airlines high paper value if they control a large number of slots at significant airports.

Navigation and air traffic control

The technical services which are provided on the ground to assist and control aircraft while in the air and in landing and taking off are not normally seen as part of the tourism industry. However, their role is a key one in the operation of aviation services. Air traffic control (ATC) has the function of guiding aircraft into and out of airports, giving pilots (usually in the form of continually updated automatic recordings) detailed information on ground conditions, windspeed, cloud conditions, runways in use, and the state of navigation aids. ATC will instruct pilots on what height and direction to take, and will be responsible for all flights within a geographically defined area.

In Britain alone, it is estimated that at any one time during daylight hours there are some 200 aircraft in the skies; aircraft movements (take-offs and landings) in Britain are expected to rise from around 2 million annually in 2001 to some 3 million by 2016, and older ATC systems would be incapable of handling this volume of traffic. ATC systems have therefore been updated throughout Continental Europe to allow many more aircraft movements to take place within a given period, but the introduction of new computers has been fraught with technical problems. At the same time, this former public service has become a public–private partnership initiative in the UK, with the National Air Traffic Service (NATS) which controls the network now 46 per cent owned by a consortium of airlines.

Improvement in altimeters on board newer aircraft has reduced the margin of error from 300 feet to 200 feet. This has allowed airlines to halve the vertical distance between aircraft at cruising speed, from 2,000- to 1,000-foot intervals. Initially introduced on transatlantic routes, this ruling was controversially extended to the European mainland in 2002, virtually doubling the number of flights operating at between 29,000 and 41,000 feet. The present horizontal distance apart which aircraft must maintain, nose to tail, is ten minutes' flying time (at this same cruising height), with aircraft held at least 60 miles apart laterally. If these lateral gaps could also be halved, this would permit an eight-fold increase in the number of flights operating, although the problems of congestion at the airports themselves would remain to be solved. Landing intervals stand at 45 seconds, and London's two major airports, Heathrow and Gatwick, are experimenting with cuts to allow intervals of 37 seconds – again, not without controversy.

Airline services

The services provided by airlines can be divided into three distinct categories: scheduled services, non-scheduled or charter services (in US parlance, supplementals), and air taxi services.

Scheduled services

Scheduled services are provided by some 650 airlines worldwide, of which around 270 are members of IATA. They operate on defined routes, domestic or international, for which licences have been granted by the government or governments concerned. The airlines are required to operate on the basis of their published timetables, regardless of passenger load factors (although flights and routes which are not commercially viable throughout the year may be operated during periods of high demand only). These services may be publicly or privately owned, although there is now a global movement among the developed nations towards private ownership of airlines. Where fully state-owned airlines continue to operate, as in the case of Emirates and Singapore Airlines, as well as in many developing countries, the leading public airline is often recognized as the national *flag-carrier*. In the UK all airlines are now in the private sector, although British Airways, privatized since 1987, is still seen by many as the national flag carrier. Privatization is not always seen as the best solution, and in one case, that of Air New Zealand, the government of that country reversed earlier privatization by bringing back 80 per cent of the carrier into public ownership after the 9/11 disaster. The importance of air transport within the national economy is such that even a government committed to private air transport, as is the US, voted public funds in the form of compensation and loans to aid the ailing US carriers in the wake of that crisis.

Airlines operating on major routes between hub airports within a country are known as *trunk route* airlines, while those operating from smaller, often rural airports into these hubs are referred to as *regional* or *feeder* airlines. In the case of the USA and certain other regions, these may also be termed *commuter* airlines, as their prime purpose is to serve the needs of commuting business people, many of whom regularly use these routes. The growing development of 'hub-and-spoke' routes will be discussed later in the chapter.

As was discussed earlier in this chapter, the growth of no-frills carriers, more correctly known as LCLF (low cost low fare) carriers, has been the major development in scheduled service operations in the past decade. These airlines have been successful by a combination of efficient operations and low cost, and have as a result sharply cut into markets formerly held by the traditional full-cost carriers, even where business traffic is concerned. A total of 80 million people travelled on European no-frills carriers in 2004, up from 47 million in 2003. LCLFs will typically employ aircraft like Boeing 737s on high-density short-haul routes with one class seating. Virtually all bookings are taken direct, over the Internet. Tickets are inflexible, and generally non-refundable. Passengers turning up late or failing to show lose the entire value of their tickets, often even including taxes – a highly profitable ploy by the airlines. Bookings are usually made and paid for well in advance to take advantage of lower prices, providing helpful cash flow to the companies. If routes prove unprofitable, the carriers pull out quickly. By operating out of secondary, less congested airports, low-cost carriers can reduce times on the ground and operate more flights per day; one study found that easyJet, for example, could employ its aircraft for 11 hours a day, while British Airways on comparable flights achieved only 8 hours[2]. Staff costs are also substantially lower than those of the traditional full-service carriers; one source[3] put British Airways' staff costs in 2001 at 27.85 per cent of their total, compared with those of Ryanair at 12.77 per cent. Similarly, the marketing costs of the two carriers were very different, at 14.56 per cent for BA and 2.43 per cent for Ryanair. The introduction of 'no frills' flights has resulted in a very pared down service where not only meals and drinks are charged for, but the airlines do little to aid passengers delayed or missing flights. Extra charges are made for the carriage of items like skis, golf clubs and surf boards. Ryanair has taken this to extremes, and is proposing at the time of writing to make a charge for baggage carried in the hold. In 2004 the company lost a court case in which they had imposed a charge for providing a wheelchair for a disabled passenger.

The arrivals and departures of new low-cost carriers are now becoming so frequent that any attempt to list current operators would inevitably date this text before it came to print; some 50 European no-frills carriers have been created in the five years up to 2005, although not all survived (one report in 2003 estimated that no fewer than 36 no-frills airlines were in operation that year). Suffice to say that throughout the European Union, in North America, the Far East and Australasia new low-cost airlines like JetBlue in the USA, Tango in Canada, Virgin Blue in Australia, Freedom Air in New Zealand, Air Berlin and Germania in Germany and Wizzair in Hungary (Eastern Europe's largest LCLF carrier) are coming on-stream to challenge the longer-established carriers. By no means all will survive; many will merge or be taken over by competitors, as has been reported earlier in the case of Go and Buzz, others will go under when faced with the cut-throat tactics of better established and more efficient carriers.

Example   Duo

Birmingham Executive Airways was formed in 1987, later becoming Birmingham European Airways and a division of Maersk, the Scandinavian carrier, before adopting its final name of Duo. The airline failed in 2004. Reasons given at the time for the failure were largely centred on weaknesses in marketing: it had inadequate funds to promote the brand, and its failure to become part of a GDS was also a serious weakness for its distribution. The airline sought a difficult niche to fill, somewhere between a no-frills and full service, thus failing to define the product clearly. Bookings were almost entirely direct, with the result that passengers were not protected by an ATOL in the event of failure.

By contrast, the demand for premium priced services has been volatile since the 9/11 crisis, but is showing signs of recovery at the time of writing. British Airways' strategy has also changed markedly in this period; first, by distancing itself from the no-frills carriers by focusing on their premium price market, then reversing its stance to slash economy prices in an effort to compete with the low-cost carriers. Many full-cost airlines are profiling their premium price seats which convert to flat beds on long-haul first and business class flights, in an effort to win back this market. An interesting development in late 2005 was the approval for two premium priced transatlantic services, EOS and MAXjet, to operate out of London (Stansted), with premium fares which were designed to undercut substantially those of BA.

Another direction has been taken by new so-called 'boutique' airlines, which are choosing niche markets on routes where they can similarly attract higher fare-paying passengers. A number of these operate in the USA, and a few have followed suit in the UK, including Lyddair and Flykeen. Their appeal is chiefly to business travellers, for whom superior service and speedier airport check-ins are important. A slightly different approach has been taken by Club Airways, the world's first members-only airline. Again appealing to the business traveller, the airline operates scheduled flights for its members from Britain to the European mainland and includes a number of unusual benefits for executives, including the use of private terminals to speed up check-ins. Lufthansa and Air France have also experimentally offered all-business class flights.

Charter services

Charter services, by contrast with scheduled services, do not operate according to published timetables, nor are they advertised or promoted by the airlines themselves. Instead, the aircraft are chartered to intermediaries (often tour operators) for a fixed charge, and these intermediaries then become responsible for selling the aircraft's seats, leaving the airlines only with the responsibility for operating the aircraft. The intermediaries can change flight departures, or even cancel flights, transferring passengers to other flights. The major tour operators now all have their own charter airlines (see Chapter 16 for a fuller discussion of this relationship), and some, like Monarch Scheduled, now operate scheduled services, too. This is making the former distinction between scheduled and charter services less clear-cut. The growth of seat-only sales on charter aircraft is a clear indication of the direction in which the market is moving, and the trend to direct bookings via the Web is further blurring the distinction. A number of scheduled carriers also operate their own charter subsidiaries.

Air taxi services

Air taxis are privately chartered aircraft accommodating between 4 and 18 people, and used particularly by business travellers. They offer the advantages of convenience and flexibility; routings can be tailor-made for passengers (for example, a feasible itinerary for a business day using an air taxi might be London – Paris – Brussels – Amsterdam – London, a near-impossible programme for a scheduled service), and small airfields close to a company's office or factory can be used. There are some 350 airfields suitable for air taxis in Britain alone, and a further 1,300 in Western Europe (see Figure 12.2), compared with only about 200 airports receiving scheduled services. In the US, where there are over 5,400 small local airports catering principally for private and business planes, 98 per cent of the population is said to live within 30 minutes' driving distance of an airport. The attractiveness of air taxi services using these airports is that flights can be arranged, or routings amended, at short notice, and with a full flight the cost for chartering can be commensurate with the combined business class fares for the number of staff travelling.

Aircraft in use range from helicopters like the Bell Jet Ranger, or the piston-engined Piper twin Comanche (each seating three or four people, with a range between 350 and 900 miles), up to aircraft such as Embraer's Bandeirante, which is capable of carrying 18 passengers up to 300 miles, and to top-of-the-market Gulfstream V aircraft costing over $40 million. Larger aircraft can also be chartered as needed. The world's fastest private jet is the Hawker 400XP, a seven-seat aircraft capable of 538 mph, which has been a popular alternative for the super rich since the demise of Concorde. Most air taxi journeys are in the range of 500–600 miles, and therefore these aircraft are ideal for many business trips within Europe. In the UK alone, some 150 air taxi companies are available to meet the needs of the market.

Some corporations which formerly ran their own fleet of executive aircraft have switched to using air taxis, as purchase is difficult to justify unless the aircraft concerned have a very high usage. However, one recent innovation can reduce the cost of ownership: the concept of fractional ownership.

Example   Fractional ownership

Fractional ownership is a form of aircraft time-share which gives a corporation access to a certain number of flight hours each year, dependent upon the overall share of the aircraft purchased. This is proving a popular alternative to air taxis for many companies. One company – Netjets – operates a fleet of 550 aircraft, and owners can buy flight time, with a minimum of 25 hours flying time each year. On this basis, costs come down to a level justifying the expense for busy top executives.

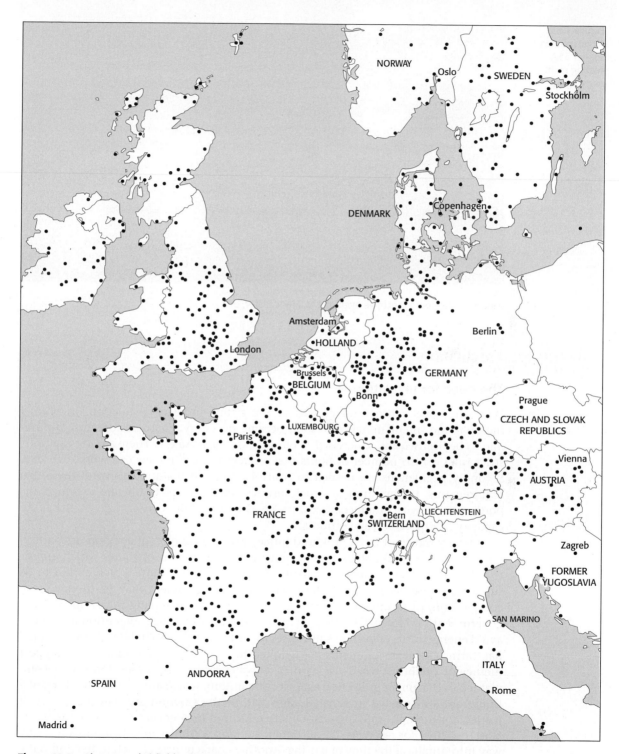

Figure 12.2 Airports and airfields of Europe

Figure 12.3
Air taxi: Gates
Learjet 35A,
seating eight
passengers

(Courtesy: Northern Executive Aviation Ltd, Manchester, UK)

Air transport regulation

The need for regulation

With the development and growth of the airline industry, regulation on both a national and international scale soon became necessary. First and foremost, airlines had to be licensed and supervised to ensure passengers' safety. There are, for example, strict rules on the number of hours that aircrew and cabin crew can work each day. Secondly, regulations are needed to control noise and pollution. Beyond these two requirements, the question of which airlines are permitted to operate to which airports, and in what numbers, becomes an issue of public concern, given the finite capacity of airports and air corridors.

Since air transport has a profound impact on the economy of a region or country, governments will take steps to encourage the development of routes which appear to offer prospects of economic benefits, and to discourage those which appear to be suffering over-capacity. While the policy of one government may be to encourage competition, or to intervene where a route monopoly is forcing prices up, another government's policy may be directed to rationalizing excessive competition in order to avoid energy waste, or even in some cases to protecting the profitability of the national flag-carrier. Some governments are tempted to provide subsidies in order to support inefficient publicly owned flag-carriers; private airlines in Europe have long complained of this unfair protection against competition, which are contrary to EU regulations, but still survive in isolated cases within the Community. The EU Court of Justice, for example, ruled against Olympic Airlines (62 per cent owned by the Greek State) in 2005 for receiving illegal public aid, and a similar investigation was under way into Alitalia at the time of writing. Another characteristic of such protection is the *pooling* arrangements made between airlines operating on certain international routes, whereby all revenue accruing on that route is apportioned equally between the carriers serving the route. This may appear to circumvent competition on a route, but is also one means of safeguarding the viability of the national carrier operating in a strong competitive environment. In developing countries, where governments are anxious to earn hard currency, the support of the national carrier as an earner of hard currency, through arrangements such as this, may be justifiable. Pooling arrangements are often entered into in cases where the airlines are not of comparable size, in order to safeguard the smaller carrier's capacity and revenue. By rationalizing schedules, pressure is reduced on peak time take-off slots, and costs are reduced. Financial arrangements between the pooled carriers usually limit to a fixed maximum the amount of revenue transferred from one carrier to the other, to reduce what may be seen as unfair government support for an inefficient carrier. Increasingly, such pooling arrangements are no longer acceptable, and may indeed be illegal, as is the case in the USA.

In some areas, air transport is an essential public utility which, even where commercially non-viable, is socially desirable in order to provide communications with a region where geographical terrain may make other forms of transport difficult or impossible (New Guinea, Alaska or the Hebrides in Scotland are cases in point). This can result in a government subsidizing one or more of its airlines in order to ensure a service is maintained. Airlines themselves often argue that they provide vital channels of communication for business, trade and investment essential for the well-being of communities, and therefore that even profitable routes should be exempted from taxation (aviation fuel, for example, is currently exempted).

Systems of regulation

Broadly speaking, air transport operations are regulated in three ways:

1 Internationally, scheduled routes are assigned on the basis of agreements between governments of the countries concerned.

2 Internationally, scheduled air fares are now subject to less and less control, and in both North America and Europe airlines are free to set their own fares. However, governments can still intercede where predatory pricing is involved. Theoretically, governments protect carriers by permitting fares to fluctuate between acceptable maxima and minima, but such constraints have been largely abandoned in the developed countries, as low-cost airlines attract passengers with rates which can fall so low that only taxes and administration charges are paid for advance booked seats. In developing areas, however, the extent of regulation is often far greater, with airlines agreeing fares which may then be mediated through the traffic conferences of the International Air Transport Association. Agreed tariffs arrived at in this way are then subject to ratification by the governments of the countries concerned. Generally, less direct control is exercised over domestic fares.

3 National governments approve and license the carriers which are to operate on scheduled routes, whether domestically or internationally. In the UK, the Civil Aviation Authority (CAA) has this responsibility and is also responsible for the licensing of charter airlines and of tour operators organizing package holidays abroad.

European countries which are members of the EU are now largely subject to EU regulations and negotiations regarding the carriage of passengers by air. The EU, for example, has introduced legislation to protect passengers in the event of delays or denied boarding (in the case of an overbooking, for instance) with compensation payable to those affected, but to date the airlines have shown considerable skill in using *force majeure* rules to avoid pay-outs.

| **Example** | **British Airways** |

In 2005, BA was subjected to a strike by their contracted-out catering services, Gate Gourmet, during which some of their own staff came out in sympathy. Services were severely disrupted, but the airline claimed that strikes affecting the operation of an air carrier were 'extraordinary circumstances beyond the airline's control', limiting compensation. This remains a grey area in EU legislation, although the EU is attempting to tighten up enforcement of their compensatory laws. However, it can be argued that the process of contracting out services limits a principal's control over their own operations, and weakens management, making it susceptible to such events.

The worldwide trend is to allow market forces to determine the shape and direction of the airline business, and regulation is today less concerned with routes, frequency, capacity and fares, and more concerned with aspects of safety. However, disagreements between governments over the regulation of routes or airlines can at times lead to major conflict, as is the case with the long-standing dispute between the British and US governments regarding traffic rights across the Atlantic, which is discussed below.

Air transport regulations are the result of a number of international agreements between countries dating back over many years. The Warsaw Convention of 1929 first established common agreement on the extent of liability of the airlines in the event of death or injury of passengers, or loss of passenger baggage, with a limit of $10,000 on loss of life, and similar derisory sums for loss of baggage (compensation is payable on weight rather than value). Inflation soon further reduced the value of claims, and liability was reassessed by a number of participating airlines, first at the Hague Protocol in 1955, where the figure was increased to $20,000, and again at the Montreal Agreement in 1966, at which time the United States imposed a $75,000 ceiling on flights to and from the USA, and it was agreed that the maximum liability would be periodically reviewed. In 1992, Japan waived all limits for Japanese carriers, and in the following year, the UK government unilaterally required British carriers to increase liability to a limit of 100,000 SDRs (Special Drawing Rights, a reserve currency operated by the International Monetary Fund, and equivalent to about $140,000). Finally, in 1995 IATA negotiated an *Intercarrier Agreement on Passenger Liability* which was designed to enforce a blanket coverage for all member airlines, whereby any damages would be determined according to the laws of the country of the airline affected. However, not all airlines agreed to implement this.

The five freedoms of the air

Further legislation concerning passenger aviation resulted from the Chicago Convention on Civil Aviation held in 1944, at which 80 governments were represented in discussions designed to promote world air services and to reach agreement on standard operating procedures for air services between countries. There were two outcomes of this meeting: the founding of the International Civil Aviation Organization (ICAO), now a specialized agency of the United Nations, and the establishment of the so-called *five freedoms of the air*. These comprise the privileges of:

1   flying across a country without landing;
2   landing in a country for purposes other than the carriage of passengers or freight, e.g. in order to refuel;
3   off-loading passengers, mail or freight from an airline of the country from which those passengers, mail or freight originated;
4   loading passengers, mail or freight on an airline of the country to which those passengers, mail or freight are destined;
5   loading passengers, mail or freight on an airline not belonging to the country to which those passengers, mail or freight are destined, and off-loading passengers, mail or freight from an airline not of the country from which these originated.

These privileges were designed to provide the framework for bilateral agreements between countries and to ensure that carriage of passengers, mail and freight between any two countries would normally be restricted to the carriers of those countries.

The move to greater freedom of the skies

Other freedoms not discussed by the Convention, but equally pertinent to the question of rights of operation, have been termed the 'sixth and seventh freedoms'. These would cover:

■   carrying passengers, mail or freight between any two countries on an airline which is of neither country, but is operating via the airline's own country
■   carrying passengers, mail or freight directly between two countries on an airline associated with neither of the two countries.

These various freedoms can best be illustrated using examples (see Figure 12.4).

While a handful of countries expressed a preference for an 'open skies' policy on regulation, most demanded controls. An International Air Services Agreement, to which more than 90 countries became signatories, provided for the mutual exchange of the first two freedoms of the air, while it was left to individual bilateral negotiations between countries to resolve other issues. The Convention agreed not to regulate charter services, allowing countries to impose whatever individual regulations they wished. Few countries, in fact, were willing to allow a total open skies policy for charters.

1st Freedom
A US aircraft flying from New York to Venezuela overflies Mexico

USA   Mexico   Venezuela

2nd Freedom
A British aircraft flying from London to Delhi refuels in Bahrain

UK   Bahrain   India

3rd Freedom
A British aircraft flies from London to Stavanger

UK   Norway

4th Freedom
A British aircraft flies from Stavanger to London

Norway   UK

5th Freedom
An Indian aircraft flying from Delhi to New York stops over in London to pick up passengers bound for New York

India   UK   USA

6th Freedom
Singapore Airlines flies between London and Sydney, stopping over in Singapore.
It uses rights London–Singapore and Singapore–Sydney to carry passengers through from London to Sydney

UK   Singapore   Australia

7th Freedom
A British aircraft carries passengers between Vienna and Budapest on a shuttle service

Austria   Hungary

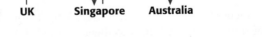

NB Reference is also made to the possibility of an *8th Freedom*, which would allow a foreign aircraft to operate on a cabotage route. An example would be:

A British aircraft is permitted to operate a shuttle service between New York and Chicago

USA   USA

Figure 12.4   Some examples of the freedoms of the air

The Anglo-American agreement which took place in Bermuda in 1946, following the Convention, set the pattern for many of the bilateral agreements which followed. This so-called *Bermuda Agreement*, while restricting air carriage between the two countries to national carriers, did not impose restrictions on capacity for airlines concerned, although this was modified at a second Bermuda Agreement reached in 1977 (and ratified in 1980), in line with the tendency of many countries in the intervening years to opt for an agreement which would ensure that a percentage of total traffic on a route was guaranteed for the national carriers of the countries concerned. It was Britain's intention, in this renegotiated agreement, to avoid over-capacity on the route by restricting it to two British and two American carriers. A further agreement in 1986 extended the agreed capacities across the Atlantic, following a three-year moratorium on new services by the British and American governments. However, in line with the policy of deregulation which both the North American and European nations have introduced, the tight control over capacity has been relaxed and new routes have been agreed. The concept of *reciprocity* remains important, however, with the British government only willing to concede new routes for American carriers if reciprocal routes are granted to British carriers. The latter are also concerned that the US restricts foreign ownership of American airlines to a minority shareholding, thus effectively restricting operational control to US ownership. Negotiation on routes and carriers is now in the hands of the European Commission, which legislates on behalf of all member countries on matters of international transport. Talks held between the EU and US officials in 2004 to develop an open skies policy foundered, and at the time of writing, the long-standing conflict between American and British air interests across the Atlantic is unresolved. The EU is pressing for the limitation on foreign ownership of US carriers to be raised to 50 per cent, and rights granted to European carriers to fly on domestic American routes, in exchange for opening up inter-European routes to US carriers, but to date the US is refusing to accept these terms. Carriage on routes within the national territory of a country (the so-called *cabotage* routes) is normally restricted to the national carriers of the country concerned. In some cases, however, this provides opportunities for a country's national carriers to operate exclusively on international routes, in cases where these countries have overseas possessions. This is the case, for example, on routes out of the UK to destinations such as Gibraltar, or on services between France and Réunion Island, or the islands of Guadaloupe and Martinique in the Caribbean. Under the EU's programme of liberalization of the air within member countries, the cabotage regulation, the final barrier to total freedom of operation, was dropped in 1997. Any airline of any member country can now file to operate services between cities within another member's borders; the British carrier Virgin Express currently operates flights between Brussels and Nice, while Air Berlin offers connections between the UK and Spain. While this liberalization should, in theory, have opened up competition and encouraged a wealth of new services throughout the EU, in practice the difficulty of getting slots at congested airports, as well as delaying tactics by some governments attempting to support their own national carriers, have meant that it has taken time for the LCLFs to build up competition in some areas, and very few are operating out of hub airports.

The role of IATA

For many years, effective control over air fares on international routes was exercised by the International Air Transport Association, a trade body whose membership today is around 270 airlines making up some 95 per cent of all airline traffic. The aims of this organization, which was restructured in its present form in 1945 but traces its origins to the very beginning of air transport in 1919, have been to promote safe, regular and economic air transport, to provide the means for collaboration between the air carriers themselves, and to cooperate with governments, the ICAO and other international bodies for the promotion of safety and effective communications. In the past, IATA also had a role in setting tariffs, in effect operating a legalized cartel. Fares were established at the annual tariff-fixing Traffic Conferences by a process of common agreement between the participating airlines, subject to ratification by the airlines' governments. In practice, most governments merely rubber-stamped the agreements. Critics argued that, as a result, fares became unnecessarily high on many routes, and competition was stifled. Often, the agreed fares were the outcome of political considerations in which the less efficient national flag-carriers pushed for prices unrelated to competitive costs. IATA also controlled many other aspects of airline operation, such as the pitch of passengers' seats, which dictated the amount of legroom they could enjoy, and even the kind of meals that could be served on board. As a result, the airlines were forced to concentrate their marketing effort on such ephemeral aspects of the product as service, punctuality or even the design of cabin crew uniforms, rather than providing a genuine measure of competition.

It was widely felt that this had led to inertia among the participating carriers, with agreements resulting from a desire to avoid controversy among fellow members. Nor had the cartel ensured profitability for its members, since they faced open competition from non-IATA carriers which successfully competed both on price and added value.

Led by the United States, and soon followed by other countries, airlines chose to withdraw from this tariff-setting mechanism, and as a result IATA was restructured in 1979 to provide a two-tier organization: a tariff section to deal with fares, for those nations wishing to continue this role, and a trade section to provide other benefits which an international airline association offered. IATA's role in tariff agreements has become steadily less important (although some 100 members still take part in this), and airlines now largely determine their own service and catering arrangements. An interlining agreement also allowed passengers freely to switch flights to other member airlines – an advantage when they were paying full fares for their tickets, but in an age of low-price tickets for all air services this no longer has the same appeal. The principal benefit offered by IATA today is its central clearing house system, which makes possible financial settlements between members, in the same manner as the British clearing banks. Tickets and other documents are standardized and interchangeable between IATA members, compatibility is established between members in air fare constructions and currency exchange rates, and other procedures, such as the appointment, through licensing agreements, of IATA-recognized travel agents, are also standardized throughout the world. The computerized Bank Settlement Plan, introduced in the UK in 1984, permits the monthly settlement of accounts with appointed agents through a single centre rather than with each individual airline, and has enabled financial transactions to keep pace with the enormous growth in airline travel.

British regulation of air transport

In the UK, the Civil Aviation Act of 1971 led to the establishment of the Civil Aviation Authority, which has five regulatory functions:

1   Responsibility for regulating air navigation services (jointly with the Ministry of Defence), through Britain's Air Traffic Control services.
2   Responsibility for the regulation of all British civil aviation, including air transport licensing, the award of licences (ATOLs) to air travel organizers, and approval of air fares.
3   Responsibility for the airworthiness and operational safety of British carriers, including certification of airlines, airports, flight crew and engineers.
4   Acting as adviser to the government in matters concerning domestic and international civil aviation.
5   A number of subsidiary functions, including the research and publication of statistics, and the ownership and management of eight airports in the Highlands and Islands of Scotland.

Prior to the Civil Aviation Act, no clear long-term government policy had been discernible in respect to aviation in the UK. As governments changed, so attitudes to the public or private ownership of carriers changed. With the aim of providing some longer-term direction and stability a committee of enquiry into civil air transport, under the chairmanship of Sir Ronald Edwards, was established. The report, *British Air Transport in the Seventies*, appeared in 1969. The Edwards Report, as it became known, recommended that the government should periodically promulgate civil aviation policy and objectives, that the long-term aim should be to satisfy air travellers at the lowest economically desirable price, and that a suitable mix should be agreed between public and private-sector airlines. The state corporations (BOAC and BEA) were confirmed in their role as flag-carriers but were recommended to merge and to start charter and inclusive tour operations. The idea of a major second-force airline in the private sector, to complement and compete with the new public airline, was proposed, as was the suggestion that a more liberal policy be adopted towards the licensing of other private airlines. Finally, the report proposed that the economic, safety and regulatory functions carried out by the previous Air Transport Licensing Board, the Board of Trade and the Air Registration Board should thereafter come under the control of a single Civil Aviation Authority.

The Civil Aviation Act which followed publication of this report in 1971 accepted most of these proposals. BOAC and BEA were merged into a single corporation, British Airways, while British Caledonian was confirmed as the new second-force airline, following the merger of Caledonian Airways and British United Airways, and the new Civil Aviation Authority was formed.

The CAA is financed by the users of its services, which are mainly the airlines themselves. Any excess profits are expected to be returned to the users through lower charges for its services. A subsidiary of the CAA is the Air Transport Users' Council (AUC), which acts as a watchdog for air transport customers. An international body with similar aims, the International Foundation of Airline Passenger Associations (IFAPA), is headquartered in Geneva.

UK government policy, 1971–1987

In its proposal to introduce a second-force airline in Britain, the Edwards Report clearly saw this as a mechanism to compete with the publicly owned flag-carrier across the North Atlantic routes. After the formation of British Caledonian, the government granted the carrier North Atlantic routes in 1973. Within two years, however, government policy had changed to 'spheres of influence', with the second-force airline licensed for complementary rather than directly competitive routes. Ignoring British Caledonian's claim that two British carriers on the North Atlantic routes would increase the British share of the total market by taking away business from American carriers, the CAA redistributed routes, giving British Caledonian South American routes, and restricting the North Atlantic largely to British Airways. A White Paper in 1976, *Future Civil Aviation Policy*, indicated the prevailing policy to end dual designation – a policy later overturned by the Conservative government during the 1980s as support for a totally deregulated air transport system gathered momentum. An open skies policy being favoured by both the US and British governments in the 1980s led to effective deregulation of fares and capacity across the Atlantic, as well as on domestic routes in both countries. British Airways was privatized in 1987, and the subsequent redistribution and licensing of routes for smaller British carriers set the scene for liberalization throughout Europe.

Deregulation of air transport

Deregulation, or 'liberalization' as it has come to be known in Europe, is the deliberate policy of reducing state control over airline operations and allowing market forces to shape the airline industry. The US led the way with the Airline Deregulation Act of 1978, which abolished collusion in air pricing. The US regulatory body, the Civil Aeronautics Board (CAB), progressively relinquished control over route allocation and fares, and was itself disbanded at the end of 1984. Market forces were then to take over, the government expecting that inefficient large carriers would be undercut by smaller airlines with lower overheads and higher productivity.

In fact, the actual outcome was very different, and caused advocates of deregulation in Europe to reconsider the case for total freedom of the air. The opening years of deregulation saw a rapid expansion of airline operations, with a three-fold increase in new airlines. Among the established airlines, those that expanded prudently, such as Delta, prospered, while others, such as Braniff, became over-ambitious and committed themselves to a programme of expansion which, as fares became more competitive, they could not support financially. While a few routes saw substantial early rises in fares, especially on long-haul domestic flights, on the whole fares fell sharply, attracting a big increase in passengers. This growth was achieved at the expense of profitability, forcing airlines to cut costs in order to survive. New conditions of work and lower wage agreements were negotiated, with some airlines abandoning union recognition altogether. Some airlines reverted to propeller aircraft on short-haul routes to cut costs, and worries began to emerge about safety, in the belief that airlines were cutting corners to save on maintenance. Indeed, air safety violations doubled between 1984 and 1987.

Within a decade of deregulation, more than a hundred airlines (including two out of three of the newly launched airlines) had been forced out of business or absorbed, as profits changed to losses. Poor morale among airline crew, due to uncertainty about their future job security, led to indifferent service.

Supplementals, as the charter operators are known in the USA, were particularly badly hit, as scheduled services dropped their fares. They had neither the public recognition nor the marketing skills to compete openly with the scheduled services, and many simply ceased to operate. In the longer term, the 'mega-carriers' were the major beneficiaries; these comprised some ten leading airlines, of which the 'big three' – Delta, American and United – held the lion's share of the air travel market. Far from expanding opportunity, deregulation led to smaller airlines being squeezed out, or restricted to less important routes, by the marketing power of the big carriers. In 2001 (prior to the 9/11 catastrophe) American Airlines took over TWA, which had been operating under Chapter 11 bankruptcy rules.

A second consequence of deregulation was the development of 'hub and spoke' systems of operation, in which feeder air services from smaller 'spoke' airports provide services into the hubs to connect with onward long-haul flights of the mega-carriers. This pattern initially enabled the airlines to keep prices down, and New York, Chicago, Atlanta, Fort Worth/Dallas and St Louis became major hubs for domestic and international flights, some dominated by a single carrier.

Developments in North American air traffic since 1990

In the early 1990s, the struggle to survive became more acute. Famous names such as Pan American disappeared, and between 1991–93 five airlines were forced to operate under America's Chapter 11 bankruptcy code, which permit an airline to continue to operate although officially bankrupt, while restructuring their finances. The huge losses sustained by even the biggest airlines led to cancellations of new aircraft orders, the sale of assets, and finally to the formation of alliances with major international carriers, a trend which has become of major importance in the early years of the twenty-first century. Airline retrenchment led in turn to great difficulties for manufacturers of aircraft, which experienced widespread cancellations of orders in favour of leasing, or the purchase of second-hand equipment, while the traditional leasing market in turn dried up.

Hub-and-spoke development, after its initial success in the United States, was challenged by new, low-cost regional carriers operating city-to-city on less significant routes. Some of these have been particularly successful, notably Southwest Airlines, a low-cost airline offering 'no frills' flying at budget fares on some 60 routes, and operating medium-size aircraft spoke-to-spoke in direct competition with the dominant hub-and-spoke operators.

By the start of the twenty-first century some stability had returned, with a pattern emerging of powerful US mega-carriers (which have become known as the 'legacy carriers') on key domestic and international routes seeking alliances with leading foreign airlines in order to offer truly global air services. Most smaller airlines opted to concentrate on niche services, but the growth of no-frills airlines in the US was initially limited, partly owing to effective marketing by the leading carriers, and partly owing to public concern over safety issues (the fatal 1996 crash of no-frills carrier Valujet did nothing to reduce this concern). The big carriers established their own low-cost operations (Delta created Delta Express and, more recently, Song Air; American Airlines, its Eagle division; United, Ted), while the much-criticized practice of 'bracketing', in which larger carriers lay on cut-price flights shortly before and after those of rival cheap carriers, threatened the survival of many of the new airlines. Only where the airline had sufficient resources to pack a route with flights (as was the case with Southwest Airlines) did this tactic prove impractical.

The terrorist attack on New York's Twin Towers on 11 September 2001 quickly unseated the airlines' economic recovery. In the aftermath, United sought bankruptcy protection in December of that year, Canada 3000 in the preceding month. US Airways followed in 2002. Even the largest carrier, American, came close to filing by March 2003, while Air Canada entered Chapter 11 in 2003 and Hawaiian Airlines filed in the same year. In the four years that have followed that disaster, the legacy carriers have all struggled to survive, let alone return profits – and with the consequent downturn in business generally following the crisis, the no-frills carriers, led by Southwest Airlines, benefited at the expense of the mega-carriers. At the time of writing, the American economy was showing signs of slow long-term recovery, but when the US airline business as a whole will return to profitability is impossible to estimate. The 'big six' cannot raise fares, owing to the competition they face from the no-frills carriers, but at the same time they are faced with high wages (which are difficult to renegotiate with strong unions, although United successfully negotiated a five-year contract with its ground workers in 2005, slashing wage costs), escalating oil prices which are likely to remain high for the foreseeable future, and added costs for the extra security they have had to put in place since 9/11. One result has been a cut-back in service levels, with economy passengers now paying for food and drink on board, and refurbishing of aircraft interiors undertaken less frequently. In the latter half of 2005, with United and US Airways both in Chapter 11 since 2002, both Delta and Northwest, third and fourth largest of the legacy airlines, also filed for Chapter 11 protection. US Airways has been able to emerge from Chapter 11 only through amalgamation with America West Airlines – an amalgamation that may also prove to be the best way forward for Delta and Northwest.

European liberalization

Elsewhere in the developed countries, governments have also supported the steady erosion of state regulatory powers over the airline industry. In Australia, liberalized air policy led to the establishment of new airlines, and for the first time a competitively priced domestic air service. Europe's airlines were also moving slowly towards a 'market forces' policy, although in those countries where the state retained a financial investment in its airlines the liberalization policy of the European Commission was resisted; Iberia and Air France continued to receive public subsidies long after these became technically contrary to EU regulations. The EU eased the transition towards liberalization by phasing this in over three stages between 1987 and 1997, after which all EU carriers became free to fly anywhere within the EU, including cabotage routes, at fares they had determined. However, the lack of availability of slots at principal airports continued to hinder competition. Later, liberalization was also introduced outside the EU, in Switzerland, Norway and Iceland.

Airline deregulation in Britain had preceded that of other EU countries, following a number of individual bilateral agreements with fellow EU members, notably Ireland and the Netherlands. This policy led to a substantial growth in the number of domestic carriers, as well as the numbers of passengers travelling. No-frills airlines were already springing up in Britain by the 1990s, operating chiefly out of regional and secondary airports, especially Luton and Stansted, which had slots available for expansion and charged lower fees. Regional airports in particular are often also willing to subsidize start-up airlines or others developing new routes, with landing charges waived for an initial period and support for advertising the new routes. High start-up costs for operators joining dense routes, high marketing costs to establish a new name in the public eye, and the success of frequent-flyer programmes among the large carriers constrained small carriers from direct competition with the larger carriers, and low prices made levels of commission less attractive to agents, making distribution difficult. However, this encouraged the budget carriers to sell their product direct, coinciding with the advent of the World Wide Web and easier direct distribution. Not all were successful, as we have seen, but the leaders were soon undermining even the largest carriers, notably easyJet, and Irish carrier Ryanair which successfully competed head-on with Aer Lingus. Inevitably, the large carriers were forced to retaliate, first by launching their own low-cost carriers, and subsequently by slashing prices of economy tickets.

One side effect of liberalization has been the virtual demise of the 'bucket shops' – non-appointed travel agents who sold off illegally discounted airline tickets dumped on the market at short notice by airlines with spare capacity. Their place has been taken by brokers, who may legally contract with the airlines for spare capacity and sell this cheaply through travel agents (who were formerly forbidden to deal with the bucket-shop operators). Increasingly, however, airlines are selling off unsold seats cheaply through the World Wide Web network, and the growth of Internet companies with programmes designed to handle these products is one of the leading characteristics of the airline business at the beginning of the new century. This will be examined later in the chapter.

The potential explosion of passenger traffic resulting from liberalization is, as we have seen, severely curtailed by problems of congestion. Government statistics indicated a likely increase in passenger journeys out of the UK from 200 million in 2003 to 470 million by 2030, the bulk of this increase arising from demand out of South Eastern airports. Mainland Europe, too, is rapidly approaching saturation. There are limits to the number of aircraft movements that can be handled at an airport within a given time, and runways and terminals are already stretched to the maximum at peak times. Air corridors are also overcrowded in Europe, and the 'stacking' of aircraft above airports prior to landing is costing airlines huge sums of money in wasted fuel. Earlier, we explored ways in which the productivity of air corridors can be boosted by reducing height intervals between aircraft on some routes, and it may be possible to reduce lateral and nose to tail intervals as technology improves and air traffic control systems in Europe are better coordinated. The easing of restrictions on night flights would be a further aid to growth, but local resistance, organized into powerful lobbies, has to be overcome first. Building larger aircraft may prove to be a solution in the short term, although as we have seen earlier in this chapter Boeing is not convinced that there is a market for the superjumbos, pointing to the trend to smaller aircraft to maximize yield. Such aircraft are likely to be introduced only on the most heavily travelled routes, such as high-density domestic routes in Japan, services across the North Atlantic, and those between London and Far Eastern hubs like Singapore or Tokyo. Dubai has declared its intention to become a major force in the airline business and is expanding tourism massively, with Emirates having been one of the first to place a major order for the A380s. However, the problems of enplaning and deplaning up to 800 passengers, as well as cleaning and refuelling, in a short space of time will have to be overcome. While the development of new, fast rail services between the European capitals may offer some help by reducing demand for air travel on routes of up to about 500 miles, the overall growth in demand for air services poses severe problems for the industry in the long run.

One further worry about the results of liberalization should receive a mention: the issue of air safety. Cost competition is driving some airlines to use older aircraft, or aircraft registered outside the UK. While the CAA has imposed restrictions on British scheduled airlines using foreign aircraft, there are no restrictions on UK tour operators chartering such aircraft to operate into and out of the UK, nor is any firm control exercised over the use of foreign aircraft registered in other EU countries. Pressures to meet targets on air traffic controllers, and the new compensation regulations introduced in 2005 by the EU against delayed flights have led to further concerns about passenger safety within the EU.

Example The Joint Aviation Authority and Turkish airlines

Thirty-nine countries in Europe belong to the JAA, which sets higher safety standards for civil aviation than those set by the ICAO in maintenance, operations and the training of pilots.

Turkey joined the JAA in 2001. However, in some cases their control is more lax than that operating within the EU; for example, Turkey accepts the ascribed weight allowance per passenger on holiday charter flights to be set at 70 kg, while the European norm is 76 kg (children 32 kg). This, when multiplied by a typical payload of 200 passengers, allows the airline to carry an extra ton of fuel, giving it scope to fly direct and non-stop between the European capitals and the Anatolian coastal resorts. Two Turkish airlines used on charter flights, Fly Air and Onur Air, have been refused permission to use airports in certain European countries, owing to perceived inadequacy in safety standards[4].

The impact of 9/11 on European carriers was as keenly felt as on those in the US, coming as it did on top of an economic downturn which was already depressing airline profitability. Several airlines have collapsed, only to return in a new, privatized form, including Sabena, the Belgian flag-carrier (now SN Brussels) and Swissair (now simply Swiss, and owned by Crossair). Air France and KLM merged their operations, becoming the largest non-US carrier in the world. However, it has been the no-frills carriers, once again, which have gained most from the economic climate, undercutting their rivals, opening up new routes and finding new markets for air transport.

The economics of airline operation

The development of an airline route is something of a catch-22 situation. Airlines require some reassurance about traffic demand before they are willing to commit their aircraft to a new route, while air travellers in turn look for regular and frequent flights to a destination in order to patronize a route. There is usually an element of risk involved in initiating any new route, especially since seat prices are likely to be high to compensate for low load factors (the number of seats sold as a percentage of total seats available) and high overheads (for both operating and marketing) before traffic builds up. When a route has proved its popularity, however, the pioneer airline is faced with increasing competition, as other airlines are attracted to the build-up of traffic – unless governments decide to control market entry. In an open-market economy, the original airline faces lower load factors, as the market is split between a number of carriers, requiring it to either increase fares or reduce profit margins; yet it may well have kept prices artificially low initially, in order to build the market and recoup launch costs later. Key routes such as those across the North Atlantic attract levels of competition which can make it difficult to operate any services profitably, and many airlines operating on these routes have suffered losses and low load factors on these routes for many years.

The development of 'hub-and-spoke' systems

Major airlines in the United States recognized that attempting to serve all airports with maximum frequency city-to-city flights was uneconomic, and developed the concept of the *hub-and-spoke* system. The hub airports provide transcontinental and intercontinental services, while the spokes are designed to offer connections from regional airports to meet these long-haul services. The latter services can be provided in aircraft that are smaller and cheaper to operate (often turboprops) by low-cost carriers, often working in strategic alliances with the major carriers. Flights are then banked into complexes, and in theory greater efficiency is achieved; a hub with 55 spokes can create 1,500 'city pairs' in this way. Larger aircraft can be used between hubs, and higher load factors and better utilization of aircraft are achieved. Some 40 hubs were soon established in the US alone, serving 25 of America's largest cities. Within a few years of their introduction, passengers taking advantage of hub-and-spoke systems accounted for three-quarters of the total at Atlanta airport, and half at Chicago, Denver and

Dallas/Fort Worth. Similarly, in Europe the hub-and-spoke system was brought into operation by leading airlines, notable among them KLM which, with Schiphol Airport as its hub, had soon built up some ten waves of spoke flights a day to feed into its European and long-haul services. In this way, the airline was able to attract traffic from UK regional airports to connect with its major routes, in direct competition with long-haul flights from London's airports. Sabena and Air France similarly developed hub-and-spoke systems based on Brussels and Paris.

Such systems are generally better suited to feed long-haul flights, as the additional stopover time called for by joining via a spoke is only a small proportion of the total journey. However, it later became apparent that there are also diseconomies in operating these systems. The organization of hub-and-spoke flights requires the establishment of frequent waves of closely spaced banks of arrivals and departures, resulting in peaks and troughs at the hub airports, which puts further pressure on congested air and terminal space, and leads to delays. It also requires larger numbers of ground handling staff during peaks, and involves further peaking expenses. Obviously, on-time performance becomes even more significant under these circumstances, and if airlines are forced to delay departures while waiting for delayed inbound flights, costs also rise. Some airports are clearly better suited than others to this problem; Schiphol has benefited by hub-and-spoke flights being based in the same terminal, so that delays in connection are less catastrophic than at Brussels airport, where connections have to be made between terminals by airport bus.

There is now growing evidence that in some circumstances, airlines remaining outside the hub-and-spoke system can be more profitable, by charging a higher fare for non-stop services, so that smaller demand may still be equally profitable. This applies particularly to business flights, where non-stop services are seen as critical. We have noted elsewhere the success of Southwest Airlines, particularly, in gaining market share by flying city-to-city within the USA. However, there are clear limits on the extent to which city-to-city services can be viable, based on passenger demand and the distances to be travelled.

The growth of strategic alliances

As the problems arising from open competition are obviously going to be long term, a huge global restructuring exercise has been taking place for the past decade, as airlines jockey to be among the survivors in a war of attrition. We have noted that observers expect perhaps as few as a dozen global mega-carriers, of which only three or four will be European, to survive beyond the early years of the twenty-first century.

European airlines had seen, and taken account of, developments in the North American market; they recognized that size, providing economies of scale and economies of scope, would be crucial to survival in the future. They also noted that US domestic carriers were expanding into transatlantic routes, some benefiting from fifth freedom rights in Europe, posing further threats to market share. The way forward for the European carriers was seen as either mergers and takeovers, or the development of strategic alliances with US carriers.

Alliances were easier to establish, but experience showed that they could prove less durable. Political differences and differences of management style frequently hindered effectiveness. The short-lived relationships between British Airways and United Airlines, and between Lufthansa and Air France were cases in point, while the much-vaunted attempt in 1993 to form an alliance between Swissair, Austrian Airlines, SAS and KLM, known as Alcazar, also foundered before being implemented, owing to failure to agree on a US partner. The movement of airlines between the various alliances to gain competitive edges also demonstrates the highly fluid nature of these alliances.

Evidence now points to the success of strategic alliances as being dependent upon expansion in three stages. First, there is a need to secure a dominant share in the home market. British Airways undertook expansion especially through franchising, absorbing 100 per cent of Brymon Airways and soon holding six franchises in the UK, as well as a further four overseas. Air France absorbed a number of domestic French carriers, as did KLM Dutch carriers. The second step is to gain a strong foothold in the main European countries, especially the UK, France and Germany. This was achieved, for example, by SAS, which controlled 40 per cent of British Midland by the early 1990s, and by KLM which purchased Air UK. BA established a German carrier, Deutsche BA, and bought minority interests in GB Airways and French carrier TAT. The final stage is the globalization of the carrier, especially through investments in North America and the Asia/Pacific region. Again, BA became a leader in this strategy, taking a minority investment in Australian carrier Qantas in 1992, and seeking similar investments in US carriers, although with little success to date, given the US anti-trust laws and European Commission fears of monopoly power.

The new global alliances are now seen as the way forward. These embrace key airlines in Europe, North America and the Asia/Pacific region. While the specific membership of each of these changes quite frequently, the picture in early 2005 was as follows:

1 *One World* (formed 1998) with current members British Airways, American Airlines, Qantas, Cathay Pacific, Iberia, Finnair, Aer Lingus, Lan Chile.

2 *Star Alliance* (1997) with Air Canada, Air New Zealand, ANA (All-Nippon Airways), Asiana, Austrian Airlines, bmi, LOT, Lufthansa, SAS, Singapore Airlines, Spanair, Thai Airways International, United Airlines, US Airways, Varig.

3 *Skyteam* (2000) with Aeromexico, Air France/KLM, Alitalia, Continental Airlines, Czech Airlines, Delta, and Korean Air, NWA. Agreements have been drawn up to give membership later to Aeroflot and China Southern.

Two other former alliances, Wings and Qualiflyer, have become defunct as airlines merged or were driven out of service in the wake of the 9/11 crisis.

Globalization is an inevitable consequence of the growth of the international airline business. A strategic alliance offers opportunities for rapid global growth, coupled with marketing benefits that cannot be achieved as an individual airline. For example, it allows domestic spokes to be tacked on to international routes, as the long-standing alliance between the US carrier NWA (Northwest Airlines) and Dutch carrier KLM demonstrated; it increases the viability of marginal routes, and it allows carriers to compete on routes where separately they do not hold rights. Alliances enable companies to reduce costs by using larger aircraft to meet overall demand, and by sharing operational costs such as counter space at airports and baggage handling. Marketing costs such as advertising may also be shared.

Alliances may range from the marginal, such as having an interline agreement to accept one another's documentation and transfer of passengers, to marketing agreements such as joint frequent-flyer programmes and operational agreements such as blocking space on one another's aircraft to sell their seats. However, the most common advantage to be gained is that of code-sharing.

Code-sharing

Domestic code-sharing was in practice within the United States as long ago as 1967, but was first introduced internationally in 1985, when American Airlines and Qantas agreed to share codes on routes across the Pacific. Under a code-sharing agreement, two airlines agree to share their codes on through routes, for example between New York and San Francisco and from San Francisco to Sydney. This has the marketing advantage of appearing to be a single through flight, but there are also very concrete advantages for passengers, in that flight timings are coordinated, transfer times between stopovers may be reduced (and carriers will often hold connecting flights for up to 20 minutes for passengers connecting from flights which are code-shared), and baggage can be checked through to final destination, reducing baggage loss. Carriers can sell each other's flights as if they were their own, and will frequently block off space to do so. A further advantage is that code-shared flights are featured on computer reservations systems before other connections, as these offer the passenger 'best choice'. They may also benefit from multiple listing on the CRS, since they will be listed under both carriers' services.

The establishment of code-sharing across the Atlantic has been crucial to the successful marketing of long-haul travel, and has been extensively used by European carriers to gain access to US domestic destinations. European airlines recognize that US airlines will continue to dominate the global market-place, partly owing, of course, to the huge demand for both domestic and international travel by American travellers. Success for the European carriers depends upon establishing close links with at least one of the leading US carriers.

An indication of the size of the world's leading carriers is given in Table 12.1, based on IATA figures before the Air France/KLM merger.

Airline costs

The selection of suitable aircraft for a route is the outcome of the assessment of relative costs involved (both capital and operating) and the characteristics of the aircraft themselves.

Capital costs

When supply exceeds demand, as is the case where there are many second-hand aircraft on the market, the competition for sales among manufacturers enables airlines to drive very hard bargains when purchasing new equipment. It must be remembered that costs for new aircraft are usually a package embracing not only the sale of the aircraft itself, but also the subsequent provision of spares and possibly servicing.

Table 12.1 Leading airlines of the world, 2005

Airline	International and domestic passenger-kilometres flown (millions)
American Airlines	195,815
United Airlines	176,048
Delta Airlines	152,661
North West Airlines	115,913
British Airways	99,123
Air France	98,541
Lufthansa	93,643
Continental Airlines	91,040
Japan Airlines	83,196
Singapore Airlines	74,172

Note: Adding KLM figures to those of Air France puts the new merged airline into third place, and the largest non-US carrier, with 157,435 million passenger kilometres flown.
Source: IATA

According to forecasts made by the ICAO in 1997, the global growth in demand for passenger services between 1997 and 2016 was expected to exceed 5 per cent annually, while in the Asia/Pacific region it would reach 7 per cent. In spite of the hiatus resulting from the post-9/11 collapse in travel, in fact, growth has continued to average around 6 per cent per annum, and investment in aircraft over the next two decades is still likely to exceed $1 trillion. Attractive loan terms are likely to be a key factor in closing sales, and some manufacturers are willing to offer very favourable trade-ins on old aircraft in order to sell their new models. However, a number of airlines have cut back on orders for new aircraft, leasing rather than purchasing (sometimes selling their existing aircraft and leasing them back, in order to release capital). A crucial decision, as was discussed earlier in this chapter, is to determine which type and size of aircraft to buy. The cost of the new superjumbo A380 is such that an order for a number of these will add up to an investment of many billion dollars, so getting the figures right is vital for the airlines' top management.

Operating costs

Mile for mile, short-haul routes (up to 1,500 miles) overall are more expensive to operate than are long-haul, although this is not simply due to the cost of fuel used. While the greater frequency of take-offs and landings on short-haul flights will mean high initial fuel consumption on each leg as aircraft gain height, recent research[5] has shown that an aircraft travelling long distances in a single hop can consume more fuel than one stopping three times during the same route. The example given was of a 9,000-mile flight which, flown non-stop, consumes 120 tonnes of fuel, while an aircraft taking three 3,000-mile hops will need only 28 tonnes for each hop, a total of 84 tonnes. The explanation for this is that long-haul aircraft need more fuel in order to carry the weight of the extra fuel needed for the longer journey. However, when factoring in the additional costs of crewing and landing fees for both forms of travel, shorter-haul costs will rise higher than those of long-haul, and force up ticket prices. Short-haul aircraft also spend a proportionately greater time on the ground; aircraft are only earning money while they are in the air, and depreciation of their capital cost can only be written off against their actual flying time. For this reason it is important that they are scheduled for the maximum number of flying hours each day. According to the efficiency of the airline, and of the airports into which the airline operates, productivity can be increased without impairing the (legally determined) minimum service and maintenance time required (Boeing 747 servicing entails 35–60 work-hours, with a complete overhaul involving 10,000 work-hours, after 6,000 hours of flying). Here, the American carriers appear to be more successful than the European, with the big three US carriers flying at least ten hours per day on short- and medium-haul flights, against a European average of only seven hours (although there are marked differences between the productivity of the various airlines within Europe). In the USA, aircraft turnarounds (time spent on the ground between landing and take-off) can be as low as 30 minutes, while in Europe a minimum of 45 minutes is the norm. Budget airlines, however, perform significantly better than the traditional carriers, owing in part to their operating out of less congested airports.

Long-haul aircraft normally operate at a ceiling of 30,000–40,000 feet (supersonics at 50,000–60,00 feet), while short- and medium-haul aircraft will operate at lower ceilings. While the cost of getting the long-haul aircraft to its ceiling will be higher, once at these heights there is little wind resistance and the rate of fuel burn falls considerably.

Improving technology is constantly extending the distance which aircraft can fly non-stop. Singapore Airlines introduced the world's longest non-stop flights in 2003, when they started operating Airbus A345s between Singapore and Los Angeles (16 hours out, 18.5 hours back) and Singapore–New York (18 hours). The customer appeal of travelling direct, and reducing overall travel time, is high, but may be off-set by concern over very long, uninterrupted flights and growing awareness of the potential dangers of deep vein thrombosis (DVT). Recent research is pointing to a 12 per cent increase in the likelihood of developing DVT among long-haul passengers compared with others.

Costs can be subdivided between the direct costs of operating and indirect costs. The former will include flight expenses (salaries of flight crew, fuel, in-flight catering), plus maintenance, depreciation, aircraft insurance, and airport and navigation charges. Airport charges will include landing fees, parking charges, navigation charges (where these are passed on to the airline by the airport) and a per capita cost according to the number of passengers carried. Navigation charges vary according to the weight of the aircraft and the distance flown over a particular territory.

After 1998, the notional weight of passengers on EU services was increased, adding to costs. The previous 75 kg for males and 65 kg for females was replaced by a notional weight of 84 kg per capita for scheduled flights, and 76 kg for holiday charters, in recognition of the trend to increased body weight internationally. This higher figure had already been adopted by US and some other carriers, but in fact the US opted for a still higher figure in 2005, moving from 185 lb (84 kg) to 200 lb (nearly 91 kg) for males, and a slightly lower figure for females. The US allows a further 5 lb per passenger in winter, in recognition of the need for higher fuel burn in summer. These figures, however, include carry-on bags, unlike regulations in Europe. Japanese airlines operate on a notional body weight of 73 kg (regardless of the nationality of those carried), which enables Japanese carriers to gain advantage over others by providing more seats. The tendency towards obesity among the populations of the developed countries is causing concern for airlines anxious to control their costs, as the average extra weight carried increases fuel costs considerably.

Example   No-frills airlines

The no-frills airlines have taken steps to recover costs associated with the increasing weight of their passengers. Maersk Air have introduced three seat sizes: basic fares are paid for the smallest, with a pitch of 70 cm on their Boeing 737-700s. For a slightly higher fare, passengers can book a medium seat with an 80 cm pitch, and an upgrade to an X-large seat can follow with additional payment. Southwest Airlines, on the other hand, require obese passengers to purchase two seats (a delicate matter for booking and check-in staff to determine how obese one must be before imposing the extra charge!). The test of obesity is whether or not the armrest between passengers can be dropped – something one would assume would be debateable until the passenger is actually on board.

Depreciation is the cost of writing off the original purchase price of the aircraft against the number of hours it flies (which may be as high as 4,000 hours per year). Total depreciation periods vary; in the case of smaller, relatively inexpensive aircraft it may be as short as eight to ten years, while wide-bodied jets may be depreciated over periods as long as 14 to 16 years. A residual value of typically 10 per cent of the original purchase price is normally allowed for. In some cases, it might be considered prudent to write off aircraft more quickly, because obsolescence can overtake the operating life, and airlines must keep up with their competitors by re-equipping at regular intervals. However, with falling profits, few airlines find it easy to re-equip, and the tendency is to extend depreciation time. On top of this, insurance costs will range around 3 per cent per annum of the aircraft's purchase price.

Indirect costs include all non-flight expenses, such as marketing, reservations, ground handling, administration and other insurances such as passenger liability. These costs will vary very little however many flights are flown, and large airlines will clearly benefit from economies of scale here.

Fuel costs globally are quoted in US dollars, and will therefore vary not only according to changing oil prices but also according to changing currency exchange rates. Airlines can contract to buy fuel in advance if they fear rising costs. Typically, it is the larger airlines with bigger financial reserves which are best placed to do so, but budget airlines most concerned to control costs have also 'hedged'; in 2004 Ryanair bought forward its fuel needs until 2007, hedging against what were at the time wildly fluctuating prices. Hedging does not necessarily save money, but it does smooth out cash flow and reduce volatility.

Other ways of trimming costs have included reducing the labour force, while renegotiating wage levels and conditions of service (often at the expense of good staff–management relations), and moving activities to countries where costs are lower. Several companies have moved their accounts to India, while others have renegotiated contracts with other low-cost countries for maintenance or cleaning services. Savings can also be achieved by forming low-cost subsidiaries, a move taken by several traditionally high-cost European and American carriers. Above all, distribution costs can be trimmed, given new means of reaching the passenger direct. This will be discussed later on in this chapter.

Aircraft characteristics

These will include the aircraft's cruising speed and 'block speed' (its average overall speed on a trip), its range and field length requirements, its carrying capacity and its customer appeal. In terms of passenger capacities, airline development tends to occur in leaps; thus, with the introduction of jumbo jets, the number of seats on an aircraft tripled, and with the new generation of superjumbos there will be a further sharp increase in capacity. While average seat costs fall sharply as seat numbers are increased, this can only be reflected in lower prices to passengers if sufficient seats are filled.

Carrying capacity is also influenced by the *payload* which the aircraft is to carry, i.e. the balance between fuel, passengers and freight. An aircraft is authorized to 'take off at MTOW (maximum take-off weight)', which is its empty operating weight plus fuel and payload. At maximum payload, the aircraft will be limited to a certain range, but can increase this range by sacrificing part of the payload – i.e. by carrying fewer passengers. Sacrificing both fuel and some passenger capacity may allow some aircraft to operate from smaller regional airports with short runways.

Cost savings can be made in a number of ways when using larger aircraft. It is a curious fact that the relative cost of pushing a large aircraft through the air is less, per unit of weight, than a small one (incidentally, this principle also holds true in shipping operations, in that large ships are relatively cheaper per unit of weight to push through the water). Larger aircraft experience proportionately lower drag per unit of weight; they are more aerodynamic. They can also use larger, more powerful engines. Equally, maintenance and cleaning costs per seat are lower.

The marketing of air services

Aside from economic considerations, the customer appeal of an aircraft depends upon such factors as seat comfort and pitch, engine quietness and the interior design of cabins. In a product where, generally speaking, there is a great deal of homogeneity, minor differences such as these can greatly affect the marketing of the aircraft to the airlines, and in turn the appeal the airline can make to its prospective passengers.

It is for the marketing division of an airline to determine the destinations to be served, although these decisions are often influenced by government policy and regulation. Marketing personnel must also determine levels of demand for a particular service, the markets to be served and the nature of the competition the airline will face.

Routes are, of course, dependent upon freight, as well as customer considerations, and a decision will have to be reached on the appropriate mix between freight and passengers, as well as the mix of passengers to be served – business, holiday, VFR etc. An airline can be easily panicked into changing routes unless it recognizes that circumstances can provide opportunities as well as threats. A good example is seen in the collapse of the so-called tiger economies in Asia at the end of the 1990s. In spite of the economic depression experienced by many of these countries, air traffic to the region actually rose, as Western travellers took advantage of currency collapses to increase their leisure travel to the area.

Flight frequencies and timings will be subject to government controls. For example, it is common to find that governments will limit the number of flights they will allow to operate at night. Where long-haul flights, and hence changing time zones, are involved, this can seriously curtail the number of flights an airline can operate. Traffic congestion will have an additional 'rationing' effect.

It is particularly important for business travellers to be able to make satisfactory connections with other flights. To gain a strategic marketing advantage over competitors, an airline will want to coordinate its flights with complementary carriers, with which it must have interline agreements (allowing the free interchange of documents and reservations). In planning long-haul flights, the airline must also weigh up whether to operate non-stop flights, or to provide stopovers to cater for passengers wanting to travel between different legs of the journey (known as 'stage' traffic). Stopovers will permit the airline to cater for, or organize, stopover holiday traffic – which might be particularly attractive for passengers across the Pacific, for instance, allowing additional duty-free shopping. However, it may dissuade business passengers from booking, if their prime interest is to reach their destination as quickly as possible, and an alternative non-stop flight exists. Tahiti experienced a sharp downfall in visitors when the stretched 747-400 was introduced on the transpacific route, and it first became possible to fly non-stop between Australia and North America.

Yield management

Following the planning stage, the airline must determine its pricing policy. Fixing the price of a seat is a complex process, involving consideration of:

■ the size and type of aircraft operating

■ the route traffic density and level of competition

■ the regularity of demand flow, and the extent to which this demand is balanced in both directions on the route

■ the type of demand for air service on the route, taking into account demand for first or business class, economy class, inclusive tour-basing fares and other discounted ticket sales

■ the estimated break-even load factor (the number of seats which must be sold to recover all costs). Typically, this will fall at between 50 and 60 per cent of the aircraft's capacity on scheduled routes. The airline must aim to achieve this level of seat occupancy on average throughout the year. Budget airlines will set a much higher load factor as the norm.

The last two points are critical to the success of the airline's marketing. The marketing department is above all concerned with *yield management*, the overall revenue which is to be attained on each route. Yield can be defined as the *air transport revenue achieved per unit of traffic carried*, or the total passenger revenue per revenue-passenger mile. It is measured by comparing both the cost and revenue achieved per available seat mile (ASM). Balancing the proportion of discounted seats and those where full fares can be charged, whether in economy of business class, is a highly skilled undertaking, since there is a need to ensure that any reduction in full fare will lead to an overall increase in revenue. This is achieved through a combination of pricing and the imposition of conditions governing the fares.

Business class, for example, will achieve much higher levels of profit than economy or discounted tickets; an airline with 10 per cent of its seats given over to business class may achieve 40 per cent of its income from the sale of these seats. However, expected demand for seats on a particular route will call for fine judgement. Discounted tickets must attract a new market, not draw higher paying passengers to save money, so they must be hedged with conditions making them unattractive to prospective business class passengers. Good yield management can in some cases even result in full service airlines undercutting their budget rivals, since the former can charge much higher fares for reservations taken close to departure times, which helps to off-set discounts given for early bookings.

The growth in bookings using the World Wide Web is a huge bonus for airlines' yield management, as passengers are now paying directly to the airline when they book, helping cash flow. Previously, payments would be made to travel agents, and payment through the airlines' clearing house could take up to two months.

Airlines have determined that in many cases they can increase yield by downsizing their aircraft, and often at the same time increasing flight frequency. This increased frequency can also build new passenger traffic, leading to still greater yield, especially where business traffic is concerned. Shuttle services for business travellers were pioneered at one time by Eastern Airlines in the USA, operating at half-hour intervals between Boston, New York and Washington. These required no advance reservations, and guaranteed that a seat would be available (although these services were later superseded by no-frills carriers). Similar flights are now under consideration for services between Hong Kong and Chinese mainland airports.

Boosting yield through frequent-flyer programmes

In order to boost overall yield, many airlines introduced the concept of frequent-flyer programmes, by which passengers purchasing airline tickets were entitled to extra free travel, according to the mileage covered. This marketing campaign has been a victim of its own success; over 90 million members worldwide now collect these benefits. At the end of 2004 it was estimated that the worldwide stock of airline loyalty schemes, or frequent-flyer programmes, was above 14 trillion miles, worth over $700 billion (making them the second largest convertible currency in the world after the US dollar).

American Airlines were the first to introduce an FFP in 1981 with their Aadvantage scheme. It is now the biggest scheme in operation, with over 45 million members. Others quickly followed: British Airways' Executive Club, United's Mileage Plus, Virgin

Atlantic's Flying Club. The programmes were later extended to allow miles to be accumulated on the value of products purchased at other outlets associated with the airline, including shops, hotels and petrol stations, as well as partner airlines within the strategic alliances. The popularity of these schemes has led to so many free seats being offered that airlines are now imposing limitations on their use (United Airlines at one point found that virtually all passengers on its Hawaii-bound flights were frequent flyers, virtually eradicating yield on this route). While frequent flyers can normally only make use of seats that would otherwise be vacant during the flight, each seat occupied costs the airline the price of the food and fuel consumed, and in total this adds up to a substantial cost for the airline.

Deep discounting

All scheduled services operate on the basis of an advance reservations system, with lowest (APEX) fares being available on routes where the booking can be confirmed some time in advance of departure. This allows the airline to judge its expected load factors with greater accuracy. To fill up seats not pre-booked, the airline offers stand-by fares, available to passengers without reservations who are prepared to take their chance and turn up in the expectation of a seat being free. On many routes, particularly business routes, the chances of seats being available are good, because business passengers frequently book more than one flight, to ensure they can get back as quickly as possible after the completion of their meeting. Airlines will overbook to allow for the high number of no-shows (up to 30 per cent on some routes), but must exercise caution in case they end up with more passengers than they can accommodate. If this occurs, they can upgrade to a better class, or compensate the overbooked passengers financially, while providing seats on another flight, but this may not be sufficient to satisfy the irate business passenger. EU plans for high levels of compensation for bumped passengers may cause some airlines to rethink their strategy in permitting business tickets to be refunded without question.

The airline distribution system

The distribution system consists of two elements, the reservation (or booking), and the issue and delivery of a ticket, where pertinent. Air tickets were traditionally sold and distributed through travel agents at an agreed rate of commission, with a proportion also sold direct by the airlines to their passengers (in the USA, the high volume of air travel allowed many more airlines to sell direct through branch offices in the larger cities). The development of the World Wide Web has now changed this pattern of distribution, with a far greater proportion of sales (and in the case of some no-frills airlines, all sales) being made through the Internet, either direct with the airlines or through Internet intermediaries' own websites.

In the face of the crises impacting on the airline industry over the past few years, airlines have re-evaluated their distribution systems, seeking to cut costs wherever possible. The first to suffer in this process of re-evaluation has been the travel agent, with commissions first being trimmed, then cut savagely and in many cases now discontinued entirely, requiring agents to charge their customers a fee for providing the service. Such a move, however, may further deter customers from booking through intermediaries. As most leading airlines have tended to follow the no-commission route, threats by agents to switch-sell air products have had little effect.

Example British Airways

British Airways has been equivocal about agency sales for several years, gradually reducing and eventually eliminating commissions paid to agents. Agents then were obliged to impose a fee for bookings they made on behalf of their customers. In 2005 the airline announced its intention to charge a booking fee of £1 for all passengers booking on-line, and a £15 fee to book long-haul flights over the telephone – in effect, ensuring that any passenger will now be obliged to pay for the distribution of their flight arrangements. BA declared that this was part of the airline's policy to charge customers the cost of their chosen method of booking.

Electronic ticketing (commonly referred to as 'e-ticketing') and so-called ticketless travel are also making real inroads into cost. This further encourages airlines to push direct sales, with a consequent worrying (for travel agents) fall in the number of airline tickets booked through intermediaries. Airlines are also moving to corporate self-booking for key business travellers, with carriers installing the necessary equipment in larger companies to allow customers to book direct via the Internet. There is little doubt that the challenge represented by these moves (which will be echoed increasingly by other travel suppliers in the future) will require agents to reconsider their whole rationale and means of operation. However, electronic booking systems pose by far the greatest threat to agents, and their simplicity in use, coupled with the low fares offered to customers willing to use the systems, will encourage more passengers to book direct in the future.

Example British Airways

BA announced in 2004 that they were generating 15 per cent of their revenue via the Web, aiming to raise this to 30 per cent by 2007, with a commensurate reduction in sales by agents. Their selling costs as a percentage of revenue fell from 17.5 per cent in 1995 to around 9 per cent in 2004. Two years previously, a study by Commerzbank estimated that BA's selling costs were running at nearly five times those of easyJet's, and represented 10.9 per cent of the average ticket price.

The earliest step in the introduction of high technology in airline distribution systems was the computerized reservations system (CRS), which provided agents and their clients with a fast and accurate indication of flight availability and fare quotations, coupled with an on-line reservations service. The next step was the introduction of the global distribution system (GDS), in which leading airlines themselves held major shareholdings. These rapidly spread to embrace worldwide hotel, car rental and other reservations facilities, and the leading GDSs battled for market leadership among travel agents worldwide. The US systems, notably Sabre, Apollo and Worldspan, either competed against or integrated with the two leading European systems, Galileo and Amadeus.

The importance of dominance in this field lies in the way in which agents make use of the information displayed. Access is made through the system to a large number of major world airlines, and 75–80 per cent of all bookings are made from the first page of information. Formerly, bias in the way information is displayed was declared illegal under US and EU law, but the US Department of Transportation ended restrictive regulations on the GDSs in 2004, as the airlines gradually reduced their stock sold through this system in the wake of the 9/11 disaster, preferring to sell direct via their own websites. In the following year, it became EU policy to allow airlines to have commercial agreements with the GDSs which will result in their favouring certain carriers. However, while the US carriers no longer have a stake in the GDSs, European carriers do still hold interests in Amadeus. The GDSs are in turn having to face the challenge of new websites, either those of the airlines themselves, or intermediaries like Expedia.com, Ebookers.com and Travelocity.com selling their services. These electronic retailers, the so-called e-tailers, have become a major force in the distribution system, particularly for the sale of late availability. The GDS companies argue that the establishment of websites by intermediaries is unnecessary, given that they themselves are coming to utilize the World Wide Web to provide the same range of travel products, but the intermediaries are successfully challenging these well-established and proven systems.

Apart from their own websites, airlines have also come together to organize joint websites for interactive reservations and information. The US website Orbitz was established in 2000 by five US carriers – American, Delta, United, Northwest and Continental, while the European Opodo network (initially launched by nine European airlines, and now part of Amadeus) followed in 2001. These offer access to hotels and car hire, in addition to airline flights. The extent to which on-line bookings are replacing traditional channels of distribution may be judged when it is revealed that the leading no-frills airlines are becoming almost totally dependent upon sales via the Web, and promote this medium prominently.

Future developments in the technological revolution are likely to involve the expansion of digital television in the home, which will provide channels for consumers in their own home to communicate with the airlines direct, and book their airline tickets. This must inevitably lead to a further shrinking of sales through the more traditional distribution outlets.

The role of the air broker

One comparatively little known role in the airline business is that of the air brokers. These are the people who act as intermediaries in the control of seats, rather than merely their sale, between aircraft owners and their customers. They provide a level of expertise to business clients, travel agents or tour operators who may not have the time or the knowledge to involve themselves in long negotiations for the best deals in chartering aircraft seats. They maintain close contact with both airlines and the charter market, and can frequently offer better prices for charters than tour operators could themselves obtain. They play an important role in securing aircraft seats in times of shortage, and in disposing of spare capacity at times of oversupply. The broker takes charge of the entire operation, booking the aircraft and taking care of any technical requirements, including organizing the contract and arranging any special facilities. In their role as so-called *consolidators*, they purchase seats on scheduled airlines on demand, at discounted rates, and can sell these on to agents at usual rates of commission. Leading companies in the UK include Gold Medal Travel, Travel 2 and Travel 4. Flight-only operators buy blocks of seats, or a whole aircraft, to sell wherever they can find a market. Avro is the leading UK company in this field, with over a million passengers every year. These roles are all ones which may be challenged by electronic direct booking systems.

Notes

1 It's Time to Follow Stelios and Bail Out of easyJet, *Sunday Times*, 1 December 2002
2 Chris Tarry, Airline Analyst at Commerzbank, reported in *The Times*, 3 December 2002, *Flights of Fancy*, T2/7
3 Estimates obtained from *The Observer*, 11 November 2001
4 En Turquie, une tolérance risquée, *Le Figaro*, 29 July 2005, p 7
5 Based on an airline study by BA, Airbus and Boeing and cited in Ben Webster, Long Haul Flights on Way Back to Earth, *The Times*, 17 January 2002

Websites

Air Transport Users' Council   www.auc.org.uk
E C Directorate-General for Energy and Transport (on compensation)
                              http://europa.eu.int/comm/transport/air/rights/info_en.htm
ebookers   www.ebookers.com
a flight.to   www.aflight.to (includes charters and no-frills)

Questions and discussion points

1   This chapter explains that BA is introducing a policy of having their customers pay for the costs of their chosen methods of distribution. Most manufacturers and retailers of other products either absorb these costs or build them into the prices charged to their customers. Argue the case for BA's approach to recovering their distribution costs.

2   Does the growth of direct selling via the World Wide Web appeal equally to leisure and business passengers? Which, in your opinion, is more likely to make use of the travel agent in the future, and why? How can the agent seek to retain the business of either of these markets?

3　What marketing strategy would you recommend leading airlines to adopt to compete with the no-frills airlines? Do they, in fact, need to compete with them, or can both coexist peacefully?

4　In 2005, BA announced its intention to introduce a voluntary 'green fee' that passengers would be asked to pay, depending upon the distance travelled, to offset air pollution. The sums collected would be spent on projects that help developing countries to reduce their carbon emissions. How willing do you think passengers will be to make this voluntary donation? Should it be compulsory, or should carbon emissions be offset in some other way? (NB: BA research, as this book goes to press, reveals that in its first year of operation, fewer than 0.5 per cent of passengers have expressed a willingness to pay this voluntary subsidy.)

Assignment topics

1　As an analyst for an airline with global routes (you may determine which airline), examine the competition between Airbus and Boeing for the new generation of airliners, and draw conclusions about the relative demand for the Airbus A380 and the Boeing 787 Dreamliner. Present a written report to your company marketing director, which considers whether the two aircraft are competitive or complementary, on which routes they are likely to be in demand, and which would be most suitable for the routes on which your airline operates. What are the advantages, and drawbacks, of each?

2　As a member of staff of a no-frills airline, you are invited as a guest speaker to address a group of undergraduates at a university, on the theme of yield management.

Prepare a set of notes for your lecture, outlining how your company can increase its yield, and the factors it must take into account in attempting to do so.

13 Water-borne tourist transport

Objectives

After studying this chapter, you should be able to:

- identify each category of water-borne transport, and the role they play in the tourism industry
- understand the economics of cruise and ferry operations
- be aware of principal world cruise routes, and the reasons for their popularity
- be familiar with other forms of water-borne leisure transport, and their appeal to tourists.

Introduction

You like doing your own thing and you'd rather dress down than up when you go away. You're adventurous, a bit of a thrill seeker – not the usual cruise holiday type. Relax. Ocean Village is no ordinary cruise. Informal and easy-going, it's for thirty-to-fifty-somethings who want to explore new places without the formality of traditional cruises. Welcome to a different sort of holiday.

Ocean Village brochure, Summer 2005

Air travel has become far the most popular means of travel for tourists. However, very few treat travel by air as anything other than the most convenient means of getting from A to B, and certainly the frustration of this form of travel, with its accompanying airport delays, queuing, congestion on the ground and in the air and the relative lack of comfort while airborne tend to detract from the idea that flights are an enjoyable part of the holiday. Transport by water, on the other hand, can be enjoyable in its own right, and for many it will be the dominant element in the holiday, such as when cruising, where the intention is not to arrive at a particular destination but to enjoy getting there. Whether travelling by sea, or inland on lakes, rivers and canals, a water-borne holiday has never been more popular, and shipping in all its forms plays an important part in the travel industry. Travelling by water is inherently relaxing, whereas air

348

transport's appeal is largely that of speed – often critical when travelling to a long-haul destination.

Cruising, in particular, has staged a revival after many years of decline, and now enjoys a popularity not seen since its heyday in the first half of the twentieth century. The advantages of this form of travel are total relaxation and a price which includes all food and entertainment (some cruises now even include drinks and gratuities). Cruises allow the passenger to be carried from one destination to another in comfort and safety, in familiar surroundings, and without the need constantly to pack and unpack. Short-sea (ferry) vessels have also achieved new levels of comfort and speed on many routes, to a point where they now attract tourists not just as a means of transport, but as an enjoyable 'mini-cruise' with food and entertainment to a standard that a few years ago could be found only on a luxury cruise liner. Technological developments have helped to reduce high operating costs, while new forms of water borne transport have been developed, such as the hovercraft, jetfoil and the twin-hulled catamaran ferry. These have provided rapid communication over short sea routes and sometimes, as in the case of the hovercraft, across difficult terrain.

The pleasure that people find in simply being afloat has spawned many recent tourist developments, from yacht marinas and self-drive motor craft to dinghy sailing in the Mediterranean and canal barge holidays in Britain and on the European mainland. The continuing fascination with older means of propulsion has led to the renovation and operation of lake steamers in England and on the Continent of Europe, and paddle steamers plying the rivers of the USA.

In this chapter, we will investigate the appeal and operation of these various forms of water transport. It is convenient to divide these into five distinct categories:

- 'line voyage' shipping
- cruise shipping
- short-sea shipping, more familiarly known as ferries
- inland waterway and excursion vessels, and
- privately chartered or owned pleasure craft.

These categories will be considered in turn.

The ocean liners

Line voyage services are those offering passenger transport on a port-to-port basis, rather than as part of a cruise. Ships plying these routes are known as 'liners'. This form of transport has declined to a point where very few such services exist any longer, and those that do tend to be seasonally operated. The reasons for this decline are not hard to identify.

From the 1950s onward, advances in air transport enabled fares to be reduced, especially on popular routes across the Atlantic, to a point where it became cheaper to travel by air than by ship. The shipping lines, which until the advent of aircraft had no competition from alternative forms of transport, could not compete: they faced rapidly rising costs for fuel and labour in a labour-intensive industry. The gradual decline in passengers, as these switched to the airlines, led to losses in revenue for the shipping companies which made it impossible to consider renovating ageing fleets or replacing them with new vessels. By 1957, more passengers were crossing the Atlantic by air than by sea, and the demise of the worldwide passenger shipping industry was imminent. Leading routes, such as Cunard Line's transatlantic services, P&O's services to the Far East and Australia, and Union-Castle and British India Lines' services to South and East Africa, were either withdrawn or reduced to a skeleton service. The resulting shake-up in management led to attempts to regenerate traffic, mainly by employing the ships on cruises; but vessels built for fast line-voyage services are not ideally suited to alternative uses, while at the same time the appeal of cruising was beginning to decline. A small but loyal demand for sea transport remained among those, usually older, passengers who feared to fly, or who enjoyed sea voyages and were willing to spend time en route to their destinations. A very few lines were able to continue to operate to serve these markets. Today, only Cunard Line, among the major carriers, continues to provide a regular summer service across the Atlantic, between Southampton and New York, having introduced a new liner in 2005, the *Queen Mary 2*, for this express purpose. Outside of the summer months, this vessel also cruises, although its sheer size (at 151,400 tons it is the largest passenger vessel afloat at the time of writing) limits the ports of call.

Example   Measuring the size of a ship

The size of all vessels is based on their gross registered tonnage, but it is inaccurate to refer to the 'weight' of a ship. This is because *gross tonnage* refers to the internal volume of the vessel, rather than its weight or displacement. One ton is equal to 100 cubic feet (a measure formally laid down in the Merchant Shipping Act, 1854). Net registered tonnage is the internal volume devoted to passenger and cargo space only, excluding any non-earning space, such as the engine room, crew accommodation, etc.

The *RMS St Helena* is one the very few cargo–passenger liners still operating. At 7,000 tons and carrying just 128 passengers, it was built with a British government subsidy to provide a lifeline to the island dependencies of St Helena and Ascension – the former presently has no airport – and the government continues to subsidize the route, experimentally shifting its home port between the UK and South Africa in an effort to lift its appeal, calls at Lüderitz and Walvis Bay (Namibia) en route to Ascension and St Helena. This service has been more important for its freight capacity than its passenger, but the switch in bases reflects the recognition that passengers can be more easily attracted to shorter sea voyages, with more opportunities for packaging different tours around each leg of the voyage. The vessel is expected to be withdrawn from the route when an airport planned for St Helena is opened around 2010. A handful of other passenger-cum-freighter services exist around the world, such as the Mauritius Shipping Corporation's services between Mauritius, Reunion Island and South Africa; services from Tahiti carrying up to 60 passengers to the Marquesas islands and Tuamoto atolls in the South Pacific, and vessels, some carrying nearly 1,200 passengers, operated and subsidized by the Indian government, which connect the mainland to the Andaman and Nicobar Islands.

Most of the remaining passenger-carrying liner vessels operating around the world are built essentially to carry cargo. A maximum of twelve passengers is carried on such vessels (the limitation is due to the requirement of the International Maritime Organization that the crew include a doctor if more than twelve passengers are carried), while some vessels are fitted only with an owner's suite, carrying two passengers, but they are all clearly designed for lovers of sea travel for its own sake. Freight demand means that neither departure dates nor ports of call can be guaranteed, nor can it be certain that passengers will be allowed to disembark to visit the destinations en route. Entertainment is limited on board, and passengers dine with the ships' officers. These vessels do not offer a cheap alternative for long-distance travel – on the contrary, fares on cargo–passenger liners can be as expensive as those on cruise ships – but they nevertheless attract an enthusiastic market, and often passengers have to waitlist their requirements a year or more in advance.

The decline of line voyages was not due solely to the rise of air transport. Enterprise was for many years restricted by the so-called 'conferences', such as the Transatlantic and Transpacific Passenger Conferences, which governed the operation of fleets worldwide and restrained open competition. Shipping management must also bear much of the blame for its failure to adapt the product to meet changing needs. Ships were built without air conditioning or adequate numbers of cabins with en suite facilities – both essential requirements to attract the American market. The vessels' specifications and size made them inflexible and unsuitable for routes other than those for which they were built, and little attempt was made to adapt them for their new purposes. Shipping managers failed to recognize the extent of the threat posed by the airlines, and were too slow to move into that sector themselves; those that eventually attempted to do so found the necessary capital investment beyond the resources of their company.

Traffic conferences were not finally swept away until the 1970s, by which time the market was to all intents lost, and the negative image of cruising appealing only to the old and infirm had become firmly ingrained in the minds of the new generation of travellers. Whether the long-term decline of line voyages anywhere in the world can ever be reversed is debatable; apart from tentative plans to build budget ships for transatlantic crossings, research has also been undertaken to test the feasibility of developing jetships travelling at 40 knots or more, which would allow transatlantic crossings within 90 hours, and a Danish prototype, the DK/A1500F, has been constructed promising a speed of 45–50 knots, which would reduce the crossing to around two and a half days. The reality is, however, that nothing tangible has emerged that would be capable of sustained speed over such periods of time, in the years since jet ship technology was first muted. Meantime, on the North Atlantic route, the *Queen Mary 2* continues the long tradition of line voyages for at least part of the year.

Cruising

After the 1950s, the passenger shipping industry shifted its emphasis from line voyages to cruising. Initially, this transformation proved difficult; vessels in service at the time were for the most part too large, too old and too expensive to operate for cruising purposes. Their size was a limiting factor in the number of ports they could visit, and they were built for speed rather than leisurely cruising. Fuel bills can be cut by operating vessels at slower speeds, but ideally cruise ships should be purpose-built to achieve their maximum operational efficiency. During the 1960s and 1970s, this meant ships of 18,000–22,000 tons, carrying some 650–850 passengers. However, changes in demand and advances in marine technology have enabled recent cruise ships to be purpose-built in a variety of sizes. Providing there is sufficient demand, optimum profits can be achieved by employing larger vessels, and the trend since the 1980s has been to build ships of steadily increasing tonnage, first in the range of 50,000–70,000 tons, and later in excess of 100,000 tons, and capable of carrying up to 3,800 passengers. There now appears to be a polarization of cruise ships, between very large vessels and much smaller vessels operated by niche companies. This trend to larger size is putting a strain on port facilities, and requires significantly increased investment, especially in the Caribbean, the cruise market's most important destination.

There are more than 250 cruise ships operating worldwide, carrying more than 10 million passengers. At the time of writing, a total of 86 new cruise ships were built or contracted to be built between 2000 and 2009, and there is some danger that supply will outstrip demand as new vessels come on-stream, although withdrawal of some older vessels will help to compensate. Competition has driven current prices down to 1980s' levels, enhancing load factors but putting pressure on profits. Recent estimates expect passenger numbers to increase to around 18 million by 2010, and to 20 million two years later[1]. More than half of all cruises operate out of US ports, and Americans represent more than four out of every five cruise passengers, at around 8.8 million passengers annually. The UK owns roughly a 5 per cent share of the world's cruise ships – a marked decline over earlier years, although in recent years the British government has lowered the taxation rate on British shipping to help reverse this decline in tonnage. In terms of passenger demand, Britain takes second place after the USA, with a little over one million passengers (and growing rapidly), followed by Germany with 551,000 in 2004, and rather fewer from Italy and France (see Table 13.1). All the

Table 13.1   The largest markets for cruising

USA	8,900,000
Britain	1,028,937[a]
Germany	551,000
Italy	400,000
Spain	300,000
France	222,000
Other European	Under 100,000

(a) excludes river cruising
Source: www.discover-cruises.co.uk based on statistics from PSA-IRN

developed countries are experiencing a marked increase in demand for cruising, after a long period of decline, and growth in this market has averaged between 9 and 15 per cent per annum since the early 1990s. Even more encouraging, extrapolations by the Cruise Lines Industry of America (CLIA), which represents 19 of the world's major cruise lines, forecast a potential long-term market for cruising of around 35 million passengers, which will continue to drive the ship-building boom that began during the 1990s.

The majority of cruise liners are built today by just four West European yards; Fincantieri in Italy, Kvaerner Masa-yards in Finland, Aker Yards' Chantiers d'Atlantique in France and Meyer Werft in Germany (passenger shipbuilding in Britain having gone into terminal decline in the 1970s) – although other prominent yards exist in South Korea and Japan. Competition from these Asian yards will be fiercer in the future, since the withdrawal in Europe of state subsidies in 2003, under EU regulations.

Most new-built vessels will be larger than 60,000 tons, and some will carry close to 4,000 passengers. The largest ship afloat, at 151,400 tons, is the *Queen Mary 2*, but this ship is essentially a liner, with reduced passenger capacity of just 2,620 passengers. By contrast Royal Caribbean Line's *Freedom of the Seas*, currently under construction and due into service in 2006, is dedicated to cruising. At 158,000 tons this will briefly become the world's largest passenger vessel; capacity will be around 3,600 passengers and 1,360 crew. Costa Line's Concordia, also expected in 2006, will carry even more passengers, with an expected 3,780 berths, while P&O have ordered a new vessel, the *Ventura*, which they claim will be the largest afloat when launched in 2008, with 3,100 passengers. Operating costs of even these giants are only marginally greater than conventional ships, while the addition of 500 cabins with an associated increase in on-board spend boosts overall profitability. With building costs that can go as high as $550 million, twice that of a superjumbo aircraft, these ships represent a huge capital investment for their owners, and are something of a gamble, given the volatility of fuel prices – the recent escalation of fuel costs led to a 5 per cent increase in costs for the shipping lines. There have been long-term plans to build a 250,000-ton giant, to be called *America World City* and carrying up to 6,200 passengers, but efforts to raise the necessary capital have been frustrated. Allowing for the anticipated withdrawal of older ships, the net increase in supply is still expected to exceed the growth in demand for cruising, posing questions over the future profitability of shipping companies. Trends evident in the early twenty-first century anticipate further programmes of rationalization and integration among the largest companies.

The whole concept of a cruise holiday has changed from its traditional image; cruise ships are coming to be seen as floating holiday resorts which conveniently move from one destination to another, offering new scenery every day and non-stop entertainment on board. The very large tonnage allows not only a vast range of public rooms, which, on the newest ships includes facilities for climbing walls and even ice skating rinks, but also ensures that passengers have the widest conceivable choice of acquaintances to meet and make friends with on board (see, for example, Plate 14).

At the other end of the scale, a market has opened for vessels of typically 3,000–10,000 tons, carrying around 100–200 passengers. The smaller of these provide a 'yacht like' form of cruising for those who are prepared to pay the higher prices these vessels are obliged to charge. Such ships are able to enter harbours far smaller than would be possible for the traditional cruise ships, opening up new ports of call for cruising, such as Seville on the Guadalquivir River in Spain, Chicoutimi on the Saguenay River in Canada or the further reaches of the Amazon River, to Iquitos in Peru. Small ships can also negotiate constricted canals, such as the Corinth Canal in Greece and the Panama Canal, neither of which is navigable by the larger cruise vessels. Small ships with ice-strengthened hulls can penetrate deeper into Antarctica, visiting the Ross ice shelf.

There is an important issue relating to the size of cruise vessels, and that is the question of their *sustainability*. It is debatable whether building ever larger cruise ships is an appropriate strategy for the tourism business, whether or not these could be profitable. The effect on small island economies of vessels disgorging up to 4,500 passengers simultaneously at any one port, and within a strictly limited time period, must be judged against any possible benefits of visitor spend. However, the logistics and viability of putting such large numbers of people ashore and organizing shore excursions for them is another factor that will have to be weighed carefully; passengers are reluctant to queue up for two hours or more in order to go ashore or return to their vessels.

Cruise routes

Broadly, the world's major cruise routes are located in seven regions of the globe (see Figure 13.1). These are:

- Florida, the Caribbean, Bermuda and the Bahamas, including coastal towns of North, Central and South America
- the West Coast of Mexico, the USA (particularly Alaska) and Canada, plus Panama Canal transit

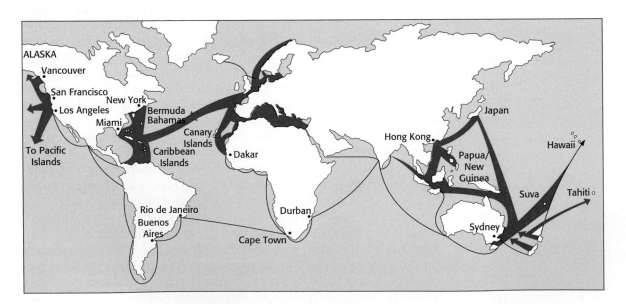

Figure 13.1   Major cruise routes of the world

- the Mediterranean, divided between the western and eastern sectors
- the Pacific islands and Far East
- the Baltic Sea, northern European capitals and the west coast of Norway as far north as the North Cape. Extensions to Svalbard (formerly Spitzbergen) are rising in popularity, as are cruises to Arctic regions like Iceland and Greenland, which are easily accessible from both Europe and North America
- West Africa and the Atlantic islands of the Canaries, Madeira and, increasingly, the Azores. Occasionally, this is extended to Cape Verde Islands
- round the world (usually permitting shorter-leg bookings).

Long-haul routes have become popular with the popularity of fly–cruises. The attractions of Indian Ocean islands is growing, to include Madagascar, the Seychelles, Réunion and Mauritius, with the principal port of embarkation being Mombasa in Kenya. Singapore is promoting itself as a major shipping hub for cruising, with interest rising in ports along the Indian coast, Hong Kong and the Indonesian 'spice islands'. The Antarctic Peninsula is experiencing strong growth, often combined with calls at South Georgia and the Falkland Islands. Vessels bound for Antarctica are often specially built for polar destinations, with reinforced hulls. Ushuaia is the main port of departure and is becoming economically important as a tourism destination in Argentina, both as a port and as a gateway to the Tierra del Fuego National Park.

In the UK, round-Britain cruising, in addition to calls at the mainland and Ireland, may include visits to the Shetland, Orkney, Hebridean and Faroe Islands, with occasional forays to remote outposts like St Kilda, which no longer has a permanent population.

Most cruising, however, continues to focus on either the Mediterranean or the Caribbean. These two regions account for over 60 per cent of all cruises, with the Scandinavian and Baltic regions accounting for a further 10 per cent. Most of these routes are seasonal, and this will mean that shipping companies may be obliged to move their vessels from one region of the globe to another to take advantage of peak periods of cruising demand. Movements for this purpose are termed *positioning voyages*, and provide lines with the opportunity to sell these sailings as long cruises, or even line voyages where transatlantic sailings are involved. The Baltic and North Cape cruises, for example, are operated during the northern hemisphere's high summer, with the North Cape cruise in particular operating in July to offer passengers the advantage of seeing the midnight sun. This is also true of Alaskan cruises, which have benefited at times when the political instability of some Mediterranean cruise itineraries is viewed as uncertain by the North American market. American cruise passengers are generally cautious about foreign travel, and have always shown a preference for cruising in their own waters, or those nearby. The on-board culture, and currency, are US oriented, and Americans are not required to carry passports for these cruises – an important selling point where only a small minority of the population owns a passport anyway. The Caribbean also benefits from the proximity of the islands to the American mainland, as well as a climate that allows year-round cruising, although the winter's more temperate climate attracts the highest level of demand. Ports in Florida, such as Fort Lauderdale, Miami/Port Everglades and Port Canaveral, have become by far the biggest bases for cruise ships; Port Canaveral alone embarks over two million passengers every year. Demand from Europe is such that charter flights from Europe now provide connections with many of the vessels which sail from Florida ports.

Fly–cruising has made a significant contribution to the growth of cruising from European countries. Passengers are carried by the cruise company on chartered aircraft to a warm-water base port from which they can directly embark on their cruise, or spend a few days at a nearby resort before or after the cruise. This overcomes the problem of poor weather and rough seas (the Bay of Biscay, off northern Spain, can be a notoriously unpleasant stretch of water to cross at any time of the year), and ensures that passengers can be enjoying the sunshine and calm seas of the Mediterranean or Caribbean from day one of their cruise holiday. Although the traditional, often older, cruise passengers at first resisted this move, it soon proved popular among an increasingly younger cruise market. However, recent years have shown a return to demand for ex-UK cruises, and companies such as Cunard, Fred Olsen and the UK tour operators are increasing their cruising from UK ports. In 2004, three out of every ten British cruise passengers chose to depart from and return to a UK port.

The search for new destinations has led to the opening up of even more adventurous cruise routes. Emulating American adventure cruises, companies like Noble Caledonia and Jules Verne pioneered Pacific inter-island cruises and voyages in the Arctic and Antarctic regions, often using smaller, purpose-built vessels. They and other specialist operators are also chartering Russian vessels with specially strengthened hulls to penetrate further south along the Antarctic shores.

However, these cruises are still largely aimed at the top end of the market, with prices starting as high as £500 or more a day. PSA, the British cruise association, categorizes the top cruise vessels as 'ultra luxury', with criteria that include passenger capacity (between 100–1,000), a crew to passenger ratio of 1:2, at least 40 square metres of space for every passenger and an average cost (in 2004) of £350 per day. A total of 17,564 passengers from Britain chose to cruise on one of these vessels in 2004.

The past decade has seen a rapid increase in the total of British passengers taking a cruise (over a million travelled in 2004) (see Table 13.2).

Table 13.2   Major destinations of the British cruise market, 2004[a]

Mediterranean	410,783[b]
Caribbean	234,696
Scandinavia/Baltic	104,929
Atlantic Isles	89,171
West Coast USA/Panama/Hawaii	23,598
Alaska	22,310
Round the world	12,690
South America/Antarctica	12,353
Far East/Australia	6,722
Other, including transatlantic and charters	111,685
River cruises	110,956

(a) 460,000 passengers embarked at UK ports. This figure includes both British and foreign residents
(b) includes cruises ex-Cyprus (22,660)
Source: PSA-IRN Annual Cruise Statistics

The large majority of cruises sold to the British are fly–cruises, although interest in sailing directly from UK ports has risen in recent years, with three out of ten now choosing to avoid flights. A total of 460,000 passengers sailed direct from the UK in 2004, and this has encouraged more ports to cater for cruise vessels; a total of 42 British ports now do so. Strong growth areas are river cruising, long-haul destinations and cheaper cruises on chartered ships marketed by tour operators. The demand for river cruising will be looked at in more detail a little later in this chapter.

The nature of the cruise market

The thought of a cruise still carries, for many holidaymakers, two distinctly negative images. On the one hand, cruise ships are thought to be peopled with conservative, rather elderly passengers who choose to spend their days at sea playing bridge, sitting on steamer chairs covered with blankets, watching the horizon and drinking cups of bouillon; while on the other hand, at the cheaper end of the market, the image is of ships as floating holiday camps, peopled by hyper-active, extrovert middle-aged passengers propping up the bars, looking for non-stop entertainment and enjoying five-times-a-day opportunities to eat, in-between shipboard romances. While undoubtedly such stereotypes exist, and some shipping lines cater for each of these, these images are far from accurate as a general picture of cruising today.

The key factors which determine cruise demand can be identified as price, length of cruise and destination, but there are a number of other factors contributing to choice, not least the efforts made by the shipping companies to appeal to niche markets through their ships, on-board activities and destinations. Interest in cruising among the population as a whole has expanded massively in recent years, and several distinct forms of cruise company have emerged. First, there are the major international cruise companies which draw on global markets and are tending to dominate the industry. The two leaders in the industry are the US-owned Carnival, by far the world's largest cruise company, which has absorbed several other leading cruise brands, including former British companies P&O and Cunard; and its competitor Royal Caribbean Cruise Line. Secondly, there are a handful of long-established lines, such as Hapag-Lloyd and Fred Olsen, which are strongly dependent upon their home markets and which attract significant numbers of repeat purchasers who tend to be brand-loyal to specific companies, and often to individual vessels. Thirdly, there are smaller companies with smaller vessels and sometimes narrower focuses, which may offer more adventurous destinations or activities designed to appeal to particular markets. These also draw intensely loyal passengers. Examples include Swan Hellenic, part of the Carnival group, which offers cultural cruises accompanied by experienced guides and lecturers; Orient Line and the World of Discovery, with their cruises to more isolated areas of the world, including the Antarctic; and Viking, whose small vessels are well suited to Baltic itineraries, and are designed to appeal to an up-market cultural audience (see itinerary and map, Figure 13.2). Expedition cruising, offering more adventurous destinations such as the Chilean fjords and Antarctica, in which landings are made by Zodiac tenders, calls for a more energetic (although not necessarily younger) market. These ships are often chartered or part-chartered to specialist tour operators that search out and organize ever more adventurous holiday destinations.

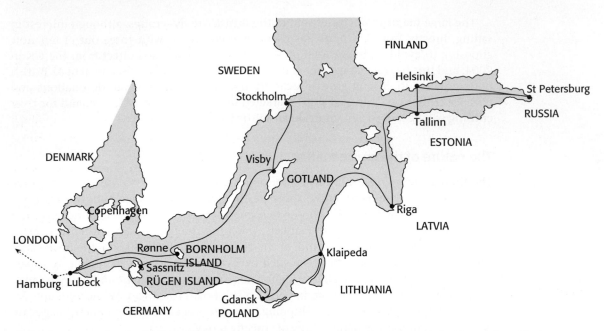

Figure 13.2 Scandinavia and the Baltic 'milk run'. The Baltic itinerary given as an example in this map is an ideal niche-marketing programme. The Swiss/French-owned ship operating the programme is only 3,000 tons, carrying 180 passengers. The two-week itinerary allows the ship to call at nine different countries, with only one day at sea without a port of call. The trip is sold as a 14-day round-voyage, or as a week-long cruise with connecting flights out of and into St Petersburg. The market is predominantly British, Swiss and German

Cruising appeals on a number of levels. The all-inclusive nature of a cruise, in which unlimited – and often excellent – food is on offer, the general ambience on board, the high levels of security that isolation on a ship can provide, the attraction of travelling with 'like-minded people' with whom it is easy to make friends, being thrown together within a confined space, the absence of constraint on the amount of baggage carried (other than on fly–cruises), all offer significant benefits. Indeed, for those with a real fear of flying, cruising directly from home ports provides the only means of travelling abroad.

While the concept of a floating hotel has become of importance in selling cruises, most passengers still expect ships to look like ships. A great deal of care goes into the design of a modern cruise liner, to provide the illusion of greater space, as well as maximum revenue-earning opportunities for the shipping company in the form of shops, hairdressing facilities, casinos and bars. Design also takes account of the nationality of those travelling; cruise ships aimed predominantly at the US market tend to make greater use of plastics, gilt stairways, mirrors, neon lights and bright colours, while the more traditional European, and particularly British, market will expect greater use of wood (although safety standards at sea encourage the use of more fire-retardant materials today) and quieter, more refined decoration.

The image of cruising as an older person's holiday is beginning to fade, as companies like Carnival, Island Cruises and Ocean Village encroach on the traditional cruise market and reach a younger group of holidaymakers. Indeed, Carnival claims an average age of 45 for its fleet overall, with a much younger average on its 'disco' ships operating short cruises in the Caribbean; the average age on Ocean Village, which describes its on-board regime as 'casual', is only 42, and predominantly British. This compares with an average age on Carnival's Holland America ships of 55, close to the average of all British cruise passengers, a quarter of whom fall between the ages of 45 and 54, according to the Passenger Shipping Association. Vessels appealing to the family market, like those operated by the Walt Disney Company, are undoubtedly contributing to a more youthful group of passengers. In the USA in particular, cruises are marketed as just another form of package holiday, comparable to an all-inclusive holiday on land. This has resulted in some 9 per cent of all Americans having taken a cruise, compared with only 2 per cent among the British.

Shipping companies have recognized the difficulty of appealing to varied markets, and varied nationalities, on the same vessel, however appealing this might be economically. Multinational passenger mixes call for multilingual announcements and entertainment on board, which will not be an attractive selling point. Passengers from different countries have differing habits and preferences in on-board food and entertainment; those from Latin countries, for instance, prefer to take dinner later than those from the UK or USA. One result of these differences is that cruise companies are tending to *niche market*, whether by price, by brand, by market or by type of cruise offered. Saga Holidays taps into the upper end of the age market, for example, catering exclusively for the over-50s. P&O's vessel *Adonia* is reserved for adults only, while their *Oceania* was designed to appeal to passengers new to cruising, both in its style and routes. *Artemis*, introduced in 2005, is a smaller vessel of 45,000 tons with more traditional decor designed to appeal to a conservative market (see Figure 13.3).

Figure 13.3
P&O's Artemis

(Courtesy: P&O Cruises)

Competition encourages shipping companies to emphasize product differentiation, while striving to build the newest ships, and offer the latest on-board facilities to meet the expectations of an increasingly sophisticated cruise market. Entertainment has become increasingly varied, with Cordon Bleu cookery courses, acting classes, wellness at sea programmes and a golf academy. On its North Atlantic crossings, Cunard's *Queen Mary 2* offers opportunities for intellectual stimulus, with lectures in association with Oxford University. One noted trend is to wider variety in catering on board. P&O's *Oriana*, to take one example, has introduced a pizzeria on board, while Crystal Cruises offers a choice of Italian, Japanese and Chinese restaurants on its vessels.

The economics of cruising

In spite of the rise in popularity of cruising, it remains a highly volatile market, and is quickly affected by adverse events, such as terrorist activities or war in the Middle East. Americans in particular are cautious travellers, and seek security abroad; the perception of danger in the Mediterranean caused many to switch bookings to safer home waters in the Caribbean or Alaska, both of which experience something of a boom when bookings to the Mediterranean decline. Cruise companies can also be forced in these circumstances to reposition their vessels to the already congested Caribbean, as a result of which, even with rising demand, over-supply leads to deep discounting for all cruise ships, and profits fall.

Cabotage rights extend to shipping operations as much as they do airline operations. Vessels of foreign registry are not permitted to carry passengers between two ports within the same country, nor to carry passengers from and back to the same port without an intermediate port of call in a foreign country. American legislation is contained in the Merchant Marine Act (1920), better known as the Jones Act, which prohibits non-US registered vessels from carrying passengers between two US ports without a call at a 'distant foreign port' (Canadian ports are close, and therefore not counted as foreign for the purpose of the act).

Example   Norwegian Caribbean Line

NCl have operated cruises from the Hawaiian Islands for a number of years, and were obliged to call at a foreign port under cabotage regulations. They programmed a call at Fanning Island (Tabuaeran) in Kiribati, the nearest non-US port, even though the call had little passenger appeal. Subsequently, the company formed a new US registered company, NCI America, which sails under the American flag and allows them to operate their Hawaiian cruises without the need to make an intermediate call.

More than 40 countries around the world continue to enforce cabotage rules, including Canada, Mexico and Japan.

Cruising is both capital-intensive and labour-intensive. A modern cruise liner can easily exceed $250 million to build, with some, like *Queen Mary 2* costing in excess of $500 million (costs for a projected 250,000-ton vessel would probably exceed $1 billion). Life expectancy of a cruise ship is fortunately far greater than an aircraft, and, allowing for rebuilding and complete renovation, a 50-year productive life would not be unusual.

Fuel burn is obviously an important consideration in overall operating costs, although perhaps not as critical as one might expect; oil prices typically represent only 4 per cent of overall costs[2]. Steamships are generally less efficient than diesel-engined vessels, and most have been phased out over the past decade, as have other, less fuel-efficient vessels. At times of rapid escalation in fuel prices, operating costs will rise sharply, but competition makes a parallel rise in prices difficult to enforce.

Vessels also need a substantial number of crew, both in passenger service and below deck – a four- or five-star cruise liner would carry as many as one member of crew for every two passengers, and a ratio of one to one is not unknown among the luxury top end of the market. With such labour costs, it is not difficult to see why luxury cruises are selling at up to a thousand dollars a day. The decline in the fleets of the established maritime nations such as Britain can be partly accounted for by their uncompetitive operating costs compared with their cheaper competitors. Lower-cost nations like Greece and Russia built up their own fleets, while the more expensive nations were obliged to trim costs by registering their fleets in developing countries such as Panama or Liberia, and by recruiting crews from countries where labour costs are low, such as the Philippines, Indonesia or India – to the chagrin of trade unions representing maritime crews in the developed nations. Virtually all leading cruise companies today recruit a substantial proportion of their deck staff from the Philippines. Large companies also reduce the ratio of crew to passengers, aiming to deliver a three star, rather than four or five star, service.

Companies operating large fleets can also obtain some economies of scale, reducing the cost per unit of their marketing and administration. It has also become more economical to operate large ships rather than small ones, and the trend is to build bigger and bigger vessels, to take advantage of this and to maximize on-board spend. Five-star operators such as Silversea Cruises face a different problem, however. While high profitability is hard to achieve for these vessels when capacity is low, any increase leads to difficulties in delivering the expected high standards of service. Optimum viability for the luxury end of the market is believed to be achieved, therefore, with vessels of around 25,000 tons carrying a maximum of 400 passengers.

The largest ships are able to pare costs by providing smaller cabins, with larger areas given over to public use. This provides space for shopping and other sales opportunities which, together with shore excursions, make up around one-third of a cruise line's revenue. Dining rooms accommodate large numbers within relatively confined spaces either by having two sittings for meals, or by providing only large tables; tables for two are rare on board ships. However, some companies have capitalized by designing their ships to permit all passengers to be accommodated in the restaurant at a single sitting – an attractive marketing advantage.

The global political situation has not only led to higher fuel costs; ships and seaports also now need heightened security, just as do aircraft and airports; passengers and their luggage have to be checked more carefully as they board, and the vessels must be guarded around the clock, while in port and under way.

Another feature of shipping which is shared with the airline industry is the highly fluid pricing structure which the industry now finds it necessary to adopt. Deep discounting has become the norm for nearly all cruise lines, with discounts for early bookers, last-minute bookers, loyal clients, even for readers of certain newspapers and magazines. Identical cabins will be sold at different fares in Britain, on the Continent, and in North America – the result, the shipping companies insist, of market conditions, although website searches by passengers are reducing this differential. Most cruises are still sold through travel agents, and they, in turn, offer discounts and incentives to secure the booking, on top of any discounts by the principal.

A useful rule of thumb in judging the relative luxury and spaciousness on board ship is to ascertain the size to passenger ratio (SPR), sometimes referred to as the passenger–space ratio (PSR). This is based on the vessel's gross registered tonnage divided by the number of passengers carried. If this amounts to 20 or less, the ship is likely to appear crowded, while a figure approaching 60 would be considered luxurious, and command high daily rates (see Table 13.3). Tonnage alone is not a good guide to the amount of space per passenger; *World of Cruising* magazine points out that the *Lirica*, at 60,000 tons, has a PSR of 25.42, while the *Discovery* at 19,900 tons offers a PSR of 32.6 – yet both are classed as four-star ships.

Further economies are obtained by calling at a greater number of ports on any itinerary, and spending more time in port, both of which help to reduce fuel burn while at the same time increasing the passengers' satisfaction. A reduction in speed also saves on fuel, but if vessels are to travel slowly and also call at numerous ports, it is essential that these ports are grouped closely together. For this reason, the Caribbean, with its many islands of differing nationality, makes an ideal cruise destination.

Table 13.3 Comparisons in size and comfort between some leading cruise ships

Ship	Tonnage	Star rating	Space ratio	Passenger to crew ratio
Grandeur of the Seas	74,137	****	38.00	2100/760
Oriana	69,000	****	37.80	1830/760
MSC Lirica	60,000	****	25.42	1600/760
Island Escape	40,132	***	26.50	1600/612
Black Watch	28,500	****	37.45	761/310
Emerald	26,431	***	26.60	1100/420
Marco Polo	21,000	****	24.10	800/356
Discovery	19,900	****	32.60	600/325
Braemar	19,900	****	26.10	727/320
Black Prince	11,000	***	26.69	412/200

Source: Modified from Voyages of Discovery brochure, 2005, based on Sept 2004 edition of *World of Cruising*

Example Cunard's transatlantic service

One example of effective cost reduction in the shipping operations is demonstrated by Cunard, which in 1996 took the decision to extend the journey time for its *Queen Elizabeth 2* between the UK and New York from five to six days. While this achieved significant savings on fuel burn, reducing average speed from 28.5 knots to 23 knots, it also offered other advantages, in marketing terms; higher on-board spend was encouraged, while the passengers themselves saw an additional day's cruising as an added benefit; it also allowed the ship to arrive at a more convenient time of day for those with onward travel arrangements.

Further economies can be achieved by putting passengers ashore by tender (ship's launches), rather than tying up alongside. This may be a practical alternative when islands are pushing up mooring fees; however, it does delay disembarkation, and will be a less attractive selling point.

Cruise lines have to ensure that their ships are used for the maximum amount of time during the year (just as airlines do) – although this does not necessarily mean their use for cruising only. Some companies charter cruise ships to tour operators, while others have successfully chartered ships for use as floating hotels when accommodation pressures force tourist destinations to find alternative accommodation for special events; Cunard was even successful in chartering its largest vessel, the *Queen Elizabeth 2*, for a period for Japan to use as a hotel; this represented a substantial saving to the company on operating costs, as it required no use of fuel for transport.

Example *The World*

The World, a £182-million investment project by ResidenSea, represents a new concept in cruising. Apartments, priced between £1.5 million to £5 million, were sold off to wealthy investors as second homes, to be used mainly for their own pleasure; owners could join the ship at any point during its continuous round-the-world itinerary. Initial sales were slow, and it was decided that some of the apartments would be sold for short legs only, while others would be made available for commercial rent to cruise passengers. Prices were set at the highest end of the scale, but resident owners were disappointed at the resultant mix of private ownership and commercial rental.

Distribution is all-important in this competitive sector, and although cruise operators have made full use of the World Wide Web to market their products, slightly more than 80 per cent of all cruise bookings in the UK are still made through travel agents. However, the complexity of cruising makes it difficult for sales staff to acquire adequate knowledge of the variety of accommodation and ships available without gaining first-hand experience. In recent years, the PSA, the marketing arm of the passenger shipping business in the UK, has attempted to overcome this problem by mounting special campaigns to train agents, and has successfully trained staff in more than 1,000 branches to provide a professional cruise sales service to their clients.

The larger shipping companies tend to receive greater support from travel agents, who find it easier to deal with companies owning a greater number and variety of ships, and therefore a larger choice of both sailings and destinations. A growing number of agents, seeking ways of specializing as commission for other services is reduced, have switched their focus to the cruise sector, obtaining advantageous commission rates and developing their competence in selling this sector. A Leading Cruise Agents' Alliance has been formed to bring these specialists together.

The cruising business

Although demand has been rising strongly for more than a decade, it has been outpaced by the growth in supply, not only in the number of vessels but also their overall size and capacity; 34 ships entered the cruise market between 2002–04 alone, adding 65,000 berths to the availability (see Table 13.4). This has led to fierce competition in

Table 13.4 Leading cruise operators and their ships, as at mid-2004

Shipping line	Number of vessels
Carnival Cruises	19
RCI (Celebrity, Island Cruises*)	19
Princess Cruises (P&O)	18
Norwegian Coastal Voyage	12
Norwegian Cruise Line (RCI)	11
Celebrity Cruises (NCL)	9
Costa Line (Carnival)	9
Royal Olympic	7
Festival Cruises	6
P&O Cruises (Carnival)	4
SilverSea	4
Airtours Sun Cruises	4
Mediterranean Shipping Co	4
Radisson SevenSeas	4
Crystal	3
Cunard Line (Carnival)	3
Fred Olsen	3
Disney	2
Thomson Cruises	2
Star Cruises (NCL, Orient)	2
Hebridean Island	2
Island Cruises*	2
Swan Hellenic (Carnival)	1
Ocean Village (P&O)	1
Orient Line (NCL)	1

* Island Cruises was established as a joint RCI and First Choice venture.

Figure 13.4
Interior (atrium)
of P&O's *Aurora*

(Courtesy: P&O Cruises)

the industry and deep discounting. Profits slimmed, and, as has been the case with so many other sectors of the tourism industry, this has led to greater market concentration. Two companies, Carnival Cruise Line and Royal Caribbean International are now coming to dominate the cruise market, together controlling about 75 per cent of the global market share. Carnival Cruise Line deserves special mention because of the way in which it has changed the face of cruising since the mid-1970s. The company was formed in 1972, and has been noted for its string of acquisitions, which since 1989 include Holland America Line, Seabourn, Costa Line, Cunard Line, P&O and Princess Cruises, Windstar Cruises, Ocean Village, Swan Hellenic and Aida. By early 2005, the company was operating 78 ships under 13 different brands, and had another 12 vessels on order. Together, they control 48 per cent of the US market, 35 per cent of the British market and 27 per cent of the German market (which at the time of writing formed about half the size of the British market for cruising).

Carnival has in particular been able to attract a much younger than average market for its major division, Carnival Cruises, which offers relatively cheap cruises of short duration, using large vessels of typically 70,000–100,000 tons or more. Its most recent vessels accommodate typically between 2,000 and 3,000 passengers. The fanciful names of the ships (e.g. *Paradise, Ecstasy, Sensation* and *Imagination*) are pointers to the expectation of their passengers as to the kind of experiences these cruise ships promise. They are sold as 'fun cruises' offering a wide range of on-board facilities, including shops and casinos (Carnival has claimed that some 14 per cent of its total revenue is on-board spend). A recent launch is the *Carnival Miracle*, a vessel of 88,500 tons with 16 themed lounges and bars, including a sports bar named after the cruise film *Jerry McGuire*, a night club in the shape of a gothic castle and another entitled Dr Frankenstein's Lab. Not perhaps to every cruise passengers' taste, but the market for which it is designed, overwhelmingly American, has responded favourably. The company has been particularly successful in attracting young, relatively high-spend passengers.

Carnival has also identified smaller niches. Its Fiesta Marina division of Hispanic-oriented tours was developed to tap into Spanish- and Portuguese-speaking markets in the US and Latin America, based on a home port of San Juan, Puerto Rico, an island commonwealth of the US. Food, wine and entertainment on board were designed for Hispanic tastes, and dining hours are later than usual, in accordance with Hispanic preferences.

Smaller niche markets are being tapped by specialist operators around the world, often using chartered vessels. Spanish operator Gheisa Tours ran a successful charter cruise for nudists on the *Flamenco* in 2004, and US operator Atlantis Events caters for the gay market with cruises on ship charters like *Celebrity Constellation*.

Over-tonnage in American waters has forced cruise companies to turn to the European markets to fill ships. Many carriers now offer free flights to the Caribbean to join cruise ships based there, as an incentive to attract this market.

Health and safety

Health and safety issues are controlled by the International Maritime Organization (IMO), which requires ships and ports to conform to internationally set standards. These are constantly being tightened up; new rulings on environmental pollution came into effect in 2004, with further amendments in force by 2010, leading ship owners either to have to invest substantially in upgrading, or withdrawing, their older vessels. Illegal cleaning of tanks at sea, discharge of oil and pumping of raw sewage into the oceans are of increasing concern for their effect on the environment – it has been pointed out that a single cruise liner can pump up to 130,000 litres of sewage into the ocean every day[3]. New ships are required to conform to the new standards immediately, while older ships have been given time to come up to standard. The dominance of the Americans in the world cruise market, and American concern with both safety and hygiene, have also resulted in strict standards being imposed on all foreign flag-carriers operating out of, or calling at, US ports. All such ships are subject to unannounced inspections from the US Vessel Sanitation Program. Vessels are rated for the quality of their water, food preparation, cleanliness, storage and repairs. An acceptable rating is 86 points out of 100, but it is not uncommon for even leading cruise ships of the world to be given grades considerably lower than this. Owners are then required to raise their standards. Adverse publicity in the press is a further incentive not to fail these tests. In the period November 2002 to September 2003 there were eight serious outbreaks of contagious diseases on board cruises ships, ranging from viral gastroenteritis to the Norwalk virus, and these outbreaks get maximum publicity in the world's press.

Owners are also required to be bonded against financial collapse. More recently constructed vessels incorporating higher standards of safety can attract lower insurance premiums. These vessels are also more technically advanced, and have lower operating costs, with the result that older ships find it difficult to compete. In this respect, the shipping and airline businesses are experiencing similar problems. Medium-sized operators are likely to be absorbed over the next few years by the three or four largest companies, leaving only the niche market cruise operators to remain as independents in the field.

Tour operator cruising

While cruises are sold as package holidays in the United States, and tour operators there have also played a part as intermediaries in bringing the product to the notice of the travelling public, British tour operators have been slower to move into the cruise market. During the 1970s, some operators, including Thomson Holidays, did charter or part-charter cruise ships which they incorporated into their programme of inclusive tours, but these attempts ran into a number of problems. Efforts to bring down the overall prices of cruising led to dissatisfaction with standards of service and operation. Later, Airtours, now MyTravel and one of Britain's leading operators, introduced its own ship, *Carousel*, selling Mediterranean cruises at lead-in prices of £399, and marketing them as merely alternatives to the traditional package holiday but with all meals and entertainment thrown in, for little more than the price of a package holiday. The popularity of the product soon brought another two leading operators, Thomson Holidays and First Choice, into cruising. In 2000, Royal Caribbean International bought a 20 per cent stake in First Choice, aiming to form a joint cruise company and with the clear intention of using the operator's retail outlets to push cruise sales in the UK. In 2004 MyTravel, facing a number of financial difficulties (see Chapter 16), abandoned its own cruise operations, although it continues to sell cruises.

The entrance of these tour operators into the mass-market cruise business changed the face of British cruising. Not only was the average age of cruise passengers reduced, but also a whole new market was introduced to cruising; 80 per cent of the Airtours passengers were first-time cruisers. Tour operators also helped to popularize the short cruise in the British mass market, which brought down cruise prices, and the seven-day, or shorter, cruise has since enhanced the appeal of this form of holiday for both European and American passengers. Ocean Village cruises introduced a less formal style of cruising in 2003, hoping to attract the 35–55 age group. Three-quarters of its first year passengers were indeed under 55, and half were first-time cruisers. A Cyprus-based company, Louis Cruises, further boosted the appeal of short cruises by offering two-night voyages from Limassol to Egypt and The Lebanon, mainly as excursions for

368 ■ Water-borne tourist transport

holidaymakers staying on the island. In 2005 the company, which also charters ships to Thomson, expanded its programme of short cruises to include sailings from Genoa, Piraeus and Marseilles.

It is still likely, however, that most cruising will retain an up-market image in the UK. Middle-priced cruising has experienced an equally sharp rise in demand. The market for this price bracket is very loyal – both P&O and Cunard have claimed 60–70 per cent of their market to be repeat bookings. The future of the cruise industry looks healthy, in terms of the growth in numbers booking, if less so in terms of profitability. According to the PSA, fewer than one in 60 passengers has ever taken a cruise, compared with one in 40 among the US population, which suggests considerable scope for growth. Less than 5 per cent of inclusive tours currently sold in the UK are cruises. In spite of the rapid growth in cruising among British holidaymakers, to over a million every year, this would have to rise a further 50 per cent before British cruising reaches the levels of that in the USA. However, the PSA is predicting growth to 1.3 million by 2008, and cruising is likely to be boosted by yet another innovation introduced in 2005: easyCruise.

Example easyCruise

In 2005, easyJet owner Stelios Hadji-Ioannou announced the launch of his latest venture, easyCruise. This is an entirely new concept in cruising, in which customers can make their own connecting flight arrangements or are charged extra for flights to and from their departure points. Additional payment is made for all meals on board, which are taken cafeteria-style. *easyCruise 1* is a small ship, at 2,840 tons, and the product is typical of the easy group's approach to holidays; the maiden voyage attracted passengers with an average age of just 35. Cabins can be booked for any variety of legs between ports around the Mediterranean, with a minimum of two nights on board. Cabins, which are very small, were initially sold at a rate of just £29 per double per night, with a supplement for housekeeping. The ship is also scheduled to operate in the Caribbean during winter periods, and plans are already advanced for a second vessel for the fleet.

Whether the launch of this new style of cruise will herald a new age for cruising, attracting an entirely new market, or whether it will be viewed with hindsight as a disastrous miscalculation, can only be speculated upon at the time of writing, although the Ocean Village concept has been successful in attracting a younger, budget-conscious market, as have ships in the Carnival fleet. It nevertheless represents a considerable gamble, and rather more so than the launch of budget flights, for which there was very clear demand. The area of greatest growth in ex-UK cruising in 2004 was in fact luxury cruising (at prices in excess of £250 a day per person), up 70 per cent over the previous year, and in spite of deep discounting, this is seen as offering the best opportunity for future profitability in cruising.

Brand loyalty is strong among cruise passengers, and great efforts are now made to differentiate individual ships as well, rather than depending upon discounting to sell unsold cabins. Certainly Carnival, with its niche-marketing among the younger holidaymakers in the US, has led the way in this direction, while other companies have focused on theme-cruising to survive (cruise lines now offer a huge variety of special-interest cruises, ranging from botanical cruises to 'classical civilizations' cruising in the Mediterranean accompanied by specialist, often well-known, guest lecturers, and from classical music cruises to jazz cruises, with on-board orchestras). Some shipping operators have experimented with new types of vessel. Radisson, for example, introduced twin-hull catamaran vessels, while both Windstar Cruises and Club Méditerranée offer luxury sail-assisted ships to widen the appeal of cruising. Small luxury ships are also in vogue: Society Expedition Cruises offer luxury cruising for around a hundred passengers to exotic destinations like the Amazon and Antarctic, while the similarly small (4,260 gross tons) Sea Dream Yacht Club ships offer unparalleled luxury to more traditional destinations in the Caribbean and Mediterranean for just 110 passengers, with a crew of just 90 and a retractable platform at the stern from which passengers may swim, snorkel or sail while the ship lies at anchor.

While the expansion of the cruise business is to be welcomed for the benefits it can bring to holidaymakers and companies alike, there are downsides which have to be taken into account, too. The emphasis on on-board spend and the creation of ships which are virtually leisure complexes in their own right, with all the amenities provided at an 'all-inclusive resort', means that destination countries suffer from the same drawbacks experienced from the growth of those resorts. Bigger on-board spend equates to less spend ashore, less money going into local shops, bars and transport companies. Some companies have purchased their own, frequently deserted, islands on which they can land their passengers for barbecues and lazy 'beach days', ensuring once again that no expenditure goes into the local economy. At the same time the growth in size of cruise vessels, as we have seen, threatens massive congestion at small island ports. Leisure transport generally is also beginning to draw criticism for its pollution effects. Large cruise vessels are fuel-hungry (if not to the same extent as thirty years ago), and one estimate has suggested that marine engines in total account for about 8 per cent of all the world's nitrous oxide emissions – admittedly a large proportion of this would be accounted for by the enormous growth in private ownership of luxury motor yachts, but cruise vessels must bear their share of responsibility for increasing atmospheric pollution, as must passenger aircraft.

Ferry services

The term 'ferry' is one which embraces a variety of forms of short-distance water-borne transport. This includes urban transport, in cities such as Stockholm, where outlying suburbs and surrounding towns are reached by water from the city centre. Ferries of this type also attract tourists, either as a convenient form of local transport or as an original way to view the city. Some ferries, such as the Staten Island ferry, which links Manhattan with the borough of Staten Island in New York, and Hong Kong's Star Ferry, have become world famous and a 'must' for visiting tourists. Other notable ferry rides which serve the needs of both locals and tourists include the Bosporus ferries linking Europe and Asia in Istanbul, the many island ferries in Greece and Indonesia, the Manly ferry between Sydney and Manly in Australia, the Niteroi ferry crossing Guanabara Bay in Rio de Janeiro, the Mersey ferry in Liverpool (immortalized in pop music), the Bainbridge Island ferry in Seattle, the Alameda–Oakland ferry in San Francisco, the Devonport and Waiheke inland ferries in Auckland, New Zealand and the Barreiro and Cacilhas ferries crossing the River Tagus in Lisbon. Most of these, of course, are designed primarily to provide essential communications for local commuters, but inevitably they also provide important attractions for tourists either wishing to get a different view of a city or planning to visit more remote areas of a country, often where convenient links by air may not be possible; examples of the latter include the Greek islands, or the Hebrides off the west coast of Scotland, the Isle of Wight off the south coast of England, and crossing the Strait of Messina, between Italy and Sicily.

However, the key ferry routes for tourists are those major links between countries separated by water, such as across the English Channel, between countries in the Baltic Sea, between Corsica and Sardinia and across the Adriatic between Italy, Greece and the Balkan countries. These routes may be vital for those wishing to take their car on holiday, and also provide an attractive alternative to flying for those with time to spare. Additionally, there are many places in the world where transport is dependent upon good national ferry services, owing either to the number of islands belonging to the territory or the difficulty of reaching coastal destinations by air or sea. A notable example is the west coast of Norway, where small towns cut off from land routes and air connections depend upon the *Hurtigruten*, or 'fast route', where daily ferries call at dozens of ports between Bergen and the North Cape. This itinerary has become so popular with tourists that full-size cruise vessels now ply the route. Other popular routes include the west coast of Canada and Alaska and the Hebridean islands off mainland Scotland's western coast.

The significance of the short-sea ferry market can be appreciated when it is learned that by the end of the last century some 2,150 ro–ro (roll-on–roll-off) ferries were estimated to be in operation worldwide; in the UK alone some 50 million passengers travel by ferry each year, more than half of these crossing to the Continent, while services out of British Columbia in Canada carry some 24 million passengers a year. Of course, not all these will be counted as tourists, and this is an important point to remember; typically, ferry services are designed to provide a communication network for local populations, while taking advantage of visitors to boost numbers and become profitable.

The growth of short-sea voyages within Europe during the past two decades can be hailed as a major success story. The rise in demand for ferries over this period can be partly attributed to the general growth of tourism and trade in the region, especially in trade between European Union countries, but growth of private-car ownership and independent travel also played a significant part in raising demand. France in particular has always been a destination with a strong attraction for independent British holiday-makers travelling with their cars, although the relative strength of the pound to the euro will be a key factor in influencing demand between the UK and the Continent. There has also been a steady rise in coach transport between Britain and the Continent, as coach companies introduced long-distance coach routes linking London with the capitals and cities of Continental Europe. In spite of the challenge offered by the

Channel Tunnel linking Britain and France since 1994, Dover remains by far the most important of the ports serving the Continent, with three ferry lines, P&O, SeaFrance and Hoverspeed all operating on this route.

Good marketing by the ferry companies has played a part in stimulating traffic over the years. New routes have been developed to tap regional markets and to provide greater choice, so that passengers have been able to choose to travel to the Continent from a variety of ports along the south coast of England (see Figure 13.5). Not all new routes have proved viable, as price competition attracts tourists to the most popular, even if not the most convenient, routes. The generally high prices charged by ferries out of Kent to the Continent (claimed to be the highest fares per mile anywhere in the world) have been challenged by a new Danish company, Speedferries, which is opening up competition across the Channel, while Eurotunnel has also slashed prices to attract more passengers to the land-based link with the Continent.

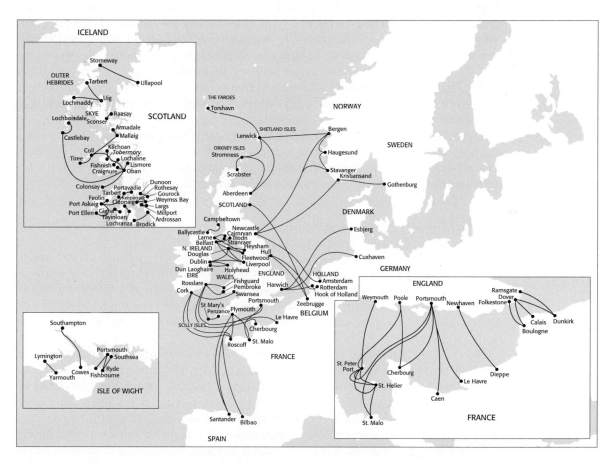

Figure 13.5   Major passenger/car ferry services from ports in the British Isles
(Courtesy: Travel Weekly)

From Britain, routes can be conveniently grouped into four geographical regions:

- English Channel (short-sea crossing) routes, including services from ports such as Ramsgate, Dover, Folkestone and Newhaven
- Western Channel routes, including services from Portsmouth, Southampton, Poole, Weymouth and Plymouth
- North Sea routes, including services from Newcastle/North Shields, Hull, Felixstowe, Harwich and Sheerness
- Irish Sea routes, including services from Swansea, Pembroke, Fishguard, Holyhead, Liverpool, Stranraer, Cairnryan and the Isle of Man.

It should be stressed that while these have been identified as key ports, services operating out of these ports do vary from time to time, as competition forces out some companies and others attempt to operate new routes in their place. The expectation that a route, once announced, will continue to operate for many years is no longer true; recent years have seen a number of companies' routes fail, including the Brighton–Fécamp route, Eurolink's Sheerness–Vlissingen service, Sally Ferries' Ramsgate–Dunkirk service and Brittany's Poole–St Malo route. Other leading companies like Stena Line and P&O have withdrawn services or reverted to alternative ports. Even one of the oldest ferry routes, between Newhaven and Dieppe, with a history of service stretching back to 1825, was briefly without a ferry connection until new services were introduced earlier this century.

In addition to Britain's ferry connections to Continental European and Irish ports, a number of important smaller ferry services provide internal links to the Hebridean islands of Scotland, the Orkney and Shetland islands, and to the Isle of Wight, the Isle of Man, the Scilly Isles and Lundy Island in the Severn Channel.

The economics of ferry operating

As with cruising, operating short-sea ferry routes is expensive in both capital invest-ment and in direct operating cost. Modern ferries on many routes are now nearly as large and sumptuous as cruise ships, and building costs can run into hundreds of millions of pounds. Within the European Union, ferries are expected to be written off over a 27-year time-span, although Greece has traditionally operated its ferries for as long as 35 years.

Profitability is achieved through a combination of maximum usage of equipment, plus on-board sales. The termination in 1999 of duty-free sales within the European Union had a significant impact on cross-Channel revenue (which had accounted for up to 50 per cent of ferry companies' turnover), forcing ticket prices up. Rapid turnarounds in port at the end of each journey are essential, as are round-the-clock sailings, with ideally an even volume of business all year round and a balanced flow of demand in both directions. In practice, this is, of course, impossible to achieve, and in winter, when much of the pure holiday traffic dries up, the ferry services become very dependent upon freight to contribute to their costs.

Figure 13.6
Ferries leave
Dover Harbour
en route for the
Continent

(Photographed by the author)

The shorter sailings to France, Belgium and Holland attract much better market demand than do the longer routes to Scandinavia, Germany and northern Spain, although the ferry companies on the latter routes have achieved considerable success in marketing the longer (24 hours or more) sailings as mini-cruises. Their success is modelled on the enormously popular service between Stockholm, Sweden and either Turku or Helsinki, Finland, which, in addition to providing one of the most scenic routes anywhere in Europe for a ferry service, also attracts customers through the sale of relatively cheap on-board drinks, in a region where alcohol is prohibitively expensive. As a result, the ferry market between these two countries has grown to a point where the two major carriers, Silja Line and Viking Line, can support a string of super-ferries, the largest of which, at 60,000 tons, is capable of carrying in excess of 3,000 passengers (see Figure 13.7). By including a stop at the Finnish-owned Åland Islands, which have special status within the European Community, duty-free goods can continue to be sold on board these vessels, retaining their popularity for the short-break market.

Off-peak sailings on shorter routes can be boosted by low fares, with a wide range of discounted prices aimed at differing market segments. Quick round-trips on the same vessel, or short stopovers of one to three nights have expanded, while shopping expeditions to the French hypermarkets for food and alcohol prove popular, especially in the run-up to Christmas. While the termination of duty-free goods on these routes cut

Figure 13.7
The superferries:
Silja Line's *Silja
Symphony* at
Helsinki

(Photographed by the author)

the market for short trips to France initially, the removal of customs barriers on duty-paid goods within the European Union, and the relatively low cost of duty-paid alcoholic drinks in France compared with Britain, helped to boost sales on cross-Channel vessels.

At extreme off-peak periods, and for night sailings which attract fewer bookings, some ferry companies will price their sailings to make a contribution to fixed costs, rather than to cover all costs on every crossing. Low fares will stimulate on-board spend, making a useful contribution to total revenue. The ferry companies have increased their general shopping facilities in their newer ships in order to boost duty-paid sales. While this has not fully made up for the loss of duty-free revenue, it has helped to reduce the impact of the withdrawal of this facility.

Leading ferry companies have made strenuous efforts to cut their operating costs in recent years, particularly their labour costs. New labour practices were introduced to increase the efficiency of crewing, but only after serious confrontations with the seamen's union. As with cruising, more staff from the Third World are now taken on. At the same time, the SOLAS (Safety of Life at Sea) regulations which came into effect at the end of 2004 following the Stockholm Agreement signed in 1997 between Great Britain and six northern European countries, have substantially added to building costs. The objective of these regulations was to increase the safety and stability of ro–ro ferries, following the disastrous *Herald of Free Enterprise* sinking at Zeebrugge in 1987, in which nearly 200 died, and the subsequent sinking of the ferry *Estonia* in the Baltic in 1994 with the loss of 850 lives. The Stockholm Agreement requires vessels operating into and out of ports in the seven countries to be capable of remaining upright in waves up to 4 metres high and with 50 centimetres of floodwater on the car deck. It called for transverse bulkheads to be fitted on all ships to improve stability in rough seas, but these obligatory modifications can reduce car capacity and slow down the loading and unloading of vessels, leading to delays in turnarounds.

The Channel Tunnel and the ferry services

The Channel Tunnel was viewed initially as the single greatest threat to cross-Channel ferries since their inception. Opened to passenger traffic in 1994, the Tunnel has attracted the lion's share of the cross-Channel market, but has failed to drive the ferries out of business, and is itself under threat under the weight of its capital debts. The background to this problem is described more fully in Chapter 14, but here we should take account of the impact of the land link upon ferry services.

Eurotunnel, operators of the Channel Tunnel, suffered a number of setbacks in building and operating the Tunnel, including repeated delays in opening, delays in obtaining equipment to run through the Tunnel, and a disastrous and costly fire in a freight wagon at the end of 1996. Eurotunnel's original estimates of passenger numbers proved wildly optimistic, but nonetheless the company achieved a 51 per cent share of the Dover Straits traffic (Dover/Folkestone to Calais/Boulogne) within its first five years of operation. Eurostar, which offers rail connections between London, Lille, Paris and Brussels, also succeeded in diverting a substantial number of air travellers back to rail on these routes.

The ferries were forced to retaliate. P&O and Stena invested heavily in their short-sea operations, and merged their services on the short-sea route between Dover and Calais, following investigation by the Monopolies and Mergers Commission (now the Competition Commission). Improvements in passenger-handling facilities at Dover were introduced, which allow passengers to check in just 20 minutes before sailing. A 'turn up and go' service obviated the need for reservations, while, curiously, Eurotunnel itself withdrew this same benefit, obliging its passengers to hold a reservation before arrival at the terminal. New, faster ferries were introduced, with the crossing between Dover and Calais reduced from 90 minutes to 75 minutes. Marketing emphasis shifted to selling the crossing as part of a holiday, with time to relax and unwind on board. The land-link opposition was disparaged as offering no more than 'a toilet and a light-bulb'. Larger, more luxurious ships on the route helped reinforce the concept of a mini-cruise, with the result that the short-sea routes held up reasonably well, although other longer routes suffered badly from the competition. On the medium-distance crossings, a new generation of fast ships and catamarans came on stream; this resulted in the crossing time from Portsmouth to Cherbourg, for example, being reduced from five hours to two hours forty-five minutes.

The worry for the ferry services must be as to whether they can attract sufficient trade during the winter months, when the Tunnel is coming to be seen by many passengers as a preferable choice to a rough sea crossing, even if only 75 minutes long.

New modes of crossing

In spite of the introduction of the new fast ferries, alternative and still faster forms of water transport are becoming popular on many short- and medium-range routes. Hovercraft, hydrofoils, and finally catamarans, have entered service with the benefits of speed and a certain degree of novelty. Hovercraft were used to initiate the first fast ferry crossings across the Channel as early as 1968. They offered several advantages over the traditional ferries: riding on a cushion of air just above the surface of the water, and able to travel over land as well as water, they avoided the usual capital costs associated with dock facilities, as the craft could simply be beached on any convenient and obstacle-free foreshore. Unfortunately, they also offered their passengers a somewhat bouncy and noisy ride by comparison with the more traditional ferries, and could not operate in seas greater than 2.5 metres. The vessels also suffered many technical problems in their development and throughout the years of their operation, and were finally withdrawn from service in 2000, to be replaced by catamarans. The hydrofoil offers better prospects for future development, even though it, too, suffered technological teething problems (which led directly to its withdrawal from the Brighton–Fécamp route). This vessel operates with a conventional hull design, but when travelling at speed the hull is raised above the surface of the water on blades, or 'foils'. This enables the vessel to travel at speeds of up to 60 knots. Recent models have been powered by jet engines (jetfoils) but their unreliability on open waters and inability to contend with high waves have hindered their adoption in British waters.

The most promising recent development in ferry operations appears to be the high-speed wave-piercing catamaran (WPC). These have been operating on cross-Channel services since 1991, and have now replaced the hovercraft. They are mainly twin-hulled vessels large enough to accommodate cars, travelling at speeds up to 40 knots. Although suffering from technical difficulties when first introduced, this type of vessel has been refined, and now operates successfully from Britain to Ireland and the Continent, and has been introduced on such key routes as the Dover–Calais and Harwich–Hook of Holland routes. Catamarans have also proved popular on routes across the Baltic Sea and other key European routes. The popular Seacats (twin-hull)

Figure 13.8
P&O's new fast
catamaran ferry

(Courtesy: David Neale)

and Superseacats (monohull) offer a valuable service for passengers wanting the fastest possible crossing to the Continent but who might find the Channel Tunnel claustrophobic. The latest HSS (high-speed sea service) twin-hull ferries introduced by Stena have further stretched capacity, carrying up to 1,500 passengers and 375 cars. The downside, however, is the higher fuel burn of all these craft, and constraints still remain on their operation in rough weather – waves above 4 metres (3.5 metres on earlier Seacats) lead to cancellations, a serious constraint in winter months. What is becoming clear, however, is that for a great many holidaymakers the trend is to choose faster surface vessels which can compete with the Tunnel on time.

Another interesting development is that of the Solar Sailor, a 100-passenger catamaran ferry which went into service in Sydney Harbour in 2000. This vessel operates with solar and wind power, with a back-up electric motor running from batteries which store the energy the craft collects while running on alternative energy sources. It is silent, smooth, creates no pollution whatever, and its photocells are boosted by 20 per cent by the sun's reflection in the water. A similar vessel equipped with solar panels, the *Helio*, is in operation as a ferry on Lake Constance between Germany and Switzerland. Further development of this form of vessel may well encourage its operation across the Channel.

Work on still more advanced vessels is under way; in France, a quadrimaran, operating on four hulls which offer a much smoother ride, has been under development since the early 1990s, while a five-hulled pentamaran is similarly under test at the time of writing. Capable of speeds in excess of 40 knots, these vessels are seen primarily as freight carriers, but they have the potential to be developed later as passenger carriers. Foil-catamarans, a hybrid of the jetfoil and hovercraft, have also been tested to prototype stage. Capable of speeds of 30–40 knots, their low resistance in the water leads to 30 per cent greater fuel efficiency, and they would therefore make a very useful contribution in the competitive UK ferry market. Another type of fast ferry, the Hoverplane, combines elements of catamaran, hovercraft and wing-in-surface-effect (WISE) in its design. WISE operates on the principle that a stable cushion of air is generated by a wing flying close to ground or water; by travelling on this dense layer of air, the craft benefits from reduced drag and increased lift, thus achieving high fuel economy. Speeds of up to 100 mph are anticipated, at one-fifth of the normal fuel cost of a ferry, which should enable prices to be much lower than at present. Crafts should be capable of carrying between 80 and 150 passengers over distances of up to 250 miles. An added advantage of such a vessel is that it requires neither runway nor port in the accepted sense of the words.

Other European ferry operations

While this text has focused primarily on connections between the UK and its Continental neighbours, the continuing importance of other routes, especially within Europe, must be recognized. In the Mediterranean, ferries provide not only vital connections to travellers on a port-to-port basis, but also the opportunity to package these routes as mini-cruises calling at a variety of different countries. By way of example, services are available in the eastern Mediterranean between Venice, Dubrovnik, Piraeus, Iraklion and Alexandria, or between Istanbul, Piraeus, Larnaca, Lattakia (Syria) and Alexandria. Other important routes include those between Patras (Greece) and Ascona (Italy) and between Nice and Corsica. Tourists who traditionally think only of travel by air to Majorca may be unaware of the alternatives of travel from Barcelona by catamaran with Transmediterranea.

The Greek economy is heavily dependent upon its shipping interests, with some 10 million passengers using ferries within the country each year. The significance of this area of the economy to Greece was such that EU cabotage restrictions were permitted to remain in place until 2004, although the disastrous sinking of the poorly main-tained and elderly ferry *Express Samina* in 2000 led the Greek government to withdraw the licences of some older vessels and bring deregulation forward by two years. Vessels from other countries are now allowed to operate freely in Greek waters (although few have taken up this challenge to date). This has spurred Greek shipowners to invest heavily in new equipment, as well as expanding their own activities outside the coun-try; for example, the Greek Superfast Ferries, offering the first direct service between Scotland and the Continent, have been in operation between Rosyth and Zeebrugge since 2002.

Ferry operations in the Baltic call for special mention. Services here connect the Scandinavian countries, and in turn provide vital connections for travellers between these countries and Germany. Independence for the three Baltic states of Latvia, Estonia and Lithuania, the entry of these countries into the European Union, the rebuilding of the historical port of Gdansk (formerly Danzig) in Poland and the reunification of Germany have all renewed interest in these destinations for tourists, and both cruise ships and ferry crossings have achieved considerable growth in this

Figure 13.9
The popular
Stockholm–
Tallinnservice

(Photographed by the author)

Figure 13.10
The world's fastest ferry: Silja Line's *Finnjet*

(Photographed by the author)

area. The benefit of having St Petersburg in Russia as a major port in the Baltic has further stimulated interest in the region. With the enormous popularity of Tallinn as a tourist venue since EU accession, the short ferry service between Helsinki and Tallinn, just 1 hour and 40 minutes by fast ferry, has become a key route in the Baltic, providing tourists with the opportunity for an attractive mini-cruise coupled with bargain priced shopping. Another prominent route is that between Stockholm–Helsinki, an overnight sailing which is also treated as a mini-cruise, with 60,000-ton superferries carrying up to 2,800 passengers at a time. The obvious success in this region in selling what were originally merely transport connections as luxury mini-cruises has established a trend which other ferry operators are keen to emulate.

Coastal and inland waterways tourism

The attraction of water offers many other opportunities for tourist activity, both independently and in forms which have been commoditized and packaged for the tourist. Inland waterways – in particular, lakes, rivers and canals – provide exceptional opportunities for recreation and tourism, and in Britain the renovation of former canals, derelict locks and similar watersites has added in recent years to the many opportunities for river and lake recreational travel.

The major waterways of the world have long attracted the tourist. The Nile River, in Egypt, has provided inland waterway cruising for many decades, and in recent years the popularity of this stretch of waterway led to an enormous expansion in the number and size of cruise ships operating as package holiday products up to the early years of the 1990s. However, the volatility of the tourism business is well illustrated by the collapse of the Egyptian inland cruise market in the mid-1990s when the country was hit first by terrorism in which tourists were targeted explicitly, and then by drought, which caused navigational difficulties in the upper Nile region. In 2000 the Nile came back into favour briefly, until the advent of 9/11 and the Iraqi war once again discouraged tourists from travelling to the Middle East. Popular European river cruises include the Rhine/Danube (between Amsterdam, Holland, and Passau in Germany, thence to Constanta in Romania), the Douro in Portugal and the French rivers Seine and Rhone (see Table 13.5). Elsewhere, rivers with strong tourist appeal include the Mississippi in the USA (where traditional paddle wheelers offer a nostalgic cruise experience) and the Yangtze and Li Rivers in China, while the Volga and Russian waterways linking St Petersburg with Moscow, the Italian river Po, the German Elbe are all increasing in popularity. The Guadalquivir River in Spain allows small passenger craft to travel from the port of Cadiz as far inland as Seville, and this has become one of the most recent innovations in river cruising. In South America, the Amazon River is sufficiently large to allow ocean-going ships to navigate as far inland as Iquitos in Peru. All of these river journeys have been packaged as tours and sold to tourists throughout the world.

Public craft are employed on coastal trips as well as on inland waterways. Excursion boats such as the paddle steamer *Waverley* (Figure 13.11) and *Balmoral* carry tourists on coastal trips in Britain during the summer from ports in Scotland, South Wales and the West Country.

Others travel across Scotland on the Scottish lochs and the Caledonian Canal. The lakes steamer remains a familiar sight in many parts of the world, providing an important tourist attraction in the US and Canadian Great Lakes, the Swiss and south German lakes, the islands of southern Sweden around Stockholm and the Scottish lochs and English Lake District in Britain. Many of these are elderly craft which are restored and kept in tiptop condition because of their appeal to tourists; the Swiss, for instance, have recently restored their classic (1909 built) *Stadt Rupperswil* and *Stadt Zürich* operating on the Zürichsee (see Figure 13.12), while the Bodensee (Lake Constance) has 34 lakes steamers owned by five different companies operating

Table 13.5 Most popular rivers for UK passenger cruising, 2004

1	Rhine and tributaries	25,594
2	Nile	22,661
3	Danube	11,069
4	Rhone and Seine	9,082
5	Russian rivers	6,598
6	Elbe	5,449
7	Po	1,324
8	Other Europe	13,886
9	Far East/China	13,096
10	Other e.g. Mississippi, Murray	2,197

Source: www.discover-cruises.co.uk based on PSA-IRN Cruise Statistics

Figure 13.11
The *Waverley*, Britain's last paddle steamer, still operates excursions from coastal resorts

(Courtesy: Dr Ron Mulroy)

Figure 13.12
A lakes steamer on the Zürichsee, Switzerland

(Courtesy: Guido and Cornelia Rohr Schlumpf)

between the ports of Germany, Switzerland and Austria. Both these lakes employ steamers essentially as regular transport for residents, but their appeal as iconic tourist symbols makes them as important as a form of transport for tourism, as are the famous red double-decker buses of London.

However, it is the growing attraction of rivers and canals for the independent boating enthusiast which perhaps holds the greatest potential for development over the next few years. The networks of rivers and canals in countries such as Britain, Holland and France have been redeveloped and exploited for tourism in recent years, and canals such as the Burgundy canals and the Canal du Midi in the South of France, and the Gota Canal in Sweden are being discovered by British tourists in growing numbers.

Britain itself is particularly well endowed with canals and rivers suitable for navigation. In the mid-1800s, the nation could boast of some 4,250 miles of navigable inland waterways, many of which had been developed for the movement of freight. As these became redundant with the advent of the railways, they fell into disrepair, and many stretches became no longer navigable. However, in recent years the British Waterways Board (BWB) has encouraged the development and use of these waterways for pleasure purposes and, in partnership with private enterprise, aided by voluntary bodies, it has helped to restore and reopen many formerly derelict canals. Today, some 2,200 miles of navigable British waterways are open and maintained by the BWB (see Figure 13.13 and Plate 15), and the Board licenses 25,000 boats to use their network.

Example   Reopening the canals

In 2005, the British Waterways Board was awarded funding amounting to £575,000 by the South West RDA to conduct feasibility studies into the reopening of six miles of the Cotswolds Canal. Once completed, it is hoped that further funding from the RDA and the Heritage Lottery Fund will allow this important stretch of water to reopen, conserving 30 historic structures and creating multi-user trails. Total cost would amount to some £25 million, but the re-opened canal is expected to generate 1,200 new jobs and attract 215,000 extra visitors annually to the area around Stroud, acting as a catalyst in the redevelopment of the entire area.

There are hopes that eventually well over 4,000 miles of the network can be reopened. BWB have estimated that these waterways attract over 10 million visitors a year, spending £1.5 billion and supporting 54,000 jobs. Visitors include 2 million powerboats, 1.5 million unpowered boats and 2.6 million anglers. Additionally, the Norfolk and Suffolk Broads offer 125 miles of river cruising, and have been catering since the early twentieth century for thousands of holidaymakers in private or hired vessels every year. The reopening of many formerly derelict waterways has made it possible for boat hire companies to organize packages which allow enthusiasts to follow a circular route during a one- or two-week holiday, without the need to travel over the same stretch of water twice.

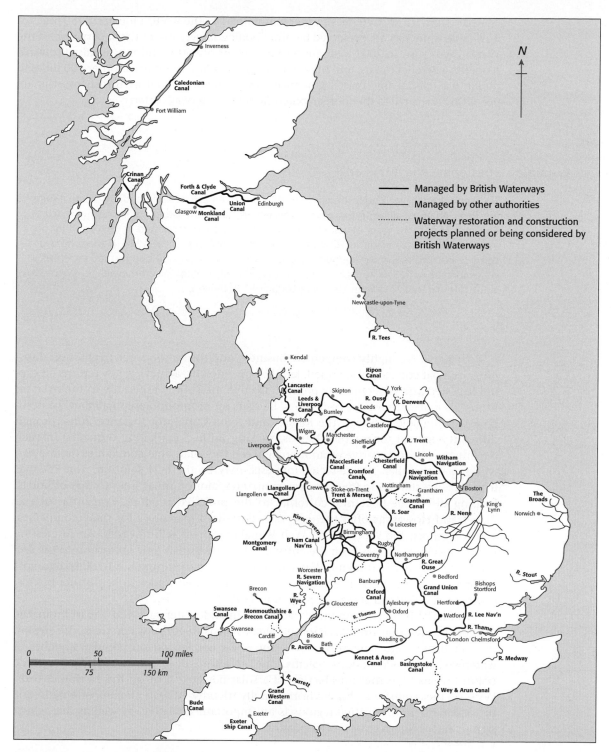

Figure 13.13 The inland waterways of Britain
(Courtesy: British Waterways (www.britishwaterways.co.uk))

Apart from those stretches of water maintained by the BWB, a further 1,250 miles of navigable waterway are preserved by other bodies, largely under the supervision of the Waterways Trust. In 2002 a long-term investment of £500 million was raised towards reopening derelict canals, and nine schemes are in place to return another 300 miles to public use, under the Trust's guidance. Now foreign as well as British tourists are becoming attracted to the tourism potential these waterways offer.

Example The Kennet and Avon Canal

The Kennet and Avon Canal stretches 87 miles between Bristol and Reading, where it joins the River Thames, allowing the passage of narrow boats and other small craft right across England. After many years of voluntary labour, the canal was reopened in 1990, and further improvements were made in 2002 to the long flight of locks at Caen Hill, Devizes, to overcome leaks. The reopening supports employment for around 2,600 people, and produces a yearly income of £28 million. One estimate gives the investment in commercial development along this waterway between 1995 and 2003 as £350 million.

Boat rental is a highly competitive business, and the season is relatively short. Most pleasure-boat companies are small, family-run concerns, achieving low returns on capital invested and generally low profits. Effective marketing, especially to the overseas tourist, is a problem where companies' budgets for promotion are small and the destination being sold is linear (the Kennet and Avon Canal, for instance, runs through different regional tourist board areas, making unified marketing difficult). In such circumstances, cooperative promotion between the small-boat companies themselves, working with other private-sector interests, may be the best solution. The ETC has introduced a star rating for boat hire companies, along similar lines to that of hotels, helping direct the boat hire customer to the preferred product. Consortia such as Blakes and Hoseasons offer the power of centralized marketing for small companies, and for others, the World Wide Web is making direct selling easier. An interesting recent development has been the entry of a leading British tour operator into the sector; First Choice has an Inland Waterways division, marketing some 1,100 boats across Europe and in the USA. The products are differentiated under three distinct brands: Connoisseur, Emerald Star and Crown Blue Line.

Sustainability is an important factor in inland waterways too. Apart from the dangers of pollution from fuel and oil leaks in sensitive freshwater areas, the erosion of river banks caused by powerboats, and sheer congestion on popular stretches of waterway, create additional problems. One interesting development to help overcome pollution has been the introduction of a solar-powered boat on the Norfolk Broads. With no fuel emissions, this environmentally friendly 12-seater boat operating in one of England's most sensitive regions is an important initiative, as well as one which significantly reduces costs for its operator.

Watersite development

In a similar fashion, the closure and subsequent dereliction of many of Britain's major docklands offered another opportunity for redevelopment of these sites for recreation and tourism. Although primarily a consequence of urban redevelopment policy, the restoration of waterfront property in sites such as the Cardiff and Brighton marinas, Bristol's Historic Floating Harbour (Plate 9), Salford Quays, Liverpool's Albert Docks, Southampton's Ocean Village and, of course, the London Docklands, has in turn generated tourism to these sites, following the construction of their marinas and the subsequent introduction of attractions like waterbuses and ferries, scenic cruises, floating restaurants and other leisure facilities. Lottery and millennium funding in Britain has spurred on the development of watersites, notably in Birmingham and Manchester, where disused waterways edged by derelict warehouses have become smart residential communities linked by waterbuses, and hence popular places for tourists to visit.

Figure 13.14
Waterbuses on Birmingham's canal network are popular means of transport and sightseeing for tourists

(Photographed by the author)

Similar developments have also taken place abroad, especially within the USA and Canada. The astonishing success of Baltimore's Inner Harbor development sparked off similar schemes in New York, San Francisco, Boston and Toronto, all of which now attract tourists in large numbers. In Europe, Stockholm and Oslo have both restored their decaying harbour sites; Sydney's Darling Harbour in Australia, and the waterfront in Cape Town, South Africa, have likewise been the subject of extensive renovation, making these areas honey pots for tourism. While most of these sites are of course planned for multiple use, including shops, offices and residential communities, the leisure use of the sites will inevitably attract the tourist and generate additional income for the cities concerned.

Seagoing pleasure craft

This chapter would not be complete without some mention of the growing demand for holidays aboard seagoing pleasure craft, a demand which is now being met by the travel industry. It has been estimated that there are more than 400,000 boat owners in Britain, and some 2 million people sail for pleasure. This is naturally leading to demand for institutionalized boating holidays. Specialist operators and hire companies are now offering package holidays aboard small chartered sailing ships or steamboats, with facilities ranging from the luxurious, where the passengers are guests, to the more basic, where passengers play an active part in crewing the boat. Tour operating companies also cater for this growing demand for boating holidays with flotilla cruising holidays, especially in areas where there are many small islands where sheltered anchorage and fair weather conditions can be found. The Greek islands and certain Caribbean islands, such as the Windward and Leeward groups, offer ideal conditions for these types of package, in which individually hired yachts sail together in flotilla formation from island to island. In this manner, the tourist has the benefits of independent use of the yacht while enjoying the social life of the group when together at anchor.

As with much larger ships, fractional ownership is now emerging as a new means of owning leisure craft for holiday-taking. Luxury yachts cost many millions, and require expensive upkeep, but owning a share of one will cost only a fraction of the price, and will enable the owner to buy one or more weeks each year to enjoy holidays on board a luxury yacht with a fully-staffed crew. One company, for example, offers a one-eighth stake in a £7 million yacht, and owners may rent out some or all of their weeks to earn income.

References

1 Tony Peisley, Numbers on the Up, *Travel Weekly*, 25 March 2005
2 Frank Kane, On the Good Ship Carnival, *Observer Business*, 27 February 2005, p 16
3 Cruise Ships Must Clean Up Their Act, *The Observer*, 28 March 2004

Websites

PSA Statistics	www.discover-cruises.co.uk
Department for Transport	www.dft.gov.uk
World Shipping	www.worldshipping.com
RMS St Helena	www.rms-st-helena.com
Cruise information service	www.cruiseinformationservice.co.uk
Seatrade magazine	www.seatrade-global.com
Exclusive collection (cruises)	www.exclusive-collection.co.uk
British Waterways Board	www.britishwaterways.co.uk
Inland Waterways Association	www.waterways.org.uk
Waterway holidays	www.waterwayholidaysuk.com
Staten Island ferry	www.siferry.com
Gheisa Tours	www.gheisa.es
Atlantis Events	www.atlantisevents.com

Questions and discussion points

1 This chapter makes it clear that cruising has enjoyed unprecedented expansion in demand from British tourists in recent years. What accounts for this, and can this expansion be realistically maintained?

2 The success of Speedferries in bringing in heavily discounted fares on the route between the UK and France is widely acknowledged: yet low price comes with questionable service. The company offers no toilet facilities at Boulogne (awkward for the customer who may have driven for several hours to reach the ferry), and while both sterling and euros are accepted on board, the company does not accept euro coins, and change is given in sterling only. Can such weaknesses be justified by low fares? Compare this lack of customer orientation with the no-frills carriers, who adopt a rather similar policy.

3 Which form of transport would you prefer when travelling between the UK and France: by car, using the Channel Tunnel, a fast ferry such as a catamaran, or a regular ferry? Give reasons for your choice, and indicate what part price and other factors would play in determining your choice.

Assignment topics

1 Working in the Planning Department of a leading tour operator, you have been asked to examine opportunities for expanding package holidays into cruising. The company is considering chartering a vessel of between 5,000–10,000 tons, and wants to avoid direct competition with other operators' cruise programmes. Your manager has asked you to present him with a report which would identify potential new ports and routes. Present a report which outlines the shape of the industry in Britain at present, the major players, the popular routes, and the markets served. Make recommendations on destinations and the markets to which they would appeal, and indicate whether fly – cruises would take precedence over sailings from a home port. Include some discussion in your report about the relative merits of chartering versus purchasing a second-hand vessel for the purpose.

2 Excursion boats remain popular among British tourists, but vessels in service are elderly, expensive to maintain and are nearing the end of their lives. You have been approached by a business partner who wishes to invest in the purchase of a new or relatively recent second-hand vessel to use for excursions either on British rivers or around coastal waters.

Undertake a programme of research among your local population to find out how much interest there would be in days out by excursion boat operating in their region, what ports and routes would be most popular, and what passengers would like to experience on board during their trip. Collate your information in a manner which will allow you to develop a customer profile for this type of leisure trip, and present a report to your manager making recommendations for his action.

14 Tourist transport on land

Objectives

After studying this chapter, you should be able to:

- understand the role and scope of railways, and their place in tourist travel
- be aware of the role and significance of the coach industry in tourism
- recognize the importance of the private car to tourist travel
- understand the role of car hire in domestic and foreign tourism
- be aware of the increasing significance of tourist travel by bicycle and on foot.

The role of the railways in tourism

The train made modern Britain and the railways are carved into the national imagination just as they lattice the landscape.

Ben Macintyre, *The Times*, 16 September 2005

Considering their early lead in time over other forms of public service transport, it may be thought surprising that railways have been so slow to take advantage of the growth of mass-market tourism following the World War II (1939–45). It is all the more surprising, given the important role played by the railways in their hundred years of existence up to that point, when rail transport was the principal means by which people took their annual holidays, travelling either to the coasts of their own countries or across the face of Europe to the Mediterranean. Rail transport's decline in popularity paralleled the rise in ownership of private cars, and rail companies appeared content to focus on what they saw as their prime markets, commuters and business travellers, and of course, freight. Even before the outbreak of war, the decline in tourist travel by rail had been noticeable, and the process accelerated in Britain after 1947, when the railways were nationalized. Improvements in coach transport, as public road vehicles became more comfortable, faster and more reliable, and the significant gap in price between the two forms of transport, encouraged those without private vehicles to

389

switch to road transport for their holidays, while the better-off made increasing use of their private cars. Instead of fighting back, the railways retrenched, cutting services and routes and concentrating on the main intercity routes. Unprofitable branch lines were closed, especially in Britain following the Beeching Report in the 1960s, and as a result many smaller coastal resorts and other destinations that could have attracted tourists became inaccessible by rail. The alternative of coach services linking with rail termini makes tourist travel inconvenient and time-consuming, and this, coupled with continuing disparities in fares and the declining cost of car travel, soon made the railways an unattractive choice for many destinations. Privatization of the railways in Britain in the late twentieth century, which resulted in higher fares and inferior service, and the previous long-term lack of investment in track and signalling under public ownership, all made rail travel still less attractive for tourists. Rail travel cannot be dismissed as unimportant to tourism, however, and the growing investment in infrastructure on the Continent and, more recently, in the UK may enable the railways to resume a key role for tourism over short- and medium-length routes. Railways continue to transport domestic tourists from the major conurbations to key English resorts such as Brighton, Bournemouth and Torquay, while faster services, especially on the Continent, are making rail an attractive alternative to air travel.

Sharp fuel price increases, such as those that occurred after 1973 and again at the beginning of the current century, have helped to win back some domestic tourists from private car travel, while rail companies have become more marketing-oriented, targeting tourists, often with the aid of specialist tour operators. Rail and hotel packages in Britain have proved popular for the short-break market, particularly to London and other capital cities. Efforts to entice rail travel enthusiasts have also met with some success, even though on a limited scale. Nostalgic day trips and excursions using old steam engines have become popular, as have short breaks using fast trains between major cities, and packages aimed at the over-55s. Recognizing that unsold off-peak seats represent substantial lost revenue, the railways have used variable pricing policies and promotions, sometimes in cooperation with well-known retail stores, to attract the tourist and excursionist back to the railways.

Tickets offering unlimited travel by train, marketed to inbound tourists and sold only before departing from their own countries, have been a popular means of boosting rail travel. These include the Britrail pass within Britain, and Eurailpass on the Continent. A Scandinavian rail pass offered unlimited travel within that region and a 50 per cent reduction on interconnecting ferry services. Such schemes have proved highly popular with independent tourists visiting Europe, especially the young backpacker market. Similar Railpass schemes are on offer on Amtrak services in the USA, and in Australia.

The privatization of rail transport

Towards the end of the twentieth century it became clear that action would have to be taken to improve the railway systems, both in Europe and North America. Heavily subsidized, and lacking adequate investment over many years, railways were in a parlous state. Two alternatives presented themselves; either for the state to move railways out of public ownership, or to agree to a programme of massive state investment to increase the appeal of the railways as a form of public transport. In Britain, the Conservative government then in power took the decision to denationalize the railways. Private companies were to be allowed to bid to run parts of the British Rail system, while the maintenance and operation of all track, signalling and stations was to be sold off as a separate company, called Railtrack. The government's belief was that a privatized railway system would be more efficient, would end the drain on government funds through subsidies and would compete effectively against other forms of transport by new private investment which would attract travellers back on to the railways. Privatization was initiated in 1993, and by early 1997 25 train-operating units in the UK had replaced the former monolithic rail system, and a further three companies were formed to control rolling-stock.

While passenger traffic did increase on most services, partly as a result of better marketing, passengers became confused about the range of choice facing them, and journeys involving the services of more than one rail company became more complex. Competition between the rail companies led to passengers not being fully informed about the range of services available or the cheapest fares for their itineraries. Concern rose over the lack of promised investment by the rail companies and the impact of cost-cutting by some companies in order to boost profits, which in some instances led to safety violations, and even accidents. Some disastrous mishaps arising from broken rails forced Railtrack into expensive investment in updating track and signals, severely disrupting mainline services. Distribution systems for rail tickets also suffered. Travel agents were already abandoning the sale of rail tickets as unprofitable before the advent of privatization; this has been hastened by the additional complexities of dealing with a score of different rail companies.

The rail companies have been less innovative in seeking improvements in their distribution systems. A computerized reservations and ticketing system, ELGAR, was introduced, initially to handle bookings for the Channel Tunnel's Eurostar service and later extended to all members of the Association of Train Operating Companies (ATOC). Eurostar's marketing and distribution was strongly criticized; onward bookings beyond Paris and Brussels could no longer be made to any European destination, but were limited to the major railway stations. Systems to sell tickets to the public via the Internet have replaced the role of many travel agents, with companies like thetrainline.com (owned by Virgin Rail and the National Express bus group) acting as electronic intermediaries for the sale of rail tickets.

Continued criticism of the rail services in Britain has led to changes in the structure of the organization. Network Rail has replaced Railtrack as owners of track, signals and stations, and at the time of writing 27 rail companies operate franchises to run the rolling-stock, usually under contracts of 5–8 years, although some have been extended to up to 20 years. Investment cost overruns have resulted in cutbacks to the more ambitious schemes to improve electrification and operate high-speed trains in the UK. The planned upgrade of the West Coast main line escalated from an initial £2 billion to £12 billion, but the idea proposed in 2002 of a dedicated TGV-style track between London and Glasgow, which would cut the journey time from six hours to three, was shelved. However, a new proposal for an ultra high-speed railway between London and Edinburgh to replace the plans for upgrading the East Coast Main Line was raised in 2005. At an estimated cost of £33 billion, this would have to depreciate over at least a 50-year period (as for TGV lines on the Continent) rather than the 30 years current in Britain. If the decision went ahead, it would cut the journey time from four and a half to two and a half hours, and be competitive with no-frills airlines. Whether this is just another pipe dream, to be cancelled when the government faces the reality of the need for public financing, will have to be seen. At present, the only truly modern high-speed rail line in Britain to be recognized by the Union of International Railways is the new 46-mile route for Eurostar between Folkestone and North Kent.

Nevertheless, the high-speed rail services on the London–Manchester and London–Newcastle routes have attracted a large part of the market back on to rail, leaving the air services between these points largely to serve as feeders for onward flights.

Although the potential exists for a greatly expanded market for rail travel within the European Union, the full potential for this is only just beginning to be tapped in Britain, with Eurostar's connections to the new high-speed train services onwards from Brussels and Paris. Marketing agreements between the European train operators, and the interest in high-speed trains, is changing attitudes to rail travel. Examples include the agreement between Eurostar and the Thalys international rail network, which has boosted rail travel between London and Amsterdam. Through trains are also now running between London and Avignon, France, during the summer months to bring tourists to the Mediterranean area, while other trains aimed at the winter-sports market bring tourists to the Alpine resorts in winter.

The Channel Tunnel and the railways

In Chapter 13 we examined the impact of the Channel Tunnel on ferry operations from the UK. Here, we must examine its impact on other transport services in Britain and mainland Europe.

The Channel Tunnel is one of the great engineering feats of the twentieth century – although, contrary to popular belief, not the longest underwater rail tunnel in the world: Japan's Seikan Tunnel, stretching 53.9 kilometres between Tappisaki, Honju Island and Fukushima, Hokkaido Island, has been carrying rail traffic since 1988. The first direct rail link between Britain and France was completed and opened to traffic in 1994, after frequent delays. It offers passengers the choice of two forms of transport: passenger travel on Eurostar from London to either Paris or Brussels, calling at Ashford in Kent and Lille in northern France (with opportunities to transfer to high-speed trains for onward travel in Europe), and Eurotunnel's vehicle-carrying rail service operating between Cheriton (near Folkestone) and les Coquelles (near Calais), a distance of some 50 kilometres, of which 37 kilometres is under the Channel itself. Cars are driven on to double-deck carriages (higher cars, those with trailers, and coaches are accommodated in single-deck carriages). These are then transported across the Channel and can be driven off to connect directly with the French motorway in a little over 30 minutes after leaving England.

Rail connections between London and the Continent have been firmly pitched at the business traveller. A fast line through Kent, which opened in 2003, allows Eurostar to operate at up to 186 mph on this stretch, cutting the overall journey time between

London and Paris by 20 minutes to a total of 2 hours and 35 minutes. This will be cut to 2 hours and 15 minutes (and just over two hours to Brussels) when the final section of the Channel Tunnel Rail Link opens in 2007/8. A journey time of around 3 hours between city centres, compared with closer to 4 hours by air (when allowance is made for check-in time and the inevitable delayed departure), has made rail a viable alternative for the business traveller; the route has absorbed virtually all of the leisure market while flights between London and the two Continental cities are now largely booked as feeder services to connect with long-haul traffic. A 2-hour trip from London Waterloo to Lille also enables the leisure tourist to connect with the French TGV (*Train à Grande Vitesse*) high-speed trains for onward travel to southern France or contiguous European countries; Lille–Bordeaux is a 5-hour trip, while Calais to Marseille is of similar duration. This brings Marseille within 7 hours of London, making the journey competitive with air travel (typically 5 hours including connections to and from local airports). Lille itself, heavily promoted as a destination in its own right, has become an important city-break market for British tourists to France.

At the insistence of the Conservative government, the Tunnel was privately financed, with no public contribution. Its construction involved leading-edge technology, and the project ran into delays and huge cost over-runs, leaving the parent company, Eurotunnel, with debts amounting to some £9 billion. Over-ambitious estimates of traffic and revenue were not realized, but this is not to say that the Tunnel has been a failure. Within two years of operation, it had made sufficient inroads into the share of the short-sea market to badly worry the ferry companies, which were obliged to slash prices to compete. A fire in the Tunnel in 1996 was a serious setback, but in spite of this Eurostar was carrying 66 per cent of all passenger traffic between London and Paris by 2003, while Eurotunnel itself has made similar inroads into the cross-Channel car market between Dover and Calais. Eurostar's passenger rail services are now in the ownership of a consortium of rail, road and air transport businesses, with National Express coaches holding 40 per cent of the company. In 2006, the minimum usage charge paid by Eurostar to Eurotunnel, agreed in the initial contract with the company, will be abandoned, substantially reducing the former's costs, which should enable it to price seats even more competitively against those of its rivals. However, it has been estimated that Eurotunnel will lose between £40 and £60 million each year as a result.

With a stop at Ashford in Kent, the high-speed line in England threatens to add to congestion in south-east England. Already, popular tourist destinations such as Canterbury and Leeds Castle, brought into reach for day excursions and short-break visitors from the Continent, face rising pressure from tourism, and the prospect of coaches connecting with more rail passengers at Ashford to tour the Kent countryside is a nightmare scenario for those local authorities whose task it is to manage congestion in the towns and on the roads of the county. To make matters worse, Kent (and particularly its coastline) has also been identified as one of the key areas of growth for house building over the next decade.

By the beginning of 2005 Eurotunnel owed £6.2 billion to its creditor banks, and was engaged in attempting to restructure its debts at the time of writing. The previous year, angry shareholders in France succeeded in dismissing its board and putting new directors in place to renegotiate its financing and revitalize the company's marketing.

Figure 14.1
The Eurotunnel
train

Source: Corbis

At this point, the company's future is far from certain. However, the banks, as major creditors, could not allow the company to collapse, and if it did so, this would be the ferries' worst nightmare, competing with a mode of crossing the Channel which would have the bulk of its capital costs erased and its operating costs set far lower than that of any shipping company. If Eurotunnel succeeds in drawing the cross-Channel market away from both the airlines and ferry companies, long-term demand will rise substantially, to a point where capacity in the present tunnel could even be reached by 2025; plans for a second tunnel are already submitted, should this prove necessary. This could be a road tunnel with the option of an additional rail link, but at far greater cost, and the question of how funding could be raised for such a massive new investment, given the crisis over the cost of building the initial link, remains unanswered.

Investment in the European rail network

The contrast between investment in the public railways on the Continent and the lack of investment in Britain's private railways is marked. In 1990, the EU approved the formation of a Trans-European Network for transport (TEN-T) of high-speed road and rail links, the bulk of which were to be in place by 2005 (the full network to be completed by 2020). The initiative was supported by the European Commissioners in the expectation that rail would account for more than 23 per cent of all passenger kilometres travelled in Western Europe by 2010, alleviating the pressure on air and road services. Total investment in rail services will approach 225 billion euros, 80 per cent of which will be found from EU and national budgets, with the balance raised privately. By completion, nearly 94,000 kilometres of rail track will be in place throughout the EU.

In France alone, SNCF, the publicly operated rail service, and RFF, which is responsible for building and maintaining tracks, invested more than £22 billion of public money to build its 300-kph TGV service. Payback on the investment is unlikely to be realized for up to 50 years (and local lines have been starved of funds while the new high-speed network was established); however, there are savings to be achieved by improved connections and communications, and switching passengers and freight from road and air services to freight will help to meet the EU's target to reduce CO_2 emissions.

Germany found £54 billion to build its own network of 280-kph ICE (Intercity Express) trains with an even faster route between Cologne and Frankfurt, allowing the ICE3 330-kph train to halve the previous journey time. Italy introduced its *Pendolino* 250-kph tilt-body train on the Milan to Rome route, while Spain's AVE (*Alta Velocidad Espagnola*) offers a high-speed, 2 hours and 15 minutes service between Madrid and Seville which within 6 years was carrying 80 per cent of all passenger traffic on the route, leading on to a Madrid–Barcelona service with speeds of up to 350 kph. Thalys, a consortium of Belgian, French and Dutch rail interests, began developing similar high-speed links between its member countries and Germany, with the popular Paris–Brussels route coming down to a mere 1 hour and 25 minutes. Sweden's hugely successful X2000 high-speed train has reduced the journey between Stockholm and Gothenburg to less than 3 hours, increasing rail's share on this route from 30 per cent to over 50 per cent and leading to the extension of the service to other Swedish cities as well as to Oslo, in Norway. In the latter country, the *Signatur* tilting train, introduced between Oslo and Kristiansand in 1999, gained sufficient popularity to ensure other routes were opened up throughout Norway. High-speed services into and through the Netherlands will join the network in 2007. Greece, too, prompted by the Olympic Games held in that country in 2004, is introducing fast intercity services; its Pathé Line between Athens and Thessaloniki, due to open in 2008, will reduce the time taken from five and a half hours to just two.

The advent of these high-speed networks is changing the face of European transport. Even allowing for the success of the budget airlines, rail services are finding that if they can provide the reliability, comfort and speed at the right price, they can attract markets from other modes of transport. Attractive low fares have been introduced on TGV services between Paris and Marseille which compete head-on with the no-frills airlines on routes to the south of France, which has helped to persuade easyJet to withdraw from this route and the Thalys service between Paris and Brussels has eliminated air competition, cutting more than 30 flights a day from the route. Research in France indicated that for journeys of up to two hours, rail could be expected to capture some 90 per cent of all traffic, while for journeys of up to three hours, rail would still capture 75 per cent. A bonus was that a significant minority of the market for TGV services were found to be people who had previously not tended to use rail travel. Today, virtually all travel between Paris-Lyon and Paris-Bordeaux is by rail, where speed is fully competitive with air services.

Bridge building is making its own contribution to the rail networks of Europe, especially in Scandinavia. In Denmark, bridges across the Great Belt and across the Øresund

Figure 14.2
One of
Germany's fast
new trains

(Photographed by the author)

between Denmark and Sweden have now opened up continuous rail travel between London and Stockholm or Copenhagen, and provide the opportunity for substantially increasing international tourism to the formerly somewhat isolated region around Malmö in southern Sweden.

Improved equipment and service, rapid connections between major cities, and the avoidance of delays in congested airports are making European rail services appear increasingly attractive to the tourist market, and there is little doubt that rail services will figure prominently in the future of European tourism.

Classic rail journeys around the world

In Britain, nostalgic rail enthusiasts are being given the opportunity to enjoy rail services which conjure up a period when travel by train was in many cases a luxury for the well-heeled. Among others on offer in recent times have been:

■ The Shakespeare Express, between Birmingham and Stratford
■ The British Pullman, between London and Bath
■ The Cathedrals Express, between London and Salisbury (and other cathedral cities)
■ The Jacobite, between Fort William and Mallaig.

**Figures 14.3
(a) and (b)**
Two high-speed
train services:
(a) Japan's
Shinkansen
(Bullet Train)
(b) France's
*Train à Grande
Vitesse* (TGV)

(a)
Source: Steve Allen Travel Photography/Alamy

(b)
Source: © 2000 Topham Picturepoint

Figure 14.4
The 'Royal
Scotsman' at
Kyle of Lochalsh,
Scotland

(Photographed by the author)

In Scotland, another successful venture has been the introduction of the 'Royal Scotsman' (see Figure 14.4). Although without benefit of a genuine pedigree, the 1920s'-style train has been packaged with success in the American market, offering a very up-market tour of the Scottish Highlands. These enterprises demonstrate that market niches exist for unusual rail programmes, which can undoubtedly be emulated in other tourist regions.

Classic train journeys are generally provided in reconditioned or reconstructed period coaches drawn by steam engines. The *Venice Simplon-Orient-Express* is a leader in such nostalgic journeys, operating not only in the UK, but also on the Continent as well as in the Far East and Australia.

Recent years have seen a sharp increase in the number of similar opportunities on the European mainland. One popular example is the *Al Andalus Express*, a vintage luxury train composed of twelve carriages built in the 1920s and 1930s, operating between major tourist centres in southern Spain like Seville, Jerez and Granada, during spring and autumn. This itinerary, and others like it, are featured in upmarket programmes of specialist tour operators like Great Rail Journeys and Travelsphere. Hungary has introduced the *Royal Hungarian Express*, employing carriages built originally for the use of high-level party members under the communist regime, as a feature to attract tourists to destinations outside Budapest.

Further afield, countries in which steam engines still operate, such as India and China (although sadly these have been largely phased out), attract both independent travellers and package tourists. Regular steam services in India may be mostly a memory, but *The Palace on Wheels* proves a notable alternative to those still anxious to experience the classic trains of imperial India. In the Far East, a few steam-hauled trains still operate in Cambodia's highlands, while luxury trains designed to cater for the growing flood of tourists to Vietnam include the *Victoria Express* between Hanoi and Sapa and the *Reunification Express* from Hanoi to Saigon. In South Africa, the *Union Limited* is still steam-hauled, and the famous *Blue Train* continues to cater to the top end of the market, while Rovos Rail's *Pride of Africa*, a train with 1930s' carriages, is chartered out to tour operators to provide an equally luxurious service between East and South Africa, via Victoria Falls. A popular and more modest-priced addition to the tourist trail, the *Outeniqua Choo-Tjoe* is a 1920s' steam-hauled train operating between George and Knysna which travels through the scenic Wilderness National Park. Australia has extensively promoted its famous trains, the *Indian Pacific* (a three-day service across the country between Perth and Melbourne) and *The Ghan* (from Adelaide across the red centre to Alice Springs, now extended to Darwin), while the Orient-Express company has introduced another luxury tourist train, the *Great South Pacific Express*, which operates between Cairns and Sydney. The tilt train between Brisbane and Rockhampton is also proving popular with tourists visiting the resorts of the East Coast and the Great Barrier Reef. Longer rail journeys across the Continents of Europe and Asia, while far from luxurious, fulfil the ambitions of true rail aficionados, who can choose between the *Trans-Mongolian Express*, the *Trans-Manchurian Express* and the *Rossiya*, or *Trans-Siberian Express*, and these too have been incorporated into programmes of the specialist operators. Finally, worthy of mention is the service from Morocco via Western Sahara to Mauritania. Essentially a service to carry iron ore, it is supposedly the world's longest train, at well over a mile in length. Tourist interest encouraged the authorities to put on a single passenger carriage, and intrepid explorers are now booking this very basic service between Nouadhibou and Zouerat to experience the Sahara Desert by rail.

In North America, rail travel in the 1960s and 1970s declined in the face of lower air fares and poor marketing by the railway companies themselves, which chose to concentrate on freight revenue at the expense of the passenger services. The continuing losses suffered by most US rail companies, and the importance of the rail network in social communications, led the government to integrate rail services in the country into a centrally funded public corporation known as AMTRAK. This organization has achieved some success in reversing the decline of passenger traffic, and has benefited from a rise in bookings by Americans nervous about flying since 9/11 – although additional security measures commensurate with those offered on airline flights have added to journey time. While many of the famous names of the past, such as the Santa Fé *Superchief* and the *20th Century Ltd*, have gone for ever, the mystique of rail is maintained, at least in name, by others which have survived, including the *Capitol Limited* from Washington to Chicago, the *California Zephyr* between Chicago and San Francisco, the *Empire Builder* between Seattle/Portland and Chicago and the *Coast Starlight* between San Francisco and Los Angeles. The only transcontinental service remaining is the three times a week *Sunset Limited*, which travels between Orlando and

Los Angeles via Atlanta and New Orleans. North American railways pass through some of the finest scenery in the world, and both the United States and Canada exploit this in their rail journeys. Rail journeys to the Rockies already form an important element in excursions for those booking cruises out of west coast North American ports; and *The Canadian*, operating between Toronto and Vancouver, has been restored to its original 1950s' style, with an observation dome on the rear carriage giving tourists spectacular views of the passing scenery. Tourists are also attracted to the restored or reconstructed nineteenth century trains operating within the regions, notably in the Far West, such as the Silverton and Durango Railroad's steam train to Durango, and the steam-hauled Grand Canyon Railway's trains.

By no means period or traditional, but nevertheless offering tourists memorable transport experiences, the *Talgo* tilting express travels from Seattle down the West Coast, while on the eastern seaboard, the *Acela* high-speed rail link between Boston, New York and Washington cuts the journey between Boston and New York from five hours to just over three. Even Mexico has entered the market for tourist passengers, the privately run *Maya Express* in Yucatan taking tourists between Cancun and other popular coastal resorts.

In Japan, the *Shinkansen* (popularly known as the Bullet train; see Figure 14.3(a)) has changed the face of high-speed transport, and its reliability and high levels of service have proved immensely popular with tourists. The journey between Tokyo and Osaka, for example, takes three hours city-centre to city-centre by train, compared with an hour's flying time between airports, and 80 per cent of all passengers now use the train for this journey. Japan takes immense pride in its bullet trains, on which delays are counted in seconds rather than minutes, and the technical specifications of these trains are being constantly improved. The most recently developed model is the Nozomi Series 800, introduced in 2004 and designed to travel at 260 kph, slightly slower than the earlier 500 series which holds the record for normal operations at 300 kph.

In the future, there is the promise of trains travelling at even higher speeds. Magnetic levitation (MAGLEV) offers the prospect of rail journeys at speeds of up to 360 mph, but the cost of building these is prohibitive. An experimental route was built in England, linking Birmingham station with its airport in 1983, but unreliability led to its closure in 1995. Since then, the Germans and Japanese have been leading the research. A German company has built the 270-mph route between Shanghai's Loyang Road Station and Pudong International Airport, covering the 19 miles in just eight minutes. The company estimates that 20 per cent of its passengers are coming aboard purely for the ride. Plans to extend this to Hangzhou, 100 miles to the South, are in abeyance, however, although there are hopes eventually that the track can be extended to Beijing, some 800 miles north. Building costs would be high, but are estimated, per kilometre, at less than half of that of building the Channel Tunnel. Central Japan Railway's MLX-01, which in 1997 broke the world speed record for a train, at 280.3 mph, is capable of speeds up to 360 mph, and there are proposals to build this between Tokyo and Osaka, a distance of 300 miles. Building costs would be 30 per cent higher than for the Shinkansen, and electricity costs three times as high to run, but, against this, maintenance costs would be extremely low and the speed would enable the line to compete with air services. Construction, though, will depend upon the availability of public finance.

In the USA, rail authorities have tested the Cybertran, a cross between a high-speed train and a light railway system, which is designed to provide fast, non-stop service at speeds of up to 150 mph between US cities. A system even more advanced than the MAGLEV is under test in New Mexico. The Hypersonic Upgrade Programme (HUP) is supposedly capable of speeds up to 6,500 mph (and has achieved a speed of just 20 mph short of this in tests conducted in 2004) but the development and application of such a project for commercial use lies obviously some way in the distance.

Russia and America have held talks to discuss the construction of a 50-mile tunnel under the Bering Strait and a 4,600-mile rail track to provide a surface transport link between the two countries. While designed primarily as a means of competing with shipping across the Pacific for the carriage of freight, it would also enable the rail enthusiast to travel by rail between London and New York in 14 days. However, the costs of all these developments are substantial (the US–Russian project is estimated at £27 billion alone), and they are unlikely to materialize until much later this century. Several of these initiatives will provide strong competition for short-haul air services, particularly on major business routes. In view of the existing congestion within many air routes, and growing concern about aviation's pollution of the atmosphere, the development of alternative high-speed land routes is vital if trade – and tourism – are to prosper.

The 'little railways' as tourist attractions

With the electrification of the railways in Britain, nostalgia for the steam trains of the pre-war period has led to the re-emergence of many small private railways. Using obsolete track and former British Rail rolling-stock, enthusiasts have painstakingly restored a number of branch lines to provide an alternative system of transport for commuters and travellers as well as another attraction for domestic and overseas tourists. In Britain alone, there are over 250 railway preservation societies, and more than 50 private lines are in operation (see Figure 14.5), with many other projects either in hand or under consideration. Some of these depend largely upon tourist patronage, while others principally serve the needs of the local community; their profitability, however, is often dependent upon a great deal of voluntary labour, especially in the restoration of track, stations and rolling-stock to serviceable condition. Since these services are generally routed through some of the most scenic areas of Britain, they attract both railway enthusiasts and tourists of all kinds, and undoubtedly enhance the attractiveness of a region for tourism generally. Notable examples include the Ffestiniog Railway and the Romney–Hythe service in Kent.

Figure 14.5 The private railways and railway transport museums of Britain and Ireland. Over 50 private railways offer tourists pleasure trips of up to 20 miles

(Courtesy: Heritage Railway Association and Ian Allen Ltd)

Figure 14.6
The Snowdonia
Mountain
Railway, popular
with tourists
since the
nineteenth
century

(Photographed by the author)

Coach travel

Coach operators today offer a wide range of tourist services to the public, both directly and through other sectors of the industry. These services can be categorized under the following headings:

- express coach routes, both domestic and international
- private hire services
- tour and excursion operations
- transfer services.

Long-distance coach services provide a cheap alternative to rail or air travel, and the extension of these services both within the UK and from the UK to points in Europe and beyond has drawn an increasing number of tourists at the cheaper end of the market, particularly among the younger age groups. Younger passengers have in the past also been attracted to adventurous transcontinental coach packages which have provided, for a low all-in price, both transport and minimal food and lodging en route (often under canvas). These services have been severely curtailed in recent years, however, due to political problems in transit countries such as Iran and Iraq. An alternative

Figure 14.7
A coach loads passengers in the Highlands of Scotland

(Photographed by the author)

is the Rotel sleeper-coach, an innovation scarcely known in Britain, although on the Continent, particularly in the German market, this is a popular form of budget long-distance coach holiday. In this form of transport, the coach pulls a sleeper trailer which at night can accommodate all the passengers in sleeping bunks (see Figure 11.9(c)).

Apart from these exceptions, for the most part coach travel remains the mode of transport of the older traveller, and the highest proportion of coach holidays are taken by those aged between 55 and 64; two-thirds of all coaching holidays booked in the UK are taken by the over-45s. This is in spite of efforts by the coach operators themselves to attract a younger market. This is perhaps unsurprising, given the advantages which coach services offer to the older market – not just low prices (reflecting low operating costs vis-à-vis other forms of transport) but the convenience of door-to-door travel when touring, overcoming baggage and transfer problems, and courier assistance, especially in overseas travel where the elderly avoid problems of language and handling documentation. Additionally, coach operators frequently make arrangements to pick up and drop off passengers at points convenient to their homes. One result of this is that coach companies traditionally benefit from high levels of repeat business, supported by loyalty benefits such as National Express's Advantage cards, which have helped that company to build up a strong client base. Coach companies are now taking the view that their marketing efforts are best spent on raising the frequency of sales to the older market, rather than trying to attract a new younger market; the former market is expanding rapidly, as more people retire early. The most popular holiday destinations for British clients are Germany's Rhineland and Bavarian regions, the Austrian

Tyrol and the Swiss Alps. While the long-distance coaching market on the Continent is holding up reasonably well, the trend is towards short-break holidays by coach, in keeping with the growth of short-break holidays in general.

The operation of coach tours is a highly seasonal one, however, and companies are often forced to lay off drivers and staff out of season, unless they can obtain sufficient ad hoc charters or contract work (such as school bussing, useful for the bus companies in that these commitments do not coincide with their busy holiday periods). However, other out of season opportunities have been successfully marketed, notably Christmas-market trips to Germany, pre-Christmas shopping trips to major cities and across the Channel, pantomime visits in the early part of the New Year and, of course, bank holiday trips.

Most coach companies specialize in certain spheres of activity. While some operate and market their tours nationally, others may concentrate on serving the needs of incoming tourists and tour operators, by providing excursion programmes, transfers between airports and hotels, or complete coach tours for overseas visitors. These coach companies must build up close relations and work closely with tour operators and other intermediaries abroad or in the home country.

Legislation in the coach business

In Britain, under the terms of the Transport Act 1980, in order to set up or operate a coach service, an operator must apply for a coach operator's licence. This is granted by the Traffic Commissioners, with conditions which limit the operation to a specified number of vehicles. Licences normally run for five years, although under some conditions the term can be shorter. Before granting a licence, the Traffic Commissioners must be satisfied that the applicant has a good financial record and adequate resources to operate the number of coaches for which the licence has been requested. At least one responsible member of the company must hold an individual transport operator's licence, which is essentially a certificate of professional competence based on management experience and appropriate educational qualifications (for example, membership of the Chartered Institute of Transport). The Commissioners must also satisfy themselves that the operator will provide satisfactory maintenance facilities (or in lieu, a contract with a supplier of such facilities), and the operating centre where the vehicles are to be garaged must be specified.

Coach operating conditions now fall into line with EU Directives, which are designed to ensure adequate safety provisions for passengers. The concern with safety has been highlighted by recent incidents in the coaching industry, most notably a series of serious accidents on the Continent involving holiday coaches. The EU regulation governing drivers' hours (No. 543/69) dictates the maximum number of hours' driving permitted for each driver per day. These regulations apply automatically to all express journeys by coach with stages over 50 kilometres. The controversial tachograph, introduced in the EU in 1970 and adopted by Britain in 1981 following the Passenger and Goods Vehicles Recording Equipment Regulations 1979, provides recorded evidence of hours of operation and vehicle speeds by individual drivers. While there can be little doubt that implementation of these regulations has led to higher safety standards in the industry, the effect has also been to increase the cost of long-haul coaching operations, making it more difficult to compete with rail or air services. To permit through journeys without expensive stopovers, two drivers must be carried, or, more commonly, since rest periods must be taken off the coach, drivers are exchanged at various stages of the journey. With the constraint of a limited number of seats on each coach, this has the effect of pushing up costs per seat by a significant amount.

The financial security of coach operations has been increased since the Confederation of Passenger Transport UK, which represents bus, coach and light-rail companies, insist that members be bonded for 10 per cent of their touring turnover, as insurance against financial collapse.

Deregulation and its aftermath

Substantial changes occurred in the UK coach industry following the 1980 Transport Act, which ended the licensing regulations affecting express coach services on routes of more than 30 miles. Prior to this, the licensing system favoured the development of national and regional oligopolies; the trunk routes in England and Wales were effectively controlled by the state-run National Bus Company (NBC), although a few smaller firms ran some regional and local routes. Companies wishing to compete with the established carriers had to apply for a licence to the Traffic Commissioners, who were generally prepared to consider granting one only where a new service was envisaged, or a new market tapped. Applications could be refused on the strength of existing operators' complaints that their business would suffer. This obviously inhibited competition, and there was little incentive for creative marketing. Similar restrictions applied to all coach tour operations (with the sole exception of tours operated by coach companies on behalf of overseas tour operators on which all passengers had been pre-booked abroad).

With the ending of regulation, a spate of new coach services of all types was introduced in 1981. A period of intense competition followed, in which the NBC emerged as the chief beneficiary, using the 'National Express' brandname. Its dominant size allowed it to gain at the expense of its rivals by offering greater frequency of service and flexibility. With its huge fleet of coaches and a national network of routes, it was able to replace a defective vehicle at short notice with little inconvenience to its passengers, an advantage denied to its smaller rivals. While smaller companies operating newer or unusual vehicles (such as luxurious foreign-built coaches) were still able to compete with the larger companies in the short term, over time most found that, given the prices they were forced to charge to recover their investments, they simply could not generate adequate demand for the luxury coaches, and consequently lost money.

A general concern about coach standards and quality control led in 1985 to the formation of the Guild of British Coach Operators, a commercial body whose aim was to promote high standards of service, safety and maintenance, and to reassure the travelling public of the continuing benefits of travel by coach. The 1985 Transport Act set the scene for almost total deregulation of Britain's bus industry the following year. This required the break-up and privatization of the NBC, providing small bus and coach operators with greater scope to compete, and many new companies emerged. However, the privatized National Express soon reestablished its lead in the long-distance market as the National Express Group, establishing a partnership with Continental operators to create Eurolines (which it purchased in 1993), operating long-distance services between Britain and major cities in mainland Europe. The company also invested in the UK railways (including a share in Eurostar) and North American coach operations. A second beneficiary was Stagecoach, a small private company which through aggressive acquisitions became one of Britain's leading bus and coach companies, with interests in trams and ferries as well as the largest rail franchise in the UK, South West Trains. The company has also launched a popular low-budget coach service, Megabus, in the UK. A third company, First Bus (later renamed FirstGroup) acquired prominent local bus companies and also successfully bid for train franchises, including the operator First Great Western, to become the third member of the triumvirate. All three have interests in overseas transport services.

With the arrival of two other medium-size operators, five organizations now effectively control the scheduled bus and coach industry in the UK. This process of concentration in transport, both at home and abroad, is the direct outcome of the move to privatization – a move which has been watched with interest by companies and governments abroad, several of which have their own plans to move transport to the private sector. In common with the US airline industry a decade earlier, deregulation of the bus and coach industry appears to have had the opposite effect to that intended, with the growth of a handful of powerful oligopolistic scheduled carriers. Additionally, there are coaching companies which do not offer scheduled services, but specialize in the inclusive-tour markets.

Coach tour operating companies

In spite of its rather archaic image, coach tours are still popular in the UK, with about 8.2 million forecast for 2005, 5.9 million in the UK and 2.3 million abroad. Operators best known for organizing package tours by coach have also tended to concentrate since deregulation, with two market leaders emerging from the string of takeovers, Wallace Arnold and Shearings. After an unsuccessful takeover bid in 1997, the Coach Holiday Group, holding company of Wallace Arnold (and also of National Holidays and Caledonian Travel), eventually took over its rival in 2005 to become known as W A Shearings. This company is now by far the largest coach tour operator in Britain, with over a million passengers a year, 447 coaches and 45 hotels. The company packages tours throughout Europe and in North America, Australia and New Zealand.

The new company is typical of the movement towards horizontal integration among the coach companies, and diagonal integration between the coach companies and the hotels they use. Smaller companies are finding it more difficult to compete, and will have to find niche markets to survive.

Example   Guide Friday

A good example of a niche operator, Guide Friday set out to become the leading local bus tour operator in cities throughout Britain. Starting up in Stratford on Avon, it now operates in 29 different locations. Older open-top buses were purchased to keep costs down and reduce depreciation. As a result the company can remain profitable even when operating through just three busy months of the year.

Figure 14.8
A line-up of coaches from seven countries at Oslo's famous Vigeland Sculpture Park

(Photographed by the author)

Another example of specialism is reflected by those companies arranging coach charters. These are often very up-market vehicles, fitted out for long-haul trips or executive use. One interesting example is that of Sleepercoaches, one of the few companies to provide on-board sleeping arrangements, thus making their vehicles ideal for charter to pop bands and others undertaking 'celebrity' tours. Their vehicles are considerably more luxurious than those available for sleeping accommodation on the Rotel coaches mentioned earlier.

The growth of shuttle services between Britain and the Continent, led by the Eurolines service, has been a prominent feature of budget travel for tourists within Europe. These international stage journeys travel as far afield as Poland, Hungary, Greece, Finland and Turkey, their success varying according to the relative strength of sterling against other European currencies, and the differential between air and coach fares.

Coach operations in North America have become equally concentrated. For many years, two powerful coach companies, Greyhound Lines and Continental Trailways, dominated the domestic coach market in North America, and their low fares enabled them to compete successfully against both the huge network of domestic air services and the private car. However, in 1982, road passenger transport was also deregulated in the USA, leading to a flood of small, low-priced coach companies, against which neither of the two giants could compete. Trailways cut services in an effort to remain profitable, but ultimately merged under new management with the Greyhound Corporation in 1987. After further restructuring and the introduction of new vehicles,

Figure 14.9
A city tour bus
operating hourly
tours of Lille,
France

(Photographed by the author)

including minibuses, Greyhound rose once again to dominate the market until challenged by a newcomer, US Bus, launched in 1998 with smaller, more comfortable vehicles. Greyhound was rescued from financial collapse in 2000, and now faces a battle to compete with both low-frills budget airlines and AMTRAK rail services which have become much more sensitive to price in their recent marketing.

Finally, mention should be made at this point of the Gray Line organization, an American franchise offering coach excursions and tours not only within the USA and Canada, but also in numerous other countries. Franchising globally on this scale is relatively uncommon within tourism, but offers a pointer to the possible direction which the industry will take in the future, as large companies go multinational.

Outside of franchises, many small independent operators are employed in small-scale enterprises including transfers between airports and hotels, local excursions and city tours (see Figure 14.9).

Before leaving the coach sector, we must look at one other aspect of public vehicles in use for tourists. In many countries, vehicles in common use for local residents are attractions for visiting tourists, too. Just as the ferries across the world are must-see attractions, so famous local services will bring tourists just to sample the experience. Examples include London double-decker buses and vintage buses in countries like Malta and the Philippines, but are by no means limited to buses and coaches. The San Francisco cable cars, tram and gondola rides to mountain tops in Hong Kong and Cape Town, black cabs in London, yellow cabs in New York, tricycles and rickshaws in the Far East – these are all essential elements of the tourist experience at the destination, and contribute to tourism revenue as well as forming the ideal way in which to see the sights of the city. However, for every country with a well-developed tourism market,

Figure 14.10
A specially
equipped 4WD
safari excursion
bus designed to
tackle the sand
dunes of
Doñana National
Park, Spain

(Photographed by the author)

there are many others which make little effort to bring their local bus and coach services to the attention of visitors. Buying bus and tram tickets can be a daunting experience for ingénues visiting a foreign city for the first time, where tickets often have to be purchased in advance from kiosks, then punched in a machine on board the vehicle, yet all too often instructions are only available in the local language. Promoting public transport encourages tourists to stay longer, since they can be told how to visit attractions away from the town centre, transport costs are often very cheap and they never need fear being overcharged. In Finland, Helsinki has successfully marketed the internationally renowned Arabia ceramic factory, museum and showroom located out of town on the end of a tram route; by contrast, visitors to Tallinn in Estonia are offered no guidance in a foreign language on how to use public transport, in spite of the rapid growth in their numbers. Similarly, visitors to Beijing in China receive little guidance on the use of local buses, in spite of their cheapness and frequency of service.

The private car

Undoubtedly, the increase in private-car ownership has done more to change travel habits than any other factor in tourism. It provided families in particular with a new freedom of movement, with increased opportunities to take day excursions as well as longer trips. Since the 1950s onwards, the costs of motoring have been falling in relative terms, and car owners also tend to take into account only the direct costs of a motoring trip, rather than the full cost, which would include depreciation and wear and tear. Thus, car transport has long been favoured over public transport.

The effect of this preference on the travel industry has been considerable. The hotel and catering industry responded by building motels, roadside cafes and restaurants, while formerly remote hotels and restaurants suddenly benefited from their new accessibility to the tourist. Car ferry services all over Europe flourished, and countries linked by such services experienced a visitor boom (France remains, for the British, the leading holiday destination, being seen primarily as a destination for the independent and mobile tourist). Camping holidays also boomed, and tour operators reacted by creating flexible self-drive car packages, including packaged camping holidays in tents or mobile homes. The rented cottage industry took off, with *gîte*-style holidays in France, soon followed by cottage and villa rentals in many other countries. Fly–drive and rail–drive packages were introduced. The railways, too, adapted to meet the needs of the motoring tourist, introducing motorail services which allowed tourists to take their cars by rail with them on longer journeys, such as to the south of France and Spain.

In the twenty-first century, the desire for greater flexibility suggests that the demand for motoring holidays is unlikely to fall, providing energy costs do not increase dramatically (and rapid fluctuations in petrol prices since 9/11 have threatened this expansion). However, this growth is by no means entirely beneficial for tourism. The need for new roads to cater for the explosion in car ownership has meant that many bypasses have been built, sidelining towns and villages. Apart from the environmental damage sustained by the countryside, this also has the effect of discouraging the impulse visitor from stopping and spending money in the towns. At the same time, the expansion of motoring and private car ownership in a small country such as Britain is leading to enormous problems of pollution and congestion. By 2005 car ownership in Britain exceeded 30.6 million, double the number registered in 1975, and the figure is rising by 600,000 per annum[1]. Back in 1996 it was estimated that Britain possessed 67 vehicles for every kilometre of road in the country, far higher than the EU average: today, the figure is in excess of 130 vehicles. Small resorts and scenic attractions cannot expand sufficiently to meet the demand for access and parking facilities without damaging the environment which the motorist has come to see. The growing interest in our society for ecologically friendly tourism will inevitably discourage motorists from taking their cars to such destinations. Greater control can be expected in the future through developments such as 'park and ride' schemes, already provided at congested resorts like Bath, Oxford, and St Ives and Polperro in Cornwall, where visitors are encouraged, and sometimes required, to park their cars outside the resort and either walk or use public transport to travel into the centre. Rationing by high prices for car parking (as has been introduced in Oxford) or by limiting access or denying facilities for car parking (as occurs at the more popular US National Parks and is now finding favour in some of the British National Parks) will inevitably become a characteristic of future tourism destinations when demand rises to a point where there is insufficient physical space to accommodate all who wish to arrive in their private cars. Many towns in the UK now adopt a variable pricing policy for parking, with comparatively low prices for parking up to two or three hours to encourage shoppers and short-stay visitors, but rising sharply thereafter to discourage commuter parking. Prices then drop in the evening to encourage leisure visitors after the business traffic has left. More drastic action has proved necessary in London, where congestion charges are now introduced for cars entering the city centre. Originally set at £5 a day and increased in 2005 to £8, the income earned is ring-fenced, dedicated to the improvement of public transport services; the change has led to a drop in private transport entering the city. Plans are in hand to extend the congestion zone by 2007, and other severely congested cities are expected to follow suit. The next development to discourage car use is likely to be road pricing, with drivers paying a set fee per mile of the roadways they drive upon. Tentatively, officials in Britain have talked of figures of £1.30 per mile in the cities, with a nominal figure of perhaps two pence in rural areas.

A move familiar in many parts of Europe to encourage use of public transport in more isolated rural areas is the use of the postbus, which not only delivers mail but carries fare-paying passengers on the mail routes. These have been employed for many years in Austria (where the service is owned by the Austrian Railways) and Switzerland, and there are now more than 230 such services in the UK, mainly in rural Scotland. This service is vital in regions like the Shetland Islands, and vehicles in use range from 4-passenger Land Rovers to 14-seat minibuses. In Australia, similar services are provided by the mail planes. Tourists travelling on foot are finding these useful means of getting about where other forms of public transport are limited or non-existent, and in turn these transport services are learning to attract visitors as well as locals; mail services in Australia have gone as far as packaging tours around their mail runs in the remote Flinders Range to include accommodation and meals.

Caravanning holidays

There are some 3,500 caravan parks in the UK, and 500,000 privately owned mobile caravans. While still popular, caravanning holidays have been falling relative to other forms of holidaymaking, largely as a result of the introduction of cheap air fares to the Continent. Nevertheless, around 17.3 million camping and caravan holidays were being taken by British residents in 2002, the most recent figures available. In the USA, sales of trailers (the American term for a caravan) have declined as motor-homes or campervans (motorized caravans) found favour. These vehicles are widely known in the USA as RVs (recreational vehicles); originating with the invention of the Curtiss Aerocar in the 1930s, they have steadily grown in popularity to a point where today more than 25 million Americans make use of them each year. The industry responded by providing new and more luxurious camping facilities, with the franchise company Kampgrounds of America ensuring water and electricity were available on all sites. RVs are widely available for rental, and are popular among European visitors touring the States, especially in the Far West. While not cheap to rent, they are luxurious by any standards, with amenities that compare with many hotel rooms, including en suite showers. While some have been imported into the UK, their sheer size makes them unsuitable for use on most British roads. However, there are specialist holiday companies which rent out campervans (see website addresses at the end of this chapter) and they are becoming popular on the Continent, where in many countries roads are less crowded and there are adequate facilities to park overnight.

The car rental business

It has been estimated that there are over 1,000 car hire companies operating in Britain, with more than 130,000 cars available for hire (many being fleet cars on hire to private companies). The car rental business owes a substantial proportion of its revenue (and in many resorts, virtually all its revenue) to the tourist. While in total only 30–40 per cent of car hire is associated with leisure, small companies and local car hire operators get a disproportionate share of this, while the large corporations have the lion's share of the business travel market.

Car rental companies can be divided into two categories:

■ large international companies, or franchise operators
■ small, generally locally based, independent hire companies.

Most of the larger companies charge broadly similar prices, but offer a choice of cars, hiring locations and flexibility (for example, the ability to pick up a car at one location and drop it at another). This flexibility and convenience makes them more attractive to business travellers, who are less sensitive to price, but who insist on speed of service, reliability and a more luxurious standard of car. Contracts with suppliers generally tie them to favouring a particular make of car, on which they are given advantageous prices.

Both Hertz and Europcar are owned by car manufacturers, who are more interested in car sales than in profits on car hire. Avis, which also owns Budget Rent-a-car, is the largest car hire company in Europe. Owned by travel conglomerate Cendant in the US, which licenses use of the name in Europe, it has more than 8 million clients, with 3,100 sites (including 75 at airports) in 107 countries. Avis has a working agreement with British Airways as favoured car rental company.

On the other hand, there are literally hundreds of small local car rental companies, who generally offer limited choice but low price and the convenience of a local pick-up – although perhaps from only one or two locations. Because of their reliance on the leisure market, these companies work in a highly seasonal business, where they may be unable to maximize their opportunities for business in summer because they have insufficient vehicles. In addition, there are a handful of specialist car hire operators who provide very luxurious vehicles, high-powered sports cars or even classic vehicles, for a small upmarket leisure or business clientele.

The competitive nature of the industry has once again resulted in good marketing playing a key role in the success of individual car rental companies. The expansion of outlets has been greatly aided by the introduction of franchising in the 1960s, a means of distribution now followed by all the large corporations. Three other factors have been critical:

1   Contracts with airports and railways. This allows the car rental company to maintain a desk at the airport or rail terminal. Opportunities for business which are provided by desk space in these locations make contracts very lucrative, and they are fought for between the major corporations, occasionally changing as competitors offer higher bids at the termination of a contract agreement.

2 Links with airlines and hotels. This establishes good relations with, and hence referrals from, hotel chains and larger airlines, generates huge volumes of business, and is critical for maximizing sales opportunities for business travel bookings. Large hotel chains may also offer desk space for the car rental company in their reception area.

3 Computer reservations systems (CRS). The development of a good CRS (and increasingly global distribution systems, GDSs), together with accessibility through the websites of major airlines or intermediaries, plays an increasingly important role in the success of the larger car rental companies, which cannot afford not to be linked to major systems. Equally, these information providers need car hire as an adjunct to their flight and accommodation sales via the Web. One company to recognize this is on-line agency lastminute.com, which acquired the fast-growing leisure rental company Holiday Autos to complement their website.

Car rental companies also court travel agents, who provide a good proportion of advance sales for business and leisure travel. Attractive rates of commission of 15 per cent or more are still on offer to gain agency support. However, car rental through the trade is less common in the UK than in the USA. The growing seat-only airline reservations market helped to expand the demand for car hire overseas, as has the huge demand generated by second-home owners travelling to their holiday homes across Europe.

Trading conditions for the car rental companies have been particularly difficult in the face of continuing high levels of competition in the trade, and in the aftermath of 9/11, which cut demand by Americans visiting Europe. ANC Rental, owners of Alamo and National car rental, went into Chapter 11 bankruptcy at the end of 2001, followed six months later by the collapse of Budget Rent-a-Car (now in the ownership of travel giant Cendant). While profits are thin for the leading franchises, others, including those associated with, or owned by, air carriers, have benefited from the introduction of low-cost air fares within Europe, which now makes it cheaper for tourists to fly to their destination and hire a car there, rather than driving all the way.

A recent development – and the direct outcome of website distribution – has been the introduction of private transfer companies. With the growth of independent travel, more holidaymakers are putting together their own packages by searching the Web, and this includes arranging transfers to their hotel abroad. Specialist companies are arranging transfers by taxi, mini-coach, private limousine – even helicopter – to customers on their arrival at airports abroad. These services can also be incorporated into dynamic packaging programmes by agents.

Cycling and tourism

Since the end of the last century, holidaymakers have shown much greater interest in cycling holidays, which are seen as ecologically friendly. The Cyclists' Touring Club boasts some 70,000 members in Britain, and several specialist holiday firms have been established in recent years to cater for those seeking organized cycling holidays in Britain, on the Continent and even further afield. These include both leisure and sporting activity (off-road) pursuits, reflecting the growth in ownership of hi-tech equipment such as mountain bikes. Tour operators like Cycling for Softies, which specializes in cycling holidays in France, provide vehicles for the transfer of cyclists' baggage between accommodation stops, leaving their clients to travel light; this form of touring has proved very popular.

Rural destinations, particularly those in relatively flat but attractive landscapes, have recognized the growing popularity of cycling as an activity for visitors, and have encouraged cyclists by providing suitable trails and informative leaflets about the surrounding countryside. Small businesses such as cycle hire companies have sprung up to serve these visitors. An example is that of the village of Worpswede, north of Bremen in Germany, which is a popular venue for domestic cycling tourists. The village lies on the edge of the famed Teufelsmoor, a nature reserve, and the *Worpswede Radtour* offers five themed cycle rides through the region, ranging in length from 19 km to 45 km. France, too, has long popularized holidays by bicycle.

Example   The Loire Valley

French enthusiasm for cycling is high. For years, local authorities in the Loire Valley region of France have closed off a section of the Loire River levee between Angers and Saumur to allow a one-day celebration of cycling, the Fête de Vélo. All other road traffic is banned, and more than 20,000 cyclists are attracted from all over France for the occasion. Similar initiatives are now being taken by local authorities in Britain.

The success of this festival has been such that a regular cycle path extending 161 kilometres has now been established between Tours and Angers, via Chinon and Saumur. Known as the Loire à Vélo Trail, the route forms an initial part of what it is hoped will eventually become an 800-km trail between Cuffy in the East and St Brévin-les-Pins on the west coast. Small companies serving the needs of cycling tourists have sprung up along the path, including bicycle rental companies and aquacycle rentals. Cycling for Softies is among British cycle touring companies offering tailor-made itineraries along the trail. There are hopes that funding will eventually become available to extend the cycling trail all the way to Budapest.

Websites: www.loire-a-velo.fr
www.cycling-for-softies.com

The interest in off-road biking has led to tour programmes catering for mountain bike tours in distant countries. Morocco, South Africa, New Zealand, the United States, Kyrgyzstan and Kazakhstan are just a few of the countries now catering for mountain bike adventure tours.

Example Llanwrtyd Wells, Powys

In Wales, the town of Llanwrtyd Wells established the World Mountain Bike Bog Snorkelling Championships competition in 1985. Contestants in wetsuits pedal mountain bikes under water, using snorkels (tyres are weighted, to keep contestants and their bicycles below the water). Introduced as an amusing pastime, the game caught on and now attracts tourists in large numbers.

Website: http://llanwrtyd-wells.powys.org.uk/eventbogbike.htm

There are fears that the rise in car numbers on rural roads, resulting from drivers seeking relief from the growing congestion on trunk roads in Britain, will make cycling far more dangerous on roads where there is no dedicated cycle path, and this discourages the individual cycling holiday. Britain is now following the lead of other European countries like the Netherlands and Denmark, in providing dedicated paths for cyclists in and around towns, and new traffic-free long-distance cycle routes are also being established. Millennium Commission lottery funding of more than £43 million was made available to the charity Sustrans to open a National Cycle Network consisting of 10,000 miles of dedicated cycleways, designed to cater for more than 100 million journeys each year. These will parallel similar cycle routes across Europe. The full UK network is shown in Figure 14.11. Nevertheless, cycling still accounts for less than 2 per cent of all trips in Britain, compared with 18 per cent in Denmark and 11 per cent in Germany. Efforts are being made to increase cycle use, both as a means of local transport and in tourism.

In the interests of improving the environment, efforts are being made to improve opportunities for cyclists in Britain to take their cycles on trains, which would encourage rural tourism by bike. While train services in Britain have offered this facility in the past, commercial concerns are making rail companies more reluctant to allow bicycles to be carried free, and rules governing their carriage differ with each of the 27 railway companies and on every route, discouraging the practice. Integrated transport planning should include and facilitate this opportunity too, but the privatization of the railways has made this more difficult to enforce.

Tourists on foot

In examining the role of transport, it is important not to forget the significant role played by tourists who travel mainly on foot, and the destinations which draw such tourists were outlined in Chapter 9. Walking holidays in the mountains have a long tradition, and hiking and trekking have both grown in popularity in recent years. Ramblers' associations represent the interest of these long-distance walkers, taking steps to ensure that rights of way are protected over both public and private land in Britain. The European Ramblers Association was established in 1969, and since that

Figure 14.11
The UK National
Cycle Network

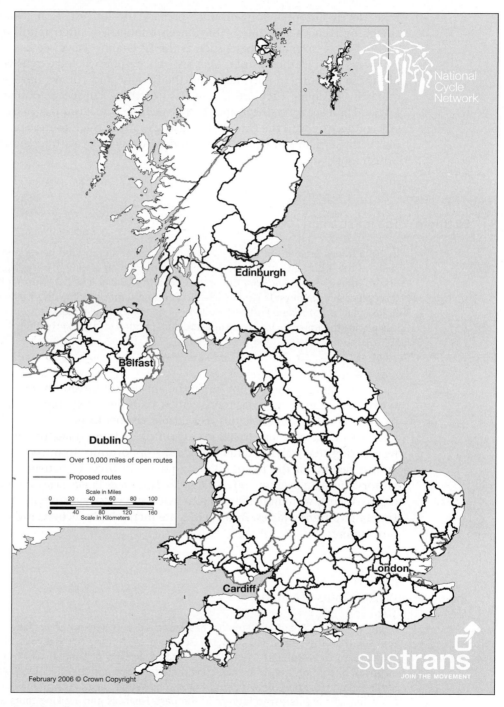

(Courtesy: Sustrans)

time eleven European long-distance paths – the longest, from Norway to Turkey, stretching some 4,500 miles – have been established, often refurbished from long-existing routes. Some of these, such as the E2 Grande Traversée des Alpes or the five pathways through the Austrian Alps, are well maintained and extensively used; others, like those in southern Italy, Romania, the Ukraine and Turkey, have yet to be opened officially, although they are in use. Two of these European footpaths extend into England and Scotland, the route E2-GB stretching from Stranraer to Dover and eventually connecting with the Grande Traversée des Alpes. Such routes are particularly popular with German and Dutch hikers, and are expecting to attract growing numbers of British tourists.

Example   The Iron Curtain Trail

In 2005 it was announced that a 4,250-mile tourist trail would be developed to follow the route of the 'Iron Curtain', a term denoting the border separating the West from the former Soviet Empire. Stretching from the Arctic Ocean to the Black Sea, the former border snakes through scenic countryside lending itself to development for cycling and walking holidays. EU funding will be provided, and each country along the route will make its own contribution to developing the infrastructure and superstructure needed to support the trail.

By contrast, we should not forget the appeal of tourism on foot for those visiting towns and cities. In popular tourist cities, trails are often marked out by symbols on pavements, just as markers on trees enable visitors to find their way in forest trails. Apart from the obvious attractions identified by these trails, promotional bodies are recognizing that walking tours provide the opportunity to introduce tourists to little known regions of the town, allowing poorer districts to benefit from the influx of visitors. Liège, in Belgium, offers a ten-day *Festival de Promenade* for tourists visiting the city in August, with more than 40 different walks of varying lengths and appealing to a variety of differing tastes. British cities are increasingly recognizing the value of such programmes.

Example   Walking tours of London

Regional Tourist Board VisitLondon has launched a collection of walking maps to draw tourists to off-the-beaten-track parts of Bermondsey, Notting Hill, Belgravia and Soho, while the London Development Agency has identified districts of London which are in the early stages of becoming 'trendy' by attracting the arts crowd and their followers. Among districts identified are Deptford, Brixton, King's Cross and Wood Green – none of which would have been thought of interest to tourists in the past. Festivals and walking tours are planned to enhance this appeal.

Figure 14.12
A signpost near London directs walkers

(Photographed by the author)

Notes

1 Webster B, More Than 30 Million Cars – and Nowhere to Park Them, *The Times*, 18 April 2005

Websites

The Trainline	www.thetrainline.com
Sleeper coaches	www.sleepercoaches.co.uk
Motorhome rentals:	
Hemmingways	www.Hemmingways.co.uk
International Motorhome Hire	www.international-motorhome-hire.com
Resort taxis (airport transfers)	www.resorttaxis.com
Holiday taxis	www.holidaytaxis.com
Resort Hoppa	www.resorthoppa.com
easyCar	www.easyrentacar.com
National Cycle Network	www.nationalcyclenetwork.org.uk
Cycling holidays in the Loire Valley	www.loire-a-velo.fr
World Mountain Bike Bog Snorkelling Championship	http://llanwrtyd-wells.powys. org.uk/ eventbogbike.htm
Cycling for softies	www.cycling-for-softies.co.uk

Mountain bike touring:
Exodus Cycling   www.exodus.co.uk
KE Adventure Travel   www.keadventure.com
Mountain Beach   www.mountainbeach.co.uk

Further reading

Penn, R, *A Place to Cycle: Amazing Rides from Around the World*, Conran Octopus, 2005

Questions and discussion points

1   The Mayor of Paris has announced plans to eliminate cars from a three-square-mile central zone in the city by 2012, allowing entry only to residents, buses, delivery vehicles and emergency services. The decision is based on the fact that 50 per cent of traffic is in transit through the centre. He also points to the success of Rome, where restrictions on cars in the centre have reduced traffic by 25 per cent. Discuss how this is likely to impinge on tourism to the centre. What are the pros and cons for the tourist? Would you advocate this approach in preference to London's congestion charging, or argue that the free movement of cars to the centre serves the tourist's interest better?

2   How can coach travel be made more attractive to the younger market?

3   Given that cycling and caravanning tourists make less of a contribution to local economies, should these forms of tourism be encouraged by destinations?

4   With the growth in second-home ownership, how will travel patterns of owners affect national and international statistics, and particularly transport movements, within Europe?

Assignment topics

1   As an employee in your local authority's leisure and tourism department, you have been asked to research the area and produce a set of cycle trails which will attract a variety of different tourists to the area. Prepare a report for your Chief Executive describing and justifying these trails, along with a set of maps showing your proposals, and recommendations as to how best to promote these.

2   As a researcher employed by a major railway company, you have been asked to do some research into rail travel and holiday-taking. Undertake a research programme involving a questionnaire to determine your local resident population's attitudes towards travelling by train on holiday, both in your own country and abroad. Analyze the nature of this market according to the frequency of travel, what determines the choice of transport mode, the market profile most likely to travel by train, and reasons why those choosing other means of transport avoid train travel. Prepare a presentation which will be made to the railway board to reveal your findings and recommendations for action.

Part III Intermediaries in the provision of travel and tourism services

15 The structure and role of the public sector in tourism

Objectives

After studying this chapter, you should be able to:

- understand the part played by local and central governments and their agencies in the planning and promotion of tourism in a country
- recognize the growing importance of the public sector in all aspects of tourism and its role in public/private partnerships
- define the term 'social tourism' and understand its significance for disadvantaged populations
- explain how governments and local authorities in Britain and elsewhere supervise and exercise control over tourism
- detail the structure and organization of public-sector tourism in Britain.

Introduction

Earlier in this text, tourism was revealed to play an important part in a nation's economy by providing opportunities for regional employment, by contributing to the balance of payments and by stimulating economic growth. On the other hand, countries that experience an influx of large numbers of tourists also suffer the environmental and social consequences of mass tourism, unless care is taken to plan for and control the flow of tourists. Any economy that has become overly dependent upon tourism can be massively weakened by a single political or natural disaster – as the chaos created in Bali following the terrorist strike there has shown: tourists in the generating countries were 'strongly advised' against travel to Indonesia for a whole year after the event, and as a result tourism virtually came to a halt. Neither does it necessarily benefit from switching labour and other resources away from, say, agriculture towards tourism. For both economic and social reasons, therefore, governments cannot let market forces rule, and must take a direct interest in the ways tourism affects their country. The more dependent a nation becomes on tourism, whether domestic, inbound or outbound, the more likely it is that the government will intervene in the industry's activities.

423

The nature of government involvement

A country's system of government will of course be reflected in the mode and extent of public intervention. At one end of the scale, centrally planned economies may choose to exercise virtually complete control, from policy-making and planning to the building and operating of tourist facilities, the organization of tourist movements and the promotion of tourism at home and abroad. Since the collapse of the Soviet empire, such central control is now limited to a very few countries, and even some of those nations still ostensibly operating centrally planned economies – China, Cuba and Vietnam, for example – recognize and accept the importance of private enterprise, and the benefits of private investment, in their tourism planning. China, ostensibly a centrally controlled economy, happily cooperates with privately owned American hotel interests to establish chains of hotels in popular tourist destinations throughout the country, and accepts the independent movement of tourists on programmes tailor-made by Western operators. Only North Korea and Turkmenistan still control tourism so rigidly that independent travel around either country is impossible.

Most other nations have mixed economies in which public and private sectors coexist and collaborate in the development of tourism within their borders; only the balance of public versus private involvement will vary. Thus the United States, with its belief in a free enterprise system and a federal constitution, delegates much of the responsibility for overseas promotion of the nation either to individual states or even to private organizations created for the purpose. Central government intervention in that country is limited to measures designed to protect the health and safety of its citizens (such as aircraft safety and air traffic control). The United States even disbanded its public tourism body, the US Travel and Tourism Administration, in 1996, allowing private enterprise to fund overseas marketing. The public body has been replaced by the privately sponsored Travel Industry Association of America (TIA) which markets the United States abroad under a number of brands, including the Visit USA Association, Discover USA and Discover America, in some cases maintaining an office abroad to serve the trade's (but not the public's) needs.

Public ownership of transport is declining, as rail and air services are denationalized, but in some developed countries there are still examples of widespread public ownership. The French Government, to cite one example, owns 100 per cent of SNCF, the French rail network, 100 per cent of Aéroports de Paris, 44.6 per cent of Air France and has shares in SNECMA aero engines and aircraft manufacturer EADS. Public ownership of the railways undoubtedly made it easier to invest in the hugely expensive TGV network for which the country is now famous.

The *system* of government is not the only factor dictating the extent of state intervention. If a country is highly dependent upon tourism for its economic survival, its government is likely to become far more involved in the industry. Spain, for example, has a Ministry of Trade and Tourism, Ireland a Ministry of Tourism, Transport and Communications. In South Africa, tourism is the responsibility of the Ministry of Environmental Affairs and Tourism, while in Kenya, the Ministry of Tourism and Wildlife takes on this responsibility. In these countries, tourism as an economic activity will feature prominently in policy-making and planning directives. Britain, where tourism is important but to a lesser extent than in the Mediterranean countries, appointed a Minister of State for Sport and Tourism in 2003 within the Department for Culture, Media and Sport. This government department has been much criticized by the travel industry for its failure to include tourism in its title. The ministerial role was more senior than that of the previous undersecretary which combined tourism, broadcasting and the media, but it still shared responsibility with an activity only marginally related to the interests of the tourism industry. In 2005, with the announcement of London's award of the Olympic Games in 2012, tourism was reshuffled, and the responsibility is now in the hands of a Minister for Media and Tourism.

Countries where tourism has only relatively recently become a significant factor in the economy, and where this sudden growth has become problematic, are likely to exercise stronger control over tourism development than are those where tourism is either in its early stages of development or has developed slowly over a long period of time. Mauritius, for example, recognized that the wave of visitors it experienced in the early 1980s could soon lead to the country being swamped by tourism, destroying the very attractions that had brought the visitor to the islands, unless the country took steps to control such key activities as hotel construction. Tunisia, too, learned the lesson and introduced control over hotel and other tourism construction early in the development of mass tourism to that destination. Unfortunately, however, the potential for quick riches can exercise a greater influence than the long-term interests of the country, and there are all too many examples of countries which have suffered from lack of sufficient control over building and development, leading eventually to a drop in visits as tourists turn to less exploited destinations. Over-building in Spain was held up as an example in the late 1960s, and could have influenced subsequent development in other Mediterranean countries to which tourists turned en masse somewhat later. Nevertheless, the 1980s and 1990s witnessed in turn over-development in key regions; first in Greece, then in the Portuguese Algarve, and later (in spite of initial efforts to control hotel-building) in Turkey. Corruption and nepotism – the significance of having influential 'connections' to overcome planning controls should never be underestimated – are very real enemies of sustainable tourism policies.

All countries, however, require a sound infrastructure in order to encourage tourism in the first place, and this will inevitably involve local and central government. Adequate public services, roads, railways, harbours and airports must all be in place before the private sector can become interested in investing in the equally necessary superstructure of hotels, restaurants, entertainment, attractions and other facilities which will bring in the tourists.

Example   St Helena

St Helena is a British dependency in the Atlantic, 1,200 miles west of Angola. One of only 13 remaining UK overseas territories, the island has a population of around 3,900, and has suffered economic deprivation for many years, owing to its isolated setting and lack of an airport. Its sole regular link with the outside world is a government-subsidized cargo–passenger

▶

ship operating out of Cape Town. With better communication links, it would have good prospects to develop tourism – with a rocky, semi-desert coastline but an attractive tropical interior, and two national parks. Its most notable feature is Longwood House, Napoleon's home during his final years of captivity.

The construction of an airport has been under consideration for a number of years, and in 2004 the Department for International Development invited proposals for a public–private partnership (PPP) to improve transport links and tourism development for the island. Initial proposals were rejected on the grounds of 'unacceptable levels of financial and other risks and uncertainties' and the Government's consultants eventually put forward plans entailing construction costs beyond what a PPP would accept as financially viable. The Government, at the time of writing, is seeking new partners to build and operate the airport, which will include the operation of a scheduled air service with a five-year contract. It is planned for the airport to be operational by 2010, when the present subsidized sea link will be withdrawn. The cost will be substantial, given that the planned runway is to be big enough to accommodate long-range Boeing 737–800s and Airbus A320s; this will call for a runway some 2,250 metres in length, in a small country with very little flat land. However, the resultant improvement in communication will allow the expansion of trade of all kinds, as well as tourism, which should result in a reduction of the subsidies (currently running at £13 million each year) that fund the island's budget. The St Helena administration has welcomed the scheme, although it has not found universal acceptance among the islanders; even the director of tourism has expressed concern that the development of an airport and up-market resort could easily lead to the island being swamped by tourists, losing much of its present charm.

Developing nations may have a further incentive for government involvement – private developers may be reluctant to invest in speculative tourist ventures, preferring to concentrate their resources in countries where there is already proven demand. In this case, it may fall to the government either to aid private developers, in the form of grants or loans for hotel construction, or even to build and operate the hotels and other tourist amenities which will first attract the tourist. Where the private sector can be persuaded to invest, it is often companies from the generating countries that first show interest, with the result that most of the profits are repatriated rather than benefiting the local economy. There is also the danger that private speculators will be more concerned with achieving a quick return on their investment, rather than the slow but secure long-term development which will benefit the country most.

The state is called upon to play a coordinating role in planning the provision of tourist amenities and attractions. Supply should match demand as closely as possible, and the state can ensure that facilities are available when and where required, and that they are of the right standard.

As tourism grows in the economy, so its organization, if uncontrolled, can result in the domination of the market by a handful of large companies. Even in a capitalist system, the state has the duty to restrict the power of monopolies, to protect the consumer against malpractice such as unfair constraints on trade or exorbitant prices.

Apart from these economic reasons for which governments become involved in tourism, there are also social and political reasons. In many countries, especially in developing nations, national airlines are state owned and operated. While of course the income accruing from the operation of the airline is important to the state, there is also the political prestige of operating an airline, even if the national flag-carrier is economically non-viable. In other situations, certain airline routes may be unprofitable, but if they may provide a vital economic lifeline to the communities they serve, they will need to be subsidized by the government.

Governments also have a duty to safeguard a nation's heritage. Buildings of historical or architectural interest, particularly UNESCO World Heritage sites and others of international importance such as Angkor Wat and its surrounding temples, a complex of magnificent twelfth-century ruins of Khmer culture in Cambodia, have to be protected and maintained, as must landscapes of exceptional merit. The state will therefore fund national heritage agencies (such as English Heritage, Historic Scotland, and CADW in Wales) and establish National Parks to protect sensitive sites and buildings.

Example   Protection versus development – the case of Twyford Down

Sometimes governments are caught up in a conflict between the need for economic development and the obligation to protect a cherished building or landscape. This occurred when bottlenecks on a major road in Hampshire required a new section of motorway to be built at Twyford Down, which would slice through one of the most attractive landscapes of Southern England. In spite of an outcry from conservationists and lobbying to suggest tunnelling (at far greater expense), the hill site was eventually bisected in 1993 with the construction of a motorway extension, destroying a cherished English beauty spot.

The long search for a third London airport was extended by several years while the government weighed up the relative merits of the economic benefits of a particular site and the environmental damage which the development would cause. Still more recently, a long-running conflict emerged in the UK between conservation and economic development over the construction of a fifth terminal at London's Heathrow Airport. Economics won out, but not before the construction had been delayed for many years, undermining the strategic importance of the airport vis-à-vis its competitors on the Continent. Needless to say, the power of political lobbying may be the critical factor in any decision taken by the public authorities, as was the case with London's third airport.

We can sum up by saying that a national government's role in tourism can be manifested in the following ways:

■ in the planning and facilitating of tourism, including the provision of financial and other aid

■ in the supervision and control of the component sectors of the tourism industry

■ in direct ownership and operation of components of the industry

■ in the promotion of the nation and its tourist products to home and overseas markets

■ in supporting key tourism interests in a time of financial crisis.

These issues will be examined in the remainder of this chapter.

Planning and facilitating tourism

Any country in which tourism plays a prominent role in national income and employment can expect its government to devise policies and plans for the development of tourism. This will include generating guidelines and objectives for the growth and management of tourism, both in the short and the long term, and devising strategies designed to achieve these objectives.

British government policy on tourism has fluctuated considerably in recent years, wavering between the need to create employment, which favoured investment in tourism, and pressures on public spending, which inhibited it. The Conservative government's approach was initially to support tourism through grant aid and other strategies, but by the 1990s the government took the view that they had established the necessary 'pump priming', that the industry was now 'mature' and that further investment should be left to the private sector. It was also the government's intention to interfere as little as possible in tourism planning and development, which were to be overseen by the British Tourist Authority (now VisitBritain) and the regional bodies. In practice, however, governments have been tempted time and again to 'recommend' approaches which were not necessarily those favoured by the tourist boards – the devolution of power from the English Tourist Board to the regional tourist boards in the 1990s is a case in point.

VisitBritain, as a quasi-autonomous national government organization with the responsibility to promote Britain abroad, had as its aims not just an increase in the total number of tourists to Britain but also a more even spread of visitors throughout the regions and across the months, to avoid the congestion of demand in the south and during the summer months. In Spain, since demand had already been created by the private sector for the popular east coast resorts and the Balearic and Canary Islands, national tourist office policy has focused on promoting the less familiar northwest coast and central regions of the country, while coastal development became subject to increasing control.

Tourism planning calls for research, first to assess the level of demand or potential demand to a particular region, second to estimate the resources required in order to cater for that demand, and finally to determine how these resources should best be distributed. As we have seen, demand is unlikely to be generated to any extent until an adequate infrastructure and superstructure are in place, but it is not sufficient simply to provide these amenities. Tourists also need staff to service the facilities – hotel workers, travel agents, guides – trained to an acceptable level of performance. Planning therefore implicitly includes ensuring the availability of a pool of labour, as well as the provision of apprenticeship schemes or training through hotel, catering and tourism schools and colleges to provide the skills and knowledge the industry requires.

In some cases, providing the facilities which tourists want can actually have a negative impact on tourism to the region. To take one example, while the building of airports on some of the smaller islands in Greece opened up these islands to larger flows of tourists, it made the islands less attractive for the up-market high-spending tourist, who preferred the relative isolation when accessibility was limited to ferry operations.

Government control over entry

Much earlier in the text, we examined the need for accessibility as a key factor in the development of tourism. This depends not only on adequate transport, but also the absence of any political barriers to travel. If visas are required for entry to a country, this will discourage incoming tourism. At the beginning of the 1990s, the UK imposed a visa requirement on citizens of Turkey seeking to enter Britain; the Turks retaliated by imposing in turn a visa requirement on British visitors to their country. However, the flow of tourists is almost entirely one way, and the Turks emerged as the clear losers, as the visa requirement dissuaded tourists from visiting their country.

Example   Entry to the USA

In 1988, the USA abandoned visas for many visitors from Western Europe (albeit with some limitations which continued to hinder the free flow of tourism), having recognized the barrier that this bureaucratic constraint exercised at a time when other factors, such as relative exchange rates, were favouring the rapid expansion of tourism to North America. Political panic which followed the 9/11 disaster changed attitudes, and the US government tightened entry requirements, including the need for computer-scanning of passports. Biometric data (initially, fingerprinting; later, planned iris-scans) were to be taken upon entry, and visas, where required, became more difficult to obtain, with prospective tourists having to travel long distances to attend interviews at US embassies. A report[1] early in 2005 indicated that visitor numbers to Florida, the most visited State in the US, were down 16 per cent year on year, in spite of a significant strengthening of the pound against the dollar.

The ending of visa requirements for the Baltic States following the collapse of Communism in Russia and the satellite countries led to a substantial increase in tourist visits. Russia, by contrast, continued to insist on visas, with associated costs raised to £100 in 2004. The predictable result has been a drop in visitors to Russia while the Baltic States have enjoyed a significant rise, accelerated since entry to the European Union. Ukraine and Georgia have both since abandoned visas for EU nationals, which will further reduce demand for visits to Russia. Maximizing revenue from inbound tourism flows is always a temptation among governments, but it is a practice which can backfire if visitors can simply switch to alternative destinations offering similar attractions. Arguably, long-haul travellers will be more willing to accept reasonably high visa costs when travelling extensively in a country, but such costs are off-putting for short-break visits or calls by cruise liner – and St Petersburg has become an important port for cruises in the Baltic region.

In 2005, Britain signed an agreement with China for Approved Destination Status (ADS), which allows Chinese visitors to enter Britain for reasons other than business or education. Given that 20 million Chinese took trips abroad in the previous year, and up to 100 million are forecast to do so by 2020, Britain hoped by signing the agreement to attract around 1 per cent of the market, estimated to be worth over a billion pounds each year to the British economy if realized. At the same time, however, Britain has pushed up the cost of visas to visitors from £36 to £50, a 38 per cent increase, while on the Continent, the Schengen Agreement gives visitors access to all EU countries who are signatories to the agreement for the equivalent of just £15 for a 30-day stay. Arguably, Britain, which has dropped from fifth to sixth place in destination popularity, cannot afford to antagonize its potential visitors from outside Europe.

Taxation policy

Government policy on taxation can impact on tourism, whether the taxes are applied directly to tourism (such as an entry or exit tax), to the industry (such as a tax on hotel accommodation) or indirectly (such as VAT or sales taxes which discourage shopping and benefit lower taxation countries). High airport taxes were introduced in 1997 both into and out of the state of Florida, increasing the cost of an airline journey for a family of four travelling to Disney World by some £70 – a substantial percentage of their total flight costs. Even within the European Union, variations in taxation can impact on tourism flows. In 1993, Greece increased its airport departure tax threefold, to 5,200 drachmas (roughly £15), sufficient to antagonize tour operators and to persuade the 'marginal' tourist to switch to other Mediterranean destinations. The British government's imposition in the 1993 budget of an airport departure tax of £5 in the European Union and £10 elsewhere was widely criticized in the press; the decision to double this rate from November 1997 provoked fury in the trade. If the revenue raised by such taxation were reinvested in the tourism industry, there would be less a sense of outrage, but if introduced purely as a convenient means to raise taxation, the British traveller feels a sense of injustice. When one sets such figures against the new low-cost fares offered within Europe by carriers such as easyJet, it is apparent that airport taxes can account for as much as 25 per cent of the air transport costs. However, there is no tax on aviation fuel, although governments have talked of introducing a so-called pollution tax as part of a sustainable policy to reduce unnecessary air travel.

Example   The Balearic Islands eco-tax

In 2002, the Balearic Islands government, composed of a coalition of Socialists and Green parties, introduced an eco-tax as a means of discouraging low-cost visitors, and funding enhancements of the islands' infrastructure to attract more up-market visitors. The local government was concerned that the islands were attracting some 7 million visitors a year, swamping the resident island population of 600,000.

The tax was imposed on hotel accommodation, ranging from €0.25 to €1.00 per night for hotels up to four-star category, €2.00 for five-star category. There was an immediate negative reaction from the tourist trade abroad, which argued that sales for flights and package tours would drop, and that it had been introduced too quickly for tour operators to incorporate the tax into their brochures. There were also complaints that the tax was unfair, as it applied only to hotels, and not to unlicensed accommodation, villas, B&Bs or privately owned second homes. As a direct result, the tax was eventually organized to be collected directly from passengers at their hotels.

A year later the tax was scrapped, when a new centre-right government was voted into power. However, during the time in which it was in operation it is estimated that the tax raised more than £25 million to help fund tourism projects. While the overall number of visitors to the Balearics did drop 7 per cent over the previous year, this could not be ascribed solely to the effect of the tax (visitors to the Canary Islands dropped a similar amount), and visitors from the UK actually increased by some 8 per cent.

Facilitating training

Another important factor determining tourism flow is the attitude of nationals of the host country towards visitors in general, and towards visitors from specific countries in particular. Governments in countries heavily dependent upon tourism must mould the social attitudes of their populations, as well as ensuring that those coming into contact with tourists have the necessary skills to deal with them. Customs officers, immigration officials, shopkeepers, hotel staff, bus and taxi drivers must not only be competent in their jobs, but must also be trained to be polite and friendly; first impressions are important for long-term image-building of a country. The USA is one of several countries which have found it necessary to mount campaigns to improve the politeness and friendliness of officials dealing with incoming visitors, while some Caribbean governments have run training programmes to reduce xenophobia among the local populations and to make residents aware that their economy depends upon incoming tourism. In Britain, the government has supported industry moves to improve social and personal skills in handling foreign tourists, with training programmes like Welcome Host, International Welcome Host and Welcome Management. Encouragement has also been given to learning foreign languages, a major weakness among personnel in the UK tourism industry.

Central and local government responsibilities

The very complexity of tourism makes its administration difficult, since it does not sit easily in any one sector of government. Although tourism in Britain comes (at least, presently) within the area of responsibility of the Department for Culture, Media and Sport (DCMS), there are clearly other departments with a direct interest in the industry, including the Department of the Environment, Food and Rural Affairs (DEFRA), the Department of Transport, Local Government and the Regions, the Department for Education and Skills and the Department of Trade and Industry (whose responsibilities include the Regional Development Agencies, competition and consumer affairs). In practice, coordination between these various departments is difficult to achieve, hindering the overall planning of tourism within the country.

The responsibilities of central and local governments will also differ with respect to issues affecting tourism. In Britain, local authorities were given responsibility for developing tourism in their areas under the Local Government Act 1972. This included responsibility for planning and infrastructure, and encouraged tourism to be considered when drawing up local planning policies. In consequence, local authorities have direct responsibility for a number of issues which directly affect visiting tourists, including the provision of car and coach parking, litter control, maintenance of footpaths and promenades, public parks and gardens and, where appropriate, beach management and monitoring of sea water for bathing. These responsibilities are to some extent split between city and county councils, and conflicting views may appear between local authorities, as well as between local and central government. Local authorities are, of course, greatly influenced by the views of their ratepayers, who are often unsympathetic to the expansion of tourism in their area, particularly if that area is already popular with tourists. A weakness of the Act was that it did not impose any legal obligation on local authorities to include tourism in their plans, and when under financial pressure, local authorities have tended to concentrate their planning and resources in areas where there is a legal obligation. Local authorities in Britain have cut their financial support for regional tourist boards, which has led to the closure of some tourist information centres. Other facilities to have suffered cuts in recent years include public toilets.

Financial aid for tourism

Governments also contribute to tourism growth through financing development of new projects. On a massive scale, tourist resorts have been constructed around Cancun on Mexico's eastern coast, while in the 1970s the Languedoc-Roussillon area in the south of France was the subject of development which included draining swampland and eradicating mosquitoes in order to build five new tourist resorts, including the now well-established Cap d'Agde and la Grande Motte. The success of these ventures demonstrates the effectiveness of large-scale private/public-sector cooperation in building new tourism resorts from scratch, with the public sector providing the huge funds necessary for land acquisition, mosquito eradication and infrastructure. On a smaller scale, governments may also provide assistance to the private sector in the form of financial aid, offering loans at preferential rates of interest, or outright grants, for schemes which are in keeping with government policy. One example of the way such schemes operate in developing countries is for loans to be made on which interest only is paid during the first few years, with repayment of capital postponed until the later years of the project, by which time it should have become self-financing. Other forms of government aid include subsidies such as tax rebates or tax relief on operating expenses.

Government support is also necessary at a time of catastrophe. The recovery of popular Asiatic resorts following the disastrous Tsunami in 2004 depended upon a programme of massive international government aid, supported by direct contributions from millions of ordinary people around the world. In Britain, after the devastating foot-and-mouth outbreak in 2001, the Government stepped in to offer financial aid to small tourism businesses in rural areas, which were granted 95 per cent tax relief; the Welsh Assembly extended 100 per cent rate relief to Welsh businesses with higher rateable values. Central government grants were also made available in the affected areas for marketing and for investment in information technology.

Apart from financial aid from a country's own government, public-sector funds are also available from sources overseas. Within Europe the European Investment Bank (EIB) provides loans at commercial rates of interest to small companies (normally those employing fewer than 500 staff). These loans have been provided for up to 50 per cent of fixed asset costs, with repayment terms up to eight years. Interest rates may be slightly lower in the EU's designated 'Assisted Areas'. The European Regional Development Fund offers financial assistance (usually up to 30 per cent of the capital costs) for tourism projects generated by public-sector bodies within the Assisted Areas. This money can be used not only as pump-priming for direct tourist attractions such as museums, but also for infrastructure development to support tourism, such as airports or car parking facilities. *Objective 1* status provides support for severely impoverished areas. In Britain, this had meant that funding has been provided to tourism projects in four regions: West Wales, Merseyside, South Yorkshire and Cornwall. In the UK a total of some £6.5 billion has been committed to the assisted regions for the period 2000–2006. However, with the admission to the EU of ten new, poorer countries in 2004, development funding is being switched to their support. Under current regulations (in which support can only be offered to regions with incomes lower than 75 per cent of the EU average) only Cornwall would now fall within the limits for aid. *Objective 2* status defines support available for deep rural areas (which includes parts of Devon, for example) or depressed urban areas. Tourism projects in both the Irish Republic and Northern Ireland have greatly benefited under the terms of these funds, especially in small projects such as theatres, art galleries, waterways, parks and nature reserves, and the establishment of tourist offices and visitor centres. European tourism may also benefit, under some circumstances, from the European Social Fund or the European Agricultural Guidance and Guarantee Fund.

Developing countries can receive aid from the International Development Association, a subsidiary of the World Bank, which provides interest-free or low-rate loans, while another World Bank subsidiary, the International Bank for Reconstruction and Development, offers loans at commercial rates of interest to countries where alternate sources of funding may be difficult to find.

Social tourism

One little known aspect of public-sector support for tourism is to be found in the encouragement offered by way of *social tourism*; little known, at least in Britain, because there it has been largely disregarded. Social tourism is defined as the 'furtherance of the economically weak or dependent classes of the population', and is designed to provide aid for low-income families, single-parent families, the elderly, handicapped and other deprived minorities within a population. Aid may be offered in the form of finance (grants, low-interest loans and the like) or in direct support through the provision of free coach trips or holiday accommodation. Under this generic term one might also include the public funding of health tourism, which has been the practice of some countries' governments to subsidize as part of the general public health and well-being of the populations.

Social tourism is of course more likely to benefit from countries whose governments have planned economies. Holidays are seen by these countries as necessary to maintain the health and well-being of the working population. In mixed economies like those in Europe, several countries have been active in providing subsidized tourism for their deprived citizens, led by Belgium, France and the southern countries of the EU. The Brussels-based International Bureau of Social Tourism (BITS) has been active since 1963 as a base for the study and debate of social tourism issues, and maintains a data bank, issues publications and conducts seminars on the subject. There are well-established programmes of aid on the Continent for holidays for the mentally, physically and socially handicapped, although financial pressures are reducing these opportunities. The French government, for example, terminated its programme of welfare-funded spa holidays in 1999, a severe blow to the spa tourism industry, which hosted over 600,000 French visitors who had been able to recover up to 70 per cent of their costs through the social security system in that country. However, other now well-established programmes of social tourism remain in place.

Example   French social tourism

France promotes sponsored holidays for employees with its programme of 'chèques-vacances', a holiday voucher scheme operated through the Agence Nationale pour les Chèques-Vacances (ANCV). This public, industrial and commercial organization supervised by the Ministries of Tourism and of the Economy, Industry and Finance, sells vouchers to some 20,000 organizations in France whose employees can spend these on a variety of holidays in France, its dependencies and the EU. In 2005, some one billion euros were invested in vouchers, enabling around 5.6 million employees to enjoy a holiday that many would otherwise have had to forego.

Little support of this kind is provided in Britain for the disadvantaged, although Britain has over 6 million registered disabled people. Responsibility for providing this service is delegated to local authorities (the Chronically Sick and Disabled Act 1970 imposed a statutory duty on local authorities to fund holidays for the disabled). Many authorities provided coach outings for the elderly and other disadvantaged groups, but over the past 20 years cutbacks in local authority funding have sharply reduced these services, and the number of those receiving financial help from local councils slumped. The result has been that social tourism has largely become the responsibility of the private sector. Sponsored by the then English Tourist Board, and with the full support of the travel industry in the UK, the Holiday Care Service was set up in 1981, essentially to provide information about holiday opportunities for the disadvantaged. Later, this was expanded to include training programmes for members of the tourism industry. A number of specialist operators then turned to catering to the needs of these groups, or providing discounted holidays for those with limited means. These responsibilities are now vested in the Tourism for All, which is a national charity. The Travel Foundation also provides help for disadvantaged holidaymakers with the financial support of the industry.

Example   The Family Holiday Association

A third national charity, the Family Holiday Association, promotes holidays for disadvantaged families. Poverty is the principal reason why one out of three people in the UK take no holiday at all, and the FHA was set up 1975 to provide grants which would make a holiday possible for this group. Each year, the Association enables around 1,150 families to holiday, and over 100,000 people have been helped since its foundation. The Association has a high profile in the industry, with strong support from ABTA and AITO. It is funded largely by individual donations, but is also helped by trusts, corporate donations and income received from fund-raising events.

Website: www.fhaonline.org.uk

Holidays are also organized by the trade unions in Britain, which have established holiday homes and subsidize holidays for their members; other bodies arranging holidays for the disadvantaged include Mencap, the Red Cross, the Multiple Sclerosis Society and the Winged Fellowship Trust. Both SCOPE (formerly the Spastics Society) and the Spina Bifida Association own holiday homes where holidays can be provided for those suffering from these illnesses.

UK government involvement in helping the disadvantaged is largely restricted to ensuring adequate access to tourism attractions, hotels etc. for the disabled. The Disability Discrimination Act (1995) has had a profound effect upon tourism facilities in the UK, necessitating substantial investment to meet the conditions of the Act. Services (including the provision of information for, e.g. the blind and deaf) have had to be accessible to the disabled since the final part of the Act came into effect towards the end of 2004, although there are exceptions granted in the case of heritage buildings which are impractical to convert.

Control and supervision in tourism

The state plays an important part in controlling and supervising tourism, as well as helping to facilitate it, where it is deemed necessary. It will, for example, intervene to restrain undesirable growth or unfair competition, or alternatively help to generate demand by improving infrastructures or encouraging hotel construction (as the Development of Tourism Act did in Britain in 1969). Governments also play a role in maintaining quality standards, and protecting all consumers (in this case tourists) against business malpractice or failure.

A government can act to restrain tourism in a number of ways, whether through central directives or through local authority control. Refusal of planning permission is an obvious example of the exercise of control over tourism development. However, this is seldom totally effective, since if an area is a major attraction for tourists, the authorities will be unlikely to dissuade visitors simply by, say, refusing planning permission for new hotels; the result may simply be that overnight visitors are replaced by excursionists, or private bed-and-breakfast accommodation moves in to fill the gap left by the lack of hotel beds. Cornwall has had measures to control caravan sites since 1954, but the local authority has still found it difficult to prevent the growth of unlicensed sites.

Failing to expand the infrastructure is another option sometimes taken by local authorities. This can be partially effective, but unfortunately it impacts equally on local residents, whose frustrations with, say, inadequate road systems may lead to a political backlash. The price mechanism can also be used to control tourist traffic. Venice has a severe problem due to the influx of visitors, its waterways becoming so crowded that it introduced a two-tier transport pricing structure, with visitors paying eight times as much for transport as locals; however, such variable pricing would now be ruled illegal under EU legislation. This would not apply in other parts of the world, however; India, for example, sharply increased entry prices in 2001 for foreign visitors to its principal attraction, the Taj Mahal, in order to control numbers and reduce wear and tear in the building. As prices are relatively inelastic for such key attractions, moves such as this have the added advantage of raising revenue for the government or local authority – although they are unlikely to reduce visitor numbers to the desired extent without the imposition of some form of rationing. Selective taxation on hotel accommodation or higher charges for parking can also be imposed, but some criticize this as a regressive tax, affecting the less well off but having little effect on the wealthy.

Rationing, i.e. limiting entry through some form of visa or licence is another practical alternative; or access can be denied to tourists arriving by private car, a measure that has been employed within the Lake District to encourage the use of public transport. Elsewhere, the use of public transport may be enforced; for example, where traffic has reached saturation, it is now common to find *park and ride* schemes, which require the visitors to leave their cars and proceed into the centre by public transport. Ports can limit traffic very easily, by simply refusing permission for cruise ships to dock. Bermuda, a small but popular island destination, exercises close control over the number of visitors permitted to land. It imposed a ceiling of 10,000 beds on the island, and a maximum of 150,000 cruise-ship passengers are permitted ashore each year. Florence, perhaps the most congested of Italian cities, limits permits to 500 coaches and 50,000 visitors a day, and has steadily increased taxes payable for each coach that enters the city. Remote areas impose even more stringent rulings: in Costa Rica, only 100 visitors are allowed at a time into the Monteverde Cloud Forest, while Bhutan limits tourists to a few thousands a year, each paying a substantial daily sum for the privilege. Thus control by licence simultaneously restricts tourists and provides the government with useful revenue.

Up to a point, planning for the more extensive use of existing facilities can delay the need to de-market certain attractions or destinations, but it is undoubtedly true that some tourist destinations are victims of their own success. Only in extreme cases are tourists totally denied access to destinations or attractions. In France, the prehistoric cave paintings at Lascaux have been so damaged by the effect of countless visitors' breath changing the climate in the caves that the French government has been obliged to introduce a total ban on entry to the site. However, an artificial replica has been built on an adjacent site, which continues to attract many visitors.

Perhaps a more acceptable form of control is exercised through effective marketing, concentrating publicity on less popular attractions or geographical regions, and promoting the off-season. Thus VisitBritain might stress the appeal of the north-east of England in its marketing abroad, making little reference to the south-west, which already attracts a high proportion of domestic tourists. However, attempts to do this may be frustrated by private-sector promotion. Airlines, for example, may prefer to concentrate on promoting those destinations for which they already have strong demand (although credit must be given to the no-frills carriers which have opened up new areas by flying into small provincial airports). There is always a danger that if the public-sector strategy is too successful, and tourists are siphoned off to the new regions, the amenities and attractions at more popular sites could suffer a downturn in business. London has always been the principal attraction for overseas visitors to the UK, but on occasions even London has experienced downturns in visitors, affecting theatres, taxis and other amenities that depend upon tourist support. Owing to the high cost of living in the city, hotel accommodation has tended to move up-market, since the high costs of building and running a hotel can only be viable when high room charges are levied. The result has been a serious dearth of good quality, modern, budget hotels for the price-conscious tourist – a problem which could eventually lead to overseas tourists and operators switching their travel arrangements to other, less expensive capitals like Rome or Berlin. Some tourism experts have called for a new government-sponsored initiative in the UK, similar to the 1969 Act discussed later in this chapter, to pump more public funds into the hotel industry, in effect subsidizing the building costs in order to retain tourists, but few governments in a free market economy would be willing to go as far as subsidizing the industry.

Britain is only now beginning to follow the example of some of its other European neighbours in attempting to stagger holidays by legislation, with some local authorities introducing a five-term school year with a shorter break in the summer. This would greatly aid the tourism industry, and help to avoid the worst peaking problems of the summer months. On the Continent, not only educational holidays but also industry holidays are staggered. In Germany, the *Länder* (individual states) are required to take their holidays on a rota basis over an eleven-year cycle, thus avoiding the holiday rush which is common in Britain at the end of the school summer term. Factories, schools and businesses all plan their closures in keeping with the rota. France, too, divides the country into three zones, each of which takes the summer holiday at a different time. While this helps to avoid national peaking, it is not without drawbacks (for example, the mass exodus of German holidaymakers clogging the motorways from their particular *Land* when their turn arrives!).

Sometimes governments exercise control over tourism flows for economic reasons. As we saw earlier in this text, governments may attempt to protect their balance of payments by imposing currency restrictions or banning the export of foreign currency, in an attempt to reduce the numbers of its citizens travelling abroad. The last significant control of this kind in Britain occurred in 1966, when the government of the day imposed a £50 travel allowance, and France also imposed restrictions on the amount of currency that could be exported in the early 1980s. There is little evidence to suggest that these controls are particularly effective in preventing the outflow of foreign currency, and since the advent of the free movement of currency within the European

Union, the right of its members to travel within the EU can no longer be restricted. Whatever the individual's views are of the euro, its introduction has benefited all tourists, including the British and others who remain outside the common currency agreement, but who no longer have to change their holiday money as they move from one euro country to another.

Concern over safety is a government responsibility, and all governments will take measures to enforce standards of safety, and prosecute breaches of safe practice (a recent example being the Hatfield rail enquiry, set up to investigate a crash in 2000 which the enquiry found was triggered by a broken rail). Transport companies are obliged to meet necessary criteria to obtain licences to carry passengers, and tour operators are also subject to certain controls through the imposition of Air Travel Organizers' Licences (ATOLs). In the mid 1970s the government introduced an Air Travel Reserve Fund (the name was subsequently modified, the fund being overseen first by the Air Travel Trust Committee, and then, in 2000, by the Air Travel Insolvency Protection Advisory Committee – ATIPAC) to protect consumers against possible collapse of package-holiday companies, funds provided by ABTA being seen as insufficient for the purpose. While tourists do not currently have to contribute to this fund, the CAA had proposed substituting a new central holidaymaker protection fund for the existing fund and bonding schemes, with a small levy imposed on each booking to protect tourists in the event of industry failures. This proposal, however, was rejected by the government in 2005.

In many countries (although not yet in the UK), travel agencies are required to have a government licence to operate, and in others, tour guides are licensed by the government or a local authority. In France, motorboats must also be licensed, even in the case of visitors from abroad, following a spate of accidents caused by poor navigation.

EU legislation protects tourists in a variety of ways, taking precedence over national laws. Legislation introduced in 2005, for instance, requires airlines to pay compensation to passengers for delayed flights, with the extent of compensation varying according to the length of the flight. Prosecution would be enforced through the CAA.

Governments will intervene where it is thought that the takeover or merger of large companies could result in the emergence of a monopoly. In Britain, the Competition Commission exists to investigate such situations, but in general it has taken a relaxed attitude towards horizontal integration on the grounds that tourists have not been disadvantaged by the moves. The EU, however, has tended to take a stronger line on this issue, and has interceded in a number of cases in recent years, notably that of the proposed merger between British Airways and American Airlines.

Perhaps the most common form of government supervision of the tourism industry in all countries is to be found in the hotel sector. Apart from safety and hygiene requirements, many governments also require hotels to be compulsorily registered and graded, prices are required to be displayed, and the buildings are subject to regular inspection. Camping and caravan sites may also be subject to inspection to ensure consistent standards and acceptable operating conditions.

Finally, the government's concern with quality will lead to setting up systems of inspection, where safety is concerned, or training programmes and other means to enhance quality where it is seen as substandard. Again, Britain has recently promoted schemes leading to publicly recognized standards of quality, including the National

Quality Assurance Schemes (NQAS) and Visitor Attraction Quality Assurance Scheme (VAQAS). The British government has recognized that tourism research statistics are inadequate and is encouraging improvements, notably through the collection and evaluation of data by the regional development agencies (RDAs). Local authorities are encouraged to support the collection of tourism data, but again, without legal enforcement.

The organization of public-sector tourism

Having looked at the various ways in which public-sector bodies concern themselves with tourism, we can now usefully summarize their main activities below.

For the most part, government policies and objectives for tourism are defined and implemented through national tourist boards (although, as we have seen, in many cases other bodies directly concerned with recreation or environmental planning will also have a hand in the development of tourism). These boards are normally funded by government grants, and their functional responsibilities are likely to include all or most of the following:

Planning and control functions

■ product research and planning for tourism plant and facilities

■ protection or restoration of tourism assets

■ human resources planning and training

■ licensing and supervision of sectors of the industry

■ implementation of pricing or other regulations affecting tourism.

Marketing functions

■ representing the nation as a tourist destination

■ undertaking market research, forecasting trends and collecting and publishing relevant statistics

■ producing and distributing tourism literature

■ providing and staffing tourist information centres

■ advertising, sales promotion and public relations activities directed at home and overseas markets.

Financial functions

■ advising industry on capital investment and development

■ directing, approving and controlling programmes of government aid for tourism projects.

Coordinating functions

■ linking with trade and professional bodies, government and regional or local tourist organizations

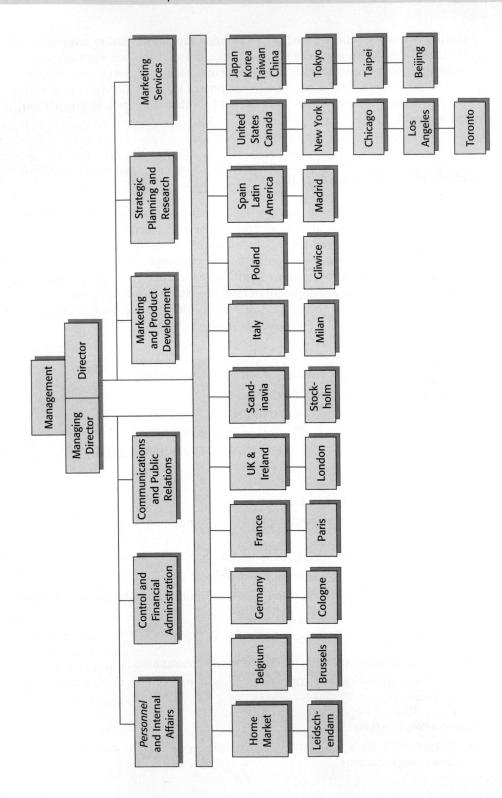

Figure 15.1 Organization chart, Netherlands Board of Tourism
(Courtesy: Netherlands Board of Tourism)

- undertaking coordinated marketing activities with private tourist enterprises
- organizing 'workshops' or similar opportunities for buyers and sellers of travel and tourism to meet and do business.

In some countries, some of these activities may be delegated to regional tourist offices, with the national board coordinating or overseeing their implementation.

National tourist boards will generally establish offices overseas in those countries from which they can attract the most tourists, while their head office in the home country will be organized along functional lines. This is demonstrated in Figure 15.1, taking the example of the Netherlands Board of Tourism.

Public-sector tourism in Britain: a historical overview

Britain has long been at the forefront of international tourism, both as a destination and a generating country, though before 1969 tourism played little part in government policy making. Forty years earlier, the government of the day had provided the first finance for tourism marketing, by funding (to the tune of £5,000) the Travel Association of Great Britain and Northern Ireland, in order to encourage travel to Britain from overseas. During the inter-war years this evolved into the British Travel Association, which was given the additional task of promoting domestic holidays for British residents. No clear policies were laid down for its activities, however, and its powers were limited.

Voluntary tourist boards were established in Scotland in 1930, and in Wales in 1948, the same year in which a board was first established in Northern Ireland. It was to be more than 20 years, however, before a coordinated framework for public-sector tourism was to be established in the United Kingdom as a whole.

The Development of Tourism Act and UK national tourism bodies

By the late 1960s, following the rapid growth in popularity of Britain as a tourist destination, it was clear that a new framework for tourism was needed in the country. This was manifested in the Development of Tourism Act 1969, the first statutory legislation in the country specifically concerned with tourism.

The Act, in three parts, dealt with the organization of public-sector tourism, with the provision of financial assistance for much-needed hotel development, and also provided for a system of compulsory registration of tourist accommodation. The last part of the Act, which was designed to include rights of inspection by government officials, has never been fully implemented, although the compulsory display of prices was subsequently introduced. The accommodation sector preferred to follow a system of voluntary classification and grading of tourist accommodation, persuading the government not to enforce a compulsory system. The result was a mixed success, as the voluntary system fails to embrace a substantial amount of the stock of available accommodation in the UK; however, the implementation of the first two parts of the Act was to have far-reaching consequences for tourism in Britain.

That part of the Act dealing with financial assistance for the hotel industry was designed in the short term to improve the stock and quality of hotel bedrooms, in order to meet changing demand and overcome scarcity. Grants and loans, administered by the three new national tourist boards, were to be made available for hotel construction and improvement until 1973 (during which time some 55,000 bedrooms were added to the stock). Unfortunately, because the Act failed to specify the location in which new hotels were to be built, much of the increased stock was located in London, leading to temporary over-capacity in the city, while areas where hotel construction involved greater financial risk, such as Scotland and the North of England, did not benefit to anything like the extent needed.

National tourism boards in the United Kingdom

The first part of the 1969 Act called for the establishment of four national boards to become responsible for tourism, and defined the structure and responsibilities of each of these. At the apex, the British Tourist Authority, to replace the old British Travel Association, was to be the sole body responsible overseas for the marketing of tourism to Britain, and would also advise ministers on tourism matters in general. Tourism issues that concerned Britain as a whole were to be dealt with by the BTA, while three further boards – the English Tourist Board, the Scottish Tourist Board and the Wales Tourist Board – became responsible for tourism development within their own territories, and for the marketing of their territories within the UK. Scotland was later given the freedom to undertake overseas marketing itself, under the terms of the Tourism (Overseas Promotion) (Scotland) Act, 1984, and Wales followed suit in 1992.

Northern Ireland was not affected by this Act, having established its own Tourist Board under the Development of Tourist Traffic Act (Northern Ireland) in 1948. Subsequent legislation, the Tourist Traffic (Northern Ireland) Order 1972, amended the Act to allow local authorities to provide or assist in the provision of tourist amenities. Similarly, the Isle of Man Tourist Board and the States of Jersey and Guernsey Tourist Committees operate independently outside the jurisdiction of the Act. Initially, both the BTA and the English Tourist Board were responsible to the Board of Trade, while the Scottish and Wales Boards were responsible to their respective Secretaries of State. All four bodies were established by the Act as independent statutory bodies, and were to be financed by grants-in-aid from the central government. They were empowered in turn to provide financial assistance for tourism projects (the so-called 'Section 4' scheme within the Act), although this scheme has since been abandoned in favour of alternative forms of funding.

Later, responsibility of the BTA and ETB passed to, first the Department of Employment and subsequently, in 1992, to the newly created Department of National Heritage, which absorbed a number of other related interests, including the royal parks and palaces, arts and libraries, sport, broadcasting and the press as well as heritage sites. This Department became known as the Department for Culture, Media and Sport when the Labour government came to power in 1997. Further structural and cosmetic changes have since occurred; in 1999, the English Tourist Board's title was changed to the English Tourism Council, and in 2003 this body was abolished as a separate entity altogether, its functions being integrated with those of VisitBritain, the new brand name for the BTA.

Following the devolution of power in Scotland and Wales, the Wales Tourist Board at first became the responsibility of the Economic Development Committee of the Welsh Assembly. However, in 2004 it was announced that the Board would be one of three Assembly Sponsored Public Bodies (ASPBs), along with the Welsh Development Agency and Education and Learning Wales (ELWa), which were to be integrated directly into the Welsh Assembly government, accountable directly to the Ministers. This change became effective in April 2006. The board's name is unchanged at the time of writing, although it has adopted the title VisitWales as its website address.

The Scottish Tourist Board became the responsibility of, first, the Department of Enterprise and Life-Long Learning, and subsequently, the Scottish Executive through the Minister for Tourism, Culture and Sport within the devolved Scottish Parliament. The Board has also adopted the name VisitScotland.

Finally, in Ireland, a breakthrough has occurred in efforts to sell the island as a whole to overseas visitors. Following the 1998 Good Friday Agreement, The Northern Ireland Tourist Board, which reports to the Northern Ireland Office, united in 2002 with its opposite number south of the border, the Irish Tourist Board, to form Tourism Ireland for marketing purposes. The entire island is now broken down into six marketing regions:

■ Cork and Kerry

■ The South-east

■ The West

■ Heart of Ireland

■ Dublin

■ North Country (the counties of Northern Ireland).

Overseas offices of both boards have been merged, although in all other respects the two boards continue to operate discretely. The IRA ceasefire announced in 2005, assuming this holds, should help to allow further joint activity between the two countries. Should self-government soon be re-established within Northern Ireland, the NITB could be expected to report to the Northern Ireland Assembly at Stormont, whose legislative and executive powers have been suspended since 2002.

The structure of public-sector tourism in Great Britain appears in Figure 15.2.

Regional development agencies and tourism

The changes in structure outlined above heralded even greater upheavals that were to affect British public-sector tourism in the twenty-first century. One of the most significant changes has been the re-routing of DCMS funds for the English board direct to the regional development agencies (RDAs), which are responsible for all economic strategy in the regions, and which have as a result become all-powerful in directing policy and resources for tourism. The nine RDAs were set up in 1998, funded directly by the Department for Trade and Industry. Theoretically, these bodies were to have been overseen by nine Regional Assemblies consisting of nominated, rather than elected, councillors, but public opinion has swung strongly against the formation of these regional bodies after their firm rejection in the North East as yet another layer of

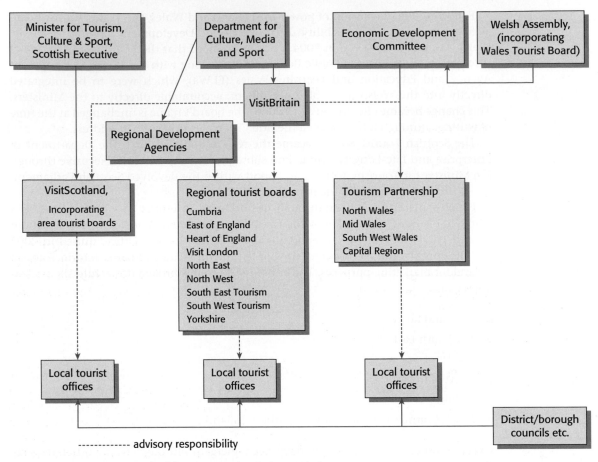

Figure 15.2 The structure of public-sector tourism in Great Britain

public control, and their future is still in doubt. The RDA areas do not coincide with those of the regional tourist boards, further complicating the administration of tourism, as the RTBs have not themselves been dissolved, although their funding has been sharply reduced.

Example The Cotswolds

The Cotswolds is one of the outstanding tourist regions in England, yet its political, administrative and economic borders are differently defined. There is a Cotswold District Council (in Gloucestershire) whose area falls within the remit of the SouthWest RDA, which funds Tourism SouthWest. At the same time, the major areas of attraction within the Cotswolds are in fact located within the area covered by the Heart of England Tourist Board – which is funded by Advantage West Midlands.

The new RDAs (some of which have adopted 'buzz' titles) are:

- South East England RDA (SEEDA)
- South West of England RDA
- East Midlands DA
- East of England DA
- London DA
- One North East
- North West DA
- Advantage West Midlands
- Yorkshire Forward.

Tourism is only one of the new RDAs' remits, but they are now responsible for developing economic strategies for their areas, including those for tourism, which the regional tourist boards are then expected to follow. Sustainability has been emphasized in the government's plans for the RDAs' development and delivery of tourism strategies in the regions.

Regional tourist boards

The 1969 Act had made no provision for a statutory regional public-sector structure for tourism. Before the Act, some attempt had been made to establish regional tourist associations, these being more advanced in Scotland and Wales than in England. However, following the establishment of the three national boards, each set about creating its own regional tourism structure. The result was the establishment of twelve regional tourist boards in England, to be funded jointly by the ETB, local authorities and contributions from local private-sector tourism interests. This number was reduced to ten during the 1990s, and later to nine, with the amalgamation of the South East and Southern boards into Tourism SouthEast (see Figure 15.3). This large and touristically important regional body decided in turn to create six sub-regions, covering:

- Berkshire, Buckinghamshire and Oxfordshire
- Hampshire
- The Isle of Wight
- Surrey and West Sussex
- East Sussex
- Kent.

Further changes are taking place, as the RDAs exercise their influence over the RTBs. In 2004, the North West Tourist Board region became the focus for the formation of four new sub-divisions, known as Destination Management Organizations. These have been entitled:

- Cheshire and Warrington Tourism
- Lancashire and Blackpool Tourist Board
- Marketing Manchester
- Mersey Partnership.

They are designed to emphasize the importance of these destinations in marketing the region.

The Wales Tourist Board established three Regional Offices in North, Mid and South Wales, which became responsible for the management of most of the tourist information centres in Wales, in conjunction with local authorities. Three Tourism Councils were also created, but their roles have been subordinated to four regional partnerships following restructuring in 2003. These are:

- Tourism Partnership North Wales
- Tourism Partnership Mid Wales
- South West Wales Tourism Partnership
- Capital Region Tourism.

Additionally, the principality has been divided into twelve Tourism Marketing Areas:

- Isle of Anglesey
- North Wales Borderlands
- Llandudno, Colwyn Bay, Rhyl and Prestatyn
- Snowdonia Mountains and coast
- Mid Wales and Brecon Beacons
- Ceredigion and Cardigan Bay
- Pembrokeshire
- Carmarthenshire, the garden of Wales
- Swansea Bay; the Gower, Mumbles and Afan and the Vale of Neath
- Valleys of South Wales
- Cardiff, Glamorgan heritage coast and countryside
- Wye Valley and the Vale of Usk.

In Scotland, the picture has become equally complex. Before the Act, regional tourism promotion was in the hands of the eight regional councils, with a separate voluntary association (Dumfries and Galloway) and a statutory development board responsible for the Highlands and Islands. This board subsequently established 15 Area Tourist Boards within its region. Under the terms of the Local Government and Planning (Scotland) Act 1982, the district councils in Scotland were empowered to set up area tourist boards which would become responsible for marketing tourism and running the tourist information centres in their region. The Highlands and Islands scheme was used as a model for the extension of the scheme throughout Scotland, and the new boards were established as a co-partnership between the Scottish Tourist

Board, one or more district councils and the tourist trade, with finance provided by grant aid and private contributions. Thirty-two Area Tourist Boards were established, with a further four district councils deciding to retain their autonomy over tourism matters, while a further six districts failed to decide whether to participate in the scheme. The Highlands and Islands retained an interest in tourism within its territory, but changed its title to Highlands and Islands Enterprise. However, scarcely had this new structure been put into place before a further revision was introduced in legislation in 1993, replacing the 32 boards with 14 new boards, all with greatly expanded territories. These were in place by 1996. Accompanying financial constraints led to the closure of a number of the tourist information centres in the country. Local enterprise companies were now given the role of operating the financial assistance programmes which were formerly the responsibility of the Scottish Tourist Board, while at the same time local authority tourism marketing was required to be channelled through the new statutory, but private-sector dominated, boards.

Further changes took place in 2005, when the ATBs were abolished and integrated into the VisitScotland structure. Their role was to be replaced by regional hubs focusing on partnership with the private sector, but details of the restructuring were still to come at the time of writing.

Northern Ireland, in addition to its forming one region within the all-Ireland marketing consortium Tourism Ireland, has also established five new regional tourist boards, entitled Causeway Coast and Glens, Kingdoms of Down, Fermanagh Lakeland Tourism, Belfast Visitor and Convention Bureau and Derry Visitor and Convention Bureau.

The distribution of the English regional tourist boards is illustrated in Figure 15.3.

Cumbria Tourist Board
Cumbria
East of England Tourist Board
Cambridgeshire, Essex, Hertfordshire, Bedfordshire, Norfolk, Suffolk, Lincolnshire
Heart of England Tourist Board
Gloucestershire, Hereford & Worcestershire, Shropshire, Staffordshire, Warwickshire and West Midlands, District of Cherwell and West Oxfordshire, Derbyshire, Leicestershire, Northamptonshire, Nottinghamshire and Rutland
VisitLondon Tourist Board
Greater London
Northumbria Tourist Board
The Tees Valley, Durham, Northumberland, Tyne & Wear
North West Tourist Board
Cheshire, Greater Manchester, Lancashire, Merseyside, High Peak district of Derbyshire
South East England Tourist Board
East Sussex, West Sussex, Kent, Surrey
Southern Tourist Board
East and North Dorset, Hampshire, Isle of Wight, Berkshire, Buckinghamshire, Oxfordshire
South West Tourism
Bath, Bristol, Cornwall and the Isles of Scilly, Devon, West Dorset, Somerset, Wiltshire
Yorkshire Tourist Board
Yorkshire, North East Lincolnshire

Figure 15.3 Regional tourist boards in England

Government policy and tourism in the UK

The intentions behind the introduction of new structures in public-sector tourism in Britain are always honourable; they include the improvement of planning and the coordination of tourism in the UK. Nevertheless, the diverse nature of tourism and its impact on so many different facets of British life make cohesive planning difficult. Tourism issues cut across the interests not only of many different government departments, but also of a number of public or quasi-public bodies whose roles also impinge in one way or another on tourism.

Example	Transport and tourism

The Department of Transport, Local Government and the Regions, quite apart from its public transport responsibilities, exercises control over certain types of signposting, and the signposting of attractions is of immense importance to the success of tourism. In January 1996, the relaxation of control over brown and white directive road signs for tourism sites led to information about these sites becoming far more readily available to passing tourists, enhancing tourist spend.

The water authorities represent one example among non-government departmental interests, and water-based recreation has come to play an important part in leisure and tourism planning. Local authorities, water authorities like the Waterways Board, and water utilities are now fully aware of the commercial leisure opportunities associated with open expanses of water. In this respect, it is interesting to note the extent to which tourism was taken into account in the planning and development of the Kielder Reservoir in Northumbria, by comparison with earlier reservoir development. Opened in 1982, Kielder is the largest man-made lake in Europe, with a shoreline 27 miles long, and is set within the largest man-made forest in Britain, Kielder Forest (which is managed by the Forestry Commission). Accordingly, the area has huge tourism potential, and facilities to attract the tourist were planned from the outset, including picnic areas, campgrounds, water sports, fishing and mountain bike hire.

Other quasi- or non-governmental bodies with interests that touch on tourism include the Countryside Agency, the Forestry Commission, the Nature Conservancy Council, the Arts and Sports Councils, the National Trust and the Council for the Preservation of Rural England, yet there is no common coordinating body to bring these interests together.

Ostensibly, tourism in the UK is the brief of the Department for Culture, Media and Sport; but quite apart from some of the interests outlined above, when one thinks of some of the issues under discussion within the government which impact on tourism, the full extent of the problem will be apparent – issues such as proposals to end daylight saving time to come into line with Continental time, legislation which ended the long-standing ban on Sunday shopping and the reform of alcoholic licensing, which has already extended drinking hours and will go further under current planned legislation. These changes have huge implications for tourism, with potentially significant increases in tourist spend resulting from each; some estimates have put standardizing European time as potentially enhancing tourism spend in the UK by some £500 million per annum.

Changing governments, changing policies: a critical overview

The period of Conservative government rule between 1979 and 1997 saw marked and frequent changes of direction in terms of tourism policy, with a noted failure to produce a clear and consistent policy. The early years of the Thatcher government were notable for outspoken support for the tourism industry, and recognition of the contribution which tourism makes to the British economy, following reviews of the industry in 1983, and promises were made to expand Section 4 grants nationwide. In 1985, the Young Report[2] promised to 'remove unnecessary obstacles' in the path of tourism development, and emphasized the role which small firms and self-employment would continue to play in the industry. Importance was attached to encouraging young people to enter the industry, and to ensure they were well trained. In the same year, the House of Commons Trade and Industry Committee proposed a radical restructuring of public-sector tourism in Britain, which although not adopted in its entirety, influenced government thinking in its later policies.

Towards the end of the 1980s, the commitment to tourism was wavering. Far from enhancing Section 4 grant aid, as permitted under the 1969 Act, this was terminated in England during 1989–90 (political considerations at the time ensured they remained in place in Scotland and Wales, but even here they were later replaced by alternative aid strategies). The Department of National Heritage review of tourism in 1992 made drastic cuts in the tourism budgets provided to the BTA and ETB, and in 1995 a total restructuring of the BTA and ETB took place which brought the two bodies closer together to avoid duplication, and combine resources. Tourism, which had already moved from the Department of Trade and Industry to the Department of Employment, was transferred to the newly created Department of National Heritage. Ministers with tourism portfolios were changed with dramatic frequency, scarcely finding time to get to grips with the nature of the industry. Often, the post was given to members of the House of Lords, further sidelining the industry. With the change in government to a Labour administration in 1997, the Department of National Heritage was given a new name, and new priorities; in spite of pre-election rhetoric, the creation of a Department for Culture, Media and Sport not only failed to incorporate tourism into its title, but continued Conservative policy of reducing support for tourism, which became the responsibility of low-profile ministers with responsibility for interests apart from tourism (as noted earlier in this chapter). It is notable that no political party has yet seen fit to make tourism worthy of a cabinet post, in spite of its importance to the British economy. Funding for the ETC was also reduced, and subsequently frozen, leading to huge cuts in staffing and activities, although more favourable resources were made available to the national boards of Scotland and Wales. The RTBs in England became responsible for their own marketing, resulting in a lack of overall coordination of the marketing function in England.

The attitude of successive governments in recent years is clearly that tourism has reached a stage in which its future funding and promotion must be the responsibility of the private sector, in spite of the fact that 90 per cent of the industry is represented by small businesses. When the regional tourist boards were established, it was the intention that these would be a means for collaboration between the private and public sectors, with a third of the income to come from the private sector, but this proved hugely optimistic, with only a small number of tourism businesses actually joining the RTBs. The role of the RTBs has been further undermined with the growth of the RDAs, which are coming to control much of those public-sector resources for tourism that remain, while the government puts its faith in public/private partnerships as its model for the future. This approach, it should be noted, is far from unique to Britain; whatever the political colour of the government in power, most developed countries take a common view that funding for tourism must come from the private sector working with the public, while the public sector itself should become increasingly self-sustaining through commercial enterprises.

The illogic of tourism policy on the part of both leading parties has been a feature of British governments for a number of years; promises of support, and recognition of the contribution which tourism can and does make to the UK economy, coupled with simultaneous cuts in government funding, lack of development grants for tourism in depressed regions while manufacturing could benefit, the withdrawal of grants in poor English regions such as Cornwall while grants were awarded in Wales and Scotland regardless of the state of local economies, the decline in support for an English national board vis-à-vis the other national boards, and its eventual absorption into VisitBritain, the transfer of funding and influence from the RTBs in favour of RDAs, all suggest a failure on the part of successive governments to think through rational policies that would give full support to tourism. Further damage is imposed on the industry by the unfavourable rate of VAT on restaurant and hotel accommodation in the UK in comparison with other countries, the imposition of passenger levies on air transport, (now seen by governments as a comparatively painless means of raising extra revenue), an inadequate transport infrastructure (notably the railways and London Underground) and the continued failure to provide an integrated transport policy which would facilitate tourism.

Against these failures, however, one can point to one clear success achieved through a public/private partnership, that of the award of the Olympic Games to London in 2012. Against what was seen as overwhelming odds favouring Paris, the PPP was able to make an effective case, based substantially on the benefits that would accrue to a deprived area of London, the new sports facilities that would become available to the population and the increase in permanent employment for locals resulting from the construction of the facilities. The long-term rejuvenation of one of the most impoverished regions of London is sufficient endorsement to justify the enormous expense that will be entailed in winning the games.

This one important success in encouraging and supporting tourism is unlikely to be emulated elsewhere. Government support to increase domestic tourism has been largely limited to exhortations, rather than hard cash. While the government advocates regeneration of seaside resorts, the costs involved are such that little is being done to halt their decline. In short, pressures on government spending will make it unlikely that the policy of self-support will be reversed, notwithstanding a substantial and ever-increasing deficit in the balance of payments on the UK tourism account.

Tourism at local authority level

We have now examined how tourism is structured at both a national and regional level. The third tier in the structure is at local authority level, where town, county and district councils, or their equivalents in other countries, may also have statutory responsibilities and interests in providing tourist facilities – or at very least, will encourage inbound tourism where the potential for it exists, as part of the economic development plans for the area. This will generally include the provision of tourist information centres.

In Britain, the Local Government Act 1948 empowered local authorities to set up information and publicity services for tourism, and this was reinforced by the Local Government Act of 1972, giving local authorities the power (but not the obligation) to encourage visitors to their area and to provide suitable facilities for them.

The organization of tourism at local level is often curiously piecemeal. Counties and districts on the whole relegate responsibility for tourism to departments which are concerned with a range of other activities, with the result that it is seldom given the significance which its economic impact on the area merits. Up until 20 years ago, fewer than half of the local authorities in England included any strategy relating to tourism in their planning, although Government Circular 13/79 had urged them particularly to consider providing for tourism in local structure plans, and the then English Tourist Board had offered guidelines for local authorities to follow when drawing up such plans. The following key points were emphasized:

- assess the number and distribution of tourists in the area
- estimate future changes in tourism flow, and implications of this for land use
- identify growth opportunities
- assess the impact of tourism on employment and income in the area
- assess the tourists' effect on traffic flows
- assess the tourists' demand for leisure and recreation
- identify the need for conservation and protection
- evaluate the contribution tourism could make to development, especially in the use of derelict land and obsolete buildings.

Local plans should take into account the impact of tourism, and the resultant need for car and coach parks, toilets, information centres, tourist attractions and local accommodation. The inadequacy of parking and toilet facilities in resorts has been a frequent topic of criticism, and cutbacks in local funding have magnified the problem recently.

By the beginning of the 1980s, tourism needs were regularly addressed within many Local Authority Structure Plans, with local authorities coming to appreciate the economic contribution which tourism could make even in traditionally non-tourist areas. Training courses such as COTICC (Certificate of Tourist Information Centre Competence), and later NVQs (National Vocational Qualifications) were developed to cover the need for basic skills among TIC staff, and some local authorities began to recruit staff with formal tourism education or experience.

The principal responsibilities of county and district authorities which bear on tourism are as follows:

1   Provision of leisure facilities for tourists (e.g. conference centres) and for residents (e.g. theatres, parks, sports centres, museums).

2   Planning (under town and country planning policies). Note that District Councils produce local plans to fit the broad strategy of the County Council Structure Plans. These plans are certified by the County Council.

3   Development control powers over land use.

4   Provision of visitor services (usually in conjunction with tourist bodies).

5   Parking for coaches and cars.

6   Provision of caravan sites (with licensing and management the responsibility of the District Councils).

7   Production of statistics on tourism, for use by the regional tourist boards.

8   Marketing the area.

9   Upkeep of historic buildings.

10 Public health, including food hygiene, and safety issues. This is taken to include matters such as litter disposal and the provision of public toilet facilities.

Local authorities may also own and operate local airports, although in many countries these are now frequently in private hands. The provision of visitor services will normally include helping to fund and manage tourist information centres, in cooperation with the regional tourist boards, which set and monitor standards. Local authorities will also fund tourist information points, information boards found at lay-bys, car parks and city centres.

Local authorities which have set out actively to encourage tourism have a number of objectives, some of which may conflict, and each of which will compete for scarce resources. Local tourist officers will need to identify the resources they require to achieve their stated objectives, and to determine their priorities. Typical objectives might include:

■ increasing visitor numbers

■ extending visitor stays

■ increasing visitor spend

- increasing and upgrading local attractions
- creating or improving the image of the area as a tourist destination
- stimulating private-sector involvement in tourism.

Local tourist officers act as catalysts between the public and private sectors and voluntary-aided bodies. As a focus for tourism in the area or resort, they become a point of reference, advising on development and grant-aided opportunities. Officers will help the local authority to determine and establish the necessary infrastructure which will allow tourism to develop, and they will carry out research and planning activities themselves. In some areas, they may become involved in the provision and training of tourist guides. In addition, they will undertake a range of promotional and publicity functions, including the preparation of publications such as guides to the district, accommodation guides, information on current events and entertainment, and specialist brochures listing, for example, local walks, shopping, restaurants and pubs. The cost of most of these publications will be met in part by contributions from the private sector, either through advertising or, as in the case of the accommodation brochures, through a charge for listing. Many resorts also now produce a trade manual, aimed at the travel trade and giving information on trade prices, conference facilities and coach parking. Tourist officers may also organize familiarization trips for the travel trade and the media, and, if the resort shows sufficient potential, they may invite representatives of the overseas trade and media. They frequently play a part in setting up and operating the local TICs (see Plate 16), and this may include a local bed-booking service. Some go as far as actively packaging holidays for inbound visitors, including activity weekends or special interest short breaks. It should be noted that all of these functions are frequently the responsibility of a very small team, on occasion no greater than a single tourist officer and a secretary.

Unlike the regional tourist boards, where responsibilities are predominantly promotional, tourism planning and sustainable development form key elements of a local authority's functions. They may consequently be as concerned to reduce or stabilize tourism as to develop it (particularly when, as is so often the case in the popular tourist resorts, local residents are opposed to any increase in the numbers of tourists attracted). In providing for leisure, the authorities must be sensitive to local residents' needs as much as to those of incoming tourists. They must convince the residents of the merits of public investment in tourist projects. The development of conference centres in popular resorts like Bournemouth and Harrogate was a controversial issue with local residents, since very few private investors are willing to put money into centres such as these, while use of public funds will greatly increase the burden of debt on the council initially. It is hard to convince local residents of the wisdom of investments that do not appear to provide a direct profit; however, conferences do generate a healthy flow of indirect revenue through additional spend by delegates in local shops, hotels and restaurants, with the added bonus that much of this revenue will accrue outside the traditional holiday season. This was the thinking behind local authority investment in the ill-fated regeneration of Bath Spa, where cost over-runs have spiralled to some £50 million through mistakes in construction, leading to a massive debt burden for local taxpayers and delaying the opening years beyond the proposed completion date.

The funding and staffing of local TICs in many countries involves public investment by both local authorities and regional tourist boards, with support funding where possible from the private sector. In addition to stocking promotional material, many of these local TICs also provide a booking service for tourists seeking accommodation in the area, and they also manage a scheme for booking accommodation from one TIC to another. In Britain, this is known as the Book a Bed Ahead scheme (BABA). If local authorities contribute directly to RTB funds, they will clearly expect to play a role in the board's policy making and serve on RTB committees. Where representatives of the private sector, such as local hoteliers, are also members of these committees, the latter's interests and objectives will often differ from those of the local authority, and this can lead to conflicts in policy making.

Public/private-sector cooperation

This chapter has provided a snapshot of public-sector tourism structure and operations. The focus has been mainly on the UK, but the picture is not dissimilar in other developed countries; due to the sheer complexity of tourism, there is frequently a lack of coordinated tourism policy at government level, while at the same time financial constraints are restricting public expenditure on tourism. Increasingly, the view is being taken that the public sector can best assist a country's prospects for tourism by reducing its role in development and promotion and entering into partnership with the private sector. In Britain, this has led to a proliferation of consultation and advisory bodies designed to ensure that private interests have a voice in public planning and policy-making, as well as active involvement in partnerships. Among these is the England Marketing Advisory Board, set up following the integration of the BTA (now VisitBritain) and the English Tourist Council. The Board, funded via the VisitBritain grant-in-aid, advises ministers on issues relating to tourism and coordinates domestic marketing within the country, liaising with the regions, RDAs and local authorities while helping to facilitate partnerships with the private and voluntary sectors. Another body, the Tourism Review and Implementation Group, serviced by the DCMS and chaired by the Minister responsible for tourism, was created with the aim of holding an annual conference which would bring together interested parties within the industry, both public and private. Yet another, the English Tourism Alliance, is the outcome of efforts by the industry to ensure its voice is heard by government policy-makers. Supported by the Confederation of British Industry (CBI), its 40-plus members include RDAs, tourist boards and trade associations. Similar bodies were established in Wales (the Wales Tourism Alliance) and in Scotland (the Scottish Tourism Forum).

The desire to turn over national tourism promotion to the private sector, or to develop partnerships with the private sector, has been led by developments in North America, where, as we have seen earlier in this chapter, the US abandoned its public-sector body in favour of the privately sponsored Travel Industry Association of America. Individual states have also gone down this road: Visit Florida is a public/private-sector partnership which is funded in part by taxation on car hire within the state and sponsorship from some 3,000 members of the industry.

Example   Tourism Canada

Canada's National Tourism Office was a public body until 1995, trading under the brand Tourism Canada. It has been replaced by the Canadian Tourism Commission, a partnership between federal, provincial and territorial governments and private-sector interests. The latter contribute around half of the total financing for the body.

Regions, sometimes trans-national, are also opting for the collaborative approach. An interesting example is that of the Øresund region, where Denmark is geographically separated from southern Sweden. The construction of a bridge linking the two countries has led to the formation of a joint marketing organization to promote Copenhagen, the surrounding region of Sjælland, Bornholm Island and southern Sweden, with privately funded support from SAS, the Scandinavian air carrier, and other regions. One notable effect of this marketing drive has been the economic improvement resulting from tourist flows into Malmø and southern Sweden, an economically depressed region. This exemplified a general move to the formation of destination management organizations, designed to form partnerships between the public and private sectors in order to promote tourism to a region more effectively.

At third-tier level, the formation of tourism marketing boards, made up of representatives from both the public and private sector interests, is becoming a popular alternative to traditional public-sector tourism organizations. In Britain, Plymouth was the first city to launch a partnership of this kind, back in 1977. The city's marketing bureau draws its members from those nominated by the city council and others elected by the private sector. The bureau is financed by a grant from the city council, by membership subscriptions and by commercial activities. Other cities and districts to have followed suit include Merseyside, Birmingham, Greater Glasgow, Sheffield and Manchester, while bodies covering larger areas, like the North Devon Marketing Bureau, are also following suit. Not all these public/private partnerships or private initiatives have proved successful – notable failures include the marketing bureaux of Chester and Bristol – but there can be no denying that the lack of collaboration between the sectors prior to the new partnerships was limiting opportunities.

The move to a more commercial approach among the public bodies has paralleled the public/private ventures. With a change in the direction of policy during the 1990s, the British regional boards became more enterprising. To cite just one example, in 1996 and with the support of the national board, Northampton TIC established a travel agency as a pilot project to sell domestic tourism products, a move soon followed by Chester TIC. If these moves are to be successful, however, they depend upon the support of the trade, unless they are to be entirely dependent upon selling direct to the public. If the industry believes that the public sector is competing with them, relationships rapidly break down. Efforts by the Wales Tourist Board to establish commercial tour operations to support tourism into Wales failed to generate the support of the retail trade, in spite of ensuring that a commissionable domestic product would be available for agents to sell. However, few travel agents appear willing to promote domestic products as enthusiastically as they do foreign holidays, and this may force the public sector to take a more proactive approach.

Lest it be thought that public funds for private tourism projects have dried up entirely, it should be stressed that many countries still offer subsidies in the form of grants, loans or other financial incentives which will help to reduce costs for entrepreneurs in tourism. Where the state remains keen to see private tourism development, and where funding for such development would not be forthcoming without direct public assistance, both central and local governments will still offer some measures of help. In Britain, this has been encouraged by the European Commissioners, who have given approval for the country's designated 'Assisted Areas' which qualify for economic aid. These areas now fall within the boundaries of the nine English RDAs, and the equivalents in Wales and Scotland. They were originally structured into three tiers, with the poorest areas of the country (in England, these constituted Cornwall and the Scilly Isles, Merseyside and South Yorkshire) falling into Tier 1. Tier 3 qualified for lower level grants for small to medium size enterprises. Since 2004, the so-called Regional Selective Assistance (RSA) grants have given way to Selective Finance for Investment (SFI) in England, with some changes to the conditions attached to the granting of subsidies. These grants (or less commonly, loans) are dispensed by the RDAs for sums up to £2 million, with DTI approval required for sums in excess of this figure.

National heritage bodies

In Chapter 10 we examined the significance of the built environment for tourism. This plays a particularly important role in Britain, with its rich heritage of monuments, historic homes, cathedrals and similar attractions which go to make up our national heritage. While many of these attractions remain in private hands, or are the responsibility of bodies like the Church Commissioners, a number of quasi-public or voluntary organizations exist to protect and enhance these heritage sites. These bodies therefore fulfil an important role in the tourism industry.

According to estimates made by the English Tourism Council, there are well over half a million sites of architectural or historical merit in England alone, broken down into categories (see Table 15.1).

Table 15.1   Listed sites in England of potential interest to tourists, 2004[a]

Type of site	Number of sites
World Heritage Sites	16
Listed buildings of architectural and historical merit	371,971[b]
Scheduled monuments	19,594
Ecclesiastical buildings	c.20,000
Historic parks and gardens	1,584
Conservation areas of architectural or natural interest	9,140
Historic battlefields	43

(a) Excluding around 1 million sites of archaeological interest.
(b) Of which around 2% are listed Grade I and 6% Grade II*.
Source: Heritage Counts 2004, English Heritage

Figure 15.4
Stonehenge:
one of English
Heritage's
responsibilities

(Photographed by the author)

One might be surprised by the very high number of valued buildings, but a walk through any country town in Britain will soon reveal a wealth of buildings worth more than a casual glance. While not necessarily open to the public, they still form an attractive backdrop to any townscape for passing tourists. Key sites such as Grade I listed buildings and internationally renowned UNESCO World Heritage sites like Stonehenge will draw people from all over the world, and are carefully protected. Many of our great national monuments were originally under the control of the Department of the Environment, but growing concern about their protection and maintenance led to the establishment of the Historic Buildings and Monuments Commission in 1983, following the National Heritage Act in that year. This body, more familiarly known as 'English Heritage', which integrates the functions of the former Historic Buildings Council for England and the Ancient Monuments Board, has a dual conservation and promotion function. The organization now looks to industry and the public to raise finance for the protection of the buildings in their care, either through sponsorship of individual buildings or subscriptions to a national membership scheme similar to that of the National Trust. Cadw in Wales and Historic Scotland share similar responsibility for historic properties in their territories.

Apart from these key quasi-government bodies, the National Trust (and the National Trust for Scotland) also plays a vital role in protecting buildings of significant architectural or historic interest. Founded in 1895, the National Trust cares for over 190 properties and a quarter of a million hectares of land, acquiring properties for the most part through inheritance. Its properties include villages, nature reserves and woodland, and it also operates a campaign, under the title Enterprise Neptune, to buy up and protect stretches of British coastline; to date, it has acquired over 500 miles of coast. Operational costs are met by subscriptions from the very large number of members in Britain, but the Trust also anticipates that properties left to them will be accompanied by sufficient money for their upkeep.

Apart from these key organizations, a great many smaller bodies exist to protect the British heritage. One of the earliest to be founded was the Society for the Protection of Ancient Buildings, dating back to 1877; other bodies include the Ancient Monuments Society, the Georgian Group, the Victorian Society, the National Piers Society and SAVE Britain's Heritage. More recent buildings are becoming valued as intrinsic to the national heritage, and the Twentieth Century Society exists to protect the best of these. To these bodies we must add a number of diverse trusts, all of which share an interest in the protection of sites of touristic appeal, including the Civic Trust, the Monument Trust, the Pilgrim Trust, the Landmark Trust and many others (over a thousand local amenity societies are known to exist in England alone). Some of these, such as the Landmark Trust and Pilgrim Trust, rent out their properties for holidays, thus playing an active part in the tourism industry.

Town twinning and tourism

No discussion of public-sector tourism can be complete without exploring the development of town twinning, even though the impact of this relationship between towns is seldom considered as an element of the tourism business. The concept of town twinning emerged in the aftermath of World War II, as a means of overcoming hostilities between the warring nations and forging greater understanding between communities in different countries. Usually, the selection of a twin town is based on some common characteristics such as population size, geographical features or commercial similarities. Local authorities and chambers of commerce arrange for the exchange of visits by residents of the twinned towns. Although conceived as a gesture of friendship and goodwill, the outcome has commercial implications for tourism, as visitor flows increase between the two twinned towns. While accommodation is normally provided in private homes, expenditure on transport, shopping and sightseeing can have a significant impact on the inflow of tourist revenue for the towns concerned – some of which may have little other tourist traffic. Friendships formed as a result of these links will also lead to subsequent travel demand. So far, no studies appear to have been made as to the financial contribution resulting from these links, but it is likely to be considerable.

Functions of the UK tourist boards

VisitBritain

As we have seen, the Development of Tourism Act empowered what was then known as the British Tourist Authority to promote tourism to Britain in overseas countries. With the agreement of the respective territories, the Authority also undertook foreign promotion on behalf of the tourist boards of Northern Ireland, the Isle of Man and the

Channel Islands. With general responsibility for tourism throughout Great Britain, the Authority acts as adviser to the government on tourism issues, and is financed by an annual grant-in-aid from the Treasury, channelled through the Department for Culture, Media and Sport.

Marketing policies over the years have included plans to extend the tourist season in Britain, to promote areas of high unemployment which can demonstrate tourist potential, and to develop new markets and market segments for inbound tourism. Most recently its core objectives have been identified as:

1   Increasing returns on investment in overseas marketing to a ratio of 30:1.
2   Increasing returns on investment in domestic marketing to 14:1 and to ensure that at least 62 per cent of the additional spend takes place outside of London.

Both aims were targeted to be achieved by the end of the 2005/6 business year.

With depleted resources, the organization maintains 27 offices worldwide, and focuses on 31 countries which are deemed best prospects for attracting tourists to Britain. In particular, VisitBritain singles out those countries offering prospects of rapid growth over the next few years. In 2005, these were South Korea, China, Poland and Russia; the following year, targets were Hungary, the Czech Republic, Thailand, Malaysia and Greece. In 2005, Britain and China also signed an Approved Destination Status (ADS) agreement, boosting opportunities to attract Chinese tourists to the UK. Forecasts are for more than 100 million Chinese to travel abroad by 2020, and the new agreement is expected to increase dramatically the number of visitors from that country. It is interesting to note that while always seeking to improve quality, the Board's policies simultaneously aim to increase the numbers of tourists it wishes to attract to Britain; as is the case with most other tourism destinations, public tourism bodies seldom suggest any finite limit to the number of visitors they can receive, either to the country as a whole or to its most popular regions.

VisitBritain also carries out research and liaises with the other national tourism bodies in the UK. The overseas offices help UK companies to reach foreign markets by, for example, circulating details of inclusive packages to travel companies bringing tourists to Britain. The organization mounts workshops, either in Britain or in major centres of population in tourism-generating countries abroad, which are designed to bring together the buyers and sellers of travel services; for the smaller British company in the travel business, this may be the most effective way to reach the overseas market with a limited budget. Typical workshops include those for European coach and tour operators, special-interest travel or English language schools. Limitations on funding, particularly within recent times, mean that the Board must necessarily restrict what it can do for travel companies, and this means that little help is available for the smaller independent companies. However, it does provide certain services at commercial rates, such as distribution abroad of a company's brochures, or advising on overseas marketing.

Other functions include the publication of sales and information guides, directories and magazines. A popular marketing approach has been to name specific years as 'theme years' as an incentive to visit Britain. The bicentennial of the battle of Trafalgar in 2005 allowed the Board to promote the theme of maritime heritage. Other marketing campaigns have included sponsorship of the annual 'Come to Britain' trophy for top new tourist attractions or facilities.

The national boards for England, Wales and Scotland

Under the terms of the Development of Tourism Act, the functions of the three national boards were established as:

- encouraging residents of the UK to travel within their own country
- encouraging the provision and improvement of attractions and facilities for tourists in Britain
- administering the Section 4 grants
- advising the government on matters concerning tourism within their territory.

As we learned earlier, Section 4 grants are no longer available, and in 2003 the English Tourism Council was absorbed into VisitBritain, giving rise to the anomaly of individual national boards for Wales and Scotland, but none for England. In its final year as an independent body, the ETC received a grant equal to 40 per cent of that of its new parent, and its integration will undoubtedly have had an impact on key functions it performed in the past, such as the collection and dissemination of research. The Wales Tourist Board's functions remain unchanged at the time of writing, in spite of major changes to its structure (we saw earlier that it is to become an integral part of the Welsh Assembly, rather than an individual agency). VisitScotland, meanwhile, reports to the Scottish Parliament.

With marketing and funding moving to regional boards via the RDAs, the functions of the individual national boards have been constrained. In the past, the boards co-operated in undertaking research and publishing a range of statistical data covering national as well as regional information, and it is uncertain how far these functions will be changing as a result of the many changes in structure undergone by the boards in current times. Reduced funding has also meant that the boards have had to become more commercial in their approach. The Wales Tourist Board, to take one example, has farmed out some of its activities by establishing private limited companies to undertake some of its functions. One example of this is the establishment of Tourism Quality Services Ltd, which acts as the Wales Tourist Board's agents in carrying out inspection of holiday accommodation and attractions, and has widened the scope of its activities to carry out inspections outside of Wales, at commercial rates. The WTB has also attempted to promote holidays to Wales commercially, by the publication of a commissionable 'Holiday Wales' tour-operating programme, for distribution through agents, but with only limited success.

Prior to the demise of the ETC, the three boards united to form Tourism UK, essentially a lobby to press the UK government for an increase in funding for the public sector.

The tourist information centres

TICs play a particularly important role in disseminating information about tourism, in the UK as elsewhere. There are well over 800 official tourist information centres in Britain, with some 600 in England alone. Funding now comes largely from the local authorities, assisted by the provision of support material and publications from the regional boards. The regional boards oversee the standards of each TIC and award them formal recognition. This has entailed, among other criteria, a requirement to employ salaried staff rather than relying upon voluntary labour, as had been the practice in some TICs. Improved access, especially for the disabled, and agreed minimum hours of opening have also become important benchmarks for recognition.

The TICs, like the boards, have been forced to become more commercial in the light of government policy, and with the decline in funding by cash-strapped local authorities, which do not, in fact, have a statutory duty to provide these services. Apart from the now well-established Book a Bed Ahead scheme, TICs are increasingly introducing commercial products for sale within their shops, while seeking ways of cutting costs to remain viable. Cafés and shops have been combined with exhibition and interpretation galleries in many information centres to attract tourists and get them to spend money in the centres.

One means of providing information cheaply is through the Tourist Information Point (TIP), unattended stands providing information about local facilities. In some parts of the world, these will include sophisticated booking systems for local hotels, either using telephone connections or computer links.

A final point to make is the valuable contribution which TICs can make to tourism through the buildings they occupy. In many cases, TICs are housed in buildings of outstanding architectural or historic interest in a city, and their careful preservation and adaptation for this purpose has ensured that the buildings are not only put to good use, but provide an additional point of focus for the visiting tourist, who is able to see the interior of a building which might otherwise be restricted. Increasingly, local authorities have come to recognize the important role which the TIC can play in drawing attention to modern design as well, whether in the traditional style and materials of local building or in a more modern concept where the new building can itself become a stimulus for tourist interest (see Plate 16).

Information technology initiatives in the public sector

The computer-linked accommodation reservation system was just the first step into IT by the public sector. The British boards have moved steadily to develop and expand their websites and provide the public with a comprehensive package of information and booking services. The BTA devised its first VisitBritain website in 1997, incorporating details of tourist attractions, events organizers and hotels, with accompanying advertisements. These have been complemented by national and regional boards' websites, and more recently the development of an all-encompassing site known as EnglandNet.

In 2000, the then Scottish Tourist Board developed its Ossian on-line booking system in partnership with the private sector, and in the following year the ETC announced its own plans to establish a website specifically to cover English resorts and accommodation, with a view to boosting tourist visits to the seaside resorts. An e-Tourism Advisory Group was set up that year to bring together public and private sector bodies in order to find new ways of using technology to promote tourism in the UK.

EnglandNet has proved to be one of the most ambitious schemes to be undertaken by VisitBritain, previously in collaboration with the English Tourist Board. Designed to provide the public with comprehensive information and booking facilities for virtually any tourist product in England, the website is open to operators and agents selling breaks, accommodation providers and the regional boards. The website is expected to be of particular value to SMEs, enabling them to reach their customers more effectively on-line. The government has provided grants totalling more than £3 million through the DCMS, and the site is still subject to further development at the time of writing. Products will be accepted on to the site subject to their being quality assessed and graded.

Example   Marketing England

With the demise of the English Tourist Council, VisitBritain now has responsibility for promoting travel to and within England through its recently launched England Marketing Advisory Board, which is working with the industry to develop closer relations with the public. A consumer database of 750,000 potential English holidaymakers has been developed, and from these, some 150,000 consumers who have requested it are receiving a monthly e-newsletter, *Enjoy England*. Research has indicated that around 40 per cent open these newsletters when they arrive in their e-mail, and more than 10 per cent take action to make enquiries or bookings through the websites of the partners included in the literature. The database of half a million regular domestic holidaymakers receives quarterly editions of the *Great Ideas* mini-guide to encourage them to visit again[3].

Website: www.enjoyengland.com

Few can doubt that the website will become one of the most popular means of accessing accommodation bookings within the space of the next few years. Some local authorities are involved with plans to allocate rooms within their districts to tour operators for package tour arrangements. Such a centrally controlled allocation of hotel rooms would enable hoteliers to reduce their individual commitments to tour operators, and therefore minimize wastage in the reservations process.

Plans are also under way for call centres to be set up within the TICs which will allow the public to make bookings direct via the new website. This has given rise to concern that the public sector will be coming into competition with private-sector websites.

One other feature that deserves mention here is the emergence of Electronic Marketing Units (EMUs) at TICs. These are databases accessible to passers-by outside the TICs, and therefore their use is not limited to the opening times of the TICs themselves. Although the range of information available through these units is limited, it is expanding and already provides the basis for interactive communication between tourists and tourist facilities, which would allow visitors to make reservations for hotels, theatres and a host of other amenities.

Functions of the regional tourist boards

It was envisaged when the structure of the regional boards was set up that they would receive their financing through a mixture of national board, local authority and private-sector funds, although private funding never achieved the levels anticipated. Additionally, the boards were to raise capital through commercial activities such as the sale of tourist products like maps and guides.

The objectives set for the regional tourist boards when they were established were:

- to produce a coordinated strategy for tourism within their regions in association with the local authority

- to represent the interests of the region at national level and the interests of the tourist industry within the region

- to encourage the development of tourist amenities and facilities which meet the changing needs of the market

- to market the region by providing reception and information services (in concert with the NTB), producing and supplying suitable literature and undertaking miscellaneous promotional activities.

Many RTBs also undertook the role of validating guiding courses for 'Blue Badge' guides within their regions.

Typically, an RTB will work with a very small staff of perhaps 10 to 15 members (although the VisitLondon, due to its importance in the tourism economy, has a larger number of employees). Coordination now has to be with a wide range of bodies, including the local authorities and tourist trade. Additionally, the RTBs are now subject to control and funding from the RDAs, as we have seen, and their policies will fall into line with the economic development plans of the RDAs.

RTBs have a particularly difficult role in their relations with local authorities. They must work with these authorities and cooperate with them in tourism planning, but their aims may be in conflict with those of the local authority, which is often apathetic or negative towards the growth of tourism in its area. Moreover, local authorities are charged with certain functions which have a direct bearing on tourism, as we have seen. They can hinder the expansion of tourism by refusing planning permission, to take one example. However, they do also play an important role in safeguarding the countryside and coastal areas within their regions.

Geographically, RTB areas are often diverse and cannot logically be promoted as a single destination. Furthermore, political regions do not necessarily embrace what the tourist understands as a 'tourist region', and the RTB's role will include the promotion of a brand image for a region which may readily cross county borders. South West Tourism, to take one example, represents counties ranging from Cornwall at its western extremity to Bristol on its northern boundary, and parts of West Dorset on its eastern boundary. It is charged with the promotion of all these regions, although Bristol's Council makes no financial contribution to the Board's funds, while the promotion of Dorset would arguably be better handled as an integral destination. Producing a coordinated strategy for the promotion and development of tourism in the face of these diverse interests is no easy matter.

Figure 15.5
National and regional tourist boards promote their territories at international exhibitions: the World Travel Market in London

(Photographed by the author)

The role of the European Union

By contrast with some European Union nations, where tourism makes an equally important contribution to the economy, Britain has chosen largely to allow the free-market economy to operate in the tourism field, with little attempt to centralize policy-making. However, as Britain becomes more closely integrated with the EU, British travel and tourism interests have become subjected to EU legislation. Most importantly, since harmonization came into force at the beginning of 1993, any constraints of trade have been largely abolished, allowing travel firms to compete within the EU on an equal footing and without legal hindrance. So far, the evidence suggests that fellow Europeans are faster in taking advantage of the opportunities that this presents than is the UK, although British airlines have continued to expand into the Continent (see Chapter 12).

Within the European Commission, at least ten of the 23 Directorates General (the Commission's departments) have some responsibilities that impact upon the tourism industry, although the Tourism Unit itself is allocated to Directorate I within the Directorate General for Enterprise and Industry. As with government departments in Britain, there is no system for coordinating tourism interests across the Directorates General.

The principal stated objectives of the EU as regards tourism include:

- the facilitation of tourist movements, through abolition of frontier controls, deregulation of transport, ease in transfer of foreign currencies, reciprocal health coverage and better information and protection for tourists themselves
- more effective promotion, through state aid and other means
- help in distributing the flow of tourists better, both geographically and seasonally, through emphasis on such features as rural tourism, and by staggering school holidays
- other measures, to include better tourism training, easing taxation etc.

Many of these ambitions were already achieved to some extent before the introduction of harmonization; the scheduled airline industry, as we saw in Chapter 12, has been fully deregulated, and there have been no controls over charter flights within the EU. Shipping has also been fully deregulated. The free movement of capital and labour promises the possibility of huge changes in the way some sectors of industry, such as tour operating and travel agencies, are run, and we are already seeing the impact of this deregulation as companies merge across borders in these sectors. While the termination of duty-free facilities within the EU was damaging for the industry, the lifting of any ceiling on duty-paid goods stimulated sales to cross-border tourists. Other EU directives which have had significant impact on the industry include the Package Travel Directive, adopted in 1992, and the move to increase compensation for airline passengers subject to delays, introduced in 2005. Although problematic and costly for the industry, the obligation on operators to bear the responsibility for virtually anything happening to their clients while abroad has marked a great advance in consumer protection for travellers within the EU. While the principle of airline compensation can also be lauded, in practice the escape clause that allows airlines to avoid paying compensation where delays can be ascribed to factors outside their control has meant that responsibility remains a grey area and consumers seldom receive the compensation they anticipate.

Notes

1 Woodbridge-Cox, C, Flexible Friends, *Travel Weekly*, 28 January 2005
2 DTI, *Pleasure, Leisure and Jobs: the Business of Tourism* (the Young Report), HMSO, 1985
3 *Enjoy England* and *Great Ideas* can be found at the website of the England Marketing Advisory Board (www.enjoyengland.com). See also VisitBritain's book website, www.visitbritainseekbook.co.uk

Websites

VisitBritain	www.visitbritain.com
England Marketing Advisory Board	www.enjoyengland.com
EnglandNet	www.englandnet.org.uk
Family Holiday Association	www.fhaonline.org.uk
Tourism For All	www.tourismforall.org.uk

Questions and discussion points

1   If we cannot compete in price, then we must compete on quality. For an island that has just 800,000 residents, our taxes cannot support eleven million tourists each year. We need the services and administration to support over ten times our population, and this tax will enable us to do that.

Tiffany Blackman, Director, IBATUR
(Balearic Islands Tourist Office)

Refer to the example given in this chapter, and argue the case for and against the imposition of such a tax on tourists, as applied in the Balearic Islands, to improve a destination's amenities. How might funding be raised in other ways for the same purpose?

2   We look at every part of the world and see what works. For example, if the main image they have of Britain is of whisky or golf, we would promote Scotland.

Michael Bedingfield, VisitBritain,
quoted in *Travel Weekly*, 1 September 2003

This suggests that the best public policy for tourism is to promote what is already known and successful, rather than to encourage travel to lesser-known destinations with potential. To what extent would you agree?

3   Sports and tourism have been separated within the ministries at the DCMS, following the success of London winning the 2012 Olympics. Shouldn't this success best be met by ensuring that the two responsibilities are brought together within a single ministry?

4   Would town twinning benefit if it became more commercial? Discuss the pros and cons of this development, and how such commercialization could transpire.

5   Is there a case for a separate tourism minister in the UK?

Assignment topics

1   As a marketing employee in your local authority's tourism section, you have been asked to undertake some research into setting up a collaborative partnership with members of the local tourism trade to improve tourist visitor numbers and spend in your region. Draw up a marketing plan for a project designed to achieve this, and assess which local organizations and companies would be best approached to collaborate and promote the project.

2   Still working with your local authority, you are given the responsibility of finding ways to boost the image of your local town to encourage tourism. Undertake research by visiting the centre of town to judge what cosmetic improvements need to be made to make the area more attractive to tourists and locals. Consider street cleanliness, paintwork on commercial buildings, floral displays, appearance of street furniture etc. and write a report to your chief executive suggesting what steps should be taken. Your report can be supported by photographs of the failings you have encountered in your research.

16 Tour operating

Objectives

After studying this chapter, you should be able to:

- define the role of a tour operator, and distinguish between different types of operator
- explain the functions of each type of operator
- understand how operators interact with other sectors of industry
- understand how the activities of operators are constrained
- understand the basic principles behind the construction and marketing of a package tour
- understand the appeal of the package tour to its various markets
- evaluate alternative methods of tour distribution, and recognize the importance of new forms of electronic reservations and sales systems for operators and their clients.

The role of the tour operator

Essentially, package holidays are the ready-made microwave meals of the travel industry.

Joanne O'Connor, Acting Travel Editor,
The Observer, 18 May 2003

For many years, tour operators have formed the core of what we understand as the travel industry, and to a large extent they can be said to have moulded the industry into the form familiar to us today. Traditionally, they formed an essential bridge between travel suppliers and customers, purchasing separately the elements of transport, accommodation and other services, and combining them into a package which they then sold direct (or through travel agents) to consumers. Their position in the tourism distribution system is demonstrated by the diagram in Figure 16.1.

Figure 16.1
The place of the
tour operator in
the tourism
distribution
system

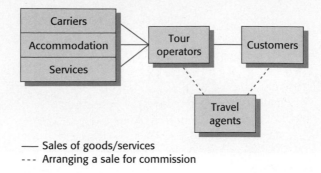

—— Sales of goods/services
--- Arranging a sale for commission

Some take the view that the tour operator is essentially a wholesaler, since they purchase services, and *break bulk* (i.e. buy in large quantities from principals in order to sell in smaller quantities). However, wholesalers are not normally known to change the product they buy before distributing it, and it is for this reason that some argue for operators to be classed as *principals* in their own right, rather than simply intermediaries. Their argument is based on the premise that by packaging a series of individual tourism products into a single whole new product, the *inclusive tour*, the operator is actually changing the nature of those products. In a sense, the operator becomes a 'light assembly' business, recognizing that the customers could well put together the same package themselves, but not necessarily at the same price, and less conveniently. The service which the tour operator provides is to buy in bulk, thus – in theory – securing considerable discounts from the suppliers which could not normally be matched by the customer buying direct. The operator is thus able to assemble and present to the customer a package – the 'inclusive tour' – which is both convenient to purchase and competitively priced.

However, recent years have witnessed a change to the ways in which travel products are bought and sold by operators. Already, some two decades ago, operators had begun to sell unpackaged 'seat only' flights to agents and customers, in order to fill their charters, and with the advent of the World Wide Web which encouraged principals to sell travel arrangements direct to their customers, operators have become far more flexible in marketing their products. Many now offer each element of their packages separately, or are giving their clients the opportunity to book their flights direct while helping them to organize the balance of their holiday programme. While traditional 7- and 14-day packages will remain a popular feature in most operators' brochures, more flexible durations as well as tailor-made arrangements and individual elements of the package are now negotiable.

This service is also valuable to the principals in the travel and tourism industry. The travel industry operates in a business environment in which supply and demand are seldom in balance; nor can supply expand or contract quickly to take advantage of changes in demand. Both the airline and hotel businesses operate in circumstances which make it difficult to adjust their capacity in the short term. A scheduled flight, for example, *must* operate regardless of whether one passenger or a hundred are booked on it. A charter airline with a single type of aircraft – say a Boeing 757 with a maximum capacity of 239 passengers – cannot expand the number of seats to take advantage of peak opportunities, nor reduce capacity if demand falls slightly (although sometimes the sale of cargo space can help to enhance passenger revenue). We say that supply is 'lumpy'; that is, it cannot be expanded by a single seat, but must be expanded in blocks of seats, perhaps as many as 150 at a time in the case of aircraft. This is most clearly evidenced in the example of shuttle airline services, in which airlines have agreed to carry every passenger who turns up for a flight to a specific destination. If one too many passengers turns up for a flight, the airline must lay on another complete aircraft. Rigid enforcement of this ruling has resulted in the decimation of shuttle services, which are now viable on only a handful of routes world wide.

In these circumstances, carriers seek ways to adjust demand to fill available seats. This is important to keep down costs per passenger, and reduce waste of resources; the aircraft costs a certain amount of money to run, regardless of the number of passengers it carries, and this fixed cost is likely to be the major element in any transport costs. Tour operators have played a very useful role for the scheduled airlines, which can offer substantial discounts on seats that they know they themselves cannot fill. Example 1 demonstrates this.

Example 1   Costing a scheduled flight

Suppose that the fixed cost of flying a 140-seat plane from London to Athens and back is £27,000 (that includes capital costs, fuel, crew's wages etc.). Suppose also that the additional, or variable, cost per passenger is £26 (to cover administrative expenses such as check-in, the e-ticket, and providing in-flight refreshments, extra fuel, and so on). If the airline wants to budget for a small profit and estimates that at a price of £275 it can expect to sell 110 seats, then the cost and pricing looks like this:

Fixed cost	£27,000
110 passengers × £26	£2,860
Cost of return flight	£29,860
Sell 110 tickets at £275 each	£30,250
Profit	£390

Of course, in the example, if only 109 passengers show up, then sales drop by £275, costs by only £26, and the airline ends up losing £141. This is a very risky business!

While this is a very simplified picture of pricing on a single route, the complexity of pricing has substantially increased since the no-frills airlines came into service, with the variation in pricing becoming far wider (see Chapter 12 for a further illustration of this). Bookings made several months in advance to a destination involving a flight of similar duration may cost as little as £10, rising 20- or 30-fold in the days prior to departure. Airlines will also overbook in the expectation that a few passengers will not turn up in time for their flight, or will cancel without refund. Airlines retain the revenue (including tax, although this is only applied if passengers actually travel, and therefore theoretically should be refundable), making a significant contribution to overall profit, especially if the seat can be resold.

This is where tour operators prove themselves so useful. By agreeing to purchase in bulk say, 25 seats, they can virtually ensure that the airline will fly at a profit. The question arises, what should the ticket price be? As far as the airline is concerned, anything above £26 a head will be profitable, as the fixed costs are already paid for. Tour operators will want the lowest price possible to ensure they can resell all 25 seats. Obviously, customers are unwilling to pay anything like the original £275 that was being asked, or they would have already booked with the airline itself. Let's say that after negotiating, the airline agrees to sell the seats to the tour operator at a net price of £150 each. The airline's budget is shown in Example 2.

Example 2 Costing a scheduled flight with tour operating support

Fixed cost	£27,000
135 passengers × £26*	£3,510
Cost of return flight	£30,510
Sell 110 tickets at £275 each	£30,250
Sell 25 tickets at £150 each	£3,750
Revenue	£34,000
Profit	£3,490

*assumes all 25 seats are sold by tour operator
Costing ignores APD or other taxes.

The airline will now be very happy: it can afford to lose some of its standard fare-paying passengers and will still be in profit. What is more, it takes no responsibility for marketing the 25 seats which the operator must sell. The operator takes on this burden, which may involve it in heavy selling costs, but as long as it sets a sensible price which will still deliver a profit for the company after paying overhead costs, the customer will still be able to buy seats which represent good value. A figure of £199 might be considered reasonable under these circumstances.

To ensure that tour operators do not poach existing passengers, airlines usually impose various conditions on the resale of the tickets. The main condition is that the tour operator must build the trip into a package, or inclusive tour, and publish a number of brochures to prove it. However, the airlines themselves may also try to sell other seats to seat brokers, whose role is merely to buy seats in bulk and sell these off to any market it can find.

As the tour operators build their markets, they can eventually decide that they will have enough customers to fill an aircraft, and can consider either part-chartering a plane with other operators, or even chartering a whole plane themselves. Eventually, they may be in a position to buy and operate their own airline to carry their customers, as do the leading tour operators in Britain and elsewhere on the Continent.

In exactly the same way, hoteliers attempt to use tour operators to fill their unsold bedrooms. They, too, have a high element of fixed costs in operating their properties, and are willing to provide substantial discounts to operators and others willing to commit themselves to buying rooms in bulk. As with airlines, once the fixed costs of the property have been covered by revenue, any price which more than pays for the variable cost will represent pure profit for the hotel, which will also then have the opportunity to sell extra services to their clients, such as drinks, entertainment and meals, whose profits will compensate for the low room rates that the operators have paid them. To this must be added the possibility that the operator, if the price is sufficiently attractive, may even be able to provide the hotel with guests during the winter period. This will mean that the hotel can retain staff year-round, possibly avoiding closing (closure means that no revenue is coming in at all, while the hotel will still attract costs for permanent staff, maintenance etc.). Hotels in the Mediterranean have found it difficult in the past to reach the North European market direct, and so have been delighted to have their marketing done for them by the tour operators in those countries. As a result, they came to depend largely, and in some cases entirely, on tour operators to sell their rooms.

In time, many larger operators started to run their own accommodation, but in practice this proved more difficult, and most operators eventually divested themselves of their overseas properties, preferring to sign contracts with overseas proprietors, often for the entire capacity of the hotel, and sometimes for several years in advance. The hoteliers' dependence upon these contracts and their inability to reach the marketplace in any other way made them overly dependent upon tour operators, which in turn used their dominant positions in the market to force down prices. The low profit levels achieved by the hoteliers meant cost-cutting in the level of service they provided, with self-service menus offering clients limited choice. The number of complaints rose as a result. Unfortunately, at least as far as British clients are concerned, there is little apparent willingness to pay higher prices for better standards of service.

The growth of independent websites is beginning to change this picture. Not only can hoteliers now market their product direct to the public at prices in competition with those they offer tour operators, they also have access to other intermediaries, like website accommodation providers. These include flight + hotel and accommodation-only on-line agencies, and both provide important booking and information opportunities for the hotel sector, which is gradually relinquishing its sales dependence on tour operators.

The move to booking on-line is also pushing back booking dates. A decade ago, 25 per cent of all summer holidays were booked before Christmas, and 60 per cent by the end of March. By 2004, only 15 per cent of bookings were taken before Christmas, seriously reducing operators' cash flow, and many bookings are now made in the run-up to departure date, to take advantage of late availability discounts. As clients become used to booking early again for the best deals on the no-frills airlines, tour operators are hoping that they will again adopt a similar policy in booking holidays.

The fastest growth has been in dynamic packaging – ABTA estimated that some 23 million dynamic packages were sold in 2004, compared with 19 million regular inclusive tours. Tour operators and their agents are adjusting to this new development, and setting up their own contacts on-line to produce dynamically packaged holidays for their customers.

The specialized roles of tour operators

The domestic operator

Tour operators fulfil a number of roles, and are not only concerned with carrying traffic out of the country, although this is the role with which we most frequently associate them. Operators also exist to organize package holidays domestically, that is, to a destination within the country in which the tourists reside. These businesses form a much smaller element of the travel and tourism industry, because it is relatively simple for tourists to make their own arrangements within their own country. In the past, it was uncommon to find a tour operator which simultaneously organized both domestic and foreign package holidays, although of course the originator of the package tour, Thomas Cook, started as a domestic holiday organizer and later expanded into foreign holidays. However, as concentration in the industry develops and competition becomes fiercer, the larger operators are tending to expand into the domestic market. Thomson Holidays, one of the leading tour operators in Britain, has been just one of several players marketing UK country cottages. The longest established domestic programmes are coach tours, operated by such well-known companies as Shearings and Wallace Arnold (now amalgamated as W A Shearings). More recently, the larger hotel chains in Britain also build their own package holiday programmes in order to help fill their rooms at weekends or in the off-peak seasons. The tourist boards in England, Wales and Scotland have strongly supported this development, and all three have at one time or another helped to coordinate programmes of commissionable domestic inclusive tours in brochures available through retail travel outlets.

Fragmentation is evident in the sector organizing domestic programmes. Most companies are relatively small in this sector, and few are members of ABTA, or indeed of any travel organization. Most deal direct with the public, and are therefore not involved in retailing through the trade.

The incoming operator

Those countries such as Spain and Greece which are predominantly destination countries, rather than generating countries, will have an incoming travel sector that is as important as the outgoing. Organizations specializing in handling incoming foreign holidaymakers have a rather different role to that of outbound operators. Some are merely ground handling agents, and their role may be limited to organizing hotel accommodation on behalf of an overseas tour operator, or greeting incoming visitors and transferring them to their hotels. Other companies, however, will offer a comprehensive range of services, which may include negotiating with coach companies and hotels to secure the best quotations for contracts, organizing special-interest holidays or study tours, or providing dining or theatre arrangements. In some cases, companies specialize according to the markets they serve, catering for the inbound Japanese or Israeli markets, for example.

In all, there are well over 300 tour companies in Britain which derive a major part of their revenue from handling incoming business. As with domestic operators, most of these are small companies, and more than a third are members of UKInbound, whose aim is to provide a forum for the exchange of information and ideas among members, to maintain standards of service and to act as a pressure group in dealing with other bodies in the UK who have a role to play in the country's tourism industry.

Incoming tour operators' services are marketed largely through the trade, and organizations work closely with public-sector bodies in marketing their services.

Other specialization

Many operators recognize that their strengths can lie in specializing in some particular aspect of operating. Some outbound operators choose to specialize according to the *mode of transport* by which their clients will travel. Although our earlier example was based on air travel, other companies focus on coach transport, some (especially those involved in providing camping holidays abroad) organize package holidays for their clients which enable them to use their own private cars, and some have chosen to specialize in holidays using the railways. Ferry companies developed their own package tour programmes to promote sea travel using their services (although in recent years the British ferry operators have preferred to divest themselves of these activities in order to allow specialist operators to organize the programmes on their behalf). Naturally, coach operators and railway companies have also sought to boost their carryings by building inclusive tours around their own forms of transport.

Finally, specialization among tour operators can be based on the markets they serve or the products they develop. The most common distinction is between, on the one hand, the *mass-market* operators, whose product – typically the 'sun, sea, sand' holiday – is designed to appeal to a very broad segment of the market, and, on the other hand, the *specialist* operator, which targets a particular niche market. By trying to distinguish their products from those of their competitors, the niche market operators are not in such intense competition as are those in the mass market, and the product is less price sensitive as a result.

In a few instances, operators have a foot in both camps – skiing holidays providing one example. Many companies specializing in this field have a charter programme through the winter using major hotels, while others offer entirely bespoke packages, restricting themselves to a limited number of small properties, and in some cases not even arranging flights, which they leave their clients to book separately.

Specialists have a number of advantages over mass-market companies in the marketplace. Most carry small numbers of tourists, and can therefore use smaller accommodation units, such as the small, family-run hotels in Greece which are popular with many tourists, but are too small to interest the larger operators. As the specialist companies generally use scheduled carriers and do not have the level of commitment to a particular destination that their larger colleagues have, they can be more flexible, switching to other destinations if the market sours for any reason. Staff can generally be expected to have a better knowledge of the products, and as the market is less price sensitive, the intense price competition found in the mass marketplace is absent, allowing companies to make reasonable profits. However, if they are successful, there is always the danger that one of the larger operators will be attracted to their market and either undercut them or make an offer that is attractive enough to persuade them to sell out. This has been a feature of the UK tour operating market in recent years, with

Figure 16.2
The specialist
inclusive tour:
safari vehicles
experience
congestion in
Kenya's wildlife
parks

(Photographed by the author)

the four largest brands buying out medium-sized niche operators and fitting them into their own specialist products division (sometimes, later dropping the brand altogether, or integrating it into their own mainstream brands).

Example   First Choice Holidays

First Choice, as one of the Big Four operators in the UK, has recognized the growth of specialist holidays at the expense of the traditional sun-sea-sand packages. It has also taken into account the strong growth in dynamic packaging and tailor-made programmes. The company has undergone a period of expansion, in part by taking over existing small specialist operators, and has reorganized its business by forming four separate divisions:

■ activity holidays
■ specialist holidays (including Meon Villas, and Hayes and Jarvis)
■ on-line destination services
■ mainstream holidays.

The company's tour operations, at the time of writing, comprise:

First Choice Holidays
First Choice Flights
Unijet Holidays

Unijets Flights
Sunstart
2wentys
Sunquest
Suncars
First4Extras
Hayes & Jarvis
Sovereign
Meon Villas
Longshot Golf
Citalia
Sunsail
Sunsail Clubs
Stardust Platinum
Crown Blue Line
Connoisseur/Emerald Star
Exodus
Waymark
Trek America
First Choice Ski
Flexiski/Eclipse Direct
Trips Worldwide
Magic of the Orient.

Source: *Travel Weekly*, 26 January 2004 and author's research

Many companies seek to specialize by geographic destination. However, this can be a high-risk decision, as exemplified by the collapse of markets due to factors affecting one country or region. The SARS outbreak in 2003 caused some operators to withdraw their entire China programmes, while the unstable political situation in the Middle East has frequently affected operators specializing in holidays to Israel and neighbouring Arab countries. An extreme example is that of Yugotours. When civil war fractured Yugoslavia in the 1990s, the company, which specialized almost exclusively in that destination, was forced not only to change its destinations, but even its brand name, in order to build a new market. It failed to re-establish itself, and the brand disappeared.

Specialization by market is common. Some companies choose to appeal to a particular age group, as do Saga Holidays, which has for many years been market leader in holidays for the over-50s. The company now faces a challenge from Travelsphere's takeover in 2004 of Page and Moy which, with four million customers, is targeting the over-45s to widen the potential market. Others target the younger markets, as do Club 18–30 and 2wenties. The singles market – fast growing, as social changes increase the proportion of divorced people in our society – is also served by specialists such as Solo Holidays. Other operators specialize by gender: WalkingWomen, as the name implies, offers walking tours for females only. Targets are becoming increasingly tightly focused, with recent additions to the marketplace targeting one-parent families, as do companies like Small Families, or One Parent Family Holidays (a non-profit organization). Obviously, there will be ample opportunity to specialize according to the specific interests, activities or hobbies of clients, and tour companies have been established to cater for such diverse needs as those of vegetarians, those with an interest in various cultural activities, golfing or angling enthusiasts, or even such highly specialized activities as textile weaving. One company which has proved itself highly successful in specific targeting is Cycling for Softies, which caters for tourists interested in using bicycles as a mode of transport but still seeking comfortable and well-equipped overnight accommodation (see Chapter 14). This company's main focus is on travel in France, and it is therefore specializing both in destination and market served.

Activity and adventure holidays are one of the fastest growing areas (Mintel estimated that 15 million were sold in 2003, with three-quarters taken in Britain).

Example   **Adventure holidays by motorcycle**

H-C Travel is an example of a company specializing by mode of transport. Founded in 1994, the company claims to be the world's number one agency for holidays by motorcycle, offering trips on several continents, as well as tailor-made holidays. Examples include two-week biker treks on Royal Enfield bikes between Kathmandu and Lhasa across the Mongolian steppes, while others include journeys across the Moroccan Sahara Desert dunes or to Yellowstone, Grand Canyon and Death Valley National Parks in the USA.

Website: www.hctravel.com

The role of air brokers

One other role should be examined here; that of those who specialize in providing airline seats in bulk to other tour operators. These specialists are known as *air brokers*, or where their business is principally concerned with consolidating flights on behalf of operators that have not achieved good load factors for their charters, they are termed *consolidators*. As with other operators, they must also now obtain Air Travel Organizers' Licences (ATOLs) from the CAA in order to operate.

Brokers negotiate directly with airlines, buying seats in bulk and arranging to sell these, either in smaller bulk blocks or even individually, to operators or travel agents. They provide the airlines, especially those companies which may find it difficult to obtain good load factors on some legs of their operations, with a good distribution service, and in return the airlines are willing to offer very low net rates to fill their remaining seats. The brokers put their own mark-up on the seats and take on the responsibility of marketing them for whatever price they can get. Their operations led to the demise of the former 'bucket shop' operators who performed a similar function but often infringed IATA regulations in 'dumping' tickets at discounted prices on the market. Deregulation on an international scale has now virtually eradicated the former illegal operations and made ticket discounting 'respectable'. Many mark-ups are very low, the broker making money on the huge turnover of seats they achieve, and in short- to medium-term investments in the money market (a source of profits shared by operators and airlines alike).

On-line intermediaries reflect the growth in modern air package brokerage, with companies such as ebookers and Opodo becoming major players in the field.

The British tour-operating scene

The structure of the outbound tour-operating business

In late 2005 there were approximately 895 licensed tour operators in the UK who are members of ABTA. However, the market is dominated by a small number of large operators, and the process of concentration into the hands of this small minority is only now beginning to stabilize and show the first signs of a decline. The four leading operators – TUI, MyTravel, Thomas Cook Group (JMC) and First Choice together held some 49 per cent of the market in 2005, based on applications for ATOL bonding. While still a significant proportion of the total ATOL-bonded IT market, it nevertheless represents a substantial fall over earlier years. Both TUI (which took over the Thomson Holidays Group) and Thomas Cook are German-owned, while the fifth largest operator, Cosmos, is in Swiss hands. This trend to horizontal integration and international concentration is also evident in other European countries. The second characteristic in the industry has been a trend to vertical integration, with the largest companies owning and/or controlling their own airlines, ground-handling agents at airports, electronic distribution channels and retail travel agencies. This trend has been slower to take effect on the Continent, at least as far as airline and tour operator links are concerned, but this picture has changed as British companies came under control of their Continental counterparts, a symptom of the third characteristic in the sector, that of internationalization of the industry throughout Europe.

The initial phases of concentration can be traced to the rapid expansion which took place in the tour operating business after the 1960s in Britain, but occurred slightly later in other parts of Western Europe and North America. Leisure activities, and holidays in particular, were seen at that time as substantial growth areas for the future, encouraging many new companies to come into the business, while those already established expanded quickly to maintain their dominance in the field. This led to a cycle in which many companies collapsed, owing to three main problems:

1   growing too fast, over-borrowing to finance the expansion and in some cases lacking the management expertise to operate larger companies;
2   making insufficient profit to survive, in the face of intense competition which drove down prices;
3   being hit by external problems such as rises in the price of fuel, political unrest in some of the destination countries, and economic recession at home. In 1974, all three of these factors occurred in a single year in the UK market.

This has been a pattern for the industry throughout the past 40 years. Even as far back as 1964, the industry's first major collapse – that of Fiesta Tours – led to tighter controls being imposed on members of ABTA. In 1974, the failure of the leading company of its day, Court Line and its subsidiary Clarksons Holidays, resulted in 50,000 passengers being stranded abroad at the height of the summer holiday season, as a direct outcome of the factors outlined above. In 1991, the International Leisure Group, owners of Britain's then second-largest tour operator Intasun, was brought down by a combination of recession at home, the weakness of the pound, cut-throat pricing against leading operator Thomson, and over-ambitious expansion, especially in the efforts of the company to develop scheduled services for its charter airline Air Europe. The collapse in 1995 of Best Travel, another company within the top seven, emphasized the continuing instability of the tour operating business, and encouraged further mergers and takeovers.

Most UK operators are very small companies, with perhaps only the top 40 being of any real significance in the market. Table 16.1 provides details of the largest companies, in terms of passenger numbers authorized by the CAA.

Although the picture of actual market shares changes rapidly throughout the year, on the basis of 28.3 million ATOL licences granted for the year ending June 2005, TUI would have held around 17 per cent of the UK market, Thomas Cook Group and the MyTravel Group around 11 per cent each and First Choice 10 per cent. In 2004/5 the top ten operators, all members of the Federation of Tour Operators (FTO), accounted for some 11 million tourists, approximately 65 per cent of the total outbound package travel[1]. This has to some extent alleviated earlier concern over oligopolistic concentration of the top four in the package tour sector.

Accurately judging potential demand when seeking seat and room allocations for the coming year is always difficult. Companies are often over-ambitious in their estimates of market share, with the result that they are obliged to offload their surplus at whatever price they can get during the season. This constant imbalance between supply and demand places severe pressures on profits in the industry, which have been meagre for the past two decades.

There is an unspoken belief among the larger operators that low-price strategies will eventually force out of the market the smaller and less efficient companies, leaving rich pickings to be shared among the remaining contenders. However, there is little

Table 16.1 Passengers authorized by CAA-bonded tour licences, 2005 (000s)
(all figures for the year ending June 2005)

TUI Group	4,762
Thomas Cook Group	3,158
MyTravel Group	3,110
First Choice Holidays Group	2,861
Cosmos Group	1,082
InterActive Corporation Group (Expedia)	851
Cendant Corporation Group	809
Excel Airways Group	773
Gold Medal Travel Group	675
Lastminute Group	602

Source: CAA figures/*Travel Weekly*

evidence from previous experience to support this view. As leading companies like Horizon and Intasun have been absorbed or collapsed, so others have risen to take their place. The demise of ILG resulted in the formation of four new tour-operating companies, each intent on picking up market share from their antecedent. While only two of these – Sunworld and Club 18–30 – were to survive the recession of the early 1990s, the growth of the former company in particular (now absorbed into the JMC brand), and subsequent rise in market share by others within the top ten, tend to suggest there is more scope for competition at the top than might have appeared to be the case. This does not refute the evidence that key market share tends to remain at any one time with three or four of the leading players.

Efforts have been made in recent years by the smaller operators to regain the high ground, by impressing on the public their more personal levels of service and greater expertise, and to distance themselves from the mass-market operators. The Association of Independent Tour Operators (AITO), with a membership at the time of writing of some 150, works closely with the independent travel agents to sell distinctive products. The appearance of TIPTO (the Truly Independent Professional Travel Organization) in 1999, launched to offset the directional selling by large agency chains of leading operators' products, reflects the concern felt among the smaller companies in the industry about the growing concentration of power in the hands of the leading companies. The new organization, currently boasting 21 members, gave as its aim at the launch to deal exclusively with a selection of around 1,000 independent travel agents. Other consortia like Advantage, Global and Worldchoice, meanwhile, have been busy recruiting independent agencies in order to build negotiating strength when dealing collectively with principals. The recent merger of these three into a single company, Triton Travel Group, will strengthen the hands of the consortia when negotiating with principals. Profit squeezes throughout the tour operating sector in the dying years of the twentieth century and beginning of the next led to frenetic activity in restructuring, collapse, takeovers and mergers, but this pattern has been followed by a calmer period, in which consolidation has become more typical of the on-line agencies than the traditional operators.

A short résumé of the most significant of these events since 1990 will be helpful here.

1990

- Owners Abroad undertakes a staged purchase of the Redwing Holidays group from BA (until 1990–91)
- ILG buys Sol Holidays, and from Granada the Quest group of brand name holidays
- Airtours forms Eurosites camping division.

1991

- ILG collapses.

1992

- Novotours, formed after the ILG collapse, itself collapses
- Midland Bank sells Thomas Cook to German operator LTU (14 per cent) and German bank WestDeutsche Landesbank (WestLB) (86 per cent)

- Dan-Air collapses
- Airtours buys Pickfords retail chain.

1993

- Riva Holidays, the second company founded following the collapse of ILG, also goes out of business
- Formation of Inspirations Holidays, which establishes a strategic alliance with Best Travel, forming Goldcrest Aviation. Inspirations develops joint venture with A T Mays chain to set up travel agencies
- Airtours attempts unsuccessfully to take over Owners Abroad, but acquires Aspro with its airline Inter European Airways and the Hogg Robinson retail chain, which it merges with Pickfords to form new agency Going Places
- Owners Abroad establishes a working relationship with Thomas Cook, which buys a 21 per cent share of the company.

1994

- Thomson Holidays acquires its first domestic operation, Country Holidays, followed by purchase of Blakes Country Holidays and English Country Cottages
- Airtours acquires Scandinavian Leisure Group and Spanair from SAS
- Owners Abroad establishes International Travel Holdings in Canada, operating under the brand Signature. The company is renamed and relaunched as First Choice Holidays; old brands Tjaereborg, Martin Rooks and Sunfare are eliminated, and new direct-sell brand Eclipse launched
- Yugotours and Ultimate Holidays collapse.

1995

- Best Travel, Britain's seventh largest operator, collapses, the biggest failure since ILG. Other collapses in the same year include Vilmar Travel, draining the Air Travel Trust Fund
- Inspirations buys the charter carrier Caledonian from British Airways
- Formation of Flying Colours Group, which purchases Club 18–30 and links this with its Sunset brand
- Airtours buys Canadian operator Sunquest Vacations
- Inspirations buys 28 branches of John Hilary Travel, giving it control over 88 A T Mays retail travel branches.
- Superbreak brought by Eurocamp (later becoming Holidaybreak).

1996

- Collapse of the Flight Company and Go-Air plunges the ATTF further into the red. Other collapses this year include All Jamaica, Sunstyle, Globespan and its airline Excalibur Airways

- Thomas Cook buys Sunworld (which also controls a Canadian operator) and Time Off
- Carnival Cruises, the leading US cruise company, buys 29.6 per cent of Airtours. Airtours buys Scandinavian company Spies.

1997

- Monopolies and Mergers Commission gives green light for expansion of takeovers and mergers
- Flying Colours launches its own airline
- Suntours, specialist tour operator to Turkey, and domestic operator Rainbow Holidays collapse (the latter later rejuvenated by First Choice Holidays)
- Airtours buys Sun International, Belgium's largest operator and owner of British operators Cresta and Bridge Travel Group, and also Suntrips, Californian tour operator
- Thomson Holidays buys specialist operator Austravel, Crystal International Travel Group, Jetsave and Fritidsresor (Sweden's second largest operator)
- Carlson Group buys Inspirations Holidays.

1998

- Thomson floats on stock exchange, buys Simply Travel, Magic Travel, domestic operator Blakes Holidays
- Airtours buys Panorama Holidays, Direct Holidays, and a minority stake in Germany's Frosch Touristik including airline and operator FTi (balance bought one year later)
- First Choice buys Hayes and Jarvis, Unijet, UK operator Rainbow, plus two regional travel agency chains Bakers Dolphin and Intatravel, with plans to build a nation-wide chain under the brand Travel Choice
- Thomas Cook buys majority stake in Carlson's UK operations, including tour operator Inspirations, Caledonian Airways and Carlson WorldChoice retail chain. Cook's Sunworld Division buys Flying Colours Group, including brands Flying Colours, Sunset Holidays and Club 18–30
- Eurocamp buys rival camping operator Keycamp Holidays.

1999

- Thomson buys Headwater Holidays, Spanish Harbour Holidays, Travel House (retailer and direct sell operator), and retail chains Sibbald and Callers Pegasus. Sets up no-frills operator Just. Fritidsresor buys leading Polish company Scan Holidays and Norway's Via Group (retail chain which includes operator Prisma Tours)
- Airtours launches hostile bid for First Choice, blocked by European Commission
- First Choice buys Sunsail Holidays and Meon Travel. Unsuccessful effort to merge with Kuoni
- Kuoni buys long-haul specialist Voyages Jules Verne

- Thomas Cook rebrands its main operating and airline divisions as JMC, drops brands Sunworld and Sunset, and integrates Inspirations into programme. Integrates Carlson WorldChoice into its retail operations under Thomas Cook banner. Establishes Thomas Cook Direct (direct-sell operation) and Thomas Cook Plus (hypermarket chain)
- Preussag, owners of Germany's leading operators, takes controlling interest in Thomas Cook
- Eurocamp rebrands as Holidaybreak.

2000

- Preussag (owner of Germany's biggest operator, TUI Group) takes over Thomson Holidays, and prepares to sell its 51 per cent share in Thomas Cook to satisfy the European Commissioners
- Airtours acquires long-haul specialist Jetset, Manos Holidays (integrated with Panorama to form Panorama Manos), Sunway Travel (coach operator), and 50 per cent of Holetur Club (hotels)
- First Choice forms strategic alliance with Royal Caribbean Cruises, which takes 20 per cent of the company. First Choice also buys Ten Tours with operations in France, Germany, Austria, Belgium and Spain, and UK company Sunquest. Further purchases include Spanish company Barcelo Group's travel interests, with hotels in Spain and a stake in Air Europa, and Swiss company Taurus Tours
- Germany's second largest operator, C&N Touristik, owner of NUR brand, buys Thomas Cook from Carlson Corporation. This becomes the Thomas Cook Group after sale to Lufthansa and department store chain KarstadtQuelle
- Holidaybreak buys Rainbow Holidays from First Choice, integrates and later drops the brand
- Germany's third largest operator, Rewe, acquires LTU and DER, integrating these into a single company holding 22 per cent of the German market
- Thomson Holidays sells its Holiday Cottages group to US-owned Cedant, the world's biggest accommodation franchiser.

2001

- Thomas Cook and British Airways Holidays merge their long-haul scheduled tour operating interests, claiming 16 per cent of the market, close to that of market leader Kuoni
- First Choice buys Sun Holidays, chain of travel agencies in Canada, also Citalia
- Thomas Cook forms a marketing agreement with website operator lastminute.com, also launches a joint venture company, Accoladia, with British Airways
- Long-haul specialists Travelbag and Bridge the World merge
- Carnival sells its 25 per cent stake in Airtours
- Superbreak buys Rainbow Holidays from First Choice. Former Golden Rail Holidays becomes Hotelbreaks.

2002

- First Choice sells its Spanish chain of travel agencies, buys adventure holiday company Exodus
- TUI changes name from Preussag, buys Nouvelles Frontières, leading French tour operator
- MyTravel sells Eurosites to Holidaybreak.

2003

- Thomas Cook relegates its JMC brand to summer holidays, with the brand to focus on family holidays. JMC airline rebranded as Thomas Cook. The company and BA drop their Accoladia venture, Cook replacing it with Thomas Cook signature
- MyTravel financial crisis leads it to sell US tour operator interests, cruise interests, Frosch Touristik in Germany and Ving and Itaka operations in Poland
- Travelocity buys World Choice Travel from MyTravel
- TUI launches Budget Holidays brand as direct sell via Internet only, aimed at the young market
- ebookers buys Travelbag.

2004

- Holidaybreak drops Eurosites name to focus on its established brands Keycamp and direct sell Eurocamp operations
- TUI buys Coventry Airport to launch its Thomsonfly.com operation (later resold). They sell 21 TravelHouse shops, half of the branches under this name
- E-travel company lastminute.com enters the high street retailing market, buying First Option, 21 travel agencies at airports and railway stations. It also buys OTC
- Cendant buys Gullivers Travel and its subsidiary accommodation supplier Octopus Travel. The company also buys on-line agencies ebookers and Orbitz
- Amadeus takes a majority stake in Opodo
- First Choice buys US company Studentcity.com
- Travelsphere buys Page & Moy.

2005

- Opodo buys French operator Karavel (owner of Promovacances)
- Travelocity (owned by GDS SABRE) buys lastminute.com
- Advantage, WorldChoice and Global consortia amalgamate into a single body, Triton Travel Group.

Integration in the industry

Nothing spells out more clearly than this list the rapid changes that have taken place and the competitive environment within the industry. Mergers and takeovers became commonplace, coupled with an increasingly international perspective in the tour operating business, as British and other European operators look abroad for opportunities to expand and dominate the market through purchasing power. The leading operators' attempts to enter the difficult and highly competitive North American markets have tended to prove abortive, although the rationale behind the move was clear: a desire to spread the seasonal flow of traffic, thus obtaining better year-round usage of aircraft. Risk would also be reduced by ensuring a more even spread of revenue between markets in North America, the UK and mainland Europe.

Even with much greater levels of concentration found in the late twentieth century, the Monopolies and Mergers Commission (later, the Competition Commission) has tended to accept that *horizontal* integration was not against the public interest, given that competition still ensured prices were kept down. After the Commission gave the industry the green light for further mergers in 1997, concentration in the hands of the big four operators rose sharply, but later tapered off, with other operators, as we have seen earlier, still managing to increase their own market share at the expense of some of the leading brands. Concentration now appears to be directed towards the e-tailing intermediaries.

The EU appeared at one point to take a stronger stand against integration, and when Airtours (as MyTravel was then known) attempted to take over First Choice in 1999, the European Commission initially stepped in to block the merger. However, this decision was later reversed by the EU Court of First Instance, suggesting that the way would now be open for further horizontal integration among the leading companies (although MyTravel's subsequent financial difficulties appears to have ended any prospect of their expansion in the immediate future).

The trend to *vertical* integration between tour operators, their suppliers and retailers has been a matter of greater concern, both to the UK Government and to the EU Commissioners. In Britain (and to a lesser extent in other European countries) operators have sought to maintain control over their transport supply in particular, usually through direct ownership of an airline. Operators need to be carrying around 400,000 passengers a year to secure the critical mass that will make it economically viable to consider establishing their own airline. This helps them to control overall standards of the package, increase overall profitability within the group, and at the same time ensure they maintain a ready supply of air seats and hotel rooms when demand is heavy (although operators often take the precaution of obtaining some of their seats through other airlines. This will enable them, when demand falls, to retain their own aircraft seats while 'dumping' other carriers' unwanted seats). There are further operational and marketing advantages in owning and controlling take-off and landing slots. However, pressure on profits in recent years has caused a number of large operators to view leasing as a more attractive proposition to purchasing aircraft.

Vertical integration *downwards* into ownership of retail outlets poses a threat of a different character. Once a tour operator has control over its own retailing chain, it can move towards *directional selling*. This implies that travel agencies owned by large operators can be encouraged to direct sales towards their parent companies at the expense of competitors. All four leading operators in Britain own their own retail outlets (all now bearing the names of the operators apart from Going Places, the travel agency division of MyTravel). Thomson, which changed the name of its retail arm from Lunn Poly to that of the parent company in 2004, claimed the move resulted in a substantial increase in sales for its own products.

The Monopolies and Mergers Commission was asked to undertake an investigation into vertical integration in the industry in 1996. They evaluated:

1   Whether agents under the control of tour operators sold those operators' programmes in preference to others, and whether they therefore offered the public biased advice on the purchase of inclusive tours.

2   Whether vertically integrated companies controlled and fixed prices of their programmes.

3   Whether these agents failed to advise their customers of their links with tour operators.

4   To what extent agents insisted that customers buy their own company's insurance policies (often at inflated prices), in order to benefit from the discounts offered on the holidays they sold.

5   Whether agents were removing, or threatening to remove, from display brochures of independent agents if commissions payable were deemed insufficient.

The MMC report recommended separation of insurance from discounting, the abolition of the status of 'most favoured customer' and that tour operator ownership of retail chains should be made clear. By 1998, companies were being informed that they could not insist that customers buy the recommended insurances, but no further ruling was imposed until 2000, when the Department of Trade and Industry, under the Foreign Package Holidays Order 2000, ruled that agents owned by a tour operator and controlling more than 5 per cent of the package tour market would in future have to publicly identify their links with suppliers, both in promotional material and in their shop displays. However, no steps have been taken to reduce directional selling by agents of their own companies' products. Thomas Cook has not been obliged to follow the new ruling, based on the curious logic that the retailer was the parent company in the relationship; neither are the links between agency consortia and operators required to be made public. The Order makes no ruling about identifying links where selling involves call centres, websites and teletext, even though these methods of distribution are growing rapidly. In these respects, the ruling has made no progress in satisfying the complaints of the independent operators and agents about unfair trading.

Because of the rapid changes taking place in the UK industry, any description of its current structure in this text is bound to be no more than a snapshot at a given moment in time, and may well be subject to modification even before this book gets into print. The picture at the time of writing is illustrated in Table 16.2, and clearly reveals the extent of integration between the leading operators, charter (and, innovatively, scheduled) airlines and retail chains in the UK.

It is significant that of the leading operators in the UK, only Cosmos has not yet developed a retail chain. Given the direction of the industry in recent years, this could be seen as a major weakness in marketing, but others would argue that this policy wins the company support among the independent agents, and allows them greater flexibility in their use of websites rather than retail agents to promote their products.

Table 16.2 Integration between the UK's leading operators, charter airlines and travel agents (mid-2005)

Airline	Tour operator	Travel agent
ThomsonFly	Thomson Holidays	Thomson Travel
MyTravel Airways ⎫	MyTravel, Airtours	Going Places
MyTravelLite ⎬		
First Choice Airways	First Choice Holidays	First Choice Travel
Thomas Cook Airlines	Thomas Cook, JMC Holidays	Thomas Cook Travel
Monarch Airlines ⎫	Cosmos Holidays ⎫	
Monarch Scheduled ⎬	Avro ⎬	

Tour operating within the European Union

The process of integration within the UK is paralleled to a large extent on the Continent, and other European companies have been actively purchasing holiday companies abroad, particularly within Britain. Investment in the tour operating business by foreign companies is nothing new (Cosmos has always been a Swiss-owned company) but as we have noted already, both Thomson and Thomas Cook are German-owned and, until sold recently, the US Carnival Corporation had a minority shareholding in MyTravel.

Germany leads Europe, both in terms of the number of package holidaymakers carried (36 million in 2004) and the strength of the industry. Composition and ownership of the leading operators in the country are complicated, although traditionally a significant share of the industry has been publicly owned through the states and the regional authorities, which control the savings banks, which in turn invested heavily in tour operating businesses. This pattern is now changing, as the banks divest themselves of their travel interests (WestDeutsche Landesbank sold their 34 per cent stake in TUI in 2004), and as the economic downturn in the country hit travel along with other sectors. TUI, owner of Thomson Holidays, is the leading tour brand in Germany, having sold just under 7 million packages in that country in the year 2003/4. The company owned 1,360 travel agencies in that year, and cooperated with a further 8,240. Their national flight operations, under the Hapagfly banner, controlled 35 aircraft, with a further 15 operating for low-cost carrier Hapag-Lloyd Express. The group as a whole served over 18 million clients across the world in 2003, and operated a total of 118 aircraft. The company took over France's second leading operator, Nouvelles Frontières, together with its airline Corse Air, in 2002. It also holds a 50 per cent stake in Spanish hotel company RIU Hotels (Palma de Mallorca), which in turn owns 5 per cent of TUI.

The second major operator in Germany is the Thomas Cook Group, formerly C&N Touristik, which was formed in 1998 as a joint venture between German air carrier Lufthansa and the Karstadt/Quelle department store organization. A third major player is Rewe, a leading supermarket chain which controls tour operator LTU-Touristik, a 40 per cent share of LTU's airline, the tour operator DERtour and some 2,570 DER retail travel agencies. In Germany, the control over travel agencies by the big players has tended to squeeze out the independents, threatening those operators without significant retail outlets.

German operators also dominate the market in Belgium, the Netherlands and Luxembourg, while MyTravel and TUI largely control operators in the Scandinavian countries. In France and Italy, there has been less foreign investment, and France's leading operator, Club Méditerranée, is regaining its position after a period of indecision. The Swiss long-haul operator Kuoni is not only the leading player in its own country, but has a strong presence in other European countries, including the UK.

As in Britain, all these operators have recognized the importance of building their numbers in order to buy at the lowest price and control the markets. Transnational mergers will become increasingly common, limited only by the anti-monopoly forces of the European Commission. Evidence of the strength of buying power among leading Continental operators can be seen in the comparative pricing structure between tour operators in Britain and on the Continent; where formerly it could pay for foreign residents to fly to Britain to begin their package holiday, there is a growing number of instances where the reverse is now the case, and standard packages can be bought at substantially cheaper prices by British customers if bought abroad.

Economic forces in tour operating

Three factors were at work in the second half of the twentieth century which encouraged the growth of the package holiday in Europe:

1   The expansion of leisure time in the developed countries.
2   This was accompanied by greater discretionary income in those countries.
3   Package holiday costs were low, both in themselves and in comparison to similar holidays in the home country. This was due to relatively lower costs for accommodation and food in the Mediterranean countries, reductions in air transport costs due to advancing technology, liberalization of air transport regulations, the introduction of year-round operations covering both summer and winter seasons, and bulk purchasing by tour operators.

The operators, recognizing the strong growth potential in the overseas holiday market, sought to expand their market shares while at the same time attempting to increase the total size of the market, by encouraging those who traditionally took domestic holidays to travel abroad. To achieve this, they slashed prices. Large companies used their purchasing muscle to drive down suppliers' prices (at some cost to quality in a number of cases); they introduced cheap, 'no frills' holidays through subsidiary companies such as Thomson's Skytours – and more recently, the same company's Just, a programme which offers no transfers, no in-flight meals and no resort representatives. Arguably, this new offering can barely be considered a package, in the traditional sense of the word. However, budget-conscious C_2D consumers (as defined in Chapter 4) have been attracted by such packages, although dissatisfaction levels are likely to be higher. Finally, profit margins were trimmed. Thomson and its leading competitors, each determined not to be undersold, engaged in the periodic repricing of their holiday programme during the selling season. Thomson, from 1983 onwards, introduced the strategy of brochure reissues with cheaper prices, and this became a regular feature of the tour operating price war; but operators always held to the hope that given the right conditions, prices could be increased rather than decreased in the later editions. Holiday prices during the period remained relatively stationary as a result, while real buying power increased greatly.

While these moves certainly expanded the market, over-optimistic forecasts of traffic growth also led to surpluses in supply; capacity generally exceeded demand each year, and operators were then forced into offloading seats at bargain-basement prices (2005 appears to have marked the first change of direction in this regard, as three of the four leading operators in fact reduced their capacity over the previous year). This factor was a key one in the growth of late bookings. Traditionally, bookings for package holidays occurred in the weeks immediately following Christmas, allowing operators more time to balance supply and demand, and aiding their cash flow – deposits paid by clients in January would be invested and earn interest for the company until its bills had to be paid, which in some cases could be as late as September or October. Demanding full balances eight to ten weeks before departure proved similarly lucrative for operators. Holidaymakers soon came to realize, however, that if they refrained from booking holidays until much nearer their time of travel, they could snap up late booking bargains. The development of computerized reservations systems allowed operators to update their late availability opportunities quickly, putting cheap offers on the market at very short notice, which made late bookings convenient as well as attractively priced. The past decade has seen the introduction of on-line booking, with websites accessible by both retail agents and the general public. This has promoted the attraction of late booking, further reducing the gap between deposits and final payments from months to a matter of weeks, or even days. Uncertainty about the forward booking position has also made tour operations management more difficult. Operators therefore set about reversing this trend, with a policy of *fluid pricing*. First introduced by Thomson Holidays in 1996 and soon copied by the other leading operators, this entailed offering holidays in the brochures at different prices, with high discounts for early booking and reduced discounts as the time of the holiday approached. Some operators (and their agents) have even quoted prices above the standard brochure price, where demand was sufficiently strong, although the legality of this move has been questioned as contrary to the Consumer Protection Act. Not surprisingly, this led to a good deal of dissatisfaction among clients who had booked earlier at higher prices. Starting in the late 1990s, there was a tendency among operators to launch brochures for the upcoming year at an ever earlier date, resulting at times in agents having to find room for brochures covering three different periods – summer and winter of the current year, and summer of the following year. More recently, some sense prevailed, and a more rational approach has been apparent. There is evidence, however, that early launches did benefit operators by boosting sales.

The long-haul market

The tendency for all mass-market operators to focus on low price rather than quality or value for money led to this type of tour moving down-market. As it did so, tourists at the top end of the market, particularly those who had travelled frequently, began to travel independently more frequently, and to more distant destinations. The demand for long-haul packages has expanded much faster than that for short-haul, even during periods of restricted growth. More than 20 per cent of all holidays are now taken to long-haul destinations annually, and this is forecast to increase. The United States, with its particular appeal of Disney World Florida, New Zealand and Australia have all witnessed mass market long-haul growth, while Thailand and Bali have successfully sold the idea of long-haul sun-sea-sand holidays. South Africa, India and the Middle East (notably Dubai), even Cuba in the Caribbean have all seen substantial growth in visitors from Western Europe. All of these increases can be directly ascribed to the huge drop in air fares relative to other prices in the past decade.

The market leader for long-haul packages is Swiss-owned Kuoni Travel, with about a fifth of the market in the UK, with the lead operators also competing strongly for these destinations with their specialist divisions.

Seat-only sales

The figures for inclusive tours by air (AIT) given in Table 16.3 also contain seat-only sales, in which passengers, although ostensibly buying a package, are in fact only using the air-travel portion of the tour. This type of 'package' was originally introduced by operators to fill surplus charter seats; technically, to abide by international regulations, some form of basic accommodation had to be included in the package, although this was seldom used. After January 1993, EU legislation swept away the requirement to book accommodation within EU destinations. Seat-only sales have now become an important feature of the travel industry, as growing numbers of holidaymakers are either prepared to find their own accommodation abroad, or are seeking flights to carry them to their second homes, time-share apartments or friends' accommodation on the Continent. Even business travellers seeking to save money during the recession are known to have made use of this facility. Subsequently, seat-only packages also became available on block-booked seats on scheduled aircraft, offering the additional benefits for clients of no consolidations and daytime flights. Sales peaked at around 20 per cent of the total AIT market, and have now stabilized. The distinction between scheduled and charter has shrunk with the introduction of the no-frills airlines, and as we have seen, lead operators have launched their own budget airlines such as MyTravelLite, while the Cosmos group has even launched its own scheduled airline.

Recent developments

There is little let-up in the volatility of the tour operating business. Political conflicts in the Balkans and Turkey at the end of the last century, wars in the Gulf and fears of terrorism which were heightened after the 9/11 tragedy, the Bali and Madrid bombings, and the London and Sharm el-Sheikh bombings of July 2005 have all unsettled global travel and tour operations. Natural disasters like the earthquake and subsequent tsunami in the Far East at the end of 2004 similarly reduced long-haul travel to the affected regions severely. In spite of this catalogue of crises, the sector has shown itself in the past to be resilient, and while in the short term cancelled bookings and hotel reservations would impact severely on these destinations, recovery from even the worst disasters would normally be expected within a year of the event.

Table 16.3 Package tours by air, 1990–2004 (000s)

Year	Total AITs
1990	11.4
1991	10.6
1992	12.6
1993	13.3
1994	15.2
1995	15.3
1996	13.9
1997	15.4
1998	17.4
1999	15.0
2000	16.4
2001	16.9
2002	16.7
2003	16.4
2004	16.5

Source: IPS/Business Monitor MQ6
NB Time series analysis cannot be applied due to changes in methodology in 1999.

European operators have sought new locations to develop, where hotel capacity was cheap and readily available, as traditional resorts began to price themselves out of the market. First, the more remote areas of Greece, then Turkey became boom destinations for the British seeking sun at rock-bottom prices. The evidence suggests that the inclusive tour market for traditional 'sun, sea, sand' destinations has now probably peaked, with now less than half of the population choosing a package when buying an overseas holiday.

Second-home ownership by the British, whether in France, Spain or Florida, has also had a marked effect on patterns of holiday-taking. Many owners disappear from the IT market, tending to take most, if not all, of their overseas holidays in their own properties. However, this has fuelled the growth of the no-frills airlines, and the benefits of travel are by no means lost to other sectors of the industry as second-home owners purchase local products and services at their destinations, invite friends and others to their homes, rent out their properties either privately or through operators, and participate in home exchange opportunities around the world.

Over 70 per cent of the UK population has now had a foreign holiday at some point in their lives, a figure which has shown little change over time. Thus, it is reasonable to assume that the first-time market has been captured, and the future growth of the IT market is likely to be concentrated on selling greater *frequency* of holidays, and with a focus on the variety of holidays offered.

The changing nature of our society is throwing up demand for new kinds of holiday, as we discussed in an earlier chapter. Growth areas include:

1 Short breaks and city breaks, especially to more exotic destinations. Reykjavik, Barcelona and even New York have become popular destinations for short-stay

tourism. The entry of the Baltic States into the EU has boosted short breaks to Tallinn and Riga, just as the earlier entry of the Czech Republic boosted Prague as the city break of choice.

2   Exotic long-haul, activity and adventure holidays. Elderly travellers are now far more active than formerly, and packages catering to their needs and interests are now common. Early retirement packages at one end of the third age, and longer life spans at the other, contribute to the trend.

3   All-inclusives are one of the fastest-growing forms of holiday. Introduced in 1976 by Sandals and Superclubs in the Caribbean, the concept has now expanded to short-haul destinations too. These are fully inclusive packages, even down to the inclusion of alcohol and all entertainment at the resort. Although popular, the sustainability of all-inclusive holidays is questionable, given that customers do not need to go out of their complex to buy anything while they are on holiday, and local shops and services fail to obtain the same benefits from the tourists.

Operators are increasing their revenue through 'add-ons' especially when customers buy no-frills packages. Operators are making additional charges for transfers, early check-in or late check-out of rooms, pre-bookable seats, meals en route, transfers by taxi, use of prestigious airport lounges, and even charges to guarantee being seated next to a friend or relative. All such techniques are now being used to increase earnings. Of course, traditional sales of excursions and car hire at the destination are also lucrative, and high cancellation charges further boost operators' profits, as operators retain the revenue while remaining free to sell the same holiday subsequently to other holidaymakers.

Consumer complaints

One inevitable consequence of the process of 'trading down' has been an increase in customer complaints. Studies revealed that some 40 per cent of complaints arose from the 'bargain basement' holidays, often based on late availability without guarantee of exactly what accommodation was to be provided. While operators were responding to consumer pressure for low-cost packages, consumers were unwilling to accept the very rational argument that they got what they paid for; minimum standards provided simply failed too often to meet consumer expectations. Even more worrying to operators was the fact that only 40 per cent of those dissatisfied were prepared to make an official complaint; others simply refrained from booking with the company again. The use by British operators of non-British-registered aircraft also led to concern over air safety. In the 1990s older aircraft registered in central European countries outside the EU were attractively priced for charter, but there was less careful monitoring of maintenance and other safety factors such as crew hours, especially where these were chartered through other EU countries. Aircraft failing to meet EU standards of safety are now forbidden from taking off and landing at any point within the EU.

One source of customer irritation was the practice of operators applying surcharges to their final invoices. IT costs are affected by changes in the inflation rate, exchange rates or costs of supplies, particularly aviation fuel, which is priced in US dollars on the world market, and is therefore affected by either increased costs or changes in the relative values of the pound and dollar. Tour operators have to estimate their costs for all services up to a year ahead of time. They can anticipate higher costs by raising prices, which may make them uncompetitive, or they can take an optimistic approach and price low, in the expectation of stable or declining costs. Until 1988, the latter was more attractive, as moderate cost increases could be passed on to customers (within established limits) in the form of surcharges. Such surcharges, however, are resented by travellers, and are in any case not applied to scheduled fares (which can respond to market prices more quickly). It also became apparent that a handful of operators were misusing this facility and adding fuel surcharges in excess of cost increases, or even when actual fuel costs had not increased at all, as a means of raising profits sliced by open competition. The leading tour operators themselves helped to phase out surcharges by guaranteeing prices for the following year. Stability in price could be obtained by 'buying forward' the fuel required for the following year, but this is only practical for the largest operators with sufficient financial reserves. While there is no formal 'futures' market in aviation fuel, negotiation is possible on future purchases of fuel on an ad hoc basis, but clearly at a premium, and purchasing forward will further affect the operators' cash flow.

The introduction in 1996 by the government of an 'exit tax' in the form of Air Passenger Duty for all flights out of the UK, amounting initially to £5 within the EU and £10 outside the EU (a rate that doubled at the end of 1997) resurrected the issue of hidden charges, with many tour operators not absorbing these taxes in their total price structures. Some claimed that to do so would make their prices unattractive against scheduled air rivals, most of whom never included the supplements. While operators are now obliged to do so, the budget airlines do not always include these taxes in their headline fares.

Complaints to ABTA totalled 14,965 in 2004/5. When seen against a background of millions travelling, this represents only a very small proportion of all holidaymakers buying a package tour. A total of 1,159 cases were dealt with under ABTA's arbitration scheme, and of these, 80 per cent found in favour of the customer.

The nature of tour operating

Let us now turn to look at how inclusive tours are operated. An inclusive tour programme, as we have seen, is composed of a series of integrated travel services, each of which is purchased by the tour operator in bulk and resold as part of a package at an all-inclusive price. These integrated services usually consist of an aircraft seat, accommodation at the destination and transfers between the accommodation and the airport on arrival and departure. They may also include other services such as excursions or car hire. The inclusive tour is commonly referred to as a package tour, and most are single-destination, resort-based holidays. However, tours comprising two or more destinations are by no means uncommon, and long-haul operators frequently build in optional extensions to another destination in their programmes – a beach holiday in Kenya might offer an optional extension to one of the game parks; or a visit to the

Chilean fjords, flying to Santiago, might offer the tourist the opportunity to extend the itinerary to Chilean-owned Easter Island. In East Asia, multi-centre holidays are very common, as many capital cities in the area are seen as meriting only relatively short stays of three to four nights. Increasingly, itineraries other than the most basic are tailor-made for clients, in terms of length of stay, accommodation, flights and activities at the resort. Dynamic packaging, which permits either operators or their travel agents to put together purpose-built tour programmes, using websites to contact suppliers, is becoming the procedure of choice for many travel consumers. Linear tours, such as those offered by coach companies which carry people to different destinations or even through several countries, were at one time the most popular form of trip, and still retain a loyal following, mainly among older clients. Even these lend themselves to tailor-made adaptation, with alternative flights to connect with the tours, and short-stay extensions at the beginning or end of the programme.

The success of the operator has usually depended on an ability to buy a combination of products, putting them together and selling them at an inclusive price lower than the customers could obtain themselves. The major international operators may be booking several million hotel beds for a season, thus negotiating very low prices from the hotel owners. Similarly, they are bulk-buying seats on aircraft, or chartering whole aircraft, at the best prices they can secure. The end result must be seen by the customers as offering value for money – either in terms of final price paid, or in time saved by shopping around. With package holidays becoming more and more a standardized product, differing little between destinations, the destination or country has come to play a lesser part in customer choice; destinations will be readily substituted if customers feel that their first choice is overpriced.

Tour operators can lower prices either by restraining profits, or by cutting costs. Cost savings are initially achieved by chartering whole aircraft instead of merely purchasing a block of seats on a scheduled flight. Further savings can be made by time-series chartering of the aircraft over a lengthy period of time, such as a whole season, rather than on an ad hoc basis – now the normal pattern of operating for the large operators. Ultimately, the largest operators reduce costs to the minimum by running their own airlines, and this also allows them to exercise better control over their operations and the standards of their product. Owning your own aircraft ensures that when demand is there, you have the aircraft to meet it at a price you can afford. Emphasis then shifts to ensuring that the highest possible load factors – the percentage of seats sold to seats available – are achieved, and that the aircraft are kept flying for the maximum number of hours each day; aircraft are not earning revenue while stationary on the ground, and parking fees can amount to hundreds of pounds every hour. This means careful planning to ensure turnarounds (time spent between arriving with one load of passengers and taking off with another) are as rapid as possible, commensurate with good standards of safety. Typically, this will result in up to three rotations in a single day, between a Northern European point of origin and a Mediterranean destination. These rotations may be made from a single point of origin (i.e. airport) to a number of different destinations abroad, from several points of origin to a single destination abroad, or from different points of origin to different foreign destinations. The latter flight plan is commonly known as a 'W' flight pattern (see Figure 16.3), which can be generally programmed to produce the maximum aircraft usage during a

Figure 16.3
A typical 'W'
flight pattern

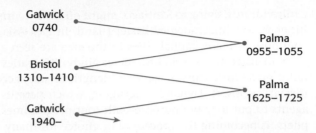

24-hour period. The operator must also factor in an empty flight at the beginning of the season, when the return flight from the destination has no passengers to bring back, and a similar empty flight at the end of the season, when there will be no passengers on the outward flight which is travelling to pick up the final group of returning holidaymakers.

W-pattern flights are not necessarily carrying the customers of a single operator (even where the carrier is owned by one of the operators). Charters can be contracted to carry the passengers of a number of different operators between the same points of origin and destination, either sharing the flights or filling different flights. This can give rise to problems, one of which will occur when different operators contract for morning, afternoon and evening flights. If one operator decides to cancel, the airline concerned has to find alternative users for the aircraft, which may mean a longer flight commitment, causing delays, or a change of flights, to passengers already booked. The knock-on effect of delays can become very apparent if air traffic controllers go on strike or mount go-slows. Tight flight scheduling, particularly into busy airports in the height of the season, can result in delays on one flight that can have repercussions on tour operator movements using the same aircraft over the next two or three days.

High load factors are achieved by setting the break-even (the number of seats to be sold on each flight to cover all operating, administrative and marketing costs associated with the flight) at a point as close as possible to capacity. This brings down the average seat cost to a level which will encourage the greatest number of people to travel. On many well-marketed charter flights, break-even is set as high as 90 per cent or higher, while actual average load factors may be as high as 96–98 per cent. The company makes its profits on the difference between these two figures, and since clearly every extra person carried is almost pure profit (virtually all costs having been covered), then substantial reductions can be made for last-minute bookings to fill these final seats, or conversely if very few seats remain, the company may even choose to inflate the price, in the knowledge that there are always a few passengers who are willing to pay for a very specific flight at short notice. Of course, if break-even load factors have not been reached, the operator will not cover all costs, but it will still be better to attract as many people as possible for the flight, because they will at least make a contribution to the fixed costs of operating the flight, even if all costs are not recovered. Passengers may also buy duty-free goods on board (if travelling outside the EU countries), which will make a further contribution to profit for the airline – or, taking a broader view, for the parent company of the jointly owned airline/tour operator. As an increasing number of short-haul airlines no longer serve food and drink free of charge, the sale of these items on board becomes another important source of revenue.

Furthermore, if the operator has contracted for a set number of beds and is committed to pay for that number, it is better to carry passengers to fill those beds than have them empty.

Productivity in airline operations can be aided, as we have seen, by the procedure of *consolidating* flights. Charter flights with unacceptably low load factors can be cancelled, and their passengers transferred to other flights, or even departures from other airports. This helps to reduce the element of risk for the operator, otherwise break-evens would have to be set at a lower level of capacity, and fares would consequently be higher. Such consolidations are not available for groups carried on scheduled airline services, and are in any case subject to considerable restrictions, such as adequate advance notice being given to the client. Inevitably, they are unpopular with clients, and many companies now try to avoid their use.

The problem of seasonality

A problem facing all sectors of tourism is the highly seasonal nature of most tourist traffic. Nowhere is this more apparent than in the demand for package holidays in Europe. This market, however, is also highly price sensitive, and longer periods of holiday entitlement over the past 20 years have helped to encourage many people to take their second holiday abroad too – often outside of the peak periods of holiday demand. This meant that operators could spread their fixed costs more evenly over the entire year, rather than concentrating them into the summer periods, helping to reduce prices further. Most importantly, it allows the operator to contract for aircraft and hotels on a year-round basis. If only a summer season is programmed, the operator is left with a 'dead leg' twice in the year – an aircraft returning empty after the first flight of the season because it has no passengers to pick up, and an empty outbound flight at the end of the season to pick up the last clients returning home. The costs of these empty flights have to be built into the overall pricing structure of the operation, but if they can be avoided by offering year-round programmes, clearly these savings can be passed on to the customers.

Operators also use marginal costing techniques to attract their clients out of season. This means pricing the holidays to cover their variable costs and making some contribution to fixed costs. This recognizes that many costs, such as those encountered in operating hotels, continue whether the hotel is open or closed, and any guests that the hotel can attract will help to pay the bills. They will also enable the hotel to keep its staff year-round, thus making it easier to retain good staff. Some market segments – pensioners, for example – can be attracted to the idea of spending the entire winter abroad if prices are low enough, and hoteliers welcome these budget clients who can still be expected to spend some additional money in the hotel bars or restaurants.

Operating scheduled programmes

Not all destinations allow charter flights to operate into their territory (often in order to protect bookings on the scheduled flights of the country's airline). Nor will there be sufficient demand to many destinations, such as those served by most long-haul programmes, to merit chartering an aircraft. For these forms of packaging, the net inclusive tour-basing excursion (ITX) or group inclusive tour-basing (GIT) fares can be used by the operator, which may in this way either contract for individual seats based on client demand (around which a tailor-made holiday can be constructed), or contract for a block of seats on flights to satisfy the needs of a brochure programme.

Airlines will allow ITX fares to be applied subject to certain conditions attached to the programmes. A minimum number of brochures must be printed, and/or the tours must be seriously promoted on a website, and the programme must consist of a package of flight, accommodation and transfer or other feature. The tour programme can be organized using one or more carriers, but approval is usually sought through a particular carrier, which will validate the programme and provide a tour code number, which is contained on each ticket issued. Tour operators in the UK making a forward commitment on seats must also obtain an Air Travel Organizers' Licence (ATOL) through the CAA.

Control over tour operating

Regulations restricting tour operators were very limiting when the mass tour market developed in the 1960s. In particular, the regulation known as Provision 1 made it impossible to price package tours lower than the cheapest regular return air fare to a destination. The sole exceptions to this rule were in the case of affinity groups, which involved charters arranged for associations whose existence was for a purpose other than that of obtaining cheap travel. Travellers were obliged to have been members of the organization for at least six months before they became eligible for low-cost flights. The rule was designed to protect scheduled carriers, and to ensure adequate profit for tour operators, but it severely hindered the expansion of the package tour business. It was also widely abused by club secretaries who backdated membership, and many spurious clubs were formed in order to provide the benefits of cheap travel.

When the CAA was established in 1971, restrictions were lifted, initially only during the winter months (leading to a huge increase in off-season travel), but by 1973 this was extended to all seasons. However, at the same time the CAA tightened up control on tour operators themselves, introducing in 1972 the requirement to hold ATOLs for charters and block-booked scheduled seats, and at the same time introducing a system for vetting operators on their financial viability. By 1995, all tour operators were required to hold ATOLs when selling any flights or air holidays abroad. Licences are not required, however, for domestic air tours or for travel abroad using sea or land transport.

Following the collapse of an important tour operator, Fiesta Tours, in 1964, which left some 5,000 tourists stranded abroad, the industry and its customers came to recognize the importance of introducing protection against financial failure. On the whole, in the UK, successive governments have preferred to allow the industry to police itself rather than to impose additional controls, and this was initially undertaken relatively effectively by ABTA on behalf of tour operators and travel agents in the UK. In 1965, ABTA set up a *Common Fund* for this purpose, anticipating legislation for the compulsory registration of tour operators. When this did not materialize, ABTA introduced its

Stabiliser regulation, under which Common Fund provisions were to apply only to ABTA members' clients, and a reciprocal agreement was entered into whereby ABTA tour operators were restricted to selling their package holidays exclusively through ABTA travel agents. In turn, ABTA agents were restricted to selling tours operated by ABTA tour operators. Many agents, however, resented having to contribute to a fund to insure operators, and it also became clear that the provisions against collapse were inadequate. In 1967, the Tour Operators' Study Group (TOSG: later to become the Federation of Tour Operators, FTO), an informal group then comprising approximately 20 of the leading tour operators, decided to establish its own bonding scheme. A bond is a guarantee given by a third party (usually a bank or insurance company) to pay a sum of money, up to a specified maximum, in the event that the company becomes insolvent. This money is then used to meet the immediate financial obligations arising from the collapse, such as repatriating tourists stranded at overseas resorts, and reimbursing clients booked to travel later with the company. TOSG's bonding scheme became a reality in 1970.

Later, ABTA itself introduced its own bonding scheme for all tour operating (and retail agency) members. The collapse in 1974, in the peak of summer, of the Court Line group brought down Clarksons Holidays, Britain's leading tour operator, and revealed once again that protection was inadequate. At this point the government stepped in to introduce an obligatory levy of 2 per cent of operators' turnover between 1975 and 1977. This levy, imposed by the Air Travel Reserve Fund Act of 1975, established the Air Travel Reserve Fund (later, this became the Air Travel Trust Fund). However, these reserves were severely depleted by collapses throughout the 1990s, particularly that of the International Leisure Group at the beginning of that decade, and the ATTF was obliged to call on the government for additional borrowing facilities when reserves ran dry.

The EU and legal issues in package holiday operations

In retrospect, Operation Stabiliser is seen to have worked effectively for its members. Its weakness lay in the fact that it failed to embrace operators outside the system, membership of ABTA being voluntary. With the collapse of several non-ABTA operators in the early 1990s, the weakness of the system was revealed.

Concern was shared by the European Commissioners, who were also looking at the problems of protecting consumers in other member countries. In 1991, the EC Directive on Package Travel was published, designed to extend responsibility to all sectors of the industry. The new regulations, which were to come into effect in 1993, covered non-air-based holidays also. The British Department of Trade and Industry (DTI) responded to the Directive with a Consultative Document to implement the Directive in the UK. The measures to be introduced included the following obligations:

- all air-based tours to be licensed
- a public protection fund to be set up, similar to that offered by the Air Travel Trust, covering other forms of package holiday
- tour operators to be required to observe certain minimum standards in brochure descriptions

- travel agents to become responsible, not only for the information contained in brochures they stocked, but for providing necessary advice to clients on booking (e.g. health requirements, passport and visa requirements, insurance needs etc.)
- restrictions on surcharges and alterations to bookings (although these were in effect weaker than those already imposed under ABTA regulations).

The imposition of these regulations brought considerable problems for operators and agents, not least because the interpretation of the regulations was unclear. In particular, it remained unclear about what exactly constituted a 'package holiday' – was this to include business trips and tailor-made holidays? Would all organizers of packages, such as clubs or schoolteachers organizing educational trips, be included? 'Occasional' organizers were to be excluded, but the interpretation of what constituted 'occasional' posed further problems. What was immediately apparent was that the long-standing Stabiliser regulation could no longer be enforced, as all operators and agents were now required to be bonded, and Stabiliser was discontinued in 1992.

The move to set up a Travel Protection Association to license surface operators was slowed by disagreements between the parties concerned about whether membership in the new body should be mandatory or voluntary. The FTO withdrew from discussions in order to implement its own scheme, and since then a number of alternative schemes have been introduced, in the form of either bonds or trustee accounts. Of these, the best-known outside of the CAA and ABTA schemes are those of the FTO, the AITO (Association of Independent Tour Operators) Trust, the Travel Trust Association (TTA) and the Association of Bonded Travel Organizers' Trust (ABTOT) for smaller operators. The Confederation of Passenger Transport (CPT), Passenger Shipping Association (PSA) and Yacht Charter Association operate their own schemes.

Initially, some believed that ABTA could no longer survive, but the significance of this body and the need to have a single body to represent the interests of tour operators and retailers as a whole has ensured that ABTA has survived, and the ABTA symbol remains a powerful sales tool for the industry, both as the public face of the industry and as a reassurance of reliability and protection. ABTA remains the organization first called upon for comment whenever a travel trade topic crops up in the news. In 2005 discussions were held between ABTA and the FTO on the possibility of integrating the two bodies, mainly as a means to provide a more effective single voice in lobbying Parliament and representing the tour operating and retailing sectors of the industry, but negotiations broke down and have not been renewed up to the time of writing.

What does appear clear is that the additional burden of responsibility placed on tour operators led to some increases in cost for consumers, as operators attempted to cover themselves against any threat of legislation. The Package Travel, Package Holidays and Package Tours Regulations (1992) imposed much greater responsibility on operators; specifically, regulation 4 penalizes the dissemination of misleading information, and provides for compensation to be paid for any loss suffered by the consumer as a result of being misled, while regulation 15 makes the tour operator responsible if hotels or other suppliers fail to provide the accommodation or services contracted for.

As mentioned above, ABTA operates its own arbitration scheme to resolve complaints by customers about its members. This is at low cost to claimants, who are successful in about half of all cases brought. AITO provides a similar scheme.

Alternatively, claims can be made through the courts under a new tracking system which entails only moderate costs for plaintiffs.

Planning, marketing and operating package tours

Planning for the introduction of a new tour programme or destination is likely to take place over a lengthy span of time, sometimes as long as two years. A typical time-scale for a programme of summer tours is shown in Figure 16.4.

In planning deadlines for the programme, it is necessary to work backwards from the planned launch dates. One critical problem is when to determine prices. These have to be established at the last minute before material goes to printing, but inevitably this will be several months before the tour programme starts, and entails a good understanding (and some luck!) with regard to the movement of currency and the foreign exchange markets in the intervening period. Assessment must also be made of what the competition is likely to be charging for similar products. The introduction of fluid pricing has eased the former inflexibility of brochure prices, although any changes immediately after publication would be frowned upon.

Market research

In practice, the decision to exploit a destination or region for package tours is as much an act of faith as the outcome of carefully considered research. Forecasting future developments in tourism, which as a product is affected by changing circumstances to a greater extent than most other consumer products, has proved to be notably inaccurate. As we have seen, tourist patterns change over time, with a shift from one country to another and from one form of accommodation to another. With the emphasis on price, the mass tour operator's principal concern is to provide the basic sun-sea-sand package in countries that provide the best value for money. Transport costs will depend upon charter rights into the country, distance flown and ground handling costs. They will also be affected by the relative demand for, and supply of, aircraft in any given year. Accommodation and other costs to be met overseas will be the outcome of exchange rates against sterling, and operators must consider these vis-à-vis other competitive countries' currency values when considering how many clients they can anticipate travelling to any one destination. Operators also have to take into account such qualitative issues as the political stability of the destination, the support given to developing tourism to the destination by the carriers, or tourist office, of the country, and the relationship between the host and destination countries. Increasingly, with an emphasis upon sustainability, today operators are encouraged (if not yet forced by government legislation) to consider the impact upon locals and the environment of any new development. Pressure groups and the media are slowly persuading companies to take more seriously the pros and cons of new developments and how these can be effectively managed by the operators, the hotels they work with and the local authorities.

Once the tour operators have narrowed the choice to two or three potential destinations, they must produce a realistic appraisal of the likely demand to these

RESEARCH/ PLANNING	YEAR 1	Summer	First stages of research. Look at economic factors influencing the future development of package tours. Identify likely selection of destinations.
		September/December	Second stages of research. In-depth comparison of alternative destinations.
	YEAR 2	January	Determine destinations, hotels and capacity, duration of tours, departure dates. Make policy decisions on size and design of brochure, number of brochures to print, date for completion of print.
NEGOTIATION		February/March	Tenders put out for design, production and printing of brochures. Negotiate with the airlines for charter flights. Negotiate with hotels, transfer services, optional excursion operators.
		April/May	Typesetting and printing space booked with printer, copy for text commissioned. Illustrations commissioned or borrowed. Early artwork and text under development at design studio, with layout suggestions. Contracts completed with hotels and airlines, transfer services etc.
		June	Production of brochure starts.
ADMINISTRATION		July	Determine exchange rates. Estimate selling prices based on inflation etc. Galley proofs from printer, corrections made. Any necessary reservations staff recruited and trained.
		August	Final tour prices to printer. Brochures printed and reservations system established.
MARKETING		September/October	Brochure on market, distribution to agents. Initial agency sales promotion, including launch. First public media advertising, and trade publicity through press etc.
	YEAR 3	January/March	Peak advertising and promotion to trade and public.
		February/April	Recruitment and training of resort representatives etc.
		May	First tour departures.

Figure 16.4 Typical time-scale for planning a summer tour programme

destinations, based on factors such as the number of tourists the destinations presently attract, growth rates over recent years, and present shares held by competing companies. The mass-market operators are unlikely to be looking at a single year's programme – any commitment to a destination is likely to be for a substantial period of time, unlike the specialist operator, which may be more flexible in switching destinations according to changing demand. Mass-market operators will be considering long-term contracts with their hoteliers abroad, or even establishing their own hotels.

Availability of suitable aircraft for the routes must be ascertained. This will in part dictate capacities for the programme, since aircraft have different configurations, and on some routes where aircraft are operating at the limits of their range, some passenger seats may need to be sacrificed in order to take on board sufficient fuel to cover the distance. In some instances, provincial airport runways may be insufficient for larger, fully laden aircraft, and, again, fewer passengers may be carried to compensate.

All planning is, of course, also dependent upon the company having the necessary finance available to operate and market the programme.

The process of negotiating

Once the decisions have been made as to destinations to be served and numbers of passengers to be carried during the season, and dates of departure have been established, the serious negotiations can get under way with airlines, hotels and other principals, leading to formal contracts. These contracts will spell out the conditions for the release of unsold accommodation or (in the case of block bookings on scheduled services) aircraft seats, or the cancellation of chartered aircraft flights, with any penalties that the tour operator will incur. Normal terms for aircraft chartering are for a deposit to be paid upon signing the contract (generally 10 per cent of the total cost), with the balance becoming due on each flight after it takes place. In negotiating with charter services, the reputation of the tour operator is of paramount importance. If they have worked with that airline, or with similar charters, in previous years, this will be taken into account in determining the terms and price for the contract. Relations between the sectors of the industry are still based predominantly on trust, since the threat of legal action, perhaps months after a dispute such as an over-booking problem arises, will do little to resolve problems which arise at the time.

A well-established operator does not wish to be at the mercy of market forces in dealing with charter airlines. In any given year, the demand for suitable aircraft may exceed the supply, encouraging the larger tour operators to form or buy their own airline, just to ensure that capacity is available to them.

Part and parcel of the negotiations is the setting up of the tour operating flight plan, with decisions made on the dates and frequency of operations, the airports to be used and times of arrival and departure. All of this information will have to be consolidated into a form suitable for publication and easy comprehension in the tour brochure.

Hotel negotiations

Hotel negotiations, other than in the case of large tour operators which negotiate time contracts for an entire hotel, are generally far more informal than is the case in airline negotiating. Small and specialist tour operators selling independent inclusive tours (IITs) may have no more than a free-sale (or sell and report) agreement with hoteliers, by which the hotel agrees to guarantee accommodation for a specified maximum number of tourists (usually at least four, although this may be higher in large hotels with plenty of availability for certain days of the week) merely on receipt of the notification of booking from the tour operator, whether by phone, fax or e-mail. This arrangement may be quite suitable for small tour programmes, but it suffers from the disadvantage that at times hoteliers will retain the right to close out certain dates. As these are likely to be the most popular dates in the calendar, the operator stands to lose both potential business and goodwill. The alternative is for the operator to contract for an allocation of rooms in the hotel, with dates agreed for the release of those unsold, well in advance of the anticipated arrival dates.

Long-term contracts, either for a block of rooms or for the entire hotel, have the attraction of providing the operator with the lowest possible prices, but they carry a higher element of risk. Some contracts have been drawn up by operators for as long as five years, and while at first glance such long fixed-term price contracts may seem attractive, they are seldom realistic, and in an inflationary period may well have to be renegotiated to avoid bankrupting the hotelier. Such an event would obviously not be in the operator's interest.

In addition to the operator spelling out exact requirements in terms of rooms – required numbers of singles, doubles, twins, with or without private facilities, whether with balconies or sea views, and with what catering provision, e.g. room only, with breakfast, half or full board – it must also clarify a number of other facts, including:

■ reservations and registration procedures (including whether hotel vouchers are to be issued)

■ accommodation requirements for any representatives or couriers (usually provided free)

■ handling procedures and fees charged for porterage

■ special facilities available or needed, such as air-conditioned or non-smoking rooms, facilities for handicapped customers, or special catering requirements such as kosher or vegetarian food

■ languages spoken by hotel staff

■ systems of payment by guests for drinks or other extras

■ reassurance on suitable fire and safety precautions (at least to EU standards, no matter where the hotel is situated)

■ if appropriate, suitable space for a representative's desk and noticeboard.

It is also as well to check the availability of alternative hotel accommodation of a comparable standard in the event of overbooking. Of course, a hotel with a reputation for overbooking is to be avoided, but over the course of time some errors are bound to occur, and will require guests to transfer to other hotels. Tour operators must satisfy themselves that the arrangements made by the hotelier for taking care of clients in these circumstances are adequate. Any operator negotiating with a hotelier will be aware that they are likely to be sharing contracted space with other operators, not only within their own country but also from other countries. It is as well to be aware of one's own standing with the hotelier vis-à-vis other companies; for example, in Spain it was not uncommon in the past to find that the German operators, which tended to pay higher prices for their rooms than did the British, would have their rooms protected in preference to British operators, when overbookings occurred. With the decline in the German economy in recent years and the simultaneous strengthening of the British economy, the subsequent reductions in the numbers of German visitors to Spain may well result in the reverse now proving to be the case.

Independent companies can find themselves squeezed out of the market for European bed stock in popular resorts, and at times even the mass-market operators become aware that greater concentration in the industry can lead to more difficulty in tying up contracts with popular hotels. For this reason, as demand rises for key Mediterranean destinations and also to ensure greater control over the major elements in the package, some operators turn to owning hotels at the destinations, or at the very least having far more say in their management. First Choice announced in 2000 its intention to play a part in designing new hotels and influencing their layout, when long-term contracts are envisaged.

Ancillary services

Similar negotiations will take place with locally based incoming operators and coach companies to provide coach transfers between airport and hotels, and any optional excursions. Car hire companies may also be approached to negotiate commission rates on sales to the tour operator's clients, and for tailor-made transfers between airport and hotel.

The reliability and honesty of the local operator is an important issue here. Some smaller tour operators in the UK may not be in a position to employ their own resort representatives initially, hence their image will depend upon the level of service provided by the local operator's staff.

If the local company is also operating optional sightseeing excursions, procedures for booking these and handling the finances involved must be established, and it should be clarified whether qualified guides with a sound knowledge of the English language are to be employed on the excursions. If not, tour operators must reassure themselves that all driver–couriers will be sufficiently fluent in the English language to do their job effectively for the company. Nationals of other countries will often want reassurance that English speakers are available, given that English is now the universal language of the travel business worldwide.

The role of the resort representative

Tour operators carrying large numbers of package tourists to a destination are in a position to employ their own resort representatives. This has obvious advantages in that the company can count on the loyalty and total commitment of its own staff. A decision must be made as to whether to employ a national of the host country or of the generating country. The advantage of a man or woman from the local community is that they will be better acquainted with the local customs and geography, fluent in the language of the country and with good local contacts, which may make it easier to take care of problems (such as dealing with the police, local shopkeepers or hoteliers) more effectively. On the other hand, they are likely to be less familiar with the culture, customs or language of their clients, and this can act as a restraining influence on package tourists, especially for those on first visits abroad. Exceptional local representatives have been able to overcome this problem, and if they themselves have some common background with their clients, such as having lived for some years in the incoming tourists' country, they can often function as effectively as their counterparts from the generating country. However, some countries impose restrictions on the employment of foreign nationals at resorts, and this is a point which must be clarified before employing representatives. This used to be a problem within the popular Mediterranean resorts, but with the freedom of labour movement within the EU now, tour operators are free to decide for themselves what should be the background and nationality of their representatives.

The representative's role is far more demanding than is commonly thought. During the season, he or she can be expected to work a seven-day week and will need to be available on call for 24 hours each day to cope with any emergencies. Resort representatives are usually given a desk in the hotel lobby from which to work, but in cases where tour operators have their clients in two or more hotels in the resort, the representative may have to visit each hotel during some part of the day. Their principal functions include:

- handling general enquiries
- advising on currency exchange, shopping etc.
- organizing and supervizing social activities at the hotels
- publicizing and booking optional excursions
- handling special requirements and complaints, and acting as an intermediary for clients, interceding with the hotel proprietor, the police or other local authorities as necessary.

These routine functions will be supplemented by problems arising from lost baggage, ill health (needing to refer clients to local dentists or doctors), and even occasionally deaths, although serious problems such as these are often referred to area managers. The representatives must also relocate clients whose accommodation is for any reason inadequate, or when overbookings have occurred, and they may also have to re-book flights for their clients whose plans change as a result of emergencies.

The representatives' busiest days occur when groups are arriving or leaving the resort. They will accompany groups returning home, on the coach to the airport, ensuring that departure formalities at the hotel have been complied with, arrange to pay any airport or departure taxes due, and then wait to greet incoming clients and accompany them in turn to their hotels on the transfer coaches. In the not uncommon situation where flights are delayed, this can result in representatives having to spend

Figure 16.5
Overseas
representative
dealing with
clients

(Courtesy: Thomson Holidays)

very long hours at the airport, sometimes missing a night's sleep. On their return to the hotels, they must also ensure that check-in procedures operate smoothly, going over rooming lists with the hotel managers before the latter bill the company. Most operators also provide a welcome party for their clients on the first night of their holiday, and it is the representatives' task to organize and host this. This provides an important opportunity to initiate excursion sales.

As operators necessarily became more commercial, they placed more emphasis on the sale of excursions. Many representatives were given targets to achieve, and they were rewarded financially for good performance in this function, which can make a major contribution to the operator's profits. This commercialization of the resort representative's role has become steadily more marked, to a point where their social and personal interaction duties became less important to the company. This led eventually to substantial reductions in the numbers of representatives employed, and in some cases to their demise entirely. The explanation for this move comes partly from the

Figure 16.6
Representatives'
notice boards
also provide
the means for
holidaymakers
to compare the
professionalism
of their
companies
against that of
competitors

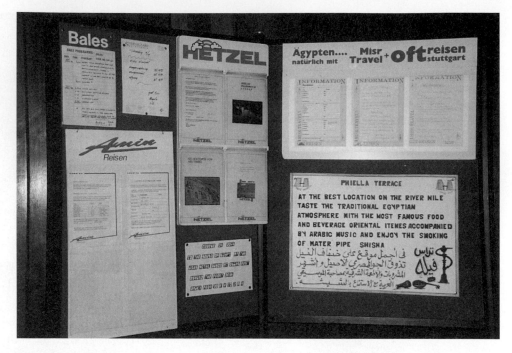

(Photographed by the author)

increasing sophistication of the customers, many of whom are well travelled and no longer feel they need to depend upon the reps' help, as long as a company rep is available at the end of a phone.

Example The resort representatives

Most of Britain's leading operators have now largely dispensed with representatives at their resorts. Thomson and Cosmos have telephone reps, with resort helpdesk hotlines for holidaymakers to make contact. Thomsons have retained reps for their new destinations, and for their Lifestyle brand, where it was found the reps' role was still in demand. Similarly, First Choice have cut reps from their cheaper range of holidays and retained them for up-market brands. Cosmos replaced the traditional welcome meeting by audio taped messages on their buses, at an estimated saving of 30 per cent on their costs. Efforts will be directed to pre-selling excursions, either direct or through the travel agent at commissionable rates.

Arguably, this development leads to two weaknesses in promoting the brand; firstly, it may reduce the opportunity for the clients to engage in commercial transactions that will benefit the company, and secondly, it devalues the image of the company, in the sense that the representative is in many cases the only personal contact the operator has with their clients, and therefore represents the brand. Smaller operators have not been slow to recognize that they now hold a significant advantage over the leaders simply by employing personable individuals to represent their company.

Where representatives continue to be favoured, they can expect to spend some time at their resort bases before the start of the season, not only to get to know the site but to report back to their companies on the standards of tourist facilities and to pinpoint any discrepancies between brochure descriptions and reality. This has become increasingly important under the regulations imposed by the EU Directive on Package Holidays, and representatives may also be expected to inform their companies if any changes occur during the season about which the clients must be notified at the time of booking. In an effort to reduce complaints and handle them at source, some operators give representatives responsibility to compensate their clients on the spot for minor claims and complaints.

Today some operators employ full-time staff who spend part of the year as representatives at the resorts, either in the summer or winter, while at other times they are brought back to head office to handle reservations or other administrative work. The job of a representative seldom offers genuine career opportunities, but for some, there is the opportunity to progress, starting with positions as children's representatives and moving on to adult representative, senior representative, area supervisor and eventually area manager. Ultimately, progression must lie back in head office, where managers having overall responsibility for resort representatives recruit and train staff, organize holiday rosters, provide uniforms and handle the administration of the representatives' department. Nevertheless, for the large majority, opportunities for employment are limited to the season.

Pricing the package tour

A key requirement for success in a tour operator's programme is to get the price right. The price must be right for the market, right compared with the price of competitors' package tours, and right by comparison with the price of other tours offered by the company.

Specialist operators which offer a unique product may have more flexibility and the freedom to determine their prices based on cost plus a mark-up that is sufficient to cover overheads and provide a satisfactory level of profit. The mass operators, however, must take greater account of their competitors' prices, since demand for package tours is, as we have seen, extremely price elastic, especially for programmes offered in the shoulder season or off-season. In the past in the UK there has been a tendency to follow the prices determined by the market leader, and economies of scale have been important in terms of reducing cost and undercutting rival prices. In the following section we will examine two alternative, but typical examples of cost-determined tour pricing. The first will consider pricing for the mass market, the second, pricing for the specialist operator.

Mass-market tour pricing

The first example is based on time-series charter travel and a two-week holiday to a destination such as Spain.

Example 1	Mass-market operator pricing		£
	Flight costs, based on 25 departures (back to back) on Boeing 737 148-seat aircraft at £14,750 per flight:		368,750
	Plus one empty leg each way at beginning and end of the season:		
		(a) out	7,375
		(b) home	7,375
	Total flight costs:		383,500
	Cost per flight:		15,340
	Cost per seat at 90% occupancy (133 seats), i.e. £15,340 ÷ 133		115.34
	Plus air charges (air passenger duty, passenger service charges):		23.00
	Net hotel cost per person, 14 nights half board:		225.80
	Resort agent's handling fees and transfers, per person:		7.00
	Gratuities, porterage:		1.00
	Total cost per person:		372.14
	Add mark-up of approx. 30% on cost price to cover agency commission, marketing costs (including brochure, ticket wallet etc.), head office administrative costs and profit:		111.64
	Selling price:	say	485.00

A small element of cost arises from VAT imposed on the relevant portion of the ground arrangements, and for operators whose company is not directly integrated with an airline, VAT must be added to the tour operator's margin under TOMS (the tour operators' margin scheme). Many companies would add a small fee, say £15, in order to build in a no-surcharge guarantee, especially in times of economic instability. Holidays which are cancelled are presently resold to the public, a source of considerable extra income, since refunds do not have to be made to the original customer (who recovers these costs from insurance, if there is a valid claim).

In estimating the seat cost for aircraft, operators must not only calculate the load factor on which this cost is to be based but must also aim to achieve this load factor on average throughout the series of tours they will be operating. This must depend on their estimates of the market demand for each destination and the current supply of aircraft seats available to their competitors. Since high-season demand will frequently exceed the supply of seats to these destinations, there is scope to increase the above price, and hence profits, for the high-season months of the year, even if this results in the company being uncompetitive with other leading operators. However, as operators have in the past tended to overestimate forecast demand, this is becoming a more risky procedure. In the off-season, meanwhile, supply is likely to exceed the demand for available packages, and the company may set its prices so low that only the variable costs are covered and a small contribution is made to the fixed costs (marketing, administration etc.), in order to fill seats.

Each tour operator must carefully consider what proportion of its overheads are to be allocated to each tour and destination. As long as these expenses are recovered in full during the term of operation, the allocation of these costs can be made on the basis of market forces, and need not necessarily be apportioned equally to each programme and destination. In practice, most operators now recover overhead costs by determining a per capita contribution, based on anticipated head office costs for the year and the total number of passengers the company expects to carry. Under this system, of course, each tour carries the same burden of office costs regardless of destination or price. However, there is a case for a more marketing-oriented approach to pricing, based on consideration of market prices and the company's long-term objectives. In entering a new market, for instance, it may be that the principal objective is to penetrate and obtain a targeted share of that market in the first year of operating, and this may be achieved by reducing or even forgoing profits during the first year, and/or by reducing the per capita contribution to corporate costs. Indeed, to some destinations the operator may introduce loss-leader pricing policies, subsidizing the cost of this policy from other more profitable routes in order to get a footing in the market to the new destination.

Detailed consideration of value-added taxation has not been included here for the sake of simplicity. However, VAT is applicable on profit margins of the operators operating within the EU countries, and the operator will also be paying VAT incorporated into hoteliers' and other services' contractual prices. Most tour operators (but not all) have agreed to pay commission to agents on revenue which includes the VAT cost (which the operator can later recover).

Specialist tour pricing

The second example is of a specialist long-haul operator which uses the services of scheduled carriers to Hong Kong, with a group inclusive tour-basing fare.

Example 2 Specialist operator pricing	£
Flight cost, based on net group air fares, per person:	370
Plus air charges:	40
Net hotel cost per person, 7 nights, twin room (HK$420 per room, = HK$210 per person; HK$14 = £1:	150
Transfers (£10 each way):	20
Sub-total:	535
Add agent's commission:	63
Total cost per person:	598
Selling prices:	
'Lead price' (offered on only one or two off-season flights):	629
Shoulder season price:	679
High season price (summer, Christmas and Easter holiday periods):	845

It will be noted that in the case of this specialist operator, prices reflect market demand at different periods of the year, and there is no equal distribution of office overheads; profits and most overheads are recoverable in the peak season prices charged to the market. The lead price gives very little profit for bookings made through the trade, but is strictly limited to one or two weeks of the year. On the other hand, high profits can be obtained over Christmas, Chinese New Year, during conferences and for other business committed to specific dates. There is a tendency to be more cautious about squeezing excess profits at periods of high demand; several Gulf States carriers are offering much lower prices to offset the need to change flights, so competition at all times of the year is quite high, and if charges are set too high operators may be left with availability during peak times.

The pricing policy shown here is common among the smaller specialist operators, which tend to use less sophisticated pricing techniques when fixing target profits. Many specialists which operate in a climate where there is no exact competition for their product could be expected to charge a price which would give them an overall gross profit of 25 per cent or more, while most mass-market operators, and some specialists, will be forced by market conditions to settle for much lower margins.

In developing a pricing strategy for package tours, operators must take into account a number of other variables in addition to those shown above. Earlier, the point was made that price had to be right compared with all competing products on the market. For example, when setting a price for departure from a regional airport, the operator will look at how much more the client will be willing to pay to avoid a long trip to a major airport. In the example given of flights to Hong Kong, numerous competitors such as Air France/KLM and SAS offer flights from regional airports with connections via their hubs which avoid passengers having to stay overnight at expensive London airport hotels, and the inconvenience of getting to Heathrow Airport on heavily congested motorways. Equally, if a flight is to leave at two o'clock in the morning, the price must be sufficiently attractive compared with others leaving during the day to make people willing to suffer this inconvenience. What special reductions are to be offered to children, or for group bookings? As seat and other costs will be unaffected, whatever reductions the company makes for these bookings will have to be recovered in profits achieved through sales to other customers.

As a general policy, FTO members standardize the date each year in which rates of exchange are fixed against the pound sterling. This usually occurs at the end of June or beginning of July in the preceding year. This ensures that the public can make meaningful comparisons between the prices of tour programmes to similar destinations, and that the mass operators are competing 'on a level playing field'. However, operators can also *buy forward* the foreign currency they will require, to protect themselves against currency fluctuations. If they are involved in exchanging large sums of money, they can buy *futures* in the international money market. Needless to say, this involves speculation and an element of risk; if the operator guesses wrong, the company's prices may end up being uncompetitive against those of other companies.

Discounting strategies

Discounts on published tour prices have become a widely accepted practice in the industry since retail price maintenance in the industry was curtailed in the 1980s.

Originally applied to late bookings, in order to clear seats, the technique has more recently been used by the larger operators to persuade members of the public to book earlier, under a system of 'fluid pricing'. Other operators prefer to rely on guarantees to early bookers against any increases in price prior to their departure.

Since a legal challenge made in 1987 by one retailer, the Ilkeston Co-op's travel agency, against operators that forced agents to sell tours at prices determined by the operators themselves, retailers have been allowed to discount tours they sold by passing on to the clients a proportion of their commission. In practice, this has meant that the largest discounts can be allowed by the largest multiple travel agencies, which can negotiate target overriding commissions well above the 10 per cent norm, and in effect can pass on to their clients almost all the 10 per cent basic commission. As this percentage represents the total commission which most independent agents receive from operators, the independents cannot match this and therefore find it impossible to compete on price. Instead, many will offer alternative benefits, such as free insurance, or an extra service such as a free taxi transfer to the local airport, to secure a sale. Heavy discounting by the market leaders, TUI Thomson and MyTravel, through their own retail chains Thomson and Going Places, were a major factor in boosting their share of the mass market. Until the Competition Commission ruled out the practice of tying sales of package tours to compulsory insurance, on which high profits were available, this was common practice with the largest chains. Given the problems which have faced the industry over the past few years and the strong competition to survive in a difficult marketplace, there is little likelihood of the industry moving away from deep discounting in the foreseeable future.

Costing the package

A tour operator, as we have noted, will normally purchase three main inputs which will comprise an inclusive tour: transport, accommodation and services. The latter will include transfers between terminals and the accommodation abroad, and possibly the services of the company's resort representative at the site. The operator will also, of course, have to cover costs which arise within the company's headquarters; these will include administration, reservations, marketing and advertising etc. Finally, the operator will have to cover the cost of commission allowed to retailers, and of servicing those retailers. A typical inclusive tour from the UK might well have the kind of cost structure outlined in Table 16.4.

Table 16.4 Typical cost structure of an inclusive tour using charter air services

Costs	Percentage of overall costs
Charter air seat	45
Hotel accommodation	37
Other services at destination	3
Head office overheads	5
Travel agency commission	10
	100

Since the profits achieved by most operators after allowing agency commissions are actually quite narrow – perhaps as little as 1–3 per cent of revenue, after covering all costs – the operator will seek to top up revenue in any other way possible. For the mass-market operator, the bulk of revenue – in excess of 50 per cent, normally – is achieved through the sales of summer holidays. Perhaps another 15–20 per cent will be achieved through a winter tour programme, and the balance of revenue is achieved through a mix of sales of excursions at the destination, the interest received on deposits and final payments invested, foreign currency speculation, and sale of insurance policies.

The normal booking season for summer holidays starts in the autumn of the preceding year, reaching its peak in the three months following Christmas, so a large proportion of deposits will have been paid by the end of March. Although the operators themselves will have had to make deposits for aircraft charters at the beginning of the season, and may also have had to make some advance to hoteliers to ensure their rooms are held, the balance of payments will not fall due until after the clients have completed their holiday. Operators will have the use of deposit payments for anything up to a year in advance, and will have final payments at least eight weeks before they themselves have to settle their accounts. This money is invested to earn interest, and in some cases this interest will actually exceed the net profits made by tour operating itself. Clearly, one effect of the growing tendency of British holidaymakers to book their holidays later, and to pay by credit card, will be a fall in earnings by the operators, which may be forced to compensate by raising the price of their holidays.

Further profits are achieved through the sale of ancillary services, such as excursions, car hire and (if the airline used is part of the parent organization) the sale of duty-free goods to non-EU destinations on board flights. One further contribution to revenue is achieved by imposing cancellation charges. These charges will often substantially exceed any costs borne by the operator which result from the cancellation, and indeed the operator may well be able to sell the cancelled accommodation again, gaining double revenue. The EU Directive on Package Holidays now allows, in theory, the substitution of names by the clients to replace cancelled bookings; however, this is impossible to enforce where many airlines do not accept name changes and where countries require arriving passengers to hold visas.

Finally, the issue of agents' commission is a key one, and will be discussed towards the end of the chapter. Given the pressure on operators to reduce their costs, the developments now taking place in seeking new means of remunerating agents have important implications for the future of the distribution network.

Perhaps the move to direct-sell operations, also discussed later in this chapter, is the most worrying trend of all for the independents, both agents and operators. The ease of booking and tendency to book direct through the Internet (and bookings through digital TV are also emerging) are proving attractive to computer-literate consumers, and with the evidence that prices are now frequently lower on the Web, sales through the traditional outlets are certain to fall still further.

Yield management

The high levels of competition for summer programme sales will require the operator to take a great deal of care to get the price of the company's packages right, so that sufficient demand is generated to fill available seats, while at the same time prices are not so cheap as to threaten profitability. This skill of *yield management* is frequently defeated by the excess capacity available on the market, forcing companies to 'dump' packages at whatever price they can realize which will, at least, help to make a contribution to the company's overheads. There is some evidence that companies are improving their skills at yield management by better forecasting or a willingness to reduce capacity in order to get a better balance between supply and demand. While such action has been taken largely through implicit agreements between the major operators, there is always the risk that the smaller operators will see this as an opportunity to steal some market share from the brand leaders, and increase their own capacity.

Example   First Choice

First Choice Holidays is held up as an example of good yield management, in the aftermath of the recent world tragedies. While other leading companies largely held on to, or only marginally reduced, their allocations, First Choice reduced their own capacity by 20 per cent following the 9/11 Twin Towers attack, and made similar sharp cuts in the lead up to the Iraqi War. As a result, their finances were in far better shape in the annual reports which followed.

If prices are set too low initially, and late demand in the season results in a 'sell-out', the company will not have maximized its profit opportunity. At the same time, if the company finds itself involved in added expenditure in the course of the summer – for example, in providing accommodation and meals for clients delayed through air traffic control strikes or go-slows (which cannot be foreseen a year in advance but occur not infrequently in Europe), what might have been a slim but acceptable profit can soon be turned into an overall loss.

Another aspect of yield management is the decision taken on when to launch the new holiday programme. Companies launching ahead of their rivals will always hope to steal a larger proportion of the early booking market, and of course have revenue which can be invested over a longer period. While the pattern in the past is for a launch in September, as we saw earlier in this chapter the larger operators have been progressively launching earlier, with some summer holidays appearing on the market as early as April the previous year. The jury is still out as to whether the advantages of early sales achieved through this means are sufficient to offset the drawbacks, not least of confusing both agents and customers through the range of choice on offer at any given time. A further issue is that publishing this far in advance gives competitors full particulars of your prices, hotels and sales techniques, allowing them an opportunity to adjust their marketing by delaying the launch of their own programmes until September.

The tour brochure

For many years, the tour operator's brochure was the critical marketing tool, and the main influence on a customer's decision to buy. Tourism is an intangible product which customers are obliged to purchase without having the opportunity to inspect it, and often from a base of very inadequate knowledge. In these circumstances – and given the limited personal knowledge of products and destinations held by travel counsellors – the brochure became the principal means both of informing customers about the product and persuading them to purchase it.

For most companies, this still means that very large sums are invested in the brochure itself, and in advertising to persuade the customers to enter the travel agent's and pick one up. In particular, the production of the brochure is likely to represent a very significant proportion of the total marketing budget for the year, with print runs, in the case of the largest operators, running into tens of millions, at a unit cost of well over £1 a copy. Accordingly, it is essential for the operator to ensure that this large expenditure achieves its intended results. In spite of this, however, there is considerable wastage. In one study undertaken by the environmental lobby Green Flag International, it was estimated that of 120 million British travel brochures printed in one year, 48 million were never used. This wastage rate, coupled with the high cost of each copy that is picked up and consulted free, was estimated to add approximately £20 to the price of the average package holiday.

The brochure is no longer the critical tool it once was, as many operators now sell directly from their websites – and, indeed, some small companies no longer print brochures at all, simply printing off relevant pages from their websites for those customers wanting hard copy of their holiday arrangements. While this trend is likely to accelerate, for the present the brochure remains an important tool, and must be considered here.

Brochure design and format

Larger companies will either have their brochures designed and prepared in their own advertising department, or they will coordinate the production with a design studio, often associated with the advertising agency they use. The agency will help to negotiate with printers to obtain the best quotation for producing the brochure, and will ensure that print deadlines are met. Other operators will tackle the design of the brochure themselves, and this process is being increasingly aided by computer graphic packages which allow desktop publishing, by which means the operator is able to produce the entire contents of the brochure, including all illustrations, on an in-house computer. The computer will organize the layout, selecting the best location of text and illustrations to minimize use of space, thus helping to reduce cost. Naturally, the financial investment in the technology necessary to undertake this work is considerable.

Smaller operators which do tackle the design of the brochure themselves are best advised to use the help of an independent design studio, which can provide the professional expertise in layout, artwork and copy that are so important in the design of a professional piece of publicity material. Most printers have their own design departments which can undertake this work for their clients, but unless the company has had experience of the standards of work of their printer, they are probably better advised to approach an independent studio for this work.

The purposes the brochure serves will dictate its design and format. A single ad hoc programme, for example to a foreign trade exhibition, may be printed as nothing more than a leaflet, or if a limited programme of tours is contemplated these may be laid out in the form of a simple folder.

Folders can take a number of different forms, ranging from a *centrefold* to more complicated folds. Larger brochures (or in printing parlance, *booklets*) consist of eight or more pages, printed in multiples of four sheets which require binding together in some manner. Smaller brochures are usually machine-bound by *saddle-stitching* (stapling through the spine), while larger brochures may be *side-stitched* with a glue-on cover, or bound as a book. It is not the aim here to discuss printing methods in detail, and the reader is referred for further reading in the subject to the many excellent books on print publicity.

Purpose-designed brochures will usually include all of an operator's summer or winter tours within a single brochure. However, many larger operators have diversified into a great many different types of holiday – long-haul and short-haul, coach tours as well as air holidays, lakes and mountain resorts as well as seaside resorts – and if all these were to be combined into a single brochure, it would run to hundreds of pages and be both clumsy to handle and very expensive to produce. There would also be high wastage, as clients who know the type of holiday they want will have to pick up the entire programme to get their particular product. Operators therefore produce individual brochures, even in some cases separating brochures by destination.

As well as overcoming the problems identified earlier, this will have the added advantage of filling more of the agents' rack space, leaving less available space for competitors. If the leading half-dozen operators produce as many as 70–80 different brochures – all top sellers for agents – this will require the agents to devote as much as half their rack space to these brands.

Example   Leger Holidays

Typically, travel brochures are A4 size today, and are designed to fit the standard racks used in travel agencies. Leger Holidays introduced an unusual shape for their Christmas Market and Festive Breaks brochure, reducing it from A4 size to a square shape. This allows the brochure to be racked in front of their main Discover Europe and Disney brochures and in the same rack, ensuring that more of the company's products are fully displayed in agencies. They also take the view that text is becoming less important in persuading the holidaymakers to book, reducing the amount of copy in favour of more illustrations. In the words of Peter Raynor, their Retail Sales Director, 'It's pictures that sell a holiday'.

Source: *Travel Weekly*, 27 May 2005

The first task of a brochure is to attract attention. Operators have therefore developed a 'house style' for the covers of their brochures which is quickly recognized by customers, when placed on the agents' racks. These are usually images of attractive models in beachwear combined with an eye-catching symbol and house name across the top of the brochure. While some might contend that there is a disappointing sameness among the leading operators' brochures today, taken individually the quality and professionalism of modern brochure design and printing is outstanding. As brochures today must also reinforce an image of quality and reliability, the text and images contained in brochures must not only be attractive but also truthful, accurate and easily understood. Good layout, high-quality photography and suitable paper are all essential if the brochure is to do its job effectively.

Obligations affecting tour brochures

As was stated earlier, the brochure must both inform and persuade the potential tourist. Tour operators are selling dreams, and their brochures must allow consumers to fantasize a little about their holidays. But it is also vitally important that consumers are not misled about any aspect of their holiday. Care must be taken not to infringe the Trades Description Act 1968, section 14 of which deals with the offence of making false statements concerning the provision of services.

In the past, operators have invoked the law of agency in claiming that within their booking conditions they act as agents only in representing hotels, transport companies or other principals. However, the provisions of the Unfair Contract Terms Act 1977 went some way towards placing the burden of responsibility on operators themselves for the services they represent, and this was enhanced by the EU Directive on Package Travel. This simplifies proceedings for the tourist, who can sue the operator for offences for which their suppliers abroad are responsible, requiring the operator in turn to sue the supplier in the destination country.

The Consumer Protection Act 1988 makes it illegal to give a misleading indication of the price of goods and services. Operators must therefore ensure that the price panels in their brochures provide full details of the tour costs. ABTA's Tour Operators' Code of Conduct also imposes specific obligations upon operators to provide honest and accurate information, an obligation which EU law strengthened.

Information required in the brochure

To satisfy not only the ITX conditions but also the clients' need for information on regular charter programmes, the operator should include the following information in the brochure:

- the name of the firm responsible for the IT
- the means of transport used, including, in the case of air transport, the name of the carrier(s), type and class of aircraft used and whether scheduled or charter aircraft are operated
- full details of destinations, itinerary and times of travel
- the duration of each tour (number of days/nights' stay)

- full description of the location and type of accommodation provided, including any meals
- whether services of a representative are available abroad
- a clear indication of the price for each tour, including any taxes
- exact details of special arrangements, e.g. if there is a games room in the hotel, whether this is available at all times and whether any charges are made for the use of this equipment
- full conditions of booking, including details of cancellation conditions
- details of any insurance coverage (clients should have the right to choose their own insurance, providing this offers equivalent coverage)
- details of documentation such as visas required for travel to the destinations featured, and any health hazards or inoculations recommended
- in the case of activity holidays, the brochure must specify how fit clients are expected to be and what sort of experience they should have had.

A booking form is usually printed within the brochure for completing a reservation. The terms and conditions of the booking should appear in full in the brochure, but should not be printed on the back of the booking form, as they need to be retained by the customer.

The e-brochure

Websites will frequently replace the traditional brochure, but their preparation has to be undertaken as carefully as that for brochures. While a website will share many characteristics with brochure work, there are important differences. Customers will read fewer words on a screen than on the printed page, so the visual element takes on greater significance. The particular advantage of the website is that it can be changed frequently, and at short notice – in fact, it is critical that the site is always up to date, as this will be expected. Staff must be trained to undertake this, and to assess what changes have to be carried out. Sometimes whole programmes will need to be withdrawn or added. Many companies use their websites to personalize their approach to their clients, giving portraits of staff and adding comments from tourists on the resort pages.

Negotiating with the printer

Printers will not expect their clients necessarily to be experts in printing methods, but those involved with the processing and production of a brochure should be reasonably familiar with current techniques in printing and common terms used. Printers will need to know:

1 The number of brochures required.
2 The number of colours used in the printing. Full colour work normally involves four colours, but some cost savings should be possible if colour photography is not to be included.

3 The paper to be used: size, format, quality and weight. The choice of paper will be influenced by several factors, including the printing process used. Size may be dictated by the industry's requirements; for example, a tour-operating brochure needs to fit a standard travel agency rack. Paper quality varies according to the material from which it is made. It may be glossy or matt, but will be selected for its whiteness and opacity. Inevitably, this requires some compromise, as very white paper tends to be less opaque, and one must avoid print showing through to the other side of the sheet. The weight of paper will of course depend upon its effect on the overall weight of the brochure, if this is to be mailed in quantity. Operators may well cut the size of a brochure if it reduces postage costs to a lower band. If 8p per brochure can be saved on a mail shot of 100,000, this represents an overall saving of £8,000, quite apart from lower printing and paper costs.

4 The number and positions of illustrations (photos, artwork, maps etc.) used.

5 Typesetting needs. There are over 6,000 typefaces from which to choose, and the style of type chosen should reflect the theme of the brochure, its subject and the image of the company.

6 Completion and delivery dates.

When obtaining prices from the printer, operators should approach several companies, as quotes can vary substantially between printers. Many operators choose to have their brochures printed abroad. Good quality work can be produced at very competitive prices for long print runs, but obviously the operator will want to compare whether British printers can match prices quoted abroad, since use of a domestic printer will reduce transport costs. Most importantly, operators must avoid cutting corners to save money, as an inferior print job can threaten the whole success of the tour programme. The progress of the printing must be supervised throughout, either by the operator itself or its advertising agency. Proofs should be submitted at each stage of production to check on accuracy and a final corrected proof should be seen before the actual print run to ensure there are no outstanding errors. As the brochure is such a crucial legal document, generally several members of staff will read it through before the final proof is passed for printing.

The printer should be asked to quote not only for the actual number of brochures that are expected to be required, but also for the run-on price for additional copies. Once a brochure is set up for printing, the cost of running off a few extra thousand is very small compared to the overall price, and it may be better to do this rather than having to reorder at a later date.

Brochure distribution and control

Tour operators must make the decision either to use all of the retail agencies available to them, or to select those whom they feel will be most productive for the company. Whatever decision is made, operators must also establish a policy for their brochure distribution to these agents. If equal supplies of brochures are distributed to every agent, many copies will be wasted.

Wastage can be reduced by establishing standards against which to monitor the performance of travel agents. A key ratio is that of brochures given out to bookings received. 'Average' figures appear to vary considerably among different operators; while one will expect to gain a booking for every three or four brochures given out (which may still mean that every booking carries the burden of some £6–7 in brochure production costs), specialist operators may have to give out as many as 25–30 brochures to obtain a single booking. The position is slightly improved when one remembers that each booking will involve typically between 2.5 and 3 persons. If figures consistently poorer than this are achieved by any of its agents, the operator should look for an explanation. The problem could be accounted for by the agent's lack of control over their own brochure distribution: do they merely stock their display racks and leave clients to pick up whatever numbers they wish, or do they make a serious attempt to sell to 'browsers'? Some agents go even further than this, and retain all stocks of brochures except a display copy, so that customers have to ask for copies of the brochures they require. This is instrumental in cutting down waste, as well as increasing sales opportunities.

It is now the practice of most operators to categorize their agents in some way, in terms of their productivity. This could typically take the following form:

Agents	Bookings per year
Category A: top producing agents, multiples	100 +
Category B: good agents	50–99
Category C: fair agents	20–49
Category D: below average agents	6–19
Category E: poor agents, producing little	0–5

Of course, for a specialist operator, the sales categories might be considerably smaller; a good agent may be producing as few as ten bookings a year. However, the principle remains the same; the operator will determine, on the strengths of these categories, what level of support to give the agent. At the top of the scale, agents can expect to receive as many brochures as they ask for, while at the other end, perhaps the operator will be willing to provide only a file copy, or two to three brochures to work with. Many new or independent agents are finding it increasingly difficult to obtain any supplies of brochures from the major operators, which are increasingly narrowing the focus of their distribution policy.

The reservations system

In order to put a package tour programme into operation, a reservations system must be developed and implemented. The design of the system will depend upon whether reservations are to be handled manually (an increasingly rare system, given the current availability of low-cost computer programs to handle bookings) or by computer, and on whether the operator plans to sell through agents or direct to the public.

Many tour operators still sell their tours principally through the high street travel agents, although direct sales through the leading operators' websites are increasing rapidly. The multiples – retail chains owned by the lead operators – are responsible for over 50 per cent of all package holidays sold by agents.

Manual systems are fast disappearing in favour of CRSs, which offer a faster, more efficient service at a much cheaper price for the operator. A travel agent needs to contact the operator quickly when serving a client at the counter. If telephone lines are engaged, or not answered for long periods of time, the agent could become frustrated and decide to deal with a competitor who is easier to contact – or the client will simply search for a holiday on a website.

Initially, the CRS operated only 'in-house', i.e. within the operator's own premises. Agents seeking to make a booking would telephone the operator, who tapped into the company's computer to check availability. It was but a short step from this to link the agent directly into the CRS, using a visual display unit (VDU) in the agent's office. Thomson, the market leader, was the first operator to decide that all bookings through agents should be handled in this fashion, forcing agents to invest in the appropriate hardware. Most other large companies rapidly followed suit.

These connections originally depended upon the use of telephone wires to link the agent's VDU to the operator's CRS. This posed problems of cost and time-wasting for the agent, if lines were busy and there was difficulty in accessing a CRS. Subsequently, agents were 'hard-wired' directly into the operators' CRSs, reducing time and allowing the agent to switch directly from one CRS to another without redialling.

Implementing a reservation

The computer will allow the agent to see whether the particular tour required is available, or if it is not, will automatically display the dates or destinations nearest to the client's needs. Once the agent has established that a package is acceptable to the client, a booking is made (sometimes an option can be taken for 24 hours, but operators are now tending to accept only firm bookings). Any late changes to the programme which are not in the brochure can be drawn to the attention of the client and agent on the screen at this time. The agent is provided with a code number to identify the booking, and obtains a completed booking form from the client, together with a deposit.

The computer booking is sufficient to hold the reservation, and booking forms are now held in the agent's files rather than, as formerly, sent to the operator with the deposit. The operator will issue an interim invoice to confirm the booking, upon receipt of the deposit, and a final invoice will be issued normally about ten weeks before the client is due to leave, requesting full payment eight weeks before departure. Changes to the programme cannot be made once the final invoice has been issued. After receipt of the final payment, the operator will issue all tickets, itineraries and, where necessary, vouchers, and despatch these to the agent, who forwards them to the client. However, e-tickets and vouchers are now dramatically reducing the amount of paperwork sent by operators to their clients.

Prior to each departure, a flight manifest is prepared for the airline, with names of all those booked. In the case of flights using US airspace, considerable personal information has now to be supplied on every passenger, a security measure introduced after 9/11. A rooming list is sent to the hotels concerned and to resort representatives where appropriate. The latter should go over the rooming list with the hotelier to ensure that all is in order prior to the clients' arrival.

Larger tour operators will have a customer relations department whose function is to monitor and handle passenger and agency complaints and ensure quality control in the operation of the tour programme. They monitor the questionnaires that most operators give to their clients to complete at the end of the holiday. These provide regular statistical analysis on which hotels are meeting clients' expectations, and which ones are failing to do so.

Late bookings

Tour operators are anxious to fill every seat in their tour programme. The ability to react quickly to deal with last-minute demand for bookings plays a key role in fulfilling this objective. Around 40 per cent of summer holiday bookings are now booked after 1 April, and a similar booking pattern has emerged for winter holidays. Coupled with the offer of last-minute discounts, many operators have introduced procedures designed to pick up these late bookings, including the rapid updating of availability on computer reservations systems, and a booking procedure which allows tickets to be collected at the airport on departure. The new dot.com agents provide an excellent new medium for selling off unsold flights and accommodation at short notice.

The distribution network

The selection of retailers

Basically, the tour operator has to choose between two alternative methods of selling its tour programmes – either through retail travel agents, or direct to the public (although websites can have a role in either of these approaches). Larger operators whose product is of universal appeal and whose market is national in scope have tended to sell the bulk of their holidays through the retail trade, but the development of websites has encouraged many more sales to be made direct – a development welcomed by the operators, who can thus cut out payment of agency commissions. Websites also aid retailers, in that agents now need to spend less time talking to their clients about the product or ordering brochures, and can therefore stress their role as the personal link which offers the client financial security. Companies with a policy of selling direct to the public will be examined at the end of this chapter.

Few operators deal indiscriminately with all retail agents. As with most products sold, some 80 per cent of package holidays are actually sold through 20 per cent of the retail agents, while a large number of agents will make very few sales (the so-called 'Pareto principle'). The cost of servicing the less productive agents is often greater than the revenue they produce – they must not only be provided with expensive free brochures, but also receive regular mailings to update their information, and are supported by sales material and even, in some cases, visits from sales representatives of the operator. Even in the era of websites, many operators still find that the personal contacts established by good sales representatives leads to more sales that do mail-shots or phone calls. The operators must therefore decide whether to vary the support they offer to different agents, or even to dispense with the services of some agents altogether. We have already seen how brochure supplies will be varied according to the productivity of the agent. It has been the practice of operators to support their best agents by offering them an overriding commission of between 1 per cent and 5 per cent, in addition to the basic 10 per cent, for achieving target sales figures. The large multiples, due to the strength of their position in the retail trade, can negotiate the highest overrides, giving them the ability to discount substantially in order to attract yet more business.

Leading operators have reduced both support and commission to their agents in recent years, and their process of directional selling has favoured sales through their own chains. This is proving a challenge for the independents, who are seeking to increase their sales of AITO and other small operators to make up for the shortfall in the sale of mass-market tours. Since only Cosmos among the leading five is now without a dedic-ated chain, independents are willing to give this operator greater support, although it would be commercial suicide to refrain from selling the products of the top four.

The smaller operators, those whose market strengths lie in certain geographic regions, or those catering for specific niche markets often involving quite a small number of customers in total, are obviously not in a position to support a national network of retailers. Most will choose to sell direct to their customers, although a handful may try to concentrate sales through a limited number of supportive agents.

Relationships with travel agents

It is customary for tour operators to draw up a formal agreement with the travel agents they appoint to sell their services. These agreements specify the terms and conditions of trading, including such issues as the normal rates of commission paid, and whether credit will be extended to the agent or settlement of accounts must be made in cash.

An ill-defined area in these agreements is that of the application of the law of agency. A contract is between the principal and the client, and this raises the question of whether a travel agent is acting as agent of the principal or agent of the client. Some agreements will suggest that the agent is the agent of the principal, but since the collapse of Clarksons Holidays in 1974, when a large amount of money had been paid by customers to agents but had not yet reached the operator, it has generally been held that this 'pipeline' money is rightfully the clients'; some agreements go so far as to specify this.

Under the terms of these agreements, the agent agrees to support and promote the sale of their principals' services. In return, the operator agrees to provide the support and cooperation necessary for the successful merchandising of the company's products, i.e. provision of adequate supplies of brochures, sales promotion material and some-times finance for cooperative regional advertising or promotion campaigns. Operators will also try to ensure that their retailers are knowledgeable about the products they sell. This will be achieved through the circulation of sales letters or mailshots, by invitations to workshops or other presentations, and by inviting selected agents on educational study trips.

The educational study trip

The educational trip (or 'familiarization trip', as it is known in North America) is a study trip organized by principals (whether tour operators, carriers or tourist offices of the regions involved). Such trips are organized for a variety of purposes; for example, members of the media, or travel writers, will be taken to tourist destinations in order for the principals to gain free – and hopefully, positive – media coverage. Travel agents are also offered opportunities to undertake trips in order to improve their knowledge of the destinations, or to encourage them to sell the region or product. Sometimes, these trips are used by operators as incentives to agents; if certain targets are reached, trips will be provided as a reward.

Visits to a destination are known to be one of the most effective means of encouraging agents to sell a particular package, and these organized trips also have a social function, enabling the operators to get to know their agents better and to obtain feedback from them. However, the cost of mounting educational trips is high, even if a proportion of the costs is met by the hotels in the destination, or the national tourist offices and carriers helping to organize the programme, and principals will try to do everything they can to ensure that the educational trip gives them value for money. This was not always the case in the past, where educational visits abroad were often treated as 'jollies', attractive as a social perk rather than an educational experience. The effectiveness of these educationals has been improved by more careful selection of candidates, by providing a more balanced mix of visits, working sessions and social activities, and by imposing a small charge for attendance, so that travel agency managers will take care to ensure that the expense is justified in terms of increased productivity and expertise among their staff.

Careful selection of candidates will ensure that all those attending share common objectives, and that, for example, senior agency managers and young counter clerks do not find themselves together on the same educational trip, to the discomfort of both. Monitoring performance, by soliciting reports from those attending and by checking the sales performance of staff from those agencies invited to participate, will help to ensure that the operators' money has been well spent.

The sales representative

Tour operators, like most larger travel principals, employ sales representatives to maintain and develop their business through travel agents, and to solicit new sources of business. The functions of the sales representatives are to call on present and potential contacts, advise agents and others of the services they offer, and support their agents with suitable merchandising material.

These representatives act as one point of contact between the agent and operator, when problems or complaints are raised, and the often close relationship that develops between representatives and their contacts is valuable in helping to build brand loyalty for the company. The personal contact enables them to receive direct feedback from the marketplace about client and agency attitudes towards the company and its products. Representatives are also likely to play a valuable role in categorizing agents in terms of their potential, and selecting sales staff for educational trips. However, making sales calls in person is expensive, and most companies have now switched to telephone sales calls to keep in touch with all but their most productive agents. As with the resort representatives abroad, however, the sales representative is another means by which the company can be distinguished from its competitors, and the appropriateness of a trend to less personal contact is questionable. It is true that many agents have mixed feelings about the merits of sales representatives, who are seen by some as time-wasting socializers. It goes without saying that if the representatives are to do their job effectively, they must be well trained; those who are not sufficiently knowledgeable about their companies' or their competitors' products will relay a poor image of the company to the agent.

Example   The role of the sales representative

'The time-honoured role of the travel trade representative is now dead', declared Richard Carrick of Hoseasons[2]. Yet not all principals agree. Libra Holidays uses its overseas reps out of season to call on agents. Ten agents are visited each day; they are given product training and helped with promotions and brochure racking, while the rep gets feedback on the company's pricing. Superbreak Mini-Holidays has a seven-strong team of sales reps, backed by three Key Account Managers, who call on agents to offer product update information, and help with training in the use of the Internet and Viewdata, problem solving and brochure merchandising and racking[3].

Direct-sell operators

Apart from those operators who will inevitably sell direct to their clients, for the reasons outlined above, a handful of larger tour operators have chosen deliberately to market their products direct to the public. This movement was spearheaded by the Danish company Tjaereborg, which entered the British market in the late 1970s with a promotional strategy that asserted that directly booked holidays, by cutting out the agents' commission, would represent a saving to the customers. However, while isolated bargains were certainly on offer, many holidays were no cheaper, and sometimes more expensive than similar packages booked through an agent. The reasons for this are not hard to understand; while travel agency commissions were saved, huge budgets were required to inform and promote to the mass public. The company had to invest millions in heavy advertising in the media, and similar high costs were incurred by the need to have a large reservations staff and multiple telephone lines to answer enquiries from the public. These costs are, of course, fixed, while commissions are only paid to agents when the latter achieve a sale. Tjaereborg soon found, after initial success which was probably the outcome of curiosity, that it was unable to achieve greater market penetration, especially as Thomson Holidays had rapidly joined the competition with a direct sell division, Portland Holidays. Tjaereborg, after turning in an indifferent performance for several years, was sold to First Choice (then called Owners Abroad), which eventually replaced the brand with another direct sell operation, Eclipse.

The evidence suggests that traditional buying patterns die hard among British holidaymakers, with many customers still seeking the assurance of face-to-face contact with an agent, even if the product knowledge of that agent may be limited. However, there are some interesting variations in the pattern of agency sales; for example, those in the London area demonstrate a higher propensity to buy their holidays direct than do other Britons, and certain types of package tour, such as ski holidays and coach tours, also experience a higher proportion of direct bookings. The advent of interactive booking of travel arrangements using the Internet is now changing this pattern dramatically, as we shall see in the last section of this chapter.

The IT revolution and its impact on tour operating

No business is being transformed by information technology faster or more radically than the business of travel, and tour operating, of all sectors of the business, is arguably the most affected by developments occurring in this field. Of course, the advent of modern technology is no longer a recent phenomenon – after all, computers were widely introduced into the trade as early as the 1960s, hastening the demise of the traditional manual booking system. However, it is the scale and pace of recent development which is proving so disruptive for the industry, as new forms of booking and information facility become available to both the trade and the customer. Even the humble telephone has become a tool for providing new techniques to book holidays, with the growth of call centres and the recent development of WAP (Wireless Application Protocol), which allows customers to download material from various information sources into their mobile phones.

The key question is not whether these new techniques will start to replace traditional methods of booking holidays, but rather how quickly this transition will occur, and how completely it will come to dominate distribution. One can only speculate on what kind of future then will remain for the traditional agency channels – or even for traditional tour operators, given that suppliers can now easily and cheaply reach their customers direct, and customers are not slow to recognize that they can put together their own packages as well as any operator. The number of holiday sales that are made on-line through the World Wide Web is growing rapidly each year, although up to the present these are largely confined to buying a package rather than the several components of a package.

Again, the leading operators are responding to retain their markets. Thomas Cook and others in the UK were quick to launch accommodation-only websites aimed at the independent traveller (not necessarily restricting sales through retailers), as well as offering tailor-made programmes dynamically packaged through the Internet. Those that have yet to do so can be expected to fall into line very soon.

Some observers in the industry are adamant that the growth of on-line booking will neither lead to the closure of tour operators nor eradicate the travel agent, and have pointed to the relatively slow take-up of this distribution system among some elements of the market. Some believe that the inherent conservatism of British consumers, the lack of IT knowledge and skills among the older generation and uncertainty about reliability of the many new dot.com companies will ensure that support remains for more traditional means of booking. Others, aware of the rise in criminal activity associated with credit cards, are becoming reluctant to reveal details of their cards over the phone. Still others believe that their independent agents will be more impartial in giving advice about travel products than will the suppliers' websites, as well as providing a wider range of expertise in recommending holidays. Undoubtedly, all of these have some validity in discouraging sales through new channels. Operators and agents are fighting back by pointing out to the independent bookers that they will have no one to turn to when things go wrong (a message strongly reinforced when the Asian tsunami struck in 2004) and that accommodation and flights booked separately will not have the level of protection offered by a package, in the event of a collapse in either of the suppliers or other disaster.

The new IT systems of distribution can broadly be described as falling into one of the following three categories:

■ information and reservations systems offered by the suppliers of travel products and available to travel agents or other retailers
■ similar systems offered by intermediaries on behalf of travel suppliers
■ similar systems offered by either suppliers, or through intermediaries, direct to the consumer.

The principal means of delivering these new systems include Internet services on the World Wide Web via the personal computer, interactive television channels and the increasingly sophisticated use of mobile telephones.

A feature of the rapid escalation of Internet on-line providers in the twenty-first century was the subsequent and equally rapid collapse of many of these same companies, largely those acting as intermediaries for the travel suppliers. Inevitably, as suppliers set up their own communication networks to service agents or the public, this has threatened to undermine the intermediaries, which depend upon the commissions received from their suppliers. However, the intermediaries' role is assured as long as they can continue to offer a wide range of products at competitive prices, and are judged by the public to be at least as impartial in providing these services as are the more traditional outlets. Whether major suppliers will be willing to continue offering their products through intermediaries if they can satisfactorily sell a sufficient majority of these direct to the public will determine the future success of the latter. What we are seeing at this point is a gradual concentration of the intermediaries, to a point where a bare handful will emerge as market leaders, just as occurred among traditional tour operators at an earlier stage. Companies like Opodo, ebookers.com, lastminute.com, expedia.com and travelocity.com are reinforcing their strong positions in the market (indeed, lastminute.com have gone further, opening their own travel agency outlets at airports and railway stations to sell travel products).

The survival of travel agents in their present form is questionable. While there are undoubtedly consumers who will still want to deal with retailers face to face, they will only do so if the agent can deliver a professional service – difficult, given the existing low salaries and poor training, coupled with the squeeze on costs resulting from commission reductions, making professional salaries even harder to attain. The likelihood is that over the next few years we will witness a sharp reduction in the number of agency outlets, and only those who can demonstrate that they are providing *added value*, through superior service, knowledge or some other aspect of the retailing function, are likely to survive. This is already leading to agents imposing service charges in lieu of the traditional commissions which have been the mainstay of their incomes.

In the meantime, rapid development of alternative channels is hindered by two further factors. Operators have been slow to realize the potential of the new technology – some are still frightened of it – and in general marketing costs remain high for suppliers attempting to sell direct to the public. Nonetheless, more and more operators are becoming aware that selling in this way will eventually allow suppliers to trim, and possibly even eradicate, their two major sources of expenditure, commission and brochures. Already much information on destinations and facilities is available for public viewing on the Internet, and before long all holiday information currently provided by operators through the medium of brochures will become accessible in this way.

Call centres, set up to take bookings over the phone, provide another convenient means of enabling operators to reach their customers cheaply while offering very competitive prices. Fluid pricing strategies introduced by operators allow holidays to be more readily retailed through these call centres than through traditional channels. As a result, call centres have already led to reductions in the number of outlets operated by the retail chains, who cannot directly compete with this form of distribution.

In the longer term, interactive television promises to have an equally significant impact on the industry. In Britain, terrestrial TV is to be replaced by multi-channel digital television by 2010. Already, shopping channels and travel channels are available through cable and satellite TV, attracting the public into searching for, and booking, their holidays in this convenient manner. Asynchronous digital subscriber line (ADSL) technology allows viewers to choose what they watch, to pause and to rewind material they wish to study more closely. Although commercial agreements with the channel owners currently prohibit direct bookings on the TV screen, this is bound to be the next stage of development in retailing travel.

The speed of development of technology in this field is too rapid to allow a thorough treatment of the subject in a textbook. Students of tour operating must keep abreast of such developments through the trade press or other media. Suffice to add that in addition to reservations systems, computers are now used widely to provide accounts and management information quickly and accurately to both operators and agents, while larger operators have also introduced accounting systems which allow direct transfer of agency payments from the agents' bank account to that of the operator.

In any examination of the influence of new technology in industry, it would be facile to ignore the counter-argument, that impersonal means of communication can only go so far in satisfying consumer needs, and that many consumers remain reactionaries in their buying behaviour. Looking at parallels in other industries, in the world of print, newspapers remain popular even though their data are available on-line; bookshops are as active as ever, attracting browsers who do not wish to spend many hours searching the World Wide Web, although many independents are feeling the squeeze from the leading chains, rather than from websites, which understand how best to meet the book-buying public's expectations. More customers are seeking help from their bank managers in face-to-face financial discussion rather than impersonal communications via e-mail or telephone. Operators would do well to look at developments in other fields and see what lessons can be learned to improve their own means of communication with their clients.

Notes

1 Merger to Add Lobbying Power, *Travel Weekly*, 11 February 2005
2 *Travel Weekly*, 26 November 2004
3 Death of Salesmen? *Travel Weekly*, 5 December 2004

Websites

H-C travel	www.hctravel.com
Small Families	www.smallfamilies.co.uk
One Parent Family Holidays	www.opfh.org.uk
Walking Women	www.walkingwomen.com
Thomas Cook accommodation only	www.roomsandhotels.com
First Choice accommodation only	www.hotelbeds.com
Cosmos accommodation only	www.somewhere2stay.com

Questions and discussion points

1   Expect JMC to be phased out in the longer term and become a marketing student's case study.

> Danny Rogers, Associate Editor, Marketing, writing in
> *Travel Weekly*, 2 December 2002

The company has since reverted to the use of Thomas Cook as its principal brand, although the JMC name has not disappeared entirely. With the benefit of four years' hindsight, discuss why the JMC brand name was chosen to replace a strong brand, and whether this was a sensible marketing move at the time. What is the case for and against name changes such as this in the travel industry? Compare and contrast this decision with that of Airtours which became MyTravel.

2   In the mini-case in this chapter, Richard Carrick of Hoseasons declared the role of the travel trade representative to be dead. How far do you agree? In what circumstances would you, as an operator, employ a representative to call on agents?

Some companies use their resort representatives as travel trade representatives in the off-season. What are the advantages and disadvantages of this practice?

3   Argue the case for and against dropping the brochure entirely and replacing it with a website to market a company's inclusive tour products. What conditions would favour such as approach?

4   Will the new Airbus A380 find favour with large tour operators? On what routes might they prove suitable?

5   If the larger tour operators are either setting up or buying out specialist divisions (as we have seen has been First Choice's practice in this chapter), how can the smaller specialists compete?

6   Would you agree with the Competition Commission that tour operator takeovers are not against the public interest as long as prices are kept down? (Comparisons with the UK supermarkets might be interesting here, with Tesco reportedly seeking to capture 45 per cent of the market and Asda challenging them).

Assignment topics

1   As an area resort representative coming to the end of the summer season, write a critical report for your General Manager on the role of resort representatives' notice boards in hotels abroad. Identify the importance of these boards, their uses and value as a means of communicating with holidaymakers, and any tips you would recommend including in future resort representatives' training programmes regarding these boards.

   Also in your role as representative, prepare two notices for your board, as follows:

   (a)   a notice advising current holidaymakers due to return home tomorrow that their flight has been brought forward from 09.30 to 06.30 due to 'technical problems'.

   (b)   A notice directed to other holidaymakers who arrived yesterday that a new excursion has become available as an optional extra, which will include dinner and entertainment *al fresco* in a neighbouring resort a 30-minute bus ride away. Bookings can be made for the tour, which will take place in three days' time. You may invent any details you wish in drawing up your notice.

17 Retailing tourism

Objectives

After studying this chapter, you should be able to:

- explain the role of travel agents as a component of the tourism industry and their relationship with other sectors
- identify the functions performed by an agent
- be aware of the qualities necessary for effective agency management and service
- understand the considerations and the requirements for establishing and running a travel agency
- be aware of the constraints and threats under which agents operate, and evaluate alternative solutions for their survival.

Introduction

The boundaries between agent and operator are becoming blurred and are likely to become more so, helped by ever-improving technology.

Ian Mounser, Sales Director, Superbreak[1]

Notwithstanding the changes we have noted in the previous chapter, most travel principals continue to rely, to a greater or lesser extent, on travel agents as an important source of distribution, and retailers continue to play a key role in the structure of the industry. However, their share of business is declining, even in the key area of inclusive tours, as the customer turns to direct booking. According to research conducted by Euromonitor in 2005, agents were responsible for just 47 per cent of all inclusive tour bookings (by value) in 2004. However, at the same time, accommodation-only bookings taken by agents have increased by 55 per cent in the same year[2]. The agent's role is changing, but there are grounds for trusting that it is far from collapsing, providing agents are willing to adapt.

Agents selling travel arrangements have been in existence for well over a hundred years; indeed, the oldest, now the tour operator Cox and Kings, traces its origins back to the eighteenth century. The Polytechnic Touring Association was set up at Regent Street Polytechnic, London, in 1888, originally as an agency for student travel, and was acquired by Sir Henry Lunn of Lunn's Travel in the 1960s. This company became Lunn Poly under Thomson Holidays ownership after 1972, until a name change to that of its parent in 2004. The agents' principal role in earlier times was to sell shipping and rail services, but with the coming of air transport and the development of the package tour business after World War II, their product range expanded.

Before the war, the shipping companies had been able to provide a good reservations and ticketing service direct to the public, with sales outlets in their city offices and at leading ports. Railways and coach operators had similarly established city centre terminals, from which they could dispense tickets direct to the public. However, when the airlines arrived on the scene, their airport terminals were situated well away from centres of population, and as a convenient network of travel agents was by that time in place, they did not face the same pressure to establish their own chain of direct sales offices in favour of appointing agents to handle their sales; however, most leading airlines did establish a main selling office in capital cities, and many also opened off-line offices in other leading cities to serve the public as well as the trade. In North America, where the volume of domestic travel by air is substantially higher than elsewhere, airline offices were opened in virtually all major cities. Travel agents in turn expanded their distribution outlets to handle the new demand for air tickets. With the advent of deregulation, and a greater willingness on the part of passengers to book direct (first by phone or fax, later via the Internet), many airlines closed their off-line offices, while agents have similarly experienced a fall in air ticket sales in the past few years.

Historically, of course, Thomas Cook originated as a tour operator, only expanding later to retail travel services. In more recent times, it was the travel agents themselves who developed the first air package tours, as we have seen in the previous chapter. A handful of retail entrepreneurs had the vision to see that if they could buy air seats in bulk and reduce the cost of air fares, a huge mass market for foreign tours would develop. The packages they developed were, in turn, sold through other agents, and eventually these became the retailers' principal source of revenue.

In mid-2005 there were about 1,400 agents affiliated to the Association of British Travel Agents (ABTA), the leading trade body representing both tour operators and travel agents in the UK. They controlled 6,131 outlets, and over 500 of these agencies were also listed as ABTA tour operators. At its high point, ABTA had nearly 3,000 members with over 7,500 offices, and the number has dwindled slightly over the past two decades. However, the composition of these agents has changed dramatically over time, with a fall in independent agencies as the travel agency chains expanded under the ownership of the major tour operators. With the growth in call centres and electronic booking, the multiples are now starting to reduce the number of their own high street outlets. As the total number of agencies falls, turnover achieved by the remaining offices increases.

Apart from those agents in ABTA, some independents operate outside the ABTA framework. Because of the regulations which formerly constrained non-ABTA agents, these were limited in earlier years to selling fringe services such as coach trips, or operated as so-called 'bucket shops' (a term referring to outlets used by airlines to dump unsold tickets on the market at short notice and at heavily discounted prices). However, as airlines were deregulated and the no-frills carriers appeared on the market with rock-bottom prices, and consolidators sprang up to wholesale air tickets, the need for bucket shops disappeared. Following the removal of Stabiliser regulations in 1992, agents became free to trade with all ABTA and non-ABTA tour operators, and are now subject only to legal requirements to carry satisfactory bonds against financial collapse. In the event, this did not lead to the wholesale withdrawal of members from ABTA; the need for a powerful association to represent the interests of tour operators and retailers remained, and many retailers chose to retain their membership. They benefit from brand recognition, as well as from the clearing house which clears payments to tour operators, and the financial protection offered by the ABTA bond is stressed in generic advertising.

The role of travel agents

The travel agent's role is dissimilar to that of most other retailers, in that agents do not purchase a product for resale to their customers. Only when a customer has decided on a travel purchase do agents approach their principal on their customer's behalf to make a purchase. The travel agent does not, therefore, carry 'stock' of travel products. This has two important implications for the business of travel distribution. First, the cost of setting up in business is relatively small compared to that of other retail businesses, and second, agents are not seeking to dispose of products they have already purchased, so will therefore display less brand loyalty towards a particular product or company. However, in the past few years negotiations between principals and agents have led to higher commissions being paid to agents that achieve target sales, and this resulted in agents becoming more commercial in their approach. This is particularly true of the multiples, or travel agency chains, which are owned by tour operators and push their parent companies' products, a process known as *directional selling*. Rather than the objective advice which customers could anticipate from an agency, it is now more common for them to be faced with a limited range of products which offer the agent the best return on sales. Some independents have tried to reverse this trend by claiming to offer objective advice, promoting the smaller, independent tour operators' products. Many of these are affiliated to one of the loosely knit associations devoted to this policy, such as the ITAA (Independent Travel Agents' Alliance). There has also been a tendency for independent agents to tie into consortia as a means of competing with the multiples, a process which will be examined later in this chapter. An international consortium has also been formed, the Worldwide Independent Travel Agents' Network (WIN), with membership in thirteen countries.

Arguably, the main role of the travel agent has always been to provide a convenient location for the purchase of travel. At these locations they act as booking agents for holidays and travel, as well as a source of information and advice on travel services. Their customers look to them for expert product knowledge and objectivity in the advice they offer, but, as we have seen, they may be disappointed, as agents choose to deal with an increasingly limited range of products on which they can maximize their revenue. In one sense, this is inevitable; the competitive nature of retail travel is such that margins are extremely thin, and agents must find whatever means they can of surviving. Nor is it realistic to imagine that sales staff – who are often young, generally inexperienced in travel themselves and poorly paid by comparison with other areas of retailing – can have a thorough knowledge of every product in the industry, with a product range of package tours alone drawn from hundreds of ATOL-holding bonded tour operators.

The range of products that an agent will choose to offer will vary, not only on the basis of the commission each earns but also depending upon the demand within the catchment area, the degree of specialization of the agency and the preferences and marketing policies of the proprietor. An agency that is attempting to provide a full range of services to the public would sell air tickets, cruise and ferry tickets, rail and coach transport, car hire, hotel accommodation and package tours (a growing number of which might be domestic). Ancillary services such as travel insurance, traveller's cheques and foreign exchange may also be offered, and some agents will also undertake to arrange travel documentation (such as procuring visas) for their clients. Some will even deal with theatre tickets.

However, these all-round agents are rapidly disappearing in the face of commercial pressures. Owing to the small amount of revenue achieved on the sale of coach or rail tickets, many agents are now forgoing the sale of these types of transport, although some agents still believe it to be better to offer a full range of services even if some are loss making, on the grounds that the customer may return to buy other travel arrangements later. Research into the relative profitability of agents who generalize and those who specialize has found that the former would generate fewer profits, supporting the specialists' policy.

Agents may specialize not only in the selection of products they offer, but in the markets they serve. The clearest distinction is between those that focus on business travel (serving the travel needs of the local, and in some cases national, business community) and those that concentrate on leisure travel.

Setting up and running a travel agency

(a) The leisure travel agency

Travel agents are located in major city centres, in the suburbs of large towns, and less frequently in smaller towns. To be successful, they tend be sited at street level and close to the centre of the main shopping districts. They compete against other agents within a catchment area which, in the case of a large city, may extend only to the surrounding streets, while in the case of an important market town the catchment may draw on residents living within a radius of 30 or 40 miles.

It is also worth noting that agents in city centres will draw their clients not only from residents in the area but also from workers employed in the area, who may find it more convenient to make their travel arrangements close to their place of work, rather than nearer to their homes. On the other hand, the agency is also faced with the likelihood that a number of workers in the area will choose to pick up their brochures from the city branch, and make their reservations at an agency near their homes, where bookings can be arranged together with their spouses. This may mean a high turnover of brochures with little return for the city agency, a problem particularly common in London.

A recent development among specialized agencies is to focus on contacting their clients through websites, or recommendation by word of mouth, thus making them less dependent upon expensive street-level offices. These agents also avoid the growing curse of 'time-wasters', people who pop in to pick up brochures from which they will later book direct on-line, or who merely wish to get quotations to compare with those obtained from countless other agencies in the area. In this sense, the independent agents are further distancing themselves from the multiples' outlets, which continue to depend upon a significant street presence.

Example   Haslemere Travel

Haslemere Travel is an English agency which is moving away from the concept of the street-level shop serving purely as a convenient location for bookings and tickets. Much of its business is achieved through promotion via its website. It also claims to have doubled its sales in one year by closely monitoring every customer who contacts its shop. All enquiries, whether in person or over the phone or website is logged and traced for progress, and where a booking does not result, staff are encouraged to follow up to find out why. This simple monitoring has resulted in an increase in bookings from 40 per cent to 75 per cent.

Website: www.haslemeretravel.co.uk

Setting up a travel agency in Britain requires little capital, for reasons already noted, nor are formal qualifications a prerequisite (unlike some other European Union members). Consequently, the business appears extremely attractive to outsiders, who see it as a glamorous occupation with wonderful opportunities for cheap travel.

Anyone contemplating opening a travel agency will have to consider the merits of buying an existing agency, or forming a new one. There are considerable advantages in taking over an existing agency. To begin with, trading figures for recent years can be examined, and the viability of the agency evaluated, in relation to the asking price. A going concern can be expected to retain its loyal clientele, if service remains comparable, but against this, if there is a strong and loyal market already, the asking price for the agency may be high, to include the goodwill. 'Goodwill' embraces the reputation of the business and the expectation that existing customers will continue to buy there. Another advantage of buying an existing agency is that licences and appointments, once granted by principals, are generally retained under the new management. Staff, too, can be retained; even in the recession, good qualified and experienced staff were not easy to find, especially for those seeking to set up a new agency.

Figure 17.1
A specialist travel agency with an attractive window display: Voyageurs du Monde, Lille, France

(Photographed by the author)

The attraction of starting from scratch is mainly a financial one; capital cost will be limited to office furnishings, fixtures, computers, phones, and perhaps a new external fascia. However, persuading principals to provide you with brochures, to offer you an appointment and to pay a commission on sales may prove difficult, especially if the area concerned is already well served by existing agents.

In recent years, prices of independent agencies were pushed up by the eagerness of the chains to expand quickly by taking over independents. As the chains have now reduced their branches, and there is also greater awareness of the difficulties of trading at a profit as an independent, the value of agencies dropped.

A popular adage has it that 'there are only three important things in setting up an agency: location, location and location'. This drives home the fundamental point that, from the customer's point of view, the convenience of the location is the main criterion in their choice of a travel agent, for those requiring little more than a simple holiday-booking at the best possible price. Increasingly, this is coming to mean a branch of one of the multiples. In focusing on this market, any agent expecting to attract casual passing trade who chooses a little-used side street away from the main shopping area, merely because rents or rates are lower, can be at a major trading disadvantage. If, on the other hand, the shop is to serve as an outlet for clients seeking a professional agency via the Internet, and who wish to progress a complex itinerary in person, a side street, or an upper floor, may serve the agent's purpose.

Equally, it can be a mistake to scrimp on floor space and decor. Clients are attracted to roomy shops with plenty of rack space and a bright, cheerful, inviting atmosphere to tempt them in. Increasingly, windows are designed not as settings to display brochures or destination publicity, but as living advertisements for the shop interior. Good lighting, warm colours, comfortable chairs, desks rather than impersonal counters, all affect the client's perception of the agency and their motivation to enter the shop. Once inside, the good agent takes advantage of the opportunity to make a sale; but enticing the client through the door is the first step in selling.

Example TUI

Thomson Travel, the retailing arm of TUI in Britain, announced two significant changes to the way they would do business in 2005. They plan to change the whole image of the travel agent, with far less clutter in their windows (allowing a fuller view of the interiors for passers-by) and a reduction in point-of-sale display in favour of a more discreet, comfortable and tasteful furnishings, in their battle for dominance in the multiples sector. They also took the decision to expand their product range, most notably by the experimental sale of property abroad to second-home buyers.

Sites need to be researched carefully. Existing pedestrian flows should be noted (usually, one side of a major shopping street – often the sunny side – always appears to attract more people than the other) as should barriers, whether physical or psychological. For instance, shops on traffic 'islands' which force pedestrians to use subways to cross the road will find it more difficult to attract the passing trade. Parking is often difficult in town centres, but if there are too many restrictions and no nearby car parks, this can be a further important disincentive to the shopper. The local planning office should be consulted to examine any plans for redevelopment in the area. Residential redevelopment in the immediate area could be an important plus for the site, while commercial redevelopment nearby may pose a threat; another travel agency could well open in competition when the site is opened, and if attractive and more accessible, could poach much of the business. It may be better, under such circumstances, to consider delaying a decision to open until renting in the new shopping plaza becomes affordable.

In law, a travel agency is an office, rather than a shop. This is important beyond mere semantics, since in the case of *Ilkeston Co-operative Travel* v. *Erewash Borough Council* (1988), it was determined that travel agents were exempt from the legal restrictions on Sunday trading applicable to retail shops, and could therefore open to trade. Sunday trading has become much more common in recent years, although often restricted to key booking periods of the year such as the post-Christmas booking season. Longer opening hours are necessary now to compete with bookings made on the Internet at any time of the day or night.

In the past, agents earned their revenue largely in the form of commission on sales. Levels of commission have varied over time and according to the travel product sold, but typically have been highest for package tour sales (between 10 and 15 per cent),

Figure 17.2
The agency
multiple: a TUI
retail shop

(Photographed by the author)

with transportation companies paying slightly lower rates and other services even less. This pattern has changed radically within the past few years, as principals sought to remain profitable by cutting costs and finding cheaper means of distributing their products. Among tour operators, Thomson led the way in reducing basic rates of commission paid to their agents, and introducing a complex reward system for greater sales effort, including directional selling. More recently, the airlines have similarly changed their payment structures to agents, with many withdrawing commissions entirely, forcing the agents to charge a service fee to their customers for the sale of tickets. This has been a noted practice of the budget carriers, led by Ryanair, whose bookings are almost entirely via the Internet, but British Airways (which now gets over half its bookings from the Internet) has moved in a similar direction, not only refusing commissions, but also withdrawing ticketing and GDS privileges for agents doing less than £50,000 worth of sales for their services. Withdrawal of commission soon became the practice of other international carriers. Even train service commissions in Britain have been shrinking, from 9 per cent to 7 per cent in 2004. The likelihood is that we shall see commissions excluded on most travel services, with agents initiating fees to cover their expenses.

Agents at first resisted the termination of the commission structure, arguing that their customers would not only be angered by attempts to charge a transaction fee, but would be more likely to book direct with the airlines. The introduction of ticketless travel by some airlines, which not only saves airlines and other travel suppliers the cost of issuing tickets, but also encourages direct bookings, has further whittled down agency revenue. Not all airlines have yet taken this approach, however, hoping their support will generate greater loyalty among agents.

Example	Virgin Airlines

Virgin continues (at the time of writing) to support agents with commission, but has redrafted its commission based on the levels of support that agents give the company. It now classifies agents by five bands, based on revenue achieved: platinum, gold, silver, red or blue. The bands determine an agent's access to net fares, the levels of training and other support offered and the extent of the agent's investment in its market. Commission structures range from 1 per cent for agents classified as blue, up to 7 per cent for platinum agents, with incentive payments of up to 5 per cent above this, depending upon factors such as location, routes, class and seasonality.

Evidence from the USA tends to support the agents in their view that service charges have been difficult to impose. Commissions were capped by the airlines there in the mid-1990s, but the public initially resisted attempts to impose fees, turning to book on the Internet. In 1995, 70 per cent of all airline tickets issued in that country were sold through agents, but this had dropped to just 30 per cent a decade later. Some 40 per cent of agents have left their jobs in the interim as a result, with many turning to working as travel counsellors from their homes to sell air travel. Virtually all US agents now charge transaction fees, while attempting to increase sales of package holidays and cruises to maintain revenues.

In the UK, package tours represent by far the largest proportion of all agency sales, although an increasing proportion of these involve some tailor-made elements. Typically, overseas holidays account for the majority of sales, with air transport a declining element. Domestic holidays, a growing area of potential sales, have been estimated to take up to 4 per cent, while the remainder is divided between cruises, rail and coach bookings and miscellaneous services. Tailor-made packages, or dynamic packaging, are steadily eroding the traditional tour operator-based package tour product for many agencies.

Value added tax (VAT) is payable by travel agencies on the 'added value' of package tours, i.e. on the commission earned by the agent. Payment to Customs and Excise is usually undertaken on behalf of the agents by the tour operators, but agents devising their own packages will make their own returns to Customs and Excise. For example:

Tour price		£400.00
Agent deducts:		
commission	£40.00	
VAT due	£7.00	
		£47.00
Agent remits to tour operator		£353.00
Agent remits to C&E		£7.00

Table 17.1 Agency branches of the Big Four, September 2005

TUI Thomson	836
Going Places	665
Thomas Cook	614
First Choice	273

Those principals who do pay commissions will generally offer higher levels to agents that are members of consortia banding together to achieve agreed sales targets, in order to compete with the multiples. This can add 2.5 per cent or more to the earnings of the agent, particularly for the sale of package tours. However, it is still rare to find an agent averaging earnings of more than 10–11 per cent on the total of the revenue achieved during the year. Since it became legal to discount the price of travel products at the point of sale, the independent agents have been under particular pressure from discounting by the multiples. These large chains, because of their substantial buying power, can negotiate higher overriding commissions with the major tour operators – some reports have put this as high as 18 per cent. Since the company also made no payments to its suppliers until eight weeks before its clients' departure, this example clearly demonstrates the power of the big distributors in the trade. It also allows the agent to pass 10 per cent or more back to its clients in the form of a discount, offering a price that few independents could hope to meet.

This helped the multiples to expand their branches rapidly – a process that is now going into reverse, as the call centres and electronic booking replace traditional high street shops. Table 17.1 reveals the retail branches of the multiples in 2005.

Additionally, the largest independent agency is the Co-op Travel Trading Group, composed of five cooperative societies which merged their travel interests in 2003 to create a single body with around 650 branches.

Out of gross profits, travel agents must pay all the running expenses of their agencies, including their own salary (see Figure 17.3). Only after these expenses have been met can they judge whether they have made a net profit or a loss for the year. One measure of the profitability, and particularly the productivity, of agents is to examine their turnover per employee. Earlier studies have generally found multiples to be more profitable than independents. However, a Benchmarking Survey carried out by PricewaterhouseCoopers in 2000 gave an overall turnover of only £271,000 per employee, and a net profit per employee of £3,574. More recent figures are unavailable, but given the commission cuts of recent years it would suggest that most agents are struggling to remain in profit.

The profitability of agents is helped by their status as 'credit' agents rather than cash agents. Agents that have credit arrangements with their principals have the advantage of simpler recording procedures and improved cash flow, since they will hold clients' payments for longer before transmitting funds to the principals.

(b) The business travel agency

Those agents whose location is close to city centres, or other centres of business and industry such as an industrial estate, may also try to capture the business travellers

Sales	1,500,000	
Gross profit (commission at average 9.4%)	<u>141,000</u>	
Expenditure		
Personnel		
Salaries, NHI, pensions	60,000	
Staff travel, training, subscriptions	<u>3,000</u>	
	63,000	(44.68%)
Establishment		
Rent, rates, water	22,000	
Light and heat	3,000	
Insurance	2,000	
Cleaning	<u>1,300</u>	
	28,300	(20.07%)
Administation		
Computers, telephone, website	10,000	
Postage	2,000	
Printing & stationery	2,000	
Hire of equipment	1,000	
Advertising and publicity	4,000	
Publications, timetables	<u>1,000</u>	
	20,000	(14.18%)
Financial and legal		
Credit cards	3,500	
Bank charges	1,500	
Auditing and accounting	4,000	
Legal fees	500	
Bad debts	<u>500</u>	
	10,000	(7.09%)
Depreciation and amortization	<u>4,600</u>	(3.26%)
Total operational costs	<u>125,900</u>	(89.29%)
Net profit before tax	15,100	<u>(10.71%)</u>
		100.00%
Note: net profit as % of sales		(1.01%)

Figure 17.3 Hypothetical operating costs of an independent travel agency

within their territory. However, this is a highly specialized market, in which staff must have greater skills and must compete against the large business travel corporations whose contacts with suppliers allow greater flexibility in negotiating prices.

Commissions earned from suppliers may have to be split with clients to retain the account, although increasingly commission payments are being replaced by management fees. Coupled with extended credit agreements, agencies may well find that the cost of servicing the business outweighs any potential profit.

If an agreement is reached, there are a number of options in drawing up a fee-based contract, the most common being:

■ a flat fee, usually payable per month

■ rebate of the agency commission and a fixed amount charged per transaction

■ a simple fee-per-ticket basis

■ variable fees charged according to the complexity of the transaction

■ a minimum fee charged per transaction with the guarantee of a minimum number of transactions per month.

It is also common to find contracts drawn up based on fees which depend upon the agency achieving a certain level of cost savings for the company. Agreements will also generally include extended credit terms, whereby accounts do not have to be settled until ten to twelve weeks after the receipt of tickets. One drawback of a system in which commission is fully rebated to the client is that the supplier, such as a hotel, gains no sales benefit from increasing its commission rates to its distributors, and must look for other strategies to gain the agency's support.

Businesses are extremely demanding customers. The level of service which an agent must offer to retain their patronage is considerable. Focusing on the business community requires not just additional skills and knowledge, but also a willingness to work long hours and provide a level of service far beyond what would be expected of counter staff in a leisure agency. Documentation such as visas may have to be arranged for clients, often at short notice, and then delivered to the client's address, possibly out of hours. Senior members of staff must be accessible at any time to arrange last-minute travel. Professional business staff will expect to be paid well above the rates paid to regular counter staff, yet margins may be slimmer to meet competitors' prices. The additional costs of handling these arrangements must be considered by the agent, particularly where credit is offered to the business house. It is not unusual for companies to delay payments until well beyond the dates due, while the agent is still obliged to make payments to principals within the agreed times; thus the agent is helping to fund the company's cash flow at its own expense. All of this makes business travel a difficult field to enter as an independent, regardless of the level of personal service it is willing to offer. However, the attraction of the larger business accounts, often exceeding a million pounds a year, will result in many agents competing for the business by offering extra levels of service, implants, fares expertise to guarantee lowest prices, and financial incentives.

Implant (or in-plant) offices are those based in the business client's own premises but staffed by the agency, specifically to handle the company's travel needs exclusively. To justify this, the company must be certain that revenue will be sufficient to cover the high costs of setting up and operating an additional branch.

Since the highest discounts can be offered by agents negotiating the best deals with their principals, this has once again led to the multiple branch agencies dominating the business house market. The Guild of Travel Management Companies is the professional body representing the leading business travel agents, and accounts for some 75–80 per cent of all airline tickets sold in the UK. Five leading brands control the market: American Express, Carlson Wagonlit, BCD, Hogg Robinson and Navigant. The Guild's role is to represent the interests of business agents and their clients, and to improve the standards and quality of travel for their members, through negotiation with suppliers such as airlines, airports and hotel chains. Some business travel agents are also members of international consortia, which offer them greater influence and purchasing power with principals. Business Travel International (BTI), is a global corporation whose members include the largest French travel chain, Havas, the German chain Hapag Lloyd, and the US agency IVI, as well as Holland International of the Netherlands, Bennett Travel of Scandinavia and National Australia Travel. With the global buying power of this group, airline and other tickets can be purchased at the lowest possible price for business house clients. Hogg Robinson owns the BTI brand in the UK.

Large companies often themselves employ specialist travel managers, who act as buyers of travel products for the employees, and therefore intermediaries between the employee and travel agency. Purchases arranged centrally in this way allow the company to benefit from increased know-how and better prices. These managers have their own professional body in the UK, the Institute of Travel Management (ITM), which seeks to use its influence to obtain better deals for its members, and acts as a mouthpiece and watchdog for this section of the industry. There is an equivalent organization in the USA, the National Passenger Traffic Association (NPTA), which has actually set up its own travel agency to make further cost savings for its members. Both the ITM and NPTA are represented in the International Business Travel Association (IBTA), which includes a number of Continental European organizations among its members.

Many of these large corporations have gone a stage further; recognizing that they have the buying power to organize their own travel arrangements without the intercession of a travel agent, they will negotiate direct with airlines for their tickets and discount agreements, cutting out intermediaries entirely. Once again, the on-line suppliers and agencies are making it easier for the customer to benefit by going direct.

Travel agency skills and competences

It follows that, owing to the extremely competitive nature of the retail travel business, two factors become paramount if the agency is to succeed: good management and good service. Good management will ensure that costs are kept under control, that staff are motivated, and that the agency goes out actively to seek business rather than wait for it to come through the door. Good service will ensure satisfied clients, help to build a regular clientele and encourage word-of-mouth recommendation, which will increase the local share of the market for the agent.

Despite the expansion of the large chains in recent years, most independent travel agents are still small, family-run businesses in which the owner acts as manager, and employs two or three members of staff. In such an agency there is little specialization in terms of the usual division of labour, and staff will be expected to cope with all the activities normally associated with the booking of travel, which will include:

- advising potential travellers on resorts, carriers, travel companies and travel facilities worldwide
- making reservations for all travel requirements
- planning itineraries of all kinds, including complex multi-stopover independent tours
- accessing relevant websites
- issuing documentation, including travel tickets and vouchers
- communicating by telephone, e-mail and letter with travel principals and customers
- maintaining accurate files on reservations
- maintaining and displaying stocks of travel brochures
- interceding with principals in the event of customer complaints.

In addition to product knowledge, therefore, the main skills that counter staff require will include the ability to read timetables and other data sources, to source 'best buy' airline fares, to complete tickets and to have sufficient knowledge of their customers to be able to match customer needs with the products available. All staff today are also required to be familiar with the latest technology, including the use of e-mail, fax and accessing websites and computer reservations systems (CRSs) of all types.

The correct construction of airline fares and issue of airline tickets is a far more complex subject than might be apparent to the uninitiated, and entails a lengthy period of training coupled with continuous exercise of these skills. A number of internationally recognized courses are available to provide these skills, including in Britain those offered by British Airways, which meet IATA requirements and can be taken up to the BA Fares and Ticketing Part II level, indicating full competence to meet any requirement for fare construction and ticketing. For most air fares, however, agents are now dependent upon quotations given by carriers or intermediaries via the CRSs and websites. The ticketing function is largely undertaken via computers, and arguably fare quotations and ticketing skills are becoming less important for most agency staff, apart from those dealing with business travel. An understanding of the principles underlying the construction of fares, however, can be helpful – for example, in explaining complex fares to customers – and of course there will be a continuing need for fares experts in the industry. The large travel agency chains have in some cases centralized this role, so that a handful of experts can quickly determine the lowest fares for a particular journey by air on request from a member of their counter staff at any of the company's branches.

In addition to counter staff functions, agency managers (who frequently spend time at the counter themselves) are required to fulfil a number of administrative functions. On the financial side, these will include:

- maintenance and control of the company's accounts
- invoicing clients

- effecting bank reconciliations
- preparing and controlling budgets
- providing an estimate of the cash flow in the company on a month-by-month basis
- controlling expenditure.

Sales records must be kept, and sales returns completed regularly for travel principals. All these 'back office' jobs can today be computerized, even in the case of the smaller independent agency. Managers also have the task of safeguarding their stock of tickets and other negotiable documents, and in addition have the usual tasks of recruiting, training and supervising office staff, and promoting their business in-shop and externally.

Finally, managers need to control and regularly up-date their websites, and oversee the preparation and distribution of e-newsletters to clients. Regular contact with clients via the Internet, or through the post, is now essential to retain business and discourage clients from booking direct on the Web.

Customer contact skills

The way in which staff communicate with clients is, together with the essential product knowledge they display, a key ingredient in the agency's success. These communication skills can be divided into three distinct categories:

- language skills
- personal and social skills
- sales skills.

There is widespread concern about the lack of basic language skills demonstrated by many British workers, and this applies not merely to a lack of foreign languages, but to a lack of competence in the way we use our own native tongue. Written communication to a client which demonstrates poor sentence construction, grammar or spelling reflects not just on the employee, but also on the company itself. When such correspondence goes out under the signature of a senior member of staff, the image of the company suffers a still more serious blow.

Personal and social skills are even more important, but fortunately it lies within our own power, to a large extent, to exercise these skills. There is still a tendency in Britain to look down upon jobs which involve serving the public, which is all too often confused with servility. We are gradually learning as a nation that if we are to compete with our European colleagues, we must be prepared to offer the same level of 'service' in our service industries as they do. The acceptance of the credo 'the customer is always right' is the first move towards creating the right atmosphere for serving behind a counter, in a travel agency as in any other shop. Customers expect to be received warmly, and with a genuine smile of greeting; staff are expected to be unfailingly cheerful whatever stress they may be experiencing during their workday. These qualities need to become second nature to counter staff (but a glance at the trade newspapers' 'mystery shopper' pages will reveal that much service is still not only incompetent, but off-hand).

First impressions weigh heavily, and staff will be judged, too, by their dress and appearance. Tourism employees must be prepared to adjust to the constraints that the job imposes, if they wish to succeed in the industry. Employers will insist on neat hairstyles, suitably discreet make-up for female staff, and overall good grooming and appearance – often to the extent that counter staff in the agency chains will be required to wear a uniform – and personal hygiene is essential.

Deportment, too, is important. The way employees sit, stand or walk says a great deal about them and their attitude towards their customers. Staff who are exposed to the clients' view will be expected to look alert and interested when addressing their clients, to avoid slouching when they walk, and to sit upright rather than slumped in their chairs. These non-verbal signals all say a lot about the attitude of the company to its customers. The scene of employees filing their nails or talking to their friends on the telephone, while customers try to attract their attention, is a common one in training videos, and one that encourages us to think about how we present ourselves in public. A warm, welcoming smile and friendly manner when greeting a customer approaching the counter will convey a positive view of the company, and make the customer feel at home and in a buying frame of mind. Attentiveness to the customer is not only polite; it ensures that vital client needs are recognized, enabling the employee to match needs with products. When talking to customers and greeting them, the employee should maintain eye contact and a manner which will breed confidence in the agency and its staff's product knowledge. Even handshakes are important cues to confidence; they should be firm and offered willingly. Use of the client's name enhances the relationship.

Even the way in which staff answer the telephone can help to generate the right image of the company. Telephones should be answered quickly and competently. As there are no dress and appearance 'cues' from which the client can make a judgement, the voice becomes the sole basis of judgement. Trainers emphasize the need to smile, even over the telephone, as an impression of friendliness can still be conveyed in the voice. If clients are asked to hold on, they should be given the reason, and regularly checked to ensure they are still holding. If the person they are trying to reach is busy, an offer should be made to call them back and there should be a follow-up to ensure that they have been called back. Similarly, if the employee cannot give an answer immediately to a problem, they should offer to call the client back with the answer in a short while, and do so. A failure to call back is one of the most common sources of frustration to clients, and one that can easily lead to a loss of business to a competitor.

The sales sequence

Travel agencies are no longer order takers; to compete, they must go out and get the business. Good social skills build the atmosphere which encourages buying, but closing a sale requires an understanding of technique. Effective selling is the outcome of four stages in the selling process, which together make up the sales sequence:

- establishing *rapport* with clients
- *investigating* clients' needs

- *presenting* the product to the clients
- getting clients to take action, by *committing* themselves to the purchase.

Below, each of these stages is examined in more detail.

Rapport

To sell products successfully, one must first match them to the customers' needs. If the clients buy a product they do not really want, or which does not provide the satisfaction they were looking for, they simply do not come back again. As no travel agency can survive without a high level of repeat business, achieving a one-time sale is clearly not enough; the customer must be satisfied in the longer term. To achieve this, the first step is to build a rapport, by engaging the client in conversation, gaining their trust and learning about their needs. This process allows the salesperson to judge how receptive the client is to new ideas, and how willing to have products sold to them. Some customers prefer to self-select, and should not be badgered into a sale, while others need and seek advice more openly.

To generate a two-way conversation, the opening phrase 'Can I help you?' has to be avoided – it simply invites the reply, 'No thanks, I'm just looking'. A more useful way of opening a conversation would be to use a phrase such as, 'Do you have a particular type of holiday in mind?', or, to a customer who has just picked up a brochure, 'That's a very good programme this year. Were you just looking for sun, sea, sand holidays, or had you something more adventurous in mind?' This forces a reply, and encourages the client to open a conversation.

Investigation

Once you have gained the client's trust, the next step is to investigate their needs more thoroughly. Once again, it is necessary to ask open questions, which elicit full answers. The sort of information needed to draw out the client will include:

- who is travelling, and the number in the group
- when they wish to travel, and for how long
- their preferred mode of travel
- their choice of destination
- what they expect to pay.

The latter is one of the hardest for junior staff. It requires almost a sixth sense to know whether the cost of the holiday is critical, and if so, what are the limits. If the customer mentions a figure, one should not take it for granted that this is the maximum they are willing to pay; the industry has encouraged holidaymakers to believe that holidays are invariably cheap, but one is doing the client a disservice not to point out that cheapness is not necessarily value for money, and that by paying a little more one might have a better guarantee of satisfaction. The good salesperson is one who can talk up the price while still reassuring the client that they are looking after that client's best interests. It is generally better to wait for the client to give an indication of their budget than to question them directly on this point.

Clients will not necessarily have the answers to all these questions. They may have only the vaguest idea about where they want to go, what they want to do, even what they expect to pay. Needs must never be assumed, even from a clear statement of intent: clients saying they do not want to take a package holiday may merely be revealing a deep-seated prejudice that such holidays are 'down-market'; alternatively, they may have had a bad experience of earlier such holidays. The salesperson's task is to tease out the real reason so that the appropriate product can be offered – for example, a tailor-made independent inclusive tour may offer the best solution, where the client would not be one of a crowd.

Sometimes it will be clear to the salesperson that the client has superior knowledge about the destination, or is seeking information about a little-known destination. In these conditions it is preferable to admit ignorance, and either to offer an introduction to another member of staff with better knowledge of the destination, or to offer to obtain more information for them.

Presentation

Once the salesperson is satisfied that they know exactly what the client needs, they may go on to the next stage, that of presenting the products that they feel will suit the client. The aim will be to present not only the features of the holiday being offered, but also the benefits:

> 'Travelling in the early spring, you have the advantage of lower prices, yet this can be the nicest time of the year in the Austrian valleys, with the blossom out and before the mass of tourists arrive in the height of the season'.

Product knowledge is, of course, critical for success in gaining the client's confidence to a point where they are willing to accept one's recommendations. Even if the salesperson feels that what they are offering is exactly suitable for their client, it is always a good idea to offer an alternative, so that the client has the opportunity to choose. If the salesperson then demonstrates just how one holiday is a better buy than the other, this will make it easier for the client to decide on the choice being recommended.

At this stage in the sales sequence, the salesperson will often have to handle objections. Sometimes objections are voiced only because the client needs reassurance, or because they have not yet fully understood the benefits being offered to them. At other times objections occur because not all the client's needs have yet been met, and here a process of patient questioning may be needed once again to draw out the possibly hidden motives for the objections.

Commitment

This final stage is the process leading to closing the sale. This means getting the client to take action – ideally to buy, but of course some clients will need more time to consider the offer. The aim of the counter clerk is to get the best possible outcome from the sales sequence – taking an option, getting the clients to call back later, or getting them to agree that the salesperson may call them later to follow up the sale. The good salesperson is always looking for the buying signals that herald that the client is ready to buy: 'Would you like me to see if I can get you a reservation for that date?' can prompt the client who is dithering to take action. Care must be taken, however, never to push the client into a sale before they are ready to buy, or they may be lost forever.

Finally, having received the deposit for a firm booking, the salesperson must remember that the sales job has not been finished. They must continue to show interest and concern for the client, helping to reinforce the sale and their commitment to return for later travel arrangements. Many agents now send a 'welcome home' card to their clients after their return from holiday, to invite them to come into the shop and talk about their experiences, and to ensure they will remember the agency in the future. E-mail is invaluable for keeping in touch with clients – communication is immediate, and there is no cost involved.

A good selling technique grows with experience, but it takes effort; effort to find out what the client really needs – effort to appear constantly friendly and interested, and effort to find the right product to match the needs.

The product portfolio

It is ironic that the travel product requires perhaps greater knowledge on the part of retail staff than does virtually any other product, while travel agents' salaries still lag behind those of others in the distributive trade. This makes it particularly hard for agency managers to attract and retain qualified staff. Agents argue that competition and discounted prices make it impossible to pay higher salaries. Principals have come to accept that their retailers cannot be expected to have detailed product knowledge of every company's offerings, and concentrate instead on providing agents with easier access to information through websites, CRSs and informative brochures.

While the apparently unbiased service provided by the independent travel agent appears to be a marketing advantage, it is questionable whether clients themselves actually deal through an agent to gain this benefit, since the proportion of sales through travel agents is highest for the standard package holidays, which could arguably be booked direct with equal simplicity. This supports the view of many that travel agents only represent a convenient outlet for buying a holiday, rather than an advisory service. One should also not dismiss the value of personal contact when making bookings; many customers are still reluctant to commit high expenditure to an uncertain fate on the Web – there is a growing fear of fraud or identity theft when offering credit card details over the Web, and agents still offer some guarantee of financial security.

The low proportion of bookings achieved by travel agents for domestic holidays owes much to the traditional pattern of booking holidays in the UK. Domestic holidaymakers have tended in the past to contact principals direct to make their holiday bookings, often by writing to resort tourist offices for brochures and details of hotels. Holidays in Britain were neither conveniently packaged, nor seen by travel agents as sufficiently remunerative to justify devoting precious rack space to brochures, or training staff in domestic product knowledge. However, two factors have tended to increase sales through agencies. First, UK holidays have risen in price vis-à-vis foreign holidays, so that sales of a holiday at home can equal or exceed the 'bargain basement' prices now offered overseas. Second, UK holidays are now better packaged by the tour operators, with the larger companies now including domestic holidays in their product portfolios.

Travel agency appointments

Membership of trade bodies

In the UK there are no legal requirements to setting up as a travel agent, but in some countries, including most of those within the European Union, governments do exercise licensing control over agencies. However, most principals license the sale of their services through a process of agency agreements, or 'appointments', which are in effect a licence to trade and to receive commission for sales achieved. Some principals dispense with this formality – hotels, for example, will normally allow commission on any sales made through a reputable travel agency, without any formal agreement.

Up to 1993, any travel agent wishing to sell the products of an ABTA tour operator had itself to be a member of ABTA, while in turn ABTA tour operators could only sell their services through ABTA retailers. This reciprocal agreement, known as Stabiliser, and allowing ABTA to operate effectively as a closed shop, is technically a constraint on trade, and as such was challenged by the Office of Fair Trading. However, the Restrictive Practices Court upheld the agreement in 1982 after appeal by ABTA, on the grounds that it was in the public interest, and certainly, ABTA's in-house scheme of protection for consumers against the collapse of a member company was recognized as one of the best in the world. A Common Fund, provided out of membership subscriptions, was held by ABTA and drawn on to allow clients of a travel agency to continue with their holidays even if the travel agency they had booked with went into liquidation before the tour operator received payment for the tour. This complemented the protection offered by ABTA against the collapse of a tour operator, details of which have been outlined in Chapter 16.

New members of ABTA were required to take up a bond to cover a percentage of their revenue in the event of their collapse. The same conditions were not imposed on long-standing members, though, and this created difficulties in the case of one or two spectacular collapses such as that of Exchange Travel, in which ABTA had to meet the costs of lost revenue without adequate bonding. This imposed a drain on the reserve fund.

Thus, membership of ABTA provided many advantages, but it also imposed obligations on its members. Premises were open to inspection, and agents were obliged to abide by a strict Code of Conduct complementing that of the tour operator. However, many earlier conditions imposed on members by ABTA, such as a prohibition on discounting, and on the sale of non-travel products ('mixed selling'), were overturned by the Restrictive Practices Court. The termination of the Stabiliser ruling and the introduction of the EU's Package Travel Directive led to much greater freedom for agents to operate outside of ABTA membership, and the Association today has lost many of its controlling functions. In 2000, the Association also removed the distinction between tour operator and retail agent membership, absorbing members into a single class.

Some key rulings remain. Members must satisfy ABTA about their financial standing and qualifications. ABTA also requires its members to have at least one member of their counter staff with a minimum of two years' experience, although this period is reduced by six months for staff holding formal qualifications.

Formal training qualifications for the industry are both diverse and confusing. Not all the plethora of courses that have been introduced are universally welcomed or understood by the industry. After numerous changes to qualifications, both professional and academic, over the past few years, training provision is now overseen by People 1st, a government-sponsored skills body. The Certificate in Travel (travel agents), formerly known as ABTAC, is among the most recently introduced programmes, and runs parallel with a similar Certificate in Travel for tour operators, both of which are generally supported by the trade. These are delivered through the trade's training body, TTC Training, which, although no longer owned by ABTA, retains close links with them. National Vocational Qualifications (NVQs) are also available, under the supervision of the City and Guilds which, along with Edexcel, are awarding bodies for travel services NVQs. Students in full-time education can follow General National Vocational Qualifications (GNVQs) or A levels in Travel and Tourism, while a raft of programmes for business travel staff has been introduced by the Guild of Travel Management Companies. ABTA itself has supported professional recognition for formal qualifications through its ABTA Gold awards for those in the industry and the award of Certified Travel Consultant and Certified Senior Travel Consultant status, according to qualifications achieved. There is widespread uncertainty within the industry of the relative values of these numerous qualifications which are, at the time of writing, undergoing the test of time to ascertain their worth in practice. Frequent changes both in qualifications and in the names of bodies delivering them has tended to confuse the industry in recent years.

ABTA remains an important association in the UK in representing the interests of both tour operators and travel agents. Given the potential conflict of interests between these two, and other conflicts that can arise between the multiples and independent agencies, continuing support for ABTA within the trade may seem surprising, but the importance of having a strong body to represent trade interests in consultations with government and other industry bodies, and the organization's role as a mouthpiece for the industry, have ensured ABTA's survival. A merger was proposed between ABTA and the FTO in 2005 which, although placed on hold at the time of writing, could further strengthen these ambitions. Other bodies have been created to serve the narrower interests of segments of this industry, such as the Multiple Travel Agents' Association (MTAA), which concerns itself with the chains' special interests. The independent agents have increasingly formed themselves into consortia to represent their interests, mainly in negotiating with suppliers, and this feature will be examined a little later in the chapter.

As agents also sell travel insurance, steps are being taken to control this side of their operations also. The General Insurance Standards Council (GISC) was set up in 2000 by the insurance industry to improve standards through self-regulation, in the wake of government moves to regulate the industry. Membership, initially voluntary, became compulsory for all agencies selling insurance in 2001, in spite of independent agents' concern about the additional burden of costs this imposes.

Bonding

A key change in the industry occurred when ABTA lost the exclusive rights to bond its members. New ABTA agents, during their first year of trading, and agents judged by ABTA, after inspection of their accounts, to be at risk financially, have been required to post a bond which indemnifies them to clients and customers against the risk of their failure. Certain principals may also require the posting of a bond, even if an ABTA bond is held – for example, if the agent plans to hold a principal's ticket stock. A significantly higher bond would normally be asked of agents without limited liability (i.e. trading as sole traders or partnerships). Additionally, a retail agent which operates tours, whether in the UK or overseas, will also be required to put up a tour-operating bond.

Bonding may be undertaken in one of three ways:

1 A sum of money equal to the value of the bond can be placed in a trust account. The agent can benefit from the interest accruing on the account, but cannot touch the capital itself. Since this could involve putting up a substantial amount of money, it is rarely chosen except by the largest corporations.

2 The agent can obtain an insurance policy for the amount required, paying an annual premium.

3 The agent's bank puts up the bond, against either company assets or, more commonly, the personal guarantees of the directors. A fee is charged which is substantially less than the premium paid for an insurance policy, but the directors become personally liable for the amount of the bond in the event of the company's failure.

As a safeguard, ABTA also has its own annual indemnity insurance policy which can provide additional funds if the bonds posted by an individual member are insufficient to cover the claims against the company in the event of its collapse.

Following the introduction of the EU Directive which made bonding compulsory for any tour operator or agent, agents now have the alternative of trading outside of ABTA, and making their own bonding arrangements through banks or other organizations. While some have chosen to do so, following a very substantial hike in the cost of bonding through ABTA itself, the brand recognition offered by the ABTA name remains a major incentive to bond with that organization. Alternatives to ABTA bonding include the Travel Trust Association, which enables member agents to use a trust account to protect their clients' funds, rather than purchasing a bond through insurance companies or banks. The association monitors its members to ensure compliance with the trust fund regulations.

Dealing with principals

Most contracts with principals are non-exclusive; that is to say, they do not prevent the agent from dealing with the principal's competitors. Occasionally, however, a contract may offer the agency the exclusive right to sell the product, and may further restrict the agent's ability to deal with other directly competing companies.

Unless expressly stated in the contract, agents do not have the automatic right to deduct their commission from the monies due to the principal. If bonus commissions are paid for targets achieved, it is generally the case that these additional sums of money are paid to the agent at the end of the season, rather than immediately following the achievement of the target. These facts must be borne in mind by the agent in estimating cash flow.

A licence is required if commission is to be paid on the sale of services of members of IATA (apart from sales of purely domestic tickets). Although IATA carriers have been reducing or eliminating commissions for agents, some are continuing to pay commissions, and it is important for travel agents that wish to offer a full range of services (and doubly so for those dealing in business house travel) either to hold the necessary IATA appointment, or to have an arrangement with another agency that does so, whereby that agent will issue tickets on their behalf. New agents are permitted to sell air tickets and earn income by sharing commission with an established IATA agent.

There were around 2,800 IATA-accredited agencies in the UK in 2004. IATA's Agency Distribution Office deals with applications for a licence, a process which can take up to 45 days. A representative from IATA's Agency Investigation Panel visits the agent to judge whether the site is easily identified as a travel centre and suitable for the sale of tickets (while proof of turnover is no longer required of agents, IATA wishes to satisfy itself that the agency has the scope to generate business). The number and competence of staff will be judged; at least one member of staff will be expected to have two years' agency experience, and preferably hold a Certificate of Travel Agency Competence, ABTAC and/or an equivalent qualification in fares and ticketing (ABTAC allows six months remission in the experience required). The representative must also be satisfied that the agency premises are secure and any ticket stock held can be safeguarded, although this is becoming less of an issue with the escalation of e-tickets. These is turn are posing new security problems, as IATA must now take steps to re-assure themselves that the agent will not issue hundreds of e-tickets and disappear with the clients' money. If approved, a bond is taken out to cover the agency's anticipated monthly IATA turnover. An entrance fee is payable, and a small annual subscription. This approval enables the agent to sell the services of all IATA members.

Approval is also required to make commissionable sales on the services of railways, National Coaches, domestic airline services and other principals such as shipping and car hire firms. Obtaining approval for most of these has been largely a formality for agents holding ABTA and IATA appointments. However, appointments to sell travel insurance will involve closer scrutiny, since the agent will be acting as a broker for the insurance service concerned; as noted above, insurance companies have tightened up on standards for their brokers, including retailers in the travel industry.

Profitability of travel agents

There are surprisingly few studies of travel agency productivity and profitability in Britain, although ABTA undertakes occasional studies of profitability among its members. Unfortunately, the sample responding to research surveys has often been quite small, throwing into doubt the results. Studies in the past have found that on average, ABTA members retained less than 1 per cent of their total turnover after expenses. That report did not make clear that success in creating high turnover may be as much a factor of location as of efficiency, nor that fast turnover is not commensurate with a professional standard of advice and sales assistance. A better pointer to profitability can be found in the trading results of the leading chains, whose negotiating power with the major principals have enabled them to offer substantial discounts on package tours, yet still raise profits above the average for the industry.

It is becoming clear that the retail sector of the industry is now moving in two, or even three, distinct directions: towards specialist business travel; or towards the fast turnover 'leisure sales shop', a feature of the multiples' approach, which is essentially a booking service offering rock-bottom prices; or towards a more specialized advisory service for complex or expensive travel arrangements, including tailor-making holidays through dynamic packaging, which will allow the agency to charge fees for their service and avoid the usual competition to discount. The latter move has its precedent in the US, where for a number of years, travel experts holding the Certified Travel Counsellor (CTC) qualification have dealt with the more lucrative end of the package tour business, often based in independent agencies. It is these agencies which seem most likely to benefit if and when suppliers move to contracts which provide for lower commissions or fee-only payments, as customers who are seeking tailor-made services will be more disposed to pay fees for the services they are rendered. Meanwhile, the traditional travel agent, attempting to provide a wide range of services with little discounting, faces a future that is increasingly uncertain as other forms of distribution arrive on the scene, and there are increasing opportunities for members of the public to book direct with the suppliers using the Internet. Euromonitor research in 2005 also concluded that there was a likelihood of some 600 agency outlets closing by 2010, leaving the big groups, on-line companies and independent specialists to compete for business.

Evidence that many sectors of travel involve greater costs to the agency than the commissions they can achieve on sales has led a number of agents to move away from selling non-profitable products. At the same time, the proliferation of brochures, and the policy of leading tour operators to produce a range of different branded products each in their own brochure, has forced agents to re-evaluate their racking policies. With the typical travel agency only having rack space for around 145 brochures, of which up to 20 per cent may be filled with the products of the leading operators, there is little opportunity for the smaller and specialist operators to get their brochures racked. While a few years ago this would have been disastrous for trading, the advent of the World Wide Web has led to these companies becoming far more dependent upon their websites to sell their products, and agents in turn are increasingly coming to use websites as a principal instrument to sell travel, in place of the traditional brochure. This improves the sales potential, since brochures can be picked up and taken away from a shop without the opportunity for counter staff to enter into the sales sequence.

So far, only a handful of independent agents have moved exclusively to niche-marketing, and those that have done so have tended to focus on the narrow long-haul and cruise markets. Some believe this may be the only way in which the independents will be able to compete with the multiples in the long run, although membership in a large consortium may offer a solution.

Figure 17.4
The fast turnover leisure sales shop. Nouvelles Frontières, a leading French operator, also owns a string of retail outlets

(Photographed by the author)

The direction in which retail travel is moving bears comparison with developments in the book trade. Companies choosing to specialize, such as Stanfords and the Travel Book Shop, attract clients for their specialized knowledge and professional service. Similarly, antiquarian bookshops have sound knowledge of their stock and offer a personal service unlike that found in the leading bookshops, which in turn have to compete with major on-line book-selling companies like amazon.com and abe.com.

The move to fast-turnover booking centres, typical of the large travel chains, is in part a recognition that salaries cannot be offered to provide the level of service demanded of a traditional travel agency. A number of developments are taking place at the beginning of the twenty-first century. First Choice has been successful in increasing profits through a supermarket approach to sales, and some others are looking to follow suit. Thomas Cook has introduced Thomas Cook Direct, a new direct sell operation for its tour operating products, while Thomson revamped many of its stores by introducing five specialist zones within the shop, each catering to a different market segment – long-haul, short breaks, summer sun, families and late bookings. Others are pushing the call centre approach, abandoning face-to-face contact with the customer to keep down costs. All four of the leading operators' chains have tried selling their products through interactive TV, although only Thomas Cook and TUI Thomson currently operate their own channels. However, this may well be a major distributive outlet in the future, with nearly half a million holidays already being sold annually in the UK via TV.

The march of the multiples

The growing fear that the multiples would expand to a point where independents would be squeezed out of the market has receded to some extent in recent years, as new forms of distribution develop and the chains reduce their branches. The market share of the leaders has in fact reduced recently, after many years in which they gradually eroded the share of the market held by the independents.

As indicated in Chapter 16, directional selling is now ensuring that the majority of sales of the larger tour operators' products is achieved through their own agencies. Some independents feel that these operators will eventually choose to retain the exclusive sale of their products through their own retail chains, reducing the independents to selling products of the smaller companies. This is thought unlikely, given the desire of the operators to increase their market shares through whichever outlets will give them support, unless the cost of distribution through those outlets becomes uneconomic.

Competing with the multiples

Although the large number of branches owned by the leading chains appears to give them an insuperable advantage over the independents, this is not always the case. Within the regions, medium-sized regional chains can provide strong competition for bookings. These chains, commonly known as *miniples*, typically control between 40 and a hundred shops. They are, however, vulnerable to takeovers, and some of the major players have been absorbed into leading operators' retailing organizations in recent years.

The independents have recognized that on their own they face an almost impossible task in competing with the multiples for the sale of mass-market holidays. They can be undercut on prices, the market has become sensitised to discounting as a result of the marketing campaigns of the leading companies, and the multiples can invest more in the latest technology and programmes of national advertising.

Independent travel agents have done what they could to cut costs or to increase turnover in order to compete, and many have realized that only through close collaboration with others will they be able to compete on price; this would allow them to negotiate for higher commissions based on greatly increased buying power. As a result, there has been massive growth in alliances, particularly through the medium of a consortium. This not only allows agents to compete with the multiples by negotiating with the mass-tour operators for higher commissions on bulk sales, but it avoids the necessity for each to have a separate mini-ATOL when putting different components of a package together in dynamic packaging. Some believe that in time this could also lead to the organization establishing its own tour operation, or even an airline (although cost has proved too daunting for the consortia up to the present).

Several major consortia have now appeared on the British market as trading alliances, and these are listed below:

Travelsavers International   Formed in the USA in 1970, introduced into Britain in 2000. Some 3,000 branches worldwide, with around 200 in the UK and Eire. Not marketed under a brand name, all agents retain their own identities, but must hold ABTA or IATA membership.

WorldChoice   Formed in 1977, formerly known as the Association of Retail Travel Agents' Consortia (ARTAC). Comprises some 700 branches, including its own travel agencies. Formed a strategic alliance with Thomas Cook.

Midconsort Travel Group   Formed in 1977, geographically centred in middle England, with some 130 branches, all ABTA or otherwise bonded.

Advantage   Formed 1978, formerly known as the National Association of Independent Travel Agents (NAITA) then as Advantage Travel Centres. Comprises around 400 companies with 800 branches. Agents may retain their independent names, but around half of the members have chosen to emphasize their Advantage brand in the name.

Global Travel Group   Formed 1993, has 1,014 branches and own bonding system.

Freedom Travel Group   Formed 2002, as trading arm of the United Co-op Travel Group. Around 65 members.

In 2005 it was announced that Advantage, WorldChoice and Global had reached agreement to unite. As the Triton Travel Group, the new body has over 1,800 branches, responsible for 15 per cent of all retail travel agency business in the UK. Although a formal merger is not on the cards at the time of writing, it will undoubtedly be the intention of the group to increase directional selling, thus maximizing profits for its members and challenging the survival of the smaller players in the sector.

Other small, mainly geographical, groupings exist, such as SWIFTA (the South West Independent Federation of Travel Agents) and Let's Go Travel. The potential buying power of these groupings of independent agencies provides them with a very real chance to compete with the large UK chains in reducing their costs, as well as ensuring that the smaller tour operating companies are represented in the high street.

Franchising has been less successful as a strategy to compete with the multiples. The first chain in Britain to attempt to franchise on a wide scale, Exchange Travel, went into liquidation in 1990, and the Canadian-based Uniglobe chain has similarly found it difficult to establish itself in the UK, in spite of a chain of offices exceeding 1,400 worldwide. The future of franchising remains uncertain. Arguably, a franchise, if it is to succeed, must offer a unique product of some kind which is not available through other distributive outlets, something which a travel franchise signally fails to deliver.

Distribution policy

As we have seen, the policy of mass-market tour operators in recent years has been directed towards selective distribution, the operator favouring a smaller number of productive agents rather than attempting to provide stock for all retail agencies. This policy has also been favoured by the multiple agents themselves, in choosing to stock the products of a few key operators which are responsible for perhaps 80 per cent of the total revenue in the mass market. Thomas Cook, to take one example, introduced a policy of racking only 400 companies, of which 30 were identified as 'premium selection'. If this tendency becomes widespread over the next few years, smaller operators will have to find other means of reaching their customers.

Multiple agents also engage in directional selling, favouring their own companies' products at the expense of any others. TUI's Thomson Travel will push sales of their operator partner, Thomson Holidays, discriminating in particular against their leading competitors. In turn, Going Places, owned by MyTravel, discriminate in favour of their parent, while First Choice and Thomas Cook will similarly favour their own operators. The Foreign Package Holidays Order (2000) requires these links between operators and their agencies to be made clear to customers; however, making clear the linkages will not necessarily work to the advantage of the independent agents, as it may encourage the public to believe that the leading tour operators' programmes can *only* be purchased from the retail branches of those operators.

The decision on what products to stock is taken not only because of what is thought will sell quickest or easiest. The introduction of tighter EU legislation over quality has forced many agents to reconsider the companies with which they deal, and while bonus commissions undoubtedly play a role in the decision, equally the service provided to the agent by the operator will be taken into consideration. Agents that encounter difficulty in getting through to operators on the telephone, or who find their e-mail communications or complaints are not answered quickly, will feel less inclined to stock that operator's products. Even companies insisting that agents use higher-cost numbers when telephoning – and keep agents waiting on-line for extended periods – can antagonize the retailers, whose telephone bills are inflated as a result.

The personal relationships between travel agency staff and their principals have become more important, at a time when electronic communication is reducing personal contacts in business. The role of a sales representative can still be of immense importance in cultivating goodwill among retailers. Here one must question the decision taken by so many principals to cut back their field representation as a cost-cutting measure (see Chapter 16). One can surmise that this is partly to fund a higher budget for selling direct.

New means of distribution

A number of notable developments in strategic marketing by retailers have taken place in the past few years, in addition to those significant developments already described above. One such change has been in the field of home selling, which has expanded rapidly. Personal travel counsellors and on-line travel counsellors who work on a freelance basis sell on behalf of an agency and earn commission from that agency. Travel Counsellors is one company that has built up a major retailing base in travel, with around 450 home-based employees in the UK.

Tour operators have become more aggressive in boosting sales through their own outlets. To cite one example, merchandisers acting on behalf of a leading operator were recruited to hand out leaflets at top resorts in Spain to holidaymakers (not necessarily their clients), offering discounts to those booking their holidays through their own retail chain for the following year. Thomas Cook was the first travel chain to introduce its own credit card to build customer loyalty, offering vouchers with the purchase of every travel product. As competition becomes fiercer, there can be little doubt that we will see an increase in such aggressive retailing and promotion.

The threat always remains of organizations outside the travel industry taking an interest in diversifying into travel retailing, especially where this is seen as a logical expansion of existing activities and the organization concerned has the ideal retailing operation to take on extra services. This has also been a threat in the past, but those who braved the market have tended to withdraw when the slim margins became evident. Both W H Smith, the newsagent and bookseller, and the Automobile Association have abandoned their sale of travel products in recent years – yet others are always ready to step in. Of the two leading supermarkets, both Tesco and Asda have invested in recent years in travel interests, as has pharmacy chain Boots. The Post Office has been selling insurance and foreign exchange for several years, and has experimentally entered the market to sell air tickets. Direct sell to readers of national and local newspapers, and cooperative marketing promotions with other products, have also reduced travel agents' sales opportunities.

The complexity of selling travel has to be acknowledged, and this may well be a factor in the decision of so many other retail organizations to avoid the travel business. Yet in the Netherlands, the sale of holidays through banks is long established, and in Germany large department stores have played a major role in travel retailing for many years. All that one can say with any certainty is that new means of distribution will arise frequently in the future, and the traditional retailers must find means of adapting their own methods of distribution if they are to survive. Perhaps the greatest threat they face in the short term is in the move to direct sell, which is now accelerating as electronic communications expand.

Direct sell

Can travel principals sell their products direct to the public at lower cost without losing sales? This is a vital question for both carriers and tour operators. Travel firms which have little alternative other than to sell their products direct (as do small coach companies, some railways, and tour operators whose total carryings are too small to be considered by a retail distribution network) do not have to take into consideration any possible retaliation of the retail trade for doing so. However, other companies which occasionally accept bookings from agents even when selling most of their product direct (and here, small hotels are a good example) usually recognize that to deliberately undermine the retail trade by, for instance, charging a lower price when accepting direct business from their customers, may jeopardize valuable marginal bookings. No principal wants to throw away bookings pointlessly.

As airlines move away from their former dependence upon retailers, the latter become increasingly dependent upon package tours, whether pre-packaged or tailor-made, for their income. However, operators, too, have made no secret of their desire to sell more of their products direct to their customers, via the Internet or call centres. There is an obvious attraction to the mass operator in selling their product direct to the public. Selling direct cuts out the high cost of servicing intermediaries and of paying commission on each sale. On the other hand, it can involve substantial capital investment to set up sales offices, and direct marketing costs can be high, especially if national advertising campaigns have to be mounted. Additional staff must be employed to operate call centres, and these must be adequately trained for the job.

If principals which presently deal through travel agents decide to sell direct for the first time, or to increase the proportion of direct sales they currently achieve, they risk antagonizing their present distributors. Therefore any effort to increase sales in this way must be handled with extreme discretion, in order to avoid any loss of sales through ill will. Currently, many products available to customers direct on the principals' websites will be offered at prices below those quoted to travel agents, leaving the customer with little incentive to book through an agent. Carriers which have withdrawn commission payments to agents will often undercut prices when selling on-line, while agents will not only fail to come up with the lowest fare, but must also charge a fee for handling the booking – hardly an encouragement to use travel agents. Similarly, the trade papers are filled with letters of complaint from agents who find they cannot offer the same products, or at the same prices, to their clients as those operators are selling on-line. Only the convenience of using an agent when making complex bookings, and when collecting tickets, remains an incentive – and is this enough?

Example Eurotunnel

When the Channel Tunnel first opened, the management of Eurotunnel services largely ignored the strength of the trade, assuming that most clients would prefer to book their crossing direct, thus simultaneously antagonizing the trade and reducing their own sales opportunities. Later, the company realized its mistake and sought trade support when sales were poor, but the damage had been done, and the ferry companies had meanwhile encouraged agency bookings.

Nevertheless, as we have seen, a large proportion of package tours are still sold through retail agents. Smaller companies, generally those offering a few thousand holidays each year, cannot afford to distribute their products through agents, nor would most agents be willing to stock brochures of these companies, in view of the small number of potential sales they would achieve. Consequently, these operators may adopt one of two distributive strategies: either to find a selection of key agents (likely to be independents rather than chains) which would be willing to stock the product, or to sell all their holidays direct to the public. The AITO Special Agents Scheme is an example of the former, in which the small specialist operators who form the membership of this association have identified some 150 specialist agencies to handle their bookings. The growth of the World Wide Web has made the latter policy a great deal easier for the smaller company, as we shall see later in this chapter.

Mass-market tour operators have additionally created products which they distribute direct to the public through specialist direct-sell divisions. These include Portland Direct, a division of TUI Thomson, Eclipse, a division of First Choice, Blue Sky Holidays Direct, a division of Thomas Cook and Direct Holidays, a MyTravel product. Saga Holidays, the largest company specializing in holidays for the over-50s, sells direct to its members through direct mail and its members' magazine.

Direct Holidays offers one example in Britain of an interesting approach. Although owned by MyTravel, whose retail chain Going Places is a key multiple, this retail agency sells its own budget holidays uniquely, dealing with no other holiday programmes, not even those of its parent.

It is significant that all the leading tour operators now have their own direct-sell divisions. Although agents might be thought to be concerned about the threat posed by these direct-sell operations, they have failed to challenge the operators on this development, perhaps in fear of jeopardizing sales of the mass-market holidays they retail. It is true that direct sales made through these divisions had stabilized as a proportion of all package tours sold in the UK, no doubt owing in part to the fact that these did not prove to be necessarily cheaper than others sold through agents (a close examination of the companies' pricing structure revealed that low prices were highly selective, rather than across-the-board), but those sold through call centres and the Internet have expanded rapidly, and it is here that the real threat to agents exists. Agents today have much more to fear from advances in technology which will allow customers to access operators' CRSs by the travelling public. This is a reality in the USA and France, and already available for business travellers in the UK. No doubt leisure travel will follow.

The impact of computer technology

The industry has been profoundly affected by developments in technology, most notably computers, over the past decade. Since innovations in this field are constantly being launched or improved, information about this sphere of travel activity tends to date very quickly, so there will be little benefit to be gained from examining the detailed merits of any existing system in this text. Suffice to say that even the smallest travel agents can today benefit from computer technology to handle their back office and front office functions – in fact, many would argue that no agent can afford to be without back-office computer aids, and in terms of making reservations, it is now mandatory to use computers rather than the telephone to make bookings with the leading companies. This final section will focus on the trends in information technology used in the industry and their impact on retailers.

The travel industry is ideally suited for computer technology. It offers products that cannot be inspected directly before purchase, but may be viewed with the use of brochures or screens; it requires some system for determining the availability of transport and accommodation, often at short notice, and the ability to make immediate reservations, amendments or cancellations; complex fares and conditions of travel must be accessed and quoted; documents such as tickets, invoices, vouchers and itineraries must be processed rapidly. The back office also needs to process an ever-increasing amount of accounting and management information quickly. All of these functions are available today to agents using computer technology.

Computer systems in travel agencies are designed to offer three distinct facilities:

- front-office 'client relations' systems enabling a counter clerk to access principals' CRSs/GDSs and websites, check availability and make reservations
- back-office systems enabling documents such as invoices, vouchers, tickets and itineraries to be issued, and accounts to be processed with principals
- management systems, producing updated figures on the company's performance to assist managers in guiding and controlling operations.

Systems have now been developed which will provide all three facilities for even the smallest independent agent, at prices which continue to fall; or equipment can be leased to reduce capital investment and spread costs.

In considering systems which are designed to access travel principals' reservations systems, one can distinguish between those developed by carriers and those developed by tour operators. In Britain, because of the importance of 'interlining' (common ticket issuing and ability to transfer bookings between carriers), any system used must be capable of booking seats on a large number of different airlines. Agents currently achieve this principally by the use of one of the four major global distribution systems, those of Galileo, Amadeus, Sabre and Worldspan. Tour operators' reservations are likewise accessed live on the computer, generally 'hard-wired', allowing agents to enter the CRS without using their telephone line to dial up separately on each occasion. Similarly, back-office systems offer not only faster means of carrying out accounting and documentation procedures, but also help to cut costs.

At the turn of the new century, technology appears to be moving in two distinct directions. First, while connections between suppliers and agents are being made simpler, agents are being forced to come to terms with constant advances in technology, providing new learning curves to master. Many of those who have embraced the technology wholeheartedly have also recognized the advantage of becoming electronic retailers, or e-tailers (the term e-travel agent is beginning to be used to describe this function). Such agencies are adapting new technology to reach their clients on-line, through the Web or even through interactive digital television (IDTV). Second, in parallel with the new intermediary on-line agencies that are being created, suppliers, notably the airlines, are creating their own websites against which the e-tailers will have to compete. More widely, there is a rapid growth in business-to-consumer (B2C) sites which are designed to cut out the intermediaries and sell direct to the public.

New high-tech distributors have come onto the scene, notably in the field of travel. After the initial explosion of new ventures, these have shaken down to a handful of surviving companies, including Expedia, lastminute.com, travelocity.com and ebookers, selling, *inter alia*, discounted and late availability travel – mainly airline seats, hotel accommodation and car rental, rather than package holidays, the sale of which by Internet is still in its infancy. The advantage of these websites to the consumer is that they are independent of the suppliers, and are viewed as unbiased in the range of products they offer, while airlines value these outlets as a means of unloading surplus stock without degrading the brand. The airlines have formed their own intermediaries, as with Opodo and Orbitz, while their own websites attract consumers with competitive prices, both of which challenge sales through agents using the traditional GDSs.

Sales via TV channels are still in their earliest days, but are already capturing a share of the holiday market, and will grow. The critical question is whether the high-street agent can survive in the face of these new methods of distribution. There are claims that while the World Wide Web offers more options to the customer, it does not necessarily replace existing forms of distribution, since answers to specific questions will need to be raised with agents. The question remains as to how agents can avoid clients coming to them to pick their brains and then going home to book their holidays through the Internet.

Opinion is confused about whether the majority of agents, or only a handful of the most adaptable, can survive the Internet explosion. Those that survive will be the most adaptable, offering a more personal service which will include expert advice. The fact remains, however, that most agents have neither the knowledge nor the resources to undertake such change. Salaries are already low in the industry, and the level of expertise among agents questionable when confronted with an increasingly sophisticated and well-travelled clientele – yet the move to cutting commissions and, in the case of the airlines, withdrawing commission entirely, must encourage many agents to transfer to a fee-charging basis. If agents are to become professionals like solicitors, as many are arguing, how do they pay the salaries and obtain the staff with the qualifications that will be required to deliver this level of expertise?

The agent as operator

There is an alternative, and it is being realized today, as agents use dynamic packaging to become tailor-made operators for their clients. The Web, which threatens their livelihoods, also offers the best prospect for their survival, if they adapt.

By accessing the websites of reliable suppliers, putting together a package of components which exactly meets their customers' needs and adding a mark-up which allows them a reasonable level of profit for the expertise they are delivering, agents are fulfilling a new role. Here, the consortia are often a step ahead; Worldchoice, for instance, has struck a deal with Thomas Cook which allows them to sell the Cook product under their own label. Members of the consortium are able to access Cook's Flexible Trips dynamic packaging operation, and are also protected under Cook's ATOL for the resultant package they create.

ATOL regulations were amended in 2003, so that agents may no longer buy the separate components of an IT and package them without possession of an ATOL. Agents are faced with the choice either of buying the components from an existing ATOL holder (such as a tour operator's dynamic packaging website), or applying for a mini-ATOL to set themselves up as package operators. If flights are not included in the package, an ATOL is not obligatory, but if bundling other components, the agent must still comply with the conditions of the Package Travel Regulations. This includes providing clear booking conditions, a rep service or 24-hour telephone assistance, and accepting liability for damages, so insurance is a must.

The situation for agents is still confusing at the time of writing, as agents can put together an unbounded package if merely booking components requested by their customer, without offering advice. This loophole is likely to be closed before long.

The future of travel retailing

It is not just the travel agent, but also the entire travel industry that faces greater uncertainty than ever before. The introduction of B2C in travel, with suppliers providing the direct interface with their clients, threatens both agents and tour operators, since if a customer is encouraged to book flights and hotels direct at a lower cost than is possible through intermediaries, how long will it be before it becomes customary for that same customer to put together their own package?

New methods of retailing travel products are continually being launched, as we have seen. Outsiders such as banks, department stores and petrol stations can be tempted to re-examine the benefits of selling travel (or of owning the industry's components), if costs can be controlled. In an effort to achieve better profit margins in an increasingly competitive business environment, travel principals will be constantly evaluating new ways to distribute their products to the public. There may be further expansion of multiple or miniple agents buying tours from operators in bulk at net prices and selling these under their own brand names (Thomas Cook has already done so), and the squeeze on independents by the multiples is not expected to slow down. Common promotional tactics of the past few years, such as 5 per cent or no-deposit bookings, are likely to become typical rather than exceptional marketing ploys. Deep discounting of holidays, a technique which favours the multiples and reduces agent profitability, is no less popular today than when it was introduced in the previous decade. Other agents are likely to follow the example set by some which recruit home-based sales staff to visit customers in their homes, taking bookings through customized laptop computers linked to the operators' reservations systems. A freelance sales force such as this, available at short notice 24 hours a day, may offer another solution to ensuring that the travel agent has a future. It also enables mature, well-experienced women agents to return to the industry on a part-time basis after having a family. It is certain that the traditional 'corner-shop' travel agent that we have known in the past is largely set to disappear. The agent of the future will be flexible, innovative, and willing to move with the times and make use of the new tools of marketing which technology has made available. They can no longer be expected to share the range of product knowledge required by an increasingly sophisticated travelling public, but must find the means to access and make this information available to their clients more effectively, and at a cost to the customer that offers value for money.

Meanwhile, a steadily increasing number of bookings will be made direct between principals and customers. The growth of broadband in the UK permits more consumers to surf the net for information about travel, and these will be encouraged to book direct. Digital TV, which will replace all analogue TV in Britain by 2012 at the latest, will have hundreds of channels available for special-interest programmes, including travel, making it an ideal marketing medium. At the same time, mobile phones will interact with the Internet and TV channels to enable travellers to call up information anywhere and at any time, check availability and make travel arrangements. The retail sector is the fastest moving sector of the industry, and is soon to be subject to the greatest changes of all.

Notes

1 All You Need to Know about Dynamic Packaging, *Travel Weekly* Special Supplement, March 2005, p 34
2 CIMTIG annual seminar, 2005, reported in *Travel Weekly*, 28 January 2005

Websites

ABTA	www.abta.com
Haslemere Travel	www.haslemeretravel.co.uk
The Travel Training Company	www.ttctraining.co.uk

Questions and discussion points

1 We would all love to see the hard-pressed workforce at the sharp end of the retail travel sector earn far more than they do now, and be treated and paid, like the professional travel advisers they are. However, as long as our industry remains discount obsessed, margins – and pay – will remain low

Paul Wellings, Director, Personal Service Travel,
in a letter to *Travel Weekly*, 18 February 2005

Discuss whether productivity can be increased by paying higher salaries. What criteria (qualities, training, experience, education) would the task demand, and would added costs be justified?

2 Should agents expand on the range of products they currently sell? If so, what should they stock or retail?

3 Are you willing to pay an agent a fee for booking an airline seat? What do you consider a reasonable charge for this service? Who do you think would prefer to use an agent than to book on-line?

4 Should agents be required to hold qualifications? Should they be licensed by governments? Or do you believe that an apprenticeship should be the best means of training staff?

Assignment topics

1 A glance into travel agency windows in any country will reveal very little difference between one agency and another, either in terms of window display or in interior design. Assuming the role of a consultant, visit travel agencies in your area, evaluating their appearance and identifying the best and worst aspects of their presentation. Which appear more professional, the independents or the multiples? Which, more inviting? Then prepare a report summarizing your findings, with suggestions for an original approach which will enable the agency to stand out from its competitors.

2 Undertake research in your local area on travel agency brochure racks, identifying:

(a) how many individual rack spaces each agency has, and the average number of spaces overall,

(b) the proportion of these spaces devoted to products of the large tour operators, and those of the retailers' own parent company,

(c) the proportion devoted to other products, including domestic holidays and specialist independent products not owned by the retailer's parent.

Present a report of your findings, and suggest how racking could be improved, either in appearance or in the range of products on display.

18 Ancillary tourism services

Objectives

After studying this chapter, you should be able to:

- understand the role of guides, couriers, insurance and financial services in meeting tourist demand
- be aware of training and education available for those in the industry
- understand the role and value of the trade press to the industry
- identify the principal sources of information in use by travel agents, and their contents
- be aware of marketing and consultancy services available to members of the industry.

Introduction

Attempts to analyze the tourism industry, as we have seen earlier, lead to the problem of defining the parameters of the industry. Some services depend largely or entirely upon the movement of tourists, but are seldom considered to be part of the industry itself; customs services or visa issuing offices are cases in point. Other services which derive much of their revenue from tourism and yet are clearly not part of the industry include companies specializing in the design and construction of hotels, theatres, restaurants and other centres of entertainment.

However, there is a further category of miscellaneous tourism services which deserves to be examined more closely here. We will call these *ancillary services*, and they are provided either to the tourist or to the suppliers of tourist services. Each will be dealt with in turn.

Services to the tourist

Guide/courier services

Unfortunately, there is as yet no term which will conveniently embrace all the mediators whose function it is to shepherd, guide, inform and interpret for groups of tourists; nor can one conveniently link their functions to one particular sector of the industry. Some are employed by carriers and tour operators; others work independently, or provide their services freelance to companies in the industry.

In an industry which is becoming increasingly impersonal, as companies grow in size, and tourism products themselves become more homogeneous, the role of those who interface with the tourist becomes more and more important. Indeed, it may be the only feature of a package tour which distinguishes one product from another; yet curiously, it is a role which is becoming progressively downgraded by the larger companies, often as a means of cutting costs. The role of the resort representative has already been discussed in this context. Here we will examine two similar roles, those of the courier and the guide.

Couriers are employed by coach companies or tour operators to supervise and shepherd groups of tourists participating in tours (either on extended tours or day excursions). As well as couriers, they may be known as tour escorts, tour leaders, tour managers or tour directors (the latter terms imply greater levels of responsibility and status). One of their functions will be to offer a sightseeing commentary on the country or region through which they are travelling, and to act as a source of information.

Some companies dispense with the separate services of a courier in favour of a driver–courier, who takes on the responsibility of both driving the coach and looking after the passengers. Many drivers, however, have neither adequate general knowledge nor the necessary training to offer a truly professional guiding service, and they should not in any case be diverted from their prime responsibility, that of driving the coach safely and expertly. Some countries frown on coach drivers who give commentaries while their coach is in motion, others forbid the practice.

Courier work is essentially freelance and offers little opportunity to develop a career. Apart from a handful of destinations which have truly year-round appeal (such as capital cities), most guiding work is temporary and seasonal, even though many professional guides choose to return to the job year after year. Some are able to find a combination of posts in summer and winter resorts, enabling them to take up paid employment throughout most of the year.

Prior experience is the principal criterion in gaining employment. While qualifications exist in many countries, they are not always essential to the role, and in Britain professional training is available but by no means obligatory. The role attracts graduates with relevant qualifications such as languages or history, but many companies prefer to recruit couriers largely on the strength of their personality, their ability to handle clients with sensitivity and tact, and their stamina, both physical and mental. In some posts, employers will lay emphasis on sales ability, as couriers and resort representatives may be required to sell supplementary services such as optional excursions. Arguably, this is changing the nature of the role, as commercial acumen replaces sociability.

Figure 18.1
A guide with tourists at Acton Court, Gloucestershire

(Photographed by the author)

Couriers differ from guides in the sense that the latter lay stress on imparting information as the most important function of their job, while couriers may attach more importance to their social and shepherding functions. Guides, or guide lecturers as they are frequently known, are retained by principals for their expertise in general or specialist subjects. Employment tends to be freelance and intermittent, with off-season jobs rare outside the large cities. Guides take pride in their professionalism, and will often have well-established regional and national bodies to represent their interests.

In Britain, the Blue Badge is seen as the mark of attainment of professional status, awarded following formal periods of training and examinations. The Blue Badge is awarded for national level 4 exams, with a Green Badge awarded for Associate status at level 3. There are approximately 2,100 members of the Institute of Tourist Guiding who hold the Blue Badge qualification, the majority based in London where guiding work is easiest to find. The ITG was formed in 2002 and represents guides in England, Wales, Northern Ireland, the Isle of Man and the Channel Islands (the Scottish Tourist Guides Association fulfils a similar function in Scotland). While the ITG does not itself run training courses, it oversees those operated in colleges and by other training providers, and sets the standard for Blue Badge and other guides. The Guild of Registered Tour Guides is the sector's professional wing, and campaigns for professional recognition and the implementation of Blue Badge standards throughout the

Figure 18.2
Animateurs,
dressed as
Roman soldiers,
pose for tourists,
Rome

(Photographed by the author)

industry. It also makes recommendations on the minimum fees to be paid to guides. However, regulations against price fixing prohibit the imposition of obligatory fees, and many companies running coach sightseeing tours prefer to recruit amateur guides without qualifications to keep down costs. The 'added value' of a qualified guide is still seen by many employers as a luxury they cannot afford in a climate where cutting costs to achieve sales is imperative.

This is a rather different picture from that in other European countries, where professional qualifications are often essential to secure a licence to operate. In France, for example, a local guide must be employed to guide in Paris, having demonstrated local knowledge in formally approved qualifications (although such qualifications can also be obtained by workers from other EU member countries, of course).

A separate category of guide is the *driver–guide*. These are professional guides who operate on a freelance basis, taking up to four individuals on tour in their own vehicles. The close personal relationship that is built up in these tours between guide and client is valued on both sides, and this form of tailor-made package is popular with wealthier visitors to the UK.

The role of the animateur

The term 'animateur' is now becoming more widely known within the British tourism industry. It applies to those members of the industry who entertain tourists, either by acting out a role, or providing entertainment or instruction. The English term 'entertainer' is not strictly comparable, as this tends to be defined as either a stage role, or is related to *street entertainers*, who are typically jugglers, acrobats, fire-eaters or – popular in leading resorts visited by mass tourists – 'living sculptures'. The French term relates to those whose task it is to interact with tourists in a broad range of roles which will enhance the destination or attraction where they work. It applies to the British role of the holiday camp 'redcoat' and to the US camp counsellor, as well as to the compère on stage in a cruise ship. Other tasks will include instructing tourists in sports or hobbies (ski instructors, surfing instructors), lecturing to cruise passengers or teaching them how to play bridge or other card games. Resort representatives are often expected to take on the role of animateurs when they form part of the evening's entertainment on stage at European camping sites. In Disney's theme parks there are a variety of animateur roles, the best known of which personify Mickey Mouse, but a host of other Disney characters are to be found on site, dressed as Alice in Wonderland, Snow White, and even the Chipmunks. These workers normally have no speaking role, and are there to make friends with younger visitors, posing for photographs etc. Others – often 'resting' actors – may be dressed as historical figures at a heritage site; for example, at Williamsburg in Virginia, a number of staff are dressed in eighteenth-century costumes, and will maintain this role if questioned by visitors. The job might be thought of as fairly basic, in terms of skills, but Continental Europeans take a different view, and animation appears on the syllabus of French tourism and leisure

Figure 18.3
Entertainers impress the crowds at Covent Garden in London

(Photographed by the author)

qualifications, to cite just one example. This reflects the seriousness with which Continental tourism employees and employers view the role as one providing just another professional service for the industry.

Financial services

This section will deal with financial services for the tourist – insurance, foreign exchange and credit.

Insurance

Insurance is an important, and very often obligatory, aspect of a tourist's travel arrangements, embracing coverage for one or more of the following contingencies:

- medical care and hospitalization (and, where necessary, repatriation – important where hospital services are of low standard)
- personal accident
- cancellation or curtailment of holiday
- delayed departure
- baggage loss or delay
- money loss
- personal liability.

Some policies are now also including coverage for the collapse of the travel agent or tour operator through which the tour was purchased – an increasingly important option in view of the growing instability in the industry, although bonded tours should be refundable in the event of a cancellation. However, the growth of budget airlines, and their not infrequent demise, point to the importance of adequate insurance, as scheduled air travel, apart from that in a package tour, is not currently protected by bonding.

Tourists may purchase insurance either in the form of a selective policy, covering one or more of the above items, or, more commonly, in the form of a standard 'package' which will include all or most of the above. The latter policy, although inflexible in its coverage, invariably offers the best value if comprehensive coverage is sought. Although most tour operators encourage their clients to buy the operators' own comprehensive policies, these are often more expensive to purchase than a comprehensive policy arranged by an independent insurance company. Travel agents may offer better-value insurance policies than those of the operator, but these too may be biased in favour of schemes paying the agent higher commissions. It is no longer legal to enforce the purchase of a particular policy, although operators can demand evidence that the customer is insured. Other retailers are now competing with travel agents to sell travel insurance, including companies such as Boots and Tesco, while cut-price annual policies are marketed direct by insurance agents, so travel agents are faced with a very competitive environment in selling this product, notwithstanding the attractive commissions paid.

Key issues in choosing a policy are to ensure that medical coverage is sufficient to meet the needs (in the USA, bills in excess of $1 million are not uncommon for serious illnesses), and that loss of any treasured individual items will be covered in full. The normal comprehensive coverage will limit compensation for total valuables, and may restrict claims for any individual item lost or stolen to a figure which will be unlikely to cover the cost of an average tourist's camera, so it is important for holidaymakers to consider covering such valuables within their house contents insurance. Insurance at reasonable cost for older travellers is becoming harder to find, as these are travelling more frequently but are also more likely to suffer medical difficulties. Doubling, or even tripling, the price of a policy is common for this group above the age of 65.

Of equal concern are the high numbers of younger travelers who fail to insure themselves when travelling abroad. A study by Sainsbury's in 2005 revealed that 1.48 million people in Britain under the age of 30 travel abroad without insurance[1], while another study by the Foreign and Commonwealth Office estimated that half of all stag and hen parties similarly fail to take out insurance for their trips.

Insurance remains a lucrative business for both operators and agents, although claims have been rising in recent years. Some reports estimate that 10 per cent of holidaymakers make claims, often fraudulent, against their policy, and this has led insurers to increase premiums to offset losses. Free insurance has consequently become an attractive incentive in marketing package tours.

Foreign transactions

Travellers today have an ever-widening choice of ways in which they can pay for services and goods while abroad. These include:

- taking sterling or foreign banknotes with them. This can lead to loss or theft, and certain foreign countries have restrictions on the import or export of their currencies
- taking traveller's cheques, in sterling or foreign currency, or in euros
- arranging for the advance transfer of funds to a specified foreign bank, or for an open credit to be made available, through their own bank, at a foreign bank
- using National Girobank postcheques
- using travel vouchers
- using credit cards or charge cards.

Credit cards such as those of Visa and Mastercard (Eurocard on the Continent) are very widely accepted throughout the world, but since transactions can take some time to filter through to one's bank account, users take a chance on the fluctuations of exchange rates. Bank charges for drawing cash abroad against both credit and debit cards can also be high. Charge cards such as American Express or Diners Club provide similar advantages and drawbacks (charge cards differ from credit cards in that accounts are due for settlement in full after receipt of an invoice from the company; credit is not extended. However, the limit on charge card transactions is generally much higher than on credit cards – indeed, the company may impose no ceiling on the amount the holder may charge to their account).

The introduction of the euro as common currency in many EU countries has made life easier for Britons and others touring a number of countries on the Continent. Leading travel agency chains in the UK operate their own foreign exchange desks, as do the high street banks, and the post office has also introduced a foreign exchange desk offering highly competitive rates.

Traveller's cheques are also still widely used, being readily acceptable throughout the world by banks and commercial institutions. They offer the holder guaranteed security with rapid compensation for theft or loss, an advantage which outweighs the standard premium charged of 1 per cent of face value. The value of the system for suppliers is that there is generally a considerable lapse of time between the tourist purchasing traveller's cheques and encashing them. The money invested in the interim at market rates of interest provides the supplier with substantial profits. Market leaders in traveller's cheque sales in the UK are Thomas Cook (whose 'circular note', the predecessor of the traveller's cheque, originated in 1873), and American Express, which first introduced the concept in 1891, but a growing proportion are being issued by the clearing-house banks. US$ traveller's cheques are useful almost anywhere in the world, and may be used as freely as cash itself within the USA.

Theft, and the fraudulent use of cards, is discouraging total reliance on plastic to make purchases and draw money when abroad, and tourists are now recommended to carry an assortment of small denomination notes, traveller's cheques and plastic cards when travelling. Sending money abroad in advance of travel is useful when planning to spend some time in the same place, but it is expensive, unless electronic transfer is insisted on – and it pays to shop around for the cheapest deal.

Travel vouchers such as Barclay's Visa and Citicorp provide for sterling prepayment for travel services like car hire and hotel accommodation. Although prepaid vouchers of this kind have been in existence in the travel industry for many years, the credit organizations have greatly boosted their use in recent years.

Apart from the popular Visa and Mastercard, there are a large number of other credit cards issued for the purchase of specific goods and services, such as car hire and hotels. Among these, mention should be made of the Universal Air Travel Plan (UATP) card, used for the purchase of IATA tickets throughout the world (although more commonly in use in North America than Europe). However, with the growth in popularity of the two leading credit card organizations, the use of other cards for international credit transactions is now limited. Since agents are required to pay a fee to the card companies when accepting credit cards in payment for travel, there has been some reluctance to accept them, but credit card sales are increasing at such a rate that no agent can afford to turn this form of business away. For the most part, however, they do pass these costs on to their clients. Payment by credit card offers the additional advantage to the traveller that funds are protected by card companies on amounts in excess of £100 in the event of the collapse of the agent, operator or airline with which they are dealing. However, the special free insurance coverage offered by some banks against the use of their cards has largely been withdrawn due to the cost of servicing claims.

The large number of foreign exchange facilities available provides the market with a very wide choice, but charges fluctuate considerably, and both rate of conversion and fixed charges need to be compared to judge what represents best value for money.

The introduction of chip-and-pin cards in Britain will shortly lead to 'smart' cards with an inbuilt microchip allowing the card to store credit. These have been use in France for some years, and have been tested in some supermarket outlets in the UK. Another alternative recently introduced to the marketplace are travel cash cards, provided by companies like Western Union, American Express, Mastercard and Fexco. These are prepaid cards loaded with a fixed sum of euros, dollars or sterling and a pin code, and they have already proved popular in the USA. They allow travellers to buy goods and services abroad to the value of the card, or to withdraw cash from ATMs. Their clear value is their relative protection against theft and fraudulent misuse; they can't be used to clear a bank account, and they also make it impossible for the holiday-maker to overspend. They are, however, rather expensive to use for withdrawing cash abroad.

Incentive travel vouchers

Incentive travel has shown considerable growth over the past few years, with companies providing their employees or dealers with attractive travel packages as rewards for achievement. One option taken up by some companies is the travel voucher, issued in various denominations, which allows the recipient to choose their own travel arrangements. This is simply monetary reward for achievement in another form, but the appeal of travel has proved to be a stronger motivator than either cash or consumer durables; it offers greater flexibility, and can be given in smaller denominations – to reward, for example, low absenteeism or the achievement of weekly targets. Some of these vouchers can only be exchanged against specific travel products, or through certain travel agents, while others can be used to pay for any holiday arrangements purchased through any agent.

Duty-free shopping

Under the category of services to tourists, mention should also be made of duty-free shopping facilities, although the subject has been discussed elsewhere in this text. The purchase of duty-free goods at airports, on board ships and aircraft, or at specially designated duty-free ports has exerted a strong attraction for tourists for a very long time. Introduced during the first half of the twentieth century, mainly to satisfy the demands of travellers on the great ocean liners, it was extended to aircraft in 1944. The first airside duty-free shopping arrived in 1947, when the Irish parliament passed the Custom-free Airport Act, giving Shannon the world's first duty-free shop. Since those days, duty-free purchases of spirits and tobacco in particular have been effectively marketed by airports and carriers alike, and the profits and sales of such items have always been substantial, accounting for large shares in the profits of many companies. Airports have achieved up to half their total operating profits through such sales, while some Scandinavian ferry companies obtain up to 70 per cent of their income in this manner.

This has led in some quarters to criticisms of profiteering, but airports reply to such criticism by claiming that without these profits, they would be forced to increase their landing charges; this would have a knock-on effect on carriers, which would then be forced to raise their fares. Without the benefit of duty-free shopping, transport fares do tend to rise appreciably; estimates typically point to increases ranging from 10 per cent to as high as 30 per cent. BAA in fact reduced its estimate of increases in charges to airlines using its airports after expanding its retail shopping outlets and forecasting rapid increases in duty-paid sales (rising congestion at airports, requiring earlier check-in times, and flight delays all tend to enhance sales in airport shops).

Tax harmonization in the European Union led to the withdrawal of duty-free privileges for travel between member states in July 1999. The full impact of this regulation on travel industry sectors has still to be assessed, but many companies were badly hit by the move; to take one example, Eurotunnel alone saw a 72 per cent fall in its retail revenues in the months following the ending of duty-free sales across the Channel. Fares on cross-Channel services were raised sharply, although heightened competition succeeded in pushing them down again, and the companies have redirected their marketing efforts to selling duty-paid goods, often at French prices, which substantially undercut those in Britain. How this new regulation is affecting travel patterns between EU and other European countries is not yet clear, although some destination switching is certain to have occurred as passengers face higher fares on some routes while others can still attract the duty-free consumer. Countries such as Tunisia, Morocco and Turkey are close enough to provide alternatives for tourists for whom this benefit is important, but with Malta and Cyprus both now drawn into the EU the scope for duty-free visits to cheap holiday islands in the Mediterranean has dried up.

Services to the supplier

Education and training

The approach to training in the tourism industry has been historically a sectoral one. In the past, each sector of the industry was primarily concerned with training staff to become competent within its own sector, focusing on narrow job-specific abilities. In an industry comprising mainly small units with entrepreneurial styles of management, the benefits of formal education and training have seldom been acknowledged. Most employees of travel agencies, tour operators and hotels were trained on the job, often by observing supervisors at work, although a handful of companies, such as Thomas Cook, were notable for their early recognition of the need for more formal, although in-house, training.

With the growing institutionalization of sectors, greater emphasis is placed on professionalism, the introduction of national standards and more formal modes of training. In Britain, the professional bodies in the industry introduced their own programmes of training and vocational education leading to membership, often carried out through full-time or part-time courses at local colleges of further or higher education. Examples of these early developments included courses offered by the Hotel and Catering International Management Association (HCIMA), the Chartered Institute of Transport (CIT) and the Institute of Travel and Tourism (ITT). However, with the rapid expansion of nationally validated travel and tourism courses in colleges of further and higher education which occurred from the 1970s onwards, there was a move to recognize formal qualifications, especially those offered by such bodies as the City and Guilds of London Institute (CGLI).

In-service training for travel agents was first formalized with the introduction of the Certificate of Travel Agency Competence (COTAC), nationally validated by the CGLI and supported by ABTA's National Training Board (now known as TTC Training). Since this date, formal training has had a bumpy ride, with frequent changes in qualification and supervisory body. Certificates in Travel (Travel Agents) and Tour (Tour Operators) replaced the former ABTA-approved ABTAC and ABTOC qualifications, but all too briefly. In 2004, the government-funded Sector Skills Council licensed People 1st as the official body to develop training programmes for the hospitality, leisure and tourism industries. This body encourages the training organizations to provide what are perceived to be the right courses for the industry. Both government and industry will provide the funding for the proposed new courses. The first of the new programmes to emerge was the Travel Destinations Certificate which, together with appropriate NVQs and key skills will form the basis of training in the new modern apprenticeships which were first launched in 1994, and which the industry hopes will overcome the perceived weaknesses in previous training. The industry has also accepted the development of the Accredited Professional Travel Qualification (APTQ) for continuing professional development, based on entry at level 2 of the NVQ plus a period of work experience.

The industry is working towards the recognition of nationally agreed benchmarks for service excellence, based on standards established originally by the British Standards Institution (BSI). National standards under the ISO 9000 scheme have given way to the programmes 'Investors in People' (IIP) and, most recently, 'Hospitality Assured' as evidence of standards achieved. At the same time, the regional tourist boards have supported customer-service training schemes under the Welcome to Excellence banner, including Welcome Host, Welcome e-Business and Welcome All (addressing customers with disabilities) programmes to upgrade personal skills for those dealing with customers in various sectors of the industry.

The difficulty of organizing day release for employees of smaller travel companies encouraged the development of distance-learning packages. British Airways fares and ticketing courses, for example, which are offered either full-time or through self-study packs, have found national acceptance as a standard for those seeking to work in travel agencies and airlines, while Lufthansa provides similar nationally accepted courses in Germany, and the World Tourism Organization (UNWTO) and International Air Transport Association (IATA) organize internationally recognized distance-learning packs for students of tourism throughout the world.

With vocational courses of this nature, the question of balance between job-specific skills and broader conceptual knowledge has long taxed employers and educationalists alike. Unlike most countries in Europe, Britain still does not hold formal qualifications in high respect, preferring to provide the job skills that are seen as essential to fulfil basic, sector-specific roles in the industry. However, public-sector colleges have offered courses since the late 1960s which were designed to provide not just essential skills, but a broader knowledge of the industry and the world of business. These were slow to achieve credibility with employers, and the new move into more vocationally oriented programmes of study, while welcomed by industry, is very different from the direction being taken on the Continent, where formal qualifications are more academically oriented.

In spite of this, Britain in 1986 was one of the first countries in the world to introduce undergraduate degrees in travel and tourism, joining the already well-established Higher National Diplomas (HNDs), postgraduate diplomas and master's degrees in the subject, so that tourism could be studied formally at all levels of post-school education. The popularity of degree-level tourism programmes led to a huge expansion of courses on offer in the new universities during the 1990s, with an output of qualified students far in excess of suitable posts available. Recent trends have led to the establishment of more specialized degrees, including the first MSc in e-tourism, for advanced students who want to take advantage of opportunities to work in positions relating to the increasing use of communications technology within the industry (figure 18.4).

Within the school system itself, GCSEs at ordinary and advanced level specializing in leisure and tourism have also been introduced, with the support of key members of the industry, in order to interest school leavers in a career in travel. Attitudes among careers counsellors in schools, however, are slow to change, and tourism continues to be seen by many as a career for the less academically able. Low salaries paid to those on the lower levels of employment tend to reinforce this attitude. The industry, especially the retail travel sector, is now agonizing over how better qualified staff can be obtained to pay the salaries that must be expected in a professional organization where fees may now have to be charged in lieu of commissions.

The trade press

In addition to specialized academic journals, there is a large selection of weekly and monthly journals devoted to the travel and tourism industry. The weekly trade papers *Travel Trade Gazette* and *Travel Weekly* provide an invaluable service to the industry, covering news of both social and commercial activities, as well as providing the heaviest concentration of advertisements for jobs in the industry (Figure 18.4).

In an industry as fast moving as tourism, employees can only update their knowledge of travel products by regular reading of the trade press. The newspapers complement the work of the training bodies, while for untrained staff they may well act as the principal source of new information. The trade press depends largely upon advertising for its revenue, as the two weeklies are distributed free to members of industry; in return, they support the industry by sponsoring trade fairs, seminars and other events.

Within the general category of the press one must also include those who are responsible for the publication of travel guides and timetables. The major publications in the field are shown in Table 18.1, and are those most commonly used in travel agencies. The task of updating the information is obviously immense, especially in view of the worldwide scope of many of these publications. Since their production becomes more complex each year, this is also a field which lends itself to computerization. Most guides now provide access for agents – and the public – electronically, and it is questionable whether there will still be a demand for hard-copy guides of this nature for very much longer.

Figure 18.4
The weekly
trade papers

(Permission of *Travel Weekly* and *Travel Trade Gazette*)

Table 18.1   Travel publications

Publication	Details
British publications	
ABC World Airways Guide (monthly)	Flight and fares information, car hire
ABC Rail Guide (monthly)	Timetables between London and all stations
ABC Shipping Guide (monthly)	Worldwide passenger and cargo–passenger services
ABC Guide to International Travel (quarterly)	Passport, visa, health, currency regulations, customs, climate etc
ABC Hotel and Travel Index (quarterly)	Hotel and trade information
Thomas Cook Continental Timetable (monthly)	Rail and passenger shipping services throughout Europe and the Mediterranean
Thomas Cook Overseas Timetable (bi-monthly)	Road, rail and local shipping in America, Africa, Asia, Australia
National Express Coach Guide (biannual)	Express coach services for British Isles
Travel Trade Directory	Directory of travel industry in UK/Eire
IATA Travel Agents' Directory of Europe (annual)	Agents, airlines, hotel groups, car hire, tourist offices
Britain: Hotels and Restaurants (annual)	BTA official guide
AA Guide to Hotels and Restaurants (annual)	Listing of 5,000 recommended establishments in the British Isles
A–Z Worldwide Hotel Guide (biannual)	Comprehensive listing of international hotels and reservations offices
Holiday Guide (annual summer and winter edition)	Identifies tour operators providing package holidays to specific hotels and resorts worldwide
Car Ferry Guide (annual)	Index of car ferry routes and operators
Cahners Hotel and Travel Index	Quarterly guide to hotels worldwide
ABTA Members' Handbook	Annual guide for agents, including country guide and full details of the Code of Conduct for agents and operators
Eurolines Directory	Annual guide to coach lines operating from the UK throughout Europe
International publications	
International Hotel guide (annual)	Worldwide guide published by International Hotel Association
Michelin Red Guides	French annual guides to Great Britain and Ireland, France, Benelux, Spain, Portugal, Italy and Germany
Europa Camping and Caravanning (annual)	Guide to campsites
Jaeger's Intertravel (annual)	Directory of world's travel agencies

Note: Many agents now buy their directories on CD-ROM or use the Internet to access directories instead of subscribing to hard-print manuals.

Example   OAG

OAG (the Official Airline Guide) was at one time virtually unchallenged as world leader in airline timetables, producing a three-volume guide listing half a million flights that are updated every month. By the mid-1990s technology was overtaking the hard-copy version, and in 2001 the company was put up for sale. Six weeks after the sale was confirmed, the 9/11 attacks paralyzed the airline industry, and airlines cut their discretionary costs, including payment to OAG. The organization recognized that to survive it would have to invest heavily in new technology, and this is under way as this text is prepared. This will enable business travellers, to take one example, to access OAG data via mobile phones, and hand-held computers, or on-line. Meanwhile, OAG Flights, its new Internet-based service, has enabled subscriptions to be cut from £599 for the hardback version to just £99. The new technology is due to come into service by 2006, although some observers question whether demand will remain, given the option of searching similar information on the Web without cost. OAG is relying on its reputation for the all-encompassing nature of the information it provides and its high level of accuracy – around 12,500 corrections to timetables are made every day – to ensure its continuing success.

Many guides are bought by both the trade and the travelling public. Corporate travel managers and frequent travellers on business are likely to want their own copies of guides, and agents may want hard copies to show to their customers when discussing alternatives. Hotel guides, of course, have always served the needs of both the trade and the public, although many are produced commercially for purchase by the travelling public. They fall into three distinct categories. Independent guides do not charge for entries, and inspections are made anonymously (examples: the *Michelin Red Guide*, the *Good Hotel Guide*); paid-entry guides make a charge for listing (examples: Alastair Sawday's *Special Places to Stay*, Condé Nast Johansen's *Recommended Hotels*); and registration guides are funded by membership fees (examples: the AA and RAC handbooks).

Travel guidebooks are enjoying huge popularity, as more and more holidaymakers travel further afield each year, and specialist bookstores like Stanfords have sprung up to cater for this growing demand. Such guidebooks must be updated frequently if they are to remain of any value, and many are produced on an annual basis. However, this again is an area which lends itself to computerization, and much of the information held in guidebooks can be readily accessed on the computer.

Example   Podcasts

Some guidebooks can already be replaced by Podcasts. Sound files can be downloaded over the Internet to a computer, then transferred automatically to an MP3 player such as an iPod. This will allow travellers to access spoken-word guides entirely for free. Virgin Atlantic was one of the first companies to offer Podcast guides, launching a guide to New York, with others to follow. The key benefit of these data is that they can be instantaneously updated, as well as being quick and easy to use.

Marketing services

A number of services exist either wholly or in part to provide marketing support to members of the travel industry. These include marketing consultants, representative agencies, advertising agencies, brochure design, printing and distribution services, suppliers of travel point-of-sale material, and research and public relations organizations. To this list must be added the organizations which provide the hardware and software for the travel industry's computer systems.

This book does not propose to discuss in depth the marketing of tourism. The subject is comprehensively covered in a companion text[2]. Other texts dealing with the topic can be found in the bibliography at the end of this book. The point to be made here is that both large and small companies in the industry can benefit by employing these specialist agencies, while in some instances their services are indispensable.

General marketing consultants in tourism

Management and marketing consultants offer advice to companies on the organization and operation of their businesses. They bring to the task two valuable attributes, expertise and objectivity. Most tourism consultants will have had years of experience in the industry on which to draw, having been successful in their own fields before turning to consultancy; but with the economic and political crises that have occurred over the past two decades, and the resultant mergers and takeovers that have led to downsizing in the industry, it was inevitable that the pool of former executives in the industry would turn to consultancy work; the consultants' group affiliated to the Tourism Society alone includes nearly 300 individuals.

Consultants, not being directly involved in the day-to-day running of the companies they are employed to help, can approach their task without any preconceived ideas. They can therefore advise companies either on the general reorganization of the business or on some ad hoc issue such as undertaking a feasibility study or the introduction of a new computer system.

Representative agencies

For a retainer or payment of royalties on sales, these organizations act as general sales agents for a company within a defined territory. This is a valuable service for smaller companies seeking representation abroad, for example. In the travel industry it is most commonly found in the hotel sector, but carriers, excursion operators and public-sector tourist offices all make use of the facility in marketing their services in other countries. As with consultants, many of the employees of these agencies will have had prior experience in the sector which they represent.

Advertising and promotional agencies

Many large travel companies, and an increasing number of smaller ones, retain an advertising agent, a number of whom specialize in handling travel accounts. Advertising agents do much more than design advertisements and place them in the media.

They should be closely involved in the entire marketing strategy of the company, and will be involved with the design and production of travel brochures. Many are equipped to carry out marketing research, the production of publicity material and merchandising or public relations activities. Some larger agencies also produce their own hotel/resort guides, using their own staff's extensive knowledge.

Travel companies may have their brochures designed by the design studio of their advertising agent, they may arrange for them to be produced by an independent design studio, or in some cases their printer's studio may undertake the work. However, a growing number of brochures are now put together in-house, with the aid of sophisticated computer software now available for desktop publishing. Advertising agents can also help and advise in the selection of a printer for the production of brochures or other publicity material.

One recent innovation in publicity material for the trade is the use of technology to replace the former hard copy of the travel brochure. Initially, this took the form of video cassettes, but these have given way to CD-ROMs and, more recently, DVDs. They are designed to help customers reach a decision on holiday destinations, facilities and services, and are sometimes produced by operators, who make them available on loan to their customers through travel agents. Production costs are borne by the principals – operators, hotels, airlines – whose services are promoted. A number of companies are now specializing in the production of these travel aids. There was some initial concern that these might come to replace the brochure entirely, but to date there is little evidence to suggest that this is occurring; holidaymakers like something tangible to flick through and refer to. With the development of direct communication between principals and consumers via the Internet and digital TV channels, if brochures are ever to be replaced it is more likely that this will be by computer-accessed text and illustrations which can be quickly updated and re-priced.

Finally, mention should be made of direct mail and distribution services, some of which specialize in handling travel accounts. Some of these companies design and organize direct-mail promotional literature aimed at specific target markets, or at travel retailers. They will also undertake distribution of a principal's brochures to travel agents in the UK.

Technical services

The rapid spread of computer use within all sectors of the travel industry has led to the establishment of specialist computer experts, who concentrate on designing and implementing purpose-made systems for their travel industry clients. Such systems include not only travel information and reservations functions, but also accounting and management information. Other computer organizations have been set up to provide networks which allow agents to access principals' computer reservations systems. With the pace of change that one has come to expect of this field, updating equipment and software is a regular function of the modern business, and these organizations fulfil a vital role in ensuring that businesses are up to date and efficient in improving their service while keeping costs under control.

Notes

1 Reported in *Travel Trade Gazette*, 5 August 2005
2 Holloway, J C, *Marketing for Tourism*, Prentice Hall, 4th edn 2004

Websites

People 1st   www.people1st.co.uk
Springboard UK   www.springboarduk.org.uk
Institute of Tourist Guiding   www.itg.org.uk
Travel Trade Gazette   www.ttglive.com
Travel Weekly   www.travelweekly.co.uk

Questions and discussion points

1 The failure of young people in Britain to take out travel insurance has been mentioned in this chapter. Why do you think so many fail to do so? Is it apathy, cost-consciousness, or simply a willingness on the part of younger people to take risks? What are your own views on ensuring you take insurance when you travel?

2 What attitudes do British people have to working as *animateurs*? Discuss between yourselves whether any of the roles outlined in this chapter would appeal to you, either in the short term or as a career, identifying the good and bad features of each role.

3 Mobile phonecards now allow users to send through the letter box personalized picture cards created from snaps taken on camera phones. The system sends information via satellite to the UK for next day delivery, together with messages of up to 60 words, to family and friends. Will this in your view replace postcards in the future?

Assignment topics

1 Undertake a search of the websites of *Travel Trade Gazette* and *Travel Weekly* (www.ttglive.com and www.travelweekly.co.uk) and compare their coverage of news with the hard copies of these papers. Write a report on the strengths and weaknesses of the websites, and which you would prefer to use for updating your knowledge of the industry, giving reasons. Search the Web for other sources of travel trade information (e.g. www.traveltrade.com) and compare these with the two trade newspapers. While browsing the Web, you will encounter pop-up advertisements for related products. Assess the value of this form of advertising spend compared with other opportunities, and include a section devoted to an analysis of the strengths and weaknesses of this medium to reach the travelling public.

2 As marketing officer for a museum which displays items which reflect the heritage of your home town or region, you are looking for new ways of reaching visitors to the area, to attract them to your site. A virtual museum, the 24 Hour Museum, funded by the DCMS, offers an on-line gateway to several thousand museums, galleries and heritage attractions. Review the site (www.24hourmuseum.org.uk) and write a report to the museum curator proposing that this site should become a key element in the campaign to attract more visitors in the coming year.

Part IV Travel and tourism management today and tomorrow

19 The design and management of tourism services

Objectives

After studying this chapter, you should be able to:

- define design and be aware of its role in the tourism business
- appreciate the need for landscaping in the layout of sites
- understand how the effective use of lighting can enhance a site
- recognize the importance of good signposting within and outside tourist sites
- be aware of the role of interpretation in tourism and how this is most effectively implemented
- be aware of the chief principles of good site management and how these should be implemented.

Introduction

Average acceptable wait time at attractions for European guests as a whole is 22 minutes.... Whilst British visitors are prepared to wait for up to 25 minutes, French guests will only happily stand in line for a much shorter length of time.

P Y Gerbeau, on Disney, Paris
Locum Destination Review, Summer 2001

This chapter will introduce the reader to issues which are often ignored or overlooked in textbooks of tourism, although some will feature in complementary studies such as museum or attraction management. Others, such as architecture and landscaping issues, are more likely to be dealt with in studies in town and country planning. The purpose of introducing them here is to increase awareness among students of tourism of the cross-disciplinary nature and complexity of the tourism business, and to encourage both students and practitioners to think more broadly about what it is that actually appeals to tourists, encourages them to visit specific sites and allows them to derive satisfaction from the experience. The discussion will necessarily have to be limited in a textbook of this nature, particularly in examining the role of features such as architecture and landscaping in tourism, but it is hoped that touching on these issues will whet the reader's appetite to learn more about them and will help to widen discussions on the nature of tourism generally.

The role of design in tourism

Architecture and design

Although all of us are affected by design, much of its effect on us is subconscious. Local architecture, the layout of our public parks, the design of signposts are all features with which we have become familiar in our own home surroundings. As a result, we see these objects in a different light from the way visitors will see them. When we in turn visit other destinations, we will be aware of and critically examine things we tend to take for granted in our own environment. Yet everything we see is designed, from the buildings to the shopfronts, from roads to lamp-posts, from street signs to ticket booths, and all these objects affect us and mould our attitude to our surroundings.

Design therefore represents a crucial element in tourism planning, whether we are designing a tourist attraction like Disneyland from scratch, or enhancing the landscape to make it more attractive or suitable for tourist use, such as a major approach road by which tourists enter a town; or even arranging for a few cosmetic changes to the housing stock of the town, by encouraging residents to do a spot of painting (Paris underwent a frenzy of fascia-cleaning of buildings in the 1960s with the encouragement of President de Gaulle. As a result the city became vastly more attractive for tourism, and Parisiens took a new pride in their city).

Design has two roles. One is *functional*, in the sense that if something is well designed, it should do its job better; the other is *aesthetic*, meaning that it should look right, in itself and in its setting, and that it should have visual appeal. However, when we refer to 'good' or 'bad' design, to some extent we are expressing subjective views. The controversy surrounding the rebuilding of Windsor Castle after the tragic fire of 1993 shows the depth of feeling about a heritage site which for some people is sacrosanct, and should be reconstructed exactly as it was (even though most architects agree that much of what was lost was no masterpiece, and the castle had in any case grown over the years into a mishmash of architectural styles). Others argued that the fire had produced an opportunity to add modern extensions reflecting the best of twentieth-century architecture. The fact that overseas tourists come to see our heritage does not rule out the potential that modern buildings have to attract their own audience, and the best of these, too, will in time become part of the heritage. Planning authorities in Britain are finally coming to recognize this truism, as they now grant planning permission for new country houses (which will become the stately homes of the future) in the modern idiom, and not merely pastiches of past glories.

Other notable new buildings which are setting standards for good design include visitor centres and reception areas of tourist attractions, which are designed not only to inform (and often to sell commercial products), but also to impress the visitor and

Figure 19.1
Yorkshire
Sculpture Park

(Photographed by the author)

reinforce the experience of the visit. Recent examples in Britain include the new reception, shop and catering block at the Yorkshire Sculpture Park near Wakefield (see Figure 19.1), and the Loch Lomond Gateway Centre (see Figure 19.2).

Restoration, renewal and 'heritage'

In the matter of architectural design, the private and public sectors often have quite different objectives. The private-sector developer is interested in good design only to the extent that it operates functionally, and that it satisfies the consumer and encourages them to return. The developer will generally try to produce the design which does these things at the lowest possible cost. They will also take a shorter-term view of the project, being less concerned about its appearance a decade hence. The public sector can, if it chooses, exercise greater control, not just by insisting on sympathetic restoration instead of rebuilding, or by requiring buildings to make use of local building materials, but by rewarding and encouraging good design. Too often, however, local authorities take a short-sighted view of their role in promoting good design; in the 1960s, for example, the developers of the Seagram Building in New York were horrified to find they would be taxed far more heavily by the City because of the added value of their building, which was designed by Mies van der Rohe and quickly hailed as a masterpiece of twentieth-century architecture. This rapidly discouraged other developers

Figure 19.2
Loch Lomond
Gateway Centre

(Photographed by the author)

from spending more than they needed to on good design. Subsequently, the city went some way to rectifying their error, when a percentage of all new building costs had to be applied to public art.

The extent to which a 'heritage building' should be restored also leads to considerable controversy, and conflicting ideals which are often summarized as a battle between restoration and conservation. When reconstruction of the medieval Barley Hall in the centre of York was completed in 1992, architectural critics were enthusiastic about the care with which the work had been carried out, and the accuracy of the reconstruction; yet the Chairman of the Society for the Protection of Ancient Buildings quickly attacked the project for producing a replica of the original building and destroying many of the later additions which had made it organic. The end result was dismissed as 'another contribution to our Disneyland heritage'. Similar attacks have been launched on reconstructions of Roman fortifications along Hadrian's Wall such as that at Vindolanda, and of the Temple at Knossos in Crete (not only over-elaborate in its reconstruction, doubts have now been cast on the authenticity of the design, although many thousands of tourists were pleased to gain an insight into the way some of the world's oldest buildings may have actually looked in their heyday).

In Britain we have been criticized for adopting a provincial attitude to new building which suggests that most of us are happier with the designs of the past. The result is that pastiche neo-Georgian or mock Tudor is more popular than the contemporary buildings that are springing up all over Europe. More legitimate criticism of modern

Figure 19.3
Finlandia Hall,
Helsinki

(Photographed by the author)

buildings is that directed not at their form, but at their construction, with unsympathetic use of material, such as raw concrete, or the fact that they are out of scale with other buildings in the area. Modern materials tend not to age attractively, while natural materials will become more attractive with the passing years (the Seagram Building, referred to earlier, is a rare exception. By coating the exterior framework in expensive bronze, the architect produced a successful modern building that aged attractively).

Some of the issues surrounding the design of modern buildings have been examined in Chapter 11, where the potential for modern hotel design to attract tourists was discussed. Certainly, issues of size and scale must be taken into consideration, as must the use of local materials in construction. On the other hand, given the right setting, and in the hands of a master architect, an uncompromisingly modern building can become the pride of its residents, and an international draw. Figure 19.3 is one such example – Eero Saarinen's Finlandia Hall in Helsinki, Finland, a country noted for the excellence of its design (which it promotes extensively to attract tourists to the country). The building succeeds in part because, set in its own landscaping and away from city centre buildings, it is not required to merge with the local traditional architecture. However, where this is required, modern adaptations of vernacular design can be undertaken and will merge sympathetically with their surroundings.

From the point of view of the tourist, the significance of such design is not only that it reflects the traditions of the local architecture and therefore merges effectively with the surrounding buildings, but it is also built on a human scale which does not dwarf the passer-by. Most visitors to a town will explore it on foot, and good street-level design is vital to retain the visitor's interest.

Figure 19.4
Modern public toilet in natural stone at Tarr Steps, Exmoor National Park, Somerset

(Photographed by the author)

Local building materials are, unfortunately, often more expensive to use in construction, but the additional cost is well justified in the long run, and may even bring in additional revenue from tourists anxious to see the construction itself. In Britain, examples may be found in the use of Bath stone in Bath, Cotswold stone in the Cotswolds, Black-and-white half-timbering in the border country, thatch in the West Country, and slate in the Lake District or Wales. Even for such mundane construction as public toilets, the use of local and natural building materials can greatly enhance the end result (see Figure 19.4) and is often insisted upon by local authority planning departments. The use of natural materials specific to the locality will help to reinforce the characteristics of the brand image which the attraction or tourist board are trying to create.

Public toilets for tourists are often treated as a peripheral issue by planners, but their inadequacies are often picked on by tourist bodies like UKInbound. Many tourist sites suffer from an inadequate supply of toilets, while others have had their toilets locked or shut down due to shortages of money for maintenance and supervision – even Bath, one of Britain's principal tourist towns, announced in 2004 a reduction in the number of conveniences remaining open for tourists. While Britain is not unique in facing this problem, it is interesting to note that in Japan, architectural competitions are promoted for public toilets, while the Chinese encourage architects to design toilets with the needs of American tourists in mind. The interest generated by the construction of the 'superloo' at Westbourne Grove in London, designed by architect Piers Gough in

1993 with an attached flower-shop, reveals just how important good toilet design can be for tourism. This particular example not only won design awards, but also was featured in English Heritage's advertisements in 1997. It should come as no surprise, therefore, that over 80 public toilets around Britain are actually listed buildings.

As we have noted in Chapter 10, shopping is a prime motive for tourism, and the design of shopfronts can do much to increase tourist satisfaction, for passers-by and window-shoppers.

In many cases, modern architecture may be actively disliked, but still provides a draw for tourists. The Pompidou centre in Paris is certainly not everybody's idea of a good modern building, but it is still a major magnet for tourists. On a smaller scale, the highly controversial Cube Houses of Rotterdam, designed by Piet Blom, and their adjoining Potloodflat (pencil flat) building have become important features to attract tourists to Rotterdam, and are now featured extensively in tourist literature produced by the city. The Netherlands is a country which has experimented extensively in modern buildings throughout the twentieth century, and this is now paying off by attracting a growing number of tourists, whether out of architectural interest or for novelty. One private house, the Rietveld-Schröder house in Utrecht, designed by Gerrit Rietveld and now restored as a museum, brings many students of architecture to visit from all over the world. Perhaps the best-known private house in the world, Fallingwater, designed by architect Frank Lloyd Wright, exercises similar appeal for tourists with an architectural interest who make the effort to visit Bear Run, in Pennsylvania, USA. This building is of such international importance that millions of dollars have been invested in recent years in bringing the house back into peak condition.

Landscape design

No building can be divorced from its setting, and just as thought must go into the design of the building itself, so the site must be landscaped attractively to maximize visitor appeal.

Part of the attraction of an English village is the way in which the houses lie in the landscape, blending as if they were made for the setting. Where a site for development is sloping, it becomes even more important to ensure that the buildings blend with the background, and if the buildings are to be exposed to view – for example, a group of self-catering chalets high in the Alps – great care has to be taken to integrate them into the landscape. Buildings should not stand out on the skyline, but if it is essential that they do, then their lines should be broken up with the use of trees and shrubs. On sloping sites, buildings can be 'stepped' or terraced up the hillside to keep their scale in harmony with the environment. Similarly, on waterside developments, buildings should be sited well clear of the waterfront itself, to allow for walkways along the banks that will attract both residents and visitors, and to ensure that those using the waterway are not intimidated by high buildings alongside.

The appeal of water is evident in the conversion of so many redundant harbours and waterways in Britain for leisure use. Here, the local authorities must determine whether the site is best retained as a dockland environment, or themed as urban parkland. Enlightened authorities have come to recognize that retention of the traditional bollards, cranes and other paraphernalia of a dockside will provide a unique setting and a better lure for the visitor, with the addition of a modest number of trees or shrubs.

In the countryside of England, boundaries are a prominent feature which give the landscape much of its character. They range from the hedges of southern England (a significant proportion of which have sadly been lost since the end of World War II, as farmers, responding to government incentives, tried to increase productivity on their land) to the dry-stone walls of the North which, using virtually no mortar, allow ferns and lichen to grow on their surfaces and soften their appearance. Fences also have characteristic local designs, particularly picket fences which are often complemented by the traditional five-barred gate; these designs can be incorporated into tourist settings, too. Public-sector grants have been made available to retain and restore dry-stone walling and hedging where these are characteristic of the local landscape.

Car parks are a particular problem for the tourism designer, since they occupy large areas of land and are visually intrusive. In the countryside, efforts are now made to ensure that the park appears as natural as possible; logs can be used to separate the bays, and substantial shrubbery planting will help to conceal the cars themselves. Good, but not intrusive, lighting is important, while the surface itself can be retained as a gravel site rather than asphalted. In some small parking areas, it may be possible to use honeycombed concrete blocks which allow the grass to grow through them, rendering the concrete surface almost invisible.

Car parks must, of course, be situated well away from any high-grade heritage sites, and this may mean that special provision must be made for the disabled. In cities, the urban setting will mean the use of more man-made materials in car park construction, but this no longer means high-rise concrete. Designs have become more fanciful in recent years, including in one case a mock medieval fortification, while parks on open land have been attractively furnished with decorative modern lamps and plenty of trees to break up the land mass. Given the high prices motorists are now resigned to paying for parking, underground car parks are often economically viable, and of course have the least impact on the surrounding environment. In Salzburg, Austria, where public parking is at a premium, the local authority went as far as to blast cavernous parking space out of the adjacent cliff faces, underground parking being impractical.

Telephone and public utility lines can mar the appearance of even the most beautiful town or village. Fortunately, in Britain local authorities have generally taken an enlightened view on hiding these ugly necessities, but a visit to Spain or Greece will soon illustrate how much visual pollution is caused by overhead wires along streets and linking into houses. The cost of burying wires is much higher, but again in the long run it is worth the investment if it leaves the site appearing much more attractive to visitors. The march of electricity pylons across the landscape in some of the most scenic parts of Britain today – and the more recent intrusion of wind-power electricity generators and mobile-phone antennae – has also been strongly criticized by defenders of the traditional countryside.

Street furniture

Street furniture is something we all take for granted, yet it plays an important part in reflecting the national landscape too. One has only to think of the classic red telephone kiosks and letter boxes in Britain, or the nineteenth-century 'pissoirs' (now sadly disappearing) and classic green boulevard chairs and tables still to be found on

Figure 19.5
A well-designed
drinking
fountain in
Zürich,
Switzerland

(Photographed by the author)

the streets of Paris, to realize that such items play a part in formulating our picture of vernacular landscapes and townscapes. In Britain, a great deal of attention has been paid in recent years to designs of public seating and litter bins, but any item of street furniture, from post boxes to telephone kiosks, from litter bins to bus shelters, from public toilets to refreshment stalls, from lamp-posts to railings, needs to be carefully designed to be in harmony with the surroundings and reflect the image of the area in which they are sited. Increasingly, they must be designed to resist vandalism and, where possible, graffiti too.

Local authorities must first determine whether to adopt a classic or modern design for their setting. Heritage sites such as York or Chester are more likely to opt for a traditional and classic design to blend with the architecture of the area. Unfortunately, this has led to the development of a ubiquitous design in cast iron with gold motifs, frequently bearing the crest of the city, which, while tasteful and elegant, does little to distinguish the city's streets from countless others in the country. However, these designs are to be welcomed over some of the products they replace, such as the plastic litter bin (all too often cracked or misshapen), in a choice of battleship grey or garish yellow. Litter bins in particular need to be big enough to accommodate the huge amounts of litter created today by take-away shops, and the council must have a policy of emptying these frequently, or the benefits of good design will be lost, as rubbish piles up around the base of the bin.

Cities on the Continent, particularly those whose centres were substantially rebuilt after the war or which wish to promote a modern, dynamic image, will adopt more modern designs. These can work equally well in the appropriate setting. Their cost may be substantially higher than more modest designs, as is the case with the drinking fountain in Figure 19.5, but they not only improve the image of the city, they will also last much longer without repair or replacement.

Providing seating in a town is a problem for the planners, as it tends to attract vagrants. However, the use of simple-to-maintain materials which will provide a brief respite for residents and tourists, but not a level of comfort encouraging longer stays, can be the answer to the problem. Individual seats, rather than benches, reduce their use by vagrants for sleeping.

Pedestrianization

Many towns popular with tourists have pedestrianized some of their principal thoroughfares. The result can greatly enhance the atmosphere of a street and encourage visitors to come shopping. Some of Britain's most attractive town centres, such as such as those of York, Brighton, Bath and Chester, and many Continental towns, feature narrow pedestrian walkways which have never been wide enough to support motor vehicles. In these towns, the narrowness of the lanes is their very attraction. Even in downtown districts where such lanes do not exist, virtually all major towns will now have areas restricted to pedestrian use; in London, for instance, Convent Garden was redesigned on this basis after the fruit and vegetable market was moved away.

However, pedestrianizing will not in itself be enough to make the street a focal point for shoppers; the shops themselves must be appropriate for the setting, and the street must be enhanced by well-designed street furniture, tree planting and the display of flowers or shrubs in tubs or other containers. When this is done tastefully, the end result can transform a street. However, the fact that it will also attract much larger numbers of pedestrians can lead to congestion and to a litter problem which the council must be prepared to tackle.

Horticultural displays

The use of hanging baskets, floral beds in the centre of main access roads, extensive tree planting along the pavements and similar horticultural displays can make a pretty village outstanding, and an ugly town bearable. Some of Britain's towns have made such a feature of their floral displays that they have become famous internationally; Bath's hanging basket displays are highly attractive features for the summer visitors, while the massed floral beds which highlight the seafronts of towns like Eastbourne and Worthing are features which draw many older visitors to these resorts year after year. As many flowers bloom in spring, they can be used as features to attract visitors before the traditional peak summer season. Aberdeen is noted for its display of formal rose beds along its main roads, while on the Continent, the flower-bedecked chalets of Switzerland and Austria are features that are indelibly associated with these countries' villages, and highlighted in all tourist brochures.

The cost of transforming a town in this way is considerable, but any town seeking to attract the tourist can at very least consider investing funds to make the main approach roads more attractive, both those carrying visitor traffic to the centre and those which provide the principal access for pedestrians to the centre from bus or train terminals. First impressions count for a lot when setting out to attract the tourist.

Art and tourism

There is a growing recognition today that art has a role to play in the tourism industry, not just through museums, galleries and arts events organized to attract the tourist, but in the everyday surroundings in which visitors find themselves. Ostensibly, 'street art' is designed to heighten the visual appeal of a town for its residents, but once again, such embellishment will add to the attraction of the destination for the visitors too, and if the work displayed is by artists of international reputation, this will widen the appeal of the destination to the international visitor. Sculptures by Henry Moore in Yorkshire or at the Serpentine in London attract a dedicated audience of overseas and domestic visitors. Cities in the United States enforce local regulations requiring a small percentage of the total cost of any new development to be spent on 'public art' at the site; and the prestigious offices of major corporations will also judge it appropriate to enhance their forecourts with sculptures by leading artists of the day. In London, prominent British artists such as Eduardo Paolozzi were recruited to design the wall tiling during the renovation of the Central London Underground railway stations.

Towns can reinforce their images by the imaginative use of sculpture or art. In Germany, for example, Hamelin has its sculpture of the Pied Piper, while Bremen has greatly enhanced its pedestrian streets with scenes from Grimms' Fairy Tales. Brussels is famous for the Minneke Pis, the tiny bronze statue of a small boy urinating, which is often the subject of tourist souvenirs and postcards. Copenhagen's major draw is its Little Mermaid statue, based on the Hans Andersen fairy tale. Recently, the city of Berlin brought back into the town centre a statue of Frederick the Great which had been deemed politically unacceptable in East Berlin before the fall of the Wall.

Britain is becoming more aware of the importance of art and the way in which it can serve the interests of the tourism industry. Notable features include two water fountain sculptures by William Pye, 'Slipstream' and 'Jetstream', commissioned by BAA at Gatwick Airport and a 130-foot long sculpture, 'Train' by David Mach, a monument to the record-breaking steam locomotive 'Mallard' and comprising 185,000 bricks, unveiled in Darlington in 1997 (to considerable local criticism but widespread national publicity). The significance for tourism of the 'Angel of the North' has already been mentioned in Chapter 10. This has not only attracted numerous tourists to visit, it has also captured the hearts and imagination of the local residents.

Lighting

External street lighting can play an important role in enhancing a town, both with respect to the design of the lights themselves and to the effect they can create at night. Again, a choice must be made between traditional and modern lamps. Some towns have reinforced their quaintness by reverting to authentic gas lighting, which has great popular appeal for tourists. In Norwegian villages in the weeks leading up to Christmas, the shopping streets are illuminated with real flares, giving visitors an impression of warmth and cosiness at a time when the long periods of darkness could otherwise easily depress.

Floodlighting major attractions, long a recognized practice for the great monuments in leading cities, has become much more widespread, and its use can encourage tourists out on to the streets at night, thus extending the 'tourist day'. White lights are normally recommended; the use of coloured lights, apart from settings where a fairground atmosphere is appropriate, such as at the Blackpool illuminations, is best avoided. The use of coloured lights to floodlight Niagara Falls, many observers feel, turned a great spectacle into an example of down-market kitsch. Limited use of coloured lighting can be helpful in highlighting horticultural displays at night, however. Care must be taken not to over-light; strong lights are particularly inappropriate in a village setting, for example.

Finally, mention might be due here of the use of fireworks displays to highlight key events such as national holidays or other days of commemoration (Independence Day, 4th July, in the USA, Bastille Day, 14th July, in France, and Guy Fawkes Day, 5th November, in Britain, are all days where fireworks commonly round off the day's events).

Signposting

All visitors look for signposts, so they become the most visible of all forms of street furniture. They serve three purposes.

1 Directional

Traffic signs direct vehicles or pedestrians in particular directions, and to specific sights. They must therefore be clearly legible, especially from a distance in the case of vehicle signs. They should be identified by use of a standard, immediately recognizable colour, and their size and shape should also be uniform. Generally, standards for road signs will be set by local authorities or government departments of transport.

Within towns, signposts directing tourists to specific attractions have received a lot of attention in Britain in recent years. Once again, a 'traditional' classic signpost has been devised, with modest variations in design, constructed of cast iron painted black with white lettering (some towns have produced a variation on this; Bristol, for example, introduced Royal Blue as the standard colour).

The more traditional black-on-white 'finger posts', the signposts we find in many UK villages, are icons of national culture, some dating back to the seventeenth century, but these are now deteriorating and local authorities are being urged to repaint them every five years before they are lost for ever and have to be replaced.

Bristol has taken a lead in location signposting for visitors, producing a clear, well-designed signpost incorporating a map of the city centre, as part of its award-winning 'legible city' initiative (see Figure 19.6).

2 Informative

These are of two types. They may be used to alert tourists passing in vehicles to a particular attraction in the vicinity, and they will also be provided at a particular site, such as a viewpoint or monument, to give information about the site itself.

Figure 19.6
Bristol's award-winning 'legible city' signposting

(Photographed by the author)

In the former case, following a long period where signposting was arbitrary and often banned from main roads, in Britain the Department of Transport introduced white-on-brown signs in 1986, with 35 different pictographs representing every conceivable variety of tourist attraction. Regulations on the use of these and other signs are complex and quite restrictive. The use of white-on-brown signs, for example, is dependent upon the numbers visiting the site (for example, historic houses must attract a minimum of 5,000 visitors a year for a road sign to be approved). This, of course, introduces a 'catch-22' situation, where already well-established attractions are favoured over newly developed ones.

Signs outside a particular attraction will also be subject to local government regulations. For example, attractions in North America, which are generally very well signposted, often adopt a standard format for imparting information about national monuments (see a typical Canadian cast-iron-with-crest 'interpretation' plaque in Figure 19.7(a)). Visitors to such sights will also need to receive information about the layout of larger sites, together with details of opening hours and price of admission. Examples of signs bearing this information are given in Figures 19.7(b) and 19.7(c). Such signs must still be clearly legible, but may have more character in their design.

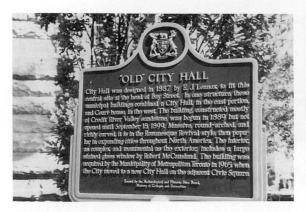

(a)

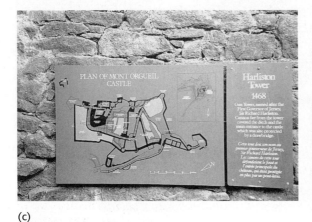

(c)

(b)

Figures 19.7 (a), (b) and (c) Three examples of informative signposting:
(a) Old City Hall, Toronto, Canada
(b) Historic Mackenzie House, Toronto
(c) Mont Orgeuil Castle, Jersey
(All photographed by the author)

Mention should be made of the traditional blue plaques which are widely in use in Britain to advise the visitor of the fact that a property has been the home of some well-known person in the past. These are invariably of great interest to foreign visitors in particular, and the fact that they are often encountered by the tourist coincidentally in walking around the streets of a city gives them added appeal.

3 Utility

These signs are designed to direct visitors to public utilities such as toilets and tele-phone kiosks. They can be smaller in scale, and will often make use of symbols, as do the white-on-brown signs – a particular boon to foreign visitors. They may have their own design and colour, but are also often incorporated into information signs in popu-lar tourist towns.

Figure 19.8
Attractive shop
signs are a
feature of
Ravensburg,
Germany

(Photographed by the author)

Within specific tourist attractions, imagination gives rein to a great variety of signs and symbols. In medieval times, as few people could read, this led to many shops hanging out symbols of their trade. These have been retained, and sometimes resurrected, by shops in tourist centres, and add visual appeal to the streets. The example shown (Figure 19.8) is one of a number of original street signs in the town of Ravensburg in southern Germany.

Politics and the need to cater for foreign visitors can often affect the layout and language of signs. In Belgium, and in parts of Canada and Wales, bilingualism is the law, so every place name or instruction must be given in two languages. In the Baltic States, although there are many Russian speakers, the hatred towards their former masters means that if any foreign language is to be used on signs, it is English. In China, Japan and Thailand, where many foreigners will drive cars but not understand the local scripts, signs in the large towns all have to be duplicated in English.

The management of tourism sites

This textbook is not the place for a detailed examination of management techniques; but anyone studying tourism needs to be aware of some of the specific issues of management that are unique to tourism, and to recognize the problems that can arise. We will examine two issues here which are central to the study of tourism: those of interpretation and of visitor management.

Interpretation

The days when visitors expected no more than to stare passively at exhibited artefacts or buildings are now over. Today, visitors to tourist sites expect to be both educated and entertained, and the managers of tourist sites, especially those incorporating 'heritage' (however we interpret this term), must find ways of getting the visitor involved, and bringing the site 'alive' for them. This implies finding ways to impart information successfully, and is seen as giving added value to any tourist visit. Given the number of foreign visitors who are also likely to visit such sites, managers have the added problem of presenting their information in a manner which can be understood by people from different backgrounds and with very little knowledge of the local language.

Interpretation has come a long way in the past few years, and whole courses of study are now devoted to understanding it. Thirty years ago, this would have involved nothing more than producing some attractive graphic design and handing out a few leaflets. Today, attempts are made to transport the visitor into another age, through the use of costumed animateurs and the careful staging of settings to make them as realistic as possible. By way of example, barmaids in period costumes will pull pints of real ale in the pubs at the Ironbridge Gorge Museum; and at Wigan Pier, an actor taking the role of a Victorian schoolmaster will invite the visitors to participate as pupils in a role-play demonstrating school life of the period. At the Blaenavon 'Big Pit' Mining Museum in Wales, visitors have to don mining helmets and lamps in order to accompany authentic ex-miners who guide them around the site; travel to the coal face is in an original mining cage, and the life and full horror of working underground are effectively communicated by the guides during the tour. In Latvia, it is even possible to stay overnight in a Soviet prison cell, with abusive guards pacing up and down outside.

Example   US Holocaust Memorial Museum, Washington DC

Arguably, one of the most emotive experiences in museum viewing is to visit the site of genocide or its interpretation. The US Holocaust Memorial Museum, commemorating the persecution and attempted annihilation of Jews and others under the Nazis, sets out to bring home the full horror of the event to visitors, especially those too young to remember, or even to have been aware of, this phase of history. Its techniques are successful in compounding the emotions aroused by the events themselves.

Upon entering, visitors are provided with a plastic identity card with a photo and name of a child. This identity card then becomes the passport to the tour of the museum. At the end of the tour the visitor receives a printout of the history of the child, which includes in most cases the date of disappearance[1].

More recently, museums and genocide sites have similarly drawn attention to events such as the killing fields of Laos and Cambodia, and doubtless others will appear in due course to drive home the point at more recent sites of genocide such as that at Srebrenica in Bosnia.

At the Robin Hood Story exhibition in Nottingham, visitors have to find out the answers to a series of questions about Robin Hood, based on information contained in the interpretation plaques found throughout the exhibition, and those answering the questions correctly receive a 'good' certificate. A museum opened in Neasden, North London, in 1993, as a direct response to local demand, with an exhibition of 'Brent people'. Visitors are able to tap into audio history tapes by telephone, photos can be called up on screens by computer, and children are allowed to dress up in costumes of the 1920s, rather than observing them at a distance on dummies. Interactive communication of this kind is ideal as a means of involving children; however, such attractions all have to face one problem – is a single form of interpretation suited to every one of the variety of markets to which the attraction appeals? Plaques designed to be read by children will be dismissed by adults as patronizing, while too much information given to those seeking the detailed background to a site will put off those enjoying an entertaining day out. The answer is to provide a variety of different forms of communication, to cater successfully for each market segment served. Stately homes often meet the need for more detailed information by providing hand-held boards for use in each room with full particulars of the contents. These are sometimes offered in two or three foreign languages also. The trend in museum interpretation today is to ensure that day-to-day life among those lower in the social scale is described and interpreted as fully as is the life of those at the top of the social scale.

Managing visitor flows

Most attractions share a common problem in managing their visitors: that of uneven flows. Demand at a particular site will fluctuate, and cannot easily be spread over time. The result is that managers face problems of scheduling and queuing to which their own preferred solutions may not be those which most appeal to the customers themselves.

Popular attractions such as major exhibitions which are mounted for a limited period of time (e.g. Tutankhamen and the Treasures of Egypt at the British Museum, the Matisse Retrospective in Paris and London) or the key attractions at a Disney theme park, where demand will always outstrip supply, pose particular problems. One solution is to require advance reservations for entry, and to determine the maximum number to be admitted at any given time (admitting too many people to an exhibition of paintings will result in enormous disappointment if people are unable to see the paintings). Many attractions in London, including Madame Tussauds, Buckingham Palace and the London Eye, as well as special exhibitions in the national museums, arrange for timed entrances which guarantee the visitor entry to the attraction. Seasonal pricing is now quite common, with lower charges applying during the winter. Variable pricing, such as inclusive pricing which allows visitors in to a number of nearby attractions for a single, discounted price, is a sensible approach to improving revenue, as is any discount offered where more than one attraction is paid for.

Other museums make special arrangements for their Friends (by subscription) and for Corporate Sponsors, who are invited to attend popular exhibitions at times when they are not open to the general public. These sites often now compete with hotels for weddings, product launches and other functions which will raise revenue and appeal to the public as an unusual location for their planned event. Galleries at the British

Figure 19.9
Not all pricing
strategies make
sense

(Photographed by the author)

Museum are particularly sought after in this respect, and wedding receptions and similar functions are popular on board the 150-year old *SS Great Britain* in Bristol, where the reconstructed main restaurant serves as the function room.

The Walt Disney attractions have years of experience in handling very large flows of tourists, and use timed entrances to handle peak demand. Their 'Fastpass' allows visitors to collect a ticket during their visit and return later in the day to join a shorter queue. They have also experimented with a 'single rider' line to top up the odd empty space on rides, but found that waiting families were angered by what they saw as 'queue-jumping' and abandoned the scheme.

Example Alton Towers

Overpricing to manipulate or reduce demand is seen by many as an injustice, and is a solution seldom enforced. However, in 2000 the Alton Towers theme park in Staffordshire went so far as to introduce two-tier pricing for its attractions, with tickets designed to be purchased in advance on the Internet which allowed higher payers to jump queues. The so-called X-celerator, priced at more than three times the regular entry fee, allowed the first 30 buyers to travel on the busiest rides without waiting. There was a predictable backlash from the public, and the very high price charged (£65) meant that take-up was seldom 100 per cent. The scheme was abandoned.

At sites where advance bookings, for whatever reason, are less feasible, queues will have to be organized, and the tedium of waiting reduced as far as possible. Very long queues form for attractions like the Crown Jewels at the Tower of London, and the management of this site must find a means of getting the right balance between their own desire to move the crowds quickly past the display and the need to avoid antagonizing their customers, who will have waited a long time and expect to take their time seeing the attraction. This can be achieved by the use of travelators, which will move viewers past an attraction at a given speed.

Example The *Pieta* at The New York World Fair

Michaelangelo's famous sculpture *Pieta* was imported from Italy to the United States as a key attraction at the time of the New York World's Fair. Its enormous popularity, and the advance publicity associated with the exhibit, caused the organizers to reject any form of restriction such as additional pricing or rationing entry. Instead, a travelator was installed, the speed of which could be adjusted according to the level of demand at any given time. While dissatisfaction arose on several occasions at the sheer speed in which viewers were whisked past the exhibit, and efforts made by some visitors to walk backwards against the crowds in order to prolong their viewing exacerbated congestion, the organizers were convinced that this solution they had introduced had been the best, given the circumstances.

Large events designed to cater for many thousands of people every day must ensure that they have the means to admit them quickly. This means sufficient numbers of ticket booths to avoid long lines queuing to buy tickets (see Figure 19.10). Where queues

Figure 19.10 Multiple ticket booths permit a smooth visitor flow at temporary exhibitions

(Photographed by the author)

Figure 19.11
Roofed
queuing area
at Baltimore
Aquarium, USA

(Photographed by the author)

are inevitable, such as on public holidays, a variety of techniques can be employed to reduce the tedium of waiting. At the aquarium at the Inner Harbour at Baltimore, an elaborate zigzag 'maze' is devised to handle the queues. This has the result of making the queue appear shorter than it is, and to be contained under a relatively small roof area as shelter from intense heat, or rain. Those queuing find themselves side by side, and can enter into conversation while they are waiting (see Figure 19.11).

Alton Towers' management has had a great deal of experience in handling queues. A variety of different approaches are taken in trying to balance supply and demand – not always successfully, as we saw above. Well-established practices include queues which are segmented to make them appear shorter, and buskers are employed to entertain those waiting. Estimates of how long they can expect to wait are given to those in line, and barriers are in place to keep the crowd orderly. As with the Baltimore attraction, the snaked queues appear shorter and allow members of the public to engage in conversation while they wait.

At popular attractions such as these, it is becoming common to sell tickets in advance on the Internet, usually at a small discount, since this is a quicker and safer way of collecting money, and it also commits the visitor in advance. These tickets generally ensure prior admission. Airlines are beginning to operate a similar check-in system, with passengers booking their seats on the net before coming to the airport.

In the case of certain forms of attraction, once the visitors are inside further problems of crowd control can arise. Many visitors prefer to tour sites in their own time, independently. This raises problems of managing the crowds (who will tend to take longer watching some displays than others) and of security – where exhibitions contain highly valuable artefacts, such as at Stately Homes, guides are normally assigned to accompany groups. Visitors who have paid high prices for entry may also want to stay longer looking at each exhibit, to get perceived value for money.

At Aarhus's Gamle By, an original means of safeguarding treasures against theft or vandalism by independent visitors has been devised; rooms are 'sealed off' with the use of huge transparent plastic screens (see Figure 19.12). Similarly, glass partitions have been pressed into use to protect key rooms on show at the chateau at Fontainebleau, near Paris.

The Gamle By represents a good example of careful attention to detail in the presentation of a historic site, while failing to protect the appearance of the site as a whole.

Figure 19.12
Room secured from public intrusion by clear plastic screens, Gamle By, Aarhus, Denmark

(Photographed by the author)

Figure 19.13
New high-rise
buildings loom
over the Gamle
By in Aarhus,
Denmark

(Photographed by the author)

The intrusion of recently constructed high-rise buildings which now overshadow this medieval site seriously undermines its appeal (see Figure 19.13).

At sites such as Jorvik in York, Tralee in Ireland and the Robin Hood Story in Nottingham, where visitors are taken around in 'time carts' on a journey through history, the carts control the flow of visitors, and determine the ceiling on the number of visitors who can be admitted. At stately homes, or sites like the Roman Baths at Bath, guides who accompany the visitors can delay or speed up the passage of visitors from one section of the building to another as the need arises. On occasions such as public holidays, greater numbers of visitors can be processed by the simple expedient of guides omitting some of the rooms usually visited on the tour, a common practice in sites that are small but very popular, such as Elvis Presley's home Graceland. While this permits greater crowd control, it fails to overcome resistance that many tourists feel towards being herded. Tourists like to feel in control of their own movements, and if they are conscious of being unduly directed, their level of satisfaction will fall. They may also feel short-changed if rooms they were expecting to visit have been clearly omitted from their tour.

Careful marshalling and stewardship of visitors is particularly important in historic sites, where damage can be done to the fabric of the building or its contents. Means should be found to minimize wear and tear, for example by placing runners across valuable carpets, sectioning off sensitive areas and ensuring visitors do not touch exhibits. At Eltham Palace, near London, English Heritage has mounted a display with samples of the fabrics they have used in renovating the building. Visitors are

Figure 19.14
English Heritage
display of
delicate fabrics
at Eltham Palace

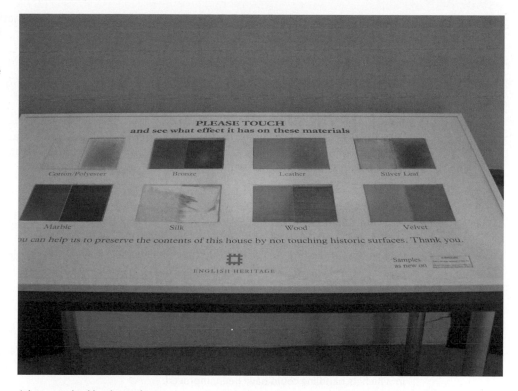

(Photographed by the author)

encouraged to touch these samples so that over time the amount of wear and tear they sustain, and the effect upon different delicate fabrics, can clearly be seen (see Figure 19.14).

We have now seen some of the problems with which managers of tourist sites must contend. Solving these problems, and the day-to-day operational difficulties associated with running any form of attraction, while delivering satisfaction and maintaining the level of quality which the tourist has come to expect, is what tourist management is about. Recognition of the importance of this aspect has led both to a more professional approach within the local authorities towards managing their sites, and in an increasing number of cases to recruitment of professional teams who advise or manage the destination or site attraction on behalf of the owners or operators; so-called destination-management organizations are taking on the responsibility for operating, controlling and marketing the destination product. This will include crisis management where severe disruption to tourism may have occurred, such as in the aftermath of an earthquake which may have devastated a particular region – or a subsequent tsunami like that which devastated South-East Asia in 2004; or sectarian strife (such as that in Fiji in the 1990s or Indonesia in the early 2000s). The supervision of safety regulations is becoming an increasingly important element in this work, as those in public transport will attest following the bomb explosions in London in 2005. In cases such as these, the support of national and regional public bodies will be essential to overcome negative publicity and re-establish tourist flows when situations return to normal.

Note

1 Reynolds, N, *An Investigation into the Underlying Motivational Constructs Towards Sites of Death and Disaster, Focusing on the Holocaust*, Unpublished BA Thesis, Swansea Institute of Higher Education, 2003, p 30. The author noted that these printouts are often then discarded in bins at the exit points.

Questions and discussion points

1 Discuss the relative importance of design in each of the following tourism services:

   (a) a travel agency
   (b) the public railway
   (c) a local museum.

   Take into account both functional and aesthetic issues of design.

2 Taking as an example any popular event which you have recently attended (e.g. special exhibition, open-air pop festival, concert), describe how well crowds were handled, and look at ways in which its handling could have been improved.

3 How important is it to include foreign languages in messages directed at tourists in Britain? Identify the difficulties of doing so, and consider why more local authorities or private operators do not do so. Taking any three settings (e.g. directional signs, tourist attraction leaflets, information signposts etc.) discuss which languages would be most important, and how many languages should be used.

Assignment topics

1 Using as your model any tourist attraction (or local museum) in your area, undertake an analysis of its relative strengths and weaknesses, in terms of:

   (a) functional design
   (b) aesthetic appeal
   (c) information and interpretation for visitors
   (d) management of visitor flows.

   Write a short report to the organization's executive in which you make recommendations for improving any of these, and determine the priority for action. Consider particularly any ways in which improved design could lead to increased revenue for the organization.

2 As an Assistant Tourist Officer for your local town, you have been asked to assess the quality of the environment for the visitor. Present a report to the Council which will include your evaluation of:

(a) the street furniture
(b) facilities for seating
(c) lighting, including any floodlighting or other attempts to improve the cosmetic appeal of the town after dark
(d) any pedestrian walkways or other attempts to improve street materials (e.g. use of coloured bricks or patterns in the roads etc.). Take into account the quality of the construction too
(e) public toilets – number, positioning, attractiveness
(f) litter control.

Your report should consider particularly the possibility of improvements to those routes used by actual or potential visitors on foot in the town. Make recommendations for action where urgent improvements are needed.

20 What future for the tourism industry?

Objectives

After studying this chapter, you should be able to:

- understand current developments in technology which will influence future developments in tourism
- be aware of changes that are affecting society, and their likely impact on travel motivation and behaviour
- recognize that, if forecasts prove accurate, climate changes are likely to have a severe impact on patterns of tourism
- distinguish between controllable and uncontrollable factors in change, and understand how best the industry can cope with either.

Can we predict the future?

Somehow, those observers who predict that future tourists will be content with a virtual reality trip back home in the living room do not understand the magic of bodily movement on the road to elsewhere. Going there in person will continue to be the most important medium of learning to be a tourist.

Orvar Löfgren[1]

We have seen in these chapters how tourism has developed to a point where it has become commercialized, institutionalized, a major industry driving the economies of many developing countries while simultaneously bringing economic benefits to developed nations. In the process, tourism has been shown to be also capable of great social benefit, in terms of health, wealth, welfare, enjoyment of life, and educational improvement. On the other hand, we have also learned that, uncontrolled, it is capable of destroying the social and cultural fabric of tourist destinations, of undermining goodwill between receiving and generating countries and of exploiting the environment of the host countries to a point where those countries can no longer support or attract tourists. Indeed, its impact is such that it threatens not merely the landscapes that tourists visit, but the climate of the globe.

The changes reflected in these chapters which have impacted on tourism in the last century are profound, and few of these could have been anticipated by the entrepreneurs who helped to develop the industry. The task of attempting to forecast events over the coming century is even more daunting – indeed, it would be a brave person to bet on the shape of tourism just 10 or 20 years hence. Forecasting the future of tourism is like imagining what the iPod – or its replacement – will look like in 2010; in the words of Donald Rumsfeld, 'there are things we know that we don't know, and things we don't know that we don't know'. No one could have foreseen the consequences of the worldwide terrorism threat that emerged after September 2001, nor could the tsunami of 2004, the SARS and Avian Flu epidemics have been prophesied.

Yet prognostication is what is expected of tourism texts, so in this final chapter, we will at least indicate where we believe current trends are taking us, and draw a very broad picture of what the shape of the industry may look like within a couple of decades. To do so, we will have to break down the elements of change into their respective parts. Some of these are controllable, others are not, but ways in which the industry must react to take account of the latter can be considered. We will examine these changes in three distinct categories: in terms of societal change, technological change and geographical change.

How will society change?

Changes in society are the result of a combination of demographic and social change. Demographic changes are easier to forecast, especially as the statisticians have done their work and have a fairly good idea of how those changes will pan out for several decades into the future in the principal developed countries, just as estimating tourism flows in the short to medium term is a relatively straightforward procedure, with uncertainties quantifiable.

The key predictable changes are reflections of ongoing changes in Western societies, and include later marriages (or as frequently, long-term partnerships replacing marriage), serial monogamy as partners are replaced throughout the life cycle, widespread acceptance of same-gender partners, an increase in the number of single-parent families and people living alone, postponement of child-bearing and fewer couples choosing to have children. The implications for tourism include an increasingly aging population of tourists, and more couples of all ages with joint incomes. In both cases, these groups will have greater disposable income for leisure activities, including travel. At the same time, there will be greater need for socially engineered group tours to bring together lone singles.

Social changes are more subtle. Sociological observers define the period in which we live as post-modern, and certainly many of the characteristics we find in contemporary tourism are symptomatic of post-modernism; most notably, in the trend to style at the expense of content, and in the confusion between reality and fantasy. We are deeply influenced by our peer groups and by our reference groups, those whose lifestyles we seek most closely to emulate. How film stars, television presenters, sports celebrities and pop idols behave on holiday, where they take their holidays and what hotels they stay at, are all faithfully and regularly reported on by the popular press; and just as the restaurants which attract the celebrities are booked for months ahead, so are tourists flooding to see the destinations, and stay at the hotels, patronized by their idols.

This paints a very superficial view of mass tourists as mindless zombies slavishly following fashion. Of course, the picture is far more complex than this. The growing number of mature tourists include many who are sophisticated and knowledgeable, demand high standards of quality and value for money, and yet who are willing to face challenges that similar tourists would baulk at just a few decades ago. Many younger tourists, too, are better educated than their predecessors, with 40 per cent and rising having attended university. They are more adventurous, even foolhardy, in their gap-year experiences and their desire to gain experience of life even in the poorest parts of the globe. Their parents, of course, never had the advantage of a gap year, and were restricted to the more conventional holiday pattern of a fortnight in the sun.

In some respects one can say that many of today's tourists are in the mould of those earlier travellers and explorers who first set out to see the world. However, it would be a mistake to carry this analogy too far – after all, transport for tourists today means little more than having to put up with some discomfort en route to their destination, and they are aided by an emergent global language, English having become the lingua franca even throughout the Third World. What is more, e-mail now allows these intrepid explorers to maintain almost daily contact with their friends en route and their families at home. A generation earlier, much travelled tourists were often mere collectors of destinations; today it would be true to say that many seek authentic and unique experiences, taking an interest in the cultures and lifestyles of their hosts, hoping to meet locals beyond the simple exchange of words with bartenders, shopkeepers and tour guides, and seeking out local foods and entertainment. In short, they are the embodiment of what it means to live in Marshall MacLuhan's Global Village.

This is more than speculation about the future; it is already happening. Long-haul travel is expanding much faster than short-haul, and consumers undertaking information searches and bookings via the Web look set to overtake those booking through agents.

Given these two very contrasting pictures of contemporary tourists, how best to define them? Perhaps by returning to Stanley Plog's model (Figure 4.8) and Valene Smith's model of adaptability to local norms (Table 6.2), reinterpreted in the light of contemporary developments to factor in age. Table 20.1 offers an alternative model of tourist behaviour.

Table 20.1 Matrix of modern tourists

C Mature unadventurous	D Mature adventurous
A Younger unadventurous	B Younger adventurous

Group A will include traditional sun, sea sand holidaymakers who will increasingly seek more active pastimes than simply swimming and lazing on the beach. Sporting activities of all kinds, entertainments in hotels reflecting examples of staged authenticity, visits to barbecue evenings at prominent sites in the area and night times spent in discos will become the new 'traditional' pattern of tourism, while the popularity of city breaks for hen and stag parties and other groups of young people will continue unabated – but perhaps on a more moderate scale than the binge drinking and anti-social behaviour that exemplifies such groups at present, as public reaction moves the authorities to crack down on such behaviour. Their preference is for familiar food, and cultural norms not too dissimilar to their own. The groups will include Britons visiting Prague, Australians travelling to Bali for surfing holidays and American students travelling to Bermuda for Easter holidays.

Group B embraces the young, carefree and adventurous, including backpackers and gap-year travellers who seek out unusual destinations. With limited funds, they will make full use of local transport and amenities, will happily consume local foods and will communicate without embarrassment with locals, regardless of language barriers. Young Australians travelling independently through Europe using rail passes, or visiting Cambodia and Northern Thailand, Americans visiting Baja California and the Maya ruins of Mexico, and Europeans flying to Tierra del Fuego to hike in the Andes all fall into this category.

Group C will include the older, traditional beach holidaymakers (although today this will include nearby foreign beaches as well as those in the home country), and coach tourists travelling abroad in the security of their glass bubble. Europeans booking more traditional cruise holidays sailing from their home ports and calling at the more popular ports in the Mediterranean, or the Canary Islands, Americans cruising in the Caribbean or to Hawaii, Australians visiting New Zealand are typical representatives of this group.

Finally, Group D will be composed of the increasingly adventurous older travellers who will purchase tailor-made programmes to Latin America, Japan and the Orient, or for the more impecunious, will visit lesser-known regions of Europe such as Galicia in Spain or the Douro Valley in Northern Portugal, staying at paradores and pousadas. Others will head for Broome or Tasmania in Australia, the Antarctic Peninsula or Guatemala and Costa Rica in Central America. This is the market for premium-priced cruising, calling at isolated islands in the Pacific or whale watching off the Alaska coast.

The world is in a period of rapid transition; the traditional tourist-generating countries are moving from an industrial stage to becoming post-industrial societies. With this change, lifestyles and values are also changing; the old desire to accumulate material possessions shows signs of abating. The prophesies of Alvin Toffler[2], that it will be our desire to accumulate experiences as avidly as we formerly collected possessions, are becoming true. However, this demand is tempered by pressures to work, and to earn sufficient to spend more on leisure time. In consequence, what we have in the generating countries is a large population of cash-rich but time-poor consumers, who are trying to compress their experiences into limited time-frames during their working lives (although they will have expectations to live longer, and to travel more extensively when they retire). The concern of the tourism industry will be to ascertain how best to tap in to this new demand for travel.

Figure 20.1
Older, adventurous tourists form the principal market for visits to Antarctica

(Photographed by the author)

How will these changing patterns of demand affect destinations? First, one can say with some certainty that tourists face an increasingly congested world, and that congestion is coming to pose a very real problem for them, because many of the world's great attractions are already overcrowded, yet there are many millions whose ambition it is to visit those very sites, if only they had the means. Increasing prosperity is going to provide those means, not just for the millions in the present generating countries, but for countless others in the emerging industrial nations. The UNWTO has forecast 1.6 billion international tourists by 2020, spending over $2 trillion per annum. In spite of the economic setbacks which South-East Asian nations have experienced since 1997, many of the so-called tiger economies have already recovered sufficiently to boost tourism from these countries. Short of war or a pandemic, it is anticipated that China alone will be sending 100 million tourists abroad by 2020, as their economy grows and the political reins are loosened. Yet this is still less than one in ten of their population.

Russia, too, has become a major generator of tourists, as a wealthy elite chooses to buy second homes abroad and holiday in the popular resorts of Western Europe. Poorer Russians, and others from former satellite countries, all eager to exercise their new-found freedom to travel abroad, have proved to be the saviour of some Mediterranean resorts which had seen a decline in their traditional markets for the past few years, as the quality of their product deteriorated.

What will be the possible consequences of a five-fold or ten-fold increase in tourists in the early years of the twenty-first century? Some understanding of the magnitude of the problem can be seen in the rapid development of tourism to the former Eastern European countries following the collapse of the Communist system in these countries.

Soon after the fall of Communism in Czechoslovakia, Prague was estimated to have been receiving some *83 million* visitors a year (admittedly, many of these were taking short trips across the border, and as few as 10 million were thought to be staying visitors). Similarly, huge numbers thronged to see the other new states, with their journeys made easy by the eradication of visa requirements. Tallinn, the attractive medieval capital city of Estonia, is a mere 1 hour and 40 minutes by sea from Helsinki, and it is common to see as many as eight giant ferries in harbour simultaneously, as Finns, Scandinavians and other Westerners throng into this small town for bargain shopping. The town is also engulfed by groups of young party-goers, attracted by low fare flights and cheap entertainment. Poland, with its long border with Germany, and Hungary, sharing a similar border with Austria, have both seen enormous increases in cross-border tourism too.

The process of urbanization is likely to continue, as workers move to the manufacturing and service-based cities seeking employment, although this may be tempered by developments in technology which will enable more people to work from their homes. In consequence, the countryside will become less crowded and more attractive to visitors seeking to get away from the congested urban centres. Some see the countryside in some countries becoming a giant 'leisure park', a fantasy world to which one can escape on weekends and for holidays, a process undoubtedly encouraged by the growth of second homes and buy-to-let homes for holiday rental. Some areas of Europe have experienced this already, including parts of the Provence in France, Tuscany in Italy and Devon and Cornwall in England.

Many seaside resorts in Britain and on the Continent are in decline. Some are desperately seeking ways to adapt their product to cater for new markets. As noted above, the demand for seaside holidays is changing. Activity patterns may also be affected by growing fear of skin cancer resulting from exposure to the sun (heightened by the depletion of the ozone layer). In the short term, this fear is more likely to affect the older traveller than the young, who have so far shown little inclination to change their holiday habits; as with smoking, many youngsters feel that the risk is too remote for it to concern them. In the longer term, the message may get home, but reaction is more likely to be to cover up and to engage in different activities, rather than to shun the traditional sunshine holiday resorts of the Mediterranean or Caribbean.

Whether the more traditional British seaside resorts can survive in an age when so many Britons choose to spend their main annual holiday abroad is debatable. Global warming may nudge up the average temperatures of our south coast resorts and improve their appeal, but in the short term only massive investment in facilities, particularly indoor entertainment, is likely to retain the domestic market. The success of Center Parcs' holiday centres in Britain has shown that if all-weather facilities are provided and the product offers value for money, the domestic market can still be attracted. If post-modern theories are correct, the way forward may be epitomized in Japan's 'Seagaia Ocean Dome' described in Chapter 9, with artificial indoor facilities to equal those found on the beaches.

An alternative in bringing the beaches to the people is the concept of the urban beach introduced first in Paris. That city created its own 'Paris Plage', a two-mile stretch of imported sand along the right bank of the Seine, incorporating potted plants, deck chairs, boardwalk hammocks and individual areas known by the names of famous

Brazilian beaches – Ipanema, Copacabana and Maracaña. While aimed predominantly at Parisian residents, the concept undoubtedly made the centre of Paris more attractive to visitors too; some four million people used the beaches in 2004, and the concept has since been copied by Berlin, Amsterdam, Rome, Brussels and Vienna. London is believed to be considering a similar area alongside the Thames.

Alternatively, destinations may build on an appeal to nostalgia and a return to the simpler things in life, by selling their attractions as recreations of the past. Such marketing has been successful for a variety of tourism products, ranging from heritage sites to steam railways, theme parks and similar attractions which emphasize their links with the past. For those markets satisfied with the artificial creation of fantasy, theme parks such as those of Disney, some popular cruise liners which provide on-board entertainment rather than ports of call as their principal attraction, and urban resorts like Reno and Las Vegas which create entirely fantasy environments will continue to appeal and to proliferate. Cost is an inhibiting factor (Universal Studios' Spiderman ride at the Orlando Islands of Adventure cost in excess of $200 million to install, and the upkeep of many interactive attractions is high), so only the largest theme parks are likely to be able to offer cutting-edge attractions of this calibre.

Changes in lifestyle will affect the traditional forms of holiday accommodation. The desire for greater flexibility, coupled with advances in 'convenience' food and more adventurous eating habits, suggest that the swing to self-catering, with more meals out for 'special occasions', will continue, and hotels and guesthouses will have to consider how they can adapt their product to win back this market. They will also have to take account of differing religious diets now in demand by clients, and the rising number of vegetarians.

A more educated population will become more curious to know and learn about everything that surrounds them. Museums and heritage sites are responding by offering combinations of entertainment and education, at levels suited to the markets targeted. This will include the appeal of dark tourism – sites of the bizarre, the macabre and the deeply depressing.

How will technology change?

As with tourism movements generally, one can divide technological advances into two categories, those which facilitate and those which motivate. Facilitators include technology which makes it easier for tourists to find information, and to travel to their destinations. Those that motivate include hi-tech attractions and transport experiences which are inherently motivating, not merely convenient means of getting to one's destination.

Technical refinements which will speed up processes in transportation are to be welcomed, although security needs tend to ameliorate the best effects of these, as more steps have to be taken to safeguard travellers against terrorist attacks. Paperless tickets will certainly be the norm within the next few years, as will improvements in automated baggage handling and keyless hotel accommodation. The Fairmont Hotels Group in the USA have already pioneered self-service check-ins at kiosks in their hotels, reducing dependency on front-office staff and speeding up the check-in process for guests. Digitally read passports which will include iris scanning, finger-print reading and probably DNA checks are all likely to arrive within a 20-year span.

Developments in information

Battle has already been joined for supremacy in the race to provide a leisure global distribution system for all forms of travel and tourism, accessible by members of the public as well as the trade. Among other services to be available on such systems, the ability to display live pictures of destinations (and print out whatever is needed in hard format) – a facility which is already available on the Web – would suggest at least a substantial decline in demand for the traditional hard-copy destination brochure, though these are unlikely to disappear entirely; many browsers still like to have access to hard print to sift through available holidays. Users of these websites can also expect to find a range of different accommodation apart from chain and independent hotels, to include gîtes, farmhouse accommodation and private villas with pools. Car rental, tourist attractions, local entertainment should all be accessible through a single site in time. However, agreement is still to be reached on the use of a global language for websites. At present, accessing the websites of destinations will all too often lead to pages available only in the country's native language – even in countries where international tourism is popular, such as the Nordic countries.

This enormous volume of information available through a single site, and the universal market at which it is aimed, will allow consumers to make their own bespoke tours at prices competitive with those offered by the intermediaries. In the meantime, pending such a development the Web will grow to support a handful of competitive sites offering access to not just leading hotel chains and airlines, but also to consortia of smaller independent products like farmhouse holidays, bed and breakfast institutions and small museum attractions, all of which will be 'bundled' into convenient sites and quickly located by the use of search engines like Google.com.

The search for 'something different' will also undermine traditional identikit destinations and hotels, which will need to position themselves more clearly and adapt their products to niche markets. Consumers have control over the transmission of information, too, with websites devoted to exchanging information about destinations and accommodation, and making recommendations. Others are devoted to complaints about specific accommodation, resorts or carriers.

With individual holidaymakers in many parts of the world being able to put together their own packages, book and pay for the booking by direct debit to their bank account, all without leaving their armchair, one can anticipate a rise in impulse booking, and demand for even more 'late availability' products, coupled with a further decline in traditional patterns of advanced booking. Indeed, if consumers can package their own holidays at home at the push of a button, conjuring up on their home TV screen all the images of the resorts they wish to choose from, the question must be asked – could this make the present tasks of operator and travel agent redundant? This is likely to be the case unless both can provide a level of service far exceeding what is offered at present. Agency counter staff in particular must be sufficiently skilled and knowledgeable to be able to offer a genuine counselling service, adding value to what is provided on-screen, but to date, there is little evidence to suggest that this will be practicable, or that the industry could pay the salaries that such skilled staff would demand. However, technology is coming to the rescue here too. The trade is benefiting from ICT programmes that allow better communication between companies and their customers, better matches between products and customer needs, and better identification of market segments. Marketing is becoming more sophisticated in targeting the travel consumer. However, the great conundrum for the industry is to guess how the present 20-somethings will choose to search for information and make a booking when they are ten years older and have children themselves.

Developments in transportation

Aviation experts agree that the development of jet aircraft has reached a plateau where productivity and efficiency are unlikely to be substantially improved, although prices may well fall further as larger aircraft like the Airbus A380, seating between 500 and 800 passengers, come on-stream.

Perhaps for students the most interesting area of speculation is in the progress towards the development of hypersonic flight. The most encouraging research is in the development of the scramjet.

Example The Scramjet

The Scramjet (the name coined from the concept – Supersonic Combustion Ramjet) is propelled by an engine which sucks in oxygen at high speeds, compresses it and feeds it into a chamber to mix with hydrogen. An early X43-a (unmanned) Scramjet achieved speeds of Mach 5 (Concorde's speed was a little above Mach 1), while research involving the co-operation of British, US and Australian scientists tested the aircraft to Mach 7-8, in excess of 5,000 mph, in 2004. Maximum speeds have been predicted of Mach 14, using available technologies and materials. In operation, this aircraft would allow travel between London and Sydney or London and Tokyo of just two hours.

NASA believes that passenger-carrying Scramjets could be in service by 2020, but others believe a 30 to 50 year time-span to be more realistic.

An ambitious scheme by a former Concorde aeronautical engineer, David Ashford, is to launch an 'Ascender' aircraft. This consists of a combination of normal jet for take-off and landing, with rocket propulsion to escape the atmosphere, permitting sub-orbital tourist flights. His belief is that this would be feasible by 2010–11. Designed to carry two passengers, the initial cost is expected to be in the range of £50,000– 100,000 per passenger, but the scheme is limited by lack of funding. A more promising development is that supported by Richard Branson and his Virgin Galactic division. Based on the success of SpaceShipOne, a two-stage aircraft which initially flies like a normal plane, but then releases a rocket into sub-orbital flight, Branson hopes to replicate this with an improved version, SS2, which will provide regular sub-orbital flights to a height of 62 miles. Up to six tourists will be accommodated at a cost of around $200,000 per trip. It is reported that some 28,000 people have already registered their interest, with the first flights optimistically planned for 2008. Many aviation observers remain sceptical that these early deadlines are achievable, and similar plans by the Russians to offer five minutes in space for tourists by 2004, using their sub-orbital M-55 aircraft, were not achieved. Nevertheless, these are the first steps towards a realistic venture into space tourism, the ambition of many, and so far achieved by no more than some half a dozen people. The American Dennis Tito claimed the title of first tourist in space in 2001, followed by Mark Shuttleworth, a South African-born Briton, in 2002 and Gregory Olsen, an American, in 2005. In each case, they paid around $20 million for the privilege. Previously, Prince Sultan bin Salman, the head of the Supreme Commission for Tourism in Saudi Arabia, became the first Arab in Space, and Toyoshiro Akiyama, a journalist for the Tokyo Broadcasting System, paid $12 million for a six-day visit to the Russian Mir space station in 1990; US Senator Jake Garn travelled on the US space shuttle in 1985, followed by Congressman Bill Nelson in 1986. Few would be prepared to pay these sums, but research carried out by a US aeronautical company Futron revealed that while only 50 people a year would be willing to spend the equivalent of $20 million for a week in space, a further 15,000 a year would be prepared to invest $100,000 for a 20-minute sub-orbital ride, supporting the applications waitlisted for Branson's project.

Less ambitious, but more practical, plans are in hand for developments which would improve flight while reducing cost and aiding sustainability. American aeronautical engineers are working on a blended wing-body aircraft which would reduce fuel burn by half that of conventional jets, owing to reduced drag. This aircraft would fly at 45,000 feet, some 10,000 feet higher than present jet aircraft, and would be windowless. The psychological consequences of this have not been researched as yet, although external views could be shown on a screen in the cabin. A similar windowless aircraft is forecast to become operative within 20 years, but as an aid to sustainability, it will be virtually silent from the ground. With engines mounted above the fuselage, this Silent Aircraft Initiative is a collaborative project between Cambridge University and the US's MIT. The plan is for a 250-seat aircraft with a range of 4,000 miles, with the potential to increase passenger capacity to 800.

Others are working on tilt-wing aircraft. A military aircraft with tilting rotors, the V-22 Osprey, was in service with the American military but withdrawn after crashing, but a civilian version, the BA609, is under test by Bell Augusta in the USA. Tilt-wing aircraft would be able to take off and land in half the distance, at half the speed of conventional aircraft, a boon where airports have limited runway space.

A more conventional approach would be development of a new era of supersonic aircraft similar to the Concorde. Airbus is among a number of aircraft manufacturers considering whether to develop a new generation of supersonic aircraft; they believe that a 250-seat aircraft with a range of 5,500 miles and speeds of up to 1,500 mph could be in production as early as 2015.

Meanwhile, amphibious aircraft are again on the agenda. The Russian Beriev Be-200 is already in operation and could easily be adapted for civilian use. Carrying 72 passengers and with a range of 2,250 miles, it would prove ideal for some European resorts, such as those on the Côte d'Azur and the Lake of Geneva. The particular advantage for the industry would be reduction in airport costs, as an amphibious aircraft requires nothing more than a jetty and a licence to use the waterways.

Another promising development is the Ground-Effect Aircraft. Flying just 20 feet above the water to reduce drag and fuel burn, this vehicle could travel at speeds of up to 240 knots, and would offer psychological reassurance for those with a fear of flying at normal heights. The Russians have taken this a stage further with the development of their surface-skimming hydrobus known as the Ekranoplane. Developed by Soviet researchers as a form of military transport in the 1980s, it has the capacity to be developed as a civilian vessel capable of carrying 400 passengers at a cruising speed of over 300 mph, with a range of up to 10,000 miles. This would make possible transatlantic journeys overnight, and at comparatively cheap fares, reaching an entirely new market. German and American interests are still examining the feasibility of building such craft for commercial purposes.

Finally, interest continues in the return of the passenger carrying airship. Work to develop a satisfactory prototype is in hand, the 100-seat Skycat 200 offering the best prospect for commercial development at present.

Research continues in other areas of advanced transport too. In shipping, work is continuing on designs for more fuel-efficient craft. Successful sea trials have taken place with vessels that complement the use of their engines with metal sails, increasing the overall speed while reducing costs – an important consideration at a time when fuel costs are rising sharply. The appeal of cruise ships that resemble floating hotels with a full range of leisure facilities is leading to the construction of ever larger vessels. Proposals have been advanced for much larger catamarans and trimarans (twin-hulled and triple-hulled vessels) capable of transporting large numbers of passengers at high speed and at far more comfort, without the customary problems of motion sickness experienced in single-hull ships. Such vessels might be constructed to cross the Atlantic in under 48 hours.

Japan is carrying out research on the use of electromagnetic thrusters for ships. Toshiba has designed a 150-ton vessel which is pushed through water by the effect of counteracting magnets. This could again lead to the development of vessels of much larger size. Sustainable transport development at sea is evident in the Solar Sailor ferry already in operation in Sydney, described in Chapter 13.

The longer-term future of the shipping industry may be boosted by new marine technology now under development, such as the SES-200 Surface Effect Ship, which rides above the surface of the sea, or superconducting electromagnetic propulsion vessels which have been tested in Japan and offer potential speeds above 100 knots. Waterjet propulsion is also under test for a new breed of container ship; the proposed 'Fastship', using a semi-planing monohull, is expected to be capable of speeds exceeding 40 knots, and may be adaptable later for cruise vessels. Such developments could further encourage the reintroduction of line voyages between major ports in the world, although this is unlikely to occur in the near future.

Sadly, none of these concepts appears to be likely to enter service in the immediate future, but over a 10–20 year cycle, possibilities rise dramatically. On land, development of new vehicles is moving even faster.

Railways in particular are making great strides. Japan's Linear Express, capable of cruising at speeds up to 300 mph, has already reached the prototype stage. This vehicle has the advantage of superspeed and super quietness; the track consists of a metal trough generating a magnetic field which repels magnets in the train, causing the vehicle to ride 10 cm above the track. There is therefore little wear and tear, and in consequence, much reduced maintenance cost. If the technology proves successful, rail services could certainly pose a major threat to air routes of distances over land up to 1,000 miles. We have seen the introduction of MAGLEV trains, discussed in Chapter 14, and even the possibility of these coming into service in the UK in time. The Government is examining the feasibility of establishing a public–private partnership (with the private sector investing 70 per cent of the cost) to build a 300 mph Ultraspeed 'Hovertrain' to operate between London and Glasgow via Manchester. Cost is estimated at £30 billion, and construction, if undertaken, would (optimistically) be completed within 12 years. Such a service would be expected to largely erase air competition on these routes.

Finally, improvements in information about transport movements are marked. Readers will already be familiar with electronic notice boards at bus stops which detail the arrival of the next bus. Moves are afoot to ensure that all transport networks will eventually be linked by global positioning software, enabling travellers to track the current location of any form of transport.

Developments in destinations

Some futurists have prophesied that there will be little need to travel away from home in the twenty-first century. Holographs are capable of reproducing any environment artificially, so that we will be able to recreate in the home any environment of our choosing to 'experience' foreign travel. This could include activity holidays such as simulating white water canoe and raft rides, winter sports or the piloting of an aircraft. BT announced in 1997 that it was working on the production of a machine which can reproduce some of the world's biggest attractions, not only on computer screens but also on wraparound screens or as holograms. Using the device, called 'Head', one can, in BT's words, 'visit Times Square or take a walk into a pyramid without leaving the room'. Whether this form of entertainment replaces travel, or only serves to whet the appetite of most of those viewing such destinations remains to be seen. What is certain is that those who cannot now travel – the very poor, the severely disabled – will for the first time be able to experience something akin to real world travel.

Example   Virtual tours

The Internet already provides opportunities for viewers to take virtual tours of key attractions around the world. Among websites currently available, one can view the Taj Mahal (www.taj-mahal.net)*, Oxford (www.seeoxford.com)* and UNESCO World Heritage sites (www.world-heritage-tour.org).

Some Disney World rides are already a half way house to virtual travel, where sitting in a theatre gives the impression of a long and often frightening journey.

(* requires installation of Macromedia)

Other forecasters predict that underwater leisure cities will be built on the seabeds adjoining our coasts, where a controlled climate will make the annual exodus to the sun no longer necessary. Some of these predictions take us into the realms of science fiction – yet, as we have seen in Chapter 11, we are already on the fringe of underwater hospitality. The untapped resources of the ocean for tourism are gradually being examined; Wildwings, for example, offers a trip in a mini-submarine to the Amundsen Plain, 4,400 metres below the sea at the North Pole for a mere £42,000, which they hail as 'the ultimate adventure challenge'.

Adventurous accommodation is also in the offing. Japanese and American companies have announced plans to build and launch hotels in space, once the vehicles are available to get the tourists there. While announced time-scales of 2015–25 might be greeted with scepticism, the current acceleration in space exploration makes such developments feasible. It is no longer a question of if, but when.

How will the world change?

We've speculated about the future of travel and stay. Geographical change is less speculative, and more predictable. On the best evidence for global warming that we have at present, we can expect, at a minimum, the following impacts on tourism within the space of 30 years.

Most European ski resorts are expected to fail within that time-frame, with a minimum snowline of around 6,000 feet (compared with resorts in the USA where the snow belt starts at around 4,625 feet). Skiing in Scotland would no longer be possible, necessitating present resorts to find a new role – or fall back on the use of expensive snow-making equipment throughout the season. In the summer, Mediterranean and Caribbean resorts would become unattractive to tourists due to their hotter climates. There are fears that this would be accompanied by water shortages akin to those already experienced in resorts in the Far East and India, accompanied by forest fires, poor air quality and even the advent of malaria. Unpredictable weather patterns are expected to develop around resorts in Australia, Florida and the Caribbean. Australia can anticipate an increase in cyclones, storms, bush fires, skin cancer and the death of one of its greatest attractions, the Great Barrier Reef; while Florida, the Gulf Coast and the Caribbean would be affected by coral bleaching, an increase in frequency of hurricanes, flooding and erosion, and the introduction of diseases more commonly found in the tropics. Countries like the Maldives could stand to lose their tourist industry entirely through rising sea levels.

Climate change can be predicted, but it cannot be controlled. The industry, already reeling from the man-made disasters of the early twenty-first century, will have to face up to far worse natural disasters in the future. This will need strategic planning, with the public and private sectors working together. In some instances, disasters can be delayed – Venice, experiencing gradual inundation of its streets and squares, is investing billions of euros to stave off the worst effects of flooding in order to continue to attract its tourists and protect its residents; while promises are that New Orleans will be rebuilt rather than abandoned following the disastrous Hurricane Katrina in 2005 – but in other cases, such as those coastal resorts and islands in developing countries where the height of the shoreline seldom exceeds 1–2 metres, there is little that can be done beyond abandoning tourism and retreating inland, or re-establishing the centres of tourism in more stable areas.

Notes

1 Löfren, O, *On Holiday: a History of Vacationing*, University of California Press, 1999, p 281
2 Toffler, A, *Future Shock*, Bodley Head, 1970

Further reading

Van Pelt, M, *Space Tourism: Adventures in Earth Orbit and Beyond*, Copernicus, 2005

Websites

Taj Mahal	www.taj-mahal.net
Oxford	www.seeoxford.com
Travel forum	www.holidaywatchdog.com
Holiday discussion forum	www.holidaytruths.co.uk
Reviews of hotels, resorts and vacations	www.tripadvisor.com
UNESCO World Heritage Sites	www.world-heritage-tour.org
Wild Wings	www.wildwings.co.uk

Questions and discussion points

1   Older, less adventurous tourists are fearful of strange cultures, and are likely to steer clear of destinations closely linked to Muslim society. Yet some Arab countries are actively courting Western tourists, and investing huge sums in their tourism developments. Dubai represents an outstanding example of this. How will the Dubai tourism authorities attract Western tourists? Which markets should they target? Can they overcome growing prejudices by the more conservative markets?

2   The chapter suggests that mature travellers are not merely collecting experiences, but also setting out to enjoy them. How does this equate with the many American tourists seeking to visit as many countries as possible, and the phenomenon of 'if this is Tuesday it must be Belgium' coach tours arranged for American tourists paying their first visit to Europe?
(The author recently encountered a fellow passenger on a cruise who was collecting his 144th cruise! Was he to be congratulated, or pitied?)

3   The biggest block to a satisfying experience in wilderness areas such as safari parks is the sheer number of other visitors. How can lesser known destinations build on this weakness, and can comparatively little known safari parks like Okavango and Chobe hope to attract tourists away from well established names like Kruger and Amboseli?

4   Given a probable shift to rejection by mature adventurous tourists of attempts at staged authenticity, what steps should be taken by hotels which presently put on local cultural displays, such as dance, singing and folk art?

Assignment topics

1   Imagine you are a journalist writing in the year 2040. You have been commissioned to write a piece for the travel pages of a national newspaper, on the subject, 'How is tourism different today than it was at the turn of the century?' Write an article of no more than 1,500 words stressing the major changes that have taken place over the previous 40 years.

2   You are asked to speak to a group of senior executives in the travel industry about what you think the industry will be obliged to do to improve the sustainability of tour operating over the next decade. Prepare a set of notes on which to base your talk.

Part V Case studies

Case study 1
The Land of Lost Content:
the appeal of the eccentric

(Prepared with the help of Stella Mitchell, Proprietor)

Figure CS1.1
Stella Mitchell in
the museum

(Photographed by the author)

This case examines the problems faced by small-scale operators of visitor attractions. SMEs make up around 90 per cent of the tourism business, as this text has made clear, and proprietors of small private collections such as this, while keen to share their enthusiasm with like-minded visitors, often fall foul of the bureaucracy involved in opening their collections to fee-paying members of the public, including planning restrictions and other issues (such as disabled access) which restrict their opportunities to trade. They may also lack managerial and marketing experience, while financial constraints limit opportunity to make contact with their prospective visitors.

The museum is located in Craven Arms, a village set in a rural area which is promoted as a gateway to the Welsh Marches, but beyond this has little to attract the visitor in its own right. However, as a base for discovering the splendid countryside surrounding it, the village proves to be a convenient centre for accommodation, and the museum (together with another visitor centre which combines an art gallery, shop and café) offers an on-site means of entertainment, particularly during inclement weather. As such, it offers comparisons with many small attractions in many parts of the world which lie in regions less frequently visited, and where careful targeting of the potential market is essential. In this respect, it bears some similarities with Case Study 4, which examines a very different form of attraction in the USA.

The case complements material discussed in Chapters 9 and 10 dealing with destinations and their attractions, and raises some of the issues of management raised in Chapter 19.

Introduction

It is an oft-repeated truism that 90 per cent of the tourism industry's businesses are SMEs, with some so small as to be staffed entirely by owner managers or their families. This case examines the smallest among these – a museum which is virtually a one-woman business. Many such enterprises depend upon the enthusiasm and dedication of their owners, and this example is no exception. Stella Mitchell is an eccentric and enthusiastic collector of twentieth century memorabilia who has, over many years, collected many tens of thousands of items encompassing the everyday life of the period, including household items and kitchenware, pop memorabilia, uniforms and other items from World War II, industrial tools, furnishings and posters. The result is a unique and invaluable source of reference as well as nostalgic entertainment.

In 1991, Stella sold her house in order to buy a twelfth century former church in the village of East Wittering, Sussex, and had long cherished the ambition to house her collection appropriately and make it accessible to the public. While satisfying the immediate need to provide display space for the collection, in many other respects the new building was quite unsuitable for its purpose as a museum. The village itself is off the main road, and therefore receives little or no passing tourist trade. The site offered parking for no more than six cars at a time, with no nearby alternative parking, nor was there any suitable approach road for coaches.

By 1995, Stella recognized that if her museum were to become viable, she would need to raise its profile, improve the parking and attract more visitors (at that point, the museum was attracting just 6,000 visitors each year). Coincidentally, she received an offer from the owner of the Birds and Butterflies Museum at Earnley Gardens to convert a greenhouse within the grounds which could accommodate her collection, and benefit from the catalyst of two museums on the same site. Attracted by estimates of a first year income in excess of £16,000, Stella agreed to undertake the renovation, and moved her collection to the new site. She adopted the title, 'Rejectamenta: the Nostalgic Centre' for the new museum, with the sub-title 'Museum of the 20th Century', fearing that giving prominence to the term 'museum' might be a disincentive to the mass market.

The move turned out to be far from satisfactory. Her new associate on the site proved to have been wildly optimistic about the anticipated income based on admission fees for joint entry to the two museums, also failing to provide the level of support and joint promotion that had been agreed upon. It was clear that a further move would become necessary by 2002, and the following year, with the sale of her bungalow for £60,000 and a £100,000 ten-year business loan from the bank, Stella was able to purchase the former Market Hall at Craven Arms, Shropshire, for the sum of £165,000.

Conversion of the hall, a three-storey building, including obligatory work on a fire alarm system and a new staircase, was completed with the convenient help of her husband, a carpenter. The new museum opened at Easter, 2003, with an entry fee structure of £5.00 for adults, £3.00 seniors and £2.50 children. The new museum was given the title 'Land of Lost Content' (an extract from A E Housman's poem *A Shropshire Lad*), and carries the subtitle, 'The National Museum of British Popular Culture'. In the first year through to Easter 2004, admissions totalled 5,700, a figure considered reasonable in the initial year of operation on a new site, given minimal publicity.

During that year, the museum operated on a shoestring. An overdraft of £11,000 helped to pay for essential running costs and advertising. Principal advertising and promotion undertaken in the first year included:

■ approximately £400 for printing 15,000 brochures, plus a run-on of 5,000
■ £700 for entry in the Premier Attractions brochure, a private consortium of attractions
■ £600 for publicity in Explore the Marches promotional literature
■ £60 for membership in Shropshire Tourism. There is a charge of £260 for entry in the annual Guide; however, as payment could not be made in advance, she could not obtain an entry in the Guide during her first year.

A Passport scheme, with an entry in freely distributed brochures, has also been arranged in cooperation with the Secret Hills Discovery Centre, another tourism attraction in Craven Arms.

Getting knowledge about the museum across to the general public is the major challenge for small attractions like this one, and lack of adequate funds to achieve this is a severe impediment. Much of the publicity for the museum is in fact achieved through word of mouth, with visitors often agreeing to distribute her brochures to others. There is a high level of visitor satisfaction, and the museum receives a significant number of repeat visitors. As Stella admits every customer personally, and takes the opportunity to talk to them individually, she has ample opportunity to obtain feedback at the door, her main source of research. From this, she is aware that most visitors are staying in the vicinity as tourists, or coming from nearby cities like Wolverhampton. Their main purpose in travelling to Craven Arms is to visit the museum.

Figure CS1.2
Interior of the
museum

(Photographed by the author)

The success of an enterprise such as this cannot be measured purely in financial terms. Stella's collection is unique and fascinating, and visitors are enchanted with what they find. Nevertheless, the museum's survival currently depends upon the unflagging dedication of its owner, who is prepared to put in seven-day weeks without holidays, with little financial reward, to enable it to remain viable. She supplements her income by opening the museum on two or three evenings a week to provide catering for groups of up to 25 people in organizations like the Women's Institute, runs nostalgia quizzes, and earns small fees by giving talks about her collection to various groups around the country. She also contributes regularly, on the theme of nostalgia, to the *Chichester Observer*. A small inheritance in 2004 has enabled her to clear her bank loan, greatly reducing running costs and offering brighter prospects for the future. Meanwhile, she has lost none of her enthusiasm for collecting, and additions to the museum occur on a regular basis as she scours the junkshops and auction houses of the country in search of the detritus of the past, and as visitors supplement her collection with their own contributions. Her collection is important, not just for tourism in the town of Craven Arms and to the industry as a whole, but also as a living archive of twentieth century life.

Discussion questions

1   Not everyone will be familiar with A E Housman's poetry. How, in fact, do you expect to pronounce the title of her museum, *con*tent or con*tent*? Does it matter? In fact, the latter is correct, but many visitors, by emphasising the prefix, give a very different meaning to the collection – some taking it as a sell-off of missing items from the former British Rail!)

2   Stella Mitchell is typical of the enthusiastic collector; someone eager to share her collection with the public, but with limited funds and a lack of commercial acumen which would allow her to recover her costs. While she is willing in the short term to give up her time and limited resources to ensuring the museum is open to the public, how might she – or more specifically the museum – survive in the longer term?

3   There are many who criticize the proliferation of museum collections. In what ways can a collection of this kind be considered important, and to whom? Who are likely to be attracted to the museum?

Case study 2
Strategies for national and local audience development at the Currency Museum of the Bank of Canada

(Prepared by Henriette Riegel, Director of Visitor Services, with the help of Caroline Roberts, Exhibition and Program Planner, The Currency Museum of the Bank of Canada, Ottawa)

While, superficially, this case has some parallels with its predecessor, there are marked distinctions, not least in the fact that this museum has the backing of a major commercial organization with a high level of management and marketing skill to draw on. However, this does not mean an infinite source of finance on which to draw, and the museum must still pursue a search for the most cost-efficient means of reaching its target audience. To this end, it has developed a sound five-year business plan, which clearly identifies the educational target market as a major prospect.

Canada is a vast country, and the difficulties of reaching a national market in a territory of this size are spelled out. Lessons to be learned from this case will be appreciated particularly by those running attractions in similar territories with widely dispersed and isolated populations. The benefits of working in partnership with similar attractions across the country for travelling exhibitions is a major theme of this case, which elaborates issues found in Chapters 9, 10 and 19.

Introduction

The Bank of Canada's Currency Museum is a small corporate museum of about 700 square metres which attracts between 30,000 and 35,000 visitors each year. The Museum is responsible for the National Currency Collection, which has over 90,000 objects consisting of an impressive selection of coins, tokens, paper money and ethnographic material from around the world spanning over 2,700 years. Although occupying a prime downtown location in the headquarters of the Bank of Canada in Ottawa, the Museum suffers from low visibility because the entrance is in the Bank's office building complex, and there are restrictions relating to exterior signage. Additionally, as a museum with a national mandate, the Currency Museum must make an impact not only with the local community, but also with educating Canadians across the country about currency and economics.

In order to meet these challenges, the Currency Museum has undergone extensive audience analysis and has taken a hard look at its strengths and weaknesses. These analyses have formed the basis for a new Five Year Public Program Plan. The Plan has three focal points for the development of new initiatives: extension programs, increased local engagement, and a strengthening of professional processes and policies.

Key to the development of new programming initiatives has been the recognition of the very strong educational experiences that a small, specialized museum offers. As Kenneth Hudson[1] has noted, it is well known that visitors like the kinds of museums that they can peruse in a few hours, especially those museums with a single theme. This enjoyment and depth of engagement has certainly been confirmed with the over-whelmingly positive visitor feedback at the Currency Museum, and by the surprisingly long average duration of stay of 90 minutes. Visitors feel safe and cared for in a small museum, and can settle down to enjoy their visit and discover the unique artefacts on display from the National Currency Collection.

Figure CS2.1
A Yap stone, a form of currency from the Caroline Islands, Micronesia

(Courtesy: the Currency Museum)

Increasing local awareness

Indeed, the Currency Museum has the reputation of being the 'hidden jewel' of the nation's capital. Over the past few years, Museum staff have worked hard to develop special activities in conjunction with other city-wide events, such as Ottawa's Winterlude and Tulip Festivals. Winterlude is one of Ottawa's most popular festivals, and features the Rideau Canal Skateway, ice sculptures and many family activities. The annual spring Tulip Festival commemorates the end of World War II and Queen Juliana of the Netherlands' gift of tulips to Canada for Canada's role in liberating the Netherlands. It is the largest Tulip Festival in the world, with millions of tulips on display, and features a wide variety of themed events and activities. The Currency Museum's Tulip Festival activities focus on the 'Tulip Mania' that occurred in seventeenth century Holland when tulip bulbs were hotly traded items. Official participation in these events allows the Museum to profit from the large number of visitors that attend area festivals and from joint marketing and advertising opportunities. These events have increased attendance, particularly with local visitors, who recognize the unique qualities of the Currency Museum and thereby spread the word to their friends.

The Museum leverages an attractive and currency-related theme to a larger audience owing to the timing of the events to coincide with a well-visited local winter festival. Recent participation in the popular National Capital Region's annual Winterlude festival (in 2005 it attracted over 800,000 visitors) has brought more local visitors to the Museum than any other days in the winter season. In 2005 the Currency Museum offered three weekends of family fun on the tempting theme of chocolate, as cocoa beans were used as currency by the Aztecs. A slew of radio, television and newspaper spots followed, as the local media featured the Museum's unique chocolate programs. Additionally, the activities were published in the official Winterlude guide. In this way, over the next few years, the Museum will offer local visitors new and exciting programs relating to the theme of money to entice them to discover the Museum for the first time and to return often. Thus the early signs of raising awareness of the Museum and increasing the visibility of one of the smaller museums in the capital have been positive.

Reach across the country

Like many other museums, the Currency Museum has used travelling exhibitions as a form of extension of the museum. Managing and developing a travelling exhibition system in a vast country such as Canada has proven to be challenging. Especially problematic has been balancing requests from host institutions all over the country with the cost of transportation; it is more cost-effective to move an exhibition between host institutions that are close to each other geographically, rather than send an exhibition across the country several times (as would be the case if each request was handled on its own). Along with the normal methods of advertising new travelling exhibitions, which include mail-outs and listings on various museum sites, Museum staff have developed contacts at conferences and participated in provincial trade shows to develop regional interest in an exhibition. Additionally, museums booking currency exhibitions are encouraged to work with other museums in their region so that a smaller regional tour becomes part of a larger travelling exhibition schedule. Certainly the more often this occurs, the easier it becomes as museums start to look beyond their own walls to partner with other institutions as a way of hosting exhibitions they may not have been able to afford on their own.

However, travelling exhibitions are only one of several extension-program vehicles being developed at the Currency Museum to reach more Canadians in all parts of the country. Three other innovative programs have been launched or are being developed with this purpose in mind. The first product has been the redesign of bilingual (English and French) Teacher Kits. These kits currently contain a lesson plan to teach students about different forms of money and exchange. The Museum was fortunate in that the new Teacher Kit launch was picked up on a website featuring resources for teachers; this led to many e-mail requests for the kits. Response to the new kits has been positive owing to the accessible and attractive design and the curriculum-friendly content. The initial success of the first Teacher Kits will now lead into further program development so that more programs can be distributed through schools via these adaptable Teacher Kits. In this way, the Museum will be able to extend on-site programs across the country. Because the kits are adaptable, a wide variety of schools and different provincial school curricula can be accommodated with the new kits. This will be an important part of the Museum's extension-program development over the next few years.

A second extension vehicle is a new DVD version of a senior high school economics program, *Inflation Busters*. This rather hip program won a national Museum Association award for excellence in programming in 2003, and has been very well received by teachers, students and the Bank of Canada. Originally it was planned that a web-based version of the program would be an effective way of offering the program to schools. However, the fast-paced group-based activities do not translate well to an Internet experience, as students are not able to interact with each other in the same way. Thus a DVD program comparable to the one offered on-site in Ottawa was developed and available for distribution in 2005.

The third example of an extension vehicle is the boxed mail-out museum program that was in the research stage at the time of writing, and was planned to be prototyped by the end of 2005. Envisaged as a combination of a more cost-efficient form of travelling exhibition with an off-site educational program, research is being undertaken as to how to design a program that can be adapted at the receiver's end. In order to be effective on a local, community level, the program must be designed so that user groups can add something of their own cultural context and experiences to complete the program. Rather than develop a generic mail-out program that cannot take into account cultural, regional and social differences, groups will be able to work with elements of the new program to form their own specific experiences. For example, each Canadian province has a different school curriculum, but the theme of money can be incorporated into a wide variety of classes. It makes sense for the teachers to add their own content to the boxed program. Thus the specificity and the powerful experiences that visitors have in the Ottawa location of the Currency Museum can be recreated at other locations.

Strengthening internal processes and policies

The Currency Museum is managed by the Bank of Canada, and benefits from the very strong processes and policies that the larger corporation has developed. This allows the Museum to approach project development with a high level of quality and with an assurance of stability of operations that may not be present in smaller, independent museums. The great strength of a small single-themed museum is in the uniqueness of the visitor experience. With the addition of a high level of quality derived from professional practices, the quality of the Museum's products increases. Thus the Museum is able to tackle the challenges of creating awareness and a broader reach with the in-depth knowledge of a very strong product base, and the abilities of specialist staff to develop and implement new initiatives. With efficient management practices and strong products, the Bank of Canada's Currency Museum is able to examine and leverage its strengths into the development of an approach that increases local engagement and national reach.

Figure CS2.2
A view of the
Currency
Museum

(Courtesy: the Currency Museum)

Discussion questions

1 The case reveals some imaginative promotional strategies linked to events in the region. What lessons might be learned by small museums in your own country, in tying in activities with other regional events?

2 Forming partnerships with other attractions is one approach taken in the Museum's strategies. Suggest two attractions within your own region which might work successfully together in such joint programmes.

3 The Museum has identified both benefits and disadvantages in reaching its customers through the Web. How effective are websites linked to museums in your region in building their customer base?

4 Are there other currency related museums in your country, or neighbouring countries? Would exchanges of exhibitions between these be an effective way of extending interest in their contents?

5 The case suggests that small museums offer benefits not to be found in larger ones. What are your own views about visiting small and large museums?

Note

1 Kenneth Hudson, The Museum Refuses to Stand Still, *Museum International* 50 (1), 1998, 43–50

Case study 3
Brilliant Weekends: the concept and development of a new holiday programme

(Prepared with the help of Richard Dennys, Managing Director, Brilliant Weekends Limited)

This case is a valuable example of how the entrepreneur can get started in the tourism business, and the importance of identifying a niche business if assets are limited. It casts light on the importance of the Internet in developing small businesses, and provides a convenient example of the new type of tour operator which is dependent upon a call-centre operation. In this respect, the location of the business becomes of minor importance, and the case offers insights equally applicable to the industry in any area of the world.

A key issue is the need to recognize the direction in which the industry is moving, and the case brings home the importance of flexibility in the face of rapid change. The case is illustrative of material found in Chapter 16, dealing with tour operators, but the sales techniques outlined in Chapter 17 also inform the critical roles of knowledge and service in growing this business.

Introduction

Richard Dennys launched Brilliant Weekends in September 2002. Working previously in the sales and marketing division of an Internet company, his role had been that of developing customer relations, and he was keen to launch an enterprise that would build on his earlier experience while offering scope for development in other directions.

His criteria for the start-up of a new business included:

- reducing dependence upon activities concerned exclusively with consultancy
- developing an Internet-based business which would incorporate a product element
- cultivating a customer base closely related to his own demographic background
- developing a niche not currently well served, but one which could ensure strong, stable demand.

Working in the tourism business was not a criterion, but he had had some experience of the industry, having acted as a resort representative with Intasun at an earlier stage of his life, and having also worked with his parents at their hotel in Torquay. A chance contact with a friend who owned an Internet portal handling stag and hen party information led to his spending two months with that organization, learning to understand customer demand, before moving with his wife to Italy in September 2002 to establish a holiday programme there (he is fluent in Italian). Setting up a website, www.stagItalia.com, and investing in limited advertising on Google, brought a satisfactory response and convinced him that there was sufficient demand to grow a stag and hen party business, with bookings starting to flow in by Christmas that year. However, he felt that he would have a stronger base back in the UK, and returned in March of 2003, putting a business plan to his bank which granted him an overdraft of £5,000, sufficient (together with his wife's income from another job) to meet his immediate needs in renting an office and taking on a single employee.

Without advertising, and based purely on customer searches on Google, he was able to grow his business within two years to a point where he was able to recruit additional staff. By the end of 2003 he was employing a total of six, three on administration and three (including himself) on the sales side. Initially, the products offered consisted of land arrangements only (accommodation and catering, spa facilities, day and evening activities), catering principally for stag and hen parties seeking short breaks in the UK and mainland Europe – most customers indicated a preference to make their own flight arrangements, using no-frills carriers, and this has helped the company to avoid the obligations and constraints imposed by the Civil Aviation Authority, although they operate a trust account and have a small business ATOL to ensure compliance with the Package Holiday Directive.

The market

A total of 65 per cent of demand is for stag and hen arrangements, with the balance made up of corporate or other group bookings. Winter-sports parties contribute substantially to off-season sales, with demand for this product arising largely from male groups. Self-catering is growing in popularity among these groups. While some clients know exactly what they are looking for, others will seek detailed advice and information before coming to a decision, and many groups have a priority criterion – they are looking for new and unique experiences.

The destinations

Demand is for destinations within two to three hours' flying time – the limit of most budget carriers. While European cities like Prague and Tallinn are always in demand for stag and hen parties, less familiar destinations have also shown remarkable growth, particularly German cities like Hamburg and Stuttgart, and Italian cities like Milan and Rimini. More recently, demand for Rotterdam in the Netherlands has increased sharply.

The company maintains good contacts in these cities for land arrangements and accommodation. Not all hotels are welcoming for groups of this kind, but those that do cater for them are well aware of the nature of their clientele, and are geared to servicing their needs. In spite of the negative publicity associated with many of these groups from the UK, the company has had remarkably few complaints. Some groups do seek representatives from the company to escort them, but this is seen as a trouble-shooting role to resolve problems rather than as a control mechanism for unruly behaviour. In many cases, transfer representatives at the destination will be employed to take on this role, both troubleshooting and offering specialized advice to the groups, such as where to go for that 'special' meal out. This personal contact is seen as a vital ingredient in the success of the programme.

Administration

Simplicity is the keynote in the operation of these programmes. The organization is geared to call-centre operations with minimal customer contact, and customers can change their arrangements on-line without recourse to the operations staff. All sales are handled either over the telephone or via e-mail, with sales staff each expected to handle around 30 calls per day.

The company is a small, close-knit team with a very good working relationship. Staff are not required or expected to have detailed knowledge of the industry, although some are recruited with prior experience of tourism; the company prefers to recruit graduates, with backgrounds similar to their clients, and will attempt to assign sales staff to customers with whom there is some affinity. Salaries are in excess of those typical of the industry, and turnover is very low, only two staff having moved on since the founding of the company in the UK. Much administration paperwork is out-sourced to allow the staff in the office to focus on their principal roles – those of selling the products and ensuring they operate successfully.

Targets are set to motivate performance. While sales are obviously the target for the sales force, organizers are motivated by three criteria:

- cash flow (ensuring customer payments are made on time)
- profits delivered are equivalent to profits sold (e.g. a group of 50 do not experience drop-outs watering down the eventual revenue)
- customer satisfaction: feedback is achieved by telephoning the clients after their return.

The company has not yet found it necessary to establish a budget for advertising and promotion. While only some 10 per cent of business results from repeat customers or word of mouth recommendation (hardly surprising, given the nature of their market), the simple listing on websites has been remarkably effective in generating new business.

Market development

Dennys estimates the annual spend of the hen and stag party market in the UK at between £300–£500 million per annum, based on research by Mintel and others. There are some 250,000 weddings every year, but only a small number of specialist operators have set out to tap the hen and stag market – he estimates his competition at just five to six companies of similar size to his own, with numerous smaller businesses posing less of a threat. The company targets sales at 2,000 bookings per annum.

In spite of healthy growth, there are weak points in the market, with only seven months of the year returning a profit. Demand from March to September is strong, while the winter ski market in the months between December and March provides scope for a strong ancillary market to summer trade, but the months of February and November are difficult.

To grow the company, and to encourage stability over the winter months, the company approached a number of private investors in September 2004, to raise capital. Of the 30 investors approached, 26 offered investment, and 6 were selected to inject £70,000 in exchange for a 6 per cent share in the company. A further £39,000 was raised through loan funding, enabling the company to invest in technology and increase staff numbers to the present total of 21.

The company next approached potential partners to grow their business. The first company approached was the carrier FlyBE, with which the operator sought help to develop new routes; negotiations resulted in the company's listing on the airline's website as an associated operator for weekend breaks. Other deals have followed, including one with easyJet, and the company has also expanded into offering coach transport options for groups. While the company is now in profit, all profits are reinvested to grow the business. Dennys's plans for the future include expansion to 50,000 movements a year, with a turnover of £3.5 million, with the intention of ensuring a stable market throughout the year. Other plans include additional investment in technology, and market development to open the product to customers with fewer than eight group members.

Discussion questions

1 Would you recommend that the company remains small, focusing on quality, or should Dennys grow the organization in order to ensure its viability in the face of competition from larger organizations?

2 If you were planning a stag and hen party, what would be the criteria you would seek when choosing the company with which to book?

3 Given the negative publicity in the media regarding stag and hen parties abroad, what do you feel are the prospects for the future of this sector? How could, or should, the company overcome the publicity and ensure proper behaviour of their clients during the trips?

Case study 4
Marketing Michigan's Heritage Route

(Prepared by Dr. Sarah Nicholls, Assistant Professor, Departments of Community, Agriculture, Recreation and Resource Studies (CARRS) and Geography, Michigan State University)

While this is essentially a marketing case study, it offers valuable insights into issues dealt with in this text. The vastness of the USA as a country lends itself to linear tourism, which is examined in Chapter 1 of the text, and as a result the initial focus is on the route between destinations and attractions, rather than the destinations and attractions themselves. The subject of the case is therefore informed by material in Chapter 14 dealing with land transport, with the car seen as the critical tool in developing tourism to the region. The case also provides an example of public-sector research-based marketing, with the State of Michigan's authorities directly involved in promoting tourism in partnership with private enterprises along the route. Both Chapter 15, dealing with the public sector, and Chapter 5, which emphasizes the importance of economic benefits to the public and private bodies within a region, inform this study, as does Chapter 7 dealing with the issue of environmental sustainability, an issue clearly taken into consideration by the local authorities in their examination of the impact of tourism on the environment resulting from the proposed development (if not the issue of sustainability of tourism using private cars!)

The Old World often tends to disparage the relative brevity of historical sites and artefacts in the New World, but countries like the USA, Canada and Australia are proud of their short histories, and are often willing to make a greater investment in preserving their heritage for the benefit of locals and tourists than are some countries in Europe with a much richer history. The economic benefits of drawing domestic tourists to such sites promoted as early interstate routes will be readily apparent to the reader of this case.

Background to the case

The Heritage Route Program, created by state legislation in 1993, is a means by which local residents, government officials, landowners and other interested groups may cooperate in order to preserve unique highways throughout the state of Michigan. There are three categories of heritage route:

- *scenic*: a state highway offering outstanding natural beauty
- *historic*: a state highway offering outstanding historic buildings and other historic resources
- *recreational*: a state highway offering an outstanding recreational driving experience.

The program recognizes that the official designation of state heritage routes offers a number of preservation, economic, social and educational benefits to the communities, landscapes and historic resources situated along them, including:

- identification, preservation, and enhancement of the state's scenic, historic and recreational resources
- promotion of greater awareness of and appreciation for these resources
- provision of an opportunity for growth management along route corridors through the encouragement of appropriate development
- provision of an opportunity to manage the impact of tourism on resources
- attraction of visitors who generate new revenues and enhance economic activity
- attraction of new businesses
- enhancement of existing jobs and creation of new jobs
- provision of a vision for the future
- enhancement of the local, regional and state image
- identification, promotion and preservation of community uniqueness and enhancement of community appeal
- enhancement of community quality of life
- provision of education opportunities for future generations
- provision of opportunities to share ideas, information, research, and lessons
- provision of an effective, hands-on teaching tool.

To date, a total of 14 heritage routes (four scenic, six historic, and four recreational) have been designated. Designation involves a nomination and application process, administered by the Michigan Department of Transportation (MDOT); routes meeting the necessary criteria are then provided with road signs (see Figure CS4.1) and other promotional materials in order to direct travellers to these resources.

Figure CS4.1
Heritage road signs for designated routes

(Courtesy: Michigan Department of Transportation)

The focus of this case study is the marketing plan, one part of a larger corridor management plan, prepared in support of the application for heritage-route designation for the US-12 Historic Heritage Trail in 2003–04.

Route US-12

What is today known as US-12 is one of the oldest and most-travelled transportation corridors east of the Mississippi River. Originally one of a network of trails created by Native Americans, in the 1820s a military road was established which, known as both the Great Sauk Trail and the Chicago Road, served as one of the most important migration routes into Michigan and on to Chicago. In the 1920s the road was paved. Officially designated a United States Highway (US-112) in 1926, this number was then changed to US-12 in 1961. Today, the Michigan portion of US-12 stretches approximately 210 miles through eight counties, from the City of Detroit in the east to the state line with Indiana in the west. The route then continues through Indiana, to Chicago, Illinois, and, ultimately, to Aberdeen, Washington. Once one of the most important routes between Detroit and Chicago, today this role has been replaced by Interstate 94 and use of the road tends to occur on a more local and regional basis.

History of the application process and the Corridor Management Plan

Formal application for recognition of US-12 as an official Michigan Heritage Route represents the culmination of a lengthy process involving local citizens, agencies and elected officials across all eight counties through which the route runs. While individual cities and townships have previously recognized the historic value of the route within each of their jurisdictions, it was not until the late 1990s that a larger, multi-county effort to nominate the entire route for state recognition began. In 2002, a committee including appointed representatives from each of the counties through which the route traverses was established. Since then, the US-12 Heritage Trail Council (HTC) has met regularly to promote and coordinate a variety of studies and plans regarding the US-12 heritage route application process. In 2003, SmithGroup JJR, an Ann Arbor-based consulting firm, was employed to prepare a Corridor Management Plan in support of the Council's application for heritage route status. In conjunction with the HTC, this firm identified *a history of movement and connection* as the key distinguishing theme of the US-12 corridor, as reflected in the slogan, 'From Pathway to Highway'. Further, seven interpretive themes, designed to emphasize the uniqueness of the US-12 corridor at multiple stages throughout its history while at the same time uniting the many communities located along it, were also identified. These included:

■ migration and settlement
■ agriculture and industry

- transportation developments
- recreation and tourism
- social, political and institutional history
- art and architecture
- 'First, most or unusual'.

The management document also incorporated a marketing plan, prepared by faculty from the Department of Parks, Recreation and Tourism Resources at Michigan State University. This plan was inextricably linked with the development of, and closely reflects, these seven interpretive themes.

The Marketing of US-12

The marketing plan developed for the US-12 HTC for use in their application for heritage route status was intended to serve as a guide – like a road map – for attracting both residents and outside visitors to the US-12 corridor. The plan consisted of two components, one for internal stakeholders (all those agencies and organizations involved in the development and marketing of US-12) and one for external or visitor markets (including both local residents and tourists). Development of the final plan was based on a series of activities, including:

1 A comprehensive inventory of the cultural and historical features situated along the entire length of the corridor.
2 Review of existing market research analyses of auto and bus-based travel both in Michigan and along/at other US heritage routes/sites.
3 A series of community meetings held in each of the eight counties through which US-12 runs, at which participants engaged in a series of activities designed to elicit local perceptions of US-12 and its cultural and historical significance. These activities included participants' adoption of the characters of historical figures (famous or otherwise) and the fictional writing of specially created postcards, as shown in Figure CS4.2.

Both the internal and external components of the plan consisted of the same series of elements:

- clear statement of the goals of the marketing plan
- a situation analysis, highlighting the strengths, weaknesses, opportunities and threats associated with the trail and its heritage designation
- identification of appropriate target markets, prioritized to reflect the HTC's limited financial resources and the amount of time available to devote to the project
- suggestion of a series of strategic marketing approaches and development of a clear marketing campaign complete with a list of specific marketing activities

Figure CS4.2
The Hartman
House, Smith's
Chapel and
Buchlen House,
Cass County

(Courtesy: Soo Hyun Jun)

- formulation of a concise positioning statement
- summary of the classic P's of marketing (product, place, price and promotion)
- construction of a timeline for the implementation of the activities suggested.

The remainder of this case study focuses on the external portion of the marketing plan, i.e. that portion concerned with attracting more visitors to US-12.

Goals of the external marketing plan

The external marketing plan had two sets of goals, one concerning visitation to US-12, and the other economic and community development along the route. The three visitor-oriented goals were to:

- make residents of the US-12 corridor aware of the heritage route designation and of the route's historical and cultural significance
- attract new/more cultural/heritage tourists to the corridor
- attract new/more bus tours to the corridor.

The three economic and community development-oriented goals were to:

- increase patronage of US-12 businesses, attractions and events by both local residents and tourists from the target markets identified (see below)
- attract new businesses to the US-12 corridor, preferably those that are not associated with any national chain but that are locally owned by corridor residents
- stimulate increased spending in US-12 communities and at US-12 sites by both local residents and tourists.

External situation analysis

The purpose of situation analysis is to recognize the strengths, weaknesses, opportunities and threats associated with a product or location. In this particular case, this included those of the US-12 corridor itself, the HTC, and, more generally, in the heritage tourism market. The strengths, weaknesses, opportunities and threats identified are outlined below:

Strengths

- Strong leadership on committee including that by local preservationists, development professionals and promotional/marketing experts
- Well-established series of special events along entire corridor
- Plentiful, historic attractions along route, including accommodations in quaint bed and breakfasts
- Existing marketing efforts in eastern portion (Auto National Heritage Area)

Weaknesses

- Heavy truck use along some portions of the route
- Relatively high speed limit does not encourage leisurely driving
- Relatively high traffic volumes in downtown areas discourages outdoor activities such as dining

Opportunities

- Current popularity of driving for pleasure, including willingness of many drivers to take longer but more interesting routes
- Continued popularity of sightseeing and shopping among tourists
- Continued growth in the cultural and heritage tourism sectors, including the search for authentic, historic, and educational experiences
- Strong interest of multiple state government agencies in corridor designation (Department of Transportation; Travel Michigan; History, Arts and Libraries)

Threats

- Commercial development is already changing the sense of place and aesthetics of the corridor, including homogenization of sights and businesses
- Strong competition from well-established Amish heritage route in northern Indiana
- Deterioration of many downtown areas, lack of agencies to assist with downtown revitalization

External target markets

Target markets were identified based on a survey of destination marketing organizations in the counties through which US-12 traverses, as well as a review of existing market analyses of current Michigan and/or cultural/heritage travellers. Key findings of these consumer studies included that the majority of Michigan visitors come from the states of Illinois, Indiana, Ohio and Michigan itself; that popular activities include driving for pleasure, shopping, exploring small towns and visiting historic sites; and, that many drivers indicate the propensity to take the more interesting route between their origin and destination, even if it is a longer drive. Based on these findings, various target markets were identified for the US-12 heritage route. These were prioritized into two categories – high (target now or soon) and medium (target in the next few years) – based on the expected amount of time, money and investment associated with their targeting.

The three high priority target markets identified were:

■ residents of US-12 counties (for day and other short trips)

■ individual car-based travellers interested in travel and auto history, and the small town experience

■ local schools and youth clubs.

Four medium priority target markets were also identified, namely:

■ travellers who currently utilize Interstates 80 and 94, the main and fastest east–west routes which run south and north, respectively, of US-12, but who might be attracted to a slower but more interesting route

■ bus tours, e.g. out of Detroit and Chicago, that focus on small town experiences, heritage travel and/or cultural tourism

■ residents of key target markets outside of US-12 corridor that are currently marketed to by the tourism agencies in the eight counties through which US-12 runs, e.g. northern Indiana, Chicago and surrounding area, Toledo

■ clubs and groups such as those interested in modern and classical vehicles (cars, motorbikes, bicycles etc.).

External marketing strategies, campaigns and activities

Once the overall goals of the external marketing component had been formulated, the situation analysis completed, and target markets identified, the key marketing strategies, marketing campaigns, and specific activities within each campaign could be suggested. The marketing strategy consisted of a four-pronged approach focusing on two types of customer or consumer (existing and new visitors to the US-12 corridor) and two types of product (the route as it currently exists, including all existing sites, businesses and communities, and new products, i.e. new sites or businesses). The strategic approach is outlined with examples below, under the four themes of:

- penetration: the easiest strategy to implement, based on creation of increased visitation among existing customers with no change to the existing product
- product development: the creation of new sites or other attractions, to be marketed to existing visitors
- market development: the search for new visitors to existing sites
- diversification: the final of the four strategies suggested to be implemented, involving the move into both new markets and the development of new products along the route.

Customer	Product	
	Existing products	**New products**
Current visitors	*Penetration* ■ More visits ■ Larger travel parties ■ Longer stays ■ More sites visited per trip	*Product development* ■ Restoration of derelict sites and their opening as new tourism attractions or accommodations ■ Creation of new parks and other natural areas
New visitors	*Market development* ■ Search for new tourist markets besides current visitors	*Diversification* ■ Development of new products aimed at new visitor markets

Beyond this broad overview of the main strategic approach to external marketing, a matrix was then developed listing each of the goals of the external marketing component, the main target market of this goal, an overall campaign theme to guide the goal, and a list of specific marketing activities. For example, under the goal of raising awareness of the US-12 heritage corridor amongst local residents, the following activities were suggested (under the campaign theme of 'US-12: A local treasure'):

- continue and expand the number and range of special events in the area
- use press releases to market special events
- work with local businesses and other organizations to use the US-12 logo developed as a part of the overall management plan
- work with local businesses, tourism attractions and other organizations to distribute information about the route, whether in the form of pictures, brochures, maps etc.)
- upon designation, utilize the special heritage route signs available from MDOT, and beautify these signs using seasonal plantings
- create a 'Friends Group' to assist with the local promotion of the route.

For each goal, campaign and set of marketing activities, a timeline was then drawn up, with each activity prioritized into one of four categories: now or soon (i.e. in 2004), 2005, 2006–08 (i.e. in 3–5 years) and beyond 2008.

Summary of the four P's of the US-12 Heritage Trail external marketing plan

Towards the conclusion of the external marketing plan, the four classic P's of marketing – product, place, price and promotion – were summarized for the HTC:

P	Description
Product	The US-12 corridor itself, and any trip (day or overnight) along any of its length
Place	The eight Michigan counties through which US-12 traverses, including multiple communities, agricultural areas, and other open spaces (public and private)
Price	Not considered at this time since the HTC is not responsible for setting prices
Promotion	Publicity and press releases; advertising; word-of-mouth communications; sales and merchandising

The final element of the marketing plan was a communications strategy. This consisted of three distinct components:

■ a promotional brochure, for distribution by mail, e-mail and at public places and tourism attractions along the route

■ a regular newsletter (four pages, available in hard copy and via e-mail), including such features as a calendar, a featured destination, a 'Did you know . . .' section, and a 'Kid's Korner'

■ a website, featuring a wide range of information about the US-12 corridor, including lists of places to visit, eat, shop and stay; learning opportunities; a photo gallery; sample itineraries; and links to other relevant sites.

All components were suggested to incorporate the newly developed US-12 logo (see Figure CS4.3) and to adopt consistent formats and colour schemes so as to maximize the building of a distinct identity as well as local and visitor familiarity with the route.

Figure CS4.3
US-12 Logo

(Courtesy: US-12 Heritage Trail Council)

References and resources

Michigan Heritage Route Program: www.michigan.gov/mdot/0,1607,7-151-9621_11041_11209---,00.html

US-12 Heritage Trail: www.us12heritagetrail.org/

US-12 Heritage Trail Heritage Route Application and Corridor Management Plan. Prepared for the US-12 Heritage Trail Council by SmithGroup JJR and Michigan State University's Department of Parks, Recreation and Tourism Resources, December 2003.

Discussion questions

1   Could route US-12 be marketed attractively to the overseas market? How might the appeal be made to visitors from overseas?

2   Could a similar initiative be launched in other countries? In which countries would this approach be most effective? A somewhat similar programme has been launched in Germany with the marketing of the Romantische Strasse. What others exist, or could be promoted? (The group could prepare a SWOT analysis on a selected route to identify suitability).

3   Comment on the effectiveness of the chosen marketing tools in reaching their targets.

4   No reference is made in the US analysis to petrol prices, or sustainability. Is this due to the date of the programme, US attitudes, the insignificance of petrol prices to travellers in the USA, or other factors? In light of experience might this be, or become, a factor in the future marketing of the route?

Case study 5
Ensuring visitor satisfaction at Warwick Castle

(Prepared with the help of Lindsay Hillman, Warwick Castle)

Figure CS5.1
Bowman
animateur
performing at
Warwick Castle

(Courtesy: the Tussauds Group)

This case provides an unusual example of a major heritage site with strong historical associations in the ownership of a commercial organization dedicated to promoting the site for tourism. What is apparent in the study is that this arrangement can work to the benefit of both preservation and tourism, when care is exercised and the importance of preservation of the site is clearly recognized by its commercial owners. Warwick Castle has long been a highly successful tourist attraction in the ownership of the Tussauds Group, an organization with a high reputation for professionalism in their attractions. The objective in the case is to focus on the minutiae of visitor attraction operations – signposting, access, litter, toilet facilities, which along with interpretation go to make up the associated elements of the product which help to deliver tourist satisfaction. Tourists responding to satisfaction questionnaires will seldom comment on these specifics, but will often refer to the 'cleanliness' of the site and similar such statements indicating their overall levels of satisfaction. The 'cleanliness' of trains in countries such as Switzerland and Denmark is often mentioned by visitors as something that strikes them, by contrast with experiences in their own countries, and many seaside resorts are acutely aware of their need to keep streets clean from litter and graffiti if they are to maintain their position in the tourism stakes. Disneyworld is a leading example of a group of attractions which aim high on these details, placing great emphasis on cleanliness at their sites, wherever they are situated in the world.

Reference to Chapters 10 (attractions) and 19 (management of sites) is appropriate in this study, and clearly once again good marketing, in the broadest sense of the term, underpins the planning, development and operation of the most successful sites.

Introduction

Warwick Castle is one of the leading tourist attractions in Britain, and is managed professionally by one of the country's leading tourism organizations, The Tussauds Group. The following are key elements in its strategy to attract and satisfy its large number of visitors.

Accessibility

The attraction is open every day from 10 a.m., apart from Christmas Day. This overcomes any uncertainty on the part of impromptu visitors about whether they will find the site open – a common problem with many heritage sites which have widely varying opening times. There are ample and clear road signs around the site, and adequate parking for cars and coaches on all but high peak days of the year. Car parks are hard surfaced and attractively landscaped.

Utilities

There are toilets for visitors strategically placed at the entry to the site and within the site. Litter bins are positioned throughout the site. It is the policy of the organization to ensure that the site is kept clean at all times, and litter is picked up constantly. Particular attention is given to catering for the elderly, and for families with young children. Staff are trained in first-aid emergency treatment.

Signposting and interpretation on site

All attractions are well signposted, and warning signs are posted outside the site if any facilities have to be closed for the day. A leaflet with comprehensive information about the site is given out with tickets. Information is also provided in other languages on key signage (State Rooms and Royal Weekend Party), guidebooks are available in French, German, Spanish, Italian and Japanese, and audio tours are also available in French, German and Japanese.

Crowd control

Visitors are directed, by additional signs, away from the most popular areas at times when queuing is likely to occur. Staff are on hand to supervise tourist flows, and queue warnings are given on peak days. Extra entertainment, such as costumed characters, is provided to entertain queues on these occasions.

Pricing

The policy is for an all-inclusive single payment for entry into every facility within the site, with the exception of the 'Warwick Ghosts' feature, which is unsuitable for under-8s and for which a supplement is payable. This has been found to achieve the highest level of satisfaction among visitors. The normal concessionary discounts are allowed, and a season ticket, the Privilege Pass, is also available for those who wish to return on future occasions.

Other features

Additional revenue accrues through the use of the castle's facilities for functions such as wedding receptions, meetings, evening events and team-building activities.

Discussion questions

1   The organization has identified a number of features which raise satisfaction levels of their customers. How do these features compare with those of attractions in your area?

2   Warwick Castle is fortunate to be able to offer sufficient parking for most customers at most times of the year. This is not true of many attractions situated in urban areas. How do these meet the needs of their customers?

3   Warwick Castle is a major heritage site in England, and one of the very few to be owned and operated commercially by a large corporation. Given their success in running this attraction, would you advocate more heritage sites being operated by large commercial concerns?

4   While concessions for senior citizens are given at this site, this is not true of many attractions or events abroad – or even within the UK. What are the arguments for and against offering discounts for seniors?

5   How would you propose the organization expands its activities to bring in more tourists during the quieter months of the year?

Case study 6
Steppes Travel: a mid-size specialist operator facing the challenge of change

(Prepared with the help of Nick Laing, Chairman, and Paul Craven, General Manager, Asia, Steppes Travel)

This is a classic example of the up-market long-haul specialist tour operator, raising a number of issues, not least that of the changing role of the tour brochure. Steppes is taking a somewhat novel approach to this in a manner which sets it apart from its rivals. The company faces the key challenge of distinguishing itself from larger brands selling similar products, and resolves the issue by its focus on quality and service. This focus in itself brings new problems, of recruiting the quality of staff it demands, and of raising expectations in its clients which it cannot meet, given the nature of some of the destinations it promotes. The company's experiences reinforce awareness of the danger in focusing too narrowly on any single destination, and the benefits of strategic marketing in which publicity rather than advertising is employed to develop awareness in a strongly competitive market. Its location on an upper floor in a small provincial market town drives home the point that modern communications and technology obviate the need for a city-centre site and face-to-face selling for specialist operations. A reading of Chapter 16 with reference to specialist tour operating will provide useful background knowledge of the setting for this case. While the case does not specifically address the sociocultural impacts of Western visitors to often remote and isolated Third World destinations, a reading of Chapter 6 will raise questions which the reader will recognize must be addressed by the company.

Background to the company

Nick Laing set out in 1989 to offer tourists something different, setting up Steppes East as a tour operation carrying clients to the then Soviet Union. Focus on a single destination always carries a high risk, and after the fall of the Communist regime Russia proved less of a draw, forcing the company to rethink its products.

The company targets up-market, and generally well-off, clients who are seeking new experiences and destinations for which tailor-made programmes provide the solution. These are mainly but not entirely cultural or adventure-based, as many clients seek a relaxing break on a beach at the end of their tours; honeymoon arrangements also form an important element in the company's products. Interest in countries tends to move in cycles based on what is fashionable, so that a country which is seen as over-exploited may come back into fashion a few years later. Russia fell out of favour for some years after the overthrow of the Communist regime, largely due to its economic crisis and perceived lack of security for visitors, but it later recovered to become popular again with the specialist market; the company, with substantial experience of the country, was quickly able to mount a major campaign and recover its market share. Similarly, the China market, popular with up-market tourists ten years ago, is showing renewed popularity at present.

Steppes has built up an organization focusing on three global regions, each of which has had its own programme and brochure up to the present. The divisions, Steppes East, Steppes Africa and Steppes Latin America will continue to retain their autonomous responsibilities, but all holiday opportunities are now integrated into a single brochure in the new (2006) season. Owing to the tailor-made nature of these holidays, no itineraries are specified in the new brochure, which is devoted to promoting the appeal of the various countries served. Additionally, the company has taken a 51 per cent share in partnership with Discovery Initiatives, a specialist operator organizing ecological tours, in order to grow this sector of the business.

The company remains small, by tour operating standards, with a staff of just 24 based in an office in Cirencester, Gloucestershire. In two decades of operation it has grown to carry some two and a half thousand clients annually, but these are offered a standard of service and advice seldom matched by other operators.

The problem

Steppes identifies its problem areas as:

- meeting the expectations of their often demanding customers
- recruiting the quality of staff that the job demands
- trying to stand out from the crowd in an increasingly competitive environment of small specialist operators
- finding ways of communicating successfully in a marketplace saturated with PR and advertising messages.

The company cannot compete with volume operators, nor does it seek to do so. It will not arrange packages comprising simply flight and accommodation; it holds no allocation of hotel rooms, neither does it hold an IATA licence, choosing in part to buy in seats through other companies which can obtain better seat prices through volume purchases, or having direct flight contracts with individual airlines. However, the company is happy to organize land programmes for tourists who prefer to arrange their own flights via the Internet, since profit margins are best achieved in the mark-ups on land programmes rather than on transport to and from destinations. Steppes Travel's orientation is quality based. Programmes are exclusively tailor-made, and are discussed with clients in considerable detail; the end package will include not only flights and accommodation, but also complex land itineraries often calling for very specialized knowledge and contacts in the countries concerned; one example of this is to be found in their programmes to Borneo, where good contacts can ensure that their clients can spend up to seven nights visiting and viewing the orang-utans, while most operators are confined to a single day's visit.

Wealthy and sophisticated travellers often make unrealistic demands, so that the sales sequence is far more complex than would be the case in a simple holiday booking. Staff have to be truthful and accurate in giving information about the countries to which they are sending their clients, and the clients must know in detail what they can expect. This can result in a mismatch between expectations and what is available; exotic destinations, for example, may be unable to provide the stretch limousines demanded by clients to transfer them between sites. Equally, where high-grade facilities are provided, these come at a price which may appear exorbitant to the client, who cannot understand why such facilities cannot be made available at a more realistic price in an impoverished country. Hotels with character are much in demand – yet these are also expected to provide high levels of service, not always realistic in developing countries. Lack of adequate infrastructure makes some destinations unsaleable to this market, regardless of demand.

Unlike other specialist agencies, the company makes no charge for the advice it provides to its clients, regardless of the time occupied in dealing with their booking. Clients will deal with one person from start to finish of their booking, and are assigned to those with intimate knowledge of the region they will be visiting. Because of the nature of the tours, considerable time is engaged in problem solving, and after-sales demand can be high, where clients travelling abroad need advice and help. The company does not depend upon an automated answering service, preferring to be available to clients on demand 24 hours a day, seven days a week to resolve problems. All this results in high labour cost, which can only be recovered if conversions from enquiries to bookings are high.

The company depends for its success on its ability to recruit sales staff who are not merely knowledgeable, but experienced and highly professional in the advice they offer. With a growing pool of young, sophisticated travellers, many interested in working in the industry, it would appear to be a simple matter to recruit talented and knowledgeable staff, but the demanding nature of the work, with often long hours and salaries which in most specialist agencies fail to match the levels of experience and qualities expected of staff, mean that only the most dedicated will commit themselves in the long term. Staff are employed based on their knowledge of the primary destinations with which they will deal, and this specialized knowledge can lead in turn to the company exploiting new areas of the globe. One typical area where mismatch can arise is in the case where staff experience of a country has been gained through backpacking and budget holidays, which can limit their knowledge of the de-luxe accommodation and facilities sought by their clients. This can be overcome in time by training, and staff are given four weeks' travel experience each year to develop and expand their in-depth knowledge of their chosen regions.

Promotion

Laing's approach was initially to grow his business by focusing on publicity, rather than advertising. In 1977 he brought in a public relations company to help develop a stronger image for the company, which resulted in a 40 per cent increase in bookings. He encourages travel journalists to experience and write about his packages, but above all, Steppes Travel depends upon repeat business and word-of-mouth recommendation, which accounts for 60 per cent of all bookings. Repeat business is further encouraged by providing discount vouchers against future bookings. Laing now takes the view that PR in this field has only limited value, with little new to be written about travel and sophisticated clients now becoming jaded with the bombardment of publicity messages to which they are exposed.

The search for the new extends to brochure design, which is constantly reappraised. The company has experimented with many different approaches in recent years, including a black and white version and a non-standard size (very little business comes through travel agents, therefore agency racking is not a criterion in design). Current brochure cover is discreet and tasteful, in line with the preferences of the clients the company serves.

Discussion questions

1 With a trend towards charging fees for counselling customers in travel agencies, would you recommend that Steppes now impose a professional fee for the advice they offer their clients? Should this be made refundable in the event of a booking being made?

2 Discuss the pros and cons of containing all a company's products in a single brochure.

3 The company's versatility in offering tailor-made dynamic packages is clearly one of its great strengths. However, could this mean that as their customers become more familiar with the Internet, they may also become confident enough to make their bookings direct?

4 Steppes finds difficulty in reaching clients, owing to the rapid increase in messages saturating the market. Yet in an earlier case (Brilliant Weekends) we learned that that company was able to grow its business almost entirely based on prospective clients searching the Web. How would you explain this apparent contradiction?

Case study 7
Ludlow Marches Food and Drink Festival

(Prepared by Liz Sharpley, Senior Lecturer, Faculty of Organisation and Management, Sheffield Hallam University)

Figure CS7.1
The Ludlow
Food and Drink
Festival

(Courtesy: Ludlow Food and Drink Festival)

This destination case study exemplifies the issues raised by event tourism which, due to restrictions of time and scale, can become a victim of its own success. The promoters recognize their need to address issues such as congestion and pressures on local accommodation as they develop and expand this noted food and drink festival. The case reveals how a faltering small town tourist destination, by identifying unique complementary products (in this case, top rated restaurants and high quality retail shopping outlets) and building on these strengths, can achieve national success and expand the tourist season. The case reveals how initial success for a destination can be extended by enhancing the original concept and encouraging repeat, and even regular, visits. This success now requires an evaluation as to where the festival is going, and whether to continue to expand demand or to stabilize it to maximize visitor satisfaction.

Many areas of the globe have honed in on their local and regional food and drink products to enhance awareness of their destination and encourage visitors. Examples from Britain include Melton Mowbray pies, Dorset Blue Vinney cheese and Arbroath Smokies (smoked herring), while the French have long traded on their success in promoting destinations associated with their wide range of cheeses, wines, liqueurs and other products. Germany has its Lübecker marzipan, now exported globally, and that country and Belgium attract tourists by associating their destinations with local beers; further afield, Canadian and US North Eastern territories promote their local maple syrups to autumn visitors. This association between food, drink and destinations is still under-exploited and offers many countries in the world growth opportunities for tourism.

A separate issue is the question of funding such events, and the solution presented here reveals that an approach to local foodstuffs suppliers can ensure sponsorship which is mutually beneficial to the funders and the event's organizers. A reading of Chapter 9 as a prelude to this case will give an insight into the nature of destinations, while Chapter 10 will give a more detailed reference to gastronomic tourism, and encourage consideration of the all-important issues surrounding accommodation associated with events tourism.

Ludlow, a small rural town of just 10,000 inhabitants, nestled close to the border which divides England and Wales, has become home to arguably the most successful Food and Drink festival in the UK (Food and Drink Festival, 2005).

The town of Ludlow is, and has been for many years, a tourist destination is its own right. A visit to the local tourism office website (Ludlow Tourism, 2005) reveals a town which is steeped in history. Impressive architecture, including a wealth of Tudor half-timbered and Georgian houses, lines the streets, a stunning castle dominates one end of the town and a range of interesting shops encircle a traditional market square. Surrounded by wonderful rolling countryside, Ludlow is an attractive place for both day and short-break visitors.

Ten to fifteen years ago, however, the economy of the town was not looking too healthy. A downturn in the UK farming and associated industries, combined with a short British tourist season in that region, had left some local businesses struggling to survive. Consequently, the morale amongst the local business community and some of the residents was poor. A strategy was needed to revive the town and the hosting of the Food and Drink Festival has proved to be an important aspect of the town's regeneration.

The idea of holding a food festival was originally conceived in 1995 when a group of local business people from the Ludlow and District Chamber of Trade and Commerce proposed the event as a bold innovation to boost the town's image and to encourage more visitors.

The idea of organizing an event with a food focus was originally a 'stab in the dark'. However, as plans for the festival developed, the committee began to appreciate the wealth of food producers who were operating within this rich agricultural area, supplying a range of top-quality meat, dairy produce, fruit, beer, cider and perry. For example, the town boasts no less than four family-owned independent butchers, all of whom are serviced by one of the last remaining regional abattoirs in the country.

The organizers needed no convincing that the town was capable of staging such an event. Ludlow was already playing host to a popular Arts and Shakespearian festival, which had been held in the town for many years, and therefore the infrastructure needed to cater for a large influx of visitors was already in place. The Arts Festival takes place each May, so by deciding to stage the food festival in September the demand for services such as hotels and restaurants was spread throughout the summer season.

The Food and Drink Festival has come a long way since its humble beginnings. In the first year the Festival took place in a hall in Ludlow College and was a small affair comprising a handful of local food suppliers promoting their goods. Now over 17,000 tickets are sold over the period of the three-day festival (2005 figures) which is always held over a weekend in early September.

The size of the event has also called for a change of venue and eleven years later the spectacular Ludlow Castle and its grounds provide the perfect setting for the event.

Marquees are erected in the outer and inner baileys of the Castle and these provide covered accommodation for the 120 local food producers who now attend the event to promote their goods. Nearly all of the producers come from the surrounding region of about 30/40 miles radius of the town. It is tempting to allow good producers from further afield to exhibit but the organizers have resisted this trend in favour of support-ing local enterprise. The Festival site also accommodates a number of 'talks' tents where cookery demonstrations and culinary talks are given throughout the weekend. A small charge is made to attend some of these talks but visitors are happy to pay owing to the quality of the lecturers and demonstrators. In 2005 these ranged from a talk about Black Pudding and Perry to a bread-making class run by a master baker. These activities add value to the event in providing both entertainment and education and differentiate the festival from a regular farmers market.

Visitors to the festival can sample many foods as they move around the site but there are also a number of concessionary stands which provide all manner of snacks and meals from paella to hog roast. Whenever possible, local businesses are used to provide this catering service.

In the centre of the festival ground an open area provides space for competitions, such as the popular Waiters' Obstacle Race, to take place. This has been a regular event for the last few years and attracts many competitors from local hotels, restaurants and pubs.

The Festival also extends its programme into the town centre. A number of food trails take place over the festival period including the famous 'Sausage Trail' which has become a popular 'high-spot' of the event. Over 1,500 tickets are sold in advance for this activity which involves the participants embarking on an early morning sampling tour of the town's butchers in an attempt to name the 'festival sausage'. Other trails include a beer tour which takes the participants on a circuit of the town's hostelries. The market square is filled each day by additional food and craft stalls and street enter-tainers; acrobats and musicians perform around the town adding value and interest to the visitor's experience by creating a carnival atmosphere.

The Festival is unusual in that it does not rely purely on formal funding from Government agencies to stage the event. A small amount of financial support is received from The European Union and Local Government departments but much of the funding is generated by ticket sales and donations from local businesses and food companies. The Festival's main sponsor in recent years has been Tyrrell's Potato Chips, a company based in nearby Leominster.

The staffing arrangements for the festival are also noteworthy. There is one paid employee, who is charged with the overall operational aspects of the event, but for the remainder of the work the festival relies almost entirely on a host of local volunteers. These willing co-workers tackle all manner of jobs from the selling of tickets at the gate to the emptying of refuse bins and the management of audiences in the tasting tents. The Mayor of Ludlow even rolls up his sleeves to help clear up the site at the end of the Festival! The event is also supported by an active 'Friends' group, some of whom are local and some of whom live at a distance. Their annual subscription allows them to enjoy certain privileges at the event, such as the provision of lunches and refreshments; but in return many of the Friends undertake duties over the weekend.

The Food Festival has undoubtedly played a significant part in the regeneration of the town and many would argue that the town of Ludlow has now become something of a culinary phenomenon. This is partly due to the success of the Food Festival but is also due to the arrival of a significant number of excellent chefs who have established businesses in or around the town. Ludlow is in the envious position of being home to more Michelin starred or listed restaurants than other town in the UK outside London. In 2005 there were seven restaurants in or around Ludlow listed in the Michelin guide. The first chef to set up an up-market restaurant in the town was Shaun Hill who established the world famous Merchant House (The Merchant House, 2005). He has now moved on to develop other food ventures but paved the way for chefs such as Claude Bosi, chef/owner of the Hibiscus (Hibiscus, 2005) which boasts two Michelin stars and Chris Bradley of Mr Underhills (Mr Underhills, 2005) which has been awarded one star. Anyone wanting to book a meal at any of the Michelin listed restaurants usually expects several months' wait before securing a table.

The town has also built on this success in becoming a flagship for the Slow Food Movement (Slow Food, 2005). In 2004 it became the first town in the UK to be awarded the title of 'Citta Slow' (Slow Food Ludlow, 2005). This is a rare honour only bestowed on those communities who demonstrate a lasting commitment to the supply of good regional food and a good quality lifestyle for their citizens. A series of Slow Food events held throughout the year include food tastings, cookery demonstrations, farm visits and Slow Food meals. These maintain interest in the concept, whilst providing entertainment and education. A highlight is the annual 'Magna Longa', held each August, a guided six-mile walk through the countryside linking food producers, pubs and farms where walkers enjoy food and drink along the way. In 2005 over 470 walkers took part in this food-lovers' event (Food and Drink Festival, 2005).

The Food and Drink Festival committee are constantly looking for ways to improve the organization of the event and one recent success has been the introduction of a Park and Ride system which buses visitors from a field on the outskirts of Ludlow into the town centre. This has eased the traffic congestion in the town centre considerably and has been well received by many of the festival-goers. The other challenge which the organizers face on an annual basis is the booking of accommodation for visitors who wish to stay overnight. Despite the fact that the town has a good offering of bed

Figure CS7.2
Visitors enjoy
the product

(Courtesy: Ludlow Food and Drink Festival)

and breakfast, hotel, pub and self-catering bed space, providing for all price ranges, much of it is booked up months before the actual festival. As the festival continues to grow this is an issue which needs to be addressed.

Until recently any research that has been carried out to support the Food Festival had done so on a fairly ad-hoc basis, primarily using volunteers at the ticket barrier. Clear data existed about the number of visitors who attended each day and there was some intelligence about where visitors had travelled from. Observation carried out by members of the committee over the festival weekend also provided some useful information to help with future planning.

The organizers, however, recognized the need to carry out a more detailed analysis of the festival and its impacts on the town. The key questions that lay at the heart of this work concerned themselves with the long-term sustainability of the festival, now that the event product is at such a mature stage. For example:

■ Can the festival maintain the size of its audience or are the numbers likely to drop as other events/attractions/activities become popular?

■ Would the organizers like the festival to grow further and if so, does the town have the space and infrastructure that will accommodate this growth?

■ Is it wise to keep the Castle as the main venue for the event or would it be more advisable to move the event to a green-field site outside the town where transport and parking may be easier?

- How can the organizers best promote the festival and to whom?

- What is the best method for communicating with visitors or potential visitors to the event regarding the festival programme, accommodation in and around Ludlow, transport arrangements, dining opportunities in the town and other associated activities?

- What impacts has the festival already had upon the town, economically, politically, socially and environmentally, and what are the likely impacts for the future?

- What are the success factors of the festival and which aspects need more fine-tuning?

In order to answer these questions it was also considered necessary to establish a good understanding of the market that is attracted to the festival, by finding out such information as visitors' home town, lifestyle, age and motivations for visiting the event. It was also considered important to investigate the amount of money that was being spent by individuals and family groups both at the festival site and within the town centre during their visit.

In order to carry out this work, a number of researchers from both Sheffield Hallam University and Greenwich University were active during the festival in 2004 and 2005 in a confidential capacity. To date, the findings of this work remain unpublished but their research findings have already played an important part in advising the festival organizers on the way forward.

It is not easy to unravel the complex set of reasons for the development of the town as such an important culinary centre in the UK and why the Ludlow Food Festival in particular has become so important to the town's revival. However, it is probably fair to assume that the combination of an attractive historic town, a stunning rural setting and an abundance of top-class local ingredients has sealed its success.

Websites

Food and Drink Festival (2005) at www.foodfestival.co.uk last visited September 2005
Hibiscus (2005) at www.hibiscusrestaurant.co.uk last visited July 2005
Ludlow Tourism (2005) at www.ludlow.org,uk last visited September 2005
Mr Underhills (2005) at www.Mr-Underhills.co.uk last visited July 2005
Slow Food (2005) at www.slowfood.com last visited September 2005
Slow Food Ludlow (2005) at www.slowfoodludlow.org.uk last visited September 2005
The Merchant House (2005) at www.merchanthouse.co.uk last visited July 2005

Discussion questions

1 This case study conveniently summarizes some of the issues faced by the organizers. One of these is the question of whether the event should be moved to a site adjacent to the town, rather than the town centre, to alleviate the congestion and parking problems. Would you recommend this?

2 How can the shortage of accommodation during these peaks be resolved?

3   Can an event such as this become a victim of its own success? For example, in the 2005 festival, it was noted that a number of visitors were dissatisfied with the long queues to buy tickets for the Sausage Trail, and the slow progress of the trail as queues built up to sample the products. Should pricing be used to ration demand?

4   Ludlow is fortunate to have been one of the first sites to organize a food festival, but these are now proliferating: prominent festivals are now organized elsewhere in Britain, including the Highland Feast, the Cumbria Festival of Food and Drink, the Nantwich Food Festival, the Manchester Food and Drink Festival, the Exmoor Food Festival and Taste South-East, held on the south-east coast of Cornwall. Does the fact that these events are widely scattered mean that Ludlow avoids direct competition?

Case study 8
Crime, safety and security: tourists' perceptions of South Africa

(Prepared by: Dorothy Ruth Queiros, Senior Lecturer, Tourism Group, Department of Marketing and Tourism Management, Business School, University of Hertfordshire, UK; Richard George, Senior Lecturer, School of Management, University of Cape Town, South Africa, rgeorge@commerce.uct.ac.za; Michele Anne Hoareau, Tourism Management Honours Student, Department of Marketing and Tourism Management, Business School, University of Hertfordshire, UK)

This final case is unique in this text, in offering a perspective on tourist demand, and should be read in conjunction with Chapter 4, which examines the nature of the tourist. Issues such as risk and fear are discussed, issues which are by no means unique to South Africa and have had to be tackled by the tourism authorities in many other countries.

Tourism is vitally important for South Africa's economy, and a reading of Chapter 5 will identify the key reasons for this, given the country's struggle to emerge from apartheid and to grow its economy in the aftermath. The country has much to offer the tourist, and is popular with visitors from the UK, but crime and the fear of crime is a critical issue for the expansion of tourism. The authorities recognize this, and are seeking to reduce crime through a number of measures which are identified in the case. Other issues deal with the question of whether crime statistics should be withheld or publicized, whether exhortations to take care, lock vehicles etc. are self-defeating in creating a sense of fear among visitors. Since the media tend to focus on reporting negative aspects of the country, should promotional budgets best be spent on attracting journalists to the country to see for themselves, hopefully generating more positive stories in the press?

The case sheds light on the nature of risk-takers versus risk-averters, but we are left to wonder whether the latter may, in fact, be avoiding travel to the country, and therefore would be less likely to figure in research on tourists carried out in the country.

While it would appear that crime against tourists in South Africa is largely the result of targeting the wealthy, in other countries tourists may be victims of crime for their politics, their nationality, their religious and cultural affiliations and even the colour of their skin. There is little evidence that tourists per se are the target in South Africa, but rather they are seen as easy victims for robbers; in other countries, tourists may be deliberately targeted merely for being 'different'. The case gives us reason to contemplate the nature of international travel in the twenty-first century and the increasing risks associated with it.

Introduction

The 'New South Africa' has emerged as a popular international tourist destination after years of relative isolation from the rest of the world. However, it is plagued by a high crime rate, which may affect international tourists' decision-making and behaviour. The issue of safety and security in tourism management is an important one. This case study, therefore, examines UK tourists who visited South Africa between 1999 and 2004, analyzing their perceptions and consumer behaviour with reference to crime safety and security. Some interesting findings emerge on the influence of crime on travel patterns and decision-making. Several crime preventative measures implemented by South African law enforcement agencies and tourism stakeholders are then reviewed.

South Africa: a popular new international destination

Tourism is of major importance to the South African economy. It is a fast-growing industry within the country and contributes approximately 7.4 per cent to the Gross Domestic Product (GDP). Tourism employs an estimated 3 per cent of South Africa's workforce, and is regarded as potentially the largest job provider and earner of foreign exchange. In 2004, foreign tourist arrivals to the country grew to a record high of 6.7 million, a growth of 2.7 per cent over 2003. Since the demise of apartheid (forced racial segregation) in South Africa in the early 1990s, international arrivals have increased steadily year-on-year (see Figure CS8.1). The release of Nelson Mandela on 11 February 1990, and the associated worldwide publicity, is one of the reasons for this increase. The transition to democracy, with the first democratic elections held in 1994, has resulted in the country possessing a positive global image and a high 'emotional pull' drawcard. Furthermore, there is good value for money compared to other destinations, and foreign currency exchange rates are favourable.

South Africa is generally perceived as a value for money, cultural, long-haul[1] holiday destination. With the current trend of tourists seeking cultural tourism destinations with a hint of the unfamiliar, South Africa has much to offer. Today's international tourists are becoming increasingly discerning and seek a variety of tourism products and activities. South Africa is well positioned to cater for the New Tourist as it has a diversity of products such as climate, natural treasures, wildlife, culture, shopping, luxurious hotels, golf courses, wine routes and nightlife.

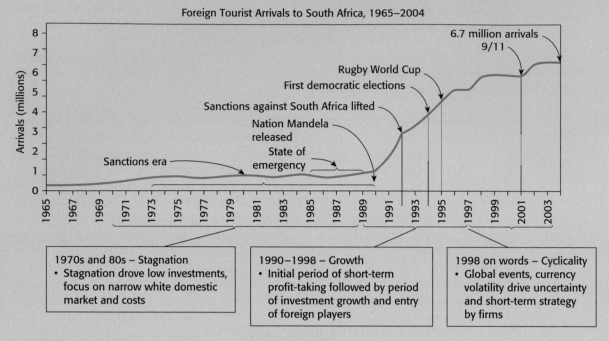

Figure CS8.1   Foreign tourist arrivals in South Africa, 1965–2004
(Courtesy: South African Tourism, 2004)

Safety and security in tourism management

The World Tourism Organization (WTO) states that safety and security are vital to providing quality in tourism, and should be an overriding objective of tourism destinations (UNWTO, 1997). The issue of safety and security is also important to the image of a tourist destination and for visitor satisfaction. Tourists will form an image based on a combination of cost, climate, scenery, personal safety and sanitation. For a tourist destination to remain successful, addressing these issues is vital.

A tourist's decision-making and behaviour is influenced by perceptions of safety, security and crime risk (Pearce, 1988). Several tourism-crime researchers, however, have suggested that residents and tourists stand an equal chance of becoming a victim of crime. For example, Prideaux (1996) proposed that in the normal course of events, tourists might expect to have at least the same probability of becoming victims of crime as residents in the area they are visiting.

Crime against tourists is not a new phenomenon, yet the link between tourist victimization and tourism demand is difficult to establish. This is because there are many exogenous factors that are involved in the tourist's decision-making process. Some of these factors include economic considerations, accessibility, climate, the extent and affect of a Destination Marketing Organization's (DMO) marketing activities, changes in consumer behaviour, and so on.

Tourists have been found to be susceptible to crime for various reasons, sometimes by chance (being in the wrong place at the wrong time), or being purposely targeted by local criminals. In 1993, in Florida, steps were taken to reduce criminal activities aimed at car rental companies by prohibiting companies from applying bumper stickers or symbols on vehicles which would identify them as rental vehicles. Incidents of tourist-related crime were reduced by implementing such preventative measures (Florida Department of Law Enforcement, 1996). Tourists are considered 'easy targets' of crime as they are clearly identifiable by appearance, language, dress codes and mannerisms. In addition, it is assumed that they carry significant sums of money and other 'portable wealth' (such as cameras, and jewellery). In Latvia, Eastern Europe, tourists are warned about high levels of street crime and told that criminals consider them soft targets. In many cases, the obvious differences in income between tourists and locals spur criminals on.

Crime rates at tourist destinations also appear to be influenced by increased population density during the defined tourist season. Conventional mass tourism results in a high concentration of tourists within certain urban and coastal environments – these are often the places with higher crime rates. Tourist locations can be 'hot spots' for certain types of crimes (Sherman *et al.*, 1989). Areas ranging from tourist resorts to transportation hubs may be considered by criminals as desirable locations for conducting crime, whether against tourists or locals. Thus, crime against tourists is more likely to occur in destinations already experiencing disproportionately high levels of crime (Schiebler *et al.*, 1996).

It has therefore been suggested that the more 'risk-taking' tourist (for example, the independent 'explorer' type) who travels off the beaten track and to less well-known destinations, may indeed be taking fewer risks than the 'risk-averse' mass tourist who travels to well-established tourist destinations and resorts. Some tourists take higher personal risks as their confidence increases, such as staying in accommodation establishments that aren't safe or taking part in 'risky business' (such as conversing with local prostitutes and drug dealers) which increases the likelihood of encountering crime. Exposure to dangerous situations may depend on where one is on Pearce's (1993) 'Travel Needs Ladder'. Tourists with a strong need for safety and security, for example, tend to travel in groups and prefer organized package tours. In contrast, a more experienced tourist may focus on higher-level needs and is perhaps more likely to take risks (Sönmez and Graefe, 1998).

Studies on the relationship between tourism and crime have been hindered by a lack of available data on tourism-victims of crime. This can be attributed to systems which do not distinguish between crime committed against tourists and crime against local residents. Certain destinations have started to make this distinction, but are reluctant to release such data, for fear of adverse publicity.

South Africa's challenge

According to the International Criminal Police Organization (Interpol) and the Crime Information Analysis Centre (CIAC), South Africa has very high levels of violent crime. This has escalated since 1994, and can cause fear among tourists, affect visitor satisfaction and give the reputation that the country is an unsafe destination. Political instability during the past, along with high levels of violence and crime, has, to a certain extent, tarnished the country's image as an international tourist destination. However, the international media tend to report the negative aspects, making crime against tourists headline news, while not reporting that the majority of visitors have an incident-free holiday.

An interesting development is that, despite crime safety and security issues in South Africa, it is now perceived by many to be a safe haven from the recent terrorism acts that have plagued major tourist centres such as New York, Madrid and London.

The National Tourism Organization (NTO) for South Africa, South African Tourism (SAT) includes the following question in its biannual Tourist Departure Survey: 'What was your most negative experience in South Africa?' According to SAT's 2004 study, 75.8 per cent of tourists said they didn't have one to report, while only 5.5 per cent mentioned theft/robbery/crime/violence as a negative experience. There is also strong evidence to suggest that although initial concerns regarding safety and security may exist, these can be outweighed by other attractive aspects of a destination (for example, value for money, warm hospitality, and diversity of cultural and natural tourist attractions).

In South Africa, most tourist activities occur within areas which already have a high-density population. These also have the highest crime rates. Figure CS8.2 shows the higher incidence of crime in cities such as Cape Town, Johannesburg and Durban, which are cities frequented by tourists.

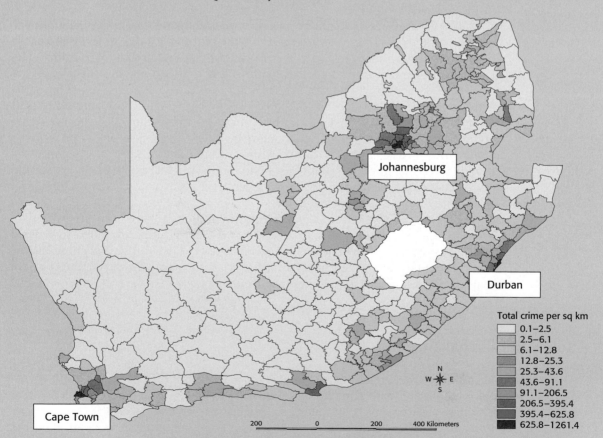

Figure CS8.2 Total crime per square kilometre over three years for each magisterial district (1998–2001)
(Courtesy: Schmitz and Stylianides, 2002)

UK tourists to South Africa

The largest share of foreign tourist arrivals to South Africa is land-based travellers from neighbouring Southern African countries (such as Mozambique, Botswana, and Zimbabwe). According to SAT data, 69 per cent of inbound tourists are short-haul, compared to the 31 per cent of long-haul tourists (see Figure CS8.3). Of South Africa's long-haul (overseas) markets, the UK is the largest with a total of 471,234 arrivals in 2004. Figure CS8.4 shows the increase in arrivals from the UK over the last five years. South Africa is increasingly seen as a repeat destination for UK travellers and, through an active brand, the UK is being targeted with the aim of continuously growing this market.

South Africa is popular amongst UK tourists for a variety of reasons. The country is popular as a winter-sun destination with a diversity of attractions. It has excellent shopping malls and nightlife, great wildlife and safari products, luxurious accommodation options, cultural and heritage attractions, and is intriguing (for those that want to know what the 'New South Africa' is like in the post-democracy phase). However, there are a number of challenges for South Africa in fulfilling demand from UK travellers. These include the need to position itself as a year-round destination and the issue of perceived safety and security (crime).

This case study includes results from a survey of UK residents' perceptions of South Africa as a holiday destination. A total of 45 per cent of respondents travelled in pairs,

Figure CS8.3
Overseas visitors by country of residence, 2003–2004

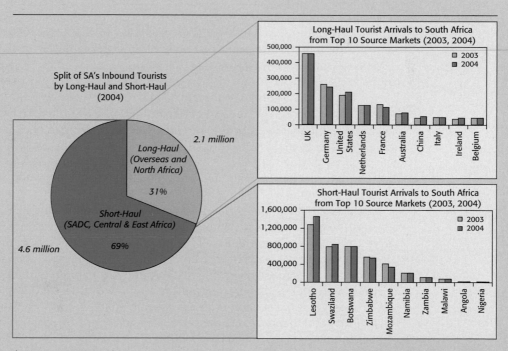

(Courtesy: SAT, 2004)

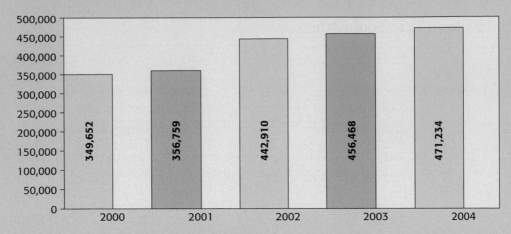

(Courtesy: SAT, 2004)

31 per cent on their own, while 11 per cent travelled with children. Over half (55 per cent) of respondents were holidaymakers, 21 per cent VFR (visiting friends and relatives), 6 per cent combined VFR with a holiday, 6 per cent were backpackers, and 11 per cent were visiting South Africa on business. These findings are consistent with South African Tourism's (SAT) 2004 visitor survey.

SAT's visitor data reveal that 72 per cent of UK tourists come to South Africa as independent travellers – putting together their own components of a tour package: airfare, accommodation, coach tours and meals. In this study, 56 per cent of respondents made use of hotels, guesthouses, self-catering units or caravan/camping facilities, while 44 per cent stayed with friends or relatives. A total of 52 per cent of respondents were visiting South Africa for the first time, while 48 per cent were repeat visitors.

When asked about how safe they felt during the daytime, 27 per cent of study respondents felt very safe and 57 per cent felt safe. However, when asked in the study, 'How safe do you feel going out at night?', only 5 per cent felt very safe, and 34 per cent felt safe. This supports the findings of George (2003) who studied tourists visiting Cape Town. He found that fear of crime was far greater at night than during the day. In this study, those respondents who felt safe were either tourists who had visited South Africa before, those staying with friends and relatives, or those who were on a package holiday. Respondents who felt unsafe were generally either younger tourists or first-time visitors to the country.

When asked about their use of accommodation establishment, the majority felt very safe (46 per cent) or safe (51 per cent), although rural hotels were perceived as the safest. City centres did not fare well, with most respondents feeling unsafe. Regarding the use of beaches, 24 per cent felt very safe and 61 per cent safe. A total of 26 per cent of respondents had made use of public transport. The majority of these tourists rated it as either unsafe or said they were unsure about how safe they felt. George's study (2003) also revealed a general wariness regarding public transport. This explains why the majority of respondents (82 per cent) made use of private rental vehicles. A total of 30 per cent of respondents had been victims of petty crime or knew someone who had.

The majority of respondents rated the presence and assistance of police and security in general, as 'good' and 'fair'. However, it must be noted that the remainder rated visibility of police poorly.

Measuring tourists' perceptions of safety is critical in attempting to improve their travel experience. This case study revealed that 72 per cent of respondents were concerned about crime and safety during their visit to South Africa. A total of 67 per cent reported that the most unpleasant aspect of their stay was linked to perceptions of safety and security issues, concerns regarding crime, and reports thereof. However, the majority of respondents (93 per cent) indicated that they were likely or very likely to return to South Africa and 84 per cent of respondents stated they were likely to recommend South Africa to friends or colleagues.

Conclusions and actions being taken

Tourists' concerns for personal safety are increasingly becoming an important issue for research and comment among stakeholders in the travel and tourism industry. If tourist destinations are to remain prosperous, the issue of tourists' safety and security is paramount.

It is interesting to note that, despite concerns and negative perceptions regarding safety and security, the majority of respondents interviewed were likely to revisit South Africa. This suggests that the positive aspects experienced by tourists while on holiday in South Africa may have indeed outweighed any negative perceptions. It appears that destination pull factors such as cultural and historical attractions, climate, world-renowned wildlife and safaris, shopping, nightlife, and value for money sway the opinions of those tourists who have visited. It may well be that visitors' perceptions also change over a course of a holiday. For example, a tourist may arrive in a city for the first time and feel very apprehensive and conscious about crime safety. Such negative feelings subside over time, and if he or she has an incident-free holiday experience, the visitor may leave feeling fine and wondering what all the fuss was about.

As with many countries, tourists need to take extra care when travelling in unfamiliar places; in many cases knowing what to do, and where to go or not to go largely decreases one's chance of being a victim of crime. A high presence of law enforcement personnel at tourist destinations is also important in deterring crime and making visitors feel safer.

Proactive crime-safety measures are currently being undertaken by the South African tourism authorities to counter the issue of crime-safety concerns. For example, tourists are warned to lock their vehicles securely, not to leave valuables in cars, not to wear ostentatious jewellery when walking about, and to take care with personal belongings at all times. Such information brochures are distributed to accommodation establishments, tourism information kiosks, and at popular tourist attractions. In addition, travel websites such as 'Backpacker Tourism SA' (BTSA), 'South African Tourism' and 'SA Venues' also provide tips and common sense crime-safety precautions to tourists visiting South Africa. However, it should be noted that such travel-safety advice and guidelines need to be provided in a way which does not worsen tourists' concerns for personal safety.

Several provinces are taking integrated and coordinated approaches to promote safety, prevent tourist crime and empower victims of crime. For example, provincial tourism authorities in the Western Cape have set up a Tourism Safety and Security Unit (TSSU) responsible for developing and maintaining proactive measures. These include:

- conducting tourism awareness and education campaigns to encourage communities to value the tourism industry
- developing the tourism media relationship and drawing attention to success stories when they occur (such as decreases in crime rates, successful prosecutions, and tourism's ability to address unemployment)
- fast-tracking courts for effective prosecution of criminals
- providing a tourist-victim hotline number with multilingual operators
- deploying Rent-a-Cops in hotspot areas (for example, Table Mountain National Park)
- installation of CCTV cameras at all hotspots in the central business district (CBD)
- encouraging the installation of safes in hotel rooms.

At a national level, the Department of Environmental Affairs and Tourism (DEAT), the country's Ministry for Tourism, has established the National Tourism Safety Network, a multi-stakeholder forum comprising the South African Police Service (SAPS), SA Tourism, Business Against Crime (BAC), and the nine provincial tourism authorities.

There have also been numerous national initiatives which have been undertaken to tackle one of the roots of crime; namely poverty. Tourism in South Africa is recognized by the government as the main socio-economic driver to assist in alleviating poverty through job creation and prosperity. Tourist guide training and general awareness programmes have also been identified as solutions to the problem of tourist crime.

Over the last few years, the townships (the previous government's planned urban settlements for Black Africans or Coloureds) have become very popular attractions for the growing number of overseas tourists who visit South Africa. Tours of townships around the country have flourished. These types of initiatives demonstrate that where local guides act as hosts, and where there are clear benefits to disadvantaged communities and entrepreneurs, tourists can have a unique cultural experience, which can contribute towards improving visitors' perceptions of crime safety.

A major national initiative to increase awareness of tourism is the 'SA Welcome' campaign. Launched in 1999, it aims to sensitize South Africans to the needs of international tourists. The logo for the campaign features a South African flag-draped 'Welcome' character, with arms outstretched in greeting (see Figure CS8.5). With the 'Welcome' logo, the core message is that 'tourism is everyone's business'. Everyone has a role to play in making South Africa an international destination of note and improving the tourist's experience.

Figure CS8.5
SA Welcome
campaign logo

Welcome

(Courtesy: South African Tourism)

References

Florida Department of Law Enforcement (1996), *Visitor Crime in Florida: the Perception vs. the Reality*. [Online] Florida, Statistical Analysis Centre. Available: www.fdlc.state.fl.us/fsac/Archives/visitor_crime.asp [Accessed 27 April 2004].

George, R (2003), Tourist's Perceptions of Safety and Security While Visiting Cape Town, *Tourism Management*, 24, 575–85

Pearce, P L (1988), *The Ulysses Factor: Evaluating Visitors in Tourist Settings*, Springer-Verlag

Pearce, P (1993), The Fundamentals of Tourist Motivation, in: D Pearce and R Butler (eds), *Tourism Research: Critique and Challenges*, Routledge

Prideaux, B (1996), The Tourism Crime Cycle: a Beach Destination Case Study, in: A Pizam and Y Mansfeld (eds), *Tourism, Crime and International Security Issues*, Wiley, pp 59–75

Schiebler, S A, Crotts, J C and Hollinger, R C (1996), Florida Tourists' Vulnerability to crime, in Pizam, A and Mansfeld, Y (eds), *Tourism, Crime and International Security Issues*, Wiley pp 37–50

Schmitz, P and Stylianides, T (2002), *Mapping Crime Levels and Court Efficiency per Magisterial District in South Africa*, [Online] Pretoria, Council for Scientific and Industrial research. Available: www.ojp.usdoj.gov/nij/maps/Conferences/02conf/Schmitz CE.doc [Accessed 14 April 2004]

Sherman, L W, Gartin, P and Beurger, M (1989), Hot Spots of Predatory Crime: Routine Activities and the Criminology of Place, *Criminology*, 27(1), 27–56

Sönmez, S F and Graefe, A R (1998), Determining Future Travel Behaviour from Past Travel Experience and Perceptions of Risk and Safety, *Journal of Travel Research*, (37) November, pp 171–7

South African Tourism (2004), Strategic Research Unit's '2004 Annual Tourism Report', [Online], Available: www.southafrica.net. [Accessed 6 September 2005]

United Nations World Tourism Organisation (1997), *Tourist Safety and Security: Practical Measures for Destinations*, 2nd edn, UNWTO

Discussion questions

1 Discuss the merits of the various steps taken by the authorities in this case study to reduce crime and its impacts.

2 There is some evidence that perceived risk is lower among visitors abroad than in their own home towns or countries. How do you account for this?

3 The case study claims that South Africa appeals strongly to the New Tourist. How would you define the New Tourist?

4 The case makes clear the difficulties facing the authorities in deciding whether, by giving out information or pamphlets warning tourists about crime, they may be contributing to perceived fear. Which course of action do you recommend?

5 Should the authorities in destinations where crime is high be obliged to publish figures separating crimes against tourists from those against local residents?

6 Would you recommend that SAT focuses its promotional spend on those areas, such as rural locations, where crime is low instead of those, such as Johannesburg, where it is high? What will they have to take into consideration if they choose this approach?

Note

1 Long-haul travel is defined as travel of six hours' flying time or more, or travel to destinations outside of Europe.

Bibliography

A note on this bibliography

The flow of tourism texts now appearing on the market is such that any attempt to offer a comprehensive listing of available and appropriate textbooks to aid the reader would be unnecessarily long, and less than helpful. Instead, in this new edition, the bibliography will for the first time extract a list of texts which will allow students to read around the topics covered in this text at a level appropriate for their courses. The texts are chosen for their suitability for those studying tourism at post-A level up to undergraduate level, and are identified according to their principal topics, apart from those texts which, in the view of the authors, offer useful supplementary reading about the nature of tourism in general – these are included under Chapter 1. Books earlier than 1980 are included only where they are classic and seminal texts or throw light on some particular aspect of tourism which cannot be readily found in more recent texts. Publications other than books are largely excluded, again except where they are deemed vital to the contemporary study of the subject.

General reference

Jafari, J (ed), *Encyclopedia of Tourism*, Routledge, 2000

Medlik, S, *Dictionary of Travel, Tourism and Hospitality*, Butterworth Heinemann, 2nd edn 1996

Weaver, D (ed), *The Encyclopaedia of Ecotourism*, CABI, 2001

World Travel Atlas, annual produced by Columbus Press, published by the World Travel Guide, 9th edn 2004

1 Introduction to tourism (and general tourism issues)

Alford, P, *E-Business in the Travel Industry*, Travel and Tourism Intelligence, 2000

Allcock, J B, Bruner, E M and Lanfant, M-F (eds), *International Tourism: Identity and Change*, Sage, 1993

Boniface, B and Cooper, C, *Worldwide Destinations: The Geography of Travel and Tourism*, Elsevier Butterworth-Heinemann, 4th edn 2005

Boniface, P, *Dynamic Tourism: Journeying with Change*, Channel View, 2001

Boorstin, D J, *The Image: A Guide to Pseudo-events in America*, Penguin, 1962

Brown, F, *Tourism Reassessed: Blight or Blessing?* Butterworth Heinemann, 1998

Burkart, A J and Medlik, S, *Tourism: Past Present and Future*, Heinemann, 1981

Burns, P and Holden, A, *Tourism: A New Perspective*, Prentice Hall, 1995

Callaghan, P (ed), *Travel and Tourism*, Business Education Publishers, 1989

Cohen, E, *Contemporary Tourism: Diversity and Change*, Elsevier, 2004

Cooper, C, Fletcher, J, Fyall, A, Gilbert, D and Wanhill, S, *Tourism Principles and Practice*, Pitman, 3rd edn 2005

Davidson, R, *Tourism*, Pitman, 2nd edn 1993

Davidson, R, *Travel and Tourism in Europe*, Longman, 2nd edn 1998

Davidson, R and Cope, B, *Business Travel: Conferences, Incentive Travel, Exhibitions, Corporate Hospitality and Corporate Travel*, Prentice Hall, 2003

Faulkner, B, Laws, E and Moscardo, G (eds), *Tourism in the 21st Century*, Continuum, 2001

Goeldner, J R, Brent, Ritchie, J R and McIntosh, R W, *Tourism: Principles, Practices, Philosophies*, Wiley, 8th edn 2000

Lavery, P and Van Doren, C, *Travel and Tourism: a North American–European Perspective*, Elm Publications, 1990

Lickorish, L J and Jenkins, C, *An Introduction to Tourism*, Butterworth Heinemann, 1995

Lockwood, A and Medlik, S, *Tourism and Hospitality in the 21st Century*, Elsevier Butterworth-Heinemann, 2002

Lumsdon, L and Swift, J, *Tourism in Latin America*, Continuum, 2001

Lundberg, D and C, *International Travel and Tourism*, Wiley, 2nd edn 1993

Medlik, S, *Understanding Tourism*, Butterworth Heinemann, 1999

Mill, R C and Morrison, A, *The Tourism System: an Introductory Text*, Prentice Hall, 2nd edn 1992

Pape, R, Touristry: a Type of Occupational Mobility, *Social Problems* 2/4 Spring, 1964

Pompl, W and Lavery, P, *Tourism in Europe: Structures and Development*, CABI, 1993

Rogers, T, *Conferences and Conventions: a Global Industry*, Elsevier, 2003

Ryan, C, *Tourism, Terrorism and Violence*, Research Institute for the Study of Conflict and Terrorism, London, 1991

Seaton, A V, Jenkins, C L, Wood, R C, Dieke, P U C, Bennett, M M, MacLellan, L R and Smith, R (eds), *Tourism: the State of the Art*, Wiley, 1994

Sharpley, R (ed), *The Tourism Business*, Business Education Publishers, 2002

Shone, A, *The Business of Conferences*, Butterworth Heinemann, 1998

Swarbrooke, J and Horner, S, *Business Travel and Tourism*, Butterworth Heinemann, 2001

Theobald, W (ed), *Global Tourism: the Next Decade*, Butterworth Heinemann, 2nd edn 1998

Toffler, A, *Future Shock*, Bodley Head, 1970

Vellas, F and Bécherel, L, *International Tourism*, Macmillan, 1995

Vukonic, B, *Tourism and Religion*, Elsevier Science, 1997

Wall, G and Mathieson, A, *Tourism: Change, Impacts and Opportunities*, Longman, 2nd edn 1997

Weiler, B and Hall, C M (eds), *Special Interest Tourism*, Belhaven Press, 1992

Youell, R, *Tourism: an Introduction*, Addison Wesley Longman, 1998

2 The development and growth of tourism to the mid-twentieth century

Adams, C, *Transport and Travel in the Roman World*, Sutton, 2003

Adamson, S H, *Seaside Piers*, Batsford, 1977

Addison, W, *English Spas*, Batsford, 1951

Alderson, F, *The Inland Resorts and Spas of Britain*, David and Charles, 1973

Bennett, T, *The Birth of the Museum: History, Theory, Politics*, Routledge, 1995

Braggs, S and Harris, D, *Sun, Fun and Crowds: Seaside Holidays between the Wars*, Tempus, 2000

Brendon, P, *Thomas Cook: 150 Years of Popular Tourism*, Secker, 1991

Burton, A and P, *The Green Bag Travellers: Britain's First Tourists*, Deutsch, 1978

Buzzard, J, *The Beaten Track: European Tourism, Literature and the Ways to Culture, 1800–1918*, Clarendon Press, 1993

CAB International, *Fashionable Resort Regions: Their Evolution and Transformation*, CABI, 1993

Casson, L, *Travel in the Ancient World*, George Allen and Unwin, 1974

Chaney, E, *The Evolution of the Grand Tour*, Frank Cass, 1998

Corbin, A, *The Lure of the Sea: the Discovery of the Seaside in the Western World 1750–1840*, Polity Press, 1994

Cormack, B, *A History of Holidays 1812–1990*, Routledge/Thoemmes Press, 1998

Delgado, A, *The Annual Outing and Other Excursions*, George Allen and Unwin, 1977

Drower, J, *Good Clean Fun: the Story of Britain's First Holiday Camp*, Arcadia, 1982

Feifer, M, *Going Places: the Ways of the Tourist from Imperial Rome to the Present Day*, Macmillan, 1985

Gordon, S, *Holidays*, Batsford, 1972

Havins, P J N, *The Spas of England*, Robert Hale, 1976

Hembry, P, *The English Spa 1560–1815: a Social History*, Athlone Press, 1990

Hern, A, *The Seaside Holiday: the History of the English Seaside Resort*, Cresset Press, 1967

Hibbert, C, *The Grand Tour*, Weidenfeld and Nicolson, 1969

Hindley, G, *Tourists, Travellers and Pilgrims*, Hutchinson, 1983

Jakle, J A, *The Tourist: Travel in 20th Century North America*, University of Nebraska Press, 1985

Löfgren, O, *On Holiday: a History of Vacationing*, University of California Press, 1999

Lloyd, M, *The Passport: the History of Man's Most Travelled Document*, Sutton, 2003

Maillet, A, *The Claude Glass: Use and Meaning of the Black Mirror in Western Art*, Zone Books, 2004

Moir, E, *The Discovery of Britain: the English Tourists 1540–1840*, Routledge and Kegan Paul, 1964

North, R, *The Butlin Story*, Jarrolds, 1962

Ousby, I, *The Englishman's England: Taste, Travel and the Rise of Tourism*, CUP, 1990

Perrottet, T, *Route 66AD: Pagan Holiday on the Trail of Ancient Roman Tourists*, Random House, 2003

Pimlott, J A R, *The Englishman's Holiday*, Harvester Press, 1976

Sillitoe, A, *Leading the Blind: a Century of Guide Book Travel 1815–1914*, Macmillan, 1995

Smith, P (ed), *The History of Tourism: Thomas Cook and the Origins of Leisure Travel*, Routledge/Thoemmes Press, 1998

Somerville, C, *Britain beside the Sea*, Grafton, 1990

Stokes, H G, *The Very First History of the English Seaside*, Sylvan Press, 1947

Studd, R G, *The Holiday Story*, Percival Marshall, 1948

Swinglehurst, E, *Cook's Tours: the Story of Popular Travel*, Blandford Press, 1982

Swinglehurst, E, *The Romantic Journey: the Story of Thomas Cook and Victorian Travel*, Pica, 1974

Walton, J K, *The English Seaside Resort: a Social History 1750–1914*, University of Leicester Press, 1983

Walton, J K, *The British Seaside: Holidays and Resorts in the Twentieth Century*, Manchester University Press, 2000

Walton, J K and Walvin, J, *Leisure in Britain 1780–1939*, Manchester University Press, 1983

Walvin, J, *Beside the Seaside: a Social History of the Popular Seaside Holiday*, Allen Lane, 1978

Ward, C and Hardy, D, *Goodnight Campers! The History of the British Holiday Camps*, Mansell, 1986

3 The era of popular tourism: 1950 to the twenty-first century

Akhtar, M and Humphries, S, *Some Liked it Hot: the British on Holiday at Home and Abroad*, Virgin Publishing, 2000

Apostolopoulos, Y, Leontidou, L and Loukissas, P (eds), *Mediterranean Tourism*, Routledge, 2000

Bray, R and Raitz, V, *Flight to the Sun: the Story of the Holiday Revolution*, Continuum, 2000

Cohen, E, *Contemporary Tourism: Diversity and Change*, Elsevier, 2004

Hodgson, G, *A New Grand Tour*, Viking, 1995

Lencek, L and Bosker, G, *The Beach: the History of Paradise on Earth*, Secker and Warburg, 1998

Middleton, V and Lickorish, L, *British Tourism: the Remarkable Story of Growth*, Elsevier Butterworth-Heinemann, 2005

Richardson, D and Richards, B, *ABTA: the First 50 Years*, ABTA, 2000

4 The demand for tourism

Apostolopoulos, Y, Leivadi, S and Yiannakis, A (eds), *The Sociology of Tourism*, Routledge, 1996

Clift, S and Grabowski, P (eds), *Tourism and Health: Risks, Research and Responses*, Cassell, 1997

Clift, S and Page, S, *Health and the International Tourist*, Routledge, 1995

Clift, S, Luongo, M and Callister, C, *Gay Tourism: Culture, Identity and Sex*, Continuum, 2002

Cohen, E, *Contemporary Tourism: Diversity and Change*, Elsevier, 2005

Davidson, R and Cope, B, *Business Travel: Conferences, Incentive Travel, Exhibitions, Corporate Hiospitality and Corporate Travel*, Pearson Education, 2003

Gullahorn, J E and Gullahorn, J T, An Extension of the U-curve Hypothesis, *Journal of Social Sciences* 19, 1963, 33–47

Hall, C M, Timothy, D J and Duval, D T (eds), *Safety and Security in Tourism: Relationships, Management and Marketing*, Haworth Press, 2004

Johnson, P and Thomas, B (eds), *Choice and Demand in Tourism*, Mansell, 1992

Krippendorf, J, *The Holiday Makers: Understanding the Impact of Leisure and Travel*, Heinemann, 2nd edn 1991

MacCannell, D, *Empty Meeting Grounds: the Tourist Papers*, Routledge, 1992

Mayo, E J and Jarvis, L P, *The Psychology of Leisure Travel: Effective Marketing and Selling of Travel Services*, CBI, 1981

Novelli, M (ed), *Niche Tourism: Contemporary Issues, Trends and Cases*, Elsevier, 2005

Pizam, A and Mansfield, Y (eds), *Consumer Behaviour in Travel and Tourism*, Haworth Press, 1999

Plog, S, *Leisure Travel: Making it a Growth Market Again!* Wiley, 1991

Rapoport, R and R N, Four Themes in the Sociology of Leisure, *British Journal of Sociology* XXV/2 June 1974

Reader, I and Walter, T (eds), *Pilgrimage in Popular Culture*, Macmillan, 1993

Robinson, M and Boniface, P (eds), *Tourism and Cultural Conflicts*, CABI, 1998

Robinson, M, Evans, N and Callaghan, P (eds), *Culture as the Tourist Product*, Business Education Publishers, 1996

Rogers, T, *Conferences: a Twenty-first Century Industry*, Addison Wesley Longman, 1998

Ross, G F, *The Psychology of Tourism*, Australian Studies in Tourism no 1, Hospitality Press, 1994

Rutherford, D, *Introduction to the Conventions, Expositions and Meetings Industry*, Van Nostrand Reinhold, 1990

Ryan, C, *Researching Tourist Satisfaction: Issues, Concepts, Problems*, Routledge, 1995

Ryan, C (ed), *The Tourist Experience*, Continuum, 2nd edn 2002

Shiller, M and Urry, J (eds), Tourism Mobilities: *Places to Play, Places in Play*, Routledge, 2004

Swarbrooke, J and Horner, S, *Consumer Behaviour in Tourism*, Butterworth Heinemann, 1999

Swarbrooke, J and Horner, S, *Business Travel and Tourism*, Butterworth Heinemann, 2001

Swarbrooke, J, Beard, C, Leckie, S and Pomfret, G, *Adventure Tourism: the New Frontier*, Butterworth Heinemann, 2003

Urry, J, *Consuming Places*, Routledge, 1995

Urry, J, *The Tourist Gaze: Leisure and Travel in Contemporary Societies*, Sage, 2nd edn 2002

Uysal, M (ed), *Global Tourist Behaviour*, International Business Press, 1994

Voase, R, *Tourism: the Human Perspective*, Hodder and Stoughton, 1995

Woodside, A, Crouch, G, Mazanek, J, Oppermann, M and Sakai, M (eds), *Consumer Psychology of Tourism, Hospitality and Leisure*, CABI, 1999

Zurick, D, *Errant Journeys: Adventure Travel in a Modern Age*, University of Texas Press, 1995

5 The economic impact of tourism (and research/statistical analysis)

Badger, A, *Trading Places: Tourism as Trade*, Tourism Concern, 1996

Buglear, J, *Stats to Go: a Guide to Statistics for Hospitality, Leisure and Tourism Studies*, Butterworth Heinemann, 2000

Bull, A, *The Economics of Travel and Tourism*, Longman, 2nd edn 1995

Clarke, M, Riley, M and Wood, R C, *Research Methods in Hospitality and Tourism*, International Thomson Business Press, 1997

Frechtling, D, *Forecasting Tourism Demand: Methods and Strategies*, Butterworth Heinemann, 2001

Go, F and Jenkins, C (eds), *Tourism and Economic Development in Asia and Australia*, Pinter, 1998

Harrison, D, *Tourism and the Less Developed Countries*, Wiley, 2nd edn 1995

Ioannides, D and Debbage, K G (eds), *The Economic Geography of the Tourist Industry: a Supply-side Analysis*, Routledge, 1998

Jennings, G, *Tourism Research*, Wiley, 2001

de Kadt, E, *Tourism: Passport to Development?* OUP, 1979

Knowles, T, Diamantis, D and Bey El-Mourhabi, J, *The Globalisation of Tourism and Hospitality: a Strategic Perspective*, Continuum, 2001

Ladkin, A, Szivas, E and Riley, M, *Tourism Employment: Analysis and Planning*, Channel View, 2002

Lennon, J (ed), *Tourism Statistics: International Perspectives and Current Issues*, Continuum, 2003

Lundberg, D, Stavenga, M H and Krishnamoorthy, M, *Tourism Economics*, Wiley, 1995

Pearce, D, *Tourist Development*, Longman, 2nd edn 1989

Pearce, D G and Butler, R W (eds), *Contemporary Issues in Tourism Development*, Routledge, 1999

Pearce, D G and Butler, R W (eds), *Tourism Research: Critiques and Challenges*, Routledge, 1992

Phillmore, J and Goodson, L (eds), *Qualitative Research in Tourism: Ontologies, Epistemologies and Methodologies*, Routledge, 2004

Ritchie, J R Brent and Goeldner, C (eds), *Travel, Tourism and Hospitality Research: a Handbook for Managers and Researchers*, Wiley, 2nd edn 1994

Sharpley, R and Telfer, D (eds), *Tourism and Development: Concepts and Issues*, Channel View Publications, 2002

Sinclair, M T and Stabler, M, *The Economics of Tourism*, Routledge, 1997

Smith, M and Duffy, R, *The Ethics of Tourism Development*, Routledge, 2003

Tribe, J, *The Economics of Leisure and Tourism*, Butterworth Heinemann, 2nd edn 1999

Veal, A J, *Research Methods for Leisure and Tourism: a Practical Guide*, Longman, 2nd edn 1997

Williams, A and Shaw, G (eds), *Tourism and Economic Development: Western European Experiences*, Wiley, 2nd edn 1991

Wong, K and Song, H (eds), *Tourism Forecasting and Marketing*, Haworth Hospitality Press, 2002

6 The sociocultural impact of tourism (and issues of general sustainability)

Ashworth, G J and Larkham, P J, *Building a New Heritage: Tourism, Culture and Identity in the New Europe*, Routledge, 1994

Bauer, T and McKercher, B (eds), *Sex and Tourism. Journeys of Romance, Love and Lust*, The Haworth Hospitality Press, 2003

Boissevain, J (ed), *Coping with Tourists: European Reactions to Mass Tourism*, Berghan, 1997

Boissevain, J (ed), *Revitalising European Rituals*, Routledge, 1992

Boniface, P and Fowler, P, *Heritage and Tourism in the 'Global Village'*, Routledge, 1993

Boniface, P, *Managing Quality Cultural Tourism*, Routledge, 1995

Briguglio, L, Archer, B, Jafari, J and Wall, G (eds), *Sustainable Tourism in Islands and Small States: Issues and Policies*, Pinter, 1996

Butcher, S, *The Moralisation of Tourism: Sun, Sand. . . . And Saving the World?* Routledge, 2003

Butler, R W and Hinch, T (eds), *Tourism and Indigenous Peoples*, International Thomson Business Press, 1996

Clift, S and Carter, S (eds), *Tourism and Sex: Culture, Commerce and Coercion*, Cassell, 2000

Cooper, C and Wanhill, S R, *Tourism Development: Environmental and Community Issues*, Wiley, 1997

Dahles, H and Keune, L (eds), *Tourism Development and Local Participation in Latin America*, Cognizant Communication, 2003

Doxey, G V, A Causation Theory of Visitor–Resident Irritants: Methodology and Research Inferences, *Proceedings of the Travel Research Association Sixth Annual Conference*, San Diego, 1975

Graburn, N H H (ed), *Ethnic and Tourist Arts: Cultural Expressions from the Fourth World*, University of California Press, 1976

Gullahorn, J E and Gullahorn, J T, An Extension of the U-Curve Hypothesis, *Journal of Social Sciences*, 19, 1963, 33–47

Harris, R, Griffin, T and Williams, P (eds), *Sustainable Tourism: a Global Perspective*, Elsevier, 2nd edn 2002

Harrison, L and Husbands, W, *Practising Responsible Tourism: International Case Studies in Tourism Planning, Policy and Development*, Wiley, 1996

Kockel, U (ed), *Culture, Tourism and Development: the Case of Ireland*, Liverpool University Press, 1994

Lane, B and Bramwell, B, *Sustainable Tourism: Principles and Practice*, Wiley, 1997

Lino, B (ed), *Sustainable Tourism in Islands, Vol 1. Issues and Policies, Vol. 2 Case Studies*, Mansell, 1996

MacCannell, D, *The Tourist: a New Theory of the Leisure Class*, Schocken Books, 2nd edn 1989

Middleton, V with Hawkins, R, *Sustainable Tourism: a Marketing Perspective*, Butterworth Heinemann, 1998

Mowforth, M and Munt, I, *Tourism and Sustainability: New Tourism in the Third World*, Routledge, 1998

Pattullo, P, *Last Resorts: the Cost of Tourism in the Caribbean*, Cassell, 1996

Pearce, P L, Moscardo, G M and Ross, G F, *Tourism Community Relationships*, Elsevier Science, 1997

Price, M (ed), *People and Tourism in Fragile Environments*, Wiley, 1996

Priestley, G K, Edwards, J A and Coccossis, H (eds), *Sustainable Tourism? European Experiences*, CABI, 1996

Reisinger, Y and Turner, L, *Cross Cultural Behaviour in Tourism: Concepts and Analysis*, Butterworth Heinemann, 2003

Richards, G (ed), *Cultural Tourism in Europe*, CABI, 1996

Richards, G and Hall, D (eds), *Tourism and Sustainable Community Development*, Routledge, 2000

Scheyvens, R, *Tourism for Development: Empowering Communities*, Prentice Hall, 2002

Smith, V (ed), *Hosts and Guests: an Anthropology of Tourism*, Blackwell, 1992

Smith, V and Brent, M (eds), *Hosts and Guests Revisited: Tourism Issues in the 21st Century*, Cognizant Communication, 2001

Stabler, M J (ed), *Tourism and Sustainability: Principles to Practice*, CABI, 1997

Sutton, W A, Travel and Understanding: Notes on the Social Structure of Touring, *International Journal of Comparative Sociology* 8/2, 1967

Swarbrooke, J, *Sustainable Tourism Management*, CABI, 1999

Wood, K and House, S, *The Good Tourist*, Mandarin, 1991

Young, G, *Tourism: Blessing or Blight?* Pelican, 1973

7 The environmental impact of tourism

Aronsson, L, *The Development of Sustainable Tourism*, Continuum, 2000

Boo, E, *Eco-Tourism: the Potentials and the Pitfalls*, World Wildlife Fund, 1990

Bramwell, B and Lane, B (eds), *Rural Tourism and Sustainable Rural Development*, Channel View, 1993

Bramwell, H, Henry, I, Jackson, G, Goytia Prat, A, Richards, G and van der Straaten, J (eds), *Sustainable Tourism Management: Principles and Practice*, Tilburg University Press, 1996

Buckley, R (ed), *Environmental Impacts of Ecotourism*, CABI, 2004

Cater, E and Lowman, G, *Ecotourism: a Sustainable Option?* Wiley, 1994

Croall, J, *Preserve or Destroy: Tourism and the Environment*, Calouste Gulbenkian Foundation, 1995

Eber, S (ed), *Beyond the Green Horizon: a Discussion Paper on Principles for Sustainable Tourism*, Tourism Concern/World Wildlife Fund, 1992

Fennell, D A, *Ecotourism*, Routledge, 2nd edn 2003

Font, X and Tribe, J (eds), *Forest Tourism and Recreation: Case Studies in Environmental Management*, CABI, 1999

Forsyth, T, *Sustainable Tourism: Moving from Theory to Practice*, Tourism Concern/Worldwide Fund for Nature, 1996

France, L (ed), *The Earthscan Reader in Sustainable Tourism*, Earthscan (Kogan Page), 1997

Hall, C M (ed), *Sustainable Tourism: a Geographical Perspective*, Longman, 1998

Hayles, J *et al*, *Guide to Green Tourism*, Victor Gollancz, 1991

Honey, M, *Ecotourism and Sustainable Development: Who Owns Paradise?* Island Press, 1999

Hunter, C and Green, H, *Tourism and the Environment: a Sustainable Relationship?* Routledge, 1995

Inskip, E, *Tourism Planning: an Integrated and Sustainable Development*, van Nostland Reinhold, 1991

Ioannides, D, Apostolopoulos, Y and Sonmez, S (eds), *Mediterranean Islands and Sustainable Tourism Development: Practices, Management and Policies*, Continuum, 2001

Neale, G (ed), *The Green Travel Guide*, Kogan Page, 1997

Newsome, D, Moore, S and Dowling, R, *Natural Area Tourism: Ecology, Impacts and Management*, Channel View, 2002

Tribe, J, Font, X, Griffiths, N, Vickery, R and Yale, K, *Environmental Management for Rural Tourism and Recreation*, Continuum, 2000

Wahab, S and Pigram, J (eds), *Tourism Development and Growth: the Challenge of Sustainability*, Routledge, 1997

Wearing, S and Neil, J, *Ecotourism: Impacts, Potentials and Possibilities*, Butterworth Heinemann, 1999

Weaver, D B, *Ecotourism in the Less Developed World*, CABI, 1998

8 The structure and organization of the travel and tourism industry

Buhalis, D and Laws, E (eds), *Tourism Distribution Channels: Practices, Issues and Transformations*, Continuum, 2001

Gee, C, Makens, J and Choy, D, *The Travel Industry*, Wiley, 3rd edn 1997

Hodgson, A (ed), *The Travel and Tourism Industry: Strategies for the Future*, Pergamon Press, 1987

Horner, P, *The Travel Industry in Britain*, Stanley Thornes, 1991

Pearce, D, *Tourism Organisations*, Longman, 1992

Pender, L, *Travel Trade and Transport: an Introduction*, Continuum, 2001

Sinclair, M T and Stabler, M (eds), *The Tourism Industry: an International Analysis*, CABI, 1991

Uysal, M and Fesenmaier, D (eds), *Communication and Channel Systems in Tourism Marketing*, Haworth Press, 1993

Weiermair, K and Mathies, C (eds), *The Tourism and Leisure Industry: Shaping the Future*, Haworth Hospitality Press, 2004

9 Tourist destinations

Ashworth, G J and Goodall, B, *Marketing Tourism Places*, Routledge, 1990

Ashworth, G and Hartmann, R (eds), *Horror and Human Tragedy Revisited: the Management of Sites of Atrocities for Tourism*, Cognizant Communications, 2004

Ashworth, G and Tunbridge, J, *The Tourist-Historic City*, Belhaven Press, 1990

Ashworth, G J and Voogd, H, *Selling the City: the Use of Publicity and Public Relations to Sell Cities and Regions*, Belhaven Press, 1990

Bachmann, P, *Tourism in Kenya: a Basic Need for Whom?* Peter Lang, 1988

Barke, M, Towner, J and Newton, M, *Tourism in Spain*, CABI, 1995

Brown, F and Hall, D (eds), *Tourism in Peripheral Areas*, Channel View, 2000

Burton, R, *Travel Geography*, Pitman, 2nd edn 1994

Butler, R, Hall, C M and Jenkins, J, *Tourism and Recreation in Rural Areas*, Wiley, 1998

Conlin, M V and Baum, T, *Island Tourism: Management Principles and Practice*, Wiley, 1995

Davidson, R and Maitland, R, *Tourism Destinations*, Hodder and Stoughton, 1997

Gabler, K, Maier, G, Mazenac, J and Wober, K, *International City Tourism: Analysis and Strategy*, Pinter Cassell, 1997

Getz, D and Page, S, *Business of Rural Tourism*, International Thomson Business Press, 1997

Goodall, B and Ashworth, G, *Marketing in the Tourism Industry: the Promotion of Destination Regions*, Routledge, 1987

Hall, C M and Johnston, M, *Polar Tourism: Tourism in the Arctic and Antarctic Regions*, Wiley, 1995

Hall, C M and Page, S J (eds), *Tourism in the Pacific: Issues and Challenges*, International Thomson Business Press, 1996

Higham, J (ed), *Sports Tourism Destinations: Issues, Opportunities and Analysis*, Elsevier, 2005

Howie, F, *Managing the Tourist Destination: a Practical Interactive Guide*, Continuum, 2001

Judd, D R and Fainstein, S (eds), *The Tourist City*, Yale University Press, 1999

Kearns, G and Philo, C, *Selling Places: the City as Cultural Capital, Past and Present*, Pergamon Press, 1993

King, B, *Creating Island Resorts*, Routledge, 1997

Kozak, M, *Destination Benchmarking: Concepts, Practices and Operations*, CABI Publishing, 2004

Law, C M (ed), *Tourism in Major Cities*, International Thomson Business Press, 1996

Law, C M, *Urban Tourism: the Visitor Economy and the Growth of Large Cities*, Continuum, 2nd edn 2002

Laws, E, *Tourism Destination Management: Issues, Analysis and Policies*, International Thomson Business Press, 1995

Lickorish, L J, Bodlender, J, Jefferson, A and Jenkins, C L, *Developing Tourism Destinations: Policies and Perspectives*, Longman, 1991

Lockhart, D and Smith, D (eds), *Island Tourism: Trends and Prospects*, Cassell, 1996

Morgan, N, Pritchard, A and Pride, R (eds), *Destination Branding: Developing a Destination Proposition*, Butterworth Heinemann, 2001

Oppermann, M and Chon, K-S, *Tourism in Developing Countries*, International Thomson Business Press, 1997

Page, S J, *Urban Tourism*, Routledge, 1995

Page, S J and Getz, D, *The Business of Rural Tourism: International Perspectives*, International Thomson Business Press, 1997

Ringer, G (ed), *Destinations: Cultural Landscapes of Tourism*, Routledge, 1998

Selby, M, *Understanding Urban tourism: Image, Culture, Experience*, I B Talaris, 2004

Shackley, M, *Wildlife Tourism*, International Thomson Business Press, 1996

Sharpley, R, *Tourism and Leisure in the Countryside*, Elm Publications, 2nd edn 1996

Sharpley, R and J, *Rural Tourism: an Introduction*, International Thomson Business Press, 1997

Shaw, G and Williams, A M (eds), *The Rise and Fall of British Coastal Tourism: Cultural and Economic Perspectives*, Mansell, 1996

Shaw, G and Williams, A M, *Tourism and Tourism Spaces*, Sage, 2004

Singh, S, Timothy, D and Dowling, R (eds), *Tourism in Destination Communities*, CABI, 2003

Soane, J V N, *Fashionable Resort Regions: Their Evolution and Transformation*, CABI, 1993

Tyler, D, Guerrier, Y and Robertson, M (eds), *Managing Tourism in Cities: Policy, Process and Practice*, Wiley, 1998

10 Tourist attractions

Ashworth, G and Hartmann, R (eds), *Horror and Human Tragedy Revisited: the Management of Sites of Atrocities for Tourism*, Cognizant Communications, 2004

Bowdin, G, McDonnell, I, Allen, J and O'Toole, W, *Events Management*, Elsevier, 2001

Dann, G and Seaton, A (eds), *Slavery, Contested Heritage and Thanatourism*, Haworth Hospitality Press, 2002

Drummond, S and Yeoman, I, *Quality Issues in Heritage Visitor Attractions*, Butterworth Heinemann, 2000

Fjellman, S, *Vinyl Leaves: Walt Disney World and America*, Westview Press, 1992

Foley, M and Lennon, J, *Dark Tourism*, Continuum, 2000

Fyall, A, Garrod, B and Leask, A (eds), *Managing Visitor Attractions: New Directions*, Butterworth Heinemann, 2003

Gammon, S and Jones, I, *Sports Tourism: an Introduction*, Continuum, 2001

Getz, D, *Explore Wine Tourism: Management, Development and Destinations*, Cognizant Communications, 2001

Getz, D, *Event Management and Event Tourism*, Cognizant Communications, 1997

Getz, D, *Festivals, Special Events and Tourism*, Van Nostrand Reinhold, 1990

Goldblatt, J J, *Special Events: the Art and Science of Celebration*, Van Nostrand Reinhold, 1990

Goodey, B (ed), *The Handbook of Interpretive Practice at Heritage Sites*, Wiley, 1997

Hall, C M, *Hallmark Tourist Events: Impacts, Management and Planning*, Wiley, 1992

Hall, C M, Sharples, L, Cambourne, B and Macionis, N, *Wine Tourism around the World: Development, Management and Markets*, Butterworth Heinemann, 2002

Hall, C M, Sharples, L, Mitchell, F, Macionis, N and Camborne, B, *Food Tourism around the world*, Butterworth Heinemann, 2003

Harrison, R, *Manual of Heritage Management*, Butterworth Heinemann, 1994

Hewison, R, *The Heritage Industry: Britain in a Climate of Decline*, Methuen, 1987

Hudson, S, *Snow Business: a Study of the International Ski Industry*, Cassell, 2000

Hudson, S (ed), *Sport and Adventure Tourism*, Haworth Press, 2003

Hughes, H, *Arts, Entertainment and Tourism*, Butterworth Heinemann, 2000

Jencks, C, *The Iconic Building: the Power of Enigma*, Frances Lincoln, 2005

Johnson, P and Thomas, B, *Tourism, Museums and the Local Economy*, Edward Elgar, 1992

Klugman, K, Kuenz, J, Waldrep, S and Willis, S, *Inside the Mouse: Work and Play at Disneyworld*, Duke University Press, 1995

Leask, A and Yeoman, I (eds), *Heritage Visitor Attractions: an Operations Management Perspective*, Cassell, 1999

Prentice, R, *Tourism and Heritage Attractions*, Routledge, 1993

Richards, B, *How to Market Tourism Attractions, Festivals and Special Events*, Longman, 1992

Richards, G (ed), *Cultural Attractions and European Tourism*, CABI, 2001

Ritchie, B and Adair, D (eds), *Sport Tourism: Interrelationships, Impacts and Issues*, Channel View Publications, 2004

Robinson, M, Evans, N and Callaghan, P (eds), *Tourism and Culture: Image, Identity and Marketing*, Business Education Publishers, 1996

Robinson, T, Gammon, S and Jones, I, *Sports Tourism: an Introduction*, Continuum, 2000

Rogers, T, *Conferences and Conventions: a Global Industry*, Elsevier, 2003

Rojek, C, *Ways of Escape: Modern Transformations in Leisure and Travel*, Macmillan, 1993

Shone, A with Parry, B, *Successful Event Management: a Practical Handbook*, Continuum, 2001

Swarbrooke, J, *The Development and Management of Visitor Attractions*, Butterworth Heinemann, 2nd edn 2002

Syme, G J, *The Planning and Evaluation of Hallmark Events*, Gower, 1989

Timothy, D and Boyd, S, *Heritage Tourism*, Prentice Hall, 2003

Uzzell, D (ed), *Heritage Interpretation: Vol 1 The Natural and Built Environment, Vol. 2 The Visitor Experience*, Belhaven Press, 1989

Walsh-Heron, J and Stevens, T, *The Management of Visitor Attractions and Events*, National Publishers, 1990

Watt, D, *Event Management in Leisure and Tourism*, Addison Wesley Longman, 1998

Weed, M and Bull, C, *Sports Tourism: Participants, Policy and Providers*, Elsevier Butterworth Heinemann, 2004

Yale, P, *From Tourist Attractions to Heritage Tourism*, Elm Publications, 1991

Yeoman, I, Robertson, M, Ali-Knioght, J, Drummond, S and McMahon-Beattie, U, *Festival and Events Management: An International Arts and Culture Perspective*, Elsevier, 2004

11 The hospitality sector: accommodation and catering services

Go, F and Pine, R, *Globalization Strategy in the Hotel Industry*, International Thomson Business Press, 1995

Lawson, F, *Hotels and Resorts: Planning, Design and Refurbishment*, Butterworth Heinemann, 1995

Lockwood, A and Medlik, S (eds), *Tourism and Hospitality in the 21st Century*, Elsevier, 2002

Medlik, S and Ingram, H, *The Business of Hotels*, Elsevier, 4th edn 2000

12 Tourist transport by air (and general transport)

Ashford, N, Martin Stanton, H P and Moore, C A, *Airport Operations*, Pitman, 1991

Barlay, S, *Cleared for Take-off: Behind the Scenes of Air Travel*, Kyle Cathie, 1994

Bell, G, Bowen, P and Fawcett, P, *The Business of Transport*, M&E, 1984

Benson, D and Whitehead, G, *Transport and Distribution*, Longman, 1985

Blackshaw, C, *Aviation Law and Regulation*, Pitman, 1991

Button, K (ed), *Airline Deregulation*, David Fulton, 1990

Calder, S, *No Frills: the Truth behind the Low-Cost Revolution in the Skies*, Virgin Books, 2003

Committee of Inquiry into Civil Air Transport, *British Air Transport in the Seventies*, HMSO, 1969

Dandel, S and Vialle, G, *Yield Management: Applications to Air Transport and Other Service Industries*, Institute de Transport Aerien, 1994

Dobson, A, *Flying in the Face of Competition*, Avebury Aviation/Ashgate Publishing, 1994

Doganis, R, *The Airport Business*, Routledge, 1992

Doganis, R, *Flying off Course: the Economics of International Airlines*, George Allen and Unwin, 2nd edn 1991

Eaton, A J, *The International Airline Business: Globalisation in Action*, Avebury Aviation/Ashgate Publishing, 1995

Graham, A, *Managing Airports: an International Perspective*, Butterworth Heinemann, 2nd edn 2003

Graham, B, *Geography and Air Transport*, Wiley, 1995

Hanlon, J P, *Global Airlines: Competition in a Transnational Industry*, Butterworth Heinemann, 2nd edn 1999

Lumsdon, L and Page, S J, *Tourism and Transport: Issues and Agenda for the New Millennium*, Elsevier Butterworth-Heinemann, 2004

Page, S J, *Transport and Tourism*, Longman, 1999

Pender, L, *Travel Trade and Transport: an Introduction*, Continuum, 2001

Phipps, D, *The Management of Aviation Security*, Pitman, 1991

Shaw, S, *Airline Marketing and Management*, Pitman, 3rd edn 1990

Wells, A T, Air Transportation: *a Management Perspective*, Wadsworth, 3rd edn 1994

Wheatcroft, S, *Aviation and Tourism Policies*, Routledge, 1994

Williams, G, *The Airline Industry and the Impact of Deregulation*, Avebury Aviation/Ashgate Publishing, 1994

13 Water-borne tourist transport

Berger, A, *Review of Ocean Travel and Cruising: a Cultural Analysis*, The Haworth Hospitality Press, 2004

Cartwright, R and Barid, C, *The Development and Growth of the Cruise Industry*, Butterworth Heinemann, 1999

Dickinson, R H and Vladimir, A N, *Selling the Sea: an Inside Look at the Cruise Industry*, Wiley, 1997

Douglas, N, and Douglas, B, *The Cruise Ship Experience*, Pearson, 2004

Peisley, T, *Global Changes in the Cruise Industry 2003–2010*, Seatrade Communications, 2003

15 The structure and role of the public sector in tourism (including planning and development)

Allcock, J B, *Tourism in Centrally Planned Economies*, Pergamon, 1990

Ashworth, G J, *Heritage Planning*, Geo Pers, 1991

Ashworth, G J and Dietvorst, A G J, *Tourism and Spatial Transformations: Implications for Policy and Planning*, CABI, 1995

Bosselman, F, Peterson, C and McCarthy, C, *Managing Tourism Growth: Issues and Applications*, Island Press, 1999

Bramwell, B and Lane, B (eds), *Tourism Collaboration and Partnership: Politics, Practice and Sustainability*, Channel View, 2000

CAB International, *Tourism in Europe: Structures and Development*, CABI, 1993

Deegan, J and Dineen, D, *Tourism Policy and Performance*, International Thomson Business Press, 1997

Edgell, D, *International Tourism Policy*, Van Nostrand Reinhold, 1990

Edgell, D, *Tourism Policy: the Next Millennium*, Sagamore, 1999

Elliott, J, *Tourism: Politics and Public Sector Management*, Routledge, 1997

Godde, P M, Price, M and Zimmermann, F, *Tourism Development in Mountain Regions*, CABI, 2000

Godfrey, K and Clarke, J, *The Tourism Development Handbook: a Practical Approach to Planning and Marketing*, Cassell, 2000

Gunn, C, *Vacationscape: Designing Tourist Regions*, Van Nostrand Reinhold, 4th edn 1997

Gunn, C and Var, T, *Tourism Planning: Basics, Concepts and Cases*, Routledge, 4th edn 2002

Hall, C M, *Tourism and Politics: Policy, Power and Place*, Wiley, 1994

Hall, C M, *Tourism in the Pacific: Development, Impacts and Markets*, Pitman, 1994

Hall, C M and Jenkins, J M, *Tourism and Public Policy*, Routledge, 1995

Heath, E and Wall, G, *Marketing Tourism Destinations: a Strategic Planning Approach*, Wiley, 1992

Jeffries, D, *Governments and Tourism*, Butterworth Heinemann, 2001

Johnson, P and Thomas, B (eds), *Perspectives on Tourism Policy*, Mansell, 1992

Leslie, D and Muir, F, *Local Agenda 21, Local Authorities and Tourism: a UK Perspective*, Glasgow Caledonian University, 1997

Montarani, A and Williams, A (eds), *European Tourism: Regions, Spaces and Restructuring*, Wiley, 1995

Morgan, N and Pritchard, A, *Tourism Promotion and Power: Creating Images, Creating Identities*, Wiley, 1998

Reid, D, *Tourism Globalization and Development: Responsible Tourism Planning*, Pluto Press, 2003

Singh, T V and Singh, S (eds), *Tourism Development in Critical Environments*, Cognizant Communication, 1999

Timothy, D J and Wall, G, *Tourism and Political Boundaries*, Routledge, 2000

Tolley, R S and Turton, B J, *Transport Systems, Policy and Planning*, Longman, 1995

16 Tour operating

Grant, D and Mason, S, *The EC Directive on Package Travel, Package Holidays and Package Tours*, University of Northumbria, 1993

Kärcher, K, *Reinventing the Package Holiday Business*, Deutscher Universitäts Verlag, 1997

Laws, E, *Managing Packaged Tourism*, International Thomson Business Press, 1997

Poustie, M, Ross, J, Geddes, N and Stewart, W, *Hospitality and Tourism Law*, International Thomson Business Press, 1999

Poynter, J, *Foreign Independent Tours: Planning, Pricing and Processing*, Delmar, 1989

Poynter, J, *Tour Design, Marketing and Management*, Prentice Hall, 1993

Yale, P, *The Business of Tour Operations*, Longman, 1995

17 Retailing tourism

Bottomley Renshaw, M, *The Travel Agent*, Business Education Publishers, 2nd edn 1997

Burton, J and L, *Interpersonal Skills for Travel and Tourism*, Longman, 1994

Coopers & Lybrand: Travel Agents' Benchmarking Survey, 1997

Horner, P, *Travel Agency Practice*, Longman, 1996

Syratt, G, *Manual of Travel Agency Practice*, Butterworth Heinemann, 2nd edn 1995

18 Ancillary tourism services

Holloway, J C, *Marketing for Tourism*, Prentice Hall, 4th edn, 2004

Pond, K L, *The Professional Guide: Dynamics of Tour Guiding*, Van Nostrand Reinhold, 1993

Reily Collins, V, *Becoming a Tour Guide: Principles of Guiding and Site Interpretation*, Continuum, 2000

19 The design and management of tourism services

Baud-Bovy, M and Lawson, F, *Tourism and Recreation Handbook of Planning and Design*, Architectural Press, 2nd edn 1998

Binney, M, *Our Vanishing Heritage*, Arlington, 1985

Binney, M and Hanna, M, *Preservation Pays: Tourism and the Economic Benefits of Conserving Historic Buildings*, SAVE Britain's Heritage (n/d)

Boer, A, Thomas, R and Webster, M, *Small Business Management: A Resource-based Approach for the Hospitality and Tourism Industries*, Cassell, 1997

Bosselman, F, Peterson, C and McCarthy, C, *Managing Tourism Growth: Issues and Applications*, Island Press, 1999

Bowdin, G, Allen, A, McDonnell, I and O'Toole, W, E*vents Management*, Butterworth Heinemann, 2001

Brotherton, B (ed), *The Handbook of Contemporary Hospitality Management Research*, Wiley, 1999

Carter, J, Goodey, B and Binks, G (eds), *Heritage Interpretation Management: Audience Characteristics, Evaluation and Impact*, Wiley, 1997

Coccossis, H, and Mexa, A (eds), *The Challenge of Tourism Carrying Capacity Assessment: Theory and Practice*, Ashgate, 2004

Crotts, J, Buhalis, D and March, R (eds), *Global Alliances in Tourism and Hospitality Management*, Haworth, 2000

Davidoff, D M, *Contact: Customer Service in the Hospitality and Tourism Industry*, Prentice Hall, 1994

Dickinson, B and Vladimir, A, *The Complete 21st Century Travel and Hospitality Marketing Handbook*, Pearson, 2004

European Tourism Universities Partnership (ETUP), *European Resort Management: Case Studies and Learning Materials*, Continuum, 2000

Evans, N, Campbell, D and Stonehouse, G, *Strategic Management for Travel and Tourism*, Elsevier, 2003

Foley, M, Lennon, J and Maxwell, G (eds), *Hospitality, Tourism and Leisure Management: Issues in Strategy and Culture*, Cassell, 1997

Getz, D, Carlsen, J and Morrison, A, *The Family Business in Tourism and Hospitality*, CABI, 2004

Glaesser, D, *Crisis Management in the Tourism Industry*, Butterworth Heinemann, 2003

Glasson, J, Godfrey, K and Goodey, B, *Towards Visitor Management*, Anthony Rowe, 1995

Gunn, C, *Tourism Planning*, Routledge, 4th edn 2002

Harrington, D and Lenehan, T, *Managing Quality in Tourism: Theory and Practice*, Oak Tree Press, 1998

Holloway, J C, *Marketing for Tourism*, Prentice Hall, 4th edn 2004

Horner, S and Swarbrooke, J, *International Cases in Tourism Management*, Elsevier Butterworth-Heinemann, 2004

Horner, S and Swarbrooke, J, *Marketing Tourism, Hospitality and Leisure in Europe*, International Thomson Business Press, 1996

Ingold, A, McMahon, U and Yeoman, I (eds), *Yield Management: Strategies for the Service Industries*, Continuum, 2nd edn 2000

Inskip, E, *Tourism Planning: An Integrated and Sustainable Development*, Van Nostrand Reinhold, 1991

Inskip, E, *National and Regional Tourism Planning: Methodologies and Case Studies*, Routledge, 1994

Inskeep, E and Kallenberger, M, *An Integrated Approach to Resort Development: Six Case Studies*, World Tourism Organization, 1992

Kotler, P, Bowen, J and Makens, J, *Marketing for Hospitality and Tourism*, Prentice Hall, 3rd edn 2003

Laws, E, *Tourism Marketing: Quality and Service Management Perspectives*, Continuum, 2002

Laws, E, Faulkner, B and Moscardo, G (eds), *Embracing and Managing Change in Tourism: International Case Studies*, Routledge, 1998

Leiper, N, *Tourism Management*, Pearson Hospitality Press, 2004

Mason, P, *Tourism Impacts, Planning and Management*, Butterworth Heinemann, 2003

Medlik, S, *Managing Tourism*, Butterworth Heinemann, 1995

Middleton, V with Clarke, J, *Marketing in Travel and Tourism*, Butterworth Heinemann, 3rd edn 2001

Mills, E, *Design for Holidays and Tourism*, Butterworth, 1983

Moutinho, L (ed), *Strategic Management in Tourism*, CABI, 2000

Murphy, P E, *Quality Management in Urban Tourism*, Wiley, 1996

Orams, M, *Marine Tourism: Development, Impacts and Management*, Routledge, 1999

Page, S, *Tourism Management: Managing for Change*, Butterworth Heinemann, 2003

Pender, L and Sharpley, R (eds), *The Management of Tourism*, Sage, 2005

Phillips, P A and Moutinho, L, *Strategic Planning Systems in Hospitality and Tourism*, CABI, 1998

Pizam, A and Mansfield, Y (eds), *Tourism, Crime and International Security Issues*, Wiley, 1995

Plog, S, *Leisure Travel: a Marketing Handbook*, Pearson, 2004

Poon, A, *Tourism, Technology and Competitive Strategies*, CABI, 1993

Robinson, M, Evans, N and Callaghan, P (eds), *Managing Cultural Resources for the Tourist*, Business Education Publishers, 1996

Rogers, H A and Slinn, J, *Tourism: Management of Facilities*, Pitman, 1993

Ryan, C and Page, S (eds), *Tourism Management: Towards the New Millennium*, Elsevier, 2000

Searle, M, *Bathing Machines and Bloomers*, Midas, 1977

Seaton, A V and Bennett, M, *Marketing Tourism Products: Concepts, Issues, Cases*, International Thomson Business Press, 1996

Shackley, M, *Managing Sacred Sites*, Continuum, 2001

Shackley, M (ed), *Visitor Management: Case Studies from World Heritage Sites*, Butterworth Heinemann, 2000

Swarbrooke, J, *The Development and Management of Visitor Attractions*, Butterworth Heinemann, 2nd edn 2002

Teare, R and Ingram, H, *Strategic Management: a Resource-based Approach for the Hospitality and Tourism Industries*, Cassell, 1993

Thomas, R (ed), *The Management of Small Tourism and Hospitality Firms*, Cassell, 1998

Tribe, J, *Corporate Strategy for Tourism*, International Thomson Business Press, 1997

Williams, C and Buswell, J, *Service Quality in Leisure and Tourism*, CABI, 2003

Witt, S F, Brooke, M Z and Buckley, P J, *The Management of International Tourism*, Unwin Hyman, 2nd edn 1995

20 What future for the tourism industry?

Löfgren, O, *On Holiday: a History of Vacationing*, University of California Press, 1999

Van Pelt, M, *Space Tourism: Adventures in Earth Orbit and Beyond*, Copernicus, 2005

Key trade, professional and academic magazines and journals of relevance to travel and tourism

In addition to the growing number of international academic and professional texts listed below, readers are also directed to the numerous magazines and journals aimed at the general public, many of which are valuable sources of material for students and practitioners of travel and tourism. These will include such periodicals as *Airline World, Flight International, Buses, In Britain* etc.

ABTA News	monthly
Annals of Tourism Research	quarterly
ASEAN Journal on Hospitality and Tourism	bi-annually
Asia Pacific Journal of Tourism Research	quarterly
ASTA Travel News	monthly
British Travel Brief	quarterly
British Traveller	monthly
Business Traveller	10 per annum
Business Travel World	monthly
Coaching Journal and Bus Review	monthly
Countryside Commission News	monthly
Current Issues in Tourism	bi-monthly
Event Management	quarterly
Executive Travel	monthly
Executive World (British Airways)	monthly
Flight International	weekly
Holiday Which? (Consumers Association)	quarterly
ICAO Bulletin	monthly
Information Technology and Tourism	quarterly

Information Technology in Hospitality	quarterly
Insights	monthly
International Journal of Hospitality and Tourism Administration	quarterly
International Journal of Tourism and Hospitality Research	quarterly
International Journal of Tourism Research	bi-monthly
International Tourism Quarterly (EIU)	quarterly
Journal of Air Transport Management	quarterly
Journal of Convention and Exhibition Management	quarterly
Journal of Ecotourism	quarterly
Journal of Hospitality and Leisure Marketing	quarterly
Journal of Hospitality and Tourism Research	quarterly
Journal of Human Resources in Hospitality and Tourism	quarterly
Journal of the ITT	quarterly
Journal of Leisure Research	quarterly
Journal of Quality Assurance in Hospitality and Tourism	quarterly
Journal of Sport Tourism	quarterly
Journal of Sustainable Tourism	bi-monthly
Journal of Tourism and Cultural Change	3 per annum
Journal of Tourism Studies	biannual
Journal of Transport Economics and Policy	Jan/May/Sept
Journal of Travel Research	quarterly
Journal of Travel and Tourism Marketing	quarterly
Journal of Vacation Marketing	quarterly
Leisure, Recreation and Tourism Abstracts (CABI)	quarterly
Leisure Studies (Leisure Studies Association)	quarterly
Motor Transport Weekly	weekly
Scandinavian Journal of Hospitality and Tourism	3 per annum
Service Industries Journal	Mar/Jul/Nov
Tourism (Bulletin of the Tourism Society)	quarterly
Tourism Analysis	quarterly
Tourism and Hospitality Research	quarterly
Tourism, Culture and Communication	3 per annum
Tourism Economics	quarterly
Tourism Geographies	quarterly
Tourism Geography	quarterly
Tourism in Focus	quarterly
Tourism in Marine Environments	biannually
Tourism Intelligence Quarterly	quarterly
Tourism Management	bi-monthly
Tourism Recreation Research	3 per annum
The Tourism Review (AIEST)	quarterly
Tourism Review International	quarterly
Tourism Trendspotter	bi-monthly
Tourist Studies	3 per annum
Transport (CIT)	bi-monthly
Transport Management	quarterly
Transport Reviews	quarterly
Travel Agency	bi-monthly
Travel and Tourism Analyst (EIU)	bi-monthly
Travel Business Analyst	10 per annum

Travel GBI	monthly
Travel Industry Monitor (EIU)	quarterly
Travel Research Journal	quarterly
Travel Trade Gazette	weekly
Travel Trade Gazette Europa (Continental edition)	weekly
Travel Weekly	weekly
World Leisure Journal	quarterly
World Travel (*Tourisme Mondiale*) (WTO)	bi-monthly

Mány of the articles from these journals are available electronically, and some journals are now produced exclusively for access electronically. The following are useful sources of electronic information:

Articles in Tourism, monthly abstracting service, Universities of Bournemouth, Oxford Brookes and Surrey

e-Review of Tourism Research an electronic bulletin for tourism research, available at http://ertr.tamu.edu

International Tourism and Hospitality Database, CD-ROM, Wiley

Journal of Hospitality, Leisure, Sport and Tourism, bi-annual e-journal

TourCD (*Leisure, Recreation and Tourism Abstracts*) CD-ROM database, CABI

Index